COMPETITION LAW DICTIONARY

COMPETITION LAW DICTIONARY

Under the direction of

Deborah Healey
Richard Whish
William E. Kovacic
Pablo Trevisán

Foreword by Linsey McCallum
Introduction by Herbert Hovenkamp

Concurrences, 2024

Paris – London – New York

106 West 32nd Street, Suite 144 New York, NY, 10001, USA
www.concurrences.com
book@concurrences.com

First Printing, Septembre 2024
978-1-939007-05-6 (Paperback)
Library of Congress Control Number: 2024937844
Cover Design: Yves Buliard, www.yvesbuliard.fr
Book Design and Layout implementation: Nord Compo

Concurrences Books

Tributes

James F. Rill, *P. Lugard, J. Taladay (eds.), Forthcoming 2024*

Eleanor M. Fox – Antitrust Ambassador to the World, *2021*

Herbert Hovenkamp – The Dean of American Antitrust Law, *2021*

Frédéric Jenny – Standing Up for Convergence and Relevance in Antitrust, (Vol. I & II), *2019 & 2021*

Albert Foer – A Consumer Voice in the Antitrust Arena, *2020*

Richard Whish – Taking Competition Law Outside the Box, *2020*

Douglas H. Ginsburg – An Antitrust Professor on the Bench (Vol. I & II), *2018 & 2020*

Wang Xiaoye – The Pioneer of Competition Law in China, *A. Emch, W. Ng (eds.), 2019*

Ian S. Forrester – A Scot without Borders (Vol. I & II), *A. Komninos (eds.), 2015*

William E. Kovacic – An Antitrust Tribute (Vol. I & II), *2013 & 2014*

Practical Books

The DMA and more – Future application and margin of manoeuvre for national jurisdictions, *G. Muscolo & A. Massolo (eds.), Forthcoming 2024*

AI & Competition Policy, *A. Abbott, T. Schrepel (eds.), Forthcoming 2024*

State Aid & National Enforcement, *J. Derenne, D. Jouve, C. Lemaire, F. Martucci (eds.), Forthcoming 2024*

Competition Inspections in 25 Jurisdictions 2nd Edition – A Practitioner's Guide, *N. Jalabert-Doury (ed.), 2024*

EU Antitrust Enforcement – Law, Economics, History, *Policy & Practice, Wouter P. J. Wils, 2024*

The EU Foreign Subsidies Regulation, *Andreas Reindl, Isabelle Van Damme, 2024*

Compendium of Antitrust Damages Action – International Chamber of Commerce (ICC) – 2nd edition, *J.W.H. Denton AO, F. Brunet, S. Williams, C. Inthavisay (eds.), 2023*

Pharmaceutical Antitrust: An Analysis of US and EU Law, *M. Thill-Tayara, G. Gordon (eds.), 2023*

Innovation Paradox in Merger Control, *G. Gurkaynak, 2023*

Antitrust and the Digital Economy, *Y. Katsoulacos (ed.), 2023 (in collaboration with CRESSE)*

Judicial Review of Competition Cases, *D. Ginsburg, T. Eicke (eds.), 2023*

Competition Law Treatment of Joint Ventures, *B. Bleicher, N. Campbell, A. Hamilton, N. Hukkinen, A. Khan, A. Mordaunt (eds.), 2022 (in collaboration with the IBA)*

Information Exchange & Related Risks, *Z. Marosi, M. Soares (eds.), 2022 (in collaboration with the IBA)*

Rulemaking Authority of the US Federal Trade Commission, *D. Crane (ed.), 2022*

The International Competition Network at Twenty, *D. Anderson & P. Lugard (eds.), 2022*

Competition Case Law Digest – 5th Edition, *F. Jenny, N. Charbit (eds.), 2022*

Competition Inspections in 21 Jurisdictions – A Practitioner's Guide, *N. Jalabert-Doury (ed.), 2022*

Perspectives on Antitrust Compliance, *A. Riley, A. Stephan, A. Tubbs (eds.), 2022 (in collaboration with the ICC)*

Turkish Competition Law, *G. Gürkaynak, 2021*

Competition Law – Climate Change & Environmental Sustainability, *S. Holmes, D. Middelschulte, M. Snoep (eds.), 2021*

Merger Control in Latin America – A Jurisdictional Guide, *P. Burnier da Silveira, P. Sittenfeld (eds.), 2020*

Competition Inspections under EU Law – A Practitioner's Guide, *N. Jalabert-Doury, 2020*

Gun Jumping in Merger Control – A Jurisdictional Guide, *C. Hatton, Y. Comtois, A. Hamilton (eds.), 2019 (in collaboration with the IBA)*

Choice – A New Standard for Competition Analysis? *P. Nihoul (ed.), 2016*

PhD Theses

The Economics of Digital Markets – Essays in Theoretical and Empirical Industrial Organization, *E. Arnaud-Joufray, 2024, Forthcoming 2024*

Abuse of Platform Power, *F. Bostoen, 2023*

Reform of Chinese State-Owned Enterprises, *X. Bai, 2023*

Competition & Regulation in Network Industries – Essays in Industrial Organization, *J-M. Zogheib, 2021*

The Role of Media Pluralism in the Enforcement of EU Competition Law, *K. Bania, 2019*

Buyer Power, *I. Herrera Anchustegui, 2017*

General Interest

Why Competition? Voices from the Antitrust Community and Beyond, *D. Crane, D. Gerard, R. Tritell (eds.), Forthcoming 2024*

Competition Law Dictionary, *D. Healey, R. Whish, W. E. Kovacic, P. Trevisán (eds.), 2024*

Great Antitrust Enforcers, *W. E. Kovacic, 2023*

Competition – How to Speak Like an Expert, *E. Combe , 2023*

Women and Antitrust – Voices from the Field (Vol I & II), *E. Kurgonaite & K. Nordlander, 2020*

e-Book versions available for **Concurrences+** subscribers

EDITORIAL NOTE

Navigating the vast and dynamic landscape of competition law requires a thorough understanding of its key concepts. The Competition Law Dictionary marks a significant milestone in legal academia. Carefully curated by leading experts in the field, this dictionary offers an in-depth exploration of competition law, serving as a cornerstone reference for legal practitioners and scholars internationally.

This Dictionary is an essential resource for comprehending the intricate language of global competition law and economics. This dynamic tool, created through a collaboration between eminent experts and practitioners, offers real-time updates, making it an indispensable guide for legal professionals, scholars, students, and anyone else wishing to delve into the world of competition law.

With a global perspective at its core, the Dictionary embodies a truly international effort, bringing together contributors from diverse corners of the antitrust realm. Esteemed experts and practitioners from various jurisdictions cooperate seamlessly, providing a rich tapestry of insights that reflect the diversity of competition law. This borderless effort ensures that the Dictionary is not confined by geographical boundaries but serves as a comprehensive guide that resonates with the nuances and practices of competition law worldwide.

This project is more than your usual dictionary. This is a collective exploration of the diverse array of competition law principles and practices across jurisdictions, allowing readers to delve into the intricacies of antitrust regulations, understand the meaning and implications of FRAND, navigate the complexities of merger control, recognize the features of a boycott, unravel the dynamics of monopoly, and explore over 230 other essential terms.

We are also privileged to have Herbert Hovenkamp authoring the Introduction and Linsey McCallum providing the Foreword of this Competition Law Dictionary. Their antitrust expertise provides enormous added value to this project and elevates the Dictionary to new heights. Professor Hovenkamp's insightful introduction and Linsey McCallum's compelling foreword not only add depth but also help us comprehend the dictionary's immense scope and complexity.

By exploring these key concepts, the Dictionary serves as a bridge, linking theoretical ideas with practical scenarios. In an age of increasingly interconnected markets, understanding the language of competition law is not only advantageous but imperative. Join this collaborative effort and let the Competition Law Dictionary guide you through the language that defines the future of competition law.

Deborah Healey, University of New South Wales
Richard Whish, King's College London
William E. Kovacic, George Washington University – School of Law
Pablo Trevisán, Instituto de Derecho de la Competencia

LIST OF TERMS

A

B

C

D

L

M

N

O

P

T

U

V

W

CONTRIBUTORS

All opinions expressed here are those of the authors and do not necessarily reflect the views of the institution to which they belong.

Alden Abbott
Gabriel de Abreu Madeira
Rafael Allendesalazar
Oles Andriychuk
Reiko Aoki
Amanda Athayde
Audrey Augusto
Tasneem Azad
João Azevedo
Grigorios Bacharis
David Bailey
Bahadir Balki
Jaime Barahona
Jonathan M. Barnett
Carl Baudenbacher
Claudia Berg
Joseph J. Bial
Friso Bostoen
Christian Bovet
Rachel Brandenburger
Irit Brodsky
Or Brook
Jacques Buhart
Eugène Buttigieg
Irene Calboli
Clara Callini
Peter D. Camesasca
Damiano Canapa
Sara Capozzi
Isabella Carcione
Alden Caribé de Sousa
Michael A. Carrier
Caroline Cauffman
Mercedes Pedraz Calvo
Laurent Cenatiempo
Carmelo Cennamo
Virender Chandel
Cindy Chang
Tomasz Chróstny
Niccolo Ciulli
Giuseppe Colangelo
Martin Coleman
Sandra Marco Colino
John M. Connor
Jorge L. Contreras
Gwendolyn Cooley
Emmanuel Coulon
Paul Csiszár
Hemangini Dadwal
Lise Damelet
Amber Darr
Fabrizio Di Benedetto
Rodrigo Rios Dordelly
Daniel Douek
Francesco Ducci
Gail Elizabeth Evans
Sean Ennis
Ercüment Erdem

Sonia Rocha Esquivel
Christina Etteldorf
Simon J. Evenett
Piero Fattori
Allan Fels
Victor Fernandes
Luís Henrique Perroni Fernandes
Stefano Firpo
Leo Flynn
Ian Forrester
Kyriakos Fountoukakos
Eleanor M. Fox
Peter Freeman
David Fruitman
Fernando de Magalhaes Furlan
Diana-Urania Galetta
David Gerber
Amira Abdel Ghaffar
David Gilo
Philipp Girardet
Aldo Gonzalez
José Carlos Gonzáles Cucho
Inge Graef
Albert Sánchez Graells
Martin Andreas Gravengaard
Łukasz Grzejdziak
Ramin Silvan Gohari
Liza Lovdahl Gormsen
Kirti Gupta
Gönenç Gürkaynak
João Otávio Bacchi Gutinieki
Michal Halperin
Martin d'Halluin
Anthony Abi Hanna
James Harvey
Michael D. Hausfeld
Deborah Healey
Sean Heather
Andreas Heinemann
Scott Hemphill
Ignacio Herrera
Simon Holmes
Tomotake Horimatsu
Liyang Hou
Clara Ingen-Housz
Jonel Mari Ibarra
María Luisa Ilharreborde Illanes
Rishabh Jain
Liana Japaridze
Léa Berthiau-Jezequel
Justin Johnson
Alison Jones
Evgeny Khokhlov
Behrang Kianzad
Katherine Kingsbury
Melanie Kiser
Timo Klein
Ioannis Kokkoris
Carsten König
Torsten Körber
Elizabeth Kraus
Carsten Krüger
Kees Jan Kuilwijk
Nicolaj Kuplewatzky
Ayberk Kurt
Dimitrios Kyriazis
Robert H. Lande
Godfrey Lam
Catrina Lam
Greg Lang

Hwang Lee
Kyle Le Croy
Claudia Lemus
Marc Lévy
Stephen D. Libowsky
Alejandro Martínez Luna
Björn Lundqvist
Alexandre Cordeiro Macedo
Fernanda Garcia Machado
Mariateresa Maggiolino
Payal Malik
Geoffrey Manne
Despoina (Deni) Mantzari
Ignacio García-Perrote Martínez
Mário Marques Mendes
Mel Marquis
Marek Martyniszyn
Marcela Mattiuzzo
Kathryn McMahon
Stefanos Merikas
Valentin Mircea
Vassili Moussis
Andreas Mundt
Willard Mwemba
Darren Brady Nelson
Caio Mario da Silva Pereira Neto
Dario da Silva Oliveira Neto
Inês F. Neves
Phedon Nicolaides
J. Nicolás Otegui Nieto
Yongama Njisane
Luis Diez Canseco Núñez
Xolani Nyali
Okeoghene Odudu
Raluca Onufreiciuc
Andrés Pérez Orduz
O. Onur Özgümüş
Tudor N. Pana
Efstathia Pantopoulou
Ricardo Ferreira Pastore
Adriana Hernandez Perez
Robert Venero Peralta
Felipe Irarrázabal Philippi
Noah Joshua Phillips
Chris Pike
Giovanni Pitruzzella
Gokul Plaha
Aurélien Portuese
Luca Prete
Alejandra Palacios Prieto
Jeffrey Prince
Lazar Radic
Claudia Georgina Brambilla Ramírez
Arno Rasek
Tilottama Raychaudhuri
David Reader
David H. Reichenberg
Agustín Reyna
Ricardo Riesco
Jani Ringborg
Juan David Gutiérrez Rodriguez
Margarida Matos Rosa
Gonçalo Rosas
Gal Rozent
Daniel L. Rubinfeld
Roberto Rustichelli
Seth B. Sacher
Rahul Saha
Quentin B. Schäfer
Till Schreiber

Margaux Seager
Martin Seegers
Eda Şahin-Şengül
Navneet Sharma
Sei Shishido
Alessandro Sia
Paulo Burnier da Silveira
Rod Sims
Athanassios Skourtis
Rhonda L. Smith
Daniel Sokol
Tina Søreide
Hanna Stakheyeva
Andreas Stephan
Richard Steppe
Kristian Helge Straton-Andersen
Ryan Stones
Julia Suderow
Gintarė Surblytė-Namavičienė
Maciej Szpunar
Yusuke Takamiya
Natasha Tardif
Fevzi Toksoy
Philip Torbøl
Pablo Trevisán
Vanessa Turner
Anna Tzanaki
Irma Urmonaitė
Georges Vallindas
Pieter Van Cleynenbreugel
Fabiana Pereira Velloso
Marcos Verissimo
Enrique Vergara Vial
José Luís da Cruz Vilaça
David Viros
Florian Wagner-von Papp
Mike Walker
Erik Wennerström
Richard Whish
Joseph Wilson
Anne C. Witt
Koren W. Wong-Ervin
Atsushi Yamada
Ya-Lun Yen
Christopher Yoo
Brian Yost
Johan Ysewyn
John M. Yun
Adriana Zabłocka-Abi Yaghi
Sabine Zigelski
Mario Zúñiga
Tania Zúñiga

FOREWORD

Studying the law means understanding the words and concepts that underlie it. How could it be otherwise when then those who create, develop or practice the law use words to design rules and express their thoughts about them.
It matters, therefore, that our legal words and concepts should be clear and easily understandable.
All the more so as the creation of the language of the law is not a linear process. It is rather a continuous one involving numerous different actors, in different places, through different instruments. It is also heavily dependent on how a certain field of law has developed over the course of the years.
In this respect, the development of competition law (and, therefore, of its language) is, in many ways, unique.
Competition law is characterized by a relatively small body of rules that has been written directly by the legislator. Its development has, therefore, always relied on the joint effort of the other "actors" involved: the judges through their judgments, the enforcers through their decisions and guidelines, and the practitioners, academics and commentators though their articles and other contributions. Moreover, competition law is also a field that is intertwined with economic analysis, with the consequence that also the work of economic scholars contributes to the creation of its language.
This multifaceted process had – and has – the benefit of allowing all actors to participate in the development of a common vocabulary, something that hardly happens when it mainly fell on the legislator. It is clear, however, that it also has its challenges, and can lead to confusion on the meaning and use of certain words and concepts.
To untrained eyes, the language of competition law can seem at times complicated, difficult to understand or even confusing. Just think about the notion of "control" under competition law, which is in many aspects different from the one used in all other fields of the law, or the definition of "online platform" which is rapidly evolving due to the work of the legislator and lawyers. It is no surprise that lawyers from other fields perceive competition law as one of the most complex!
In this context, the development of a Competition Law Dictionary by Concurrences is groundbreaking and necessary work.
In this Dictionary, written by some of the most experienced names in competition law, you will find clear definitions and explanations of the words through which the main concepts of competition law are expressed. This will be of immense help for all those approaching the study or the practice of competition law.
Moreover, by contributing to the effort of clarifying and systematising its language, the Dictionary will benefit greatly the general discussion about competition law and it is set to be a fundamental tool for all those who believe in the crucial role played by competition law in this ever-changing world.

Linsey MCCALLUM
Deputy Director-General for Antitrust and Regulation of Digital Platforms
DG Competition
European Commission

INTRODUCTION

The publication of Concurrence's Competition Law Dictionary is important for many reasons. First, it adds to a long list of high-quality and practical books that Concurrences has published on antitrust and competition law. Second, its group of accomplished and serious editors (Deborah Healey, Richard Whish, William E. Kovacic and Pablo Trevisán) is second to none. The same is true of its numerous individual contributors. Third, it has managed in the space of a single volume to assemble high-quality essays on the most important topics in competition law today, addressing them so as to describe the approaches taken by the leading competition law jurisdictions. Fourth, its scope is worldwide, although focusing mainly on the EU and the United States. Fifth, an additional feature that makes this dictionary unique is an invitation to users to contribute their own additions to the dictionary's entries, reflecting their experiences in their own countries. Subject to review by the editors, these will be included as well. As a result, this dictionary promises to grow in usefulness over time.

The treatment of topics in this volume is somewhat more like that of an encyclopedia than a dictionary. Many entries are several pages long, although none seem overly long. Even entries on technical subjects, such as Cournot equilibrium or the Lerner Index are presented in an accessible fashion readable by lawyers without extensive economics training. The entries are followed by case references and citations to more detailed literature.

The individual entries contained here are just right for most users – sufficiently detailed to go beyond the one-sentence definitions in lay dictionaries, that are too often useless for scholarly purposes, but not so long as to be tedious or hyper-technical. They are up to date in their presentation of both the law and the economics of competition policy. Most entries are accompanied by a brief bibliography that includes references to both leading court decisions and important scholarly writings.

The dictionary also includes entries covering many of the more interesting and controversial issues in competition law today, including two-sided markets, self-preferencing, potential competition, the Digital Markets Act, error costs, and FRAND. For each of these, the level of presentation is sophisticated but not overly technical. For example, the entry on relevant markets has a good but nontechnical discussion of the hypothetical monopolist test (HMT). The entry on price discrimination covers both economic price discrimination and the very different set of practices addressed by the U.S. Robinson-Patman Act.

This dictionary deserves a spot on the bookshelf of every lawyer and student who is serious about global competition law.

Herbert HOVENKAMP
James G. Dinan University Professor
University of Pennsylvania

A

ABSOLUTE TERRITORIAL PROTECTION

Mario ZÚÑIGA
International Center for Law & Economics

■ Definition

Mostly used under European Union Competition Law, the term "Absolute Territorial Protection" designates a practice by manufacturers or suppliers, according to which a single distributor obtains the rights from a manufacturer to market a product or service in a certain territory and other distributors are prohibited to sell actively or passively into this territory. In that vein, distributors cannot offer the product or service outside its designated territory and cannot respond to solicitations from consumers in other territories. Absolute Territorial Protection is equivalent to a "reinforced exclusive dealing", whereas, in addition to the exclusivity, there is a prohibition on so called "parallel imports".

■ Commentary

European Union

Understandably, given its goal of creating a single market, EU Competition Law is skeptical of practices that appear to undermine that goal, independently if they increase output. Accordingly, agreements aiming to restrict trade between Member States are in principle restrictive of competition "by object" (or "by their very nature") under Article 101(1) of the Treaty on the Functioning of the European Union (TFEU).

This apparently absolute prohibition applies not only to horizontal agreements (as would be the rule on most jurisdictions with a Competition or Antitrust Law), but to some vertical restraints that could enhance inter-brand competition and benefit consumers in the process (Ibañez Colomo, 2016). In *Consten and Grundig v. Commission*, the Court of Justice reached the conclusion that if an agreement goes beyond granting exclusive rights to a territory, imposing importing bans and preventing "parallel trade", it is considered to have "as its object" the restriction of competition.

In that vein, Article 4 of the Vertical Restraints Regulation No. 330/2010 qualifies as "hardcore restrictions" stipulations limiting "the territory into which, or the customers to whom, a buyer party to the agreement may sell the contract goods or services". It is important to bear in mind, however, that the heading of article 4 uses the phrase "have as their object"; which means that a broader agreement that contains other provisions, with other plausible goals, and with a plausible competitive justification (i.e. agreements that include investments in advertising or protection of intellectual property), could fall outside the scope of Article 4.

Moreover, Article 4 includes four exceptions to the rule:

(i) the restriction of active sales into the exclusive territory or to an exclusive customer group reserved to the supplier or allocated by the supplier to another buyer, that do not limit sales by the customers of the buyer;

(ii) the restriction of sales to end users by a buyer operating at the wholesale level of trade;

(iii) the restriction of sales by the members of a selective distribution system to unauthorized distributors within the territory reserved by the supplier to operate that system; and,

(iv) the restriction of the buyer's ability to sell components, supplied for the purposes of incorporation to customers who would use them to manufacture the same type of goods as those produced by the supplier.

United States

Under U.S. Antitrust Law, the analysis is more straightforward, especially after *Continental T.V., Inc. v GTE Sylvania.* An absolute territorial protection is analyzed as a vertical restraint and, as such, would be analyzed under the rule-of-reason standard. In Sylvania, the Supreme Court acknowledges that "vertical restrictions reduce intrabrand competition by limiting the number of sellers of a particular product", but "promote interbrand competition by allowing the manufacturer to achieve certain efficiencies in the distribution of his products". Therefore, vertical territorial restrictions merit further analysis.

Under the rule-of-reason, plaintiffs must demonstrate that the defendant has a high degree of market power, and that the restriction has negative effect on competition. Defendants can demonstrate that the restraint has procompetitive interbrand effects that mitigate the anticompetitive effects on intrabrand competition.

Competition law of other nations

The competition laws of other nations give a similar treatment to territorial restrictions, the main difference being the burden of proof. Peruvian Antitrust Law (Legislative Decree 1034) has a clear classification between unilateral practices and agreements, which can be vertical and horizontal agreements. Only horizontal agreements related exclusively to price, output, and client allocation, and bid-rigging, are under an "absolute prohibition" rule (akin to the per se rule). Vertical territorial restrictions (even "absolute", therefore, would be analyzed as a vertical agreement; and are hence subject to a "relative prohibition" rule (akin to the rule of reason). Plaintiffs, therefore, must demonstrate that the defendant has dominance in the relevant market, that the practice is unjustified, and that it has or may have negative effects on competition.

Bibliography

Gavil, A., Kovacic, W., Baker, J. and Wright, J., *Antitrust Law in Perspective. Cases, concepts and problems in Competition Policy*. Third Edition. West Academic, 2017

Heimler, A. and Mehta, K., Absolute Territorial Protection and Competition in the EU: An Economic Approach (April 15, 2014)

Ibanez Colomo, P., Article 101 TFEU and Market Integration. LSE Law, *Society and Economy Working Papers* 07/2016

Mastromanolis, E., Insights from U.S. Antitrust Law on exclusive and restricted territorial distribution: the creation of a new legal standard for European Union Competition Law. U. Pa. J. Int'l Bus. Vol. 15, No. 4 (1994)

Whish, R. and Bailey, D., *Competition Law*, Seventh Edition. Oxford University Press, 2012

See also

Agent, Distribution agreement, Vertical agreement, Vertical restraints (or restrictions)

A

ABUSE OF DOMINANT POSITION

Deborah HEALEY
University of New South Wales

Definition

Abuse of dominance is unilateral conduct using dominant market power (or a dominant position) to damage market competition and ultimately welfare. Most jurisdictions address the issue by prohibiting use of dominance or substantial market power, taking different approaches to terminology and the relevant threshold of market power. Dominance itself, or the degree of market power required by other wordings, is generally measured by the ability of an organisation to act without significant constraint, or to influence prices to exclude competition, or to profitably maintain prices above the cost of supply in the long run. Conduct which may infringe abuse of dominance and like provisions includes predatory pricing, exclusive dealing, loyalty rebates, tying and bundling, refusal to deal, and in some jurisdictions, excessive pricing.

Commentary

The distinction between acceptable conduct and conduct which will breach the dominance provisions is often difficult to draw. In most jurisdictions, no definite market share thresholds are set on a numerical basis to determine market power for assuming dominance or substantial market power. In some jurisdictions, presumptions of dominance arise based on specified market shares (for example, China, Korea), while some of these presumptions are rebuttable. The EU uses the threshold of dominance in Article 102 TFEU.

A dominant position is the power to behave to an appreciable extent independently of its competitors, its customers, and consumers *(Hoffmann-La Roche)*. Article 102 prohibits collective abuse of dominance: by "one or more undertakings" *(Airtours)*. Mere possession of the required degree of market power is not sufficient. "Abuse" is not defined but various cases exemplify this conduct in particular sets of circumstances: see for example, *(Hoffmann-La Roche; Deutsche Telekom AG, para. 174)*. Article 102 identifies, non-exhaustively, potential problem conduct in paras. (a)-(d) as: imposing unfair purchase or selling prices or other unfair trading conditions; limiting production or technical development which prejudices consumers; discriminatory conditions on trading partners; and imposing obligations which have no connections to the dealings.

The EU Commission and courts have more recently moved from a traditional form-based approach to prohibited conduct to focus more generally on the analysis of economic effects, but there is still a tendency to formalistically assess some types of unilateral conduct, particularly in the courts. A dominant undertaking has a special responsibility in the EU not to allow its behaviour to impair genuine, undistorted competition on the internal market *(Michelin, para. 70)*. It is not, however, the role of Article 102 to protect less efficient competitors *(Intel)*. If the dominant company can establish an objective justification for its conduct, such as achieving a legitimate objective of protecting or enhancing a public interest, defending its commercial interest *(United Brands)* or generating efficiencies not otherwise available *(British Airways)*, assessed on the basis of proportionality, there will be no abuse. More recently important decisions have addressed concerns in digital markets, for example *Google Search (Shopping)*.

In the U.S., the prohibition contained in section 2 of the Sherman Act is against monopolization, being the use of monopoly power with an anticompetitive outcome. Monopoly power is power characterised as significant and durable market power. The Supreme Court has held that unlawful monopolization consists of two elements: the possession of monopoly power and the willful acquisition or maintenance of the power, as opposed to its development as a consequence of superior product, business acumen, or historic accident *(Grinnell Corp)*. The law requires proof of both monopoly power and exclusionary conduct *(Berkey Photo Inc v Eastman Kodak Co)*. The courts decide the meaning of the provision. Currently, as long as there is a business rationale for the conduct, it is likely to be judged efficiency-enhancing and allowed *(Verizon Communications Inc v Law Offices of Curtis V. Trinko)*. The U.S. prefers false negatives to false positives in antitrust intervention, which means that enforcement actions are likely to be less common than in the EU. See, for example *Verizon Communications Inc v Law Offices of Curtis V. Trinko 540 U.S. 398*.

National complements

The definition and commentary above focus on the EU/U.S. points of views, or/and the author's own jurisdiction. Readers are invited to complement these from their own legal system by proposing addendum of no more

150 words per country. These national complements contribute to building a more diverse and complete project. The complements are subject to review by the Editors and the primary author before inclusion.

China

China takes a European approach, focussing on elements associated with European Union law but with some additional considerations. Singapore also takes a European approach but focuses on total welfare rather than consumer welfare and expressly refers to predatory behaviour towards competitors as one type of conduct which might constitute an abuse of a dominant position.

Hong Kong, Australia and New Zealand

Hong Kong, Australia and New Zealand set thresholds for intervening in relation to unilateral market power although with differing approaches to purpose and effect and also arguably to thresholds of "substantial degree of market power". Australia and New Zealand focus less on market shares and more on barriers to entry in determining market power. Australia has an anticompetitive purpose or effect test, while New Zealand currently has an anticompetitive purpose test. Hong Kong has an object or effect test, similar to the Australian test. All three jurisdictions focus analysis on substantially lessening or harming competition.

Bibliography

WHISH, R. and BAILEY, D., *Competition Law*, 9th Edition, Oxford University Press, 2018

See also

Abuse of economic dependence, Boycott, Collective dominance, Discriminatory practices, Dominance (notion), Excessive prices, Exclusionary practice, Exclusivity clause, Exclusive purchasing agreement, Market power, Price discrimination, Price leadership, Monopoly, Predatory pricing, Self-preference

A

ABUSE OF ECONOMIC DEPENDENCE

Vassili MOUSSIS, Atsushi YAMADA
Anderson Mori & Tomotsune

■ Definition

Abuse of economic dependence, also known as an abuse of a superior bargaining position (ASBP), is a legal concept that addresses a situation where one party to a transaction that is in a position of relative strength to another abuses such position. In contrast to abusive conduct by dominant undertakings prohibited by provisions such as Article 102 TFEU, abuse of economic dependence does not require a dominant position in any market. Instead, it requires some sort of superior position relative to the counterparty of a transaction, and aims to protect the weaker party from the abuse of such position by the party in the superior position.

■ Commentary

In contrast to abuse of dominance whereby a party that holds a dominant position abuses such position vis-à-vis another party for its own benefit and hence falls foul of provisions such as Article 102 TFEU, for abuse of economic dependence to come into play there is no need for a position of dominance to exist. This becomes particularly relevant in situations where an abusive practice may have taken place but by a party that does not hold a dominant position in the market. A typical setting where this might occur is, for example as where a large scale retailer with buying power (e.g. a supermarket chain) takes advantage of its stronger bargaining position vis-à-vis its smaller suppliers and imposes unfavorable trading conditions on them. In order to address such situations, some jurisdictions have established separate rules from abuse of dominance provisions.

Recently a trend is developing whereby this type of provision is newly introduced, or existing legal provisions are re-interpreted, in order to address growing concerns in digital markets. Often in digital markets it is difficult to prove dominance, including because of the speed of technological evolution and market innovation, which often means that regulators find it very hard to grasp what the exact boundaries of the market might be.

A number of leading jurisdictions in Asia, including Japan, Korea and Taiwan have competition law provisions that provide for abuse of superior bargaining position which corresponds to abuse of economic dependence.

In Japan, Article 2(5) of the Anti-Monopoly Act (AMA) prohibits the abuse of a superior bargaining position, referring to a situation in which a party makes use of its superior bargaining position relative to another party to take, unjustly in light of normal business practices, certain acts that are further specified in the Act and its guidelines. The abuse provision has been applied typically to a mass retailer's abusive conduct against its suppliers, such as retrospective discounts, requiring monetary contribution or the practice of requesting the dispatching of employees from the suppliers when the retailer is opening a new or refurbished store, or even the practice of compelling the suppliers to purchase products unrelated to those stipulated in the contract. Along these lines, the Japan Fair Trade Commission (JFTC) has concluded by way of its commitment procedure an abuse case against Amazon for its acts against its supplier, and also filed for an emergency injunction against Rakuten, an e-commerce platform, regarding its acts against the merchants using the platform. Both cases suggest that the JFTC has developed a strong appetite toward applying the abuse provision against digital platform operators. Further, in 2019, the JFTC took a further step by issuing new guidelines that suggest it may enforce the ASBP provision in the context of the collection and use of personal information by digital platform operators.

In Korea, Article 45(1)(6) of the Monopoly Regulation and Fair Trade Act (MRFTA) defines abuse of a superior bargaining position as an enterpriser's act of unfairly taking advantage of his/her position in trade when trading with others, and the Korea Fair Trade Commission provides further details in its enforcement decree and guidelines. In Taiwan, the abuse of a superior bargaining provision will likely violate the general competition provisions such as Article 20, or the unfair trade provisions under Article 25, of the Taiwan Fair Trade Act. Further details are provided in the Principles Governing the Application of Article 25 of the Fair Trade Act.

In Europe, while the EU competition rules do not provide for a provision addressing abuse of bargaining position or economic dependence, at EU Member State level Germany, France, and Italy provide for such a provision, and there are member states such as Belgium that have recently added such a provision.

In Germany, section 20 of the Act against Restraints of Competition (Competition Act – GWB) prohibits conduct of undertakings with relative of superior market power, addressing situations of abuse of economic dependence. Until recently, relative market power was defined as where small or medium-sized enterprises as suppliers or purchasers of certain types of goods or commercial services depend on the undertaking in a way that sufficient and reasonable possibilities of switching to other undertakings do not exist. However, as part of an amendment effective 2021, the provision is no longer limited to small or medium-sized enterprises, and consideration would be given instead to whether there is a clear imbalance vis-a-vis the countervailing power of the other companies. In France, abuse of economic dependence is addressed in Article L. 420-2, paragraph 2, of the French Commercial Code, where abuse of the state of economic dependence of a client or supplier by an undertaking or group of undertakings is prohibited, if it is likely to affect the functioning or structure of competition. This abuse may include, but is not limited to, a refusal to sell, tie-in sales or certain discriminatory practices referred to in Articles L. 442-1 to L. 442-3 of the French Commercial Code. The provision explicitly requires three cumulative conditions: (1) the existence of a state of economic dependence of one company on another; (2) the abusive exploitation of this state; and (3) an actual or potential effect on the functioning or the structure of competition in the market (such effect must be sufficiently tangible). If, however, a company deliberately puts itself in a position of economic dependence it will not be able to claim the benefit of Article L. 420-2. In addition, for an infringement it is necessary to show the absence of an equivalent solution (e.g. that there is no alternative supplier). The French Competition Authority may open a case ex officio or upon a complaint from the victim of an abuse, as was the case for Apple, which was recently fined 1.1 billion euros for abusing the economic dependence of its commercial partners. In Italy, Article 9 of Law no. 192 of 18 June 1998 provides for the prohibition of abuse of the state of economic dependence. The law provides that a state of economic dependence exists when a business finds itself in a position to bring about excessive imbalances in the rights and obligations pertaining to its commercial relations with another business, and the assessment of economic dependence also accounts for any real possibility for the weaker party to find satisfactory alternatives elsewhere in the market.

In contrast to the above EU Member States' legislation, in the U.S. there are no equivalent provisions. In its response to a questionnaire prepared by the International Competition Network (ICN) in 2008, the U.S. responded that "U.S. antitrust and related laws and regulations do not prohibit acts referred to as 'abuse of superior bargaining position' under this questionnaire." In the questionnaire, "abuse of superior bargaining position" was defined as a concept that "typically includes, but is not limited to, a situation in which a party makes use of its superior bargaining position relative to another party with whom it maintains a continuous business relationship to take any act such as to unjustly, in light of normal business practices, cause the other party to provide money, service or other economic benefits. (For example, acts such as request for provision of supplier's labor without compensation and coercive collection of contributions, exercising buying power, are considered abusive in Japan.)" A party holding a "superior bargaining position does not necessarily have to be a dominant firm or firm with significant market power." In its 2019 Final Report of the Task Force on International Divergence of Dominance Standards, the American Bar Association's Antitrust Section confirmed that "exploitative abuse is not a recognized concept in the United States, and the regulation of prices is viewed as inconsistent with the competition principles on which antitrust is based. Indeed, the [U.S.] Supreme Court stressed in the Trinko case that 'The opportunity to charge monopoly prices – at least for a short period – is what attracts 'business acumen' in the first place; it induces risk taking that produces innovation and economic growth.'"

Bibliography

ABA Antitrust Law Section, Differences and Alignment: Final Report of the Task Force on International Divergence of Dominance Standards (2019), at 9, 61-80

Bailey D. and John, L. E. (eds.), *Bellamy and Child: European Union Law of Competition* (8th edn, Oxford University Press 2018), Chapter 10

Masako Wakui M. and Cheng T. K., Regulating Abuse of Superior Bargaining Position under the Japanese Competition Law: an Anomaly or a Necessity? *Journal of Antitrust Enforcement* (2015), 1-32

Task Force for Abuse of Superior Bargaining Position, Report on Abuse of Superior Bargaining Position (ICN 7th Annual Conference, 2009)

Whish, R. and Bailey, D., *Competition Law* (9th edn, Oxford University Press 2018), Chapter 2

See also

Abuse of dominant position, As-Efficient-Competitor (AEC), Dominance (notion), Discriminatory practices, Market power, Oligopoly, Price discrimination, Price leadership

A

ACCESS TO THE FILE

João OTÁVIO BACCHI GUTINIEKI
Cabanellos Advocacia

■ Definition

Access to the file is a right of the parties which guarantees the principle of equality of arms – based on the idea that every person is entitled to equal interest and respect by an authority – and the effective exercise of the right of defense through access to data and documents related to the procedure ("file"). Access to the file can also be given to third parties interested in the outcome of a certain conduct investigative procedure or merger, in order to influence the authority's decision or use it as a basis for other procedures. There is also the concern of protecting business secrets from disclosure, as well as investigations effectiveness and the competition policy as a whole.

■ Commentary

Brazil

The Brazilian Constitution (article 37) determines that transparency is one of the principles that govern the activities of public authorities. As a result, procedures, whether judicial or administrative, have public access as a rule, and secrecy as an exception. In the procedures related to competition investigations and control of structures (mergers) it is nodifferent. The Brazilian Competition Law (Law n. 12.529/11) contains several provisions regarding the confidentiality of the records and documents produced in proceedings before the competition authority. Article 49 of Competition Law provides that the *Conselho Administrativo de Defesa Econômica* (CADE), the Brazilian competition authority, will ensure the confidential treatment of documents, information and procedural acts necessary for the elucidation of the facts or required by the "interest of society". The sole paragraph of article 49 provides that parties may request confidential treatment of documents or information, in the time and manner defined in CADE's Statutes. With the establishment of an

Administrative Proceeding, the fourth paragraph of article 70, defines that the party being investigated is assured broad access to the Court's records, assuring the adversarial principle – that to each party involved in a procedure has been given the chance to affirm their rights and expose their arguments – and the exercise of the right of defense.

The Statutes of CADE regulate access to documents in richer detail, classifying the level of secrecy into four levels of access to records, information, data, communications, objects, and documents related to all sorts of administrative proceedings (article 49 of Statutes): (i) public, the regular rule, when it may be accessed by any persons; (ii) restricted access, when access is only granted to the party that presented the document/information, to investigated parties, and other persons according to the case authorized by CADE; (iii) confidential, when access is only granted to those authorized by CADE and to the government authorities responsible for issuing an opinion or decision; and (iv) under seal, when limited access is granted only by judicial order. The first paragraph of article 51 provides that the parties are granted full access to all documents considered in CADE's decision before the end of the discovery phase of administrative proceedings to impose sanctions for antitrust violations, confirming the provision of access to documents provided for in the Brazilian Competition Law.

European Union

The Charter of Fundamental Rights of the European Union (CFR) is an extremely relevant source for the procedural aspects of EU Competition Law. Article 41 of the CFR guarantees the citizen the right to good administration, including the "right to have his or her affairs handled impartially, fairly and within a reasonable time by the institutions, bodies, offices and agencies of the Union". The guarantees include the right to be heard before a decision is made, the obligation of the administration to give reasons for its decisions, and "the right of every person to have access to his or her file, while respecting the legitimate interests of confidentiality and of professional and business secrecy".

Access to a file in cases of investigation of anticompetitive conduct, such as cartels, is, as a rule, only given to the addressees of a statement of objections. According to article 27(2) of Regulation 1/2003: "the rights of defense of the parties concerned shall be fully respected in the proceedings. They shall be entitled to have access to the Commission's file, subject to the legitimate interest of undertakings in the protection of their business secrets". The same article provides that access does not extend to confidential information, internal Commission documents and communication between national competition authorities and the Commission. In merger procedures, article 18(3) of Council Regulation n. 139/2004 (Merger Regulation) provides that: "Access to the file shall be open at least to the parties directly involved, subject to the legitimate interest of undertakings in the protection of their business secrets".

Regarding the access of interested third parties to documents and antitrust leniency agreements (mainly for damages claims), it is important to note two cases, *Pfleiderer* (C-360/09) and *Donau Chemie* (C-536/11), from 2011 and 2013, respectively. Both cases involve access to documents and statements presented in the context of leniency programs, and bring the understanding that it was possible to grant access to these documents provided that the legal interests involved were considered by the national court. Contrary to the provisions of these two precedents, the Damages Directive (2014/104/EU), subsequent to the judgments, in the article 6(6) expressly prohibits national courts to order a party or a third party to disclose leniency statements and settlement submissions.

United States

The two United States government antitrust enforcement agencies are the Federal Trade Commission (FTC) and the Department of Justice Antitrust Division (DOJ). Each of the agencies has its own competencies and procedural rules. As a general rule, during the course of an investigation, the party or parties under investigation do not have access to the case file. But it is natural that the agencies share their concerns with potential defendants, as well as their general view and understanding of the investigated facts. They cannot share confidential information submitted by third parties.

While during the course of the investigations the parties have no access to the case file, the case file is disclosed just at the moment that the investigation becomes a filed case before a judicial (in the case of DoJ investigations) or administrative court (in case of FTC investigation). At this moment individuals external to the Agency may obtain access to the files. In federal court cases the U.S. Constitution and the Federal Rules of Civil Procedure (FRCP) guarantee an extensive review of the evidence that the agency has used to build the case. For administrative litigation, the FTC's Part 3 rules guarantees similar rights to the Federal Rules of Civil Procedure.

Finally, there are a diversity of rules that protect confidential information, mainly those obtained from third parties, as competitors, which the disclosure may directly affect the course of the investigation, the agencies' enforcement activities and policies, and expose business or industrial related information and secrets.

Bibliography

CAUFFMAN, C. and HAO, Q. (eds.), *Procedural Rights in Competition Law in the EU and China*, China-EU Law Series, Volume 3, Springer, 2016

FRANZ, W., *Handbook of EU Competition Law*, Springer, 2016

INGRID VANDENBORRE, I., GOETZ, T. and KAFETZOPOULOS, A., Access to File under European Competition Law, *Journal of European Competition Law & Practice*, Vol. 6, December 2015

RODGER, B. J. and MACCULLOCH, A., *Competition Law and Policy in the EU and UK*, Sixth edition, Routledge, 2022

See also

Akzo Procedure, Statement of Objections

A

ACTUAL COMPETITOR

Gonçalo ROSAS
Morais Leitão, Galvão Teles, Soares da Silva

Definition

An actual competitor is an undertaking which is active in the same relevant product, geographic and temporal market as another undertaking or undertakings. This should be contrasted with a potential competitor (see European Commission Guidelines on the applicability of Article 101 of the Treaty on the Functioning of the European Union to horizontal co-operation agreements, paragraph 10). Most systems of competition law define actual competitor by assessing the cross-elasticity of demand and supply, barriers to entry and the conditions of competition in the market. The concept of competitor is central in competition law systems because it is the starting point for further substantive analysis. The concept is relevant in order to ascertain *inter alia* whether an agreement between undertakings infringes antitrust rules, to find and assess a dominant position and the effects of an abuse or to review the impact of a merger.

Commentary

The relation between competing undertakings is at the heart of competition law. These relations are subject to increased scrutiny from antitrust agencies as, under certain conditions, they are susceptible to cause harm to competition and to consumers.

Agreements between actual and potential competitors are regarded as horizontal agreements, and as such they will be subject to different analysis as vertical and other agreements. Competition Authorities have specific guidelines and block exemption regulations for assessing these types of agreements.

The first step to define an actual competitor is to identify the relevant economic unit, considering the relevant agreement or conduct. Given the complex nature of the CJEU's case law on the concept of undertaking, defining the boundaries of the economic unit may be a difficult endeavor.

An agreement between two subsidiaries controlled by the same parent company does not fall within the scope of Article 101 TFEU given that it is deemed to be an agreement within the same undertaking and not *an agreement between undertakings*. However, in *Sumal*, the CJEU clearly affirmed that the concept of undertaking and corporate group may not necessarily coincide. According to the CJEU, the organization of groups of companies may be very different from one group to another (*Sumal*, paragraph 45), which means that the same parent company may be part of several economic units composed of itself and of different combinations of subsidiaries belonging to the same group of companies. The CJEU considered that the crucial factor to determine whether different legal persons within the same corporate group are part of the same economic unit is whether they exercise the same economic activity (*Sumal*, paragraphs 38-47).

Nonetheless, it remains elusive whether the economic activity criterion used in *Sumal* should only apply in similar cases (i.e., to hold liable a subsidiary for the parent's infringement) or whether this criterion should apply across the board. In other words, it is unclear whether the definition of undertaking remains the same for all competition law purposes or whether it should be understood as a variable concept, although the CJEU affirmed the concept of "undertaking" cannot have a different scope with regard to the imposition of fines by the Commission as compared to actions for damages (*Sumal*, paragraph 47).

The second step in defining an actual competitor, as the European Commission states in its Block Exemptions Regulations and Guidelines, is to identify the relevant market.

A similar approach is followed in the U.S. In the case *United States v. E. I. du Pont de Nemours & Co.*, the U.S. Supreme Court first defined the relevant market in order to assess the market power of Du Pont de Nemours. The DoJ's Horizontal Merger Guidelines establish that "*market definition allows the Agencies to identify market participants and measure market shares and market concentration*" (see Section 4).

The product and geographic markets are not the only ones that are relevant. Time or seasonal constrains may change the boundaries of a market. In merger cases involving energy producers in Portugal, the Portuguese Competition Authority admitted that the geographic market may be Iberian when there are no bottlenecks in the interconnections between Portugal and Spain, and national in scope if such bottlenecks exist to a significant extent.

Although, in some cases, it may be fairly obvious that the undertakings compete with one another, in other cases, this conclusion might be harder to reach and may require an in-depth breakdown of the undertakings' activities, and an analysis of the clients targeted by them and the elasticity of demand, their location or how they are supplied.

This analysis is relevant to characterize the type of agreement or merger as horizontal or to assess if a company has a dominant position and market power (*Generics UK and others vs. Competition and Markets Authority*, paragraph 127), providing thus an important context to assess a competition law issue (in the U.S., Case *City of N.Y. v. Group Health Inc.*, Discussion, Section I).

In markets with a high rate of innovation, although their structure is often restricted by the industrial and intellectual property rights, that may rapidly change due to new developments or entrants. In the *Bayer/Monsanto* merger, the European Commission recognized the parties as innovation competitors, as they developed overlapping lines of research with similar discovery concepts and pipeline projects targeting the same product markets that, if brought to the market, would compete head-to-head against each other. This conclusion had an impact in the analysis of competition post-transaction.

Actual competition can be distinguished from potential competition by the actual and active presence both in the product and geographic market of the competitor. A potential competitor is an undertaking that is likely, within a short period of time, to undertake the necessary additional investments or other necessary switching costs to enter the relevant market. Some authors claim that if an undertaking is already perceived as a competitive restraint, even if the entry is still to occur, it should already be treated as actual competitor. The focus on (actual) competitive restraints, whether or not they come from existing competitors or potential entrants, may help to assess the substantive impact of an agreement, conduct or merger on the conditions of competition (OECD Note on Potential Competition, p. 9).

Furthermore, not all competitors are born the same. Although two undertakings may be competitors, their market positioning (e.g., if they do not target the same customers) may indicate they are not close competitors. This factor also may help to calibrate competition concerns. In the merger review field, the European Commission states in its Horizontal Mergers Guidelines that the higher the degree of substitutability between the merging firms' products, the more likely it is that the merging firms will raise prices significantly.

The concept of closeness of competition and the relevance for finding anti-competitive effects is being debated in *CK Telecoms*: Advocate General Kokott disagreed in her Opinion with the General Court finding that the merging parties have to be "particularly close" competitors for the Commission to infer anti-competitive effects (*CK Telecoms Opinion*, paragraphs 115-125). The case is awaiting the decision of the European Court of Justice and it will help to densify the "*significant impediment to competition test*" in oligopolistic markets.

In the U.S., the FTC also considers the closeness of competition as an important criterion to assess the effects of a merger. In the *Otto Bock HealthCare North America* case, the FTC considered that a merger would produce significant unilateral effects even though the merging products are not each other's closest competitors (Section VII.B.2). The forthcoming launch of a new product by the target, deemed a close substitute to the one of the Otto Block, the acquirer, was also considered a relevant factor in the FTC's analysis.

Bibliography

WHISH, R. and BAILEY, D., *Competition Law* (10th end, Oxford University Press 2018), Chapter 1, Section 5 and Chapter 5, Section 4

Block Exemption Regulation on the application of Article 101(3) of the Treaty on the Functioning of the European Union to certain categories of research and development agreement, Article 1

European Commission Guidelines on the applicability of Article 101 of the Treaty on the Functioning of the European Union to horizontal co-operation agreements, paragraph 10

Horizontal Merger Guidelines of the U.S. Department of Justice and the Federal Trade Commission

OECD Background Note on Potential Competition (2021)

See also

Anti-competitive object or effect, Potential Competition

A

ADMINISTERED PRICES

Oles ANDRIYCHUK
Newcastle University

Definition

An administered price is one that is imposed by the state or a state institution in place of a price to be set by the market. It is a requirement imposed on undertakings by governments or other public authorities. Such prices are usually driven by the intentions of regulators to remedy/prevent market failures and similar situations, which are likely to lead to undesirable macroeconomic and non-economic consequences. The prices prescribed imperatively by the public authorities, obscure microeconomic analysis as they are driven by the incentives, which are hard to internalise into equilibrium modelling. The instances of administrated prices are common and hardly avoidable as they are usually legally valid and have strong societal legitimacy appeal. For competition law, administered prices are the exogenous factors, which are capable of changing the outcomes of the assessment of anticompetitive practices.

Commentary

Administered (regulated) prices are prices for goods and services imposed on undertakings by public authorities. Also, the term may refer to prices in oligopolistic markets not responding to short-run fluctuations – unlike genuinely market prices, which react to changes in demand and supply. In this sense, administered prices may (but do not necessarily have to) be seen as the instances requiring antitrust intervention. In the latter sense, the prices are imposed by oligopolies, not by public authorities. This line of reasoning is not considered in the present analysis.

One of the foundational assumptions in theories measuring the performance of economic competition is that prices for products and services are defined by internal market processes. Such a freedom of exchange is an essential condition, which allows making substantiated conclusions about the objective economic benefits of the transactions. The price, defined by the market supply and demand forces, is one of the central parameters of competition law, economics and policy. Clearly, no agreement and no transaction in the markets are driven and defined by the autonomous wills of the private agents exclusively. Numerous external constraints and factors always have some impact on the purity of the modeling. As long as these constraints to the freedom of exchange are minor, contextual and indirect, the prices are yet assumed to be free, and the external impact is internalised into the equation, allowing a meaningful assumption of the accuracy of the equilibrium analysis.

The situation becomes fundamentally different if prices for specific products and services become regulated by the government. Such practices are systemic in the countries with planned economy. These societies do not rely on competition as the main driving force of growth, innovation and income generation. Instead, the main coordination and distribution function is assigned to the public authorities. Economic competition is seen in such countries as either suboptimal or harmful outright, and as such not requiring any particular measuring. These jurisdictions are excluded from the present analysis. The discussion of the administered prices is important only for countries, in which such situation is not a rule but an exception from the ordinary approach to pricing. It is particularly relevant for the countries with hybrid elements of planned and market economy as such administered pricing may be used by the governments of these countries as the main mechanism of dirigistic interventions.

To a different extent, all economies have either specific situations or entire sectors, requiring an administration of prices by public authorities. This could be a prescription to keep a minimum price, prohibiting going below (as would be the case in instances of protecting small and medium size producers in the markets dominated by much bigger companies capable to decrease price without operating at a loss). In other situations, the regulators may, on the contrary, require keeping a maximum price, prohibiting going above (as would be the case with some natural monopolies, essential food supply or for example opportunistic price gouging during major societal turbulences). Unlike the previous scenario, capping the prices to an imposed maximum is a measure envisaged to benefit primarily not competitors but consumers. Formally, instances of both minimum and maximum price administration allow the markets to compete on price within the permitted parameters (selling at higher price in cases of minimum price requirements or at lower in cases of maximum price requirements). There are also situations when price is set in absolute terms, allowing no deviation from the prescribed nominal. This could be the case with assigning the price for a specific pharmaceutical product or any other product or service in specific cases of public interest. On the temporal dimension the measures of administrating prices may vary from being ad hoc to permanent.

The phenomenon of administered prices is different from a phonetically similar practice of price maintenance. The former concerns situations when prices are imposed on the market players by public authorities, while the latter is related to the same cap established by the market players themselves and imposed by a stronger market player on its economically weaker counteragents. The former is an external factor, which may be taken into consideration during competition law analysis. The latter constitutes one of the central economic problems addressed by competition law. Similarly, administered prices are different from the practice of price fixing, which constitutes a substance of anticompetitive agreement between market players, and alongside price maintenance is one of the most common instances of infringing the provisions of competition law. Price maintenance takes place vertically between producers and distributors. Price fixing takes place horizontally, between competitors. At the level of unilateral conduct, various forms of price discrimination constitute the core of all price-abusive practices.

There is a difference between administered prices imposed by a regulator charged with the task of doing so and prices as a result of competition law intervention. The former scenario concerns proactive price policy, aiming to regulate administratively a specific sector of the economy. The latter situation has a different rationale, aiming primarily at remedying the consequences of an anticompetitive conduct. These remedies are relatively rare, and the pecuniary aspects of these interventions are of the secondary nature. The primary purpose of this aspect of administered prices is bringing the infringement (or its consequences) to an end.

Administered prices are common in the EU Member States, and not so much in the U.S. In the context of the EU, the phenomenon has also an important implication on establishing and functioning of the Internal Market (ANODE, 2016), as it may hinder market integration as well as have direct impact on EU trade with third countries. Another layer of complexity is added by the instances of practicing price administration by the EU itself (e.g. "Roaming Regulation" or EU Common Agricultural Policy). Giving the strong interdependency between the goals of competition and market integration policies, the negative impact on the protection of either or both is often hard to distinguish.

If leading to or imposed in conjunction with an anticompetitive behaviour, administered prices usually serve as a circumstance mitigating the severity of competition infringement. The fact that the restriction is to a different degree linked with the state interference into the market process, may lead to the softening of the liability of the infringer. Particularly, if applied in conjunction with Art 4(3) TEU, imposing upon all EU Member States a duty of sincere cooperation. Depending on the level of autonomy, the undertaking is left with under a specific administered pricing order, the liability may shift from the undertaking to the Member State (Van Eycke v ASPA, 1988): the bigger the autonomy and the room for maneuver are left for the undertaking, the higher its liability would be; the stricter the public imperative, the softer the liability (API and Others, 2014).

Bibliography

David Storer, D. and Teljeur, E., "Regulated Prices: Is the Process Right? An Analysis of Administered Prices in South Africa", Executive Report for National Treasury of South Africa, 2003

Dunne, N., "Regulating Prices in the European Union", *Yearbook of European Law*, Vol. 37, No. 1, 2018, pp. 344–394

MacCulloch, A., "State Intervention in Pricing: An Intersection Of EU Free Movement and Competition Law", *European Law Review*, Vol. 42, No. 2, 2017, pp. 190–207

Stigler, G., "Administered Prices and Oligopolistic Inflation", *The Journal of Business* Vol. 35, No. 1, 1962, pp. 1–13

Vickers, J., "Regulation, Competition and the Structure of Prices", *Oxford Review of Economic Policy*, Vol. 13, No. 1, 1997, pp. 15–26

Consolidated version of the Treaty on European Union, OJ C 326, 2012

Consolidated version of the Treaty on the Functioning of the European Union, OJ C 326, 2012

"Price Controls and Competition Law During Covid-19 In Latin America" Report, 2020

Regulation 717/2007 of 27 June 2007 on roaming on public mobile telephone networks within the Community and amending Directive 2002/21/EC, OJ L171/32, 2007

Regulation 1308/2013 of 17 December 2013 establishing a common organisation of the markets in agricultural products and repealing Council Regulations (EEC) No 922/72, (EEC) No 234/79, (EC) No 1037/2001 and (EC) No 1234/2007, OJ L347/671, 2013

See also

Prices

A

ADVISORY COMMITTEE

Rachel BRANDENBURGER
APCO Worldwide

Definition

Within the EU Merger Regulation's framework for cooperation between the European Commission and Member States, the Advisory Committee on Concentrations provides the conduit for formal consultation between the Commission and Member States for mergers investigated by the Commission under the EU Merger Regulation. The Advisory Committee on Restrictive Practices and Dominant Positions plays a similar role in relation to antitrust investigations under Regulation 1/2003. That Advisory Committee can also act as a forum for discussing (but not deciding) antitrust cases that are being handled by Member State competition authorities and can be consulted on draft Commission block exemptions, notices and guidelines.

Commentary

The EU Merger Regulation (Merger Regulation) requires the European Commission (Commission) to "act in close and constant liaison with the competent authorities of the Member States". This is the basis for the Advisory Committee on Concentrations whose members consist of EU Member States' national competition authorities (NCAs).

The Merger Regulation provides a framework of cooperation between the Commission and NCAs and, within that framework, a specific role for the Advisory Committee. The Merger Regulation provides that "[t]he Commission and the competent authorities of the Member States should together form a network of public authorities, applying their respective competences in close cooperation, using efficient arrangements for information-sharing and consultation, with a view to ensuring that a case is dealt with by the most appropriate authority, in the light of the principle of subsidiarity and with a view to ensuring that multiple notifications of a given concentration are avoided to the greatest extent possible." The Commission's powers to request information and carry out inspections under the Merger Regulation may also be exercised in conjunction with Member States.

Specifically in relation to the merger investigation process, the Commission is required to "transmit to the competent authorities of the Member States copies of notifications within three working days and, as soon as possible, copies of the most important documents lodged with or issued by the Commission pursuant to this Regulation." This includes commitments that the merging parties offer to remedy any anti-competitive effects of their merger. The Commission has an overall obligation to conduct its investigation "in close and constant liaison" with the NCAs and the NCAs "may express their views upon those procedures".

The Commission must consult the Advisory Committee on concentrations before taking a decision in relation to the outcome of a merger investigation. This applies to Commission decisions to approve, approve subject to commitments or prohibit a merger. The Advisory Committee consists of representatives of the NCAs from each Member State. Member States may appoint up to two representatives, one of whom must be competent in competition law. NCAs "should make [their] best efforts to attend Advisory Committee meetings".

Soon after the initiation of a phase two, in-depth investigation and subject to confirmation that no Member State objects, the Commission appoints a rapporteur from one of the Member States, to facilitate the Advisory Committee's preparation for, and discussions at, Advisory Committee meetings in relation to each investigation. Advisory Committee representatives attend Oral Hearings and subsequently also a meeting convened at the invitation of, and chaired by, the Commission to consider a summary of the case, together with the most important documents relating to the investigation including Commission decisions adopted during the investigation, the statement of objections and legal and economic replies thereto, the Hearing Officer's report and any commitments offered by the notifying parties, together with a preliminary draft of the decision to be taken by the Commission. NCAs may also have access to the Commission's file should they wish. The rapporteur "has the function of stimulating a probing discussion of the Commission's draft decision at the meeting of the Advisory Committee."

NCAs are permitted to attend Advisory Committee meetings in person or by video-conference or if "the issues involved are not generally regarded as substantively or procedurally contentious" by telephone. Since the Covid pandemic, NCAs may also attend Oral Hearings remotely as well as in person. EFTA States may also be invited to attend Oral Hearings and Advisory Committee meetings.

The Advisory Committee is required to deliver a single opinion on the Commission's draft decision. The Advisory Committee may take a vote, if necessary. The vote is determined by a simple majority of the Advisory Committee member present and voting (excluding abstentions). NCAs usually support the Commission's draft decision; occasionally there may be a few negative votes or abstentions. The Advisory Committee may deliver its opinion even if some NCAs are not represented at the meeting. Indeed, it is unusual for an Advisory Committee meeting to be attended by all NCAs. The opinion is not binding on the Commission: the Commission must take "the utmost account of the opinion" delivered by the Advisory Committee and must "inform the Committee of the manner in which its opinion has been taken into account". The opinion is required to be delivered in writing and appended to the Commission's draft decision.

The Commission is required to communicate the Advisory Committee's opinion, with the Commission's decision, to the addressees of its decision. The Commission is also required to make the Advisory Committee's opinion, as well as its own decision, public – after having made appropriate redactions to protect business secrets in respect of both documents.

In contrast with Commission decisions, Advisory Committee opinions are usually only a couple of pages in length. They usually record which Member State was the rapporteur in a particular investigation, how many Member States participated in the opinion (without revealing the identities of those Member States), and how many Member States agreed with the Commission's findings on jurisdiction, geographic and product market definitions, competitive assessment, remedies and conclusion in a particular investigation (also without revealing the identities of the Member States concerned). If a Member State abstains or votes against the Commission's decision, that is also recorded (without identification of the Member State).

The Advisory Committee on Restrictive Practices and Dominant Positions plays a similar role, is constituted in a similar fashion, and operates in a similar fashion in relation to antitrust investigations under Regulation 1/2003.

In addition and in contrast with the Merger Regulation's one-stop shop, under the decentralised application of EU competition law set up by Regulation 1/2003, the Advisory Committee is also able "to act as a forum for discussing cases that are being handled by the competition authorities of the Member States, so as to help safeguard the consistent application of the Community competition rules." Thus, if an NCA requests, the Commission must include on the Advisory Committee's agenda cases that are being investigated by an NCA under Articles 101 or 102 of the Treaty for the Functioning of the European Union. The Commission may also do so on its own initiative. In either case, the Commission must inform the NCA. However, the Advisory Committee must not issue opinions on cases being investigated by NCAs.

The Advisory Committee may also discuss general issues of EU competition law. It can also serve as a forum for the discussion of case allocation and be consulted on draft Commission block exemptions, notices and guidelines.

Bibliography

Commission notice on cooperation within the Network of Competition Authorities

Council Regulation (EC) No 139/2004 of 20 January 2004

Council Regulation (EC) No 1/2003 of 16 December 2002

Working arrangements for the functioning of the Advisory Committee on Concentrations

Working arrangements for the functioning of the Advisory Committee on Restrictive Practices and Dominant Positions

See also

Abuse of dominant position, Merger

A

AGENT

Alison JONES
King's College London

■ Definition

An agent is one who acts on behalf of another, the principal, either generally or in relation to a particular issue. An agency relationship exists where it is agreed that one person, the agent, may act behalf of another, the principal, either generally or in relation to a particular issue. In commerce, principals frequently engage agents to act on their behalf in return for a commission or other remuneration. In some agency relationships, agents have power to affect their principals' legal relations. For example, a supplier of goods may engage a commercial agent to negotiate and/or conclude sales agreements on its behalf. An important issue in competition law is whether, and if so when, an agent forms an integral part of its principal's business, so that arrangements between them fall outside of the scope of antitrust laws governing joint conduct between independent firms. This question has become increasingly significant as more suppliers sell online, via platforms following an agency model.

■ Commentary

Competition law systems typically draw a sharp distinction between concerted and independent conduct, with the former being viewed as more fraught with antitrust risk than unilateral conduct. The U.S. and EU systems thus contain broad prohibitions of agreements, or other collusive arrangements, between independent entities that restrain trade or restrict competition (Section 1 Sherman Act and Article 101 TFEU respectively). Neither provision extends, however, to wholly unilateral conduct, or the internal workings, of a single firm, for example arrangements between an employer and employee or other persons within a firm, or between a parent and its wholly-owned subsidiary. In the U.S., the Supreme

Court has held that since parents and their wholly owned subsidiaries always have a unity of purpose, they are incapable of conspiring with one another in an antitrust sense (the activity is viewed as that of a single enterprise, see *Copperweld Corp v Independence Tube Corp* (1984)). In the EU, where a subsidiary has no economic independence or freedom to determine its course of action on the market, but carries out the instructions issued by its controlling parent, the entities are treated as part of a single "economic unit" and agreements between them fall outside the scope of Article 101 (see *Viho Europe v Commission* (1996)).

Similarly, it has been held that arrangements between a principal and agent may fall outside of Section 1 and Article 101. The U.S. Supreme Court has held that a manufacturer that simply consigns its products through a genuine agent, disposing of its goods directly to customers and establishing the price at which it sells the product, acts unilaterally (see *United States v General Electric* (1926)). Consequently, the supplier is able to dictate the price at which the agent sells, and the territory into which and customers to whom it can sell, without creating a conspiracy. In this respect, the agent acts as its representative and an integral part of the principal's business rather than as a conspirator. Although the doctrine has had less prominence and importance since *Sylvania* (1977) and *Leegin* (2007), and their reversal of the per se prohibition of vertical territorial and price restraints (so requiring them to be appraised under a fuller rule of reason analysis), it still applies (*Valuepest* (4th Cir 2009)).

In the EU, the close economic links existing in an agency relationship may also mean that an agent is so closely interrelated with its principal that the relationship is characterised by "economic unity". Where an agent operates as an integral part of its principal's undertaking, agreements between them relating to the market on which the agent offers the principal's goods or services to potential customers, fall outside of Article 101(1) (see *Confederación Española de Empresarios de Estaciones de Servicio v Compañia Española de Petróleos (CEES)* (2006) and *CEPSA Estaciones de Servicio SA v LV Tobar e Hojos SL (CEPSA)* (2008)).

In addition to impacting on the substantive reach of Section 1 and Article 101, the doctrine also enables liability and responsibility for an antitrust infringement by an agent to be attributed to its principal in certain circumstances; in the U.S. where the agent(s) acts within the scope of apparent authority (U.S. Supreme Court, *American Society of Mechanical Engineers Inc v Hydrolevel Corp* (1982)) and in the EU where the agent forms part of the same economic unit as the parent (EU General Court, *Minoan Lines v Commission* (2003)).

Given the significant consequences that flow from the doctrine, a crucial issue is how to identify genuine agency agreements and to distinguish them from ones between independent entrepreneurs. It is clear in both the

U.S. and EU that it is not the parties' characterisation of the arrangement (the form) which is determinative (so sham agency arrangements are not able to evade application of the antitrust rules). Rather, in the U.S., it is a question to be determined by the trier of fact taking account of a range of factors, including, whether the supplier retains title to, and control of, the products, whether the supplier retains risk of loss, who insures the products and whether consignment is used as a veneer for a vast anticompetitive scheme (see *Simpson v Union Oil Co* (1964)). Likewise, in the EU, it is the "economic reality" that is decisive. Although some early cases suggest agents must act as "auxiliary organs" of the principal (and constitute independent entities if acting for a number of principals, see *VZW Vereniging van Vlaamse Reisbureaus v VZW Sociale Dienst van de Plaatselijke en Gewestelijke Overheidsdiensten* (1987)), modern cases focus on the question of whether the agent bears more than a negligible proportion of the financial and commercial risks linked to sales of goods to third parties (CEES and CEPSA).

The question of how broadly the agency concept extends is important to the question of whether arrangements in digital markets between suppliers and platforms (such as Amazon, or e-Bay,) are caught by Section 1 or Article 101. Although several publishers agreed in settlement arrangements to terminate their distribution agreements for electronic books using an agency, as opposed to a wholesale or reseller, model, with Apple (and other retailers) following European Commission and DOJ investigations (see *e-books* (2013) and *United States v Apple* (2d Cir, 2015), there is no explicit ruling in either the U.S. or EU on how such distribution agreements are to be treated. The core question arising in each of these cases was whether the publishers engaged with Apple, in a horizontal concerted practice or conspiracy to raise retail prices for e-books. The question of whether the vertical agreements relating to sales on online platforms would fall within the scope of Article 101 or Section 1 did not therefore arise. Nonetheless, applying the principles set out in the cases, it seems possible that an arrangement between a supplier and a platform could constitute a "genuine" agency one falling outside the reach of Section 1 or Article 101 where, for example, ownership of the products/services is not passed to the platform (the platform does not buy products from suppliers for resale), where contracts concluded are formed between the supplier and customer, and where the platform does not bear any of the risks related to the sale or provision of the goods or services, but receives a commission or remuneration for concluded contracts. If this is the case, some have argued that the antitrust laws may have a "platform gap", immunising potentially restrictive distribution arrangements from scrutiny under these provisions. This has led some to call of a modification or reinterpretation of agency rules.

Bibliography

Akman, P., "Online Platforms, Agency, and Competition Law: Mind the Gap" (2020) 43(2) *Fordham International Law Journal* 209

Jones, A., Sufrin, B. and Dunne, N., *Jones and Sufrin's EU Competition Law: Text, Cases, and Materials* (Oxford University Press, 7th edn, 2019), Chapters 4 and 11

Zhang, A. H., "Toward an Economic Approach to Agency Agreements" (2013) 9 *Journal of Competition Law and Economics* 553

See also

Absolute territorial protection, Distribution agreement, Vertical agreement, Vertical restraints (restrictions)

A

AGREEMENT (NOTION)

Liyang HOU
Shanghai Jiao Tong University

Definition

An (anti-competitive) agreement is one of three classic types of monopolistic conduct (together with abusing dominance and anti-competitive mergers) prohibited under competition law. Article 16 of China's Anti-monopoly Law (AML) defines anti-competitive agreements as "agreements, decisions or other concerted practices that exclude or limit competition", which is similar to the EU and the USA. The illegality of anti-competitive agreements lies in their unique structure, namely collusion. Agreements, which must involve two or more independent firms, are different from abuse of dominance that is unilateral in nature, and also different from anti-competitive mergers that aim to form one single firm in the end.

Commentary

Anti-competitive agreements took many forms in history, with most notable examples being cartels and trusts. The objective of such agreements is to limit competition between participants involved in the agreements. Common methods include fixing prices, controlling production, sharing markets, and boycotting. This notion is so important to competition law that many countries use anti-competitive agreements to denote competition law, such as antitrust law in the USA and federal cartel office (Bundeskartellamt) in Germany. Anti-competitive agreements catch most attention of competition authorities. For example, China has enforced its Anti-monopoly Law since August 2008. Till the end of 2021, Chinese competition authorities have adopted in total 407 decisions, including 263 in relation to anti-competitive agreements, 93 on abuse of dominance, and 51 blocking or conditionally approving merger notifications. Of those, anti-competitive agreements constitute 64.6%. In terms of the number of cases, anti-competitive agreements are certainly more important than abusing dominance and merger control.

Anti-competitive agreements first caught social attention at the end of the nineteenth century. However, the original purpose was not so much to limit competition, but to establish a self-saving solution among a group of firms in order to jointly get through economic crisis. Therefore, anti-competitive agreements were initially considered positive to the society, as they may stabilize prices and employment. However, it was soon discovered that anti-competitive agreements can significantly impair the market mechanism, thereby bringing more bad than good. Although legislative attempts were initiated more or less at a similar time on both sides of the Atlantic, the Sherman Antitrust Act adopted in the USA in 1890 was the first modern competition law to govern anti-competitive agreements. With the proliferation of competition laws, anti-competitive agreements are considered illegal under all systems of competition law.

Competition law differentiates two types of anti-competitive agreements: horizontal and vertical. Horizontal agreements refer to anti-competitive agreements directly agreed between competitors, or firms on the same relevant market. Vertical agreements are agreed between firms in neighboring levels on the same production chain, or in the upstream and downstream markets. The AML dedicates different articles to horizontal agreements and vertical agreements. Article 17 of the AML governs horizontal agreements, and non-exhaustively enlists five examples of horizontal agreements: pricing fixing; quantity limitation; market allocation; jointly restraint on new technology; and boycotts. Article 18 of the AML deals with vertical agreements, and give two examples, namely fixing retail prices and imposing minimum retail prices. The division of horizontal-vertical agreements can also be observed in the EU and the USA. For example, the European Commission adopted the Guidelines on the applicability of Article 101 of the Treaty on the Functioning of the European Union to horizontal cooperation agreements (OJ C 11/1, 14 January 2011), and the Guidelines on Vertical Restraints (OJ C 130/1, 19 May 2010).

The division between horizontal and vertical agreements is not so important by itself, but is relevant for competition assessment. Since the adoption of the Sherman Antitrust Act, the USA courts after *Standard Oil* (1911) have gradually developed two distinct approaches for competition assessment for agreements, i.e. per se illegal and rule of reason. Agreements subject to per se illegality are assumed to be illegal in an abstract manner. In comparison, those subject to rule of reason must be evaluated by the pro-competitive side and the anti-competitive side, in conjunction with the concrete facts in a particular case. Such a difference also exists in the EU (*Société Technique Minière*, 1966), under the terms of restriction of competition by object (equivalent to per se illegal) and by effect (rule of reason).

The distinction between per se illegal and rule of reason is not expressly included in the provisions of the AML. Chinese justice in the early cases mistakenly required all agreements to be analyzed under the rule of reason. This can be observed in *Shenzhen Anti-pest Association* (2012). The High Court of Guangdong Province reviewed a pricing fixing decision made by the Anti-pest Association in Shenzhen for its members. The court maintained that the decision was not an anti-competitive agreement because the market shares of all the participants were only about 22.32%, and hence could not affect competition in a significant way. This was corrected by the Supreme Court of China in the Provision on Several Issues in the Trial of Civil Dispute Cases Arising from Monopolistic Conduct (Judicial Interpretation 2020 Nr. 19). Article 7 of the provision requires defendants to prove the anti-competitive effect of the disputed matter falling into Article 17 of the AML. This arrangement essentially makes the analysis closer to per se illegal. So far in China, all the exemplified agreements are regarded per se illegal, and non- exemplified agreements are handled under rule of reason. This practice is comparable with the USA and the EU. Nevertheless, one difference still remains that China and the EU considers retail price maintenance as per se illegal while the USA puts it into the rule of reason category after *Leegin* (2007).

Agreements can restrain competition in one way or another. However, it is not the purpose of competition law to prohibit all agreements without regard to the extent of limiting competition. Competition law only prohibit agreements that substantially or significantly limit competition. As such, many jurisdictions adopt guidelines (block exemptions) to exclude from their applicable scope agreements that limit competition in a non-significant way. This is normally done by reference to market shares of the participants. The less the market share, the more likely it is for the agreement to be exempted. For example, China has included exemption directly into Article 18 of the AML in 2022.

In addition to block exemptions, agreements can also be exempted on a case-by-case basis. Under Article 20 of the AML, the beneficiary must prove the agreements, though limiting competition, can promote technologies or new products, improve quality, production costs and efficiency, and protect social public interests (e.g. energy saving, environmental protection and rescue relief). In addition, they also have to establish that the agreement would not significantly limit competition, and can allow consumers a fair share of the resulting benefit. Similar arrangements can also be observed under Article 101 of the Treaty of Functioning of the European Union.

Bibliography

BORK, R., "The Rule of Reason and the Per Se Concept: Price Fixing and Market Division", (1965) 74 *Yale Law Journal* 775

GERBER, D., *Law and Competition in Twentieth Century Europe: Protecting Prometheus*, Oxford 2003, Chapter 2

HOU, L., "Crossover in Categorical Analysis of Antitrust Jurisprudence: From the Perspective of Boycott", (2016) 4 *Peking University Law Journal* 1039

JONES, A., BRENDA SUFRIN, B. and DUNNE, N., *EU Competition Law: Text, Cases, and Materials*, Oxford 2019, Chapter 4

LI, J., "Misunderstanding and Clarification of the Application of Horizontal Agreements", (2014) 3 *Jurist* 128)

See also

Negative clearance, Nullity, Pay-for-delay, Price signalling

A

AI COLLUSION (ALGORITHM)

Justin JOHNSON
Cornell University

Daniel SOKOL
USC Gould School of Law

Definition

AI collusion means collusion in the presence of certain market features that are commonly associated with computers in general or algorithms. AI collusion also refers to how algorithms may learn to collude as distinct from humans, putting aside issues related to price monitoring or the ability to rapidly change prices. The idea is that algorithms may use different processes than humans in setting prices or learning about the market environment. Finally, AI collusion refers to the intersection of collusion by humans and machines, such as when market participants use an algorithm and it is designed to limit competition, perhaps serving a role in a hub-and-spoke conspiracy.

Commentary

Increasingly, competition authorities are concerned with the different facets of AI-related collusion. Actual cases have thus far been rare. Public discussion by a number of authorities such as the U.S. Department of Justice Antitrust Division, French and German Competition Authorities, and the Canadian Competition Bureau all have announced increased focus on such issues but all also show some skepticism.

AI collusion research remains in its nascent stages. Assuming that it is possible to infer agreement for purposes of antitrust liability, AI collusion raises new possible mechanisms to create collusion. However, when used as a mechanism to detect collusion via screens, AI can help to solve collusion problems. This is particularly true for certain industries that are more prone to collusion for structural reasons or where certain patterns of behavior may be more likely to yield results with an investment in AI screening technology. Overall, the literature on AI collusion has focused on theory and policy arguments rather than on empirics. Nevertheless, the study of AI collusion is significant.

It has long been thought that easy price monitoring coupled with the ability to rapidly change prices may foster collusion, even without the involvement of computers. However, AI may reasonably represent an extreme case in which prices are observed and adjusted in real time, faster than humans are able to operate. Because of the amount of data, it might be possible for collusion to be "hidden in plain sight" (such as coordinated as part of massive amounts of public information so that it is difficult to observe the collusive signals), which makes detection of collusion more difficult.

The interaction between human and computer may lead to harmful outcomes and there have been examples of humans designing algorithms with collusive intent or as part of a hub and spoke conspiracy, such as in the Topkins and Eturas cases in the United States and EU. Further, we might imagine that there might be algorithms programmed to elicit or teach cooperative behavior in competing players, be they humans or algorithms. For instance, an algorithm might be intentionally programmed to lead the market to higher prices in some manner, or to target punishments towards firms that lower their prices. In these cases, the algorithm is the agent of a human designer, who has a particular collusive desire in mind.

There is also the concern that algorithms, even if not explicitly programmed to collude as such, may learn over time to do so. Increasingly, academic work has moved beyond pure theory where AI that is not explicitly programmed to collude nonetheless ultimately sets supranormal prices. Although there are different types of learning that algorithms could employ, experimental work shows what might happen when algorithms set prices. Calvano, Calzolari, Denicolò, and Pastorello (2020) study collusion by (Q-learning) AI algorithms in a logit model of differentiated products. The algorithms they deploy are not programmed as such to collude. The algorithms interact with each other repeatedly, and the outcome of this process is prices that are elevated compared to theoretical predictions of non-collusive behavior. These collusive outcomes are supported using reward-and-punishment schemes. Klein (2021) also studies the strategies algorithms learn to utilize in a setting where firms selling homogeneous products take turns changing prices, and finds Edgeworth price cycles supporting supranormal profits.

Johnson, Rhodes, and Wildenbeest (2023) ask whether a retail marketplace platform, on which product prices are set by (third-party) sellers' algorithms, can "regulate" the market and fight against collusive outcomes, thereby intensifying competition between the algorithms and lowering prices. They find that strategic use of demand-steering policies by the marketplace, in particular policies that reward low prices with more exposure to consumer demand, can shape the learning of the algorithms and thus shape the final pricing strategies of the algorithms. Such policies can make collusion harder for the algorithms to sustain, so that lower prices arise, benefiting consumers. Under some circumstances, these same policies may also benefit the platform. Salcedo (2015) shows that collusive behavior may occur when algorithms can "decode" rival algorithms and when changing an algorithm takes time. Here the basic idea is that such conditions allow for a form of price commitment and communication of that intent, which can lead to collusion. Observe that this collusion might occur even if it is possible to change prices very rapidly, because the design of the algorithms can limit the types of pricing decisions that are made.

Brown and MacKay (2023) also examine how algorithms can serve as commitment devices. More precisely, they consider firms that compete not directly in prices but in algorithms which are in turn potentially functions of observables such as market prices. One possibility is that firms use this commitment power to soften competition, leading to higher prices. Related to this idea is that if one firm is more sophisticated than the other, in that it can more rapidly change prices, then the firm that is less sophisticated may gain by acting as a price leader. This means the less sophisticated firm sets a higher price than it might otherwise, trusting that the more sophisticated firm will respond with its own high price. These authors also provide some empirical evidence supportive of their theories.

Bibliography

Brown, Z. Y., and MacKay, A., 2023. "Competition in Pricing Algorithms." *American Economic Journal: Microeconomics*, 15 (2): 109-56

Calvano, E., Calzolari, G., Denicolò, V., and Pastorello, S., 2020. "Artificial Intelligence, Algorithmic Pricing, and Collusion." *American Economic Review*, 110 (10): 3267-97

Johnson, J. P., Rhodes, A., Wildenbeest, M., 2023. "Platform Design When Sellers Use Pricing Algorithms." *Econometrica*, 91, (5): 1841-1879

Klein, T., 2021. "Autonomous algorithmic collusion: Q-learning under sequential pricing." *RAND Journal of Economics*, 52(3): 538-558

Salcedo, B. (2015), Pricing Algorithms and Tacit Collusion, Working Paper, University of Pennsylvania, available at http://brunosalcedo.com/docs/collusion.pdf

See also

Artificial Intelligence, Collusion, Digital Markets Act (DMA)

A

AKZO PROCEDURE

Raluca ONUFREICIUC
University Paris-Panthéon-Assas

■ Definition

The term Akzo Procedure emerged as a direct consequence of a significant ruling delivered by the European Court of Justice in the case of Akzo Chemie BV and Akzo Chemie U.K. Ltd. v. Commission ([1986] E.C.R., 1965). This ruling compels the European Commission ("EC") to establish a distinctive set of procedures applicable in instances where a party seeks access to information submitted to the Commission by a third party.

■ Commentary

This procedural rule established by the European Court of Justice ("ECJ"), which was also inserted into the mandate of the hearing officer, concerns the disclosure of confidential documents or business information by the EC. In accordance with this rule, if the party that submitted the information requests that the information be regarded as commercially important (either as a trade secret or other confidential data), the EC must formally notify the company of its plan to disseminate information and the rationale for such action. Seen as a proactive step, this notification provides the submitting party with an opportunity to express any objections regarding the proposed disclosure.

In this sense, if the EC determines that the information is not protected and can be shared despite the company's objections, it is obliged to provide a rational conclusion. The company concerned is notified of this decision and has the option to contest the Commission's assessment by initiating legal proceedings before the European Court of First Instance.

The applicants (Akzo Chemie BV and Akzo Chemie UK Ltd, part of the Akzo Group) argued that before proceedings were concluded there should be a right of action for annulment against such a measure. The process could take a while, and it might even conclude without a decision on the grounds of the case (Her, 1987, p. 273). Therefore, where the parties' right to protection of their business secrets had been wilfully violated, they should have been able to pursue their claim to legal recourse (Akzo Opinion, paragraph 1). [this previous sentence is very wordy and thus not clear- needs to be rewritten] They invoked a breach of the obligation of professional secrecy laid down in Article 214 of the European Economic Community Treaty ("EEC Treaty") [Article 339 of the Treaty on the Functioning of the European Union ("TFEU")], Article 20 (2) of Regulation No. 17 First Regulation implementing Articles 85 and 86 of the Treaty (Article 28 of Regulation 1/2003 on the implementation of the rules on competition laid down in Articles 101 and 102 of the TFEU) and Article 20 (1) of Regulation 17 (Article 27 of Regulation 1/2003) (Whish & Bailey, 2018, p. 85). In essence, the primary challenge resided in the necessity of balancing confidentiality and business secret protection with file access. In this regard, Article 27 of Regulation No. 1/2003 is meant to prevent any abuse on the part of a party hiding under the guise of confidentiality stating that "nothing… shall prevent the Commission from disclosing and using information necessary to prove an infringement".

In delivering his opinion, Mr. Advocate General Lenz stated that if the application had been declared admissible, it would have created confusion between the administrative procedure and the judicial proceedings taking into consideration that the applicants' arguments in regard to admissibility were closely related to the question whether the documents were or not covered by the obligation of professional secrecy (Lenaerts, 2006. p.1475-1477; Coutrelis & Giaccob, 2006). In that sense, he noted that it would have been premature to undertake a judicial review in that respect as the administrative procedure was still in progress creating a case of incompatibility with the division of powers between the EC and CJEU. From a legal point of view, he emphasized that the EC had weighed various interests of the two parties concerning "the protection of professional secrecy, the applicants' interest in protecting their business secrets, the intervener's need for information for the purposes of the hearing and the duty of effective supervision to ensure compliance with the competition rules of the EEC Treaty" (Akzo Opinion, paragraph 2).

Considering it a "pure factual step", and not a special procedure, AG Lenz underlined that the EC established the legal boundary between the applicants' right to confidentiality of their business documents and the intervener's (Engineering & Chemical Supplies – ECS) right to information underlining that "the transmission of the relevant documents to ECS and the latter's observations thereon had advanced and accelerated the investigation of the case". In addition, he stated that the Court had held that when acts or decisions were adopted through a multi-stage procedure, especially when they were the result of an internal procedure, they could only be reviewed if they were measures that definitively established the authorities' position at the end of the procedure, rather than measures that were meant to be temporary steps leading up to the final decision (IBM, paragraph 10).

Even though the EC made reference to the regulations that govern anti-dumping actions, which in its opinion were equivalent and the judgement of Timex Corporation and Others v Council and Commission (where the Court expressly emphasized that "the principle of confidential treatment of information must be interpreted in such way that the right provided by Article 7 (4) (a) of Regulation No 3017/79 were not deprived of their substance"), in Akzo judgement the Court stated that the EC must have given the company a chance to file a lawsuit before it and in this way have stopped the documents in question from being disclosed, given the extremely serious harm that could have arisen from improperly communicating documents to a competitor (see also Hercules Chemicals NV v Commission of the European Communities).

Bibliography

Coutrelis, N., Giacobbo Peyronnel, V., Access to the file: A practioners' point of view, May 2006, *Concurrences* N° 2-2006, Art. N° 850, pp. 66-78

Ehr, T. G., The European Commission's ECS/Akzo Standard for Predatory Pricing in the E.E.C.: Deterrence or Disorder?, 17 *Ga. J. Int'l & Compar. L.* 271 (1987)

Lenaerts, K., Some Thoughts on Evidence and Procedure in European Community Competition Law, 30 *Fordham Int. Law* 5 (2006)

OECD Working Party No. 3 on Co-operation and Enforcement Access to the case file and protection of confidential information – Note by the European Union, DAF/COMP/WP3/WD(2019)44

Whish, R. and Bailey, D., *Competition Law* (9th end, Oxford University Press 2018), Chapter 3

See also

Access to the file, Hearing officer, Legal privilege

A

AMICUS CURIAE

Georges VALLINDAS
European Court of Justice

Definition

Amicus Curiae stands for "friend of the court", also known in some jurisdictions as a "third-party intervention", that is to say someone who is not a party to the litigation, but who intervenes in the proceedings to enlighten the sitting judges and influence the outcome of a lawsuit involving matters of public interest by providing their external analysis regarding questions of law or fact in their area of expertise. The entity assuming this role can be a Governmental representative, a public institution or agency, an interest group established or not as an NGO, a company, a law firm, a university professor that believes that the court's decision may affect its interests.

Commentary

Amicus Curiae, an expression whose first known use is dated in the early 17th century UK, is a concept that authorities and courts have carefully avoided to strictly determine the perimeters and conditions justifying its use. The Amicus is not a litigating party, provides information on areas of law that the court regards as complex and beyond its expertise, and can also represent third party interests that could be ignored under adversarial court systems.

The practice of submitting *Amicus Curiae* briefs is well established in common law jurisdictions, has become common practice within international cooperation organizations, within arbitral tribunals in matters of investment arbitration and is largely used in competition cases in the U.S. and more recently in the European Union. It is important to note that civil law jurisdictions do not have a tradition in using such an instrument and its introduction is mostly recent.

In the U.S. antitrust enforcement of the last decades, it is extremely interesting to notice that concerning Foreign

States' Amicus Curiae participation, the European Commission emerges as the most frequent Amicus filer in front of U.S. Courts, followed by Canada and Japan. So, it should not come as a surprise that this instrument was progressively also introduced in EU Competition Law enforcement on the initiative of the same EU institution.

Why did the use of Amicus briefs in antitrust cases flourish in the U.S.? The main characteristic of the U.S. antitrust system, as observed from abroad and more specifically from the EU, is the fact all decisional power relies in the hands of Judges and not the governmental antitrust agencies. Non-expert judges are called, since the Sherman Act, to decide complex technical and economical questions relating to industrial organization. The traditional methods of decision-making based on precedent, analogy, intuition and considerations of morality and efficiency have quickly lagged behind the increasing needs of antitrust litigation.

That is where Rule 37 of SCOTUS, referring to the year 1937 codified rules about amicus participation, started to play an important role, allowing Justices to look for technical help in understanding economic theory and interpreting empirical data on competition. Unsurprisingly, these amicus briefs receive considerable attention from the Court and influence its opinions. The Court's increased interest in amicus arguments coincided with the rise of legal realism, which rejected the idea that judges discover law as a scientist discovers physical properties of the universe. As the Court began to realize its role to be policy making, access to information about the effects of that policy became necessary to make rules responsive to social needs.

Formally, an amicus in the U.S. must get permission from either the parties or the Court to file a brief, but the Court's current practice is to grant nearly all motions for leave to file as amicus curiae when consent is denied by a party. As a result, ninety-five percent of cases filed before the Supreme Court between 1996 and 2003 included at least one amicus brief while the influence of Amicus briefs on Supreme Court decisions is considered significant and often explicitly cited in the judgment or a dissenting opinion. (*Omari Scott Simmons, Picking Friends from the Crowd: Amicus Participation as Political Symbolism, 42 Conn. L. Rev. 185, 193 (2009); Joseph D. Kearney & Thomas W. Merrill, The Influence of Amicus Curiae Briefs on the Supreme Court, 148 U. PA. L. REv. 743, 828-30 (2000)*).

This is the opposite of the rationale of EU competition law and policy, since the European Commission is entrusted with full decision-making powers, and as a governmental agency includes a full Economist Team and a well-established process of consulting the industry during the legislative phase. Once adopted, an administrative decision of the European Commission can only be appealed before the General Court of the EU in Luxembourg. This is probably the main explanation on why the amicus curiae, although introduced in EU antitrust, is not as developed nor influential. Nevertheless, in front of the EU Courts, competitors or NGO's may be permitted to introduce briefs as "intervening parties". A fundamental difference with the U.S. is that EU Courts still exercise a very strong scrutiny on the usefulness of such an intervention, while EU Members States or EU institutions can always intervene if they wish since the EU Treaties grant them directly this benefit.

The recent rise of private enforcement of EU Competition Law, in particular cartel damages claims following Directive 2014/104/EU, has resulted in the Amicus Curiae mechanism becoming crucial to the system. Article 15(3) of EU Regulation 1/2003 established it as the cooperation mechanism between the Commission, the national competition authorities and the courts of the Member States, in order to ensure the coherent application of EU competition rules in the 27 EU Member States and jurisdictions. This is part of the general principle of sincere cooperation, which is of particular importance where that cooperation involves the judicial authorities of a Member State which are responsible for ensuring that EU law is applied and respected in the national legal system. The mechanism of the Amicus Curiae gives the the European Commission the opportunity to show its good faith and sincere cooperation towards Member State's Judges.

Despite these positive theoretical considerations, national judges have so far made limited use of obtaining an Amicus brief from the Commission. An explanation could be that judges are reluctant to be advised by an administrative body, or the reluctance may be because the judge is not so familiar with the procedure. In fact, despite the crucial role given to national judges, one must still keep in mind that the final word about the application and interpretation of the EU law, including all competition rules, remains in the hands of the EU Court of Justice, via the preliminary ruling procedure established by article 267 TFEU. In fact, any national court may refer a question to the CJEU on the interpretation of a rule of EU law if it considers it necessary to resolve a dispute brought before it and national judges have a long positive experience with this procedure. Nevertheless, the Amicus mechanism is used increasingly together with the Preliminary reference, thus showing a complementarity that pursues the effectiveness of articles 101 and 102 TFEU all over the EU. However, obtaining an Amicus Curiae legal opinion from the Commission could be faster than a reference to the CJEU and probably should be more used by national judges. Indeed, the Commission, in its non-binding observations, generally refers to the case law of the CJEU and its own decisions as useful indications of the criteria and the type of evidence that have been taken into account in similar cases.

Bibliography

GERLICH, O., More than a friend? The European Commission's amicus curiae participation in investor-state arbitration, in: G Adinolfi et al. (Eds.), *International economic law*, Springer 2017, pp. 253–269

HAW ALLENSWORTH R., Amicus Briefs and the Sherman Act: Why Antitrust Needs a New Deal, 89 *Texas Law Review*. 1247 (2011)

KEARNEY, J. D., and MERRILL, T. W., "The Influence of Amicus Curiae Briefs on the Supreme Court." *University of Pennsylvania Law Review*, vol. 148, no. 3, 2000, pp. 743–855

VALLINDAS, G., Amicus Curiae: An overview of EU and national case law, 15 November 2018, *e-Competitions Amicus curiae*, Art. N° 87106

WIIK, A., *Amicus Curiae before International Courts and Tribunals* (pp. 707–734). Baden-Baden: Hart/Nomos (2018)

See also

Antitrust

A

ANCILLARY RESTRAINTS

Kathryn McMAHON
University of Warwick

Definition

The "ancillary restraints" doctrine is applied to validate restraints (including merger agreements) which are objectively necessary to implement a legitimate objective which has neutral or positive effects on competition. The restriction must be proportionate to, and directly related (strictly indispensable) to, the implementation of the legitimate objective of the agreement or merger. Ancillary restraints, including reasonable non-competition clauses, may be imposed on a franchisee, to protect the know-how and reputation of the franchise network. They may also be necessary to prevent free riding in a selective distribution system. A sporting regulatory body may impose restrictive rules on athletes' freedom of action in pursuit of a legitimate objective such as the maintenance of competitive balance among sporting teams.

Commentary

Article 101(1) TFEU prohibits agreements that have as their object or effect the restriction of competition unless they satisfy the criteria in Article 101(3). The Court of Justice has stated "not every agreement between undertakings or every decision of an association of undertakings which restricts the freedom of action of the parties or of one of them necessarily falls within the prohibition laid down in Article [101(1)] of the Treaty" (Wouters, 2002, paragraph 97).

Article 101(1) will not apply to a restriction in an agreement where it is objectively necessary to implement a legitimate objective which has neutral or positive effects on competition. The restriction must be proportionate to, and directly related to, the legitimate objective of the agreement (MasterCard, 2014, paragraph 89). These restrictions are called "ancillary restraints". The successful completion of a merger or concentration may also require undertakings to enter into ancillary restraints.

For the restriction to be classified as an "ancillary restraint" the question is asked "whether that operation would be impossible to carry out in the absence of the restriction in question" (MasterCard, 2014, paragraph 91). The restriction must be strictly indispensable to the implementation of the main operation. If the restrictions go beyond what is objectively necessary to implement the objectives or are not proportionate to the objectives they must be assessed under Article 101(1) or considered for exemption under Article 101(3).

Ancillary restraints, including reasonable non-competition clauses, may be imposed on a franchisee, to protect the know-how and reputation of the franchise network so that competitors do not benefit indirectly from the assistance provided. Territorial restraints may be necessary to facilitate entry to a new market or prevent free riding in a selective distribution system. Restrictions may also be imposed on members of a joint purchasing association, which enable members to exercise buying power vis-à-vis suppliers, preventing them from joining competing joint purchasing arrangements, if the restrictions imposed are limited to what is necessary (European Commission, 2022). The exchange of commercially sensitive information for the implementation of a legitimate Research & development agreement may be an ancillary restraint (European Commission, 2022, paragraph 152) if it is objectively necessary to implement the Research & development agreement and is proportionate to its objectives. An exchange of commercially sensitive information, including on prices, may also be necessary to implement a production agreement that provides for joint distribution or to implement a joint commercialisation agreement (European Commission, 2022, paragraphs 224-225; 376- 377).

Legitimate objectives can include the pursuit of a public policy or regulatory purpose such as the Dutch Bar Council making rules to ensure the proper practice of the legal profession (Wouters, paragraph 107). A sporting regulatory body may impose restrictive rules on athletes' freedom of action in pursuit of anti-doping rules for competitive sport to be conducted fairly and to safeguard equality of opportunity for athletes (Meca-Medina, 2006, paragraphs 43-45). The question arises whether this invites some assessment of the reasonableness of the regulatory rule.

Whether the objective is legitimate does not turn on its public or regulatory purpose. The assessment must not be made in the abstract (Meca-Medina, paragraph 42). Within the overall context of the agreement the objective must have a neutral or positive effect on competition. Whether the consequential effects restrictive of competition are inherent in the pursuit of those objectives (Wouters, paragraph 97) and are proportionate to them must then be considered.

Sustainability objectives may also be achieved through ancillary restraints. They are not a distinct category of horizontal agreement for the purposes of Article 101. The Commission has stated that the same questions of whether the objective has a neutral or positive impact on competition will apply (European Commission, 2022, ch. 9).

Ancillary restraints may also be restrictions directly related and necessary to the implementation of a concentration or merger. These restrictions are generally subject to self-assessment by the parties because the Merger Regulation automatically covers such restrictions once the concentration is declared compatible. Individual assessment by the Commission may arise for "specific novel or unresolved issues giving rise to genuine uncertainty" (Merger Regulation, recital 21). The Commission has issued a Notice which provides guidelines on compatible restrictions. For the agreement to be objectively necessary the merger "could not be implemented or could only be implemented under considerably more uncertain conditions, at a substantially higher cost, over an appreciably longer period or with considerably greater difficulty" (European Commission, 2005, paragraph 13). Examples include the licensing of patents or know-how. Non-competition clauses can also ensure that the transfer has the intended beneficial effect on competition if they are objectively necessary and proportionate to the transfer and strictly limited in duration and scope to that purpose.

The ancillary restraint doctrine also applies under Section 1 of the U.S. Sherman Act 1890 to validate restraints on competition imposed by legitimate business collaborations or joint ventures where a certain degree of cooperation is essential if the product is to be available at all. The FTC and DOJ will analyse an agreement under the rule of reason if it is "an efficiency-enhancing integration of economic activity... that is reasonably related to the integration and reasonably necessary to achieve its procompetitive benefits... even if it is of a type that might otherwise be considered per se illegal" (FTC and DOJ, 2000, 8). "However, if the participants could achieve an equivalent or comparable efficiency-enhancing integration through practical, significantly less restrictive means, then the Agencies conclude that the agreement is not reasonably necessary" (Ibid, 9).

An abbreviated so-called "quick look" to examine the context of the agreement in question is used in place of a full rule of reason analysis. Per se treatment is thought inappropriate to condemn rules where the economic impact of certain practices is not immediately obvious. The blanket licenses for copyrighted music issued to broadcast networks, for example, were not found to be per se price fixing under s1. They were considered a cost-effective method of avoiding the virtual impossibility of individual negotiation with each copyright owner, "the whole is truly greater than the sum of its parts; it is, to some extent, a different product" (Broadcast Music, 1979, 440-441).

The Supreme Court refused to apply the ancillary restraint doctrine to a joint venture between two oil companies to refine and sell gasoline at a single price because "the business practice being challenged involves the core activity of the joint venture itself – namely, the pricing of the very goods produced and sold" (Dagher, 2006, 7-8). While regulations of a sporting body that maintain a competitive balance among amateur athletic teams are generally legitimate and procompetitive the Supreme Court found that the restraints on student compensation could not be dealt with under a "quick look" but required a rule of reason analysis because the NCAA enjoyed monopsony power in the market for student athletes' labour (Alston, 2021, 15-19).

Bibliography

WERDEN, G. J., "The Ancillary Restraints Doctrine after Dagher", 8 *Sedona Conference J.* 17 (2007)

Council Regulation (EU) No 139/2004 of 20 January 2004 on the control of concentrations between undertakings (EU Merger Regulation)

European Commission (2005), Commission Notice on restrictions directly related and necessary to concentrations (Ancillary Restraints Notice), (2005/C 56/03)

European Commission (2022), Guidelines on the applicability of Article 101 of the Treaty on the Functioning of the European Union to horizontal co-operation agreement (2022/C164/01)

Federal Trade Commission and U.S. Department of Justice (2000), Antitrust Guidelines for Collaborations among Competitors

See also

Merger, Vertical restraints (restrictions)

A

ANNULMENT

Marcos VERISSIMO
University of São Paulo

■ Definition

In many jurisdictions, competition law is directly enforced by an administrative agency with no prior intervention of the Judiciary. In those jurisdictions, an action for annulment is usually the remedy granted to affected parties to challenge the legality of the agency's decisions before the courts. Grounds for annulment may include failure to observe procedural fairness, or even a misapplication of the law to the case.

■ Commentary

In Administrative Systems, an administrative agency is the body primarily in charge of applying the competition laws. In those jurisdictions, the right to question the agency's decisions before the courts commonly derives from a broader right to request the judicial review of administrative action in general.

In Brazil, CADE is that administrative agency. The right to challenge its decisions before the courts arises from article 5 of the Constitution, which is the basis for the judicial review of administrative action in general, and may be exercised by any interested party before any federal court (appellate jurisdiction may be further exercised by a Federal Tribunal, by the Superior Court of Justice, and by the Brazilian Supreme Court in certain circumstances).

In the EU, the antitrust agency is the European Commission. An interested party may challenge its decisions before the General Court (at first instance) and the European Court of Justice (at appellate level, on questions on law only), according to articles 256, 263 and 264 of the TFEU. Grounds for annulment would include lack of competence, infringement of an essential procedural requirement, infringement of the treaties or of any rule of law relating to their application, or misuse of powers (see SA Roquette Frères v Council, Maizena GmbH v Council, and Pellegrini v Commission). Violations of a defendant's right to a fair trial may also trigger a comprehensive review by the European Court of Human Rights (see, for instance, Menarini Diagnostics v. Italy).

In the United States, the DoJ and the FTC have competence to enforce competition law at federal level. The DoJ does not have direct adjudicative powers, but rather investigates cases and brings challenges before the courts when it deems necessary. The FTC, however, can exercise direct adjudicative authority, in which case a decision will be initially rendered by an administrative law judge and, then, potentially reviewed by the FTC commissioners. In the latter case, the commissioners' decision will be appealable to a federal court of appeals. This USSC recently decided that this distinct review scheme does not displace a district court's jurisdiction over claims challenging the constitutionality of the very structure or powers of the agency (see Axon Enterprise, Inc. v. Federal Trade Commission).

The right to challenge a competition agency's decision before the courts is usually exercised ex-post, i.e., after the decision becomes final. However, interim measures may be subject to immediate judicial review in certain jurisdictions, such as Brazil, the U.S. and the EU.

Actions for annulment may be narrower in scope, allowing for just a legality review (focused on procedural fairness and on the adequate use of the agency's powers or competence, sometimes complemented with a superficial scrutiny of reasonableness), or have a broader one, also including a substantive review of the correctness of the decision (comprising the competition authority's evaluation of the facts, assessment of the evidence, or interpretation of the law). The United States, Brazil and Belgium are examples of the latter (although in the U.S. determinations of fact made by the FTC are usually respected by the courts if supported by sufficient evidence). In the UK, cartel and dominance cases would trigger a broad review, and merger cases only a narrow one. In the EU, decisions imposing fines are also subject to broad review, as well as the interpretations of the law made by the Commission. In a decision rendered in 2018, the Spanish Supreme Court decided that the Spanish courts would also have a broad mandate to reevaluate the evidence used by the national competition authority.

When review is broader in scope, courts will often grant some level of deference to the legal and factual assessments made by agency. This is so because competition statutes are usually drafted in broad language, leaving considerable room for interpretation, and their application frequently requires the use of economic knowledge. In view of that, courts may consider that administrative authorities might have better resources (like a specialized staff and specific investigative tools) to determine the law and assess the facts. Economic theories applicable to competition law are also open to dispute, with some schools defending a narrower scope of intervention, and others a more aggressive one. This could be also an additional reason for deference, if courts are convinced that executive agencies are better placed to arbitrate such disputes.

Deference, however, must be balanced with other reasons that could point towards a more aggressive standard of review. Because competition authorities apply sanctions and impose restrictions on individuals, exercising a quasi-judicial role, rule of law principles could recommend that courts should have a more substantive responsibility in competition law application. Additionally, competition agencies are often at the same time the investigators, prosecutors and judges of their own cases, which could also suggest a more extensive supervision.

In the EU, the General Court usually concedes a margin of discretion to the Commission to assess economic matters, but that does not mean that it will refrain from reviewing the use of economic information by the agency (see, for instance, Commission vs Tetra Laval BV). In CK Telecoms UK Investments v Commission the General Court exercised a broad scrutiny of the factual assessments made by the Commission, ultimately deciding that it had applied a wrong standard of proof. This decision was later annulled by the Court of Justice, but the Court of Justice nonetheless confirmed that EU courts can broadly review the Commission's interpretation of economic information and its interpretation of legal concepts requiring an economic analysis (see Commission v. CK Telecoms UK Investments).

In Brazil, caselaw is not consistent as to the proper level of deference that CADE's decisions should have. In the Cascol case, the Supreme Court ruled that broad deference should be reserved to "regulatory agencies" like CADE, since those bodies deal with polycentric issues, and courts lack expertise to review political and technical choices inherent to economic regulation. That decision was nonetheless criticized because the case was related to an alleged abuse of dominance, and not to economic regulation, or to polycentric, political or technical regulatory choices. In any case, decisions rendered by other tribunals are hardly consistent with such broad deference standard (see, for instance, cases TRF1 AC 2005.34.00.015042-8/DF, TRF1 AP 0016643-24.1998.4.01.3400 and TRF1 AC 0043979-85.2007.4.01.3400, in which CADE's decisions were annulled because the court decided to review the agency's substantial assessment of the facts or evidence of those cases).

Procedural fairness is also a relevant ground for annulment actions. It relates to the disrespect to due process of law principles, like transparency, fair treatment, and the right to defense.

In United Parcel Service, Inc. v Commission, for instance, the General Court decided that the Commission's failure to disclose the methodological choices behind the econometric studies used to assess the effects of a proposed merger resulted in violation of the parties' due process rights, and thus would be grounds for annulment. In Brazil, courts have also annulled decisions rendered by CADE on procedural basis. In the Industrial Gases Case, the court annulled the imposition of roughly USD 1 billion in fines for alleged cartel offenses, by finding that the corresponding evidence would have been illegally obtained. In the Gerdau Case, another cartel conviction was annulled because CADE denied the interested party's request to produce expert evidence, which the court considered as a violation of its due process rights.

Bibliography

FORRESTER, I. (2016), Quis custodiet ipsos custodies? Assessing the judicial role in a lawful system of competition enforcement", *European Competition Law Annual 2013: Effective and Legitimate Enforcement*, Philip Lowe and Mel Marquis (Eds.)

OECD (2019), The standard of review by courts in competition cases

OECD (2018), Scoping Note on Transparency and Procedural Fairness as a long-term theme for 2019-2020

OECD (2017), Judicial Perspectives on Competition Law

OECD (2016), The resolution of competition cases by specialized and generalist courts: Stocktaking of international experience

See also

Antitrust, Competition policy, Preliminary ruling (Art. 267 TFEU)

A

ANTICOMPETITIVE MARKET DISTORTIONS

Alden ABBOTT
Mercatus Center – George Mason University

Definition

Anticompetitive market distortions (ACMDs) are government-imposed restrictions that distort market-based competition, domestically or internationally. They typically empower favored private interests to obtain or retain artificial competitive advantages over their rivals be they foreign or domestic. ACMDs comprise government laws, regulations, or practices that: lessen or entirely eliminate competition among firms; create regulatory exemptions; discriminate among firms; involve selective prosecution or non-enforcement of competition law; bestow state aids or other support on favored recipients; and allow distortions by state-owned enterprises.

Commentary

Because they often distort the treatment of different competitors engaged in international commerce, yet generally fall outside the scope of domestic competition and trade laws, ACMDs are a major impediment to international trade as well as to domestic competition.

ACMDs are recognized to be a serious global economic problem. Two major international economic organizations, the OECD and the World Bank, have spotlighted ACMDs and have encouraged governments to avoid and dismantle them. In a similar vein, the International Competition Network (ICN), established in 2001, provides support for "competition advocacy" initiatives by its member competition agencies, aimed at encouraging national governments to avoid anticompetitive public policies.

Despite this institutional attention, however, ACMDs remain pervasive, due in no small part to the fact that their costs to the general public and competitors are hidden from sight. The development of measures to estimate the costs of ACMDs could strengthen the case for rooting them out. Even more significantly, cost measures could be used to develop targeted trade sanctions calibrated to counteract specific ACMDs. The threat of sanctions and the publicized scale of the ACMD problem could also facilitate multilateral efforts to incentivize the phasing out of these pernicious restrictions.

Fortunately, since 2014 research to estimate the economic impact of ACMDs is being carried out. In 2016 Singham and Rangan published a basic econometric model for estimating the cost of ACMDs. That model included a metric that estimated the negative impact on economic welfare stemming from ACMDs' harmful effects on property rights, domestic competition, and international competition. The authors applied that model to estimate the impact of ACMDs in India, and found "that if all ACMDs in India were replaced with truly pro-competitive policies,… [D]omestic GDP would rise by a factor of 4, making India the fourth-biggest economy in the world behind only the EU, U.S., and China."

A subsequent 2019 study prepared by the Centre for Economics and Business Research (Cebr) found that a within-country trade distortion (ACMD) of 25 percent (an ACMD that prohibits one-fourth of beneficial commercial transactions between companies and consumers) reduces global output relative to the benchmark case with no distortions by around 14 percent. Research along these lines continues.

Studies finding dramatic ACMD-specific welfare losses are generally consistent with other recent quantitative research finding a strong relationship between a growth in regulation and a major decline in economic growth. Although certainly not definitive (the research deals with regulations in general, which may include some non-ACMDs), this research clearly bolsters the case for combating ACMDs as a key element of competition policy.

To be effective, an anti-ACMD strategy must come to grips with the fact that many of these distortions exist due to the lobbying of powerful organized special interest "rent-seekers," that manipulate government processes to gain competitive advantage. Accordingly, any effort to rein in ACMDs must involve international cooperation. Such cooperation might include agreements embodying robust enforcement mechanisms with credible commitments that induce like-minded market-centered nations to eliminate specific ACMDs – and to act in concert to counteract ACMDs imposed by third party nations.

ACMD trade remedies might be unilateral or multilateral. For example, a nation unilaterally might assess a duty equivalent to the size of a distortion ("tariffication") on imports that artificially benefit from a foreign ACMD and harm domestic producers. A tariffication-based trade remedy might also be imposed more broadly on a multilateral basis, and included in free trade agreements with like-minded nations, as detailed in a 2021 United Kingdom Trade and Agriculture Commission report.

Other potential unilateral remedies for ACMD violations might include, among others, penalties and fines; withdrawal of licenses in the case of licensed or regulated services; disciplines of domestic firms that receive government distortion benefits from a foreign government; prohibitions on investments in domestic firms by foreign ACMD beneficiaries; and applications of surcharges to government procurement bids by companies that benefited from a foreign ACMD.

Dealing with ACMDs that a nation uses to protect its domestic industries from foreign competition may be more complicated than imposing defensive measures, especially when the specially favored industries export little or nothing. In such cases, trade agreements might include disciplines on those ACMDs. Failure to unwind or modify ACMDs could lead to dispute settlement and the potential for retaliatory tariffs on sectors that do export.

Finally, domestic antitrust remedies might occasionally prove helpful in combating ACMDs. For example, ACMD subsidies enjoyed by an exporter could lead to charges of predatory pricing. Also, blocking a merger could prevent future harm when one of the parties benefitted from a foreign ACMD that would enable the merged entity to predate against other competitors post-acquisition.

In sum, an enhanced policy focus on curbing ACMDs appears warranted. This could involve new sorts of targeted trade sanctions and competition law initiatives. In addition, enhanced domestic competition advocacy and regulatory review efforts aimed at highlighting the pernicious effects of home-grown ACMDs could also prove helpful.

Bibliography

Singham, S. A. and Abbott, A. F., *Trade, Competition and Regulatory Policy*, 1st edition, Routledge, 2023

Singham, S. A. and Srinivasa Rangan, U., "Anti-Competitive Market Distortions: A Typology" (2018) 38(3) *Economic Affairs*

Shanker A. Singham, U. Srinivasa Rangan, Robert Bradley, and A. Molly Kiniry, "Anti-Competitive Market Distortions and Their Impact: A Case Study of India" (2016) *Legatum Institute*

"An agent-based model of trade: Market distortions and output" (2019) Centre for Economics and Business Research

OECD, "Competition Assessment Toolkit"

World Bank, "Markets and Competition Policy"

See also

Concerted practices, Economic analysis

A

ANTICOMPETITIVE OBJECT OR EFFECT

Richard WHISH
King's College London

■ Definition

Article 101(1) TFEU prohibits agreements that have as their object or effect the restriction of competition; such agreements are forbidden unless they satisfy the criteria in Article 101(3). Many other systems of competition law, in the EU and beyond, are formulated in a similar manner. Economic analysis is required to show that an agreement has the effect of restricting competition. However some agreements – for example secret price-fixing or market-sharing agreements between competitors – are so obviously pernicious that they are held to restrict competition by object: no further analysis of their economic effect is required for them to be unlawful.

■ Commentary

Article 101(1) prohibits agreements that have as their object or effect the restriction of competition.

In *Société Technique Minière v Maschinenbau Ulm (1966)* the Court of Justice stated that the words "object or effect" were to be read disjunctively; this means that where an agreement has as its object the restriction of competition it is unnecessary to prove that it will produce anticompetitive effects: only if it is not clear that the object of an agreement is to restrict competition is it necessary to consider whether it might have the effect of doing so. It is still controversial, after more than 50 years of EU competition law, what constitutes a restriction of competition by object. The Court of Justice has stated, for example in *Cartes Bancaires v Commission (2014, paragraph 57)*, that the essential legal criterion for ascertaining whether coordination between undertakings restricts competition by object is the finding "that such coordination reveals in itself a sufficient degree of harm to competition". The term "object" in Article 101 means the objective meaning and purpose of the agreement considered in the economic context in which it is to be applied; it is not necessary to prove that the parties have the subjective intention of restricting competition when entering into the agreement.

However, subjective intention may be a relevant factor in assessing whether the object of an agreement is anticompetitive *(Cartes Bancaires, paragraph 54)*. The concept of a restriction of competition by object should be interpreted restrictively *(Cartes Bancaires, paragraph 58)*. In order to decide whether an agreement restricts competition by object, "regard must be had to the content of [the agreement's] provisions, its objectives and the economic and legal context of which it forms a part. When determining that context, it is also necessary to take into consideration the nature of the goods or services affected, as well as the real conditions of the functioning and structure of the market or markets in question" *(Cartes Bancaires, paragraph 53)*.

Advocate General Kokott's Opinion in *T-Mobile (2009)* includes an interesting discussion of why Article 101(1) makes a distinction between object and effect restrictions. First, the classification of certain types of agreement as restrictive by object "sensibly conserves resources of competition authorities and the justice system" *(T-Mobile Opinion, paragraph 43)*. The fact that a competition authority does not need to demonstrate, for example, that a horizontal price-fixing agreement produces adverse economic effects relieves it of some of the burden that would otherwise rest upon it. Secondly, the Advocate General pointed out that the existence of object restrictions "creates legal certainty and allows all market participants to adapt their conduct accordingly" *(T-Mobile Opinion, paragraph 43)* adding that, although the concept of restriction by object should not be given an unduly broad interpretation, nor should it be interpreted so narrowly as to deprive it of its practical effectiveness *(T-Mobile Opinion, paragraph 44)*. Thirdly, she pointed out that, just as a law that forbids people from driving cars when under the influence of alcohol does not require, for a conviction, that the driver has caused an accident – that is to say proof of an effect – so, in the same way, Article 101(1) prohibits certain agreements that have the object of restricting competition, irrespective of whether they produce adverse effects on the market in an individual case *(T-Mobile Opinion, paragraph 47)*; such agreements will be permitted, therefore, only where the parties can demonstrate that they will lead to economic efficiencies of the kind set out in Article 101(3), and that a fair share of those efficiencies will be passed on to consumers. A competition authority is entitled to conclude that an agreement restricts competition both by object and by effect *(Hungarian Banks, paragraphs 33 to 44)*.

Section 1 of the U.S. Sherman Act 1890 characterises some agreements as per se illegal, whereas others are subject to so-called "rule of reason" analysis. Where there is a per se infringement it is not open to the parties to the agreement to argue that it does not restrict competition: it belongs to a category of agreement that has, by law, been found to be restrictive of competition. There is an obvious analogy between an agreement that is per se illegal under the Sherman Act and one that is restrictive of competition by object under Article 101(1). However there is an important difference between section 1 of the Sherman Act and Article 101 TFEU in that, even if an agreement has as its object the restriction of competition, that is to say that it infringes Article 101(1) per se, the parties can still attempt to justify it under Article 101(3). This possibility does not exist in U.S. law, since there is no equivalent of Article 101(3) in that system. In this sense a judgment such as that of the U.S. Supreme Court in *Leegin (2007)*, in which it determined that minimum resale price maintenance should be analysed under the rule of reason rather than being per se illegal, brings U.S. law into alignment with that of the EU: it has always been possible to argue that resale price maintenance satisfies Article 101(3), even though it is classified as having as its object the restriction of competition for the purpose of Article 101(1).

Bibliography

Bailey, D. and John, L.E., (eds), *Bellamy and Child: European Union Law of Competition*, 8th Edition, Oxford University Press, 2018, ch 2

Faull, J. and Nikpay, A. (eds), *The EU Law of Competition*, 3rd Edition, Oxford University Press, 2014, ch 3

Hovenkamp, H., "The Rule of Reason", *University of Pennsylvania Institute for Law & Econ, Research Paper No 17-28*, 2016

Whish, R. and Bailey, D., *Competition Law*, Oxford University Press, 9th Edition, 2018, ch 3

See also

Actual competitor, Anticompetitive market distortions, Economic analysis, Buyer power, Cartel

A

ANTICOMPETITIVE PRACTICES

Kees JAN KUILWIJK
Gateley

Definition

Competition encourages businesses to offer high quality goods and services at the lowest possible price. If a company does so, it will attract customers and expand market share. Competition also drives diversity and innovation. To compete for business, firms will try to make products that are different from those of their rivals, and more appealing to consumers. Competition thus forces businesses to be creative and innovative, for example in the design of their products or the use of technology. Anticompetitive practices are business practices that prevent or reduce competition in a market. Anticompetitive practices typically lead to market distortions resulting in higher prices, lower quality products, poorer service and a stifling of innovation.

Commentary

It has been known for centuries that anticompetitive practices have harmful economic effects. Adam Smith famously declared that "People of the same trade seldom meet together, even for merriment and diversion, but the conversation ends in a conspiracy against the public, or in some contrivance to raise prices". Cartels are indeed one of the most harmful anticompetitive practices and cause significant damage to consumers and to the economy as a whole. A cartel is basically a group of firms that colludes to behave like a monopolist by restricting output and raising price.

More than a century after Smith, Alfred Marshall popularized the concepts of consumer surplus, producer surplus and deadweight loss. Consumer surplus measures the difference between the price a consumer pays for an item and the price he would be willing to pay rather than do without it. Producer surplus is the difference between the market price and the lowest price a firm is willing to accept to produce a good. A deadweight loss is a cost to society created by market inefficiency, which occurs when supply and demand are out of equilibrium. In economic terms, the exercise of monopoly power causes an inefficient allocation of resources by restricting output below what would be achieved by a competitive market. As a result, there is a deadweight loss in welfare. In addition, monopoly redistributes gains from consumers to producers by transferring consumer surplus to profit.

Still, laws prohibiting anticompetitive practices were slow to catch on. In 1970, only twelve jurisdictions around the world had a competition law regime. During the 1970s and 1980s, numerous economic studies were undertaken to demonstrate the harmful effects of anticompetitive practices on consumers and producers alike. These studies led to a growing awareness among both developed and developing countries that regulation is necessary to protect economies and that competition law is not intended to punish companies but that these rules are healthy for businesses too, because it keeps them on their toes. Some 130 jurisdictions have now enacted competition laws and the vast majority have a competition enforcement authority actively pursuing anticompetitive practices. Particularly the European Union and the United States have well-developed competition laws and policies that aim to prevent and penalise anticompetitive practices.

Anticompetitive practices may take the form of either collusion between competing businesses, for example to set prices or limit production, or of unilateral conduct by companies with significant market power that exploits consumers or excludes competition. In the EU, collusion is caught by Article 101(1) of the Treaty on the Functioning of the European Union (TFEU) and abusive unilateral behaviour by Article 102 TFEU. In the U.S., Section 1 of the Sherman Act prohibits agreements between two or more independent entities that unreasonably restrain trade, while Section 2 makes it illegal to acquire or maintain monopoly power through improper means.

Examples of anticompetitive practices are horizontal price fixing (firms fixing prices between them, or controlling prices, discounts, rebates or credits); market division (firms dividing up customers or territories to limit the need to compete for customers); output restriction (restricting the volume of goods produced or services offered). Examples of exclusionary practices would be a dominant firm charging prices below cost; entering into a long-term exclusivity agreement with customers with no objective justification; or refusing to supply a vital input to a customer that competes with it in a downstream market.

Some jurisdictions make a distinction between anticompetitive practices which are, in U.S. parlance, "per se" illegal and those which are examined under a "rule of reason". Under the per se rule, certain conduct is presumed to violate antitrust law, which means that no further inquiry into the practice's actual effect on the market or the intentions of those who engaged in the practice is necessary. Under the rule of reason, the actual effect of the anticompetitive behaviour on competition is examined, and it requires a court to balance an agreement's pro- and anticompetitive effects.

Similarly, in EU law agreements can be restrictive of competition by "object" or "effect". Price-fixing or market-sharing agreements between competitors are examples of anticompetitive practices that are so obviously harmful that no further analysis of their economic effects is required for them to be unlawful, i.e., unless they satisfy the criteria in Article 101(3). In *Budapest Bank*, however, the CJEU held that the by-object restriction concept must be interpreted restrictively and applied to practices only if they reveal a sufficient degree of harm to competition to consider that it is unnecessary to investigate its effects. The *Intel* case demonstrates that the European Courts are prepared to annul Commission decisions if they do not undertake a thorough effects-based analysis or if their economic analysis has flaws.

Bibliography

BISHOP, S. and WALKER, M., *The Economics of EC Competition Law* (3rd edition, Sweet & Maxwell, 2007)

MARSHALL, A., *Principles of Economics* (1st edition, Prometheus Books, 1890)

OECD, *Relationship Between Public and Private Antitrust Enforcement*, Working Party No. 3 on Co-operation and Enforcement, 15 June 2015

POSNER, R., *Antitrust Law* (2nd edition, The University of Chicago Press, 2001)

WHISH, R. and BAILEY, D., *Competition Law* (10th edition, Oxford University Press, 2021)

See also

Bid rigging, Cartel, Collusion, Discriminatory practices, Economic analysis, Exchanges of information, Rule of reason

A

ANTITRUST

Eleanor M. FOX
NYU School of Law

Definition

Antitrust is the body of law that controls the creation, use and abuse of market power. In some jurisdictions, including the United States, antitrust is another word for competition law. In the European Union, antitrust denotes the part of competition law that covers abuse of dominance and anticompetitive agreements but not merger control. This entry will use the word in the more generic sense.

Commentary

Antitrust, or competition law, removes impediments to competition and thus helps make markets work better for consumers and other market participants. It focuses on three types of conduct or behavior: agreements, single-firm conduct, and mergers and acquisitions. Competition laws generally declare to be illegal anticompetitive agreements, anticompetitive conduct by dominant or monopoly firms, and anticompetitive mergers. Much weight is put on the word "anticompetitive." In some cases the inquiry – is this conduct anticompetitive? – is easy, and in some cases it is very complex. Moreover, some jurisdictions allow justifications for anticompetitive conduct and others do not.

Agreements. Under United States law, Section 1 of the Sherman Act prohibits "restraints of trade." This provision is read to prohibit anticompetitive agreements. Some agreements are clearly anticompetitive in that they remove competitive forces from the market and have no efficiency or innovation qualities. These agreements are called "naked restraints" and are classified as illegal without any further inquiry; that is, they are "illegal *per se*." Agreements among competitors to fix prices, divide markets, or allocate production ("cartels") are illegal *per se*. Agreements that are not illegal per se are subject to a rule of reason. Under the rule of reason, an agreement is anticompetitive and illegal if the anticompetitive aspects outweigh the procompetitive aspects. Efficiencies and innovation qualities are considered to be procompetitive.

In the European Union, the antitrust provisions are found in the Treaty on the Functioning of the European Union. The Treaty provision applicable to agreements invalidates agreements that have the object or effect of restricting or distorting competition unless justified by a showing that they are (in effect, this is a summary) productive or efficient and a fair share of the benefits goes to consumers. Naked cartels are agreements that restrict competition by object. Naked cartels virtually never meet the requirements for justification.

Unilateral conduct. The U.S. Sherman Act, Section 2, prohibits "monopolization" and conspiracies and attempts to monopolize. To be liable for monopolization, a firm must have monopoly power and must use that power in anticompetitive ways likely to enhance or entrench its power. The law is reluctant to condemn unilateral acts for fear that antitrust intervention will chill pro-competitive and innovative incentives and protect inefficient small firms. Accordingly, under U.S. law, a monopoly firm has no duty to deal with its competitors except under narrowly-defined circumstances. The Trinko case (*U.S. Sup. Ct. 2004*) most famously stands for this proposition. The U.S. law on monopolization does not prohibit exploitative conduct. Very high prices are an example of exploitative conduct. The law does not prohibit excessive pricing.

EU competition law prohibits the abuse of a dominant position. A firm can have dominant power at a somewhat lower level than is required for monopoly power. Under EU law, dominant firms have a special responsibility not to distort competition, for example by exclusionary conduct that blocks rivals' freedom to contest markets on their merits. Intel v. Commission (EU Court of Justice 2017) provides examples. EU law prohibits exploitative as well as exclusionary conduct.

Mergers. U.S. antitrust prohibits mergers whose effect may be to substantially lessen competition. The EU merger regulation prohibits mergers that create a significant impediment to effective competition. The difference in statutory language is not significant; both sets of laws mean to proscribe mergers that are likely to harm competition. If the merger will probably significantly create or increase market power, it is likely to harm competition. If the merger creates efficiencies that are likely to get passed on to consumers, that is a procompetitive quality and is considered in the analysis. Mergers between competitors (horizontal mergers) are the category most likely to be targeted by antitrust merger control. Mergers between buyers and suppliers, acquisitions of potential rivals, and other (conglomerate) mergers may also fall afoul of the merger law. EU law has been somewhat more aggressive than U.S. law against non-horizontal mergers.

Neither the U.S. nor the EU allows a national champion or other public interest defense to an anticompetitive merger.

What is the remedy for anticompetitive mergers? Commonly, the agency and parties agree to spin-offs of offending assets and accompanying behavioral obligations. In contemporary times, relatively few mergers are flatly prohibited, although prohibition is an available remedy, and divestiture is an available remedy for completed anticompetitive mergers (in jurisdictions where consummated mergers may still be subject to challenge).

Competition law of other nations. The competition laws of other nations are quite similar to those of the U.S. and/or the EU. EU is the more frequently followed model. Some of the more common divergences from the U.S./EU model are: Asian nations may include in their unilateral conduct laws a provision for abuse of a superior bargaining position, and they may recognize antitrust violations for unfair conduct even if the conduct does not harm the market or consumers. (Certain Western countries share these characteristics.) They are more likely to allow an industrial policy defense.

Developing countries are likely to have more expansive competition laws than the U.S. and EU. Their markets generally work less well and barriers to entry are higher, and the countries need economic development. Developing countries' competition laws often value inclusive growth, are more vigilant against exclusionary and exploitative conduct, and allow public interest defenses to help workers, small business, and historically excluded majorities. The South African case Babelegi (Court of Appeal 2020) is an example of South Africa's application of its abuse of dominance law to challenge price gouging during the coronavirus pandemic.

Bibliography

Fox, E. M. and Crane, D. A., *Global Issues in Antitrust and Competition Law* (2d ed. West Academic 2017)

Gerber, D. J., *Competition Law and Antitrust: A Global Guide* (Oxford University Press 2020)

Hawk, B. E., *Antitrust and Competition Laws* (Juris Publishing 2020)

See also

Competition policy

A

APPLICABLE LAW

Eugène BUTTIGIEG
University of Malta

Definition

The competition rules of any given jurisdiction would be found in one or several pieces of primary legislation and the accompanying secondary legislation laying down the substantive rules governing the economic behaviour of market players with a view to ensuring a competitive market and the procedural rules instituting the national organs that enforce these rules and setting the procedure to guarantee the due process of law. This legislation might be accompanied by soft law in the form of guidelines, notices and so forth that provide guidance to market players on the application of these rules. Just as important are the judgments of the local judicial bodies shedding light on the interpretation and application of these provisions.

Commentary

In the EU, the basic provisions can be found in the Treaty on the Functioning of the European Union (TFEU), specifically in Articles 101 and 102 that respectively prohibit collusive behaviour by market operators and abusive conduct by dominant undertakings, and Article 107 that while prohibiting state aid to undertakings in any form, exempts aid that is deemed justified to meet certain objectives. Moreover, Article 106 articulates how these provisions are applicable to public undertakings and undertakings enjoying special or exclusive rights granted by the Member States.

However, in addition to these basic provisions, there is a gamut of important competition rules to be found in Regulations that the Commission and the Council have adopted throughout the years under Articles 103, 105-106 and 108-109 TFEU. The EU's merger control regime is contained in Council Regulation 139/2004 that empowers the Commission to evaluate notifiable mergers and acquisitions ("concentrations") of an EU dimension and to prohibit their implementation, or to grant conditional approval, if they are found to significantly impede effective competition. Likewise, in the enforcement of the antitrust provisions (Articles 101 and 102 TFEU), Council Regulation 1/2003 articulates the investigative and sanctioning powers of the Commission while establishing the procedural guarantees of the undertakings. Moreover, it regulates the application of Articles 101 and 102 TFEU at national level, the coordination between the Commission and the national competition authorities in this enforcement, and the relationship between EU and national competition laws. Its counterpart in the field of state aid is Council Regulation 2015/1589.

The Commission has also adopted a series of so-called "block exemption regulations" that exempt restrictions in bilateral or multilateral horizontal (Regulation 2022/2455 for Research & development agreements, Regulation 2022/2456 for specialisation agreements), vertical (Regulation 2022/720) and licensing (Regulation 316/2014 for licensing for the transfer of technology) agreements between undertakings that generate offsetting pro-competitive effects from the prohibition in Article 101 TFEU. A general block exemption regulation, Regulation 651/2014, exempts various forms of aid from the prohibition in Article 107 TFEU in relation to state aid.

Each of these regulations is accompanied by guidelines to assist undertakings in the self-assessment of their agreements under the block exemptions. These guidelines add to a growing body of Commission soft law "notices" and communications that provide guidance to undertakings and national authorities on the Commission's application of the law, based on its own past decisional practice and the judgments of EU Courts in antitrust, merger control and state aid. Although these instruments do not constitute binding legislation, the Commission is expected to follow them, out of respect for legal certainty and the principle of equal treatment, unless it can show that the particular circumstances of a case justify departure. Noteworthy are the Commission notices outlining the Commission's leniency policy and settlement procedure in cartel cases, its fining policy, its methodology in defining the market for antitrust and merger purposes, its assessment of horizontal and non-horizontal mergers and its enforcement priorities in applying Art 102 TFEU. In the domain of state aid, particularly important were the "Temporary Framework" communications issued during the 2008 financial crisis, the Covid-19 outbreak and the Russia/Ukraine war explaining how the Commission intended to apply the state aid rules during these times of crisis.

In the U.S., the basic provisions are found in one of the world's first statutes on antitrust, the Sherman Act of 1890, named after the senator who promoted this bill before Congress to outlaw the powerful trusts existing in the U.S. at the time. Although it is written in rather broad and general terms, prohibiting "every contract, combination, or conspiracy in restraint of trade," over time the Supreme Court has read a per se/rule of reason distinction into this provision. Restraints are deemed lawful when their positive effects outweigh their negative effects, provided they do not fall into a category of agreements (such as price fixing, market sharing or bid rigging arrangements) that are so inherently anticompetitive and damaging to the market as to be considered per se illegal. Agreements in the latter category are deemed "per se" violations of the statute with no redeeming virtues and no defence or justification is allowed.

Throughout the years, other legislative instruments were adopted by Congress to clarify and strengthen the Sherman Act. Thus, while, the Sherman Act also outlaws, in vague terms, any "monopolization, attempted monopolization, or conspiracy or combination to monopolize", the Clayton Act passed in 1914 defines as illegal, in its second and third sections, certain specific business practices such as price discrimination, price cutting, predatory pricing and tying arrangements. The prohibition of different forms of price discrimination was further articulated through the amendments to this Act introduced by the Robinson-Patman Act in 1936. The Clayton Act in its seventh section also prohibits anti-competitive mergers and acquisitions and interlocking directorates and, following the amendments introduced by the Celler-Kefauver Act of 1950 and the Hart-Scott-Rodino Antitrust Improvements Act of 1976, provides for a proper merger control system. It requires companies to notify regulators of planned mergers and acquisitions, and bans such transactions when they may substantially lessen competition or tend to create a monopoly.

The 1914 Federal Trade Commission Act likewise complements the Sherman Act by banning "unfair methods of competition" and "unfair or deceptive acts or practices" and it established the Federal Trade Commission (FTC) to share the role of public enforcer of these federal statutes with the U.S. Department of Justice's Antitrust Division (DOJ).

Enforcement of federal antitrust laws is done mostly via civil lawsuits filed by the DOJ or the FTC or by private parties. Although only the DOJ enforces the Sherman Act, the Supreme Court has held that violations of the Sherman Act also constitute violations of the Federal Trade Commission Act. Therefore, the FTC may also bring cases under the Federal Trade Commission Act targeting the same kind of conduct that violates the Sherman Act. Consequently, both agencies regularly consult each other to avoid duplication efforts. However, in addition, the FTC is empowered to challenge practices harmful to competition that, while not fitting strictly into categories of conduct formally prohibited by the Sherman Act, are outlawed by the Federal Trade Commission Act.

The Clayton Act empowers individuals to sue for treble damages when they have been harmed by conduct that violates either the Sherman Act or the Clayton Act and to obtain a court order prohibiting the anticompetitive practices in the future. Civil cases involving violations of the Clayton Act can also be filed by state attorney generals or as class actions by groups of individuals with similar claims.

However, the Sherman Act, unlike the Clayton Act and the Federal Trade Commission Act, is also a criminal statute. Intentional violations may be investigated and prosecuted by the DOJ in criminal antitrust suits, and the individuals and companies found responsible for the infringement by the adjudicating court may incur hefty criminal fines or even custodial sentences.

Throughout the years, the FTC and the DOJ have issued various guidelines to serve as guidance on the way the federal laws are applied, foremost amongst which the Vertical Merger Guidelines and the Horizontal Merger Guidelines that set out the agencies' analytical framework for assessing such mergers and the Antitrust Guidelines for the Licensing of Intellectual Property.

As in the EU, in addition to these federal statutes, most of the states in the U.S. have their own antitrust laws that are enforced by state attorneys general or private plaintiffs. These laws mirror the federal antitrust laws, just as, in the EU, the national competition laws are modelled on the EU antitrust and merger laws.

Bibliography

Bailey, D. and John, L. E., *Bellamy and Child: European Union Law of Competition* (8th edn Oxford University Press 2018)

Elhauge, E. and Geradin, D., *Global Competition Law and Economics* (2nd edn Hart Publishing 2011)

Hovenkamp, H., *Federal Antitrust Policy: The Law of Competition and its Practice* (6th edn West Academic Publishing 2020)

Jones, A., Sufrin, B. and Dunne, N., *Jones and Sufrin's EU Competition Law: Text, Cases, and Materials* (7th edn Oxford University Press 2019)

Whish, R. and Bailey, D., *Competition Law* (10th edn Oxford University Press 2021)

See also

Arbitration, Extraterritoriality, Procedural autonomy

A

ARBITRATION

Christian BOVET
University of Geneva Law School

■ Definition

Arbitration is an alternative dispute resolution mode under which an arbitral tribunal composed of one or more – generally three – independent persons (the arbitrators) issues one or more formal decisions (awards) that aim to settle a legal disagreement outside the ordinary judicial system according to the rules designated by a contract or a treaty. Appeals against the awards may be brought before a court but only on limited grounds, such as lack of competence of the arbitral tribunal or violation of public policy. The New York Convention of 1958 generally governs the recognition and enforcement of foreign awards.

■ Commentary

Since the *Mitsubishi judgment*, the arbitrability of antitrust cases has become a standard admitted in most – if not all – jurisdictions. Arguments based on competition law first arose in connection with agreements (e.g. vertical restraints) and quite quickly extended to abuses of dominant positions. Nevertheless, in the 2019 *Shell (China) Limited v. Hohhot Huili Material Co., Ltd.* case the Chinese Supreme People's Court opted for a restrictive interpretation, excluding from arbitration civil disputes involving monopoly issues, since these are unrelated to contractual or other property rights.

Although merger control remains within the hands of competition authorities, arbitration procedures may be used in or even fully integrated into some measures relating to the implementation of remedies. For instance, the powers of a monitoring or divestiture trustee may be extended in order to allow it to render proper decisions and, as was the case in the EU Standard Trustee Mandate, give the possibility to the parties to provide for an arbitration clause. In connection with the proposed acquisition of Aleris Corporation by Novelis Inc., the buyer and the U.S. Department of Justice agreed in 2019 on the terms of a binding arbitration procedure on the question of the relevant market under the Administrative Dispute Resolution Act of 1996 (5 U.S.C. § 571 et seq.). Beyond commercial disputes, one can observe interesting developments in sports arbitration, where parties have been invoking breaches of competition law by various organizations active in this field, including sports federations or anti-doping agencies.

In the *Pechstein* case, the German Federal Court (*Bundesgerichthof*) deemed both the arbitration clause and its acceptance by skaters to be valid, although athletes had no choice but to adhere to it if they wanted to participate in a competition. More specifically, it pointed out that both the national and international associations involved in this dispute were organized according to the "*Ein-Platz-Prinzip*", i.e. they held exclusive competence over speed-skating competitions in Germany and internationally. Thus, the two federations as monopolists maintained dominant positions in their relevant markets. On the other hand, the imposed jurisdiction of the Court of Arbitration for Sport (CAS) was justified by legitimate grounds and therefore not abusive (paragraph 2 et seq.). Similarly, in *International Skating Union v Commission* (paragraph 163) the General Court accepted the argument that arbitration rules that confer on the CAS exclusive jurisdiction to review the legality of ineligibility decisions do not constitute an aggravating circumstance under the EU Guidelines on the calculation of fines. In a judgment of 2 October 2018, the European Court for Human Rights (ECHR) rejected objections pertaining to a fair hearing or a structural absence of independence and impartiality in the CAS, but admitted that the merits of the sanction imposed on Claudia Pechstein for doping required a public hearing.

Arbitral tribunals may not decline their competence and have to decide on issues pertaining to competition law, provided that these aspects are sufficiently related to the disputes covered by the arbitration clause. However, they have generally been denied the possibility to submit references for preliminary rulings to the Court of Justice of the European Union (CJEU). Indeed, the Court has consistently stated that an arbitral tribunal is not a "court or tribunal of a Member State" within the meaning of Article 267 TFEU. Nevertheless, in its 2014 order in *Merck Canada* the CJEU confirmed that it would consider: "admissible preliminary questions referred to it by an arbitral tribunal, where that tribunal had been established by law, whose decisions were binding on the parties and whose jurisdiction did not depend on their agreement" (paragraph 18). While supporting the views expressed by legal authors that the prospect of a broader opening vis-à-vis other types of arbitration tribunals is not so remote, one should also nuance this perspective. Indeed, the 2018 *Slovak Republic v. Achmea BV* jurisprudence and the 2021 conclusions of Advocate General Maciej Szpunar in the *Republic of Moldova v Komstroy* case show, at least in the context of investment arbitration, that the CJEU is still reluctant to put national courts and arbitration tribunals on an equal footing.

Eco Swiss truly sets forth the standards on judicial review of an arbitral award by a national court in relation to a recognition and enforcement application filed by one of the parties in the EU. The Court first recalled explicitly that Article 101 TFEU constituted a fundamental provision which is essential for the accomplishment of the tasks entrusted to the Community and, in particular, for the functioning of the internal market; in other words, it belongs to the provisions constituting public policy with the EU. Therefore, a national court must grant an application for annulment of an arbitration award founded on failure to observe national rules of public policy when such award does not comply with the prohibition laid down in Article 101 TFEU. This approach is consistent with the provisions of the New York Convention, since under its Article V(2)(b): "Recognition and enforcement of an arbitral award may also be refused if the competent authority in the country where recognition and enforcement is sought finds that [t]he recognition or enforcement of the award would be contrary to the public policy of that country." However, this judicial review should be limited since, as the Court emphasized: "[I]t is in the interest of efficient arbitration proceedings that review of arbitration awards should be limited in scope and that annulment of or refusal to recognise an award should be possible only in exceptional circumstances" (paragraph 35). European national courts broadly share this approach, whether at the time of an appeal or in respect of a recognition and enforcement application. This is especially the case when antitrust issues are raised for the first time before a court of appeal or, even worse, while the winning party is seeking the recognition and enforcement of the award.

This last point calls for two additional remarks regarding the arbitrators themselves: first, the parties should in principle select arbitrators who master the basic concepts of competition law; second, when arbitrators decide *ex officio* to address antitrust questions, they should obviously respect the parties' right to be heard and give them the opportunity to present all their arguments before rendering their award.

Bibliography

Blanke, G. and Landolt, P. (eds.), *EU and U.S. Antitrust Arbitration, Volumes 1 & 2* (Kluwer 2011)

Landolt, P., *Modernised EC Competition Law in International Arbitration* (Kluwer 2006)

Organisation for Economic Co-operation and Development (OECD), Arbitration and Competition 2010, Document of 13 December 2011 (DAF/COMP[2010]40)

Zuberbühler T. and Oetiker, C. (eds.), *Practical Aspects of Arbitrating EC Competition Law* (Schulthess 2007)

See also

Applicable law

A

ARTIFICIAL INTELLIGENCE

Alden ABBOTT
Mercatus Center – George Mason University

Definition

Artificial Intelligence (AI) encompasses a variety of innovative technologies that imitate or automate human cognitive functions through mechanisms like machine learning. AI applications range from the mimicking of human reasoning to the automation of specific complex tasks. AI facilitates these functions through increased analytical speed and scale of action. Generative AI, which involves the creation of new text and media content, has rapidly gained a foothold for business and personal use, through "foundation models" such as ChatGPT, Microsoft CoPilot, and Gemini (formerly Bard), to name just a few. AI model training, involving the provision of selected information to algorithms that help generate responses to queries, is key to generative AI.

Commentary

AI is attracting government scrutiny, in light of its major significance for the conduct of business. In particular, the European Union and the United States are assessing regulatory and law enforcement initiatives, aimed at ensuring that the application of AI does not undermine the public interest.

European Union (EU)

The AI Act

On 13 March 2024 the European Parliament adopted the AI Act, the first comprehensive regulatory framework for dealing with AI. The Act seeks to ensure that AI systems used in the EU are safe, transparent, traceable, non-discriminatory, and environmentally friendly. The Act establishes a risk-based framework applicable to AI systems.

- "Unacceptable risk" systems that are considered a threat to people are banned. They include cognitive behavioural manipulation of people or specific vulnerable groups; social scoring (classifying people based on behaviour, socio-economic status, or personal characteristics); and biometric identification and categorization of people. Some exceptions may be allowed for law enforcement purposes.

- "High risk" systems that will be assessed before being put on the market and throughout their life cycles. These include AI systems used in products falling under EU product safety legislation; and AI systems falling into specific areas that must be registered in an EU database (for example, critical infrastructure management and border control management).

The Act also imposes transparency requirements on uses of AI, even if they are not high risk. Thus generative AI, such as ChapGPT, has to make certain types of disclosures to avoid copyright infringement. High-impact general-purpose AI models that might pose systemic risk (such as GPT-4) will be subject to thorough evaluations and complaint monitoring by the European Commission (EC). Content that is either generated or modified with the help of AI will need to be clearly labelled as AI.

In order to help small and medium-sized enterprises develop and train AI models, the Act requires that national authorities provide companies with a testing environment that simulates conditions close to the real world.

Finally, the Act will be fully in force within 24 months (except for high risk systems, which are given 36 months), with certain key elements applicable sooner: the ban on unacceptable risk systems will apply after six months, codes of practice after nine months, and transparency requirements after 12 months.

Some scholars have expressed concern that the AI Act will stifle AI-related innovation in Europe, given its focus on risk-avoidance without assessing public benefit.

The Digital Markets Act (DMA) and the General Data Protection Regulation (GDPR)

Certain AI systems may be subject to other EU regulatory regimes. The DMA seeks to enhance competition by imposing certain interoperability and access requirements on specific large digital platforms designated as "gatekeepers." The GDPR imposes major privacy obligations on organisations that target or collect data related to people in the EU. Generative AI foundation models, that train on large databases, are subject to GDPR strictures. These include, for instance, principles of data minimization and storage limitation found in GDPR Article 5(1), and the preemptive prohibition on using special categories of personal data unless the requirements of GDPR Article 9(2) are met. The DMA is concerned with the competitive leveraging of data by gatekeepers. As such, generative AI modeling decisions conceivably could implicate DMA provisions related to contestability, fairness, and transparency. As of early 2024, the EC had not yet taken any position on the possible future application of the DMA to AI models.

EU Competition Law

In addition to ex ante regulation, AI applications may be subject to ex post EU competition law enforcement.

Algorithms may help firms respond more efficiently to real-time market conditions, allowing them to better respond to consumer preferences. At the same time, the use of price-setting AI algorithms may facilitate collusion among competitors. In a 2023 report to the OECD, the EU expressed particular concern with three types of collusion involving algorithms: (1) algorithmic facilitation of traditional collusion; (2) algorithmic alignment via a third party; and (3) algorithmic alignment (where different pricing algorithms could, without explicit instructions to do so, engage in some sort of explicit collusion with each other). The EU had doubts about whether the third category would violate EU competition law.

The EU's OECD submission also highlighted algorithmic exclusionary practices that constitute abuse of a dominant position. The submission focused on dominant platforms' use of algorithmic ranking criteria to favor their own products and services. Specific references were made to the European Commission's *Google Shopping and Amazon – Buy Box cases.*

EU merger enforcement will also take into account the effects of AI. In January 2024, the EC announced an investigation into whether Microsoft's investment into generative AI firm OpenAI comported with the EC merger regulation. More generally, In February 2024 EC Commissioner Margrethe Vestager stressed the need to evaluate AI's transformative effects in merger evaluations, with an emphasis on vertical integration and digital ecosystems.

United States (U.S.)

The U.S. Government is devoting increasing attention to AI as well, but, unlike the EU, it has not adopted a comprehensive AI regulatory scheme.

In an October 2023 Executive Order, President Joe Biden called for a government-wide effort to target a wide array of potential AI-related abuses, including fraud; discrimination; bias; disinformation; worker harm; safety and national security risks; consumer protection; and the stifling of competition. Regarding competition, the Order called for "addressing risks arising from concentrated control of key inputs, [and] taking steps to stop unlawful collusion and prevent dominant firms from disadvantaging competitors".

There is ongoing U.S. private antitrust litigation seeking damages for alleged algorithmic collusion. In two separate cases, *RealPage Antitrust Litigation and McKenna Duffy v. Yardi Systems, Inc.*, renters claim that multiple landords used the same algorithm to inflate rental prices. The U.S. Department of Justice (DOJ) asserted in a November 2023 court filing in ReaPage that "the alleged scheme meets the legal criteria for per se unlawful price fixing." The DOJ thereby signaled that it will be on the lookout for criminal prosecutions raising similar fact patterns.

Monopolization and anticompetitive mergers involving AI are also high on the list of DOJ and U.S. Federal Trade Commission (FTC) priorities. In January 2024, Assistant Attorney General for Antitrust Jonathan Kantor announced that DOJ had opened multiple probes into competition in AI. Also in January, the FTC stated that it was conducting market studies into Microsoft's OpenAI partnership, as well as investments in Anthropic by Alphabet Inc. and Amazon.com Inc.

At its first annual AI Summit in January 2024, the FTC emphasized its commitment to enforcing competition and consumer protection violations involving misuses of AI technologies. The Commission emphasized, among other topics, the actions of cloud providers, chip makers, and AI model builders. It noted software-related data security, bias, and privacy concerns. It also discussed potential relief, such as the deletion of AI models that violate the law through improper data collection or maintenance.

Other Jurisdictions

As of early 2024, various other jurisdictions were contemplating (or were already beginning to undertake) AI-related enforcement and regulatory measures. These included China, which was considering an "artificial intelligence law." The EU and U.S. approaches undoubtedly will be closely studied, as legal oversight of AI spreads around the world.

Bibliography

Marar, S. (2024), "Artificial Intelligence and Antitrust Law: A Primer." *Mercatus Special Study*, Mercatus Center at George Mason University

Prainsack, B., and Forgó, N. (2024), "New AI regulation in the EU seeks to reduce risk without assessing public benefit." *Nature Medicine*

Competition Policy International. 2024. "EU Antitrust Chief Warns of AI Impact on Merger Control Policy"

European Parliament. 2023. "EU AI Act: first regulation on artificial intelligence"

European Union. 2023. "Algorithmic competition – Note by the European Union." Directorate for Financial and Enterprise Affairs, Competition Committee, OECD

See also

AI Collusion (algorithm), Digital Markets Act (DMA), Fintech)

A

AS-EFFICIENT COMPETITOR (AEC)

Timo KLEIN
Utrecht University

Definition

The "as-efficient competitor" (AEC) principle is an analytical framework that may be employed in competition law to help distinguish exclusionary abuse of dominance from competition on the merits. Rooted in economics, it presumes that conduct by a dominant firm is anticompetitive only if it leads to the exclusion of a hypothetical, equally efficient competitor. AEC tests are mathematical abstractions of the principle, tailored to the specific conduct under consideration.

Commentary

The "as-efficient competitor" (AEC) principle is an analytical framework that may be employed in competition law to distinguish exclusionary abuse of dominance from competition on the merits. Rooted in economics, the principle presumes that conduct by a dominant firm is anticompetitive only if it leads to the exclusion of an imaginary, equally efficient competitor.

Within the EU, the principle was introduced in the 2009 European Commission Guidance on enforcement priorities in applying Article 102 of the EU Treaty to exclusionary abuse of dominance (European Commission, 2009). The objective at the time was to shift the focus of EU competition policy away from protecting competitors per se and towards the protection of competition in general (Whish and Bailey, 2015, section 5.2). This shift recognised that competition on the merits may lead to the exclusion of competitors that are less efficient. By nevertheless protecting those less efficient competitors, EU competition policy risks undermining the incentives of dominant firms to reduce costs, invest, and innovate – effectively stifling the competitive process and eventually harming consumers.

In addition to avoiding the protection of competitors per se, a key advantage of the AEC principle is that it promotes the predictability of competition law enforcement and facilitates compliance by providing a practical analytical framework for self-assessment. In particular, dominant firms would need to consider the consequences of their conduct only on a hypothetical, equally efficient competitor, rather than their actual competitors, of which they are unlikely to know the cost structures and demand.

In practice, AEC tests have been developed to translate the AEC principle into mathematical abstractions that aid in the assessment of the principle in specific cases. Exactly how the principle is applied – and hence how an AEC test looks like – depends on the specific conduct under consideration.

For example, in predatory pricing cases (e.g. Post Danmark), the AEC principle and test simply ask whether the prices set by the dominant firm are indeed lower than its marginal costs – with much of the discussion then focussed on exactly which prices and marginal costs to consider, over which time frame, and with what possible counterbalancing rationales for any below-cost pricing. In margin squeeze cases (e.g. Slovak Telekom), the AEC principle and test instead ask whether the upstream wholesale prices and downstream retail prices of a vertically integrated dominant firm are such that a hypothetical downstream competitor with the same downstream marginal cost can still make a profit if it were to buy at that wholesale price and sell at the same retail price. Again, much of the discussion is then focussed on exactly which costs to consider.

In loyalty rebate cases (e.g. Intel), the AEC principle and test instead ask whether the difference between the undiscounted and discounted price of the dominant firm is such that a hypothetical competitor with the same marginal cost can still profitably compensate customers for the loss in discount that they experience on the share of demand that they unavoidably need to buy from the dominant firm (the so -called uncontestable share of demand). In such cases much of the discussion is then focussed on which costs to consider, but also on how the rebates are exactly structured and what the uncontestable share of demand would be (Oxera, 2022).

Finally, the AEC principle (and potentially test) may also be applied in non-pricing conduct, such as bundling and tying or self-preferencing. For example, in self-preferencing cases (e.g. Google Shopping), the AEC principle asks whether the reduction in demand of a hypothetical competitor with the same marginal cost still allows it to operate profitably. A further development of this (including a suggestion on how the AEC test would look like in self-preferencing cases) is provided by Gaudin and Mantzari (2022).

While the AEC principle promotes an important focus on the protection of competition (as opposed to competitors per se) as well as predictability and compliance, it does come with its shortcomings. In particular – as also recognised in a policy brief reflecting on the 2009 Guidance ahead of drafting guidelines on exclusionary abuse of dominance (McCallum et. al, 2023) – protecting new entrants and not-yet as-efficient competitors may be vital for fostering dynamic competition in emerging markets or nascent industries.

Moreover, it is well-recognised within economic theory that even from a static perspective (e.g. ignoring changes in costs or innovation), structurally less efficient competitors can still impose an important competitive constraint on dominant firms. In such cases, a strict adherence to the AEC principle might overlook the benefits of protecting less-efficient competitors.

However, any alternative approach to exclusionary abuse of dominance that aims to remedy these shortcomings would ideally also aim to maintain as much as possible the key merits of the AEC principle – i.e. its focus on protecting competition rather than competitors per se and its positive effects on predictability and compliance.

Bibliography

Gaudin, G. and Mantzari, D. (2022), "Google Shopping and the as-efficient-competitor test: Taking stock and looking ahead", *Journal of European Competition Law & Practice*, 13(2), pp. 125–135

McCallum, L., Bernaerts, I., Kadar, M., Holzwarth, J., Kovo, D., Lagrue, M, Leduc, E., Manigrassi, L., Ramos, J.M., Pereira Alves, I., Pozzato, V., and Stamou, P. (2023), "A dynamic and workable effects-based approach to abuse of dominance", *Competition Policy Brief*

Oxera (2022), "Intel and the AEC test: 'Do. Or do not. There is no try.'", Agenda, 24 February

Whish, R. and Bailey, D. (2021), *Competition Law*, 10th edition, Oxford University Press

European Commission (2009), "Communication from the Commission - Guidance on the Commission's enforcement priorities in applying Article [102] of the EC Treaty to abusive exclusionary conduct by dominant undertakings", 2009/C 45/02

See also

Abuse of economic dependence

B

BARRIERS TO ENTRY

Fernando DE MAGALHAES FURLAN
Furlan Associados Consultoria

Definition

There are two definitions of entry barriers. The first defines them as any factor that permits firms already in a relevant market to earn higher than normal profits while simultaneously deterring others from entering and competing. An alternative definition and much narrower approach argues that the entry barrier concept should be limited to costs that a prospective market entrant must incur at the time or after the time of entry that existing market participants did not have to incur when they entered the relevant market. Barriers to entry may be structural (business conditions) or strategic (purpose of deterring entry) and must be scrutinized from a dynamic perspective. Conditions that influence entry include sunk costs, legal and regulatory barriers, economies of scale, economies of scope, capital costs, network effects, barriers to exit, vertical integration, predatory pricing, limit pricing, fidelity rebates and bundled discounts and exclusive dealing arrangements.

Commentary

In 1993, in Brooke Group, Ltd. v. Brown & Williamson Tobacco Corp., the Supreme Court has unquestionably recognized the entry barrier concept and imposed it in antitrust jurisprudence. It has not provided a clear definition of barriers to entry or clearly explained how the presence or absence of such barriers affect specific antitrust claims, though.

Some lower federal courts appear to follow ideas from economic literature that may be inconsistent with the predominant precedents. In United States v. Baker Hughes Inc. the D.C. Circuit decision rejected the government's argument that entry must be «quick and effective" to count on the ground that this requirement overlooks that potential competition, even it never resulting in actual entry, can nevertheless exert competitive pressure on the market.

The Ninth Circuit Federal Courtin Rebel Oil, a monopolization case, recognized that entry, though easy for some firms, may be insufficient to solve a competitive problem "if the market is unable to correct itself despite the entry of small rivals" and cited the Merger Guidelines "timely, likely, and sufficient" language as persuasive authority for undertaking that analysis.

The legal question involving burdens of proof is unresolved. The 1992 U.S. Merger Guidelines disclaim allocation of burdens; they describe an analytic framework adopted by the enforcement agencies, not a legal framework that should be employed by a court. Courts applying the Philadelphia National Bank presumption of anticompetitive effect from market concentration generally address entry as a rebuttal factor, designed to respond to the government's showing of concentration. This approach clearly places a burden of proof on the defendant.

On the other side of the Atlantic, most European rulings on dominance are determined around the existence of additional market characteristics, which either add to or detract from potential dominance. It is said that dominant positions raise "almost insuperable practical and financial obstacles" for actual and potential competitors. These characteristics have expanded through later case law and do not form a fully defined set.

On the one hand, in Continental Can, the European Court of Justice emphasized the importance of proving the possibilities of other competitors to enter the market, before ascertaining the existence of a dominant position. In other words, the ECJ stated that a causal relationship should not necessarily exist between the dominant position and its abuse, or that the causal relationship between a dominant position and its abuse is not necessary to ascertain the abuse of the dominant position.

On the other, in Hoffmann-La Roche, it provided a caveat in listing the factors (markets shares, price elasticity of demand, profitability measurement, barriers to entry, barriers to expansion, structural factors and behavioral factors) that may determine the existence of a dominant, which taken separately however, are not necessarily determinative.

In the 2012 AstraZeneca AB and AstraZeneca plc v European Commission , the European Court of Justice (ECJ) dismissed an appeal brought by AstraZeneca against a General Court ruling upholding the Commission's decision fining AZ 60 million euros for abuse of a dominant position on the market for proton pump inhibitors (PPIs) used for gastro-intestinal diseases. The Commission found that AZ had misused pharmaceutical marketing procedures in order to exclude competition from generic alternatives to, and parallel imports of, its Losec drug.

In Brazil, the most recent case (October 2018) involving barriers to entry was Administrative Process

N. 08012.007423/2006-27 where the Tribunal of the Administrative Council for Economic Defense (CADE) condemned the ice cream maker Unilever, owner of the Kibon brand, for limiting and harming free competition by preventing access by competitors to distribution channels. The case concerned points of sale (POS) in the ice cream market in the municipalities of Rio de Janeiro and São Paulo. During the investigation, there were indications that the company would have offered discounts and bonuses to the POS in exchange for exclusive sales, merchandising (privileged exposure) or the use of refrigerators. Cade also identified the existence of contractual provisions imposing the obligation of points of sale to sell a minimum quantity of products under penalty of fine and refund of the amount advanced upon signing the contract.

Bibliography

BAKER, J., Responding to Developments in Economics and the Courts: Entry in the Merger Guidelines. *The United States Department of Justice Archives*, August 2015

European Commission's DG Competition discussion paper on the application of Article 82 of the Treaty to exclusionary abuses, December 2005, paras. 34

Federal Trade Commission and U.S. Department of Justice, Antitrust Guidelines for Collaborations Among Competitors §3.35 (2000), reprinted in 4 Trade Reg. Rep. (CCH) 13,161

HERZ, M. and VEDDER, H., A commentary on Article 102 TFEU. In Blanke, H.-J. & Mangiameli, S. (eds.), *The Treaty on the Functioning of the European Union (TFEU)*

HOVENKAMP, H., *Federal antitrust policy. The law of competition and its practice*. 5th ed. Hornbook Series, West Academic Publishing, 2016, St. Paul, p. 50

LAZAROFF, D. Entry Barriers and Contemporary Antitrust Litigation. 7 *U.C. Davis Bus. L.J.* 1 (2006)

ROBERT O'DONOGHUE QC, R. and PADILLA, J., *The Law and Economics of Article 102 TFEU*, 2013, p.151 ff

WHISH, R. and BAILEY, D., *Competition Law*, 6th edition, 2010, p. 179 ff.

WHISH, R. and BAILEY, D., *Competition Law*, 7th edition, 2012, p. 179 ff.

OECD Policy Roundtables, Barriers to Entry. DAF/COMP(2005)42. Organization for Economic Co-operation and Development (OECD). March 2006

See also

Economic Analysis, Dominance (notion), Market power, Mobility barriers, Potential competition, Relevant market

B

BERTRAND (NASH) EQUILIBRIUM

Mike WALKER
UK Competition & Markets Authority – CMA

■ Definition

Formally, a set of strategies is called a Nash equilibrium if, holding the strategies of all other firms constant, no firm can obtain a higher payoff by choosing a different strategy. In less formal terms, a Nash equilibrium holds when each firm is doing the best they can (i.e. earning the highest profit) given what all the other firms in the market are doing. A Bertrand Nash equilibrium describes the Nash equilibrium outcome in a Bertrand model of oligopoly. Bertrand models are widely used models of oligopoly in competition economics. The great attraction of Nash equilibria is that they are stable as no firm has an incentive unilaterally to change their behaviour. It is the most widely used equilibrium concept in industrial organisation economics and was introduced by John Nash in his seminal 1951 paper.

■ Commentary

The basic Bertrand model of competition involves firms setting the price for homogeneous products. It is assumed that each firm can supply as much product as is demanded at any given price. Under these assumptions, it can be shown that the Bertrand (Nash) equilibrium is that price is equal to marginal cost (i.e. the same outcome as under perfect competition). The logic for this result is simple. Suppose there are just two firms, A and B. Suppose Firm A prices above marginal cost. Then Firm B's profit maximising price is to price just below Firm A but above marginal cost and capture all the market demand. But if Firm B does this, then Firm A can do better by pricing just below Firm B. This process of undercutting continues until price is at marginal cost. It would not make sense for either firm to price below marginal cost. The Bertrand (Nash) equilibrium is thus that price equals marginal cost.

This leads to the so-called Bertrand paradox: two firms are enough to generate the same outcome as under perfect competition. The "paradox" is that we normally assume that a duopoly will not be competitive and will price above marginal cost.

There are three ways to solve this apparent paradox. These involve relaxing one of the following assumptions:

- Products are homogeneous
- Each firm can supply the whole market
- Firms act in a short run non-cooperative fashion.

The most common way to change the model in order to get more intuitively plausible results is to assume that the firms sell differentiated products. Now firms do not lose all of their sales even if their competitors price slightly below them. This unravels the logic that leads to price equal to marginal cost in the standard (homogeneous products) Bertrand model. To see this, suppose that both Firm A and B did set their prices at marginal cost. Firm A would have an incentive to raise its price very slightly above marginal cost as it would not lose all its sales: those customers who prefer Firm A's product to Firm B's product would continue to buy it. This would increase Firm A's profits as it would make a positive profit on those sales that it continues to make, rather than the zero profit when price is equal to marginal cost. But Firm B faces the same incentives. The result is that both will raise their prices above marginal cost until the point at which a further price rise is not profitable given the price set by the other firm. This is a Nash equilibrium. The extent to which prices are above costs is driven by the extent of differentiation between products i.e. prices increase more as products become more differentiated. To the extent that more firms in the market implies less differentiation between products, this means that prices will tend to be lower as more firms enter the market. This accords with our intuition for how prices should fall as the number of suppliers increases.

The Bertrand differentiated products model is a workhorse model for merger analysis. When two firms merge in a Bertrand differentiated products setting, the competition that previously existed between them is lost. The merged entity has an incentive to raise prices because sales that were previously lost by one of the firms but captured by the other firm are now recaptured within the merged entity. The stronger the competition between the two firms was pre-merger, the more the merged entity has an incentive to raise prices. A price increase by the merged entity incentivises the other firms in the market to also raise their prices, although these "second order effects" are typically much smaller than the merging parties' price rise. This price rise is driven by the logic of the Nash equilibrium concept: if all the firms were previously doing the best they could given what all the other firms were doing, this will no longer be true if the merged entity raises its prices.

The Bertrand differentiated products model is applicable to markets where firms set prices for differentiated products and then customers choose whether or not to buy. It is therefore particularly relevant for retail markets. The UK Competition and Markets Authority review of the proposed *Sainsbury's/Asda* merger in 2019 is a good example of this. Standard empirical measures of the effect of mergers on pricing incentives, such as upward pricing pressure indices and indicative price rise indices, are typically based on the Bertrand differentiated products model.

The model is not relevant where prices are set separately for each buyer (i.e. markets involving substantial price discrimination) or where firms choose quantities rather than prices (i.e. Cournot competition).

Another way to escape the Bertrand paradox is to remove the assumption that each firm can supply the whole market. Where there are several firms in a market, this is unlikely to be a plausible assumption, at least not in the short run. The Bertrand-Edgeworth model assumes that no firm can supply the whole market. This allows prices to rise above marginal cost as the logic of the standard model (undercutting to win the whole market) no longer holds. This model illustrates another important aspect of the Nash equilibrium concept: it relates to strategies, rather than just to prices. In the Bertrand-Edgeworth model firms do not set a single price, but instead set different prices for each period based on a mixed strategy equilibrium (e.g. set a price of 10 with probably 0.2; a price of 11 with probability 0.18; etc.). This is because there is no single Nash equilibrium price in the Bertrand-Edgeworth model, but there is a Nash equilibrium set of mixed strategy equilibria. The European Commission's decision on the *Inoxum/Outokumpu* merger is a good example of the application of the Bertrand-Edgeworth model to a case.

The third way to escape the Bertrand paradox is to drop the assumption that firms think only about the outcome of period. The Bertrand paradox arises because the model is a one-period model. But suppose firms compete over many periods. Is it plausible that in each period they will set price equal to marginal cost and earn zero profits? Maybe. But where there are only a few firms it is also plausible that they will "soften" their pricing in the hope that other firms will as well.

Economists have traditionally assumed that collusion between firms would tend to be unstable as collusion was not a Nash equilibrium. The argument was that each firm has an incentive to cheat on the collusion (i.e. lower prices to win more demand) because, given what the other firms were doing, cheating is profit maximising. However, this argument is hard to square with the observed facts that cartels do exist and do manage to raise prices significantly. The problem with the standard argument is that it is very short termist. When firms compete over time, they aim to maximise profits over time, not just in one period. Fudenberg and

Maskin (1986) showed that any collusive output can be sustained as a Nash equilibrium of a pricing game when discount rates are high enough and when punishment mechanisms are credible.

Bibliography

CARLTON, D. and PERLOFF, J. 2015. *Modern Industrial Organization* Fourth edition (Pearson)

EDGEWORTH, F. 1989. "The pure theory of monopoly" reprinted in *Collected Papers relating to Political Economy Macmillan* (1925)

FUDENBERG, D. and MASKIN, E. 1986. "The Folk Theorem in repeated games with discounting and with incomplete information" *Econometrica* (vol. 54)

FUDENBERG, D. and TIROLE, J. 1989. "Noncooperative game theory for industrial organization: an introduction and overview" in *Handbook of Industrial Organization* ed. Schmalensee, R. and Willig, R. (North-Holland)

NASH, J. 1951. "Non-cooperative games" *Annals of Mathematics* (vol. 54, no 2. Sept 1951)

See also

Cournot (Nash) equilibrium, Oligopoly, Prices

B

BID RIGGING

Martin COLEMAN
UK Competition & Markets Authority – CMA

Definition

Bid rigging is a form of coordination between firms that may adversely affect the outcome of any sale or purchasing process in which bids are submitted. Such processes often, though not exclusively, relate to public procurement. Bid rigging may take a number of forms including: Bid suppression, where one or more parties agree not to bid; cover bidding, where parties agree to bid an artificially high price and bid rotation, where parties may agree to bid, or bid only at an artificially high price, in rotation according to the number or value of contracts.

Commentary

Bid rigging is an egregious form of anti-competitive behaviour, in part because it normally includes elements of other serious anti-competitive conduct such as price-fixing, the sharing of markets/customers and the exchange of confidential information between competitors. The gravity is exacerbated by the fact that it often involves public contracts with consequent loss to taxpayers and the undermining of important public purposes in areas such as defence and national infrastructure.

Bid rigging is an object infringement under Article 101(1) TFEU. In the *PreInsulated Pipes* case, for each supply contract the existing supplier would inform other suppliers participating in the arrangement of the price they intended to quote, the other suppliers would provide quotations at higher prices to ensure the maintenance of existing customer relationships. This was found by the European Commission to restrict competition by its very nature.

In the USA bid rigging is a per se violation of the U.S. Sherman Act 1890 (*USA v Javier Sanchez* (2019)). "*An agreement to interfere with competition for a transaction conducted by bid*" is a standalone infringement of the Sherman Act independent of any element of collusion which may also be present (*United States v Guthrie* (1993)).

Bid rigging is unlawful in all OECD member countries. In the EU, UK and Japan, 33% of competition authority fining decisions by volume concerned bid rigging activities; in the U.S. the percentage was 46% and in South Korea it was 89% (*Allen & Overy, Global Cartel Enforcement Report, 2020*). Bid rigging will normally fall within the scope of national criminal prohibitions on anti-competitive practices (for example, the "cartel offence" under section 188 of the UK Enterprise Act 2002). Even in jurisdictions where cartel activity is not criminalised, bid rigging may be a criminal offence. Ten jurisdictions can impose criminal sanctions exclusively for bid rigging conspiracies (*OECD Working Party No 3, 2020*). Bid rigging may be associated with other unlawful activities such as bribery, for example where a purchaser or an intermediary receives a payment to favour certain bidders or to ignore coordinated bidding practices.

Under EU law a joint bidding or consortia agreement is not unlawful if the parties to the agreement are not actual or potential competitors. It is not always easy to distinguish legitimate pro-competitive cooperation through teaming, joint bidding and subcontracting arrangements from unlawful bid rigging agreements. How public authorities choose to combine or fragment potential projects may therefore impact whether potential bidders can bid individually or whether they need to combine with others. In the *Danish Road Marking Consortium case (Dansk Vejmarkerings Konsortium)* tenders were invited for road markings in three different districts. Two of the biggest undertakings submitted a joint bid covering three districts. Each party had what was needed to bid for one lot. The Danish Supreme Court upheld a decision by the Danish Competition Council which found that the parties to the consortium agreement were actual competitors since both had the financial resources, know-how and access to the requirements concerning machines and staff in order to bid for one lot. Consequently, their bidding arrangement, which involved price-fixing and contract sharing, was anti-competitive by object thereby infringing Article 101(1) TFEU. The contracting authority had encouraged bids for all three contracts collectively but did not make this a requirement. Presumably, if the public authority had not offered bidders the option of bidding for individual road marking projects, that is if the only contract available had been for the three combined projects, the outcome would have been different if the two tenderers did not have the resources to individually bid for the combined project. A more difficult question is if the two tenderers had anticipated bids from third parties for the combined contracts, and therefore taken the view that in practice the real competition was for the combined package, should their joint bidding agreement have been considered as an object infringement?

Although they could in practice have bid for the individual contracts the economic and business reality in such circumstances was that the contest was for the combined project.

An agreement under which the bidders materially integrate their assets and resources in order to bid is, depending on circumstances. less likely to be considered to be anti-competitive by object than one where they simply allocate particular contracts or geographic areas between themselves though may still, on analysis, be anti-competitive by effect.

The impact of bid rigging on public authorities requires close cooperation between competition authorities and other public bodies to maximise the possibility of detection. In November 2019 the U.S. Justice Department announced the formation of a Procurement Collusion Strike Force (PCSF), which now includes 29 public agencies, focusing on deterring, detecting, investigating and prosecuting antitrust crimes, including bid rigging, which undermine competition in government procurement, grant and program funding. In its first year the PCSF opened over two dozen grand jury investigations across the United States spanning the range of procurement collusion and fraud matters including domestic and international investigations into conduct affecting U.S. government procurement overseas.

On the one hand, the transparency of public bidding processes makes bid rigging easier because it is harder for parties to secretly "cheat" on each other. On the other hand, detection is helped by the standardisation and digitisation of procurement processes which enable authorities to access transparent and comparable data. Many competition authorities produce guidelines to assist purchasing authorities in detecting bid rigging, for example warning buyers to look out for, changes in bid patterns, pricing irregularities and suspicious behaviour. Bid rigging screening tools may be helpful to complement other cartel detection methods (such as encouraging leniency, whistleblowing and intelligence functions). The UK CMA was one of the first competition authorities to develop a digital bid rigging screening tool in 2017. After encountering some initial difficulties when applying the tool it was withdrawn to allow further work on its effectiveness. Several other authorities have introduced, or are developing, bid rigging screening tools, for example, the Spanish competition authority has established a specialised new economic intelligence unit which conducts market screening activities and targets in particular potential bid rigging in public procurement activities.

The end date of a bid rigging scheme matters in order to determine the limitation period and the size of any penalty. In *Kilpailu- ja kuluttajavirasto* (2021), the European Court of Justice held that a bid rigging scheme ends on the date that the infringing company signs a contract with the party that put out the tender (not when tenders are submitted or when the price is paid in full). The financial consequences of such activity may have a longer term effect and might be taken into account in any damages action.

Bibliography

Allen & Overy, Global Cartel Enforcement Report, February 2020

Sander Løjmand, H., The Danish Supreme Court's Ruling in the "Road Marking Case": The End of a Joint Bidding Era, How to Crack a Nut, 28 November 2019

Justice Department Announces Procurement Collusion Strike Force: a Coordinated National Response to Combat Antitrust Crimes and Related Schemes in Government Procurement, Grant and Program Funding, 5 November 2019, Press Release Number: 19-1,189 and speech by Assistant Attorney General Makan Delrahim, "Here I Go Again": New Developments for the Future of the Antitrust Division, 12 November 2020

OECD, Working Party No. 3 on Co-operation and Enforcement Executive Summary of the roundtable on Criminalisation of cartels and bid rigging conspiracies Annex to the Summary Record of the 131st Meeting of Working Party No. 3 on Co-operation and Enforcement 9 June 2020

OECD, Ex officio cartel investigations and the use of screens to detect, 7 July 2014, DAF/COMP(2013)27 and see also: M Huber and D Imhof, Machine Learning with Screens for Detecting Bid-Rigging Cartels (2018) University of Fribourg Faculty of Social and Economic Sciences Working Paper Series No 494

See also

Cartel, Anticompetitive practices, Price-fixing agreement, Public procurement

B

BLOCK EXEMPTION (REGULATION)

Inês F. NEVES
University of Porto

■ Definition

An instrument issued by the competent authorities, with erga omnes effects, specifying the conditions under which certain types or categories of agreements, decisions or concerted practices are automatically presumed to be valid and enforceable. In the European Union, when an agreement falls within a block exemption adopted by the Council or the Commission pursuant to an enabling Council Regulation, it is presumed to satisfy the conditions of Article 101(3) TFEU without the need to determine whether the conditions for the application of Article 101(1) TFEU are met. In some jurisdictions there are no block exemptions or safe harbour provisions. However, sector-specific rules may end up superseding competition rules.

■ Commentary

Article 101(3) TFEU lays down the conditions under which the provisions of Article 101(1) TFEU may be declared inapplicable to certain agreements, decisions or concerted practices. Article 2 of Regulation 1/2003 provides that the legal burden of proof rests on the party claiming the benefit of Article 101(3) TFEU. A block exemption Regulation ("BER") is based on the presumption that restrictive agreements, decisions or concerted practices that fall within its scope fulfil the four conditions set forth in Article 101(3) TFEU; a BER therefore provides a "safe harbour" for certain categories of behaviour. According to the Court of Justice in Pedro IV Servicios SL v Total España SA (2009, paragraph 36), where an agreement is caught by a BER, there is no need to incur a complex economic and legal assessment to determine whether the conditions for the application of Article 101(1) TFEU are met. When a block exemption Regulation is available, companies should focus on i) determining whether the agreement in question falls within its general scope of application; ii) checking the market share thresholds defined therein; and iii) assessing whether the agreement, decision or concerted practice contains any hardcore or excluded restrictions. In this respect, even though Article 2 of Regulation 1/2003 does not expressly rule on the burden of proving that the conditions of a block exemption are fulfilled, the general rule seems to apply, so it will be on the party claiming the benefit to prove such conditions (*JCB Service v Commission of the European Communities* (2004), paragraph 168).

The fact that an agreement is not block-exempted does not mean that it is caught by Article 101(1) TFEU (*Auto 24 SARL v Jaguar Land Rover France SAS* (2012), paragraph 22) or that it does not fulfil the conditions of Article 101(3) TFEU: this will require a separate assessment.

When a BER is *prima facie* applicable, it is legally possible for the Commission or a National Competition Authority ("NCA") to withdraw the benefit of a block exemption, where the specific behaviour it covers has certain effects that are incompatible with Article 101(3) TFEU. According to Article 29(2) of Regulation 1/2003, an NCA can do this only where the negative effects of the behaviour occur in the territory of a Member State, or in a part thereof, which has all the characteristics of a distinct geographic market. The Guidelines on the application of Article 81(3) (now, Article 101(3)) of the Treaty (paragraph 37) state that the courts of Member States have no power to withdraw the benefit of block exemption regulations. In any case, the benefit of a block exemption can be withheld only when the agreement has already been concluded at the time of the withdrawal decision, which means that there is no withdrawing for future agreements. Finally, it is also possible for the Commission to declare by Regulation that a block exemption is inapplicable in certain circumstances.

In the system of Regulation 1/2003, only the Council and pursuant to an enabling Regulation under Article 103(2) b) TFEU, the Commission have the power to adopt block exemption regulations regarding the application of Article 101(3) TFEU. The block exemptions may concern, among others, specialization agreements, research and development agreements, vertical restraints, motor vehicle aftermarkets, technology transfer agreements, agreements in the field of transport by rail, road, and inland waterway, as well as agreements relating to the joint operation of liner shipping transport services, when entered into in the context of consortia between vessel-operating carriers. Even though most block exemptions currently in force have been adopted by the Commission (with the authority granted by the Council), the Council has itself provided block exemptions for certain agreements, for instance, between small and medium-sized undertakings in the road and inland waterway sectors. The block exemptions share a typical format, and they all contain an expiry date before which the Commission reviews and consults on the functioning of the exemption about to expire. There is no presumption in favour of renewing a block exemption.

Besides increasing legal certainty for companies and relieving antitrust authorities of the burden of assessing individual agreements, decisions or concerted practices, block exemption regulations also express the Commission's policy towards the behaviours to which the exemption applies. As a consequence, and having regard to the general prohibition of agreements, decisions and concerted practices restricting competition in Article 101(1) TFEU, provisions derogating therefrom in a certain BER must, by their very nature be strictly and narrowly interpreted (*Automobiles Peugeot SA and Peugeot SA v Commission of the European Communities (1993)*, paragraph 37). Also, its direct applicability does not confer upon national courts the power to modify the scope of the exemption, by extending its sphere of application to agreements not expressly covered by it or further than necessary for the protection of the interests which it is intended to safeguard (*Stergios Delimitis v Henninger Bräu AG (1991)*, paragraph 46).

In many jurisdictions, there are no block exemptions or safe harbour provisions (the United States is an example, even though a number of industries benefit from legislative exemptions from the antitrust laws therein). Sector-specific rules, which apply as lex specialis, derogating the application of competition rules to specific sectors of economic activity, are present in many jurisdictions (such as Brazil, Colombia, Czech Republic, among others). In other countries, the National Competition Act specifically provides for certain exemptions (for instance, Australia's Competition and Consumer Act, New Zealand's Commerce Act and Russia's Federal law on protection of competition). Finally, so-called "statutory" or "legal" exemptions are also possible in those cases in which a certain behaviour is imposed or specifically authorised by law and therefore automatically exempted from the competition law scrutiny (among others, Spain, Israel and New Zealand). In many European Union Member States, National Competition Acts include dynamic referrals to the existing EU BERs, these being applicable to cases limited to the national territory without requiring a European dimension (as in the case of Germany and Portugal, for instance). The same connection is also present when the provisions of "national" block exemptions are based on those provided for in the respective EU Regulations.

Bibliography

Bailey, D. and John, L. E. (eds.), *Bellamy and Child: European Union Law of Competition* (8th edn, Oxford University Press 2018), Chapter 3

Faull, J. and Nikpay, A. (eds.), *The EU Law of Competition* (3rd edn, Oxford University Press 2014), Chapter 3

Sokol, D. D., Crane, D. and Ezrachi, A. (eds.), *Global Antitrust Compliance Handbook* (Oxford University Press 2014)

Tuytschaever, F. and Wijckmans, F., *Vertical Agreements in EU Competition Law* (3rd edn, Oxford University Press 2018), Chapter 2

Whish, R. and Bailey, D., *Competition Law* (10th end, Oxford University Press 2021), Chapter 4

See also

Consortium, Exclusive distribution, Hardcore restrictions, White clause, Withdrawal of the benefit of a block exemption

BOYCOTT

Sonia ROCHA ESQUIVEL
Mexican Competition Authority

Definition

Boycott refers to an orchestrated refusal to deal that is used to exert pressure, on a third party, which may be a competitor, supplier, or customer. The aim is to exclude or to force the third party to behave in a particular way. A boycott may be orchestrated by an individual who indirectly harms a third party through the support of a group of firms. The firms themselves may decide directly, in a concerted manner, to refuse to deal with a third party. This practice may be illegal per se in certain jurisdictions.

Commentary

Boycott is a practice that has been scrutinised as a per se violation of antitrust laws in the United States. For instance, in Fashion Originators' Guild of America v. FTC (1941), the U.S. Supreme Court declared "it was not error to refuse to hear the evidence offered" [to the Federal Trade Commission]. In the European Union, it is unclear how a boycott may be pursued. One interpretation is that article 101(1) TFEU prohibits concerted boycott as expressed in Dansk Rørindustri A/S and Others v. Commission of the European Communities and others (2005, paragraph 21) which considered a boycott as part of the arrangements that "may together be regarded as forming an agreement prohibited by Article 85(1) of the Treaty" [nowadays article 101(1) TFEU]. However, whilst Article 101(1) condemns some violations as per se, there is scope for an efficiency defence under Article 101(3).

In the U.S., per se illegality may implicitly consider that the orchestrator group or individual of a boycott has an important position in the market or possesses unique access to a necessary input to compete as suggested by the U.S. Supreme Court in Northwest Wholesale Stationers v. Pacific Stationery and Printing Co. (1985) who declared that "the Court of Appeals failed to exercise the requisite care, and applied per se analysis inappropriately".

Similarly, a boycott can be examined under the rule of reason. For example, in the United States itself it is also possible to find this kind of scrutiny as can be seen in U.S. FTC v. Toys "R" Us Inc. (2000) and Northwest Wholesale Stationers v. Pacific Stationery and Printing Co. (1985). Hence, it is not entirely clear what treatment a boycott case will receive on U.S. Courts.

In Mexico, boycott is expressly typified and evaluated under the rule of reason, as 1) substantial market power or joint dominance is required and 2) a theory of harm explaining the object or effect of restricting competition must be constructed for it to be considered unlawful. Another jurisdiction that has expressly typified boycott is Germany but there the concerted refusal to deal with the aim of unfairly harming other firms is per se unlawful as can be seen from Section 21 of its Competition Act.

Boycott typically involves a group refusal to deal. However, the group of firms instrumenting the boycott may be persuaded to engage in this practice without seeking to do so. In other words, there is an individual or group of firms who are interested in the result that the collective refusal to deal is going to achieve, but they are not necessarily the ones exerting the pressure over a third party. An example of this situation is depicted in U.S. FTC v. Toys "R" Us Inc. (2000). The Mexican competition law contemplates this scenario when typifying boycott.

Authors such as Posner (2003) suggest that boycott cases involve "an extraordinarily heterogenous body of practices, many of which are not exclusionary". In this respect, a concerted refusal to deal may be orchestrated and implemented by a group of firms to provoke a vertically related third party to behave in a certain way. For example, a group of firms may expect the third party to respect a price policy (e.g. a lower price if it is a supplier and a higher price if it is a customer). This type of boycott is referred to as "collusive" by some authors, such as Baker et al. (2017), who note that collusive boycotts "result in collusive effects, i.e., those that directly fix the output, or the prices charged by the colluding firms". Therefore, justifications for orchestrating this type of boycott may not be accepted. Accordingly, other authors such as Hovenkamp (2021) describe that the per se analysis is reserved for the so-called naked boycotts "when no case can be made that the refusal is ancillary to any legitimate joint activity."

Another type of boycott is called "exclusionary". An exclusionary boycott occurs when an individual or group orchestrator aims to force a competitor out of the market through the intervention of other parties (suppliers or customers) who refuse to deal with the boycotted party. Firms themselves may refuse to deal with a competitor in a concerted way, as can be the case involving a trade association. For Baker et al. (2017), it is more difficult to characterise an exclusionary boycott because "(1) its effects may be less obvious and (2) its potentially legitimate justifications can be more varied". Consequently, some exclusionary boycotts may be justifiable under the antitrust scrutiny. For example, a boycott may be aimed at preventing free riding. As the U.S. Supreme Court stated in Northwest Wholesale Stationers v. Pacific Stationery and Printing Co. (1985), "The mere allegation of a concerted refusal to deal does not suffice, because not all concerted refusals to deal are predominantly anticompetitive." A case involving this type of boycott in Mexico is the one where a trade union association of taxi guilds in Los Cabos exerted pressure on tourists to not use other touristic transportation foreclosing them of the market (2006); this case was fined.

In this category, it is also possible to find that the boycott is implemented as a mechanism of retaliation, when there is a deviation from an agreement on prices or quantities. If a competitor does not respect a cartel agreement, the other members of the cartel may punish the cheater by orchestrating a boycott to force it out of the market. This behaviour may therefore be indicative of the existence of a cartel and may be analysed as such.

Bibliography

Baker, J., Gavil, A., Kovacic, W., and Wright, J., *Antitrust Law in Perspective: Cases, Concepts, and Problems in Competition Policy*, (3rd edn, West Academic Publishing 2017), Chapters 2 and 4

Emperanza Sobejano, A., *El boicot como acto de competencia desleal contrario a la libre competencia* (Tirant Lo Blanch 2000), Chapter 1

Hovenkamp, H., *Principles of Antitrust* (2nd edn, W West Academic Publishing 2021), Chapter 5

Hylton, K. N., *Antitrust Law: Economic theory and common law evolution* (Cambridge University Press 2003), Chapter 9

Posner, R., *Antitrust Law* (2nd edn, University of Chicago Press, 2001), Chapter 7

See also

Anticompetitive practices, Abuse of dominant position, Cartel, Exclusionary practice, Refusal to deal

BRAND COMPETITION

Laurent CENATIEMPO
AIM – European Brands Association

Definition

Brand competition refers to the strategies employed by brands to differentiate themselves from competitors in a market or industry in order to gain the attention, trust and loyalty of consumers. While brand competition can benefit consumers by promoting lower prices and better quality or service, it can also harm competition and consumers.Competition authorities are particularly concerned about the potential for dominant brands to engage in anti-competitive behaviour and about the impact on competition of a merger between two or more brands. Brand competition strategies are typically examined through the prism of two core concepts: *inter-brand competition* (competition between different brands or products) and *intra-brand competition* (competition between different sellers of the same brand or product), which form the basis for assessing and regulating brand competition.

Commentary

Competition law regulates brand competition to ensure that it benefits consumers and promotes fair competition between companies. As an essential component of market competition, brand competition can be defined as the rivalry between brands or products that are designed and differentiated on the basis of specific characteristics, mainly in the form of inter-brand competition And intra-brand competition.

Inter-brand competition refers to the rivalry between different brands or products that serve the same purpose or function. In this type of competition, companies compete for market share by differentiating their products through factors such as price, features, quality, design, brand image and reputation, innovation, comparative advertising and marketing strategies. This form of competition promotes diversity and innovation within industries.

Intra-brand competition, on the other hand, refers to the rivalry between sellers of the same brand or product. In this type of competition, sellers compete to attract customers to their specific products by using strategies such as product line extensions, product variations, product bundling, packaging and presentation, price differentiation and customer experience differentiation. This form of competition encourages innovation in marketing and consumer engagement.

Beyond these fundamental concepts, other important aspects of brand competition include:

- Generic competition, where brands compete with unbranded or generic products within the same category
- Private label competition, where brands compete with private label products offered by retailers within the same category,
- Substitute competition, where brands compete with alternative products or services that perform similar functions, and
- Category competition, where brands compete for consumer attention, preference and market share within a specific product category or industry.

Brand competition encompasses a variety of strategies to gain a competitive advantage in the marketplace by satisfying unmet demand or creating demand:

- Price competition (e.g., positioning, matching, promotions, bundling, dynamic pricing),
- Product differentiation (e.g., quality, components, features, design, size, portability, packaging, presentation, sustainability, customisation, performance, cultural relevance),
- Brand visibility (e.g., advertising and promotional campaigns),
- Market positioning (e.g., distribution channels, geographical availability, online presence),
- Commercialisation strategies (e.g., product line extensions, product variations, product bundling),
- Customer experience quality (e.g., ease of purchase, customer support, warranties, after-sales services),
- Innovation and research and development,
- Brand loyalty programmes,
- Patents, trademarks and copyrights,
- Partnerships with other brands,
- Market and competitive intelligence, and
- Commitment to corporate social responsibility

The complexity and diversity of brand competition underline the dynamic nature of the marketplace and the evolving expectations of consumers. Indeed, brand competition is a multi-faceted landscape characterised by a variety of strategies used by brands to differentiate themselves, adapt to market demands and secure consumer loyalty.

The competition law implications and significance of brand competition practices depend on a number of factors, including the structure and dynamics of the market, the potential anti-competitive effects and the factual circumstances of each situation.

For example, inter-brand competition is likely to be restricted when a dominant undertaking engages in anti-competitive behaviour such as price fixing, market sharing or refusing to supply products to competitors, while intra-brand competition is likely to be restricted when a dominant undertaking engages in anti-competitive behaviour such as imposing unfair conditions on its distributors or preventing them from selling to certain customers. Such restrictions may also result from a collusive agreement between undertakings.

Another important concern of competition law in relation to brand competition is the protection of intellectual property rights. While companies have the right to protect their trademarks, patents, and other intellectual property from infringement, the exercise of this right must be balanced against the need to ensure that consumers have access to a wide range of products and services. Accordingly, competition law typically prohibits intellectual property from unduly restricting competition in the marketplace.

Brand competition plays a key role in enhancing consumer welfare by enriching the landscape of options across several dimensions, including brands, products, and prices, thus enabling and empowering consumers to choose products that meet their preferences, needs, and budget constraints. The more competitive a marketplace is, the more it encourages brands to continuously innovate and improve the quality of their offerings to stand out in a crowded field and respond to consumer demands, and the more consumers are well served, informed, and empowered.

The legal frameworks that govern brand competition in different jurisdictions seek to strike a balance between protecting legitimate competition and preventing anti-competitive practices. These frameworks typically include antitrust laws, which regulate practices to ensure fair competition, but may also include unfair trading practices laws, intellectual property laws and consumer protection laws.

In the EU, the legal framework for brand competition is primarily shaped by competition law, which aims to ensure fair and undistorted competition in the Single Market.

Articles 101 and 102 of the Treaty on the Functioning of the European Union deal respectively with anti-competitive agreements and abuses of dominant positions, while Regulations 2022/720 (Vertical Block Exemption Regulation) and 2023/1066 and 2023/1067 (Horizontal Block Exemption Regulations) exempt certain types of agreements and practices from the general prohibition of anti-competitive behaviour under Article 101 TFEU.

Regulation 139/2004 (Merger Regulation) provides for the control of concentrations between undertakings to ensure that they do not significantly impede effective competition within the Single Market. While the Regulation is more directly related to overall market competition than to specific brand competition, its implications have an impact on how brands operate in the competitive landscape. Indeed, the main objectives of the Merger Regulation are relevant to brand owners:

- Preventing the creation or strengthening of a dominant position that

could impede effective competition with other brand owners,
- Preserving consumer choice and the incentives for brands to innovate and differentiate,
- Encouraging market entry and expansion to support a diverse and competitive marketplace, and
- Protect small and medium-sized enterprises, which may be disproportionately affected when larger companies consolidate and create dominant positions.

EU case law has consistently emphasised the importance of maintaining competition not only on price but also on parameters such as quality, variety, and innovation. EU courts have shown a nuanced approach, taking into account the impact of distribution practices on market access, brand reputation, and the overall competitive environment, and have also highlighted the challenge of striking a balance between brand protection and the promotion of fair competition, particularly in the context of online sales and selective distribution networks.

In *Consten and Grundig*, the German brand Grundig offered exclusive distribution to the French distributor Consten, potentially restricting intra-EU trade. The Court disregarded potential positive effects on inter-brand competition and focused on the establishment of absolute territorial protection. This decision demonstrated a cautious approach to territorial restrictions and their effects on market access.

The *Metro* I judgment emphasised that competition goes beyond price and endorsed selective distribution networks based on qualitative criteria. This marked a shift, recognising that product differentiation leading to higher prices could be compatible with EU competition law if it promoted competition on non-price parameters such as quality, variety, and innovation.

Pronuptia de Paris recognised that franchise agreements could restrict intra-brand competition by allowing franchisors to select franchisees and impose restrictions to protect brand reputation. The case highlighted the importance of protecting brand identity within a franchise network by recognising the transfer of intellectual property rights and know-how.

The Pierre Fabre case clarified that maintaining a prestigious image is not a legitimate objective for restricting competition. The decision focused on the prohibition of online sales restrictions in selective distribution networks. The ruling underlined the need to strike a balance between brand protection and the promotion of competition, and challenged broad restrictions based on brand image protection.

Maintaining healthy brand competition faces challenges, including intellectual property disputes, counterfeiting, and the evolving landscape of online marketplaces. Counterfeiting threatens brand integrity and consumer trust, while online marketplaces present both opportunities and challenges. Future trends in brand competition include the growing influence of e-commerce, with digital platforms shaping consumer behaviour. The impact of social media on brand visibility and consumer engagement is a notable trend. In addition, sustainability practices are becoming a key factor, influencing consumer preferences and shaping brand competitive strategies towards environmentally responsible practices. Navigating these challenges and embracing emerging trends will be critical for brands seeking sustainable success in the competitive marketplace.

Bibliography

Fox, E. M., "Parallel Imports, The Intraband/Interbrand Competition Paradigm, and the Hidden Gap Between Intellectual Property Law and Antitrust", *Fordham International Law Journal*, Volume 25(4) (2001)

Lianos, I., "Brands, Product Differentiation and EU Competition Law", *CLES Research Paper Series* 7/2014 (2014)

Sharp, B., Dawes, J., Victory, K., "The market-based assets theory of brand competition", *Journal of Retailing and Consumer Services*, Volume 76 (2024)

Weber Waller, S. and Desai, D., "Brands Competition and the Law", *BYU L. Rev.* 1425 (2010)

See also

Economic analysis, Selective distribution

B

BUNDLING

Alden ABBOTT
Mercatus Center – George Mason University

■ Definition

Bundling and tying arrangements are widespread in the modern commercial economy. Bundling is the practice of selling a number of separate products together in one bundle at a single price. It is related to tied selling, whereby a seller requires that the purchaser of the "tying" product also must purchase a separate specified "tied" product or products. In "pure bundling," the seller only offers the individual products in a package. In "mixed bundling," the products are offered in a bundle and also separately, with the bundle sold at a discounted price. Bundling may combine complementary items or non-complementary items.

■ Commentary

Bundling may have both positive and negative effects on consumer welfare and competition. It may generate consumer-friendly cost-reducing efficiencies, which allow the bundle to be sold profitably at a price lower than the aggregate price of its components sold separately. Bundling may in theory, however, allow a firm to leverage its dominance in one market into other markets, thereby denying other firms the ability to compete effectively in those markets. The extent to which such "anticompetitive leveraging" is a serious problem and harms consumer welfare is highly contested. While bundling may involve particular price discount schemes, it may also arise in the mandatory technological integration of multiple products into a package without explicit price discounting.

United States antitrust case law assesses bundling practices under the antitrust rule of reason. European Union (EU) competition law is somewhat less favourable toward the practice, which it evaluates both in unilateral dominant firm conduct cases and in merger cases where the acquisition may bring about bundling. Price discounted-related bundling cases and technological bundling cases are analysed separately.

Bundling with Explicit Discounting: United States Decisions

Two distinct frameworks are employed to assess bundling involving discounts in United States case law, which is largely centered on applying Section 2 of the Sherman Act (monopolization). Unless and until the Supreme Court intervenes, the status of bundling discounts under U.S. law will remain uncertain.

Several U.S. Circuit Courts of Appeals follow the logic of the Third Circuit's *Cascade Health* (2009) decision, holding that mixed bundling is legal as long as the prices of the "competitive" product or products in a bundle are above an appropriate measure of cost. This determination is made by allocating all of a package's discount to the "competitive" (leveraged) products. Some have critiqued this "discount attribution standard" as difficult to implement (because determining and applying the appropriate cost measure is hard). Certain "pro-enforcement" critics find that it may foreclose or exclude equally efficient rivals even in the case of above cost pricing (by analogy to tying). In contrast, other commentators believe that it underplays the importance of economies of scope and thereby may disincentivize efficient, procompetitive behavior.

In *Lepage's* (2003), the Third Circuit Court of Appeals analogized bundled rebates to tying and applied a modified rule of reason approach. 3M, a dominant transparent tape supplier, had bundled its private label tape (which competed with LePage's tape) with other products not offered by LePage's. Lepage's claimed that 3M's conduct amounted to Sherman Act monopolization by inducing many of LePage's major customers not to buy LePage's tape. The Third Circuit, without examining whether 3M's prices were above cost, held that 3M's conduct was anticompetitive foreclosure that could lead to higher prices and reduced output. Adissenting judge argued that LePage's was a less efficient producer than 3M. Various critics have excoriated the *LePage's* decision, arguing that its failure to focus on efficiencies could preclude many pro-consumer bundling arrangements from being introduced into the marketplace. Critics have also decried *LePage's* failure to provide a discernible standard for determining the legality of a bundling arrangement.

Bundling with Explicit Discounting: European Union Decisions

Bundling involving discounting faces close scrutiny in the European Union (EU). European courts have accepted a foreclosure-based approach , applying Article 102 of the EU Treaty (abuse of a dominant position). Once a threshold of dominance (lower than the U.S. test for monopolization) is reached, EU competition law generally condemns retroactive bundled discounts that make it difficult for rivals to enter the market, without any objective economic justification. Recently however, EU Courts have increasingly focused on the actual effects of bundling conduct. EU Courts have clarified that, where a dominant firm produces evidence that rebates (or exclusivity) could not have an anti-competitive effect, the European Commission (EC), or national competition authority, must address that evidence. The EU Courts also have stressed that Article 102 foreclosure analysis is concerned with protecting the interests of as-efficient competitors (AECs), not less efficient competitors.

In *British Airways* (2007), the EU Court of Justice, upheld a Commission finding of an Article 102 infringement, but implicitly modified earlier case law that suggested all dominant firm loyalty-inducing discounts within the EU are anticompetitive. The *British Airways* court adopted a slightly different approach that balanced a rebate system's anticompetitive foreclosure effect against advantages bestowed upon consumers.

Subsequent judicial decisions underscore the concern of EU Courts with the need for evidentiary backing and economic analysis supporting findings of anti-competitive foreclosure. In *Intel* (2017 and 2022), EU Courts first questioned then annulled the EC's condemnation of Intel's conditional rebates on microprocessors, criticizing the Commission's analysis of Intel's substantive conduct and its failure to adequately address certain Intel arguments. In *Unilever Italia* (2023), the EU Court of Justice faulted the Italian Competition Authority for not assessing evidence submitted by Unilever regarding its exclusivity clauses, citing the 2017 *Intel* decision's discussion of evidentiary analysis in the context of rebates. Finally, in *Qualcomm* (2022), the General Court set aside the EC's condemnation of Qualcomm's incentive payments to Apple, citing massive procedural irregularities by the Commission.

Bundling Through Technological Integration: U.S. and EU Approaches Compared

U.S. antitrust enforcers have had less luck than European enforcers in challenging the technological bundling of complementary products by monopolists, in particular, "high tech" companies.

Microsoft is a prime example of a high tech company that over time progressively has bundled additional component features into its Windows operating system. Such features have included the Internet Explorer browser (1995), the Windows Media Player (WMP, 2000), among others.

United States case law has been reluctant to condemn the "zero additional cost" bundling by high tech companies of new technological features that add value to a service or product offering. (An example is a court's failure to condemn outright Microsoft's "free" bundling of Windows in litigation over two decades ago.) The U.S. courts' intuition appears to be that new bundled technological features may substantially enhance consumer welfare and should not lightly be interfered with by the courts.

The European approach is different. In *EC v. Microsoft*, the EU Court of First Instance (now the General Court) upheld the European Commission's finding that Microsoft abused its dominant position by bundling Windows with WMP on all client PCs. The Court agreed with the Commission that this practice inevitably damaged third party media players and that Microsoft had not presented an objective justification for the practice. As a remedy, Microsoft was required to sell some of its Windows software without WMP. Consumer demand, however, for the WMP-less software proved to be negligible.

Since *EC v. Microsoft*, the "zero cost" technological bundling of separate functionalities by dominant high tech platforms has continued to stimulate successful European Commission enforcement actions, but has not inspired similar initiatives in the United States. European courts, however, have begun to closely assess the reasoning of the Commission in finding competitive harm. Indeed, they have been willing to reduce fines in cases where the Commission's economy analysis was found to be partially flawed.

In *Google Android*, for example, the EU General Court reduced the Commission's record 4.3 billion euro fine against Google for bundling Google Search, Google Play, and Chrome with Android. The Court agreed with the Commission's decision that the pre-installation of these features gave Google a significant competitive advantage, by creating a consumer "status quo bias" that sellers of competing features could not overcome. The Court affirmed that "the practice in question had led to the strengthening of Google's dominant position on the market for general search services, while deterring innovation, in so far as it had limited the diversity of the offers available to users." The General Court, however, reduced the fine to 4.1 billion euros, because it did not agree with the Commission's analysis of certain revenue-sharing agreements.

Bibliography

Brandenburger, A., Nalebuff, B., Waldman, M., Pil Choi, J., Stallings Williams, M., and Sibley, D. S., "Bundling and Tying" (2021) 1 *Antitrust Chronicle* 1

Crane, D. A. and Wright, J. D., "Can Bundled Discounting Increase Consumer Prices Without Excluding Rivals?" (2009) 5 *Competition Policy International* 209

Economides, N. and Lianos, I., "The Elusive Antitrust Standard on Bundling in Europe and in the United States in the Aftermath of the Microsoft Cases" (2009) 76 *Antitrust Law Journal* 483

Maziarz, A., "Tying and bundling: Applying EU competition rules for best practices" (2013) 3 *International Journal of Public Law and Policy* 263

See also

Abuse of dominant position, Exclusionary practice

B

BURDEN OF PROOF

Pieter VAN CLEYNENBREUGEL
Liege Competition and Innovation Institute

Definition

Allegations of (potentially) anticompetitive behaviour need to be proven. Legal provisions or case law precedents on the burden of proof determine (1) in general terms which party has to produce relevant facts and evidence in competition/antitrust law procedures (the burden of production of evidence) and (2) the extent to which specific evidence has to be offered by that party in order to be sufficiently persuasive to meet the standard of proof required to establish the pro- or anticompetitive nature of the behaviour (the actual evidential burden). Article 2 of Regulation 1/2003 is the clearest example of a burden of proof provision.

Commentary

Explicit legal provisions or case law precedents accompanying competition law frameworks generally determine who has the obligation to produce factual and legal evidence to establish the existence of (potentially) anticompetitive behaviour. Those provisions or precedents are necessary tools to ensure that competition law investigations take place in a predictable manner. In their essence, burden of proof norms or principles determine which party bears the risk of facts remaining unresolved or allegations unproven (see also Opinion of Advocate General Kokott in CJEU Case C-8/08, *T-Mobile*, EU:C:2009:110, para 80). Competition law frameworks therefore classically determine who has to prove what in general terms. In addition, the courts generally recognise short-cut rules to fast-track certain cases and to allow infringements/liability to be established on the basis of certain assumptions or evidentiary presumptions. Those presumptions may in turn shift the burden to prove the absence of anticompetitive behaviour or effects on a different party.

The general principle that the claimant bears the burden of producing relevant evidence (*actori incumbit probatio*) stands in both EU and U.S. law. In European Union law, Article 2 of Council Regulation 1/2003 states that the burden of proving an infringement of Article 101(1) or of Article 102 of the Treaty shall rest on the party or the authority alleging the infringement. The undertaking or association of undertakings claiming the benefit of Article 101(3) of the Treaty shall bear the burden of proving that the conditions of that paragraph are fulfilled. In merger control, it follows from Articles 2(2) and (3) of Regulation 139/2004 that the Commission bears the burden of proving that an envisaged concentration would produce a significant impediment to effective competition (see also General Court, T-399/16, *CK Telecom*, EU:T:2020:217, para 107). In U.S. antitrust law, it is in principle also the claimant who needs to adduce the relevant evidence. In per se infringements, the government or plaintiff needs to produce evidence that the behaviour falls within one of the per se categories (U.S. Supreme Court, *Ohio v American Express*, 138 S. Ct. 2274 (2018), 9). The same goes for merger review under Section 7 of the Clayton Act. In such cases, "[t]o establish a prima facie case, the Government must (1) propose the proper relevant market and (2) show that the effect of the merger in that market is likely to be anticompetitive" (*FTC v. Penn State Hershey Med. Ctr.*, 838 F.3d 327, 337-38 (3d Cir. 2016).

Despite those general rules or principles, courts have come to accept so-called short-cut rules and evidentiary presumptions that in practice result in alleviating or shifting the actual evidentiary burden ordinarily falling upon the claimant.

Short-cut rules allow a claimant to assume that anticompetitive behaviour is in place on the basis of proof of certain types of behaviour or other elements, without having to show more conclusively the anticompetitive object or effect of the behaviour in question. An example in EU law is the assumption that pricing below average variable costs by a dominant undertaking is anticompetitive (CJEU, Case C-62/86, *Akzo*, EU:C:1991:286) or the assumption that certain behaviour meets U.S. per se standards. Short-cut rules alleviate the burden of proof resting on the claimant, who can successfully bring a claim based on evidence assuming anticompetitive behaviour. The defendant is generally unable to refute or contest the claim where such assumptions apply.

Evidentiary presumptions allow the decision-maker to infer, on the basis of evidence offered, that anticompetitive behaviour is present. The defendant may then proceed to rebut those presumptions on the basis of more specific evidence to the contrary. Examples of evidentiary presumptions are the presumption of parental liability (CJEU, C-97/08 P, *Akzo*, EU:C:2009:536), the presumption that contacts between undertakings behaving in a parallel fashion allow the inference of the existence of a concerted practice (although not automatically an anticompetitive practice) under Article 101 TFEU (CJEU, C-49/92 P, *Anic*, EU:C:1999:356, para 121) or the presumption of dominance on the basis of (excessively) large market shares. The U.S. rule of reason framework also establishes a burden-shifting evidentiary presumption framework. According to the U.S. Supreme Court, "the plaintiff has the initial burden to prove that the challenged restraint has a substantial anticompetitive effect that harms consumers in the relevant market. [...] If the plaintiff carries its burden, then the burden shifts to the defendant to show a procompetitive rationale for the restraint. [...] If the defendant makes this showing, then the burden shifts back to the plaintiff to demonstrate that the procompetitive efficiencies could be reasonably achieved through less anticompetitive means" (U.S. Supreme Court, *Ohio v American Express*, 138 S. Ct. 2274 (2018), 9-10). Evidentiary presumptions in practice thus shift the evidentiary burden from the claimant to the defendant. The latter will have to offer the evidence of absence of anticompetitive behaviour or of procompetitive advantages justifying and outweighing anticompetitive effects.

Although short-cut rules and evidentiary presumptions exist in both EU and U.S. law, two factors currently mitigate against their unbridled expansion. First, at a more individual level, shifting the burden to or disabling a defendant to prove innocence is difficult to align with fundamental rights such as the presumption of innocence. Someone accused of anticompetitive behaviour cannot simply be held liable or condemned on the basis of assumptions against which no reasonably justified defence can be introduced. Second, and more generally, competition/antitrust systems increasingly pay attention to effects-focused analysis: in order to prove anticompetitive behaviour, the anticompetitive effects of such behaviour on the structure and operations of the market need to be established to a sufficient extent. Short-cut rules and evidentiary presumptions allowing fast-track analyses make it easier for claimants to establish liability without fully proving the presence of such effects. It appears that reliance on those shortcuts or presumptions to meet the standard of proof is no longer unequivocally tolerated by courts. As a result, an apparent overall decline of both short-cuts and evidentiary presumptions in favour of a more coherently applied *actori incumbit* probatio burden of proof standard can be seen in both EU and U.S. (case) law (by way of recent example, General Court, T-286/09 *RENV*, EU:T:2022:19, para 165-166).

Bibliography

FERNANDEZ, C., "Presumtions and Burden of Proof in EU Competition Law: The Intel Judgment", 10 *Journal of European Competition Law & Practice* (2019), 448-456

GAVIL, A., "Burden of Proof in U.S. Antitrust Law", in 1 *Issues in Competition Law and Policy 125 (ABA Section of Antitrust Law)* (2008), 125-156

GAVIL, A. and SALOP, S., "Probability, Presumptions and Evidentiary Burdens in Antitrust Analysis: Revitalizing the Rule of Reason for Exclusionary Conduct", 168 *University of Pennsylvania Law Review* (2020), 2107-2143

KALINTIRI, A., "The Allocation of the Legal Burden of Proof in Article 101 TFEU Cases: A 'Clear' Rule with Not-So-Clear Implications", 34 *Yearbook of European Law* (2015), 232-256

VOLPIN, C., "The Ball is in your court: evidential burden of proof and the proof-proximity principle in EU competition law", 51 *Common Market Law Review* (2014), 1159-1186

See also

Judicial review

B

BUYER POWER

Ignacio HERRERA ANCHUSTEGUI
University of Bergen

■ Definition

Buyer power describes the bargaining position of a buyer with respect to its supplier(s) of goods or services. Through purchasing strategies, the buyer, unilaterally or through coordination with other buyers, can decrease the purchasing price of its input below the supplier's standard selling price, above or below the competitive level. Two sub-types of buyer power are distinguished: first, monopsony power, which implies a withholding effect, being inefficient and dubbed the reverse of monopoly power; and second, bargaining (or countervailing) power, in which tactics other than withholding may be used to the benefit of the buyer to reduce the input's price. Bargaining power tends to be welfare enhancing as supra-competitive profits kept by the supplier are passed on to the buyer and eventually to the end consumers if there is competition in the retailing market.

■ Commentary

Introduction – Buyer power is an often-neglected topic in the theory and practice of competition law. Buyer power is economically and legally complex. This is due to its dual nature as either a usually efficiency-enhancing purchasing behavior (bargaining power) or as an inefficient one (monopsony). Buyer power interacts and affects two markets. First and foremost, the upstream market, where the purchases are made; secondly, the retailing market in which the buyer acts as a retailer. Anticompetitive concerns prompted by buyer power have arisen across the whole spectrum of competition law: including agreements, abuse of market power, and concentration cases.

Monopsony power describes the situation in which the supply side of a market is perfectly competitive, represented by an upward-sloping supply curve, and in which a sole buyer is present. The buyer will exercise its market power by withholding purchases (i.e., buying less) to decrease the purchasing price it pays for a good/service below the level that would emerge in a competitive market. The price is set by the buyer fixing a purchasing price it is willing to pay for the input, in a take-it or leave-it offer, or by refusing to negotiate on price. In such a setting, the monopsonist becomes a price-maker. This approach to buyer (monopsony) power is essentially the reverse or mirror image of monopoly power. Monopsony is only possible when the buyer faces an upward-sloping supply curve, i.e., the more you buy, the more expensive the marginal unit becomes. Monopsony power exertion also implies suppliers selling below their marginal costs; if this is the case, the suppliers will be eventually driven out of the market. Monopsony cases tend to be rare. Buyers often try to exercise their purchasing power not through a reduction in purchases but by obtaining more favorable conditions However, a few demand withholding examples are found in the case law. Among them, the alleged imposition of abnormally low purchasing prices of film licenses by a dominant buyer (*CICCE v Commission*), agreements between buyers limiting the amount of durum wheat that macaroni producers would include in the formula (*National Macaroni Manufacturers Association v. Federal Trade Commission*) or fixing minimum purchasing prices for grapes for cognac (*BNIC v Clair*).

Bargaining power, often labeled as the "new" approach to buyer power, describes the strength in bilateral negotiations of a buyer regarding its supplier(s). Bargaining power allows the buyer to obtain a concession (be it in the form of price and/or non-price terms) from the supplier by, for example, threatening to acquire goods from a different party or simply having the upper hand in the negotiation. Unlike monopsony power, bargaining power does not involve withholding demand or acquiring goods below the competitive price. Instead, it increases trade and neutralizes seller market power by transferring supra-competitive profits from the supplier to the seller that may be passed on eventually to the end consumers. This is because bargaining power can only be exercised where the price is above the supplier's marginal cost. Therefore, bargaining power tends to be welfare enhancing, being this a reason why there are few anticompetitive cases involving this form of purchasing. That said, bargaining power may raise anticompetitive concerns; these are usually linked to exclusionary effects. Leverage of buyer power to obtain advantages in a subsequent downstream market through the offer of particularly beneficial (and loyalty enhancing) purchasing conditions was discussed extensively in *British Airways v Commission* through the grant of some "reverse" rebates. Additionally, predatory buying has also been reviewed in the case law and found to be a plausible theory of harm, for instance, by the U.S. Supreme Court in *Weyerhaeuser Company, v Ross-Simmons Hardwood*

Lumber Company, Inc. Bargaining power is often used as a procompetitive argument to justify a conduct and render it compatible with competition rules. Prime examples of this situation are buying alliances that pool buyer power, leading to lower input prices and higher output, as discussed, for instance, in *Gøttrup-Klim and Others Grovvareforeninger v Dansk Landbrugs Grovvareselskab, or Northwest Wholesale Stationers, Inc. v. Pacific Stationery Printing Co.*

Countervailing buyer power, or the ability to sufficiently neutralize opposing market power based on the buyer's bargaining strength in a commercial relationship, has been a topic of discussion in concentration and abuse of dominance cases. While often invoked, practice shows that meeting the sufficiency requirements for countervailing buyer power to effectively prevent seller market power exertion is rare. This neutralizing power must benefit not only the large buyer exerting it but also spill over to other (smaller) buyers, as discussed in *Enso/Stora*.

The type of harm required for EU competition law to be applicable to buyer power cases has also been analyzed by the case law. European courts have found that buyer power liability arises without requiring direct evidence of end consumer harm (e.g.: *British Airways v Commission*, as well as the spill-over effect requirement in countervailing buyer power cases, such as *SCA/Metsä Tissue*). This means that harm that can be proven and has taken place in the upstream market in and by itself is sufficient for competition law to apply; not that this necessarily implies that inefficient suppliers are protected, or that end consumer harm is irrelevant. A narrower approach that focuses on the effects on the output market and, therefore, also direct end consumer harm appears to be adopted in the USA in *Weyerhaeuser Company, v Ross-Simmons Hardwood Lumber Company, Inc.* This narrower approach assumes that buyers always compete in the same upstream and downstream markets, which is not necessarily the case.

The EU Competition law's scope of application has been defined regarding which purchases are controlled by it and, therefore, determining which exercises of buyer power (or by whom) could be illegal. Not all purchases by an entity imply an economic activity, a defining factor for EU competition law to be applicable. In *FENIN v Commission*, the ECJ stressed that establishing whether purchasing constitutes an economic activity "must be determined according to whether or not the subsequent use of the purchased goods amounts to an economic activity".

The topics of unfair purchasing practices, gatekeeping and economic dependence have recently brought rare attention to buyer power. Discussions on fairness, relative market power, and exploitation of small suppliers by large buyers combine issues related to antitrust, contractual equilibrium, and fair competition. Most instances of unfair purchasing practices (e.g.: delisting, slotting allowances, etc.), typically related to the food retailing sector, will fall outside the scope of antitrust rules as buyers tend not to be dominant. Regulatory solutions to unfair purchasing practices have been adopted in various countries, including most EU member states and the USA. Legislative interest and concern in the matter led to the Directive (EU) 2019/633 on unfair trading practices in business-to-business relationships in the agricultural and food supply chain in April 2019. Gatekeeping, or the ability of buyers to create entry or exit barriers to either the upstream or downstream market, is another buyer power topic enjoying a renaissance because of the discussions on the regulation of digital markets. Examples related to unfair purchasing, gatekeeping, and economic dependence are found in the case law and EU Commission's practice, such as the *Kesko/Tuko* concentration case.

Bibliography

CARTENSEN, P. C., *Competition Policy and the Control of Buyer Power: A Global Issue*. Edward Elgar, 2017

CHEN, Z., "Defining buyer power." *Antitrust Bulletin*. 53 (2008): 241

HERRERA ANCHUSTEGUI, I., IGNACIO, *Buyer Power in EU Competition Law*, Concurrences (2017). Winner of the 2017 Concurrences PhD Award

KIRKWOOD, J. B., "Buyer power and exclusionary conduct: Should Brooke Group set the Standards for Buyer-Induced Price Discrimination and Predatory Bidding?" *Antitrust Law Journal* 72, 2004: 625

VAN DOORN, F., The Law and Economics of Buyer Power in *EU Competition Policy*, Eleven International Publishing, 2015

See also

Anticompetitive object or effect, Concentration indexes, Dominance (notion), Market power

C

CARTEL

Kyriakos FOUNTOUKAKOS
Herbert Smith Freehills

Definition

A cartel is an anti-competitive agreement or concerted practice between two or more rival firms aimed at coordinating their competitive behaviour on the market or influencing other parameters of competition through practices that include but are not limited to: the direct or indirect fixing of prices or other trading conditions; the limitation or control of production, markets, technical developments or investment; the sharing of markets or sources of supply, including bid-rigging; restrictions of imports or exports, or a combination of these practices. Exchange of competitively sensitive information can also be treated as cartel conduct in certain circumstances.

Commentary

Cartels involve collusion among rival firms to distort, limit or eliminate competition, primarily in pursuit of higher prices and profits, without producing any countervailing benefits. As such, cartels are considered among the most harmful forms of anti-competitive conduct and their prosecution is a priority among competition authorities. It is estimated that in 2021, competition authorities worldwide imposed cartel fines totalling approximately USD 4.6 billion (EUR 4 billion). Cartel participation may also give rise to individual criminal liability in certain jurisdictions as well as private damages actions by harmed undertakings and/or consumers.

Cartels involve collusion between firms and can therefore be distinguished from unilateral conduct capable of infringing competition laws (i.e. an abuse by a dominant firm of its position of market power).

A cartel typically involves secret meetings or contacts between cartel participants over a sustained period of time (although in certain jurisdictions a one-off meeting may provide a sufficient basis for a cartel). Such arrangements may take many different forms: cartels can be based on written or oral agreements, whether formal or informal in nature, or, in the absence of a concluded agreement, a common understanding by which the parties consciously commit to a common scheme (*Monsanto*, pages 465 U.S. 752, 768; *Suiker Unie*, paragraph 26).

Cartel participants generally compete in the production and / or supply of a relevant set of products or services. However, organisations such as trade associations and consultancy firms may also be found guilty of cartel conduct if they knowingly facilitate cartel meetings, contacts or the exchange of competitively sensitive information between competitors.

A cartel may result from an isolated event, a series of acts or from continuous conduct. Many cartels are complex and last a long period of time. During the entire duration of the cartel, some firms may be more active than others: some may abandon the cartel but subsequently re-join, others may attend only a handful of meetings. If a cartel operates on a global basis there may also be a number of sub-agreements covering different products or services and jurisdictions. For these reasons, competition authorities have found ways to ensure that a related series of anti-competitive actions may be treated as a single, overreaching cartel.

In the EU, for example, the concept of a "single and continuous infringement" (SCI) enables a competition authority to group together a series of infringements of Article 101 of the Treaty for the Functioning of the EU (TFEU) and treat these as forming part of the same cartel conduct, on the ground that they pursue a single overall plan. The U.S. has developed a similar concept, known as the "single versus multiple conspiracies" doctrine. Under these concepts, it is necessary to determine whether the cartel arrangements are sufficiently linked to be considered part of one unified cartel, instead of a number of smaller, independent collusive practices.

Practices commonly found in cartel arrangements, such as price-fixing, output restrictions and market-sharing, are treated as among the most serious types of competition infringement. For example, in the EU such arrangements are characterised as restrictions of competition "*by object*", while in the U.S. they are treated as *per se* violations under Section 1 of the Sherman Act. The important practical consequence of such categorisations is that there is generally no need for competition authorities to establish the actual effect of the cartel on any specific market in order to conclude that there has been a competition law infringement; harm to competition is self-evident given the nature of the activities involved (*Cartes Bancaires*, paragraph 51).

Most forms of cartel activity entail exchanges of information among rivals. The exchange of certain types of information between competitors can provide a standalone basis for a cartel finding. Competition authorities are particularly concerned with the exchange of so-called "competitively sensitive information" (CSI) that may enable undertakings to predict each other's future behaviour and to coordinate their behaviour on the market by reducing uncertainty as to the operation of the market in question, with the result that competition is restricted (*T-Mobile*, paragraph 35). CSI may include future prices, marketing strategies, quantities, commercial terms with particular customers or suppliers, costs, operational plans, production levels and utilization, capacity reduction/expansion plans and technical information. The exchange of CSI may be unlawful where it is part of a mechanism for enforcing or monitoring a cartel or as an infringement in itself.

Competition authorities generally have extensive powers to investigate suspected cartels. These typically include powers to request information directly from firms and to conduct surprise inspections (so-called "dawn raids") at business or private premises to search for electronic or physical documents and conduct interviews. These wide-ranging powers of investigation are generally limited by legal professional privilege and the privilege against self-incrimination (with the availability, precise nature and scope of differing forms of privilege capable of varying between jurisdictions).

A fundamental feature of cartel enforcement worldwide is the power for competition authorities to impose significant sanctions, with the related aims of punishing firms that participate in cartels and deterring firms from forming cartels in the first place. Most competition authorities can impose substantial administrative fines on cartel participants. In 2021, the largest cartel fines were imposed by the European Commission (totalling around USD 2 billion; EUR 1.7 billion), South Korea (USD 865 million; EUR 763 million), Brazil (USD 656 million; EUR 578 million), China (USD 268 million; EUR 263 million), the United States (USD 150 million; EUR 132 million) and India (USD 117 million; EUR 103 million).

Parties harmed by cartel conduct can and increasingly do bring actions for damages. In certain jurisdictions (like the EU) a competition authority's findings can be relied on as evidence without the claimant needing to prove the existence of the cartel.

Many jurisdictions, such as Australia, Canada, Brazil, Chile, Denmark, France, Germany, Hungary, Israel, Italy, Japan, Mexico, Poland, Romania, South Africa, South Korea, the UK and the U.S., also have powers to impose criminal sanctions against individuals involved in cartel activity. These sanctions may lead to imprisonment in cases of serious infringement. In most of these jurisdictions, criminal cartel offences are investigated and prosecuted by a public prosecutor and criminal sanctions imposed by the national criminal courts. One notable exception is the UK where both the Competition and Markets Authority (CMA) and the Serious Fraud Office (SFO) have the power to investigate and prosecute criminal cartel offences. However, only the UK's criminal courts can impose criminal sanctions against individuals.

One of the most successful tools to detect and prosecute cartels is the use of leniency programmes, whereby cartel participants that report the existence of a cartel to a competition authority and hand over evidence are granted either total immunity (in principle to the first undertaking to come forward) or a reduction from fines. Leniency programmes have been adopted in most jurisdictions worldwide.

Bibliography

BAILEY, D. and JOHN, L. E. (eds.), *Bellamy and Child: European Union Law of Competition* (8th edition, Oxford University Press, 2018), Chapter 5

BRODER, D., *U.S. Antitrust Law and Enforcement* (3rd edition, Oxford University Press, 2016), Chapter 3

JONES, A., SUFRIN, B. and DUNNE, N., *EU Competition Law: Text, Cases, and Materials* (7th edition, Oxford University Press, 2019), Chapter 9

WHISH, R. and BAILEY, D., *Competition Law* (10th edition, Oxford University Press, 2021), Chapter 13

See also

Anticompetitive object or effect, Anticompetitive practices, Bid rigging, Boycott, Concerted practices, Price-fixing agreement

C

COLLECTING SOCIETY

Adriana ZABŁOCKA-ABI YAGHI
University of Gdansk (Department of Economics)

Definition

The collecting societies (CSs) are primarily private, non-profit membership organizations that manage copyrights. Their economic function is to collect and distribute royalties and monitor the use of copyrighted works on behalf of the right owners and holders. Since CSs are primarily organized as national monopolies bound by a complex network of bilateral agreements, so their practices were of interest to competition authorities. However, technological changes are the stimuli for a pro-competitive shift in the collective management system.

Commentary

The CSs enable the functioning of markets for the use of copyright works, especially when it is impossible for right owners (holders) to contact users of their work directly. By managing bundles of rights on behalf of their members, CSs obtain significant economies of scale and scope in administering, licensing, and enforcing copyrights. These economies reduce transaction costs that are too high to make the individual enforcement of copyrights economically feasible. The economies, the territorial nature of copyrights, and traditional forms of copyright mass use made CSs national, natural monopolies. In some countries, the market position of CSs is strengthened and accepted by additional functions fulfilled by CSs, such as the provision of social benefits or cross-subsidizing less popular music categories. Another feature of national CSs is their linkage through reciprocal representation agreements. The primary purpose of the agreements is to offer licenses for a broader range of copyrighted works (domestic and non-domestic) and to protect domestic copyrighted works in another territory.

CSs activities' features and conduct were a trigger to proceedings conducted by national competition authorities and the European Commission (EC). They focused mainly on the relationship of CSs with users and their members and on reciprocal representation agreements.

Pricing policy was one of the critical issues concerning relationships between CSs and users. The principal case on this issue is the *Tournier case* (1989). The European Court of Justice (ECJ) stated that a national copyright-management society imposes unfair trading conditions when the charged royalties are appreciably higher than those in the other Member States. Therefore, any differences in the rates of royalties charged by national CSs must be justified by referencing objective and relevant dissimilarities between CSs in question (*Tournier*, paragraphs 36-46).

The ECJ judgment in the *Tournier case* also addressed issues regarding the relationship between CSs and users. Firstly, a CS may only refuse direct access to its national repertoire for users from the other Member States for efficiency reasons (*Tournier*, paragraph 24). Secondly, the refusal to grant the user access only to part of the repertoire (the foreign one) does not restrict competition if it entirely safeguards the interests of right owners without increasing the costs of management and monitoring of copyrighted work use (*Tournier*, paragraph 33).

The legal framework of the relationship between CSs and their members was set up in the EC decision concerning the German collective management organization, *GEMA* (1971). The EC stated that the requirement to assign existing and future members' rights entirely to GEMA could constitute abuse of a dominant position (*GEMA*, part II, paragraph C). Therefore, the EC obliged GEMA to amend the rules of its statute, allowing members to assign all their rights to GEMA or divide them by category and assign them to various CSs (*GEMA*, article 1). Moreover, the other amendments to the statute rules should allow members to withdraw the administration of specific rights categories without incurring penalties while maintaining membership (*GEMA*, article 1). The EC also indicated that the statutory provisions that discriminate against CS members regarding income distribution and voting rights should be withdrawn (*GEMA*, article 1). Moreover, any discrimination on nationality must automatically be regarded as an infringement of art 102 TFEU (ex Article 86 TEEC) (*GEMA*, part II, paragraph C).

Reciprocal representation agreements were of interest to the ECJ in *Tournier* and *Lucazeau, and others* (1989) cases. The Court stated that such agreements at that time were economically justified due to the requirements of physical monitoring of copyright usage, and as such, did not fall under art 101(1) TFEU (ex Article 85(1) TEEC) (*Lucazeau and others*, paragraphs 13-14). However, the development of the digital network environment has changed the possibilities of exploiting copyrighted works allowing for its worldwide reach and monitoring at a distance. These changes have renewed the EU institutions' interest in reciprocal representation agreements. An agreement between CSs to grant international copyright licenses to radio and TV broadcasters wishing to make musical works available to the public via the Internet posed a challenge to the EC (*IFPI Simulcasting* case (2002)). Ultimately, a new product brought to the market (simulcasting licenses for the use of licensed right in more than one country), benefits to consumers, and opening up CSs to competition (*IFPI Simulcasting*, paragraphs 84-95) were decisive factors in granting an individual exemption for this agreement under Article 101(3) TFEU until 2004. In turn, the provisions of the model reciprocal agreement concerning the exploitation of musical works on modern platforms (Internet, satellite, and cable) were the subject of a complaint to the EC against CISAC (*CISAC*, 2008). The EC found that the exclusivity clause concerning CSs' members' acceptance, license issuing, and the territory of intervention resulted in geographic market segmentation and thus infringed Article 101 TFEU (ex Article 81 TEC) (*CISAC*, paragraphs 250-252). However, due to the lack of sufficient evidence, the Commission's claims were rejected by the EU General Court (*CISAC v Commission*, 2013, paragraph 182). Shortly after the Court's ruling, the EU adopted a legislative solution in the form of Directive 2014/26, which requires CSs to take steps to adapt their licensing activities to the digital age.

The music licensing landscape in the U.S. is different from the EU. Although the performing rights organizations (PROs) in the U.S. are similar to CSs, their activity concentrates on certain rights. Antitrust concerns related to the activities of PROs led to the adoption of specific regulations. An example is antitrust consent decrees that restrict activities of the American Society of Composers, Authors and Publishers (ASCAP) and Broadcast Music, Inc (BMI).

Bibliography

Gervais, D., The economics of collective management, in: *Research Handbook on the Economics of Intellectual Property Law.* (Edward Elgar Publishing, 2019).

Guibault, L. and Van Gompel, S., Collective Management in the European Union, in: Daniel Gervais (ed.), *Collective Management of Copyright and Related Rights*, second edition (2nd edn, Alphen aan den Rijn: Kluwer Law International, 2010), pp. 135-167.

Handke, C., *Joint Copyrights Management by Collecting Societies and Online Platforms: An Economic Analysis* (March 11, 2016).

Kretschmer, M., "The aims of European competition policy towards copyright collecting societies" (2005) *Serciac. Montreal* 7-8.

Miernicki, M., *Collective Management of Copyrights between Competition, Regulation, and Monopolism.* (Nomos, 2017).

See also

Copyright, Intellectual property right

C

COLLECTIVE DOMINANCE

Liza LOVDAHL GORMSEN
British Institute of International and Comparative Law

■ Definition

Article 102 of the Treaty on the Functioning of the European Union (TFEU) is the statutory provision governing the abuse of dominance in the European Union. The provision captures both single and collective dominance. Article 102 TFEU states that any abuse by one or more undertakings of a dominant position within the internal market or in a substantial part of it shall be prohibited as incompatible with the internal market in so far as it may affect trade between Member States. Certain markets – oligopolistic markets – lend themselves to collective dominance due to the market structure with a small number of operators who can observe each other's competitive actions. Both Article 102 TFEU and the European Union Merger Regulation capture collective dominance.

■ Commentary

The conduct of several operators can approximate that of a single dominant firm and if they are found to be collectively dominant such behaviour could fall under the prohibition of abuse of dominance. The notion of collective dominance under Article 102 TFEU was first accepted by the General Court in Italian Flat Glass (1992). In the Compagnie Maritime Belge (2000, paragraph 45) the Court of Justice of the European Union stated that collective dominance is a position "held by two or more economic entities legally independent of each other, which from an economic point of view, present themselves of act together on a particular market as a collective entity".

Collective dominance is also a known concept in merger cases. The leading case is Airtours (2002, paragraph 62) where the General Court established a three-prong test for a finding of collective dominance. First, each operator must have the ability to monitor the behaviour of the others as to whether they are adopting a common policy.

This means there must be a certain level of transparency. Second, the situation of tacit collusion must be sustainable over time. Third, the reaction of actual or potential competitors (countervailing competitive pressure) and consumers (countervailing buyer power) must not jeopardise the results of the common policy. The Court of Justice of the European Union confirmed the Airtours test in Impala II (2008, paragraph 251) and held that the three Airtours criteria can also be established indirectly.

Airtours confirmed collective dominance under merger control. Laurent Piau (2005, paragraphs 109-111) clarified that the assessment of collective dominance under Article 102 TFEU and merger control should be based on the same principles. If collective dominance is proved, each individual undertaking is in principle subject to the special responsibility of dominant firms under Article 102 TFEU. One collectively dominant company can commit an abuse even if not acting jointly with the others, but the General Court held in Irish Sugar (1999, paragraph 66) that conduct must be "one of the manifestations of such a joint dominant position being held".

National competition law follows European competition law and collective dominance is no exemption. On the national level, most of the cases concerning collective dominance arise in the context of merger control rather than abuse of dominance. It appears from national case law that certain industries such as the media, telecommunications, banking and energy are more likely to create collective dominance concern than others, although collective dominance allegations might arise in any other sector. National case law follows the legal standard developed by in Airtours although the UK Competition Appeal Tribunal held in Brannigan (2007, paragraph 106) that it is not always necessary to show that there is price transparency in the relevant market. In AEM/ASM Brescia (2007), the Italian Competition Authority considered that post merger the structural links between the second and the third largest electricity supplier may induce them to coordinate their behaviour regardless of the presence of a dominant market leader – ENEL. The competition authority did not consider the market characteristics and the ability of the firms to monitor, detect and punish deviations from the collusive outcome.

Bibliography

O'Donoghue, R. and Padilla, J., *The law and economics of Article 102 TFUE* (2th edn, Hart Publishing 2013)

Petit, N. and Neyrinck, N., "Collective dominance: An overview of national case law", *e-Competitions* N° 39129, October 2011

See also

Dominance (notion), Group purchasing organization, Monopoly, Oligopoly

C

COLLECTIVE REDRESS (CLASS ACTION)

Grigorios BACHARIS
London School of Economics and Political Science

■ Definition

The term collective redress indicates proceedings where multiple claimants with similar or related interests group together against the same defendant(s), usually concerning harm caused in the same or a similar way. Collective redress encompasses several distinct types of actions including representative, class, and group actions and involves different remedies, injunctive and compensatory. Collective (or "mass") actions are used widely and increasingly frequently to enforce competition law, mostly to deal with the issue of dispersed economic harm.

■ Commentary

Collective redress schemes in competition law differ significantly between jurisdictions with some, most prominently U.S. law, having a long history and permitting them in a large range of claims, and others only making use of them in limited circumstances. Recently there has been growing pressure in the EU and the UK, to provide effective ways for bringing collective actions, resulting in significant legislative and caselaw developments.

Generally, collective redress procedures are designed to offer access to justice for claimants who would find it impracticable or economically unviable to pursue their claims individually. They also aim at maximizing the deterrence potential of private enforcement regimes. Aggregating claims saves administrative and litigation costs and promotes legal certainty by establishing uniform precedents. At the same time, it creates risks linked with opportunistic or strategic litigation as the threat of massive damages awards can lead to the deterrence of legitimate business activity.

Collective actions might be brought by businesses, consumers, and other organizations. They exhibit a wide variety of forms and purposes. On the one end, so-called "group" litigation amounts to an aggregation and collective management of separate claims and is common in most jurisdictions. Inversely, "representative" actions denote actions brought by qualified entities on behalf of groups of claimants, such as actions brought by NGOs or consumer associations. Finally, the term "class action" describes proceedings commenced on behalf of a defined class of individuals each with their right of action who do not commence their own actions. The class members are largely unidentified and might never be identified. They are represented by a "representative plaintiff" who might or might not be personally affected by the events giving rise to the class action. In all forms of collective redress, remedies can range from injunctive relief or personal damages to aggregate damages awarded to the class, to a sum awarded to a third party.

Significantly, collective actions might operate under an opt-in regime, requiring claimants to actively join the action to be eligible for any awarded damages. This differs from an opt-out system, whereby claimants are automatically included in the action unless they specifically withdraw. Opt-out collective actions are used in competition law and are considered more effective in ensuring deterrence and compensation; however, they exacerbate the excessive litigation risks associated with collective redress.

Lastly, many procedural changes and facilitations are associated with collective proceedings, many necessary for achieving their aims. Separate damages proceedings, case management, lead counsel arrangements, and structured settlement procedures are ubiquitous in class action litigation and essential to its functioning. In addition, litigation funding schemes, fee-shifting rules, award distribution rules, and specialised law firms also form a critical part of the collective redress apparatus, as complexity and costs are often prohibitive without the necessary funding and expertise.

United States

Class actions are a significant part of the U.S. legal system, especially in federal and state antitrust cases. Despite facing judicial and legislative backlash over the past decades, they remain prevalent and a distinctive characteristic of the U.S. enforcement regime. To be certified as a class, plaintiffs must meet specific criteria under Rule 23 of the Federal Rules of Civil Procedure. This includes showing that there are too many members for joinder, that common legal or factual issues exist, that the main plaintiff raises claims typical of the class, and will adequately represent the class. Additionally, damages must be measurable on a class-wide basis. If a class is certified, the potential liability for the defendant can be enormous, often leading to settlements even when valid defences might exist. Notably, the Illinois Brick caselaw shields defendants from the scope of collective indirect purchaser actions.

European Union law

EU Member States exhibit several regimes of collective redress, and the Damages Directive did not cover this issue. Germany allows for certain authorized representative associations to initiate proceedings, but only on an opt-in basis. These mechanisms have seen limited use, primarily due to civil procedure rules that hinder the consolidation of claims and "model declaratory actions" and assignment of claims to special purpose vehicles might present more viable alternatives. France also permits opt-in class actions by authorized entities, but few actions have progressed far. Contrariwise, the Netherlands is well-known for its collective redress mechanisms, reinforced by a 2020 Act (WAMCA). Various entities can initiate damages actions on behalf of a class, and Dutch law permits an opt-out system. Other jurisdictions, like Portugal, also boast new opt-out class action regimes and have experienced a recent rise in litigation activity. Significantly, in 2020, the new EU's Representative Actions Directive (RAD) introduced uniform standards for collective redress. The RAD requires Member States to establish procedures for collective redress but grants them leeway as to procedural matters, such as opt-in or opt-out systems, criteria for qualified entities and certification, third-party funding, and discovery procedures. Representative actions can be brought against traders by qualified entities, typically public authorities, or consumer organizations. The RAD provides safeguards against abusive mass litigation such as "loser pays" rules on costs and allows courts to summarily dismiss unmeritorious actions. However, it focuses on areas like data protection, financial services, and consumer law and not competition law. Notwithstanding this, the RAD alongside the new DMA collective proceedings provisions might soon inspire changes to make competition collective redress more appealing.

United Kingdom

The UK presents arguably the most developed collective actions forum in Europe, with actions proliferating over the last decade. Collective redress mechanisms include both opt-in and opt-out mechanisms. The pioneering framework for collective proceedings was introduced by the Consumer Rights Act 2015 and competition claims are heard in the Competition Appeals Tribunal (CAT), that determines whether these claims will be brought as opt-in or out. Certification for these claims requires authorisation of the class representative and eligibility of the claims for collective proceedings (identifiable class, common issues, suitability), with the leading Merricks v Mastercard case clarifying (in a claimant friendly way) how these conditions can be met. The Competition Act allows for aggregate damages awards, departing from the compensatory principle. This unique aspect, combined with the CAT's experience and the UK legal and litigation funding industry makes it attractive for claimants pursuing class actions, as evidenced in a slew of recent class action filings. Conversely, as the ruling in Lloyd v Google demonstrates, there are stricter criteria for other types of collective actions, requiring for instance damages to be quantifiable on a basis common to the class.

Conclusion

Collective redress mechanisms are gaining traction in Europe and continue to thrive in U.S. law. Certain jurisdictions in Europe are pioneering new forms and developments warrant close monitoring. Particularly, UK caselaw could yield significant insights on matters such as the calculation of aggregate damages, the appropriate theory of harm as well as the overall practicability of similar regimes. Other European jurisdictions remain more cautious, but many of them could potentially emerge as forums for these matters in the future.

Bibliography

AMARO, R., AZAR-BAUD, M.-J., CORNELOUP, S. *et al.*, CORNELOUP S et al, "Study commissioned by the European Parliament, Collective redress in the Member States of the European Union" (2018)

ASHTON, D., *Competition Damages Actions in the EU and the UK: Law and Practice* (Edward Elgar Publishing 2023) Ch 15 and 16

NAGY, C., "Collective redress and aggregation of claims" in BJ Rodger & MS Ferro & F Marcos (eds), *Research Handbook on Private Enforcement of Competition Law in the EU*, Ch 13 (Edward Elgar Publishing 2023)

SALIM, R., FAIRGRIEVE, D. (2023), "Improving collective redress in Europe: implementing the Representative Actions Directive" (2023) 42(1) *Civil Justice Quarterly* 52

SANGER, C. and WICKHAM, P. (eds.), *The Class Actions Law Review* 7th edition (Law Business Research Ltd 2023)

See also

Damages, Private Enforcement

C

COLLUSION

Gal ROZENT, Irit BRODSKY
Barnea Jaffa Lande

Definition

Collusion is an anticompetitive business practice that firms perform in a coordinated manner to obtain benefits at the expense of consumer welfare. A distinction exists between explicit collusion, concerted practice, and tacit collusion. Explicit collusion between competitors, which includes communication and agreement with respect to core elements of competition, is illegal worldwide. Other practices that involve less explicit arrangements, such as information exchange, are known as "concerted practices." These are also illegal if they might restrain competition. Tacit collusion, a practice where a competitor unilaterally follows the behaviour of other competitors, is not illegal in and of itself.

Commentary

One of the basic assumptions of competition law is that rivalry between competitors is necessary to maintain effective competition and to benefit consumers. Collusion is a conspiracy meant to eliminate or reduce such rivalry (or have such effect) by manipulating prices, quantities, product features, innovation, or other market conditions, thus benefiting the colluders at the expense of consumer welfare. Collusion by definition is bilateral or multilateral conduct, as opposed to unilateral anticompetitive conduct such as abuse of dominant position. The classic form of collusion usually deals with colluding competitors, but collusion can also occur between parties who operate in different levels of the supply chain (such as manufacturers and distributors). Nonetheless, the aim of collusion is usually to eliminate or reduce competition between actual or potential competitors. Therefore, that is the focus of this definition.

Competition laws and economic literature distinguish between explicit collusion, tacit collusion, and concerted practices. Explicit collusion occurs when express communication and agreement (sometimes a mere understanding will suffice) exist, with the purpose or outcome of the reduction of competition. When carried out between competitors with respect to core elements of competition, the practice of explicit collusion is generally known as a "cartel". Cartel practices may include direct or indirect fixing of prices or other commercial conditions, market allocation (including bid-rigging), limitation of production or technical development, and other practices that have a similar anti-competitive effect. Price fixing, bid rigging, market sharing and output restrictions are generally known as "hard core cartels" and in many jurisdictions these practices are treated more strictly than other collusive practices.

Tacit collusion occurs when competitors behave in a parallel manner without explicit collusion. This phenomenon, sometimes referred to as "conscious parallelism", is a unilateral practice in which a competitor matches its behaviour to that of other competitors without engaging in any form of communication or agreement. An example is increasing prices following a price increase by another competitor. Tacit collusion is considered to arise mainly in oligopolistic markets where a small number of operators act in a parallel manner due to the characteristics of that market, e.g., the existence of market leader(s), market transparency that allows the monitoring of competitors' behaviour, high entry and transfer barriers, homogenous products, and diffused customers.

Concerted practices reside somewhere between explicit and tacit collusion. They are situations in which a supra-competitive outcome is achieved with direct communication (such as the exchange of competitively sensitive information) or even subtle forms of signalling (such as public statements), but without an express agreement.

Explicit collusion between competitors is illegal pursuant to competition laws in jurisdictions worldwide.

Article 101(1) of the TFEU prohibits all agreements between undertakings, decisions by associations of undertakings, and concerted practices, whose object or effect is to restrict, prevent, or distort competition. Both explicit collusion and concerted practices may thus serve as independent infringements of Article 101(1). In particular, cartelistic practices such as price fixing, limiting production, control of production, and market sharing are considered unlawful. Arrangements forbidden by Article 101(1) may nevertheless be permitted under Article 101(3), if the parties demonstrate they will lead to economic efficiencies and that consumers will share in the resulting benefits. Cartelistic practices are usually impossible to justify.

In the U.S., Section 1 of the Sherman Act 1890 prohibits any arrangement or conspiracy that unreasonably restricts competition in a relevant market. Typical forms of explicit collusion (i.e., cartels, price fixing, bid rigging and market allocation) are considered inherently anticompetitive in nature and thus "*per se*" illegal, regardless of any possible justification. While in the EU cartels are subject to administrative enforcement, in the U.S. they constitute a criminal offense for which the punishment might be imprisonment for the individuals involved.

Tacit collusion, i.e., conscious parallelism, is not generally considered unlawful in itself. To determine the existence of a cartel, competition laws in different jurisdictions usually require at least some form of agreement, mutual understanding, or concerted practice between competitors. Concerted practice is somewhat akin to tacit collusion in the sense that it does not require much evidence of explicit coordination. However, it does require an effective breach of a firm's obligation to determine its market behaviour independently that must go beyond mere tacit collusion, such as direct communication between competitors.

Article 101(1) TFEU applies to written contracts, oral agreements, non-binding arrangements and understandings, and other types of informal collusion, including concerted practices. Some type of "concurrence of will" is nevertheless required, and therefore mere tacit collusion is not generally deemed to constitute a violation of Article 101(1). In *Sukier Unie* (1975, paras. 173-174), it was held that the requirement of each economic operator to independently determine its competitive policy "does not deprive economic operators of the right to adopt themselves intelligently to the existing and anticipated conduct of their competitors". The Court, however, held that the independence requirement strictly precludes "any direct or indirect contact between such operators, the object or effect whereof is either to influence the conduct on the market of an actual or potential competitor or to disclose to such a competitor the course of conduct which they themselves have decided to adopt or contemplate adopting on the market." In *Ahlström Osakeyhtiö* (1993, paras. 70-72), the Court held that parallel conduct cannot be regarded as furnishing proof of concertation unless concertation constitutes the only plausible explanation for such conduct. However, this is not to imply that tacit collusion in itself can be considered to be cartelistic behaviour, but rather that under extremely strict conditions, parallel behaviour may be evidence establishing classical explicit collusion under EU competition law.

Section 1 of the Sherman Act prohibits "every contract, combination in the form of trust or other-wise, or conspiracy". In *Interstate Circuit* (1939 p. 226), it was held that an express agreement is not a prerequisite to an unlawful conspiracy, and thus a concerted practice may constitute a conspiracy in itself. However, conscious parallel behaviour itself is not considered a conspiracy and does not suffice to establish a claim under Section 1. In *Twombly* (2007, p. 557), the U.S. Supreme Court ruled that "when allegations of parallel conduct are set out in order to make a §1 claim, they must be placed in a context that raises a suggestion of a preceding agreement, not merely parallel conduct that could just as well be independent action".

Israel

Israeli competition law resembles European law in the sense that it generally prohibits any bilateral or multilateral arrangement that may restrict competition, unless permitted due to the economic efficiencies it entails. Cartelistic practices are presumed to be inherently anticompetitive and thus illegal. As in the U.S., a cartel constitutes a punishable criminal offense. Concerted practices such as information exchange may also be deemed illegal if they might restrict competition, but are more likely to be enforced by administrative measures, unless their aim was to restrict competition between competitors. Tacit collusion, i.e., mere parallel conduct, is not considered illegal in itself.

Bibliography

EZRACHI, A., *EU Competition Law: An Analytical Guide to the Leading Cases* (7th edn, Oxford: Hart Publishing 2021), Chapter 3

FAULL, J. and NIKPAY, A. (eds.), *The EU Law of Competition* (2nd edn, Oxford University Press 2007), Chapters 3 and 8

HARRINGTON JR., J. E., "A Theory of Tacit Collusion" (2012) *Economics Working Paper Archive* 588, The Johns Hopkins University, Department of Economics

HOVENKAMP, H., *Federal Antitrust Policy, The Law of Competition and Its Practice* (6th edn, Hornbooks 2020), Chapter 4

WHISH, R. and BAILEY, D., *Competition Law* (10th edn, Oxford University Press 2021), Chapters 3, 14

See also

Anticompetitive practices, Artificial intelligence, AI Collusion (algorithm)

C

COMITY

David GERBER
Chicago-Kent College of Law

Definition

The term "comity" is used in public and private international law to urge or demand that the institutions of one jurisdiction take the interests of one or more other jurisdictions into consideration in making legal decisions. Two levels of meaning may be relevant to competition law. One uses comity as a general concept to inform decisions. In this use it is not an element of enforceable law. In some countries, however, the concept has a second level of meaning in which it is an element of enforceable law that requires legal decision makers to take foreign interests into account in specific ways in specific situations.

Commentary

The distinction between these two uses of the term often goes unrecognized, but it can be highly significant.

As a general concept

The comity concept is often overlooked or dismissed where it is not an element of enforceable law and therefore does not have a defined effect on specific legal decisions. It can, however, play important roles in understanding trans-border dimensions of competition law. There are two such roles.

First, the idea of giving weight to the interests of foreign laws and institutions often influences relationships among competition law institutions. Respect for the interests of other jurisdiction is typically necessary where these institutions seek transnational cooperation – for example, where a competition authority in one state seeks information from a foreign competition authority. Some institutions pay significantly more attention to this concept than others, and there is often value in recognizing the weight given to comity considerations by the participants. For example, it can identify factors that are likely to influence the success or shape of negotiations regarding cooperation. Sometimes comity-based cooperation principles are embodied in agreements among the governments involved or between the relevant competition authorities themselves. For example, the competition authorities of the U.S. and the EU are obligated by an international agreement to cooperate in specified ways in the sharing of particular types of information. Uses of this general concept by diverse states can also structure issues related to global competition law convergence and cooperation. This, in turn, will shape the future of competition law in the global economy.

Second, as discussed below, comity is often a conceptual basis for specific doctrines and rules in areas such as international private law (known in the U.S. as conflicts of law) and the transborder jurisdictional reach of national laws. The concept may not be mentioned, but awareness of its content and roles often helps interpret and predict the application of specific rules.

As an element of applicable law

The general comity concept described above is an element of applied law in several contexts relevant to competition law.

Jurisdictional reach of antitrust laws

It has been particularly prominent in shaping the jurisdictional reach of U.S. antitrust law. For several decades after the Second World War its role was central in applying U.S. antitrust law beyond U.S. territorial borders. Its role has diminished significantly since then, but decisions from that period still influence outcomes in U.S. courts. Moreover, its influence has molded thinking in many countries about the role of the U.S. in the global antitrust law arena.

The basics of this story are necessary for grasping the role of comity in the U.S. antitrust context. Near the end of World War II U.S. courts claimed jurisdiction over conduct outside the United States that caused harm either within the U.S. or to certain U.S. interests. The claim extended the reach of U.S. antitrust laws beyond what had previously been accepted as legitimate under international law. As a result, many states rejected the legitimacy of the jurisdictional claim, and some protested vigorously that it represented an attempt by the U.S. to force other countries to accept "U.S. capitalism". Nevertheless, the U.S. government vigorously promoted antitrust law as a means of protecting competition and thereby averting concentrations of economic power that were thought to have led to the disasters of the first half of the 20th century.

Responses to U.S. jurisdictional claims led U.S. courts to turn to the concept of comity to limit the reach of U.S. claims. In this context, it played a central role from the 1960s into the 1990s. The courts applied a balancing of interests test in which they were expected to weigh the potential harm to a foreign state from application of U.S. law against the interests of the U.S. in applying the law. In 1994 the U.S. Supreme Court curtailed the role of the comity concept, holding that it would not curtail

U.S. jurisdiction unless its application would create a "true conflict" with the law of another jurisdiction. Courts have differed in assessing the current status of the comity principle. In a 2018 case the U.S. Supreme Court declared that U.S. courts should give "respectful consideration" to a foreign jurisdiction's interpretation of its own laws, but that they are not bound by that interpretation. The courts have also referred to the comity principle in considering the extent to which U.S. pretrial discovery procedures can demand presentation of foreign materials in U.S. courts.

Comity concerns were incorporated into a Federal statute in 1982, and this legislation remains the primary basis for determining the reach of U.S. antitrust law. The U.S. also has agreements with some foreign countries that include a role for the comity principle.

Jurisdictions outside the U.S. seldom refer to the comity concept in determining the reach of application of their competition laws. They typically rely on statutes to delimit the range of jurisdictional competence of their courts. The comity concept is, however, often implicit in the relevant statutes.

There are many reasons for the differences between principles of extraterritorial application of the antitrust laws in the U.S. and in most other countries. Two factors are prominent: 1) The concept of "jurisdiction" in the U.S. legal system is exceptionally broad, and it provides courts with the authority to impose obligations on litigants for failure to comply with a court's dictates. Few other jurisdictions provide courts with such extensive authority and discretion in applying their laws extraterritorially, and 2) U.S. courts are authorized to "make law" in ways that are seldom found outside the U.S. – i.e., their decisions regarding jurisdiction are understood as law and evaluated accordingly.

Private international law (conflicts of law)

In numerous countries, the comity principle is a component of the laws and principles governing the application of foreign law in their courts. These laws specify situations in which domestic courts must apply the law of a foreign jurisdiction or may not do so. In some jurisdictions the comity-based rules are specific, while in others they involve interest balancing by the domestic court. These principles are sometimes relevant to the application of competition laws.

Positive comity agreements

In addition to the basic concept of comity discussed above, there is a concept referred to as "positive comity" which occurs in a limited number of international agreements, typically bilateral agreements. Such provisions provide that on request of one party another party should apply its law to punish a violation of the requesting party's competition law. Positive comity provisions are seldom applied.

Bibliography

BASEDOW, J., *Limits and Control of Competition with a view to international harmonization* (Kluwer, 2002)

DODGE, W. S., International Comity in American Law, 115 *Colombia Law Review* 2071 (2015)

GERBER, D. J., *Global Competition: Law, Markets and Globalization* (OUP, 2010, 2011)

PAUL, J. R., "Comity in International Law," 32 *Harvard International Law Journal* 1 (1991)

PAUL, J. R., The Transformation of International Comity, 71 *Law & Contemp. Probs.* 19 (2008)

See also

Applicable law, Cooperation between competition authorities, International cooperation

C

COMMISSION (EU) COMMUNICATION

Anne C. WITT
EDHEC Business School

Definition

A Commission Communication is a recommendation within the meaning of Article 288(4) TFEU. It is a soft law instrument that has no direct legal effect but is capable of significant effects in practice. In the area of competition law, the Commission commonly issues Communications to provide guidance on its understanding of key legal concepts and its approach to applying these concepts in practice. Communications often take the form of interpretative guidelines.

Commentary

The European Commission has used Communications to provide guidance on key legal concepts to the business community since the earliest days of EU competition law. Its first Communications on the interpretation of Article 101 TFEU date from the 1960s (e.g., Première communication relative à l'application de l'article 85 du traité à certains accords de distribution exclusive, [1962] OJ 113, 2627–2628, or Communication relative aux accords, décisions et pratiques concertées concernant la coopération entre entreprises, [1968] OJ C75, 3-6; no English versions available). However, it is not until the mid- to late 1990s that the Commission started to employ Communications systematically to spell out its understanding of the key substantive provisions (e.g., in the four sets of guidelines on Article 101 TFEU or the merger guidelines) and important procedural tools (e.g., the first leniency Notice) of EU competition law. Communications have since become a key tool in the Commission's enforcement strategy, aimed at increasing legal certainty, facilitating compliance and enhancing the uniform interpretation of EU competition law at the national level.

Commission Communications have no direct legal effect. Article 105 TFEU in conjunction with Article 292(4) TFEU empower the Commission to issue Communications explaining its administrative practice and give recommendations on EU competition policy as part of its responsibility for maintaining and developing a system of undistorted competition in the European internal market (Case C-226/11 Expedia Inc v Autorité de la Concurrence and Others ECLI:EU:C:2012:795, para 29). However, according to Article 288(4) TFEU such recommendations and opinions have no binding force. According to longstanding case law, therefore, Commission guidelines and other Communications are not binding on undertakings, the national enforcement authorities and courts, or on the European Court of Justice itself (Case C-360/09 Pfleiderer ECLI:EU:2011:389, paras 21, 22; C-428/14 DHL, ECLI:EU:C:2016:27, paras 29-44; C-23/14 Post Danmark v Konkurrencerådet, ECLI:EU:C:2015:651, para 52). The Court of Justice has not hesitated in the past to interpret the law differently than spelled out in a Commission Communication. In Expedia, for example, the Court ruled that restrictions by object had to be considered appreciable per se, despite meeting the quantitative thresholds spelled out in the Commission's former de minimis Notice (Case C-226/11 Expedia, ECLI:EU:C:2012:795, paras 14-38). The Commission amended the Notice accordingly.

Nonetheless, Commission Communications are powerful soft law instruments that have significant influence in practice. Businesses have a strong incentive to abide by the guidance set out in Commission Communications if their aim is to avoid legal proceedings. Moreover, even though Commission Communications have no direct legal effect, the Commission itself may not deviate from the approach spelled out in its guidelines in individual cases. The principle of equal treatment and the protection of legitimate expectations, both general principles of EU law, require that the Commission not deviate from an established enforcement practice in individual cases without legitimate reason. This also applies to rules of conduct that the Commission has published with the express intention of henceforth applying to relevant cases (Case C 167/04 P JCB Service v Commission ECLI:EU:C:2006:594, paras 207 and 208; Case C-189/02 P Dansk Rørindustri and Others v Commission ECLI:EU:C:2005:408, paras 209–211). Communication Notice are thus indirectly binding on the European Commission until such time as it publicly revokes them for all future cases. Finally, even though national competition agencies and courts are not legally required to follow the principles spelled out in Commission Communications, they are of course free to do so. In practice, national authorities often rely on important Communications when interpreting EU or even national competition law (e.g., Autorité de la Concurrence, decision no 22-D-13 of 21 June 2022 – Google, para 134). Even the European Court of Justice occasionally relies on the principles set out in Commission Notices, including interpretative guidelines, in support of its interpretation of the EU competition rules (see e.g., Case C 680/20 Unilever Italia, ECLI:EU:C:2023:33, para 51).

In the past, the European Commission has succesfully used Commission Communications to introduce significant changes to the interpretation of the law. This was the case in the late 1990s, for example, when the Commission embarked on a 10-year process of introducing a more economic approach to the interpretation of Articles 101 TFEU, 102 TFEU and the EU Merger Regulation by means of Communications. It read a consumer welfare aim into Articles 101 TFEU and EU merger control by means of interpretative guidelines and reduced the scope of both provisions accordingly (see Witt, "The European Court of Justice and the More Economic Approach to EU Competition Law – Is the Tide Turning?", (2019) 64(2) Antitrust Bulletin 172-213). For Article 102 TFEU, it took a more indirect way and – formally at least – merely modified its enforcement priorities (Guidance on the Commission's enforcement priorities in applying Article 82 of the EC Treaty to abusive exclusionary conduct by dominant undertakings, [2009] OJ C45, 7–20). A reinterpretation of Article 102 TFEU in line with the other two provisions would not have been compatible with the case law of the European Court of Justice at the time.

Over the following 15 years, the European Court of Justice gradually embraced core elements of the Commission's Article 102 TFEU enforcement priorities – occasionally even going beyond the changes introduced by the original Communication – and integrated them into its interpretation of Article 102 TFEU, prompting the Commission to embark on a process of recalibrating the approach in guidelines on Article 102 TFEU (Call for evidence – Ares(2023)2189183). Despite not being legally binding acts within the meaning of Article 288(1)-(3) TFEU, Commission Communications are therefore influential enforcement tools that are capable of steering and even changing the established interpretation of the law.

Bibliography

Cosma, H. and Whish, R., "Soft Law in the Field of EU Competition Policy", (2003)14(1) *European Business Law Review*, 25-56

Oona, Ş., "European Competition Soft Law in European Courts: A Matter of Hard Principles?", (2008) 14 *European Law Journal*, 753-772

Witt, A. C., "The Commission's Guidance Paper on Abusive Exclusionary Conduct – More Radical than it Appears?" (2010) 35 *European Law Review* 214

See also

Competition policy, Direct effect, Guidelines

C

COMPETITION POLICY

Greg LANG
Canadian Competition Bureau

■ Definition

Competition policy governs how businesses interact with both consumers and each other. A country's competition policy is the sum of its competition laws, which proscribe anti-competitive behaviour, and the effect that its public policy may have on competitive processes in the economy. Sound competition policy is central to a country's prosperity, as it drives lower prices, greater consumer choice, and high levels of innovation and economic productivity.

■ Commentary

The competitive process is the driving force of consumer and business outcomes in a market economy. In the economic model of perfect competition, businesses seek to undercut each other on price and offer ever-more valuable products to attract consumer purchases. This competitive process maximizes economic welfare, and leads to lower prices, greater consumer choice, and high levels of innovation. (*Church & Ware*, Chapter 2)

Outside of this theoretical world, however, markets can fail to achieve the outcomes associated with perfect competition. Businesses, governments, and economic realities can impede the competitive process through myriad factors, such as exclusionary business conduct, marketplace regulation, and economic barriers to entry. (World Bank) The main inspiration of competition policy is to correct for, or reverse, restraints on the competitive process, with the goal of influencing market outcomes closer to those that would be delivered by a perfectly competitive market.

The heart of a country's competition policy lies in its competition law. Competition laws prohibit certain types of economic behaviour that are generally agreed to be anticompetitive in purpose or effect. For example, modern competition laws typically forbid cartels, monopolistic business practices, and mergers that have an anti-competitive effect (International Competition Network, pages 3-6). Nearly all advanced economies have competition laws that are enforced by one or more national (or multi-national) competition agencies.

Competition policy, however, extends beyond competition law enforcement and into the wider realm of public policy. Public policy can often encourage, or even require, businesses to act in a manner that affects the competitive process. Domestic price controls, burdensome administrative policies, and restrictions on foreign investment are all examples of government actions that can chill legitimate competition (OECD, page 4). Pro-competitive public policy stimulates a healthy competitive process to deliver effective marketplace outcomes.

Sound competition policy is not an end in itself, but rather is a key determinant of prosperity. Competitive markets increase economic opportunity by acting as a key driver of innovation and productivity (*Canada*, pages 3-5). For example, pro-competitive competition policy reforms implemented by Australia in the 1990s are estimated to have increased that country's real GDP by 2.5%, resulting in AU$20 billion in unlocked economic value (*Australia*, page XVIII).

Bibliography

Church J. and Ware, R. (2000) *Industrial Organization: A Strategic Approach*

Australia Government Productivity Commission. (2005) *Review of National Competition Policy Reforms*

Canada Competition Policy Review Panel. (2008) Compete To Win

International Competition Network. (2014) The Origins and Aims of Competition Policy

OECD. (2021) Competition

International Competition Network. (2014) Major Characteristics of Competition Policy

OECD. (2018) Indicators of Product Market Regulation Brochure

World Bank. (2017) A Step Ahead: Competition Policy for Shared Prosperity and Inclusive Growth

World Economic Forum. (2019) The Global Competitiveness Report

World Bank. (2021) Markets and Competition Policy

See also

Comity, Commission (EU) communication, Independence and impartiality, Industrial policy, International cooperation, International Competition Network (ICN)

C

COMPLAINT

Valentin MIRCEA
Mircea & Partners

Definition

An act of informing a competition authority about possible infringements of the competition rules; complaints are often made in writing and in standard formats prescribed by the recipient authority. The competition authority that receives a complaint might decide to open an investigation into the alleged wrongdoing and it must motivate its decision in case it decides to reject the complaint. In the EU, where a complaint is lodged by an entity that has a legitimate interest in bringing the claim – such as being damaged by the alleged wrongdoing – its author enjoys certain procedural rights during the investigation.

Commentary

The complaint is the main instrument whereby an aggrieved party, affected by anticompetitive behaviour, may bring its situation to the attention of a public enforcement agency. The persons who lodge such complaints must, as a rule, justify an interest in the opening of an investigation, such as the existence of damage produced by the behaviour. Even if the investigation is opened pursuant to a complaint, it is always conducted ex-officio by the competition agency; complainants may enjoy certain procedural rights, such as the right to receive a copy of the statement of objections (investigation report) and the right to be heard by the adjudicating board, before a final decision is taken in the case and, consequently, to challenge the decision in a court of law if the result is not deemed satisfactory. In all jurisdictions, complaints are an important source of information about the operation of markets; competition authorities often have specific provisions for the handling of the complaints, including designated templates.

See also

Burden of proof

COMPLIANCE PROGRAM

Clara INGEN-HOUSZ
Stellantis

■ Definition

Compliance programs refer to the range of internal rules and tools companies develop and implement to ensure they conduct their business activities in line with competition rules. Typically, they include prevention, detection, and remediation measures – including policies and guidelines explaining the rules and sharing good practices; trainings for at-risk employees; audits to spot issues and identify improvement areas; and processes to alert, investigate and cure potential infringements. In addition, compliance programs require two key ingredients to be truly effective: an unambiguous engagement from the management to spread the compliance culture across the organisation; and a skilled, resourceful, and business-minded compliance function.

■ Commentary

The rise of corporate social responsibility (CSR) in recent years has led companies to take steps towards better accountability vis-à-vis their stakeholders and the public at large. Business ethics, of which compliance is a core pillar, often appears as a priority goal on materiality assessments, alongside carbon footprint reduction or health and safety. This trend is shaping the modern approach to compliance and concerns the promotion of fair competition as much as other areas such as the fight against corruption or the protection of personal data. This approach to compliance brings about rich, multi-dimensional strategies helping companies drive their key regulatory risks (carrying high reputational, financial and even criminal impact) and achieve accountability.

This means competition compliance programs are increasingly organized as structured and dynamic schemes with clear accountability. That being said, because competition law is deeply fact-based and behaviour-dependant, the approach cannot be as processed and automated as in other fields of compliance, and agility to tailor solutions remains of the essence.

In the past two decades, competition authorities have shown an increasing focus on competition compliance, both through advocacy and enforcement practice. Regulators globally and international organisations (International Competition Network, OECD) have contributed to this trend.

On the advocacy front, the focus has been on explaining the benefits of competition, issuing guidance or recommendations (including to specific target groups such as small-and-medium enterprises), and publishing sometimes very innovative materials (videos, templates, brochures).

On the enforcement front, as compliance programs are usually not considered mandatory, the issue has focused on whether their existence should be credited or not in enforcement actions. Here there is wide disparity. Some leading authorities (European Commission, French Competition Authority) explicitly refuse granting fine reductions on the basis that programs should only be assessed as regards their effectiveness. In a different approach, agencies such as the United States, Canada, Germany or Brazil credit effective programs by way of fine reductions. In 2019, the United States reinforced its policy with new guidance and recognition of effective existing programs in criminal antitrust investigations both at the charging and sentencing stages. Finally, some authorities have engaged in compliance program evaluations (e.g., the Korea Fair Trade Commission) but the trend remains limited due to the significant resources required to conduct assessments.

Ultimately, authorities carefully balance the pros-and-cons of rewarding compliance programs. Indeed, strong fine reductions could undermine incentives to self-report, at a time when leniency applications have significantly decreased. Yet, they remain a much-needed detection and enforcement tool.

What are the standards to consider a compliance program is effective? As emphasized by various agency publications (such as the 2019 U.S. Department of Justice guidance), compliance programs should be comprehensive, structured and dynamic in order to be effective. They should be constantly enriched, developed and adapted on the basis of lessons learned from their own implementation. With regards to the core elements of the program, they should encompass the following elements.

Management engagement. Because competition law awareness often remains weak within business (as noted in the 2021 OECD Study), a strong commitment from top management in favor of competition compliance is critical. Such support will carry much more weight than any message from the legal or compliance function. This requires that management be kept informed regularly on compliance matters (legal developments, incidents…) and communicate frequently on the stakes, expectations and implications of deviant behavior (including zero-tolerance). KPIs should be developed to keep track of management engagement over time.

Compliance function. The resources and positioning of the compliance function are a strong marker of senior management commitment. In recent years, many large organizations have internalized the expertise needed to cover the competition law risk. This is a welcome development in so far as this allows a more calibrated risk management than if the task is entirely delegated to outside counsel. However, two challenges must be considered. First, the design and implementation of competition compliance requires a high degree of antitrust expertise, so it begs the question of who should be in charge when the legal and compliance functions are distinct. Second, given the growth of competition law regimes globally, close attention should be paid to the adequate geographical footprint of such internalized functions.

Risk assessment. To ensure effectiveness, the compliance function should seek to identify antitrust risks related to business operations, personnel involved, countries and markets concerned. Rooted in an intimate knowledge of the firm's activities, this assessment should be enhanced by interviews and documents review. further evaluation may be needed at certain junctures: when entering a new market, going through an economic crisis, conducting M&A due diligence, or integrating a recently acquired business. Appropriate risk assessment will duly inform which internal guidance to provide, whom to train as a priority, where to conduct audits, etc. Based on objective factors, each organization may determine the depth of risk assessment it is prepared to undertake.

Policies and procedures. Issuing internal policies and procedures is now a common and legitimate expectation. Why so? Following a logic of accountability, organizations should be transparent towards their employees about what is expected of them (and the consequences of deviant behavior). Since competition law can be complex and possibly counter-intuitive, guiding principles should be communicated to raise better awareness, provide practical guidance, and maintain a coherent approach over time across the organization. Multinationals should pay attention to the way group rules are adapted locally and made available and understandable to employees.

Training and awareness. It is commonly good practice to train all staff exposed to the identified risks. Natural target groups include managers, sales, marketing and purchasing staff, but also members of the HR, finance, strategy and possibly R&D communities. Training should take place upon onboarding and then on a recurrent basis. Training materials should not be "off the shelf": in-person, small-scale workshops are always the most effective option but realistically, they can hardly cover all concerned employees in large organizations. Thus, multinationals develop tailored online programs to reach scale. SMEs, in turn, may not have the resources to ensure adequate training and sometimes rely on training materials provided by local competition agencies.

Monitoring and auditing. The effectiveness of the program should be monitored on an ongoing basis. The compliance function may collaborate with the organization's internal audit department to conduct various checks (e.g., deployment and awareness of the policies). For deeper dives, the compliance function may collect and review training evaluations, organize surveys or interview key people. Finally, the compliance function may mandate outside counsel to conduct dedicated audits, which can be particularly appropriate when assessing finely specific situations (a recent acquisition, country with a new regulation).

Incident management. Beyond risk assessment and auditing, the compliance program should provide a secure framework to discover and handle incidents. Typically, a confidential, effective, and accessible whistleblowing line affording due protection against retaliation should be set up, open to all within and outside the organization. The program should also anticipate what to do in case of an incident, including crisis management protocol, internal investigations guidelines, and various remedial options (disciplinary action, possibly leniency application). While the remediation strategy must be case-specific, a predefined framework will dramatically secure the process and improve the outcome.

Though the effects of improved compliance on antitrust enforcement actions are hard to quantify, the trend towards more sophisticated programs is not about to slow down. Indeed, no one questions that such multi-level initiatives lead to less infringements, and besides, such trajectory is aligned with CSR objectives and the rise of responsible business conduct. That said, improving compliance programs' "productivity" is necessary. While many options exist, we chose to mention three.

Scalability. Various avenues can be explored to improve the program's reach and effectiveness, for instance: easing accessibility (on smartphones) and format (games) of online trainings; using more plain English and less legal jargon. Also, more accurate evaluation of third parties could increase efficiency (refining clauses in commercial contracts; raising due diligence standards in M&A transactions).

Technology and compliance by design. Competition compliance will gradually evolve towards compliance by design and data-driven compliance. Subject to adequate governance and safeguards (privacy, confidentiality/trade secrets, algorithmic coordination…), better access to data across organizations will enable more speed and proactivity in preventing core risks and designing remediation strategies. At this stage though, firms are varying levels of maturity regarding data governance, which could unlevel the playing field.

Incentives alignment. Finally, the topic of proper management alignment is on the rise. A developing literature considers incentives for managers to engage in or facilitate illegal conduct based on a cost-benefit analysis. Solutions are proposed, both at policy level (effective criminal sanctions, disqualification…) and at company level (conditional compensation, bonus reversibility, career advancement setback).

Bibliography

CMA's guidance as to the appropriate amount of a penalty, December 2021

European Commission, Compliance Matters, February 2013

French Competition Authority, Framework Document on Compliance, May 2022

OECD Competition Compliance Programmes, 2021

U.S. Department of Justice Antitrust Division, Evaluation of Corporate Compliance Programs in Criminal Antitrust Investigations, July 2019

See also

Competition policy, Corruption

C

COMPULSORY LICENSE

Behrang KIANZAD
University of Copenhagen

■ Definition

Compulsory licensing refers to a situation in which a non-exclusive license of an intellectual property right ("IPR") can be granted by a competent authority to a third party to make, use or sell an invention, where remuneration is paid to the right-holder and the right-holder maintains its legal intellectual property rights. Thus, Compulsory Licensing represents an exception to the normal exclusivity enjoyed by a right-holder. The legal basis for compulsory licensing is found in the TRIPS Agreement, the Paris Convention, but also in national systems of intellectual property law. As compulsory licensing represents an intrusive act by the Government into property rights, there are varying views on the economic and legal implications of the concept. In exceptional circumstances it may be that a competition authority may order the licensing of intellectual property (or analogous) rights where a refusal to licence them amounts to an abuse of a dominant position.

■ Commentary

The term compulsory licensing characterizes a situation where regulatory bodies or the government can issue a mandatory license of an IPR (for example patent rights for a specific pharmaceutical product) against the wishes of, and without the consent of, the right holder.

The term compulsory licensing in its modern international codification can be dated back to article 5A(2) of The Paris Convention on Intellectual Property Rights (Paris, 1883), stating: "Each country of the Union shall have the right to take legislative measures providing for the grant of compulsory licenses to prevent the abuses which might result from the exercise of the exclusive rights conferred by the patent, for example, failure to work".

In a normal case, the legal owner of an intellectual property right (such as patents, copyright, trademark, design right etc.) enjoys freedom with whom to conduct business and to license. However, compulsory licensing is a situation where a competent authority enforces a non-exclusive licence right to the protected property to be used by a third party, although consent of the right-holder is lacking.

This exception from exclusivity of intellectual property rights and freedom to deal is constitutionally codified under different names, nationally and internationally, such as Government Use, Crown Use and Compulsory Licensing. The ratio legis for Compulsory Licensing might be construed either via exceptional situations (see e.g. UK Patent Act of 1977 Section 55(1)(a); German Patent Act of 1980, Section 13) or that the right-holder does not make use of his invention within reasonable time or at affordable pricing (See e.g. Indian Patent Act, Section 84; Belgian Code de droit économique, Art. XI.37; Dutch Patent Act of 1995, Art. 57). In response to a WIPO study on compulsory licensing, the most cited grounds for grant of compulsory licensing included non-working or insufficient working of the patented invention, refusal to grant licenses on reasonable terms, public health, national security, anti-competitive practices and/or unfair competition as well as national emergency and/or extreme urgency (WIPO, 2014).

The United States, in contrast with most other jurisdictions, does not have a general compulsory licensing rule in its Federal legislation, beyond the possibilities available under 28 U.S.C. § 1498. The statute enables right-holders whose intellectual property rights have been used by the federal government or any of its contractors without permission of the right-holder to bring claims for "reasonable and entire compensation" in the U.S. Court of Federal Claims. The Bayh-Dole Act of 1980 in turn offers a "March-in Right" as per 35 U.S. Code § 203 for the federal government with regards to patents if the invention was made possible through some federal funding.

The most important international legal basis for compulsory licensing, related requirements for granting of such a license and the rights of the right-holder during such a process are found in the TRIPS Agreement of 1995 (Trade-Related Aspects of Intellectual Property Rights), a protocol to the founding document of the World Trade Organization. Compulsory licensing according to TRIPS must be notified to the TRIPS council and the parties have right to appeal to the WTO Dispute Settlement body.

The corresponding article and the legal content mimicking Article 5A (2) of the Paris Convention is found in Article 31 TRIPS, defining compulsory licensing as "Other Use Without Authorization of the Right Holder" under specific provisions given in Article 31 (a-l). However, the TRIPS Agreement does not specifically list the reasons that might be used to justify compulsory licensing, nor does it require a "national emergency". More recently anti-competitive abuses of intellectual property rights have been debated as grounds for compulsory licensing.

The enactment of the TRIPS Agreement in 1994 and harmonization global protection of IPRs elevated the debate on compulsory licensing, coinciding with HIV / AIDS crisis and fears indeveloping world of increased pharmaceutical spending resulting from protection of patents.

India, for example, did not protected patents on medicines until 2005, thus creating a vibrant generic industry which reverse-engineered patented medicines and acted as "Pharmacy of the Third World". This changed with the enactment of the TRIPS Agreement where members could be target of WTO-sanctions if they failed to protect IPRs such as patents. Least Developing countries were nevertheless allowed a period of transition (now extended to 2033) and rules on compulsory licensing on TRIPS and grounds for issuance were updated post the Doha Ministerial Declaration on TRIPS and Public Health in 2001. It was reaffirmed that each member had the right to grant compulsory licences and the freedom to determine the grounds upon which such licenses are granted. (Doha Ministerial Declaration, 2001, Para 5b).

Nevertheless, as Article 31 (f) TRIPS states that compulsory licensing shall be authorized predominantly for the supply of the domestic market of the Member authorizing such use, and since many developing countries lacked the know-how as well as manufacturing capacities required, the Doha Declaration paved the way for export to these countries. The TRIPS agreement was subsequently amended in 2017 to incorporate the new regime.

As the European Union, beyond individual member states, is a member of the TRIPS Agreement, in theory the European Commission should be able to initiate a process of compulsory licensing. Nevertheless, European Commission has regularly held that such an approach is not feasible, due to the national character of IPRs. The legal basis for granting compulsory licenses in the EU beyond TRIPS Agreement is found in the 1998 Biotech Directive regarding plant variety rights and, in view of implementing Art. 31bis TRIPS, the EU Regulation No. 816/2006 with regard to the manufacture of pharmaceutical products for export to countries lacking manufacturing capacities.

As a matter of competition law, it may be that a refusal to grant a license of an IPR could, in exceptional circumstances, amount to an infringement of competition law; for example of Article 102 TFEU which prohibits the abuse of a dominant position. In its *Magill* decision the European Commission issued an order similar to a compulsory licensing of the copyrighted works at issue. On appeal, the appellant questioned the legal mandate of the Commission, as only national jurisdictions originally granting the copyright would have the power to impose an obligation of compulsory licensing on the appellant. This view was rejected by the CJEU, holding that after finding an abuse of dominant position, the Commission was entitled under Article 3 of Regulation No 17 (now Regulation 1/2003), in order to ensure that its decision was effective, to require the appellants to provide the copyrighted material to the requesting party. In the *IMS case* the Commission again ordered a license of an IPR, but this was annulled following an appeal to the General Court in Luxembourg. In the *Microsoft case* Microsoft was required by the Commission to make interoperability information available to producers of software producing software that could interoperate with Microsoft's.

Although compulsory licensing has been debated mostly in relation to developing countries, the recent decade indicates a growing use and threat of compulsory licensing by developed countries such as Germany, United Kingdom, Israel, Russia and U.S.

Compulsory licensing has been subject of fierce debate as it represents an invasive public authority infringement on exclusive legal rights alongside rather broad concepts such as "public health", "national emergency" and so on. Where the protagonists forward compulsory licensing as a necessary legal tool to combat certain abuses of intellectual property rights, the antagonists point to the chilling effect such intervention might pose to investments and incentives.

Bibliography

Hilty, R. M. and Liu, K.-C. (eds.) *Compulsory Licensing*, Springer, 2015

Kianzad, B. "Excessive Pharmaceutical Prices as an Anticompetitive Practice in TRIPS and European Competition Law," in *New Developments in Competition Law and Economics*, ed. Klaus Mathis and Avishalom Tor, Springer, 2019

Qunaj, L., Kaltenboeck, A. and Bach, P. B., "Compulsory Licensing of Pharmaceuticals in High-Income Countries: A Comparative Analysis", *The Milbank Quarterly*, 2022

Risenfeld, S. A., "Compulsory Licenses and United States Industrial and Artistic Property Law", *California Law Review*, 1959

Whish, R. and Bailey, D., *Competition Law* (10th edition, 2021, pp 837-842)

World Intellectual Property Organization, "Exceptions and Limitations to Patent Rights: Compulsory Licenses and/or Government Use (Part I) – Prepared by Secretariat", 2014

See also

FRAND, Intellectual property right, Licensing, Remedies, SEP

C

CONCENTRATION INDEXES

Ricardo RIESCO
Chilean Competition Authority

Definition

Concentration indexes are a set of measures aimed at calculating the level of concentration existing within a relevant market. Alongwith other evidence, they are used as initial indicators of the degree and/or intensity of competition. In principle, a large concentration index value is indicative of a concentrated market with a low intensity of competition due to the presence of only a few firms making most of the sales within the relevant market. The concentration indexes are predominantly used as the initial indicators of the likely effects of a merger in a relevant market, as a first screening tool to assess whether or not a transaction raises potential competitive concerns and would therefore merit closer scrutiny.

Commentary

Market shares and concentration levels are helpful in providing indications of the market structure and of the competitive relevance of market players. Antitrust agencies commonly use concentration indexes to measure the concentration level of a relevant market. The Herfindahl-Hirschman Index ("HHI") is the most common tool. The HHI is equivalent to the sum of the squares of the individual firms' market shares. The HHI is based on the premise that industry structure correlates with the behavior of its players, which justifies the paradigm of structure-conduct-performance. Other commonly used concentration indexes are the Concentration Ratios ("CRN'"), which refer to the sum of the market shares held by the N largest firms in the relevant market.

According to the OECD (2008), concentration indexes do not consider the relative size of the firms in the relevant market and could thus be less suitable as an initial assessment tool of the potential effects of a merger. However, the HHI proportionately gives greater weight to larger market shares and hence can provide an accurate, initial measure of the degree and/or intensity of competition in a relevant market.

Market concentration and concentration indexes are predominantly calculated based on market shares. However, as recognized in several merger guidelines (§19, EU Merger Guidelines and §5.3 Market Concentration, U.S. Horizontal Merger Guidelines), the impact of a merger in a relevant market should also be evaluated alongside other evidence of the merger's potential effects on competition, such as the evaluation of recent or potential entry with a small market share that is not representative of its future development; the existence of "maverick" firms or relevant innovators, which may not be reflected in current market shares; the existence of significant cross-shareholdings among market participants (that could be more accurately assessed with the modified HHI developed by O'Brien & Salop, 1999) or the existence of past or ongoing coordination and/or facilitating practices among market players.

The use of HHI is recognized in merger guidelines throughout competition jurisdictions as a first screening tool to identify competition concerns arising from a merger, including in the EU and U.S. In general, high HHI levels, in combination with high projected variations of HHI levels as a result of a merger or delta, are usually considered to be an initial indicator of competition concerns that likely merit a closer scrutiny of a merger in a relevant market. The European Commission ("EC") considers that concerns are unlikely to be raised in markets with a post-merger HHI below 1.000 points. In Sherwin-Williams/Valspar, the EC considered that a low projected variation of the HHI arising out of the merger [100-200 points], regardless of the plausible product market definition, would be indicative of a transaction that would not have significant impact on the market structure. However, that initial finding that a merger is not likely to lessen competition based on post-merger HHI variations does not give rise to an imperative, legal presumption of either the existence or the absence of such concerns.

In the United States, both the DOJ and FTC consider that an HHI below 1.500 points corresponds to unconcentrated markets, an HHI between 1.500 and 2.500 points is indicative of moderately concentrated markets, and highly concentrated markets have an HHI of above 2.500 points (§5.3 Market Concentration, Horizontal Merger Guidelines). The U.S. guidelines consider that small changes in concentration (i.e., post-merger HHI variations of less than 100 points) are unlikely to generate adverse effects in a relevant market and ordinarily do not require further analysis. On the other hand, a rebuttable presumption of likely potential effects is established when mergers taking place in highly concentrated markets (i.e., HHI above 2.500 points) generate a post-merger HHI increase of more than 200 points. While the guidelines presume such mergers to be likely to enhance market power, such presumption may be rebutted by persuasive evidence showing otherwise. In FTC v. Staples, Inc., the Court stated that, although the Merger Guidelines were not binding to them, they do provide "a useful illustration of the application of the HHI". In using said illustration, it was considered that high levels of pre and post-merger HHIs showed a "reasonable probability" of the anticompetitive effects of the proposed merger.

In the United Kingdom, the CMA also uses certain measures of concentration as an initial screening in order to identify – as the start of a more substantive assessment – whether a merger has the potential to raise competition concerns in the absence of more compelling evidence. For instance, in Masstock Arable (UK) Ltd / Dalgety Arable Ltd, the CMA considered that the low increment of the post-merger HHI suggested that the merger raised no competition concerns. Concentration indexes are considered to be a useful indicator of the merger resulting in a prospect of a substantial lessening of competition. However, for purposes of measuring market concentration, rather than HHI the CMA Merger Assessment Guidelines strongly rely on traditional market shares and the number of effective, post-merger competitors.

Although the HHI has become a common tool in antitrust analysis, it does not work for every setting. The logic behind the HHI derives directly from the Cournot oligopoly model (i.e., when the number of firms decreases, the competitive equilibrium price increases and the HHI increases), which, in turn, is based on quantity competition, suitable for markets where products are homogeneous. When the market is characterized by differentiated products, other technical approaches are more appropriate, since a structural analysis based on concentration indexes could lead to inaccurate predictions, especially when assessing unilateral effects of mergers.

Bibliography

ELHAUGE, E. and GERADIN, D., *Global Competition Law and Economics* 2nd ed., Hart Publishing 2011, Chapter 7

KWOKA, J., Merger Control and Remedies: a retrospective analysis of U.S. policy, *The MIT Press* 2014

O'BRIEN, D. P., & SALOP, S. C. (1999). Competitive effects of partial ownership: Financial interest and corporate control. *Antitrust LJ*, 67, 559

PARKER, J. and MAJUMDAR, A., *UK Merger Control* 2nd ed., Hart Publishing 2016, Chapter 11

OECD (2018). Market Concentration, Issues paper by the Secretariat

See also

Buyer power, Hart-Scott-Rodino Filing (US), Marker power, Market share

C

CONCERTED PRACTICES

Amira ABDEL GHAFFAR
Central Bank of Egypt

Definition

The term "concerted practice" is a form of anticompetitive market coordination without an agreement necessarily being reached. It may be defined as the coming together of two factors joined by a link of causality, based on the coordination between the parties through a way of contact whether direct or indirect, and the modification of the normal conditions of the market. A concerted practice has the purpose of harming competition where commercially sensitive information, such as an undertaking's planned future pricing or output or capacity, is exchanged between actual and/or potential competitors.

Commentary

The term "concerted practice" was used in Article 85 of the Treaty of Rome of 1957 (Article 101 TFEU). This term can be found in numerous competition laws of EU Member States, but also in many other jurisdictions worldwide, such as Singapore, Malaysia, or Australia.

The concept of a concerted practice, as it has been developed through the jurisprudence of the Court of Justice of the European Union, refers to a form of coordination between undertakings by which, without having reached the stage of a true agreement, a cooperation between competitors is knowingly substituted for the risks of competition. (Dyestuffs)

The parallel behaviour may not by itself be identified as concerted practice. It may however be considered evidence of such practice if it substitutes cooperation between competitors for the risks of competition in the market, having regard to the nature of the products, the size and number of the undertaking, and the volume of the said market. This is especially the case if the parallel conduct enables those economic operators, for example, to stabilize prices at a level different from that which normal competition would have led. (Dyestuffs)

Acting independently is the normal conduct that each undertaking shall adapt in the decision-making process. As the Court stated in the AC-Treuhand AG case, each economic operator must determine independently the policy which he intends to adopt in the market (AC-Treuhand AG and Anic Partecipazioni). This means that a competitor should not be influenced by other competitors while making decisions about future behaviour in the market, for example, about future prices and strategies. (T-Mobile)

The existence of a way of contact or communication, either direct or indirect, between the competitors with a possibility of affecting their independence while making decisions, is a required element to prove the infringement. (Suiker Unie)

The contact or communication which does not occur directly between competitors may happen in form of exchange of commercially sensitive information through third parties, for example, trade associations, distributors or from one retailer to another through their supplier may be considered as an infringement. The English Court of Appeal found that the exchange of information through an intermediary amounted to an infringement by object. (Argos Ltd & Littlewoods and Umbro Holdings Ltd)

In the Cimenteries case, the Court set a requirement of having "reciprocal" behaviour. However, a unilateral disclosure of information may be considered an exchange by one undertaking if it expresses its future intention or conduct, it has received a request from another undertaking with a wish to receive such information, and/or the receiving undertaking accepts the information exchanged. (Cimenteries)

Taking the same approach, the Court stated in Treuhand AG that if an undertaking does not wish to participate in a concerted practice it must oppose the invitation in a clear manner, otherwise tacit acceptance will suffice. (AC-Treuhand). Thus, by not distancing itself publicly from anti-competitive conduct an undertaking will be part of the stated behaviour. This approach tends to affirm that attendance at a meeting can violate Article 101(1) when the receiving undertaking does not make a clear objection. (P. Aalborg Portland)

Information considered harmful to the competitive process typically involves strategic data, such as prices, discounts, rebates, interest rate levels, increases or reductions in prices, volume, capacity, marketing plans, risks, investments, and the customer base. Such information can facilitate collusion by reducing independence in decision-making. (EU Competition Rules on Horizontal Agreements Guidelines 2011)

The distinction between individualized and aggregated data is important. (Jones and Sufrin EU Competition Law – fifth edition (2014), p. 699). The level of details increases the likelihood of coordination between competitors. This means that if precise cost or demand information is exchanged this facilitates collusion, particularly if it is commercially sensitive. (Case AT.39850 – Container Shipping para. 35 and 51). Additionally, both specific and the periodic information exchanges are likely to be anti-competitive (P. Aalborg Portland)

The case-law clearly illustrates that an agreement or concerted practice also infringes Article 85(1) of the Treaty if it has the purpose (and not necessarily the effect) of restricting competition. (Judgment of 12. 7. 2001 – joined cases T-202/98, T-204/98 and T-207/98)

To establish concerted practices within the meaning of Article 101 TFEU, it is sufficient to show that competition has been restricted, and unnecessary to prove that it has been prevented. (Suiker Unie)

The mere fact that a party does not fully abide by an agreement or concerted practices, which is manifestly anti-competitive, does not relieve that party of responsibility. (Replica Kit and Toys)

Bibliography

Black, O., *King's College London* Cambridge University Press, 2005

Jones, A. and Sufrin, B., *EU Competition Law*, 5th edition, Oxford University Press, 2014

Page, W. H., *Facilitating Practices and Concerted Action Under Section 1 of the Sherman Act. Antitrust Law and Economics.* (2008)

Whish, R. and Bailey, D., *Competition Law*, 8th edition, Oxford University Press, 2015

Australian Competition and Consumer Commission – Guidelines on concerted practices (August 2018)

See also

Anticompetitive market distortions, Cartel, Price signalling, Anticompetitive object or effect, Anticompetitive practices,

C

CONCESSION

Rodrigo RIOS DORDELLY,
Claudia GEORGINA BRAMBILLA RAMÍREZ
Mexican Competition Authority – COFECE

■ Definition

A concession is an act through which the government, at any level, grants an undertaking or an association of them, the right on a non-exclusive basis to provide certain public services or to exploit state-owned assets while transferring operational risks and receiving the corresponding benefits. A concession title defines and regulates the service or asset involved, the conditions under which it must be provided, and the period granted, the pecuniary benefits (income) obtained, among others, all set in a type of long-term contract. Typically, concessions are granted in the mining, telecommunications, transport, water, or energy sectors, in one or several production chain links, and at different government levels, as the government seeks to positively impact large numbers of users and citizens.

■ Commentary

Concessions are often confused with permits or authorizations; for example, those about licenses or regulations to carry out certain economic activities or professions (occupations) according to some standards. Each jurisdiction establishes what should not be deemed as a concession as well as the positive scenario.

However, crucial aspects are the transference of operational risk to the undertaking(s) and that they are seen as an alternative for the government to privatize the provision of goods and services. Through concessions, the government seeks to take advantage of the experience, knowledge, and efficiency of the private sector, especially in activities either intensive in capital or knowledge.

To fully take advantage of the potential benefits that the participation of the private sector might bring, the concession-granting government must keep in mind that granting concessions is a process vulnerable among others, to poor design failures, fraud, corruption, and collusion.

In this regard, an integrated approach at different stages of the concession granting process is necessary to shield it from such vulnerabilities.

For instance, before granting a concession, well-defined, transparent, and clear rules must be present either at a federal, central, or local government level along with a myriad of economic and non-economic elements that must be met, such as: the value of the concession, the conditions applicable to the transmission of the rights granted, technical and expertise requirements, the length of the contract, and an appropriate design and allocation (competitive auction design, depending on the number of contestants, if relevant).

It is crucial to pay attention to competition for the market as well as in the market. When dealing with the bidding or public tender to award a concession contract, the granting entity must be aware of collusion risks, opening the space for competition authorities to play an important role in either ex-ante or ex-post.

Ex-ante – this may be achieved through their advocacy powers in different stages of the concession granting process, such as the collusion risk assessment tool of the Canadian Competition Bureau aimed at helping authorities sort this particular risk when dealing with the procurement process. Ex-post – this may be achieved by monitoring and prosecuting any anticompetitive conduct, exercising enforcement powers.

An example of this can be found in the Directive 2014/23/EU of The European Parliament and of The Council on the Award of Concession Contracts (Directive). It provides specific provisions that must be observed at the Union level and locally when dealing with such contracts to gain in clarity and certainty for the members of the Union and the undertakings, while respecting the principles of the Treaty on the Functioning of the European Union such as non-discrimination, transparency, free movement of goods, establishment and provision of services, among others. One member of the Union is free to enact legislation concerning the award of concessions insofar as it is aligned with the Directive complying with the above principles allowing any member the opportunity to operate in any other member jurisdiction.

In the United States of America, concession awarding contracts can occur at different government levels in sectors or activities such as transport, energy, infrastructure, water, and mining. The normativity is diverse depending upon the nature of concession, as states can have their own legislation.

Mexico´s normativity considers concessions regarding public services, infrastructure, mining, telecommunications, broadcasting, energy, and water, which can be granted by different levels of government according to the nature of the service or good involved. This is set out in the Political Constitution of The United Mexican States and other diverse regulations.

The principles in the awarding of concessions are: accountability, social and environmental responsibility, public interest, efficiency, quality, transparency, and the protection of public interest, amongst other matters. These principles seek to ensure that concessions are granted and managed in a fair, transparent, and efficient manner and that they serve the public interest. Finally, it is worth noting that, once this process has been successfully implemented and the undertakings are exploiting the concession, they can still violate the competition normativity of the jurisdiction.

Mexico

Pursuant to the Mexican competition law, the Federal Economic Competition Commission analyses public tender documents issued by the granting authority in certain regulated sectors. The aim is to ensure the exclusion of any anticompetitive requirements, the presence of clarity and transparency to provide legal certainty to potential participants, and that the allocation design will promote competition for the market.

In certain cases, sectoral regulations may also require undertakings to obtain a prior favorable opinion from the Commission to participate in the public tender procedure. These opinions are granted based on competition principles. The Commission has had several cases that involved collusion in public procurement that, if it is not by itself a concession, involves a contract with the government.

Bibliography

Holmes, W. and Mangiaracina, M., (2023) *Antitrust Law Handbook*

Klemperer, P., How (not) to run auctions: The European 3G telecom auctions, *European Economic Review*. Volume 46. Issues 4–5, 2002. Pages 829-845

Directive 2004/18/EC of the European Parliament and of the Council of 31 March 2004 on the coordination of procedures for the award of public works contracts, public supply contracts and public service contracts

Directive 2014/23/EU of the European Parliament and of the Council of 26 February 2014 on the award of concession contracts

International; Kluwer Law International 1976, Supplement No. 439, February 2021 pp. BG.L.I -105 – BG.L.I-152.58. Bulgaria: Concessions Act

Organisation for Economic Co-operation and Development. Competition Policy and Concessions. Policy Brief. 2007

See also

Licensing, Public procurement

CONSORTIUM

Victor FERNANDES, Fabiana PEREIRA VELLOSO
Brazilian Administrative Council for Economic Defense (CADE)

■ Definition

A consortium is a strategic alliance formed by independent entities to achieve a common objective in a specific project. Consortia established by competing firms are recognized as valid business collaborations and may be subject to scrutiny under competition law where they involve horizontal agreements between competitors. The application of Article 101 of the Treaty on the Functioning of the European Union (TFEU) within EU Competition Law needs to be considered when firms enter into consortium agreements. Consortia in public procurement necessitate enhanced regulatory oversight due to their potential to facilitate bid collusion; however bidding consortia may enable entities with limited capabilities to participate in joint tenders and provide more competitive bids. While this entry focuses primarily on bidding consortia in the context of public procurement, one should note that consortia can take various forms and exist in different industries, each with its own specific regulatory considerations.

■ Commentary

Consortia can be formed for various purposes, such as research and development, production, or service provision. For example, in the shipping industry, liner shipping consortia are subject to a block exemption under EU competition law. The Consortia Block Exemption Regulation allows shipping lines to cooperate in consortia to provide joint cargo transport services, subject to certain conditions. This type of consortium is distinct from bidding consortia and highlights the diverse applications of consortia across different sectors.

Joint bidding and consortia have garnered increased scrutiny within competition law, with ongoing debates centering on how such collaborations might constitute anti-competitive practices, especially in the context of bidding processes. This complexity calls for meticulous procedural design by procurement entities and rigorous oversight by competition law regulators. Not all consortia are collusive by nature, prompting the necessity for detailed, situation-specific analysis. This level of examination is further influenced by the applicable public procurement laws of each jurisdiction.

Under the framework of the European Union (EU) Competition Law, consortia are subject to evaluation in accordance with Article 101 of the Treaty on the Functioning of the European Union (TFEU). According to the Guidelines on the applicability of Article 101(1) of the Treaty on the Functioning of the European Union to horizontal co-operation agreements of 2023, it is stated that a bidding consortium agreement does not impede competition "if it allows the parties to participate in projects that they would not be able to undertake individually". This includes scenarios where companies offer services that complement each other, as well as instances involving major or intricate projects (§352). The factors used to evaluate the potential of individual parties to compete include: the requirements included in the tender rules; and a realistic assessment if each party would concretely be able to pursue the contract on its own (§ 353).

As outlined in paragraph 358 of the 2023 Guidelines on the applicability of Article 101 of the Treaty on the Functioning of the European Union to horizontal cooperation agreements, a tendering consortium agreement among competitors, subject to Article 101(1), may satisfy the provisions of Article 101(3). Such cooperation may result in efficiencies, including lower costs, better quality, a wider selection, or quicker availability of the products or services that are the subject of the tender.

Fulfilling these efficiencies requires adherence to the additional conditions of Article 101(3), such as being indispensable, benefiting consumers, and not eliminating competition. In tender procedures, these conditions typically interrelate, enabling efficiencies from a joint bid to be transferred to consumers through lower prices or improved quality, as long as competitive dynamics for the contract award are preserved with the participation of other effective competitors. Even though companies can bid individually or participate in the tender in a consortium with fewer parties, the agreement could also fall under the exceptions of Article 101(3) TFEU.

The European Commission's Notice regarding measures to deter collusion in public tenders provides guidance on scrutinizing procurement consortia, which might suggest collusive behavior, as detailed on page 26.

Authorities across European states, particularly within the European Economic Area, consider such consortia as potential manifestations of bid-rigging and market allocation cartels. The EFTA Court's decision in the case involving joint tender submission by two rival Norwegian taxi firms, which had agreed on a price to the procurement entity, was adjudged to have an anti-competitive objective. (Ski Taxi/ Follo Taxi) Denmark and Sweden's competition authorities have similarly enforced stringent measures, judging consortia on whether the involved parties could feasibly submit separate bids. A positive determination led to the classification of the consortium as anti-competitive, foregoing any need for further analysis of how such actions affected the overall competitiveness of the bidding process.

Beyond the EEA, consortium activities within bidding frameworks have not escaped the vigilant eyes of European competition bodies, as they aim to protect the integrity of competitive practices. The French competition overseers, for instance, censured a group of public transport enterprises in 2016. This collective, which had joined forces to tender for educational transport contracts, was declared superfluous, given the individual competitive capabilities of the companies. The French regulator identified this as a direct constraint on competition, observing that the consortium's creation not only diminished the pool of bids but also carved up the market amongst the consortium members.

In a similar vein, Italy's antitrust authority imposed sanctions on a consortium comprising the top five urban waste management companies in 2015, who together controlled a majority of the market. The punitive measures were a response to evidence suggesting that the firms' collaborative pattern throughout multiple bids amounted to a segmentation of the market and impeded free competition. The consortium's rationale, which was based on the distribution of financial risks, did not hold up against the regulatory framework, affirming that such risks, whether intrinsic, regulatory, or due to demand variability, do not justify breaches of competition law.

Conversely, in 2018, the Italian antitrust body concluded an investigation into a supposed cartelization attempt by Kedrion and Grifols, both contenders for a national plasma-based pharmaceutical contract. Notwithstanding preliminary doubts and the fact that both firms could have pursued solo bids, the authority concluded that being individually equipped to satisfy tender stipulations does not inherently disqualify a collaborative bid as being anti-competitive. In the United States, the situation is less definitive as the Antitrust Guidelines for Collaborations Among Competitors stop short of explicitly addressing consortia. The legal framework for assessing joint bids remains ambiguous, with uncertainty prevailing over whether they should be considered through the rule of reason or inherently illegal due to the scarcity of guiding literature. Within the realm of corporate takeovers, joint bidding has come under the microscope for potential antitrust violations.

There are some cases where U.S. courts have discussed whether consortia could be renderd illegal under the Section 1 o f the Sherman Act. In the rule of reason or considered per se illegal. In the context of corporate acquisition, there is evidence that joint bidding practices could raise antitrust scrutiny. (The Court in Dahl v. Bain Capital Partners LLC (No. 07-12388, 2008 WL 5206990 (D. Mass. Dec. 15, 2008) In addition, a decision of the District Court for the Eastern District of California stated that a clause forbidding parties to bid independently, in the context of a joint venture, was per se illegal since it fixed the bid amount. (American Medical Response, Inc. v. City of Stockton)

In Brazil, the competition authority (Portuguese Acronym CADE) has established that such consortia should undergo a rule of reason analysis. In scrutinizing a consortium involving prominent telecommunications firms, CADE's stringent approach was evident. It posited that the consortium's legitimacy hinged on two factors: the operational synergies between the companies or their collective inability to fulfill contractual obligations individually. (PA Teles) In a more recent case, however, CADE has considered additional economic grounds in assessing a consortium created by fuel distributors for port area auctions. It took into account the tender's stipulations for a minimum cargo threshold, which was beyond the capabilities of the companies on their own. This case reflects an effects-based analytical methodology akin to that of the European Guidelines. (IA Raízen/ Petrobras/ Ipiranga)

Bibliography

Kjaer-Hansen, E. and Alsing, J., Danish Court: Consortium Agreement and Joint Bidding Permissible under Competition Law, in 10 *J. Eur. Comp. L. & Prac.* 245 (Gianni de Stefano & Pablo Ibáñez Colomo eds., 2019)

Petr, M., Joint Tendering in the European Economic Area, 20 *Int'l & Comp. L. Rev.* 201 (2020)

Sanchez-Graells, A., Ski Taxi: Joint Bidding in Procurement as Price-Fixing?, 9 *J. Eur. Comp. L. & Prac.* 161, 162 (2018)

Thomas, C., Two Bids or Not to Bid? An Exploration of the Legality of Joint Bidding and Subcontracting Under EU Competition Law, 6 *J. Eur. Comp. L. & Prac.* 629 (2015)

Danish Competition and Consumer Authority, When Companies Bid Jointly (2020)

See also

Block exemption (Regulation), Horizontal cooperation agreement

CONSUMER PROTECTION

Allan FELS
University of Melbourne

Definition

"Consumer protection" refers to laws and regulations aimed (or said to be aimed) at protecting consumers from misleading, unsafe, or exploitative behaviour.

Commentary

Consumer protection is varied in its instruments, form, and substance, more so than competition law.

As regards the instruments, consumer policy has a conventional enforcement element (that is most marked in respect of misleading and deceptive conduct). Misleading conduct may harm consumers, but it can also harm honest competitors. An example arose in *ACCC v Reckitt Benckiser* (RB). RB marketed a standard general pain relief pill. It then began to market specific pain relief pills for back pain, migraine and other specific pains charging about double the price for the standard pill, even though each specific product was the standard pill. Aside from the harm to consumers, there was harm to honest competitors by diverting sales away from them.

Consumer policy, however, also covers weights and measures, product quality and safety standards, industry codes of conduct, the regulation of behaviour in individual professions and occupations, and consumer ombudsman and dispute resolution mechanisms.

While there are some important consumer protection instruments that are economy-wide, they are usually paralleled by an extensive assortment of sector- or market-specific instruments. These rely on a broad range of enforcement instruments and in some cases (such as information and consumer education) are very "soft" forms of regulation.

Consumer policy and competition law generally share a common purpose and, in that regard, reinforce one another.

Broadly, as a general matter, competition law and policy aims at protecting and, where appropriate and efficient, extending the range of choices available for the consumer. For example, where firms operate in competitive markets, they have incentives to develop and protect a reputation for being good quality suppliers, as this allows them to secure repeat business and reduce marketing costs. In that sense, ensuring that a market is competitive can help meet one of the central concerns of consumer policy.

The same applies to many consumer policy interventions. For example, policies that ensure that advertising and product descriptions are honest and reasonably informative, that contract terms and the obligations they involve are understandable and not disproportionate, and that consumers can reasonably expect products to be safe and fit-for-purpose, will both make consumer choice a more effective discipline (thus directly strengthening competition) and will force firms to compete on the merits (rather than on the basis of fraudulent or misleading claims or of unfair contract terms).

Each of these instruments can, however, create challenges for the other. For example, opening a previously highly regulated market to competition may well raise new issues for consumer protection:

- Many countries faced new consumer protection issues as a result of the liberalisation of financial markets, which, however beneficial it may have been, exposed consumers to new risks and difficulties.
- Equally, the introduction of competition into some public utility markets (such as electricity and telecommunications) has created challenges in terms of regulation of service quality and of issues such as the management of churn, of customer complaints and of disconnection for non-payment. It has also raised questions about the ability of consumers to understand what are often complex pricing schemes and exercise choice between them.
- Finally, liberalisation of professional services poses complex questions about balancing competitive pressures (for example, in terms of pricing and marketing, including advertising) with the protection of consumers in situations characterised by potentially large information asymmetries and substantial error costs.

Moreover, when a market becomes more exposed to competition than it was (say, because of the removal of trade barriers), the incentives of market participants may change in ways that raise consumer protection concerns:

- For example, incumbent firms, faced with customers that are more mobile, may seek ways of locking customers in, including by building termination penalties into customer contracts. While those arrangements can be fully reasonable in some instances, they may raise both competition and consumer protection concerns in others.
- At the same time, the liberalised market may attract fly by night operators, whose unscrupulous practices undermine consumer confidence in the market as a whole,

reduce consumers' willingness to rely on information firms in that market provide, and thereby erode the incentives for all firms to act honestly. Moreover, those firms that do act honestly will be forced to bear additional costs in so doing (as they seek to signal to consumers the higher quality of the information they provide), increasing prices and reducing both consumer and producer surplus.
- Finally, the advent of the digital world has opened up a mass of consumer protection issues, many traditional, some relatively new for competition regulation e.g. privacy, data use and misuse, non-disclosure of data use, non-cancellable subscription services, "take down" orders.

In the same way, consumer protection policies, however well-intentioned, can have adverse consequences for competition, with the ultimate outcomes being contrary to the goals that both consumer and competition policy should seek. Classic cases include prohibitions on comparative advertising, mandatory product standards that exclude low-cost entrants and products, and transparency and posted price requirements that facilitate collusion.

It is not surprising that substantial numbers of countries around the world integrate in one organisation the operation of the two policies (at least to some extent) whilst a substantial number do not. Indeed, where the policies are brought together, it is usually not a full integration. The most frequent are laws prohibiting false or misleading conduct ("false advertising"). At the other end of the spectrum laws about weights and measures are left with consumer protection bodies or other parts of government. In countries with multi-level government characteristics such as federations, much consumer protection is left in the hands of lower levels of government, other than where there are substantial national issues.

Overall, there are a number of respects in which gains can be achieved by locating responsibility for both competition policy and consumer policy in a single institution. Those gains include:
- Benefits in terms of better policy coordination, and in particular, in the selection of policy instruments to meet the needs of particular fact-situations;
- A better understanding by policy-makers and enforcers in each area of the role and limitations of the other; and
- The ability to secure economies of scope in access to resources and in the efficacy of monitoring and accountability processes.

However, there are also inherent limits to the possibilities for integration:
- The nature of the tasks involved in implementing consumer policy differs greatly from those involved in the administration of competition policy, reducing the economies of scope achievable through their integration; and
- It is an inherent feature of any effective policy of consumer protection that it will involve a range of agencies, and (especially in federal countries) span several territorial levels of administration.

Bibliography

FELS, A., PARKER, D., COMLEY, B. and BERI, V. (2001) – Occupational Regulation, in *The Anticompetitive Impact of Regulation*, eds Guiliano Amato, Laraine L. Laudati, Edgar Elgar, pp 104 to 115

FELS, A. and ERGAS, H.: Institutional Design of Competition Policies, OECD Competition Committee, 17-18 December 2014

MURIS, T. (2002), The interface of competition and consumer protection', Prepared remarks at the Fordham Corporate Law Institute's 29th *Annual Conference on International Antitrust Law and Policy*; and SYLVAN, L. (2004), Activating competition: The consumer-competition interface', 12 *Competition and Consumer Law Journal*

See also

Consumers' associations, Damages

C

CONSUMERS' ASSOCIATIONS

Vanessa TURNER, Agustín REYNA
The European Consumer Organisation (BEUC)

Definition

The European Consumer Organisation – BEUC, is an umbrella organisation representing national consumer groups across Europe. Its role is to protect and promote consumers' interests at EU level. This includes the participation in competition policy development and competition cases before the European Commission and the EU courts. Due to its unique position as an independent consumer body, BEUC provides the consumer viewpoint in investigations concerning products and services offered to consumers to ensure that competition investigations lead to real improvements for consumers. BEUC has recognised standing to intervene in cases before the European Commission and the EU courts.

Commentary

The "Bureau Européen des Unions de Consommateurs" (BEUC) was created on 6 March 1962 by consumer organisations in Belgium, Luxembourg, France, the Netherlands, Italy and Germany. Today, BEUC represents 45 independent consumer organisations from all 27 EU Member States as well as Iceland, North Macedonia, Norway, Switzerland and the United Kingdom. It is the only consumer association operating at the pan-European level with recognised standing to intervene in competition cases. BEUC's main role is to represent its members' interests to the EU institutions and to defend the interests of European consumers in the elaboration and implementation of European Union policies and case law.

BEUC, the European Consumer Organisation, was one of the first lobbying organisations set up in the European capital in a bid to influence decision-making processes. Many others followed, and the number of lobbyists rose exponentially to the present-day figure of over 15,000. The intense pressure brought to bear on decision-makers from this multitude of lobbyists working on behalf of commercial interests, regional representations, trade unions and many others, highlights the need for BEUC to have a strong presence in Brussels.

BEUC has been an active player in the enforcement of EU competition, internal market and trade law. Case law related to BEUC's right to access documents and to be heard in proceedings before the European Commission can be traced back to antidumping proceedings in the 1980s and 90s in *Bureau Européen des Unions de Consommateurs v Commission of the European Communities* (1991 and 2000) and *Bureau Européen des Unions de Consommateurs and National Consumer Council v Commission of the European Communities* (1994). In *Peugeot SA v Commission of the European Communities* (1990), BEUC was recognised as having standing in a competition proceeding concerning interim measures.

EU competition law gives BEUC as a consumer organisation, an opportunity for standing to intervene in both antitrust and merger cases before the European Commission where it can show a "*sufficient interest to be heard*". For antitrust cases see Article 27(3) of Regulation No 1/2003, Article 13 of Regulation No 773/2004, Article 5 and Recital 12, second sentence, of Decision 2011/695/EU, which provides that "*[c]onsumer associations that apply to be heard should be generally regarded as having a sufficient interest, where the proceedings concern products or services used by end consumers or products or services that constitute a direct input into such products or services.*" For merger cases see Article 18(4) of Regulation No 139/2004, Articles 11(c) and 16 of Regulation No 802/2004.

Most recently, the standing of BEUC in competition cases before the EU courts was confirmed by the General Court in the appeal brought by Google against the Commission's decision in the Google Search (Shopping) case. Despite Google's opposition to BEUC's intervention in the proceedings, the Court by order of the President ruled that BEUC had "*a direct, existing interest in the result of the case*" and thus the right to intervene since competition rules are likely to have an impact on consumer interests and BEUC's object is "*to promote, defend and represent the interests of European consumers*".

In recent years, BEUC has participated in a number of cases before the European Commission regarding competition in technology markets (*Intel, Google Search (Shopping), Google Android, Amazon Marketplace*), market integration and geo-blocking (*Cross-border Pay-TV*) and exploitative pricing in pharmaceutical markets (*Aspen*). BEUC has also provided input into merger control proceedings where the acquisitions were likely to impact consumers. Recent cases include Apple/Shazam and Google/Fitbit with BEUC being formally admitted as an interested third party in the latter case. BEUC has also intervened in EU court proceedings in support of the European Commission in the *Google Search (Shopping), Google Android, and Cross-border Pay-TV* appeals.

BEUC's objective in competition law enforcement is to ensure that markets deliver for consumers not only in terms of competitive prices but also as regards choice, product quality and innovation. BEUC provides input to the European Commission and the EU courts on the direct and indirect impact of anticompetitive behaviour on consumers. Enhancing consumer welfare in the internal market through enforcement is and should remain a priority for the European Commission and the national competition authorities in Europe. In this regard, it is important to ensure that when looking at practices that could fall within Articles 101 and 102 of the Treaty on the Functioning of the European Union (TFEU) through the lens of consumer welfare, a holistic approach is taken. While consumer welfare is a concept that is anchored in the EU's unique normative system, it needs to be applied in a way that reflects the reality of consumers in today's markets. Or, in the words of former DG Competition Director General Johannes Laitenberger "*we must take an empirically driven view of consumer welfare and recognise that some consumer harm is not readily visible in price and output effects*". This is something particularly relevant when assessing practices in digital markets.

Consumers do not behave in the same way in all markets and this needs to be recognised not only in how competition law is enforced but also in other areas of law such as consumer and data protection law. Consumer organisations can provide authorities with important insights into this in consumer-facing markets.

At national level in the EU and in the context of the implementation by Member States of the new European Competition Network (ECN+) Directive, BEUC aims to ensure stronger, structural and mutually beneficial relationships between Member States' national competition authorities and consumer organisations. The objective is to create channels of communication between consumer organisations and national competition authorities to allow consumer organisations to take a more proactive role in national enforcement, alerting competition authorities to examples of consumer harm caused by anticompetitive practices and giving competition authorities feedback and data that can assist in competition cases. Against this background, best practice at national level includes the conclusion of Memoranda of Understanding between competition authorities and national consumer groups. These exist, for example, between the Dutch competition authority (the ACM) and BEUC's member, Consumentenbond and between the Greek competition authority and the Greek consumer organisations.

BEUC is a founding member of the Trans-Atlantic Consumer Dialogue (TACD) which groups U.S. and EU civil society organisations to develop and agree on joint consumer policy recommendations to the U.S. government and the European Union to promote consumer interests in EU and U.S. policy-making.

BEUC also cooperates with consumer organisations across the globe in the context of Consumers International. In the U.S., Consumer Reports is a non-profit consumer organisation dedicated to product testing, investigative journalism, consumer-oriented research, public education, and consumer advocacy. In Australia, CHOICE is the leading consumer organisation. Both Consumer Reports and CHOICE are members of the International Consumer Research Testing organisation (ICRT) together with several BEUC members.

Bibliography

DOCTER, K., "The Early Years of the European Consumer Organisation BEUC, 1962-1985" in Hans-W. Micklitz (ed.) *The Making of Consumer Law and Policy in Europe*, (Hart Publishing, forthcoming)

HILTON, M., *Prosperity for All. Consumer Activism in an Era of Globalisation* (Cornell University Press, 2009)

IOANNIDOU, M., *Consumer Involvement in Private EU Competition Law Enforcement* (Oxford University Press, 2015)

LAITENBERGER, J., "EU competition law: relevance anchored in empiricism" (CRA Conference, 5 December 2018)

BEUC, "The Role of Competition Policy in Protecting Consumers' Well-being in the Digital Era" (Report, October 2018)

See also

Consumer protection, Damages

C

CONTROL (CHANGE)

Amanda ATHAYDE
University of Brasília

Luís HENRIQUE PERRONI FERNANDES
Pinheiro Neto Advogados

■ Definition

Control is the power or ability of one or several undertakings to exercise decisive influence of key competitive variables over another undertaking, by means of rights, contracts, or any other means. The change of control is the modification in terms of the owner of the power, and refers to an alteration in the ownership or governing structure of a company. The change in control can be the result of a de jure or a de facto modification of the power. This change of control is generally implemented by a change in a company's ownership or management that results in the decision-making capacity of that entity being exercised by a different group of shareholders and/or directors. When there is change of control, transactions may be assessed as concentration in terms of competition law depending on the jurisdictions considering that in many acquisitions two companies come under common control or the acquisition of less-than-full control may affect key competitive variables decisions at the target firms.

■ Commentary

Control over entities can be analyzed through various lenses, and different jurisdictions have distinct criteria and frameworks for determining control and change of control. The requirement or not for filling [is this filling or should it be "filing"?] a change of control as a merger for antitrust purposes also vary from jurisdiction to jurisdiction.

The concept of control, as elucidated by classic North American authors Berle [incorrect spelling of name] and Means, manifests in five primary types: 1) control through almost complete ownership; 2) majority control; 3) control without majority ownership; 4) minority control; and 5) management control. This framework is particularly relevant in countries where capital market ownership is typically diluted.

In the North American context, the Hart-Scott-Rodino (HSR) Act plays a pivotal role in defining control, drawing distinctions between corporations and non-corporate entities. For corporations, control is established through ownership of 50% or more of voting securities or the contractual right to appoint 50% or more of directors. Non-corporate entities define control by having rights to 50% or more of profits or assets upon dissolution. While the U.S. does not mandate notification for a change of control unless the acquired entity is non-corporate, merger control necessitates an acquisition of voting securities or controlling assets. For merger control to apply, an "acquisition" of voting securities, controlling non-corporate assets, or assets is required. If such an acquisition occurs, even a temporary change of control may require notification (although under the HSR Act a change of control is not necessary for the filing obligations to apply). But depending on the specific situation, it is possible that a temporary change of control may not be considered an "acquisition" covered under the HSR Act.

Brazilian authors Comparato and Salomão Filho provide an alternative perspective, emphasizing four major types of control in countries with concentrated capital market ownership: 1 total control; 2) majority control; 3) minority control; and 4) management control. For minority or management control, a meticulous analysis of rights and vetoes is crucial to ascertain the extent of control. Unlike the U.S., Brazil's Competition Act does not explicitly define control, relying on CADE's understanding that it involves the ability to interfere with a company's activities, either through equity interest or contractual arrangements. Notably, the change of control is not a prerequisite for mandatory pre-merger review in Brazil. CADE's Regulation 33/2022 sets forth that acquisitions of minority interest carried out by the controlling shareholder that already holds sole control of the target company are not subject to mandatory notification, even when the turnover thresholds are met. In the European Commission, control denotes the ability to exercise decisive influence on a company's strategic commercial decisions. This influence can arise from rights, contracts, or other means, either individually or in combination. Control can stem from rights (shares or assets), contracts or any other means which, separately or in combination, by law or by fact, give the possibility of exercising such influence. In case of multiple shareholders, veto rights of a minority shareholder regarding decisions that are essential for the strategic operation of the business – in particular the appointment of the management, the adoption of business plan and budget and major investment – can grant a minority shareholder control.

The concept of "control" set out in Article 20(5) of Regulation (EU) 2022/2560 mirrors the one used under Regulation (EC) 139/2004 on the control of concentrations between undertakings. The Commission provides detailed guidance on the definition of control and change of control. The change of control is a prerequisite for mandatory pre-merger review in EU. The Commission provides guidance on how this criterion is assessed in case of successive transactions in its Consolidated Jurisdictional Notice. The Merger Regulation defines the concept of a concentration in such a manner as to cover operations only if they bring about a lasting change in the control of the undertakings, and therefore does not deal with transactions resulting only in a temporary change of control. Temporary changes, as in situations with a pre-existing plan for asset splitting within a short period, may not trigger the need for Commission notification. An example of a temporary change of control is a situation in which one or more parties acquire control over a target undertaking but have a binding pre-existing plan to subsequently, within a short period of time usually not longer than one year, split the assets among themselves. In that case, the initial transaction would not lead to a change of control on a lasting basis and would hence not need to be notified to the Commission. By any definition, change in control is commonly instigated by mergers, consolidations, or acquisitions resulting in a shift of more than 50% ownership or a significant alteration in management. Transactions like the sale of substantial assets or changes in shareholders with the right to elect over 50% of the board also fall under this purview. It is imperative to recognize that the definition of control can vary across legal domains, encompassing antitrust, corporate, educational, among others. The considerations outlined herein primarily pertain to antitrust regulations.

In conclusion, control is a nuanced concept subject to diverse interpretations across jurisdictions. Understanding the intricacies of control types, change of control and regulatory frameworks is crucial for entities navigating transactions, mergers, or changes in ownership structures. The divergent approaches underscore the need for a comprehensive understanding of jurisdiction-specific regulations and requirements, ensuring compliance and facilitating seamless business operations in an increasingly interconnected global landscape.

Bibliography

Berle, A. A. and Means, G. G. C., Gardiner *Gardiner Coit. The modern corporation and private property*. Transaction publishers, 1932

Comparato, F. K., *O poder de controle na sociedade anônima*, 3" ed., São Paulo, ed. Forense, 1983

2023 Merger Guidelines (December 18, 2023). Justice Department and Federal Trade Commission

See also

Control (notion), Economic analysis, Merger, Merger (sole control), Minority shareholdings

C

CONTROL (NOTION)

Fevzi TOKSOY
ACTECON

Definition

Control is defined as the right of one or several undertakings to exercise decisive influence over another undertaking. Control is a key concept that is relevant for the assessment of concentrations. When there is no change of control, transactions are not assessed as concentrations in competition law. For the control to be deemed to occur, it is sufficient that one party acquires the power to exercise decisive influence over strategic decisions of another company through an acquisition of shares or assets, contracts, transfer of the IP rights, strong economic dependence, or through any other means.

Commentary

A notion of control and its interpretation serves as a starting point of any concentration control analysis, as a concentration should be deemed to exist in case a change of control takes place. Whether the control of an undertaking is acquired or not is determined on a case-by-case basis. The essence of the definition lies in the words "decisive influence on an undertaking" (Article 3(2) EUMR), i.e., its strategic decisions such as business plans, budget, investments, appointments of management, etc.

Control of an undertaking may be acquired by a single undertaking leading to a sole control, or jointly by two or more undertakings leading to a joint control. Sole control is acquired on a legal basis where an undertaking acquires a majority of the voting rights of a company. It is not in itself significant that the acquired shareholding is more than 50% of the share capital or that it is 100% of the share capital. An acquisition which does not include a majority of the voting rights does not normally confer control even if it involves the acquisition of a majority of the share capital. Sole control might also result from the acquisition of a "qualified minority" of the share capital with ability to veto strategic commercial decisions. Joint control exists where two or more undertakings have the power to block strategic commercial decisions of an undertaking. Therefore, joint control is characterized by the possibility of a deadlock situation resulting from the power of two or more parent companies to reject proposed strategic decisions. It follows, therefore, that these shareholders must reach a common agreement in determining the commercial policy of the JV.

Control, whether sole or joint, can be exercised on a de jure or de facto basis. While de jure control requires review of shareholdings (more than 50 per cent), de facto control is a much broader concept, which looks at other possible influence over the undertakings that would result in control. There are various factors which may be relevant in deciding whether de facto control exists. The ability to appoint the majority of the board of directors, which is in charge of the company's strategic decisions, is one of the most common forms of de facto control. This is true for the situations where a shareholder is highly likely to achieve a stable majority at shareholders' meetings or if the remaining shares are widely dispersed. In *Electrabel* although holding close to 50% of CNR's shares, due to the wide dispersion of the remaining shares and past attendance rates at CNR's shareholders' meetings, Electrabel enjoyed a stable majority at such meetings. In *Vivendi/Telecom Italia*, the transaction consisted of the acquisition of control by a minority shareholder over a listed company with a widely dispersed share capital.

Usually these are the cases where a minority shareholder has the right to manage the activities of the company and to determine its business policy; minority shareholders may have a strong common interest which means that they would not in practice act against each other. A veto right on the approval of the business plan, the budget and the appointment of the senior management are considered to be sufficient to have a control over an undertaking. De facto control occurs in a situation of economic dependency, through economic and other links between the two undertakings and regardless of the size of the shareholding concerned. In *J&J/Actelion* there were strong economic links between J&J and Idorsia on a long-term basis: J&J was to provide to Idorsia a 10-year loan, a 15-year credit facility, as well as access to IP rights through the cross licensing arrangement. These economic links were coupled with a structural link, with J&J acquiring between 16% and 32% of Idorsia's share capital while all the other shareholders would each hold less than 5% of the shares. The interpretation of control under the Turkish Competition Law resembles the EU approach, in that control may be acquired through rights, contracts or other instruments which, separately or together, allow de facto or de jure exercise of decisive influence over an undertaking. In particular, these instruments consist of ownership rights or operating rights over all or part of the assets of an undertaking, and those rights or contracts granting decisive influence over the structure or decisions of the bodies of an undertaking.

As in the EU, de facto control under the Turkish Competition Law can occur in various ways. Long-term supply agreements concerning an essential component for the business of an undertaking might give rise to decisive influence over management actions, and thus control might be acquired on a de facto basis. Another example of de facto control can be seen in a certain circumstance where a minority shareholder is likely to have the majority at the shareholders' meetings, e.g. when taking into consideration the share proportion, the voting pattern at past shareholders' meetings and the position of other shareholders.

Control can be conferred through a contract. In AstraZeneca LP, the transaction did not include a transfer of shares, but the TCA considered the "Agreement on Common Offers" enabling change of control allowed joint control of Amylin by Bristol and AstraZeneca, even though 100% of shares remained under the control of Bristol. In practice, the most common example of control through a contract is through a long term lease agreement.

Transfer of intellectual property rights might enable control, but only where an intellectual property right constitutes a business with a market turnover. This is particularly so in the situations when transfer of related brands plays an essential role in activities which enable the undertaking to acquire market share and generate a turnover.

Finally, control may arise through appointment of professionals. In *Medya Holding Sabah* the changes in the board of the company were considered sufficient to establish a change of control. Change in the positions on the boards of the four companies was implemented by the withdrawal of the directors representing Sabah Group and the subsequent appointment of new directors among the nominees, who were assumed to be "bound to MTM group."

Bibliography

Toksoy, F., Balki, B., Stakheyeva, H., *Merger Control in the EU and Turkey: A Comparative Guide*, 2019, Wolters Kluwer, Book – International Competition Law Series

Communique on Mergers and Acquisition Calling for the Authorization of the Competition Board (Communiqué No 2010/4), Turkish Competition Authority, 2010

Council Regulation (EC) No 139/2004 On the control of concentrations between undertakings, 2004

Guidelines on Cases Considered as a Merger or an Acquisition and the Concept of Control, TCA, 2013

Merger Control in the EU and Turkey: A Comparative Guide, F. Toksoy, B. Balki, H. Stakheyeva, 2019, Wolters Kluwer, Book – International Competition Law Series

See also

Control (change), Minority shareholdings, Merger (sole control)

C

COOPERATION BETWEEN COMPETITION AUTHORITIES

Alejandra PALACIOS PRIETO
USC Sol Price School of Public Policy

■ Definition

Refers to the voluntary collaborative endeavors, formal or informal, between two or more competition agencies. Formal collaboration is conducted under legal instruments or formalities (e.g. cooperation agreements, waivers of confidentiality), whereas informal collaboration occurs without these formalities. Cooperation may be related to competition enforcement procedures or may concern non-enforcement efforts such as technical assistance, exchange of experiences and best practices. Cooperation may increase familiarity between agencies and mutual understanding (e.g. about respective laws, procedures, practices) which can foster trust and facilitate further interactions. Challenges for cooperation may relate to practical issues (e.g. language, time differences), legal limitations (e.g. for sharing confidential information) and lack of resources (e.g. personnel, budget).

■ Commentary

Increasing economic integration and the rapid digitalization of markets requires more and better cooperation between competition agencies around the world. The following sections provide cooperation experiences of the Mexican Federal Economic Commission (COFECE), with its counterparts from the United States (U.S.) and the European Union (EU), which illustrate how the relationship with these agencies has been strengthened over the years, through better mutual understanding and increased trust.

Cooperation with U.S. antitrust authorities

Since the negotiations of the North American Free Trade Agreement (NAFTA) in the 1990s, trade between Mexico and the U.S. has increased to such an extent that Mexico became the

U.S.' largest trading partner in 2020. This agreement has not only laid the foundation from which complex production value chains have been built, making both countries an attractive region for investment from around the world, but was instrumental in the establishment of competition policy in Mexico.

In order to comply with the terms established in NAFTA regarding the enforcement of the competition laws in the countries of the region, the governments of Mexico and the U.S. signed an agreement in 2000 that establishes the grounds for cooperation between their competition agencies. Thereafter, cross-border merger control has been a forefront cooperation issue between COFECE and its counterparts, the Federal Trade Commission (FTC) and the Antitrust Division of the Department of Justice (DOJ). This cooperation has been carried out mainly by formal means, particularly through confidentially waivers provided by the merging parties. Two examples worth highlighting are the cooperation in the Continental/Veyance operation (2014), where agency collaboration was key when crafting extraterritorial remedies, which were imposed jointly by COFECE and the DOJ, that contemplated divestiture in the Mexican State of San Luis Potosi and in Fairlawn, Ohio. The other relevant case is the ChemChina/Syngenta merger (2017), in which COFECE coordinated with the FTC to ensure decisions were taken within similar timeframes.

COFECE has also cooperated with the U.S. authorities in cases related to anticompetitive conducts. In these types of cases cooperation has been carried out formally through the use of waivers (only in cases with leniency applications). However, some of the most beneficial results have been achieved through informal cooperation, mainly by general discussions unrelated to particular cases regarding, for example, investigation strategies followed by other jurisdictions, publicly available market information or competition analysis methods. A case worth highlighting is the international cartel investigation in the global market of air conditioning compressors, where the Commission had an ongoing cooperation with various jurisdictions, but mainly with the DOJ.

Informal cooperation in enforcement cases is crucial to COFECE because there are important impediments in the Mexican competition law to: disclose confidential information without a waiver; disclose information during the investigation stage; and grant access to the case file during the trial-like procedure to those that do not have legal standing in the procedure. Therefore, all cooperation with foreign authorities regarding a case must occur through waivers or informally without disclosing information on the specific case. In order to address these hurdles, the Commission is currently exploring the possibility of entering into second-generation agreements that would enable the possibility of engaging in investigative assistance activities.

Non-enforcement cooperation with the U.S. authorities has been extremely fruitful, particularly that related with technical assistance provided by the FTC, the DOJ and even the Federal Bureau of Investigation (FBI), to the Commission's staff. Another type of cooperation which has greatly benefitted the Commission is the advice received from the FTC and the DOJ to improve the Commission's procedures. For example, the drafts of the regulatory provisions for client-attorney privilege and leniency program received important feedback from these authorities, which allowed the strengthening and alignment of these documents with best international practice. It is worth highlighting that the regulatory provisions for client-attorney privilege fulfil the recognition of this principle, which was recently included in the new U.S.-Mexico-Canada Agreement (USMCA), that entered into force in 2020, substituting NAFTA.

Cooperation with the competition authority of the European Commission

Mexico is amongst the largest trade partners of the EU, mainly since 2000, when their economic relations were facilitated by the European Union-Mexico Economic Partnership, Political Coordination and Cooperation Agreement. This agreement includes specific provisions for cooperation and coordination in competition enforcement and policy between Mexico and the European Community. In 2016, the parties began negotiations for the modernization and update of the agreement. The proposed draft includes a new competition chapter, which defines anticompetitive business practices, provides for cross-border cooperation and coordination between the parties, amongst other provisions. Although the legal revision of the new EU-Mexico trade agreement has been finalized, its signature is still pending.

On a bilateral level, in 2018, the Directorate-General for Competition (DG Competition, the EU's Competition Authority) and COFECE signed the Administrative Agreement on Cooperation in the Field of Competition Law and Enforcement. The scope of the agreement extends to the coordination of enforcement activities between COFECE and DG Competition, which is increasingly relevant, for example, in the assessment of global mergers and acquisitions subject to review in diverse jurisdictions. This agreement also includes a provision related with cooperation on technical matters, for instance, through capacity building or the exchange of officials.

COFECE and DG Competition have cooperated in several cases, especially comparing approaches and issues of common interest, and in the design of remedies for cross-border mergers. COFECE considers that the most beneficial means to conduct this cooperation are regular calls to exchange information and views regarding the status of the ongoing merger investigation, markets involved, substantial theories of harm, and information on potential remedies. To facilitate cooperation in this process, waivers of confidentiality granted by the merging parties have been instrumental.

For example, in the Dow/DuPont merger (2017), the parties offered COFECE a remedies proposal that consisted in complying with those imposed by DG Competition. COFECE considered that these effectively resolved any competition concerns in Mexico; and only requested the parties to prove that they complied with the remedies imposed by the European Commission.

In the 2019 merger between Nidec and Embraco (Whirpool's refrigeration compressor business), COFECE also relied on a remedy imposed by DG Competition, which consisted in the divestiture of one of the parties' businesses (compressors for commercial applications).

Final remarks

COFECE's bilateral cooperation experiences with its U.S. and EU counterparts are an example of how ongoing collaboration on enforcement cases and technical assistance strengthens the relationship of trust between the authorities' staff, which helps to further enhance the benefits of future collaboration efforts between these agencies. Participation in international organizations, such as the ICN, OECD and UNCTAD also strengthens these relationships; such organizations provide an important platform to forge potential bilateral and multilateral relationships for future collaboration on international enforcement cases.

Bibliography

Administrative Agreement on Cooperation in the Field of Competition Law and Enforcement between the Directorate-General for Competition of the European Commission and the Federal Economic Competition Commission

International Competition Network

OECD's International Co-operation in Competition Webpage

The Agreement between the United States of America, the United Mexican States, and Canada

UNCTAD's International cooperation under section F of the Set of Multilaterally Agreed Equitable Principles and Rules for the Control of Restrictive Business Practices: Adoption of the guiding policies and procedures

See also

Applicable law, International cooperation, International Competition Network (ICN)

C

COPYRIGHT

Scott HEMPHILL
NYU School of Law

Definition

Copyright is a form of intellectual property that grants exclusive rights to a creator's original expression. Protection applies to a wide variety of creative work. Copyright prohibits not only simple copying but also the development and distribution of nonidentical works that incorporate protected expression. Most individual copyrights fail to confer market power. Moreover, the exclusionary force of a copyright is limited by various doctrines internal to copyright law. Concerns about anticompetitive collusion or exclusion may arise from the licensing in tandem of multiple copyrighted works. Innovation in distribution may intensify or ease these concerns over time.

Commentary

Copyright is a form of intellectual property that grants exclusive rights to a creator's original expression. The underlying ideas expressed in a work, however, are not protected. Protection applies to a wide variety of creative work, ranging from books and music to film and computer programs. Copyright prohibits not only simple copying but also the development and distribution of nonidentical works that incorporate protected expression.

Copyright law is in some tension with competition law – antitrust law, as it is known in the United States. It permits certain conduct that might ordinarily raise antitrust concerns. For example, the assertion of a valid, infringed copyright against a rival is legal, even if the resulting exclusion raises prices and reduces output. However, most individual copyrights fail to confer market power. Just as with real property, the legal power to exclude does not necessarily imply the ability to exclude rivals in any economically meaningful sense. Moreover, as discussed below, the exclusionary force of a copyright is limited by various doctrines internal to copyright law. In any event, copyright does not grant a broad privilege to act anticompetitively, any more than ownership of a hammer confers a right to break storefront windows.

When multiple copyrighted works are licensed in tandem, concerns about anticompetitive collusion or exclusion may arise. These concerns are illustrated by antitrust enforcement in the music and film industries. In the United States, licensing in both industries historically has been constrained by court-administered consent decrees.

Collusion. Antitrust concerns about collusion can arise when separately owned copyrights are consolidated and licensed as a bundle. For example, songwriters have the exclusive right to authorize public performances of their work by radio stations and other downstream music users. The writers typically grant licenses to a performing rights organization (PRO), such as the American Society of Composers, Authors and Publishers. The PRO packages the rights into a blanket license that is offered to downstream users at a price set by the PRO. The arrangement reduces price competition among the writers while also producing a valuable benefit: an administrable mechanism for compensating writers and making available a wide repertoire to users.

In assessing antitrust liability, one relevant question is whether PRO licensing might be accomplished in a manner that preserves the benefits of centralized administration while avoiding the suppression of competition. This inquiry is often framed as an assessment of less restrictive alternatives. For example, instead of offering only a blanket license, the PRO might offer a per-use license. Technological advances have made such licenses easier to administer. In this respect, innovation in distribution has intensified antitrust scrutiny over time.

Exclusion. Concerns about exclusion may arise when a licensor conditions access to one copyrighted work on the acceptance of a license to additional works. For example, historically, movie studios licensed their films to theatres as a package. Such "block booking" has been criticized on the ground that, by forcing the theatres to accept unwanted films alongside the preferred ones, the distribution of independent films would be foreclosed. Defenders have argued that the practice reduces transaction costs and results in significant economies of scale.

The film example illustrates how innovation in distribution sometimes lessens antitrust concerns over time. For more than 70 years, block booking was prohibited in the United States under a consent decree. The rise of Internet-based streaming eased concerns about foreclosure, as did the increased prevalence of multiplex theatres equipped to show movies from different distributors on different screens. In light of industry evolution, the prohibition was retired in 2022.

Mergers. When a single movie studio or music label controls a large set of important copyrights, it may become a "must-have" content provider for downstream distributors. For example, if consumers expect a music streaming service to offer a comprehensive catalogue, the must-have label might be in a position to bargain for higher prices. If a merger of two labels confers must-have status and thereby increases the bargaining power of the merged firm, an antitrust enforcer might be moved to challenge the combination.

Matters might be different if both labels are already must-have. In that instance, access to one label's music makes access to the other more valuable. The labels, though rivals, are offering complementary products from the standpoint of the distributor. When complements are separately owned, each firm charges a higher price, failing to fully take into account the price charged by the other firm. The result is higher prices and inefficiency. Thus, a merger of must-have labels might be viewed as beneficial. The argument is a variation on the elimination of double marginalization as a procompetitive justification. An argument of this kind supported a U.S. enforcer's decision in not to challenge a four-to-three merger of major labels.

The role of copyright doctrine. The discussion thus far has explored how antitrust law protects competition in the licensing of copyrighted works. In addition, copyright doctrine itself shapes competition by placing limits on the exclusionary force of a copyright. One such limit is fair use, which permits innovators to incorporate existing works as building blocks, without permission from or payment to the earlier creator. Fair use employs a multifactor analysis – aptly described by the U.S. Supreme Court ("Court") as an "equitable rule of reason" – that weighs (among other things) the innovative and competitive features of the new use. A transformative purpose counts in favour of fair use, while close competition with the earlier work counts against it.

As an illustration, consider *Google v. Oracle*. In designing the Android operating system for smartphones, Google incorporated thousands of lines of so-called declaring code from the Java programming platform. The copied code enabled programmers to redeploy their existing knowledge of Java commands in developing applications for Android. In holding that Google's copying was a fair use, the Court emphasized that the creation of a new software platform was a transformative purpose. The Court also noted, in an echo of the antitrust inquiry into less restrictive alternatives, that Google took no more than necessary to ensure the portability of programmers' investment in learning Java.

As for competition with the earlier work, the Court concluded that there was none, as Java was not a viable platform for smartphones. The Court did not consider the applicability of another limitation on the reach of copyright, which is to deny protection to user interfaces under a statutory exclusion for so-called "methods of operation." The method of operation approach, like fair use, protects the portability of third-party investments in learning a system, and potentially facilitates entry even when the innovator is a close competitor of the incumbent.

Bibliography

Areeda, P., Kaplow, L., Edlin, A. and Hemphill, C. S., *Antitrust Analysis: Problems, Text, and Cases* (8th ed. 2021)

Hemphill, C. S., *Intellectual Property and Competition Law*, in Oxford Handbook of Intellectual Property Law (Rochelle C. Dreyfuss & Justine Pila eds., 2017)

Hemphill, C. S. and Suk, J., The Fashion Originators' Guild of America: Self-Help at the Edge of IP and Antitrust, in *Intellectual Property At The Edge: The Contested Contours of IP* 159 (Rochelle C. Dreyfuss & Jane C. Ginsburg eds., 2014)

Hemphill, C. S., Less Restrictive Alternatives in Antitrust Law, 116 *Columbia Law Review* 927 (2016)

Kaplow, L., The Patent-Antitrust Intersection: A Reappraisal, 97 *Harvard Law Review* 1813 (1984)

See also

Collecting society, Intellectual property right

CORRUPTION

Tina SØREIDE
Norwegian Competition Authority

Definition

Corruption refers to a form of collusion between parties that exchange benefits for the sake of distorting a decision. It describes trade in decisions that should not be for sale. In a market context, corruption refers to private players' *active* or *passive bribery* of decision-makers on the side of government or in other firms, to distort decisions for corporate profit and/or personal gain. The benefit offered, i.e., the *bribe*, can be anything of value to the decision-maker, including a financial transaction, objects of value, rights in action, privilege of any sort, a promise to influence somebody else, or a promise to provide a benefit in the future.

Commentary

Corruption circumvents principles of fairness and honesty, and harms societies in numerous direct and indirect ways, depending on the decisions which are distorted in exchange for which benefits. As corruption generates illegal gains for those involved, it seriously undermines competition in markets. Although it may harm any part of the economy, it is particularly a concern in sectors where firms are subject to comprehensive regulations, privatization and/or concession contracts, such as sectors that provide basic services, including transport, electricity, telecoms, water & sanitation, as well as services with substantial health and safety components. The risk is considered high in public procurement, and especially where contracts are large, complex and/or shrouded in secrecy, such as construction projects and defense sector acquisitions. Bribery has a direct impact on competition when targeted at the outcome of tenders, competition law enforcement, regulations related to entry barriers, taxation of specific firms, access to credit, or biased enforcement of the law. Beyond such direct impacts, corruption harms markets and society in many ways as it typically leads to unfair allocation of benefits and higher expenses for citizens, firms, and public institutions. It demotivates innovation and investment, and facilitates other forms of crime, corporate crime included. The consequences of corruption are normally more severe, the more discretionary and high-level authority is corrupted, and the scarcer the benefits in question. These are the factors that drive up the size of bribes as well because they are associated with more profitable outcomes. When extensive, corruption reduces trust in government institutions and increases income differences in society.

The more profitable the benefits in question, and the higher the bribes, the trickier it is to eradicate the problem. Societies, therefore, apply a broad spectrum of measures to control corruption. In countries all over the world there are conflict of interest regulations, rigorous auditing requirements, ombudsman arrangements, revenue control as part of tax law, procedural rules for recruitment, public procurement legislation, access to information laws, whistleblower protection, ethical guidelines, and in most countries, mechanisms intended to bolster democracy. In addition to the plethora of state institutions with an oversight responsibility (and the multilateral cooperations they are part of), there are civil society groups, journalists, and researchers in most countries who contribute to monitor how such integrity mechanisms are recognized and enforced.

Given the serious consequences, and the importance of sustaining the many integrity mechanisms in society, corruption is regulated by criminal law. In fact, many jurisdictions define *corruption* in their penal code only. Typically, corruption is here described as improper influence and extortion, while the law also lists the thresholds for enforcement. Many countries introduced corruption as a new concept in criminal law in the years after the turn of the millennium, as part of an impressively rapid evolution and harmonization of anti-corruption law, driven by international anti-corruption treaties. These treaties included in particular the United Nations Convention against Corruption (UNCAC), the Inter-American Convention against Corruption, the African Unition Convention on Preventing and Combating Corruption, the criminal law and civil law anti-corruption conventions of the Council of Europe /GRECO, and the OECD Anti-Bribery Convention that forbids bribery in a foreign country.

Under these reforms, business leaders as well as civil servants and elected officials can be imprisoned for their involvement in corruption. Many countries, including all OECD member countries, can hold corporations criminally liable for bribery, or have legislation functionally equivalent to criminal liability. Corporate sanctions for bribery tend to reach high levels. On top of law enforcement, corporations involved in bribery face claims for damages by different categories of victims, including victim societies, government institutions, and business partners. They risk exclusion from public procurement and pension funds, as well as serious collateral damage.

With respect to law enforcement, however, there is substantial variation across countries. Some countries, such as the United States, actively enforce their foreign bribery regulations, and impose heavy sanctions on American firms or firms that operate in U.S. markets if they have paid bribes abroad, while in other countries, such rules have not been enforced in any cases, despite serious allegations of wrongdoing. The OECD Working Group on Bribery keeps track of enforcement patterns and operates a solid system for peer review evaluation of enforcement practices across the signatories to the OECD Convention. Their cooperation, combined with research in law and economics, and pressure for enforcement from the most active enforcers, have driven cooperation between countries towards more efficient and incentive-based law enforcement, more mutual legal assistance, better whistleblower protection in corruption cases, joint efforts for asset recovery, and recently, recommendations for the use non-trial resolutions in cases of corporate criminal liability.

While there are still numerous serious challenges in this area of law enforcement, firms that are involved in corruption and related offences increasingly rely on the enforcement system in question to reduce sanctions substantially if they report their own offences and cooperate with enforcement agencies.

Bibliography

ARLEN, J., 2020. The potential promise and perils of introducing deferred prosecution agreements outside the U.S. In Søreide and Makinwa (Eds) *Negotiated Settlements in Bribery Cases*. Edward Elgar Publishing

AURIOL, E., HJELMENG, E. J. and SØREIDE, T., Deterring corruption and cartels: In search of a coherent approach, February 2017, *Concurrences* N° 1-2017, Art. N° 82670

OECD. 2016. The Liability of Legal Persons for Foreign Bribery: A Stocktaking Report. Paris: OECD

ROSE-ACKERMAN, S., 2010. The law and economics of bribery and extortion. *Annual Review of Law and Social Science* 6: 217-238

SØREIDE, T., 2016. *Corruption and Criminal Justice: Bridging Economic and Legal Perspectives* Edward Elgar Publishing

See also

Collusion, Compliance Programme

C

COST-BASED ACCESS

Darren BRADY NELSON
Center for Freedom and Prosperity

Definition

Cost-Based Access (CBA) has its origins in United States antitrust case law on the Essential Facilities Doctrine (EFD). According to the background note in a 1996 OECD paper, that examined this from the perspectives of the U.S., Europe and Australia, EFD: "specifies when the owner(s) of an 'essential' or 'bottleneck' facility is mandated to provide access to that facility at a 'reasonable' price." However, the OECD noted: "The variance in [access] definitions is great." The OECD highlighted that: "In the Australian example, essential facilities are limited to natural monopolies and...the safeguard to an overly broad finding of a duty to deal is provided, rather than by a market test, by a cost structure test." The Australian approach most clearly links EFD to CBA and, therefore, is the focus of this entry.

Commentary

There are multiple CBA regimes in Australia, across various industries, at federal, state and territory levels. The prime one is the *National Access Regime* (NAR) under Part IIIA of the *Competition and Consumer Act 2010* (CCA). Access is defined under section 44AA as: "promot[ing] the economically efficient operation of, use of and investment in the infrastructure by which services are provided, thereby promoting effective competition in upstream and downstream markets". The access criteria under section 44CA refers to "at the least cost compared to any 2 or more facilities" which "includes all costs associated with having multiple users of the facility" as well as "the effect on... investment" plus "administrative and compliance costs".

The Australian legal institutions of most relevance to the NAR, in provision order under the CCA, are the: Australian Competition and Consumer

Commission (ACCC) under Part II; National Competition Council (NCC) under Part IIA; Australian Competition Tribunal (ACT) under Part III; and Federal Court of Australia under Part IIIA Subdivision F. Part IIIA and the NCC both have their origins in the *Competition Policy Reform Act 1995*, that resulted from National Competition Policy (NCP). NCP was initiated by the Hilmer Review that reported on August 1993 to the Heads of Australian Governments at federal, state and territory levels. NCP culminated in April 1995 with three intergovernmental agreements of the *Competition Principles Agreement* (CPA), *Conduct Code Agreement and Agreement to implement the National Competition Policy and Related Reforms*. Clause 6 of the CPA provided for the establishment of a NAR.

The ACCC describes the current NAR as: "set[ting] the legal right for third parties to gain access to certain infrastructure services, with terms and conditions that are reasonable"; via "declaration", "voluntary undertaking" or "state access regime". A key term and condition is price. In this regard, the *Hilmer Review* foreshadowed that: "Policy judgments are involved as to where to strike the balance between the owner's interest in receiving a high price, including *monopoly rents* that might otherwise be obtainable, and the user's interest in paying a low price, perhaps limited to the *marginal costs* associated with providing access." In a March 2022 case, the NCC expanded upon this as follows: "The *floor price* should reflect the lowest price at which the operator could provide the relevant services without incurring a loss and the *ceiling price* should reflect the highest price that could fairly be asked by an operator for provision of the relevant services."

Section 44ZZCA of the CCA requires for NAR: "that regulated access prices should be set so as to generate expected revenue for a regulated service or services that is at least sufficient to meet the efficient costs [and] include a return on investment commensurate with the regulatory and commercial risks involved". In an April 2022 case, the ACT highlighted how this is applied: "The *Building Block Model* [BBM] is to be used to calculate the *Maximum Allowable Revenue* [MAR]." They added that: "The inputs to the [BBM] are limited to: the regulated asset base [RAB;] actual capital expenditure [CapEx;] interest incurred [INT;] forecast inflation [CPI;] forecast depreciation [DPN;] useful life of assets [ULA;] weighted average cost of capital [WACC;] forecast capital expenditure [CapEx;] forecast operating expenditure [OpEx;] [and a] Material Change Event [MCE]." All of these components typically come together under BBM as follows:

BBM = { ⌊ CPI – X] x MAR }
where: CPI = consumer price index;
X = efficiency x-factor;

MAR = { OpEx + Return *of* Capital (RFK) + Return *on* Capital (RNK) }
where: OpEx accounts for INT, MCE and TAX; RFK = [RAB – DPN]; RNK = [RAB x WACC]; RAB and DPN both account for ULA;

> **WACC** is a function of the Cost *of*, or Return *to*, both EQUITY and DEBT where: EQUITY is based on CAPM = Re = { Rf + [β x Rm] } where: Re = expected return; Rf = risk-free return; β = systemic risk; Rm = market risk premium.

A CCA and ACCC related institution is the Australian Energy Regulator (AER), who produced a November 2017 overview of the BBM, including formulas consistent with those above. Their overview states that the "objectives of regulation" are "to promote outcomes in the long term interest of customers" thus "revenue should reflect *efficient costs* and an appropriate level of service quality". They add that "various regulatory models could be used to achieve these objectives" yet "the regulatory process we follow [is a] building block model". BBM is used as the standard benchmark for NAR-related pricing by the ACCC and NCC, as well as other CBA-related pricing in Australia at federal, state and territory levels. The AER provides a pie chart of some typical "building block proportions" where "return *on* capital" is "52.8%", "operating expenditure" is "29.9%", "return *of* capital" is "11.1%", "tax allowance" is "4.0%" and "revenue adjustments" are "2.2%". Because of both materiality and complexity, capital has increasingly been the focus of any CBA process. In the AER's example, capital represents 63.9% of the BBM cost pie, with "return on capital" being 82.6% of that. Thus, CBA nowadays has largely become all about RAB, WACC, CAPM and the components thereof.

An AER related institution is the Australian Energy Market Commission (AEMC), who undertook a 2009 stakeholder survey of the *pros and cons* of the BBM. They firstly defined it as an: "approach [that] involves the determination of forecasts of efficient costs to set revenue and/or prices using the [above] types of costs or "building blocks" for each year of a regulatory period" and one "commonly adopted by most Australian jurisdictions in setting prices and revenues." In terms of *pros*, AEMC found that BBM: "is considered to be a relatively straight-forward, stable, certain and understandable process which yields sufficient incentives for service providers to seek cost efficiencies." But the *cons* were: "that it fails to cater adequately for innovation, there is a risk that the regulator may set the level of efficient prices too low leading to insufficient returns and that the regulator is exposed to information asymmetry." The AEMC also noted that: "*direct costs* incurred ranged from $2 million to $5 million [per] regulatory assessment", "*indirect costs* could amount to as much as $15.7 million", however, the "*overall...cost* to a service provider...generally accounted for 0.01% to 0.3% of total revenue over a five year regulatory period." Studies since suggest higher.

The Productivity Commission (PC) has reviewed the NAR twice, reporting in September 2001 and October 2013 respectively. In the latter one, the PC stated that: "the empirical evidence on the effect of the [NAR] in practice is limited. It has therefore not been possible to quantify the economic effects." But they noted: "However, government intervention also has costs." These include "significant administrative costs", such as those "incurred by the NCC have ranged from about $2 million to $4 million annually." On balance, however, they recommended the NAR "should be retained" as it "can address an enduring lack of effective competition, due to natural monopoly, in markets for infrastructure services where access is required for third parties to compete effectively in dependent markets."

Bibliography

Australian Competition and Consumer Commission (ACCC), How Access to Infrastructure Services is Regulated

Australian Energy Market Commission (AEMC), Perspectives on the Building Block Approach, Published July 2009

Australian Energy Regulator (AER), The Building Block Model: Consumer Information Session, Published November 2017

National Competition Council (NCC), National Competition Policy Website, Viewed November 2023

Organization for Economic Co-operation and Development (OECD), The Essential Facilities Concept, Published February 1996

See also

Essential facility, Prices

C

COURNOT (NASH) EQUILIBRIUM

Timo KLEIN
Utrecht University

Definition

A set of strategies is called a "Nash equilibrium" if no agents can obtain a better outcome by choosing a different strategy, given the strategies of others. A Cournot Nash equilibrium describes a Nash equilibrium in a Cournot model of oligopoly, in which firms choose how much to sell (i.e. quantities) and prices are determined through market clearing. This contrasts with Bertrand competition, in which firms directly compete on price. Economic theory shows that the Cournot equilibrium can reflect a situation in which firms first set capacity and then compete on price. This may make Cournot a more appropriate assumption than Bertrand in some cases, even under price competition.

Commentary

The Bertrand and Cournot models are the two basic and fundamental economic models aimed at capturing strategic interaction between a limited number of firms active in a particular market (i.e. oligopoly competition). Where the Bertrand model (Bertrand, 1883) assumes that firms compete on price and subsequently produce whatever quantity is demanded, the Cournot model (Cournot, 1838) assumes that firms determine the quantity that they want to sell to the market, and prices are subsequently determined based on a presumed process of market clearing.

This commentary first discusses the theoretical justifications behind the Cournot model relative to the Bertrand model, so as to subsequently link the respective models to their use in competition policy practice. For a comprehensive introduction to oligopoly theory more generally, see, for example, Shapiro (1989).

As discussed by Walker (no date), the basic Bertrand model of price competition with homogeneous products leads to the counterintuitive result that equilibrium prices will always be equal to marginal costs, and firms will never make any profit on their products sold. This is considered to be a paradox, as in reality we observe price-setting competitors enjoying positive gross margins. To resolve the paradox, the basic model would need to be extended by allowing for differentiated products, capacity limitations, long-run repeated interaction, or imperfect information.

In contrast, the basic Cournot model of quantity competition leads to the intuitive result that equilibrium prices are higher when markets are more concentrated. The basic intuition is as follows: the market-clearing price is inversely related to the total supply of a product in a particular market (higher total supply leads to a lower market prices, and lower total supply leads to higher market prices). When there are fewer firms active in a market, any one firm will have a larger influence on the market-clearing price. Each individual firm has a higher incentive to restrict its output somewhat in order to push up the market-clearing price. Conversely, when markets are less concentrated, each individual firm has a smaller incentive to restrict its output, as its influence on the market-clearing price is smaller. Equilibrium quantities are lower and market prices (and hence margins) higher in more concentrated markets. In fact, it can be shown that in a linear Cournot model with homogeneous products, the Hirschman-Herfindahl Index (HHI) for market concentration is one-to-one related to market power as measured by price-cost mark-ups (i.e. the Lerner Index) – justifying the use of HHI as a measure of market power in such cases.

Importantly, economic theory also shows that under relatively mild assumptions, the theoretical outcome under Cournot competition between firms mimics the theoretical outcome of a two-stage model in which firms first choose their capacity level of production and subsequently compete on price (Kreps and Scheinkman, 1983). As such, the Cournot model may still be a better reflection of market competition even if firms compete on price, provided that they first invest in a particular capacity level and cannot readily change these levels (so-called "capacity-then-price" competition).

Bertrand and Cournot models of competition are used in the academic economics literature (theoretical and empirical) to analyse how different market characteristics or interventions may be expected to affect market outcomes. Similarly, these models are used in competition policy practice to provide economic insights on the potential effects of mergers, coordinated behavior, or unilateral conduct. For example, in complex merger cases, a Bertrand or Cournot model may be calibrated using real-world data on margins and diversion ratios to estimate the changes in the theorised equilibrium prices and output post-merger. Such an analysis combines economic theory with data to produce a type of economic evidence that may complement other evidence on the potential competitive effects of a merger (quantitative or qualitative). Bertrand and Cournot models are also used, for instance, in antitrust damages proceedings to help inform an economic expectation of harm following a cartel infringement.

To choose between a Bertrand or Cournot model of competition means to choose between two different ways in which firms are assumed to behave in the market. Bertrand competition is more appropriate when firms have unlimited capacity or when prices are difficult to adjust in the short run. In contrast, Cournot competition is more appropriate when firms can readily change prices but face capacity constraints that can only be adjusted in the longer run.

For example, in mobile telecommunication mergers, the European Commission consistently assumes that firms set prices without regard to any capacity constraints (i.e. Bertrand competition) – including, for example, in *Hutchison 3G Austria / Orange Austria* (2012), *Hutchison 3G UK / Telefonica UK* (2016), and *T-Mobile NL / Tele2 NL* (2018). This is appropriate, as network capacity is rarely binding for telecom operators and retail prices are usually fixed over the short run.

In contrast, an assumption that firms commit to prices while flexibly adjusting volume depending on demand may not be realistic in other settings. For example, in support of its *Sunweb / Corendon* (2020) merger clearance, the Netherlands Authority for Consumers & Markets (ACM) produced a merger simulation model for the market of packaged holidays that assumes that firms compete by setting quantities rather than price (i.e. Cournot competition). This choice was driven by the observation that firms active in the market for packaged holidays first stock up on flight and accommodation capacity for a subsequent season, based on estimated future demand, and then sell this fixed capacity to consumers against a dynamically optimised price aimed at fulfilling capacity. Such a competitive dynamic coincides with the capacity-then-price model discussed above.

Bibliography

BERTRAND, J. (1883), "Théorie mathématique de la richesse sociale", *Journal des Savants*, pp. 499–508

COURNOT, A. (1838), *Rescherches sur les Principes Mathématiques de la Théorie de la Richesse*, Paris: Calmann-Lévy (new edition 1974)

KREPS, D. M. and SCHEINKMAN, J. A. (1983), "Quantity precommitment and Bertrand competition yield Cournot outcomes", *The Bell Journal of Economics*, pp. 326–337

SHAPIRO, C. (1989), "Theories of oligopoly behavior", in Schmalensee, R. and Willig, R. (eds), *Handbook of Industrial Organization*, Vol. 1, Amsterdam: North-Holland

WALKER, M. (2024), "Bertrand (Nash) equilibrium", *Competition Law Dictionary, Concurrences*, Art. No. 85397

See also

Bertrand (Nash) equilibrium, Oligopoly

C

CRIMINAL SANCTIONS

Joseph J. BIAL
George Mason University – Antonin Scalia Law School

■ Definition

Criminal sanctions are the penalties imposed on those who commit crimes. Whether a sanction is criminal or civil flows not from the nature of the penalty, but from the wrongdoing it punishes (or from the law that imposes the liability). Indeed, there are similarities in the penalties imposed for criminal and civil wrongdoing. Much depends on jurisdiction, including whether the sanction seeks to punish the wrongdoer, remunerate the victim, or both, as well as how the sanction is calculated. Thus, the U.S. has criminalized certain agreements in restraint of trade, whereas certain EU Member States and other jurisdictions outside the U.S. have criminalized only bid-rigging arrangements and other egregious cartel behaviour such as horizontal price fixing: however the EU, which has not criminalized anticompetitive conduct, imposes administrative and civil sanctions.

■ Commentary

When applied to individuals, the distinction between criminal and civil sanctions is stark: in jurisdictions in which anticompetitive conduct is criminal, individuals may be sentenced to prison, but in jurisdictions in which anticompetitive conduct is a civil wrong, sanctions do not include jail time. When applied to corporations, however, the distinction between criminal and civil sanctions is less apparent. In the United States, for example, a corporation entering a plea agreement and paying a criminal fine is nonetheless subject to restitution, which is more akin to a traditional equitable remedy and form of civil penalty.

It is also the case that the manner in which criminal fines are determined often hinges on concepts imported from the civil arena. In the U.S., under the Sherman Act, corporations that commit antitrust violations are subject to fines of up to $100 million, but in the alternative the Department of Justice (DOJ) may seek to impose penalties based on the unlawful gains or losses occasioned by anticompetitive activity. That is, the alternative penalty is rooted in the damage caused or the amount by which the perpetrator is unjustly enriched, both of which are civil concepts. Likewise, when it comes to bid-rigging offenses specifically, fines are assessed based on a formula provided in the U.S. Sentencing Guidelines (the Guidelines) that starts with the "volume of affected commerce" (or VOAC). The Guidelines are largely silent as to how VOAC is to be determined, but they do explain that VOAC is a proxy for "actual gain or loss," and "actual loss" is the "reasonably foreseeable pecuniary harm that resulted from the offense." In other words, VOAC resembles in many respects the general rule for assessing civil damages and, in effect, VOAC approximates (and is a shortcut for calculating) the damage caused by the violation. The punitive element of the fine calculation is conducted after a determination of VOAC. The court calculates 20 percent of VOAC to determine a base fine, which is subsequently multiplied depending on a "culpability score" reflecting the circumstances of the particular case, including aggravating and mitigating factors.

The EU Commission, although it imposes only civil sanctions for anti-competitive agreements or abusive practices in violation of Articles 101 and 102 of the Treaty on the Functioning of the European Union (TFEU), uses a methodology similar to the DOJ. Like the DOJ, the Commission undertakes a two-step process. First, it calculates the "value of sales," or VOS, which is similar to the American concept of VOAC. VOS is the value of the undertaking's sales of goods or services to which the infringement directly or indirectly relates in the relevant geographic area. The basic amount of the fine is a percentage of VOS. The percentage used is determined based on the gravity and duration of the offense. Second, as in the U.S., in the EU the basic fine amount is then adjusted based on circumstances of the case, including aggravating and mitigating factors.

It is notable that, although the U.S. levies criminal sanctions and the EU imposes civil sanctions, when it comes to fining organizations the methodology is similar insofar as both start with an approximation of the gain from the misconduct and then add a further amount determined based on the circumstances of the case to punish the misconduct. It remains an open question whether, in the U.S., the additional assessment of restitution is redundant given the stated reason for assessing a criminal fine. Finally, irrespective of jurisdiction, a formulaic approach to assessing fines is subject to over-penalizing the wrongdoer because the calculation of VOAC, VOS and similar concepts tend to include sales that demonstrably are not impacted by the underlying conduct of the defendant. The impact of over-counting is beyond the scope of this definition but is something worthy of further deliberations by fine-assessing agencies.

Bibliography

European Commission. (2006). Guidelines on the method of setting fines imposed pursuant to Article 23(2)(a) of Regulation No 1/2003. Luxembourg: Publications Office of the European Union

European Council. (2003). Council Regulation (EC) No 1/2003 of 16 December 2002 on the implementation of the rules on competition laid down in Articles 81 and 82 of the Treaty. Luxembourg: Publications Office of the European Union

United States Sentencing Commission. (2018). 2018 Guidelines Manual Annotated

See also

Complaint, Investigations/inquiries

C

CROSS SUBSIDISATION

Payal MALIK
Indian Competition Commission

Definition

Cross-subsidisation is a pricing strategy adopted by multi-product firms when relatively high prices from one set of products or services allows a firm to set prices below cost for another set of products or services. Not all forms of cross-subsidisation are considered harmful from a regulatory perspective. Harmful cross-subsidization may take place when a firm charges excessive prices in markets where it holds significant market power. The profits generated from these markets are then utilized to offer products or services at prices below their actual costs in other markets with differing levels of competition. Thus, this involves a dual form of exploitative conduct, encompassing both excessive pricing and below cost pricing, with the former essentially financing the latter.

Commentary

Cross-subsidisation, plays a pivotal role in shaping market outcomes across various industries. Cross-subsidisation can be defined in several ways. The most general definition entails "cost transfer", where some or all costs from one product/service are shifted to another. Regardless of the definition used, cross-subsidisation fundamentally entails the transfer of resources or costs from one market segment to another within a firm.

A notable European Commission (EC) case finding cross-subsidisation as anti-competitive, is the Deutsche Post Case. In this instance, United Parcel Service (UPS) alleged that the *Deutsche Bundespost Postdienst* (DPAG) was using profits from its lucrative letter-post monopoly to support a strategy of selling parcel services in a competitive market at prices below their actual costs. In the absence of this revenue transfer from its monopoly business to the competitive business, DPAG wouldn't have been able to employ this pricing strategy. UPS claimed that this strategy had driven competitors out of the market.

Another instance of an anti-competitive conduct involving cross-subsidisation is the case of *MCX Stock Exchange Ltd. v. National Stock Exchange of India Ltd. & DotEx International Ltd.*, decided by the Competition Commission of India (CCI). In this case the National Stock Exchange (NSE) was found to be engaged in an anticompetitive behaviour by waiving off the transaction fees for all currency future trades (a new financial instrument). This waiver of fee resulted in losses to MCX (Multi Commodity Exchange of India Ltd.), a public limited company as it was also required to waive off the transaction fee to compete with NSE. CCI pronounced this practice of NSE as unfair as it was observed that the intention of NSE was to acquire a dominant position in the Currency Derivative segment by cross subsidizing this segment of business from the other segments of the Stock Exchange where it enjoyed virtual monopoly. While the Appellate tribunal upheld CCI's order, an appeal is still pending before the Hon'ble Supreme Court of India.

In the digital age, cross-subsidization has gained a novel interpretation. Multisided platforms often utilize cross-subsidisation to harness cross-side network effect. On certain platforms, attracting one side by lowering price is particularly profitable for the platform if this side creates substantial externalities on the other side. For example, media platforms usually give free content to attract users, and charge higher mark-ups to advertisers. Other examples of platforms making no or little money on one side include software platforms (Adobe Acrobat or text processing vendors that charge nothing for the readers but earn revenue from the writer; operating system platforms earn revenue solely from users and not from application developers) and videogame platforms which sell consoles at a price equal to or below their production costs, cross subsidised by game developers. Seminal papers point out that platform operators devise a pricing structure rather than a cost based pricing for each side of the market for profit maximisation.

However, the implications of this strategy has resulted in new theories of harm in digital markets, consumers may not pay with money, and are cross subsidised by the advertising side of the market, but pay an implicit price in the form of personal data Thus, data becomes a form of currency paid for "free" online services. Controlling data can confer market power in these markets, impeding competition. The rise of a cohort of a few intermediation/aggregator platforms whose business model is characterised by pricing strategies that have a flavour of cross subsidisation has allowed these platform centric markets to acquire data hegemony.

In the case of *Mr. Umar Javeed & Ors. v. Google LLC & Google India Private Limited*, Google's conduct of tying Android OS to Google Mobile Services (GMS) products for "free" was seen as "dynamic leveraging" by CCI. It was observed that this was a means to appropriate user data for monetisation in the search advertising market thereby providing Google market power.

Online retail platform Amazon has "successfully" used cross subsidization to grow, leading to its dominance across various sectors. Amazon, beyond its role as a retailer, functions as a marketing platform, a delivery and logistics network, a payment service, an auction platform, a book publisher, a producer of television and movies, a contributor to fashion industry, a hardware manufacturer, and a major player in the provision of cloud server space and computing resources.

Amazon has achieved a dominant position in some markets primarily from losses incurred and significant investments made to expand its operations, for instance, providing benefits of prime membership to consumers, at the expense of profits. Similarly, Amazon Kindle (e-reading device) was sold below manufacturing cost and also the bestseller e-books were priced significantly below cost. But at the same time, the prices charged from publishers were not dropped. Amazon has been able to forego its profits in certain lines of business due to its expansion into multiple business lines. Thus, for establishing anti-competitive conduct, the leveraging theory of harm can only be sustained if legal framework supports leveraging across unrelated/ distinct markets.

Courts typically assume that firms recoup losses by raising prices on the same goods they previously offered at a loss. However, recoupment across markets is also a strategy, particularly for firms diversified across products and services. Therefore, for assessing potential cross subsidies in any case, the regulatory agencies may perform the incremental cost test and stand-alone test to determine if a cross subsidy is present. It has been observed that as long as the prices charged fall between the stand-alone cost and incremental cost of those products, those prices would be subsidy-free. Preventing cross subsidisation and proscribing below-cost pricing may benefit smaller or more fragile rival firms, but in certain markets they may also lead to higher prices and thus harm consumers. Herein, lies the antitrust dilemma in the treatment of cross subsidization in conduct cases.

Bibliography

FJELL, K. (2001). A cross-subsidy classification framework. *Journal of Public Policy*, 21(3), 265-282

KHAN, L. M. (2017). Amazon's Antitrust Paradox. *Yale L. J.*, 126, 710

ROCHET, J. C., & TIROLE, J. (2006). Two-sided markets: a progress report. *The RAND journal of economics*, 37(3), 645-667

Data shaping firms and markets, *OECD Digital Economy Papers*, December 2022 No. 344

ERGP PL II (19) 40 Report on cross-subsidisation practices

See also

Administered prices, Prices

D

DAMAGES

Ignacio GARCÍA-PERROTE MARTÍNEZ
Uria Menéndez

■ Definition

Damages are a monetary relief available for the party harmed by a competition law infringement. The term refers to the sum of money that the claimant seeks compensation for and is causally connected to the anticompetitive conduct that injured the claimant in her business. Damages awards for competition law infringements compensate the overcharge and loss of profits caused by the infringement, plus interest. Damages can also compensate the loss of chance and, occasionally, non-material harm.

■ Commentary

Introduction

Infringements of competition law, such as cartels and abuses of dominant positions, have a double negative effect. Firstly, they distort competition and have a negative impact on social welfare in general and consumer welfare in particular, Inter alia, they cause price increases, limitations in output or the exclusion of market actors. Secondly, the price increase caused by the infringement obliges customers of infringers (direct purchasers) to pay a higher price than the one that would have been set absent the infringement. This difference, known as the overcharge, is the basis for quantifying the anticompetitive harm suffered. It must be noted that direct purchasers can absorb the effects of the infringement or, if market conditions allow it, pass it on to their own customers (indirect purchasers).

Damages awards compensate the individual harm caused by infringements of competition law. According to national tort law rules, claimants will have to prove that (i) there was an infringement of competition law, (ii) they suffered a harm, (iii) there was a causal relationship between the injury and the anticompetitive conduct and, when appropriate, (iv) the defendant's fault. Victims can claim for the following heads of damage: actual loss (damnum emergens) and the profits lost (lucrum cessans), plus interest *(Manfredi)*. Depending on the jurisdiction, claimants may also seek compensation for loss of chance and non-material harm, such as harm to its reputation, though the latter is rare.

The purposes of damages: compensation and deterrence

Damages for infringements of competition law have a two-fold purpose. Firstly, they seek to compensate the victim and put her into the position she would have been absent the infringement. Secondly, they have a deterrent effect on current or future infringers deciding whether to continue an ongoing anticompetitive conduct or to engage in one. Whereas damages are always compensatory, if emphasis is set on the latter purpose, they may become punitive.

The double nature of damages is undeniable regardless of the legal tradition of each jurisdiction. The European Union and, as a consequence of the partial harmonisation of the damages claims regime by EU 2014 Damages Directive, its Member States too are the paradigm of jurisdictions where the award seeks to compensate victims: they are built upon the principle of full compensation. Thus, passing-on arguments are accepted to grant legal standing to indirect purchasers and to allow defendants to raise the passing-on defence. Furthermore, the Court of Justice of the European Union has stated that damages claims contribute to the effectiveness of the enforcement of the prohibitions laid down in Articles 101 and 102 of the Treaty on the Functioning of the European Union (Courage, Skanska and Sumal). This is a clear recognition of a collateral deterrent effect. Norway's damages regime is aligned with the EU and the award compensates the net amount of the harm suffered.

In other jurisdictions, however, damages are primarily punitive. In the United States of America at the Federal level, section 4 of the Clayton Act allows victims to seek treble damages, i.e. an award of up to a threefold of the harm. There, the enforcement of competition law relies on private actions and encouraging them and keeping the treble damages system operating efficiently had spill over effects, such as the denial of both the passing-on defence and the legal standing for anyone who is not a direct customer of the infringer (Hanover Shoe and Illinois Brick). Punitive damages are also present in Brazil and Turkey, where courts may award double or treble damages, respectively, provided that certain conditions are met.

Quantifying damages

Quantifying damages is one of the main challenges that claimants, defendants and courts face in damages actions. The specific market circumstances of the affected market and the impossibility to observe the counterfactual scenario render it especially burdensome. Parties must nonetheless provide a quantification of the award as accurately as possible.

Therefore, the European Commission issued the Practical Guide on quantifying antitrust harm in competition law damages claims in 2013 and the Guidelines for national courts on how to estimate the share of overcharge which was passed on to the indirect purchaser in 2019. Those guidelines set forth several methods to assist parties elaborating the counterfactual scenario that will allow them to quantify the impact of the infringement and estimate the net harm suffered. With enough data, economic experts can prepare their reports and quantify the damage that both direct and indirect purchasers may have suffered: actual loss, including the share passed on, lost profits and loss of a chance, plus interest.

The guidelines are also useful for judges that need to appraise the economic reports provided by the parties and decide whether they are robust enough to present a plausible result and supported by evidence. If the report is robust and based on sound economic theory, damages may be awarded in full. If courts consider that the economic evaluation is not well founded or presents methodological issues, the result may be the dismissal of the action or a reduction of the damages awarded and its setting by judicial estimation. The latter may happen if the court considers that the claimant proved all other requirements and tried to offer a precise economic assessment, but quantifying the harm is excessively difficult or practically impossible. In these cases, courts may do an ex novo estimation of the damage or use one of the reports provided as a starting point. For instance, such has been the case for appellate judgments in the paper envelopes cartel and trucks cartel litigation in Spain.

Damages and collective redress

In the EU, the principle of full compensation requires that all victims have a right to damages. Depending on the extension of legal standing, anyone from customers of the infringers to final consumers can claim damages, as well as customers of the infringers' competitors *(Kone)* and other undertakings key to the functioning of a market that are not active operators therein *(Otis GmbH)*. Usually, the more distanced from the origin of the damage, the lower is the amount of the harm accrued and the harder its quantification becomes, especially taking into account that it should not overcompensate them.

When it comes to small and scattered (or dispersed) harm, collective redress mechanisms may become a suitable mean to foster damages claims. The issue, however, is setting the amount of damages per each victim so that they are fully compensated, especially if the action is opt-out, i.e. where victims are included in the group unless they expressly renounce to be part thereof. In these cases, the amount set is likely to be an aggregation of the harm suffered by the class as a whole (Merricks) and victims may be over- or undercompensated since the individual harm is not quantified.

Bibliography

AMARO, R. and LABORDE, J.-F., *La réparation des préjudices causés par les pratiques anti-concurrentielles*, 2nd edn, Concurrences, 2021

AMARO, R. (ed.), *Private Enforcement of Competition Law in Europe. Directive 2014/104/EU and Beyond*, Bruylant, 2021

HOVENKAMP, H. J., "A Primer on Antitrust Damages", *Faculty Scholarship at Penn Law* 1846, 2011

POSNER, R., *Antitrust Law*, 2nd edn, University of Chicago Press, 2001

RODGER, B., SOUSA FERRO, M., MARCOS, F., *The EU Antitrust Damages Directive: Transposition in the Member States*, Oxford University Press, 2018

See also

Collective redress (class action), Consumer protection, Economic analysis, Private Enforcement

D

DE MINIMIS NOTICE

Caroline CAUFFMAN
Maastricht University

Definition

Article 101 (1) TFEU prohibits agreements between undertakings, concerted practices and decisions by associations of undertakings which may affect trade between Member States and which have as their object or effect the prevention, restriction, or distortion of competition within the internal market. According to the case law of the Court of Justice (Expedia), the provision does not apply when the effect on competition is not appreciable. The De Minimis Notice is short for the European Commission's "Commission Notice on agreements of minor importance which do not appreciably restrict competition under Article 101(1) of the Treaty on the Functioning of the European Union'. In this Notice, the European Commission sets out, through the use of market share thresholds, the conditions under which it considers that the effect on competition is not appreciable.

Commentary

In 1969, the Court of Justice held in Völk v Vervaeke, that an agreement between undertakings, while being capable of affecting trade between Member States, falls outside the scope of Article 101 TFEU (then Article 85 EC) "when it has only an insignificant effect on the markets, taking into account the weak position which the persons concerned have on the market of the product in question" (para 5/7).

Since the 1970s, the Commission has published Notices specifying the conditions under which it considers the effect on competition not to be appreciable. The conditions concern market share and/or turnover thresholds and have varied over time.

An important evolution took place regarding the scope of the De Minimis Notices. Up until 2014, the De Minimis Notices applied to both restrictions by object and restrictions by effect. Völk v Vervaecke, the case that triggered the Commission to publish the Notice, itself concerned a restriction by object (vertical agreement providing absolute territorial protection). However, in its 2012 Expedia decision, the Court of Justice held that "an agreement that may affect trade between Member States and that has an anti-competitive object constitutes, by its nature and independently of any concrete effect that it may have, an appreciable restriction on competition" (para 37). Following this decision, the Commission published a new De Minimis Notice, the scope of which is limited to restrictions by effect in 2014. This Notice is still in force. It was accompanied by a Document providing Guidance on restrictions of competition "by object" for the purpose of defining which agreements may benefit from the De Minimis Notice.

Under the current De Minimis Notice, the Commission considers that agreements, decisions or concerted practices "which may affect trade between Member States and which may have as their effect the prevention, restriction or distortion of competition within the internal market, do not appreciably restrict competition within the meaning of Article 101(1) of the Treaty:

(a) if the aggregate market share held by the parties to the agreement does not exceed 10% on any of the relevant markets affected by the agreement, where the agreement is made between undertakings which are actual or potential competitors on any of those markets (agreements between competitors); or
(b) if the market share held by each of the parties to the agreement does not exceed 15% on any of the relevant markets affected by the agreement, where the agreement is made between undertakings which are not actual or potential competitors on any of those markets (agreements between non-competitors)'.

In the case of doubt as to whether an agreement is either an agreement between competitors or an agreement between non-competitors, the 10 % threshold applies.

If competition is restricted by the cumulative effect of parallel networks of vertical agreements, the market share thresholds are reduced to 5%, both for agreements between competitors and for agreements between non-competitors. However, individual suppliers or distributors whose market share does not exceed 5%, are in general not considered to contribute significantly to the cumulative foreclosure effect. Moreover, a cumulative foreclosure effect is considered unlikely if less than 30% of the relevant market is covered by parallel (networks of) agreements having similar effects.

If the thresholds set out in the De Minimis Notice are not exceeded, the Commission will not start proceedings. If the Commission started proceedings but undertakings can demonstrate that they assumed in good faith that the relevant thresholds were not exceeded, the Commission will not impose fines. While intended to provide guidance to national competition authorities and national courts, the Notice does not bind them. The Court of Justice, being responsible for the final interpretation of Article 101 TFEU, is not bound by the De Minimis Notice either.

The benefit of the De Minimis Notice no longer applies if the market shares of the parties to the agreement exceed the applicable thresholds of 5%, 10%, and 15% by more than 2 percentage points during two successive calendar years.

That the benefit of the De Minimis Notice does not apply because the applicable thresholds are exceeded, does not mean that the agreement, decision, or concerted practice in question automatically has an appreciable effect on competition (Bagnasco, paras 34–35; Whish and Bailey, 146). This needs to be examined taking into account the specific circumstances of the case. It is important to note that the appreciability of a restriction of competition is not always linked to market power assed by proxy of market shares. It may also result from the type of restriction, product, or industry (see eg., Pavlov, paras 90–97 concerning a decision by the members of a profession to set up a pension fund entrusted with the management of a supplementary pension).

Bibliography

Bailey, D. and John, L. E. (eds.), *Bellamy and Child: European Union Law of Competition* (8th edn, Oxford University Press 2018), Chapter 2

King, S., "How Appreciable is Object? The De Minimis Doctrine and Case C-226/11 Expedia Inc v Autorité de la concurrence" (2015) 11 *European Competition Journal* 1-25

Whish, R. and Bailey, D., *Competition Law* (10th end, Oxford University Press 2021), Chapter 3

See also

Agreement (notion), Concerted practices

D

DIGITAL MARKETS ACT (DMA)

Philip TORBØL
K&L Gates

Definition

The Digital Markets Act ("DMA"), Regulation (EU) 2022/1925 of the European Parliament and of the Council of 14 September 2022 on contestable and fair markets in the digital sector and amending Directives (EU) 2019/1937 and (EU) 2020/1828 (Digital Markets Act) is a rulebook providing a set of ex-ante rules in the digital ecosystem. The DMA's purpose is to maintain contestable digital markets and promote fair commercial practices with the main online market operators. In a desire to avoid that the largest operators dominate the online market excessively, the DMA provides business users and end users with regulatory safeguards through imposition of obligations on the main online market operators in the European Union.

Commentary

Purpose

The DMA's ex-ante enforcement rules complement traditional competition rules. However, as opposed to the latter, which are only enforced following an ex-post assessment of conduct and the relevant market, the DMA obligations apply objectively regardless of market definition or effect. The DMA applies without prejudice to Articles 101 and 102 TFEU.

Scope

The DMA applies to so-called "gatekeepers". Gatekeepers are market operators which provide "core platform services" ("CPS"). CPS include online search engines, online social networking services, web browsers, virtual assistants, connected television, online intermediary services (e.g., app stores, marketplaces), online advertising, video-sharing platform services and cloud computing services. A CPS provider will be designated as a gatekeeper when three cumulative requirements are met:

1. it has a "significant impact" on the internal market, presumed to be fulfilled if the CPS reaches at least €7.5 billion annual turnover in the European Union in each of the last three financial years, or at least €75 billion average market capitalization or equivalent fair market value in the last financial year;
2. its CPS is an "important gateway" between business users and end users, presumed to be fulfilled if it has at least 45 million monthly active end users established or located in the European Union, and at least 10,000 yearly active business users established in the European Union; and
3. it has or is expected to have an "entrenched and durable position" in its operations, presumed when, in each of the last three financial years, its CPS had at least 45 million monthly active end users established or located in the European Union, and at least 10,000 yearly active business users established in the European Union (Article 3(1)(a)-(c)).

The DMA establishes the rebuttable presumption that an undertaking fulfils the above-mentioned cumulative criteria when it meets the corresponding presumptive quantitative thresholds. The CPS provider is prohibited from segmenting, dividing, subdividing, fragmenting or splitting its services as a way to circumvent the quantitative thresholds (Article 13).

While an undertaking must notify the European Commission ("Commission") when it meets all three quantitative thresholds, in that event, it should demonstrate that it nonetheless does not meet all three cumulative criteria (Article 3(5)). Similarly, the Commission may determine that an undertaking qualifies as a gatekeeper by meeting the cumulative criteria, even if it does not meet the corresponding quantitative thresholds (Article 3(8)). Here, the Commission will consider the undertaking's size, number of users, scale and scope effects, user lock-in, conglomerate corporate structure or vertical integration, and other characteristics (Article 3(8)).

Impacted Practices

The DMA enumerates expectations and obligations for gatekeepers. To ensure that the catalogue of prohibited practices remains up to date, the Commission is empowered to adopt delegated acts to supplement the existing DMA obligations. The following obligations are set out in Article 5:

- *Restrictions on processing of personal data:* For example, when a third party is using the gatekeeper's CPS, the gatekeeper cannot process the personal data of end users that are using the third party's services (Article 5(2)(a)).
- *Prohibition on most favoured nation clauses:* Business users must be able to offer end users the same services through third-party intermediation services at different conditions than those offered through the gatekeeper intermediation (Article 5(3)).

- *Prohibition of anti-steering practices:* A gatekeeper must allow business users to promote offers to and communicate, contract and close transactions with end users outside the gatekeeper's CPS. This is required even if the business user initially acquired the end user through the gatekeeper's CPS (Article 5(4)).
  Its CPS must enable end users to access and use content, subscriptions, etc., by using the business user's software application, even if the end user acquired the item from the business user without initially using the gatekeeper's CPS.
- *Prohibition on interference:* A gatekeeper must not stop business users from raising issues with the relevant public authorities in relation to gatekeeper practices (Article 5(6)).
- *Anti-tying expectation:* A gatekeepercannot impose certain bundling and tying practices on business or end users (e.g., require business users to use, offer or interoperate with gatekeeper services) (Article 5(7)).
- *Transparency on prices paid for online advertising services:* A gatekeeper must provide advertisers and publishers with information concerning the price paid by the advertiser and publisher and remuneration paid to the publishers (Article 5(9)). It must also provide advertisers and publishers gratuitous information regarding the price paid for online advertising services to facilitate price comparisons between the gatekeeper's advertising services and that of an alternative undertaking.

The obligations set out in Articles 6 and 7 are subject to further clarification from the Commission. The Commission may, either on its own initiative or at a request of the gatekeeper, further assist a gatekeeper with designing suitable measures to comply with the gatekeeper's responsibilities.

- *Data access and data use:* When in competition with its business users, a gatekeeper cannot use data derived from the use of its CPS that is not publicly available and generated by the activities of its business users and their consumers (Article 6(2)). A gatekeeper must provide advertisers and publishers, free of charge, with access to the performance measuring tools of the gatekeeper and the data necessary to conduct an independent analysis of their ads published on the CPS (Article 6(8)). It must provide business users with continuous and real-time data portability (i.e. for data generated by both business and end users in the context of the use of the CPS) (Article 6(9)). A gatekeeper must provide third-party providers of online search engines with access on fair, reasonable, and non-discriminatory ("FRAND") terms to ranking, query, click and view data in relation to searches generated by end users on online search engines of the gatekeeper (Article 6(11)).
- *Interoperability:* A gatekeeper must implement interoperability (i.e. allow business users and providers of ancillary services (e.g. payment services) to access and interoperate with the gatekeeper) (Article 6(7)). A gatekeeper must not impose technical restrictions

on an end user's ability to switch between different software applications (Article 6(3) and services that are accessed using the gatekeeper's CPS (Article 6(6)). A gatekeeper must allow, more broadly, end users to uninstall any pre-installed software applications and allow the use of third-party software application and systems (Article 6(4)). Additionally, gatekeepers providing number-independent interpersonal communications services will have to ensure interoperability with these services provided by other operators (Article 7).

- *Self-preferencing:* A gatekeeper cannot preferentially rank its own product or service offerings, or those of a business user it controls, on its CPS (Article 6(5)). It must apply FRAND conditions of access to its software application store for business users (Article 6(12)).

Moreover, gatekeepers need to ensure full and effective compliance with the DMA obligations and provide the Commission with a report describing its compliance measures within six months after their designation.

Furthermore, gatekeepers must inform the Commission about intended concentrations involving another provider of a CPS or of any other services provided in the digital sector (Article 14). Finally, they must submit to the Commission an annual independent audit description of techniques used for profiling consumers that apply to or across its CPS (Article 15).

In exceptional cases, where compliance would endanger the economic viability of a gatekeeper's EU operation, the gatekeeper may request the suspension from an obligation. Moreover, the Commission may, in whole or in part, exempt a gatekeeper from a specific obligation on grounds of public health or public security.

Enforcement

Teams from the Commission's Directorate-General for Communications Networks, Content and Technology, together with its Directorate-General for Competition, oversee DMA enforcement. Pursuant to Chapter IV, the Commission may adopt a decision to open a market investigation into non-compliance, with potential assistance from national authorities (Article 16). The Commission is also entitled to adopt interim measures to prevent harm to users (Article 24), enforce binding gatekeeper commitments (Article 25) and impose fines on gatekeepers following a non-compliance decision (Article 30). It may also impose behavioural and structural remedies in cases of systemic non-compliance.

The DMA applies as of 2 May 2023, with 3 July 2023 as the notification deadline for companies that fulfil the DMA's criteria. The Commission subsequently came to a designation decision on notifying companies' gate-keeper status on 6 September 2023. A designated gatekeeper had to comply with the DMA's requirements within six months and no later than 6 March 2024.

Bibliography

European Parliament Briefing on DMA (2022)

Regulation (EU) 2022/1925 of the European Parliament and of the Council of 14 September 2022 on contestable and fair markets in the digital sector and amending Directives (EU) 2019/1937 and (EU) 2020/1828 (Digital Markets Act)

See also

Artificial Intelligence, AI Collusion (algorithm), Fintech

D

DIRECT EFFECT

Oles ANDRIYCHUK
Newcastle University

Definition

Direct effect is a concept, which is mainly used in the situations of parallel application of two or more legal systems: national and inter-/supranational or state and federal. Its rationale concerns the question of establishing legally binding and directly enforceable rights and obligations for the individuals vis-à-vis the states (vertical direct effect) and individuals vis-à-vis one another (horizontal direct effect). Usually, the principle is associated with the problems of the division of competences between the coexisting legal systems concerning the instances of a deeper and a more systematic application of the provisions of the upper legal system. The term is also relevant for purely domestic situations. For example, when deciding upon enforceability of certain constitutional provisions, which are broad and allow different (and conflicting) interpretations.

Commentary

From the purely juristic point of view, the norm can only have direct effect if it is clear, complete, precise and does not contain clarificatory references to other norms (the element of executability or ratione materiae) and if it concerns a definable group of individuals (the element of determination or ratione personae). The narrower and the better articulated the norm, the easier it is to assign to it a direct effect. In reality, the level of precision may vary. The term "direct effect" is sometimes confusingly used for defining the nature of EU legislative acts, when distinguishing the acts requiring a separate domestic implementation (e.g. directives) and those not requiring such implementation (e.g. regulations). EU regulations always have direct applicability, but not all provisions of the directly applicable (i.e. not requiring further transposition by a domestic legislative act) EU laws, are necessarily directly effective; and vice versa, even some provisions of the EU legislative acts, which are not designed to be directly applicable (i.e. EU directives) may become directly effective if not transposed by the Member State in due course. The concept of direct effect is also closely linked – but again only partially – with the principle of primacy of (some provisions of) one legal system over the other. The fact that the provisions of international or EU law may have primacy over the provisions of domestic law does not automatically imply the direct effectiveness of such provisions; and vice versa, not all directly effective provisions of EU law have necessarily the primacy over the domestic law.

The issue of direct effect is particularly relevant in the context of EU law. Historically, the Court of Justice of the European Union (CJEU) designated direct effectiveness to many provisions of EU primary and secondary law (starting with the seminar *van Gend en Loos*, 1963) paving thereby the way to a more harmonious and comprehensive European integration. In this sense, the former is instrumental to the latter.

In the context of EU competition law, the provisions of Art 101 and 102 TFEU were confirmed as having horizontal direct effect in 1973 (BRT v SV SABAM, 1974). The concept of horizontal direct effect continues to have a paramount importance in the field of private enforcement as it enables bringing stand-alone and follow-on actions against the infringers of the provisions of Art 101 and 102 TFEU. This is particularly relevant for the follow-on actions, relieving the plaintiffs from various procedural burdens related to the discovery of evidence and proof of the infringement, allowing them to focus mainly on the issues of proving harm and showing causality. But stand-alone actions are not uncommon too.

The compensatory rationale was established in a landmark 2001 *Courage v Crehan* judgment, in which the individual right to claim damages for the infringement of competition law was explicitly acknowledged (This was elaborated further by expanding the right to damages to the loss of profits in *Manfredi*, 2006). An important spillover of this ruling was a much wider and consistent use of the mechanism of private enforcement at the national courts of the EU Member States.

Direct effect of EU competition law does not answer the question of which jurisdiction – domestic or EU – has primacy over applying the law, it only stipulates conditions under which the provisions of EU competition law may be applied by individuals in cases of breach of EU competition law. The parallelism in applying the provisions of Art 101 and 102 TFEU has been reaffirmed, institutionalised and calibrated by the Modernisation Regulation of 2003. While ideally the provisions of the directly effective EU norms must be read and interpreted uniformly in all Member States, the remedies available for individuals may differ from one national legal system to the other, as the relevant norms could only be directly enforced via the substantive and procedural mechanisms of domestic legal systems, which are inherently unique and can be very different. A number of effective steps aimed at the unification of EU rules and practices related to damages in competition law cases have been introduced, though room for further improvements remains wide as the issue of damages goes to the heart of the procedural and substantive specificities of the national laws of EU Member States. One of the most problematic issues in this respect is the binding effect of national competition authorities' decisions declaring infringements of Articles 101 and 102 TFEU (Miguel Sousa Ferro). The doctrine of direct effect plays a paramount role in integrating and approximating the national legal systems of the EU Member States and contributes to the increasing role of European law in all EU Member States.

Bibliography

Craig, P., "Once upon a Time in the West: Direct Effect and the Federalisation of EEC Law", *Oxford Journal of Legal Studies*, Vol. 12, No. 3, 1992

Gáspár-Szilágyi, S., "The 'Primacy' and 'Direct Effect' of EU International Agreements", *European Public Law*, Vol. 21, No. 2, 2015

Rodger, B., Sousa Ferro, M. and Marcos, F., *The EU Antitrust Damages Directive: Transposition in the Member States*, Oxford University Press, 2018

Sousa Ferro, M., "Antitrust Private Enforcement and the Binding Effect of Public Enforcement Decisions", *Market and Competition Law Review*, Vol. 3, No. 2, 2020

Whish, R., "The Enforcement of EC Competition Law in The Domestic Courts of Member States", *European Business Law Review*, Vol. 5, No. 1, 1994

See also

Tipping

D

DISCRIMINATORY PRACTICES

Tilottama RAYCHAUDHURI
The West Bengal National University of Juridical Sciences, Kolkata

■ Definition

Discriminatory practices in competition law are understood as the imposition of different conditions to transactions of a similar nature, thereby creating a competitive disadvantage for trading partners. This also applies to situations where identical conditions are imposed on dissimilar transactions. Provisions against discriminatory practices are contained in Article 102 of the Treaty on the Functioning of the European Union (*TFEU*), s1 and 2 of the Sherman Act, 1890 along with the Robinson-Patman Act, 1936 (United States) and s4 of the Competition Act, 2002 (India). Discriminatory practices encompass a wide variety of actions including price and non-price practices. There is scope for firms to argue that the discrimination is objectively justified or enhances efficiency. The exact enforcement standard may vary based on the specific nature of the conduct and the jurisdiction involved.

■ Commentary

European Union

Under Article 102(c) of the TFEU, an abuse of a dominant position includes "*applying dissimilar conditions to equivalent transactions with other trading parties, thereby placing them at a competitive disadvantage*". This provision targets dominant undertakings that engage in discriminatory sales based on non-price conditions (*C-163/99 Portugal v Commission, C-163/99, and CASE AT.40461 – DE/DK Interconnector*) or pricing disparities (*COMP/C-1/36.91 Deutsche Post AG – Interception of cross-border mail*) among comparable customers. It also applies to cases where vertically integrated dominant undertakings favour their own operations (*C-242/95 GT-Link A/S v. De Danke Statsbaner*). Other forms of discriminatory conditions have also been recognized. The French Competition Authority penalised EssilorLuxotica (*Decision No. 21-30/395-199*), a dominant player in the wholesale corrective lenses market, for implementing discriminatory practices which hindered its online sales operation for 12 years, thereby maintaining high prices for the product in the market. Essilor had imposed discriminatory restrictions on electronic commerce operators in terms of deliveries, communication and warranties.

The aim of the prohibition against discriminatory practices in the EU is to safeguard fair competition in the internal market, including among the dominant undertaking's suppliers or customers (*CASE C-95/04 P British Airways v Commission and Case C-525/16 MEO – Serviços de Comunicações e Multimédia SA*). The prohibition is also applied to situations where equivalent conditions are applied to dissimilar transactions with other trading parties, thereby placing them at a competitive disadvantage. (*Case COMP/A.36.568/D3 Scandlines Sverige v. Port of Helsingborg*). Discrimination, while critical, is not the sole factor to establish an exclusionary abuse under Article 102(c). The legal framework requires the following to establish such abuse:

- *Discriminatory behaviour:* The determination of discriminatory behaviour requires an assessment of the differences in the treatment of various customers of the dominant undertaking and careful examination of these disparities. (Case C-52/07 Kanal 5 Ltd, TV 4 AB v. Föreningen Svenska); and
- *Distortion of competitive relationships* : Beyond identifying discriminatory behaviour, it is essential to demonstrate how the behaviour in question distorts competitive dynamics. In essence, this means proving that the conduct hampers the competitive position of some business partners in comparison to others from the perspective of the dominant undertaking. (Case C-525/16 MEO – Serviços de Comunicações e Multimédia SA)

The onus is on the dominant entity concerned to raise any plea of objective justification for discriminatory behaviour and to support it with arguments and evidence. It then falls to the Commission, which proposes to make a finding of an abuse of a dominant position, to show that the arguments and evidence relied on by the undertaking cannot prevail and, accordingly, that the justification put forward cannot be accepted (*Case T-301/04 Clearstream Banking AG v Commission [2009] ECR II-3155*)

United States

In the United States, discriminatory practices predominantly come under the realm of the Sherman Act. Under certain circumstances, a duty is imposed by §2 of the Sherman Act on monopolists to engage in non-discriminatory trading practices. One such circumstance includes when a monopolist controls an essential service or a bottleneck. (*MCI Communications Corp. v. AT&T Co., 708 F.2d 1081 (7th Cir. 1983).*

There are notable differences in the treatment of discriminatory conduct under the United States Antitrust Law, compared to the European Law. For instance, a firm in the United States with a legally obtained monopoly is free to set its prices and may even limit production to increase prices. The difference in approach is rooted in differing priorities and perspectives among competition authorities; significant differences in interpretation by courts; and divergent philosophies.

Additionally, the Robinson-Patman Act, an amendment to the Clayton Act in the United States, was specifically designed to prohibit certain types of unjust price discrimination that harm competition. The Robinson-Patman Act specifically applies to price discrimination, whereas the Sherman Act is focused on monopolisation through exclusionary conduct. As such, the approach in looking at exclusionary price discrimination cases, particularly those involving primary-line injury, under the Robinson-Patman Act has become consistent with the framework that exists for all exclusionary conduct cases under the Sherman Act (*Brooke Group Ltd. v. Brown & Williamson Tobacco Corp., 509 U.S. 209 (1993*).

There are two legal defences to alleged Robinson-Patman Act violations: (1) the price difference is justified by different costs in manufacture, sale, or delivery (e.g., volume discounts), or (2) the price concession was given in good faith to meet a competitor's price.

With the rise in discriminatory practices in the digital sector, a bill similar to the Robinson Patman Act (*The American Innovation and Choice Online Act*) has been introduced in the United States to prevent large digital platforms from indulging in discriminatory practices like self-preferencing and limiting the availability of competing products on their platform. The goal of the bill is to give equal opportunity to smaller businesses in the digital space.

India

In India, discriminatory practices are regulated under Section 4(2)(a) of the Competition Act, 2002, from the perspective of both price [under Section 4(2)(a)(ii)] and non-price [under Section 4(2)(a)(i)] related practices. These provisions declare that the imposition of "unfair" or "discriminatory" prices or conditions by a dominant entity, in the purchase or sale of goods or services, whether directly, or indirectly, amounts to an abuse of dominance. Section 4(2)(a) further provides that discriminatory conditions or prices which may be adopted to meet competition are excluded from the above.

The Competition Act, 2002, does not specifically define the term discriminatory practices, instead, the ambit and scope of the term are determined according to the facts and circumstances of each case. The legal defence available with the contravening enterprise is to demonstrate that the conduct was adopted with a view to meet the competition. (*In Re: XYZ and Association of Man Made Fibre Industry of India and Ors. (Case No. 62 of 2016) and Google LLC v Competition Commission of India, Competition Appeal (Appellate Tribunal) No. 1 of 2023)*

In practice, the Competition Commission of India (CCI) has accepted certain objective justifications as defences.

For instance, in the context of differential pricing for different customers, the CCI has found that giving better discounts to bulk purchases is an objective justification, with such conduct not being violative of the Competition Act. (*M/s ESYS Information Technologies Pvt. Ltd. v. Intel Corporation & Ors., Case No. 48 of 2011*)

In India, for a violation under Section 4(2)(a), the legal framework requires the following:

- *There must be an imposition:* The first element required under Section 4(2)(a) of the Competition Act is an imposition i.e., an element of compulsion where a party is bereft of choices. (*DLF Limited v. CCI, COMPAT Appeal No. 20 of 2011*).
- There must be a discriminatory condition: The second element required under Section 4(2)(a) of the Competition Act is that there must exist a discriminatory condition. In order to establish a discriminatory condition, two factors must be demonstrated (*Schott Glass India Pvt Ltd v CCI, COMPAT Appeal No. 91-92 of 2012*):
  - It must be shown that similar transactions are being treated differently; and
  - Harm or likely harm to competitive dynamics.

Finally, conditions or prices adopted to meet competition are not treated as discriminatory. Section 4(2)(a) of the Competition Act is more or less similar to the prohibition under Article 102(a) of the TFEU with the CCI often following a similar approach to the one adopted in the EU.

Bibliography

DUGAR, S. M., *Guide to Competition Law (Commentary on the Competition Act, 2002 MRTP Act,1969 & the Consumer Protection Act, 1986)* (8th edn, LexisNexis 2020), Volume I

HORNKOHL, L., "Article 102 TFEU, Equal Treatment and Discrimination after Google Shopping" (2022) 13 *Journal of European Competition Law & Practice* 99

VAN BAEL & BELLIS (ed), *Competition Law of the European Union* (6th edn, Kluwer Law International 2021), Chapter 8

WEBER WALLER, S., "The Omega Man or the Isolation of U.S. Antitrust Law" (2020) 52, *Connecticut Law Review* 123

WHISH, R. and BAILEY, D., *Competition Law* (10th edn, Oxford University Press 2021), Chapter 17 and 18

See also

Abuse of dominant position, Abuse of economic dependence, Price discrimination

D

DISTRIBUTION AGREEMENT

Sei SHISHIDO
Seikei University

■ Definition

Article 101 of the TFEU prohibits agreements regarding price, quantity, quality, and other conditions for sale between companies horizontally or vertically. The vertical agreement regarding a distribution condition is often called the Distribution Agreement. Distribution Agreements can be conducted in two types: Exclusive distribution and Selective distribution.

Exclusive distribution

Under an exclusive distribution system, a supplier allows only one or a few specific distributors to resale its product to a specific geographic area or to a specific customer group. It can violate the TFEU101 (1) if it gives the supplier absolute territorial protection.

Selective distribution

Under a selective distribution system, a supplier sets some criteria for selecting "authorized distributors". Once distributors meet those criteria, the supplier does not supply to non-authorized distributors. Additionally, the supplier prohibits authorized distributors from reselling the product to non-authorized distributors. It is prohibited by TFEU 101 (1) if it doesn't meet the criteria by Metro I.

■ Commentary

Since there are also entries for "Selective distribution" and "Exclusive distribution," I will mostly discuss distribution agreements in general here.

From the suppliers' perspective, distribution agreements have some benefits to prevent other undertakings from free-riding the investment by some distributors and suppliers. Such positive effects can typically be led by vertical restraints that give territorial protection to the dealers.

On the other hand, distribution agreements can lead to the foreclosure of the distribution network, which causes an anti-competitive effect in the sense of diminishing intra-brand competition in a market. Such negative effects of the agreement can be found especially in a highly oligopolistic market containing highly differentiated products. Generally speaking, this anti-competitive effect can be evaluated based on the circumstances of both intra-brand and inter-brand markets. If the inter-brand competition is not lively due to product differentiation, for example, the distribution agreement might have more tendency to reduce competition overall. In the EU, Article 101 (1) of the TFEU prohibits distribution agreements between companies related vertically if such a distribution system causes an anti-competitive effect on competition without producing enough pro-competitive effects. If such a system has a pro-competitive effect overwhelming its competitive harm, then Article 101 (3) exempts such an agreement from applying Article 101 (1).

The Guidelines on Vertical Restraints by the European Commission (2022/C 248/01) also stated that "restrictions on the territory in which, or the customers to whom, the buyer may sell goods or services covered by the vertical agreement, subject to certain exceptions that enable the supplier to operate exclusive or selective distribution systems."

Types of distribution agreements are originally defined by Regulation (EU) 2010/330 and those are now defined by Article 1 of the Regulation (EU) 2022/720 (the new Vertical Block Exemption Regulation: vBER) as follows:

- "Selective distribution system" means a distribution system where the supplier undertakes to sell the contract goods or services, either directly or indirectly, only to distributors selected on the basis of specified criteria and where these distributors undertake not to sell such goods or services to unauthorised distributors within the territory reserved by the supplier to operate that system.
- "Exclusive distribution system" means a distribution system where the supplier allocates a territory or group of customers exclusively to itself or to a maximum of five buyers and restricts all its other buyers from actively selling into the exclusive territory or to the exclusive customer group.

In evaluating whether the agreement is eligible for the block exemption by the VBER, it is first checked whether the distributor or the supplier holds more than 30% of the market share as a safe harbor. Also, vBER listed the "Restrictions that remove the benefit of the block exemption" as "hardcore restrictions.

Whether a distribution agreement is exempted under Article 101(3) is first assessed by whether it falls under the block exemption provided by the VBER. If not, one might consider if the agreement falls within the scope of Article 101(3) TFEU individually, but it is rarely approved.

In *Metro 1* (Metro v Commission (1977)), the court showed that the pure-qualitative distribution agreement presumed to be part of a competition and compatible with TFEU 101 (1), if the "resellers are chosen on the basis of objective criteria of a qualitative nature relating to the technical qualifications of the reseller and his staff and the suitability of his trading premises and that such conditions are laid down uniformly for all potential resellers and are not applied in a discriminatory fashion" (para 20), and the agreement did not go further than necessary. This so-called Metro1 criterion is still applied today (*E.g., Coty Germany v Parfümerie Akzente (2017))*.

It is important to note that the agreement does not need to meet those criteria by Metro 1 to be block-exempted by VBER. Also, the fact that the agreement is not block-exempted does not mean it violates Article 101 (1).

In the U.S., neither courts nor competition authorities rely on the two categories of distribution agreements mentioned above. Distribution agreements can be prohibited by Section 1 of the Sherman Act as a vertical restraint if the agreement harms competition overall (*Continental TV v GTE Sylvania; Leegin Creative Leather Products Inc v PSKS Inc.*). Generally speaking, distribution agreements are presumed to be pro-competitive and evaluated under the "rule of reason." That is because, partly due to the influence of the Chicago School, non-price vertical restraints are generally considered to have no anticompetitive effects that would outweigh efficiency.

In fact, most decisions by U.S. Courts after the *Sylvania* case apply the rule of reason to vertical agreements that give dealers territorial or customer restrictions. Courts generally consider (i) the purpose of the agreement, (ii) the anti-competitive effect of such agreement in a relevant market, and (iii) balance the pro-competitive effect and the anti-competitive mentioned in (ii) (See ABA, Antitrust developments 8th, pp.152-157.).

In Japan, Article 12 of General Designation defined "trading with another party on conditions which unjustly restrict any trade between the said party and its other transacting party or other business activities of the said party" as "Trading on Restrictive Terms." Such conduct is prohibited by Article 19 of the Japanese Anti-monopoly Act (JAMA).

The Japanese Supreme Court showed that a non-price vertical restraint is presumed to be pro-competitive if it is "somewhat reasonable" and it is applied to other distributors in a non-discriminatory manner (Supreme Court, 18 December 1998, 52-IX Minshu 1866 (*Shiseido case*); Supreme Court, 18 December 1998, 1664 Hanrei Jiho 14 (*Kao case*).)

"Guidelines Concerning Distribution Systems and Business Practices Under The Antimonopoly Act" by the Japanese Fair Trade Commission (JFTC) also clearly mention that adopting the selective distribution system is lawful when the criteria of selection are somewhat reasonable from the consumer's point of view, and the criteria applied are non-discriminatory to all trading parties. Notably, JFTC also uses the "Selective Distribution System" category when JFTC mentions the distribution agreement in guidelines since 2015.

Bibliography

AREEDA, P. E. and HOVENKAMP, H., *Antitrust Law: An Analysis of Antitrust Principles and Their Application*, Volume VIII, Chapter 16A and 16D.]

BAILEY, D. and JOHN, L. E. (eds.), *Bellamy and Child: European Union Law of Competition* (8th ed, 2018), paras 7.094–7.117

WAKUI, M., *Antimonopoly Law: Competition Law and Policy in Japan* (2nd ed), Chapter 6

See also

Absolute territorial protection, Agent, Exclusive distribution, Exclusive purchasing agreement, Horizontal cooperation agreement, Vertical Agreement, Selective distribution

D

DIVESTITURE

Torsten KÖRBER
University of Cologne

Definition

The term divestiture refers to the (partial or full) sale or disposal of a business unit, subsidiary, division, product line or other assets. A divestiture may be based on a voluntary management decision to concentrate on certain products or markets; it may be offered to competition authorities as a commitment in order to eliminate competitive concerns; or it may be ordered as a structural remedy to address competitive problems which already exist in a market or would be created by a merger. While structural measures like divestiture are the preferred remedies in merger control, they may be used only as a last resort in other areas of competition law.

Commentary

Divestiture is often used as a structural merger remedy. Competition authorities regularly prefer structural remedies over behavioural remedies because merger control is aimed at preserving competitive market structures and because an order to divest certain subsidiaries, production facilities or other assets does not require constant subsequent monitoring by the competition authority.

For instance, the EU Commission cleared the proposed acquisition of SABMiller, the world's second largest brewer, by AB InBev, the world's largest brewer. The Commission had found, inter alia, that the merger would remove an important competitor in the beer market in several Member States, and that it would facilitate tacit price coordination among brewers in the EEA through an increase in the number of multimarket contacts. AB InBev offered to divest the whole of SABMiller's business in France, Italy, the Netherlands and the UK to the Japanese brewer Asahi. To dispel the Commission's concerns AB InBev also offered to divest SABMiller's business in the Czech Republic, Hungary, Poland, Romania and Slovakia. In sum, the commitments were aimed at selling practically the entire SABMiller beer business in Europe. The Commission approved the merger conditional upon full compliance with these commitments in 2016.

In contrast, divestiture may be used in the EU only as a last resort remedy to address violations of the cartel prohibition or the abuse of market power. Art. 7 Reg. 1/2003 (EU) states that structural remedies can only be imposed by the EU Commission "*either where there is no equally efficient behavioural remedy or where any equally effective behavioural remedy would be more burdensome for the undertaking concerned than a structural remedy*".

This rule, which is an expression of the principle of proportionality, has sometimes been relaxed in cases in which the EU Commission has accepted (and made binding by a decision according to Art. 9 Reg. 1/2003) divestiture commitments in order to address abusive behaviour by vertically integrated undertakings.

For instance, the Commission investigated possible violations of the prohibition against the abuse of a dominant position (Art. 102 TFEU) by the German energy provider E.ON. The Commission came to the preliminary conclusion that E.ON might have infringed Art. 102 TFEU in two ways: first, by deliberately refusing to sell the production of certain power plants that was available and that it would have been economically rational to sell, in order to raise prices (withdrawal of production capacity); second, by favoring its own production affiliate. In order to address these concerns, E.ON proposed to divest itself of about 5000 MW (more than 20%) of its production capacity, and to divest itself of its transmission system business consisting of an extra-high-voltage (380/220 kV) power grid network as well as system operations currently run by E.ON Netz. This was aimed at removing the incentive of the network operator to favor a particular (vertically-integrated) supplier. In 2008, the Commission made these commitments binding by way of an Art. 9 decision.

According to established competition law doctrine, the fact that an undertaking has acquired a strong market position or even a monopoly through internal growth based upon competition on the merits does not entitle competition authorities to divest such undertaking in order to create a more competitive market structure (cf. ECJ, 6.9.2017, C_314/14 P, ECLI:EU:C:2017:632, n°133 *Intel*). Competition law is aimed at promoting competition and not at discouraging competition by punished successful undertakings.

Some systems of competition law permit, under exceptional circumstances, an "objective divestiture" of undertakings, that is to say the divestiture of undertakings which have not violated competition law or other laws. The best example of this is Part 4 of the UK Enterprise Act, which establishes a system whereby the Competition and Markets Authority (CMA) and the sectoral regulators may conduct a market investigation in order to discover whether any features of a market prevent, restrict or distort competition. If such a distortion is found, the CMA has a wide range of remedial powers which, as a last resort, include orders for an objective divestiture.

This power was applied to force the British Airport Authority (BAA) to sell three of its airports in 2009. BAA was privatised in 1987. A market investigation that had been performed from 2007 to 2009 found that BAA accounted for more than 60% of all passengers using UK airports. Heathrow, Gatwick, Stansted and Southampton accounted for 90% in south-east England. Edinburgh, Glasgow and Aberdeen accounted for 84% in Scotland. The investigation concluded that BAA's common ownership together with other features of the relevant market created adverse effects on competition. CMA evaluated the effects of the divestiture order in 2016.

Provisions analogous to those in the UK have been adopted in various countries, including South Africa, Iceland and Mexico. The German government is considering introducing a similar provision as Sec. 32f in the German Act against Restrictions of Competition (ARC) by way of the 11th amendment 2023 to the ARC.

The term divestiture is closely related to (and sometimes used as a synonym for) the term unbundling. Unbundling measures are regularly applied in the field of regulatory law. They cover a wide range of remedies that are aimed at splitting up (vertically) integrated undertakings. Unbundling measures may range from accounting and informational unbundling via functional unbundling and legal unbundling to full ownership unbundling. Accounting unbundling requires the undertakings to keep separate accounts for their transmission and distribution activities; for other activities consolidated accounts may be kept. Informational unbundling stops the information flow between the transmission (net) branch and the other branches of a vertically-integrated undertaking. Functional unbundling involves independent management in terms of organisational independence, the decision-making powers of management staff and a compliance program to ensure non-discriminatory behaviour. Legal unbundling means the setup of independent network undertakings which, however, can remain as a member of the same group of undertakings or be owned by the same owner. Ownership or asset unbundling is the strongest form of unbundling. It involves, for example, the complete sale of a transmission business, where the transmission undertaking a cannot stay in the a group of undertakings that provide distribution services. For instance, a vertically-integrated energy supplier may be required, by law or by regulatory intervention, to unbundle its network business in order to enable competition on the transportation level and thereby competition in upstream and downstream markets.

Bibliography

Whish, R. (2020), *New Competition Tool: Legal Comparative Study of Existing Competition Tools Aimed at Addressing Structural Competition Problems with a Particular Focus on the UK's Market Investigation Tool*

EU Commission Notice on Remedies Acceptable Under Council Regulation (EC) N° 139/2004, OJ 2008, C267/1

EU Commission, Staff Working Paper "The Unbundling Regime" (2010)

OECD (2019), The Divestiture of Assets as a Competition Remedy: Stocktaking of International Experiences

See also

Merger remedies

D

DOMINANCE (NOTION)

Francesco DUCCI
Western University

■ Definition

Dominance is a legal requirement to establish an abuse of a dominant position. Dominance reflects possession of a substantial degree of durable market power, typically defined as power to price above competitive levels, power to exclude, and ability to act independently of competitors and consumers. While direct evidence may be used to prove dominance, the most common approach is the assessment of market shares and entry barriers within a defined relevant market. Having a dominant position is not in itself a violation of competition law, but it is necessary for a finding of abuse. Dominance is not part of U.S. antitrust law, which instead requires possession of monopoly power.

■ Commentary

Dominance is a legal concept applied in competition law cases involving abuses of a dominant position. Possession of dominance is a precondition to establish whether unilateral practices by a firm, or a group of firms in cases of joint or collective dominance, is abusive. From an economic perspective, dominance can be equated with a substantial degree of durable market power. In the model of perfect competition, firms are price-takers with no market power and the equilibrium market price equals marginal cost. At the opposite end of the theoretical spectrum, a monopolist holds large market power, and with it the ability to restrict output and raise prices above the competitive level, resulting in a deadweight loss and a transfer of surplus from the consumers to the monopolist. These theoretical extremes, however, are rarely found in practice. Real markets are located on a continuum between perfect competition and monopoly and tend to be characterized by firms that hold at least some degree of market power – for example, due to product differentiation, switching costs, and the existence of barriers to entry. For this reason, competition law enforcement is neither limited to cases of strict monopoly nor broadly applicable to all firms with market power. It is instead based on the more specific legal notion of dominance, which reflects a substantial or significant degree of market power.

The typical legal framework on abuse of dominance across jurisdictions includes the following common requirements: a finding of a dominant position, usually within a defined product and geographic market; the assessment of a dominant firm's conduct as a potential abuse. Dominance is not condemned in and of itself, since firms may legitimately achieve a dominant position through better products and services, lower prices, more efficient production, and innovation. The legal notion of dominance serves instead as a necessary requirement for a finding of abuse. The greater the market power, the greater the potential impact of anticompetitive conduct on the market. For this reason, dominance acts as a threshold to guide competition law enforcement against unilateral practices that pose the highest risk of competitive harm.

Theoretically, proof of dominance can be either direct or indirect. In principle, metrics such as evidence of a firm's profits, markup of price over marginal cost, and demand elasticity may be used to assess dominance directly. However, precise and comprehensive data necessary for a direct evaluation of market power is often unavailable. Hence, the most common approach is to infer market power indirectly through market definition and the assessment of market shares and entry barriers within a well-defined relevant antitrust market. The Hypothetical Monopolist Test is a common tool used to define the boundaries of the relevant market and market shares are generally used as prima facie thresholds. However, market shares are not determinative of dominance alone and must typically be analyzed in conjunction with entry barriers and related market conditions. This framework is also relevant in the context of merger review, in particular the analysis of unilateral merger effects.

In United Brands, the Court of Justice of the European Union provided the following legal definition of dominance under Article 102 TFEU: "a position of economic strength enjoyed by an undertaking which enables it to prevent effective competition being maintained on the relevant market by affording it the power to behave to an appreciable extent independently of its competitors, customers and ultimately of its consumers." A rebuttable presumption of dominance applies when the market share is 50% or more, while a dominant position is unlikely below 40%. Having a dominant position does not violate Article 102 TFEU. However, the Court of Justice in Michelin held that a firm with a dominant firm has a "special responsibility not to allow its conduct to impair undistorted competition in the internal market." Decisions have also occasionally referred to positions of 90% market share or more as super-dominance (Compagnie Maritime Belge; Google Shopping), where conduct is significantly more likely to be found abusive. Once a dominant position is established, Article 102 TFEU can be enforced against exclusionary practices as well as exploitative abuses such as excessive pricing.

In contrast, the notion of dominance is not found under U.S. antitrust law. Section 2 of the Sherman Act makes it unlawful for any person to "monopolize, or attempt to monopolize, or combine or conspire with any other person or persons, to monopolize any part of the trade or commerce." A monopolization claim does not require dominance but rather possession of "monopoly power in the relevant market" (Grinnell Corp; Trinko), which in turn has been defined by the U.S. Supreme Court as the "power to control prices or exclude competition" (du Pont). Monopoly power generally demands a higher market share threshold than dominance under EU competition law: typically, it is likely to be found with at least 70% market share and unlikely below 50% market share. Unlike Article 102 TFEU, Section 2 covers both monopolization and attempts to monopolize. The latter involves anticompetitive conduct with specific intent to monopolize and a dangerous probability of achieving monopoly power.

The assessment of dominance in digital markets demands careful analysis of specific economic features not necessarily at play in other contexts. Key factors include, among others, the centrality of non-price dimensions of competition, the multi-sided nature of platforms, and the role of data and network externalities. In some jurisdictions, these characteristics have been explicitly incorporated within the legal definition of abuse of dominance. In Canadian competition law, for example, dominance has been defined by the Competition Tribunal and the Federal Court of Appeal in Toronto Real Estate Board (TREB) as the ability to control both price and non-price dimensions of competition for a significant period of time. The text of Section 79 of the Competition Act also explicitly refers to factors such as network effects, non-price competition on quality, choice, consumer privacy, and innovation as relevant factors in the determination of dominance and abuse.

Bibliography

Francis, D. and Srigman, C. J., Antitrust: Principles, Cases, and Materials (ABA Antitrust Law Section, 2023)

Motta, M., *Competition Policy: Theory and Practice* (Cambridge University Press 2004)

Whish, R. and Bailey, D., *Competition Law* (Oxford University Press, 2021)

OECD, Abuse of Dominance in Digital Markets (2020)

See also

Barriers to entry, Bundling, Geographic market, Market power, Monopoly

D

DOWNSTREAM MARKET

Ya-Lun YEN
National Cheng Kung University

■ Definition

According to the definition provided by the European Commission in the Glossary of Terms Used in EU Competition Policy Antitrust and Control of Concentrations (2002), a downstream market means "a market at the next stage of the production/distribution chain, for example, the distribution and sale of motor vehicles would be a downstream market in relation to the production of motor vehicles." A downstream firm purchases outputs of an upstream firm, utilizing them as inputs to manufacture products or provide services for sale in the downstream market. The market where transactions take place for a firm to sell its products or services to its customers is referred to as the "downstream market". The customers (buyers) of the goods or services (inputs) provided or sold by firms or input suppliers are situated in the downstream market.

■ Commentary

The downstream market refers to the market where buyers of a firm's goods or services reside. During merger reviews, competition authorities assess the impact of the merger on relevant markets, including both upstream and downstream markets, or related markets. Relevant markets can be upstream or downstream. A focus of vertical merger review is whether the merger may diminish the competitive constraint the merged entity faces from rivals in the downstream market due to unilateral foreclosure or raising a rival's costs. For instance, the European Union's Guidelines on the Assessment of Non-Horizontal Mergers demonstrate that the European Commission will examine whether the merged entity, post-merger, would have the ability and incentive to significantly foreclose access to inputs and whether such a foreclosure strategy would have a substantial anticompetitive effect on competition in the downstream market. For input foreclosure to be a concern, the merged firm, significantly powerful in the upstream market, must be anticipated to negatively influence prices and supply conditions in the downstream market by restricting access to its own upstream products or services.

The merged entity may aim to diminish the competitive constraint from downstream rivals by increasing their costs. Input foreclosure resulting from a vertical merger could lead to higher prices in the downstream market and may hinder effective competition by raising barriers for potential downstream entrants. Moreover, the European Commission will assess the likelihood of anticompetitive customer foreclosure from a vertical merger that involves integration with an important customer in the downstream market, including the merged entity's ability or incentive to foreclose access to downstream markets after reducing purchases from upstream rivals, and the significant anticompetitive effect this strategy might have on downstream market customers. According to the revised Notice on Simplified Procedure in the Merger Simplification Package adopted by the European Commission in 2023, whether the individual or combined upstream and downstream market shares of the merging parties are below 50% (or 30-35% in a flexibility clause for vertical relationships) is one factor in determining if the case can benefit from simplified treatment. Notably, the latest U.S. Merger Guidelines, jointly issued by the U.S. Department of Justice and the Federal Trade Commission on December 18, 2023, have stated that "the merger may substantially lessen competition or tend to create a monopoly in upstream markets, that loss of competition is not offset by purported benefits in a separate downstream product market."

As for the application of the essential facilities doctrine and imposing liability on a monopolist for its refusal to deal with its competitor, both an upstream market and a downstream market are required, and the essential facility is an input into the downstream market. The United States Court of Appeals for the Ninth Circuit in Alaska Airlines, Inc. v. United Airlines, Inc. (1991) and Aerotec Int'l, Inc. v. Honeywell Int'l, Inc. (2016) opined that a facility controlled by the monopolist is essential "only if control of the facility carries with it the power to eliminate competition in the downstream market." Guidance on the European Commission's enforcement priorities in abusive exclusionary conduct by dominant undertakings indicates that a downstream market is necessary for applying Article 102 of the Treaty on the Functioning of the European Union (TFEU) to refusal-to-supply cases.

The European Commission will consider imposing an obligation to supply on the dominant undertaking if the refused product or service is objectively necessary for effective competition in a downstream market, and if such refusal is likely to eliminate effective competition in the downstream market, resulting in consumer harm. Margin squeeze is another form of abuse by a dominant undertaking. In this scenario, a vertically integrated firm operating in both the upstream and downstream markets may engage in practices that increase the price of products or services in the upstream market, thereby elevating the costs for downstream market competitors to acquire essential input. This tactic is designed to hinder downstream competition, as it prevents even equally efficient competitors from trading profitably in the downstream market.

Subparagraph (c) of the second paragraph of Article 102 TFEU prohibits a dominant undertaking from distorting competition on an upstream or a downstream market by discriminatory conduct. In MEO vs Autoridade da Concorrência (2018), the Court of Justice of the EU (CJEU) held that where a dominant undertaking applies discriminatory prices to trade partners on the downstream market, and this behavior is capable of distorting competition between those trade partners, a finding of "competitive disadvantage" described in subparagraph (c) of the second paragraph of Article 102 TFEU could be established without proof of actual quantifiable deterioration in the competitive situation. In 2014, the Taiwan Fair Trade Commission made a decision that the Taiwan International Ports Corporation, while charging "building rent" at Taichung port, engaged in discriminatory treatment of essential facilities (namely warehouses) for downstream cargo handling contractors without proper justification. Such behaviour was deemed abusive conduct using a monopolist's market power, violating Paragraph 4, Article 10 (now Article 9), of the Fair Trade Act.

Specific vertical restraints or collaboration among competitors often require an assessment of their procompetitive and anticompetitive effects on the downstream market to determine their reasonableness or legitimacy. For example, while resale price maintenance might reduce competition in the downstream market and homogenous competition within brands, thus potentially serving as a tool for concerted action among firms, under exceptional circumstances resale price restrictions might have more pro-competitive effects compared with free pricing. Similarly, patent pools that increase the opportunity to use essential patents may also enhance competition in the downstream market.

Bibliography

Temple Lang, J., "Potential" Downstream Markets in European Antitrust Law: A Concept in Need of Limiting Principles' (2011) 7 *Competition Pol'y Int'l* 106

European Commission, Guidelines on the assessment of non-horizontal mergers under the Council Regulation on the control of concentrations between undertakings, OJ C 265, 18.10.2008, p. 6–25

European Commission, Directorate-General for Competition, Glossary of Terms Used in EU Competition Policy – Antitrust and Control of Concentrations (Publications Office, 2002)

European Commission, Communication from the Commission – Guidance on the Commission's enforcement priorities in applying Article 82 of the EC Treaty to abusive exclusionary conduct by dominant undertakings, OJ C 45, 24.2.2009, p. 7–20

European Commission, Communication from the Commission – Amendments to the Communication from the Commission – Guidance on the Commission's enforcement priorities in applying Article 82 of the EC Treaty to abusive exclusionary conduct by dominant undertakings, OJ C 116, 31.3.2023, p.1-5

European Commission, Commission Notice on a simplified treatment for certain concentrations under Council Regulation (EC) No 139/2004 on the control of concentrations between undertakings, OJ C 160, 5.5.2023, p. 1–10

OECD, The Essential Facilities Concept (1996)

OECD, Margin Squeeze (2009)

U.S. Department of Justice and the Federal Trade Commission, Merger Guidelines (Dec. 18, 2023)

See also

Upstream market

ECONOMIC ANALYSIS

Tasneem AZAD
Kroll

■ Definition

Economic analysis in a competition context refers principally to the use of industrial economics – a field of economics devoted to industrial organisation and market structures –, increasingly alongside other fields such as behavioural economics (which combines economics with insights from psychology), to assist in the development of a framework and/ or a set of hypotheses or theories to test. The analysis may be employed in the consideration of anti-competitive conduct, abuses of market power, merger assessments, state-aid compatibility or follow-on damages. Economics also provides a wide set of tools and techniques for use by competition practitioners, ranging from hypothetical monopolist tests to merger simulation models to difference-in-differences assessments (as may be used, for instance, in a cartel damages claim). Taken together, the economic framework, theories of harm and the practical toolkit can serve to guide and inform the construction of an economic evidence base. The oft-used term "competition economics" is generally employed as shorthand for the use of economic analysis within a competition setting.

■ Commentary

That economics is neither art nor science, that it remains inexact and that the discipline teems with theoretical dichotomies, is well documented. And yet, despite decades of examination and deliberation by academics, policy makers and practitioners alike, economics remains a cornerstone of competition policy and of its laws around the world. The inability to extricate competition policy and enforcement from the supposed vagaries of economics is, however, with good reason.

First, knowledge of industrial economics is crucial to understanding the ways in which markets are structured and how participants within those constructs operate and behave. Developing an understanding of how any given market structure might be formed, strengthened, destabilised or ultimately supplanted by another, can generally only be done through a lens of economics and its building blocks: alternative competition models, game theory, and the core economic principles of demand, supply, efficiency and consumer welfare.

Economics can in theory provide a coherent explanation of the incentives that drive firms to behave and engage with their customers, their suppliers and their competitors in the variety of ways that they do. This may include, for example, the choice of products and services that firms offer, the prices and the quality of those, the level of innovation that might be observed and how participants within a market might interact with and respond to one another, for example in relation to price changes or following market entry by new players.

Absent such a grounding in economics, competition policy makers, for example, would struggle to advance credible bases upon which to reason for reform. A well-structured narrative around the likely market impact of a change in policy would likely require economic theory to describe how each of the individual market participants and stakeholders might be likely to respond to the change and how consumers might collectively benefit (or not).

Parenthetically, much is made of conflicting schools of thought amongst economists. Take, for example, the "hipster" antitrust movement, brought into recent prominence in the U.S., arguing that competition policy has thus far failed to contain the activities of technology giants. Notably, however, the schools do not appear to differ in respect of underlying economic explanators, such as the structure of these markets. Rather, the conflict appears to arise in relation to the objectives of antitrust policy, with the hipster argument for wider standards of consumer welfare including, for example, non-price measures in respect of personal data that users exchange for the free use of platforms.

Second, in the case of competition enforcement, economics provides a theoretical framework against which to examine a case. Coherent theories can be constructed around the evolution of a market, allowing for the development of a strawman against which to examine the facts in any given case. As noted by the OECD, for example in the case of mergers, "(t)he economic framework for merger analysis provides the scaffolding on which to hang both quantitative and qualitative evidence and analysis of data, documents and witnesses, in order to build an integrated picture of how competition and efficiency are likely to be affected by a merger". Economic frameworks can assist practitioners in developing theories of harm: a set of plausible and internally consistent hypotheses for testing and validation, be it with empirical, documentary or witness evidence. Some of the objectives behind establishing such theories of harm might include (i) to determine which of a wide range of hypotheses might fit most closely with the facts of the case as observed, (ii) to ascertain which sub-set of underlying assumptions might in theory have held true given the evidence presented and (iii) to the extent feasible, to assess what range of effects might be envisaged under competing hypotheses and/or alternative scenarios.

Third, economics, together with its sister discipline, econometrics (the use of statistical techniques to analysis economic and financial issues), provides a veritable treasure chest of tools and techniques, a variety of which can be used to analyse and assess data collected as part of a competition case. For example, depending on the specifics of the case at hand, the tests might include:

- the hypothetical monopolist (or Small but Significant Non-transitory Increase in Price (SSNIP)) test to circumscribe markets,
- the Herfindahl–Hirschman index to measure the level of concentration in a market,
- econometric estimation to assess the elasticity of demand,
- merger simulation models to assess structural equilibria or the likely impacts of a merger,
- balancing tests to inform state-aid compatibility considerations, or
- price-cost margin analyses to assess unduly excessive or predatory pricing behaviour.

The 2021 Nobel prize – as won by Angrist, Card and Imbens – related to a key set of tools now widely in use in competition cases: natural experiments that could, depending on the specifics of the case, provide a view on causality rather than simply providing insights on correlation. Difference-in-differences assessments are now widely being used in the competition arena in the case of follow-on cartel damages claims for example, to examine, where possible, the potential extent of overcharges that may have been experienced by customers of cartelists (by comparing, for instance, price differences across time periods, product sets or geographies).

As competition analysis becomes increasingly sophisticated using a wider range (and choice set) of tools and with larger volumes of data being analysed, the importance of rigorous testing and careful examination by practitioners increases manifestly. For example, where specific tools may not necessarily be prescribed or where there may be multiple techniques to choose from, some practitioners may seek to assess ranges of plausible outcomes. In this context, the UK's Competition and Markets Authority (CMA) has set out its view of a series of principles for the submission of economic evidence including, for example, the need for clarity and transparency in relation to assumptions and results, the completeness of submissions with discussion around the choice of techniques and the need for the CMA to be able to replicate results using raw, underlying data.

Finally, it is this symbiosis of theory, framework, and tools and techniques that together provide a compelling foundation for competition enforcement.

Views of "but-for" worlds, theoretically untainted by anti-competitive conduct or market abuse, can be constructed and used to compare against the facts of the case at hand. Theories of harm could assist in the practical progression of a case by serving to clarify the scope of disclosure requests or by providing a roadmap and a set of priorities for collating evidence. The availability and level of granularity of data in a case could prove crucial to supporting a key tenet of a case or to advancing a sufficiently robust argument. In short, the economics evidence base that is ultimately arrived at in a competition assessment could prove to be pivotal to the outcome.

Overall, it appears economic analysis will remain a critical component of competition policy and enforcement, not least to the extent that economics itself will continue to evolve in respect of the tools and techniques used and how they may be applied to support competition assessments. To summarise, in the words of Paul Samuelson, "(e)conomics is not an exact science, it's a combination of an art and elements of science. And that's almost the first and last lesson to be learned about economics: that in my judgment, we are not converging toward exactitude, but we're improving our data bases and our ways of reasoning about them."

Bibliography

Davies, P. (2018) – Economic Evidence and Procedural fairness: lessons, *Journal of Competition Law & Economics* 14(1), April 2018

Lianos, I. (2013) – Economic and Econometric Evidence in Competition Law: an Empirical Perspective, Supported by the United Nations Conference on Trade and Development (UNCTAD) Research Partnership Platform

Competition and Markets Authority (2009) – Suggested best practice for submissions of technical economic analysis from parties to the Competition Commission. Originally published by the Competition Commission, and subsequently adopted by the CMA board (with original text retained and unamended)

OECD (2020), Economic analysis in merger investigations, 2020 OECD Global Forum on Competition Discussion Paper

See also

Dominance (notion), Abuse of economic dependence, Anticompetitive market distortions, Damages, Economic efficiency, Economies of scale, Market power, Market economy investor, Passing-on, State-aid

E

ECONOMIC EFFICIENCY

Rhonda L. SMITH
University of Melbourne

Definition

Economic efficiency is a measure of how well a market or the firms within it are performing. There are various different aspects of efficiency. Production efficiency (also referred to as technical efficiency) occurs when a firm produces a given output at the lowest unit cost of production given the technology employed. A related concept is x-inefficiency which measures cost incurred by a firm in excess of that which would be incurred in a competitive market. An example would be the "gold plating" of the CEO's office suite. The cost differential reflects the firm's ability to ignore at least to some degree market pressures, that is, its market power. Allocative efficiency refers to how well resources are allocated between productive activities in order to best satisfy consumer preferences. Firms will be allocatively efficient when consumers willing to pay a price at least equal to the marginal cost of producing the product obtain supply. Together, production and allocative efficiency are static measures as they are assessed at a point in time and so assume that key variables such as technology are given. Transaction costs, as the name implies, are costs that arise when making a sale that are additional to the cost of production. They include the cost of monitoring, controlling, and managing transactions. Decisions about whether to source inputs from the market or to self-supply are at least in part a reflection of these costs – high transaction costs provide an incentive to self supply. Arguably, ensuring that the organizational structure of a business minimises these costs is a form of efficiency. However, despite recognition of the significance of transaction costs, this is not a unanimously accepted view. Dynamic efficiency is an assessment of how quickly and completely firms adjust to change, whether on the demand side, such as a change in consumer preferences, or on the supply side, such as the adoption of new cost-saving technology. Consequently, it is closely related to R&D and innovation. Dynamic efficiency may also be increased by the introduction of better work practices. This will have the effect of lowering the long run average cost curve but additional costs associated with this may increase costs in the short run, representing a tension between short run and long run gains.

■ Commentary

Central to competition policy and law is the acceptance that in competitive markets inefficient firms will not survive. They will incur higher costs than their rivals and so will be priced out of the market or they may not be supplying product of a quality or variety that consumers want. The exit of these firms enables resources to be reallocated to other firms that will better serve the market. Given this, only conduct that excludes or deters firms that are at least equally as efficient as the firm engaged in the conduct is likely to contravene competition law. However, an entrant into a market may be production inefficient even though once it becomes established it may be more efficient than incumbent firms because, for example, it has a better product or better technology. Conduct that caused the exit of that firm or even curtailed its ability to compete effectively could damage the competitive process

Markets that are not very competitive tend to be relatively inefficient. The lack of competition means that producers are able to restrict output and charge a price above the economic cost of production (which includes return to capital). If the unit cost of production decreases as output increases, this will be production inefficient. Additionally, a monopolist is likely to be x-inefficient. In addition, the higher prices mean that consumers lose some of the benefit of transacting in the market, that is, consumer surplus decreases. This is transferred to producers as economic rents/monopoly profits. In response to the higher prices some consumers will switch to other products which are cheaper but less preferred. The increased demand for these products causes those businesses to expand production. The result is that resources move from producing the products that consumers preferred to those that they prefer less – resources are inefficiently allocated. However, if a monopolist can perfectly price discriminate, charging each consumer their marginal willingness to pay, all consumers wiling to pay the marginal cost of supply will obtain supply and this outcome is allocatively efficient.

Dynamic efficiency is the engine of economic growth and is driven by innovation. Innovation may benefit consumers by making new products available that better meet consumer preferences, by making existing products safer, and by providing more variety for consumers. Consumers benefit from innovations that provide them with better products, although they may do so at a higher price (the higher price of new medical treatments). This identifies a tension between static efficiency which focuses on price and dynamic efficiency. In addition, the cost saving associated with technological improvements may not be passed on to consumers but it does represent an increase in total welfare. The tension here illustrates the debate concerning the measure of welfare against which the efficiency producing conduct is assessed.

Innovative distribution models, such as platform businesses, while clearly providing significant benefits for consumers, have raised concerns about increased market concentration with the dominance of mega-platforms such as Google and Facebook. The efficiencies available by the development of ecosystems around the original platform may raise barriers to entry, especially for suppliers of only part of the platform's offering.

It is often said that competition policy promotes competition not for the sake of competition but because competition drives markets to be efficient and efficient markets increase economic welfare. However, if there are significant market failures this may not be the outcome. Indeed, conduct designed to overcome market failure and increase efficiency, such as the imposition of vertical restraints, may lessen competition. This creates another potential tension between competition policy and law and policies designed to increase efficiency and stimulate growth.

Under the influence of the Chicago School of economic thought, in the United States, antitrust authorities have tended to focus on promoting efficiency even if it has ani-competitive effects. Claims of efficiency benefits are used to justify conduct that is anti-competitive. Other jurisdictions are less permissive, generally balancing any pro-competitive effects from increased efficiency against associated anti-competitive effects. The detrimental effect on competition is offset by the saving in resources which increases total welfare.

Bibliography

Symposium: Recognizing Bert Foer, his AAI Founding and Presidency, *Antitrust Bulletin* 60 (2), June 2015

Symposium: The Role of Efficiencies in Antitrust Law (Part II), *Antitrust Bulletin* 60 (3), September 2015

OECD, The Role of Efficiency Claims in Antitrust Proceedings, *Best Practice Roundtables*, 2012

See also

Economic analysis, Economies of scale, AEC test

E

ECONOMIES OF SCALE

Andrés PÉREZ ORDUZ
Palacios Lleras

Definition

Refers to the situation in which the average cost of production decreases as the quantity of goods or services produced increases. In other words, as a company produces on a larger scale, unit costs tend to decrease. A large factory, therefore, will be more efficient than a small factory, because the large factory will be able to produce more units at a lower cost per unit. For example, if a factory produces only one product, then that product must bear the entire cost of establishing and running the factory activity. If the same factory produces 100,000 products, then the costs are spread over 100,000 products instead of just one.

Commentary

Economies of scale represent an economic principle that categorizes them as a form of efficiency. This is due to their association with ongoing enhancements in production efficiency as a company expands its size and operational scale. The efficiencies stemming from economies of scale typically involve (i) optimizing the utilization of resources such as labor, raw materials, and machinery; (ii) incorporating more efficient technologies, adopting best operational practices, and eliminating redundant processes; (iii) securing improved negotiation terms with suppliers, thereby enhancing efficiency through the acquisition of inputs at reduced costs; (iv) fully leveraging facilities and equipment, among other factors.

Nevertheless, economies of scale are commonly linked to acting as a potential barrier for entering or expanding into a particular market when a dominant player is present. This is due to the efficiencies gained by the dominant firm as a result of its size, leading to lower costs and increased production capacity. As a result, economies of scale serve as a barrier to entry by enabling established companies with substantial production volumes to maintain lower average costs in the long run compared to new entrants into the market.

Additional reasons why economies of scale act as barriers to entry encompass various factors: **(i)** companies that have achieved economies of scale tend to wield greater bargaining power with their suppliers, making it challenging for new entrants to secure similar favorable terms; **(ii)** new entrants may face difficulties in competing with the lower unit costs of firms enjoying economies of scale, as they must distribute fixed costs across a smaller production volume; **(iii)** new entrants typically lack immediate access to the efficient production and operational expertise developed by established companies, along with the specialized skills acquired by their employees; **(iv)** matching the investments in advanced technology made by large incumbents may be a struggle for new entrants, placing them at a disadvantage in terms of operational efficiency; **(v)** entering and establishing a significant market presence is more difficult for new entrants, given that those with economies of scale often hold a dominant position in distribution channels and maintain strong relationships with retailers and distributors; lastly, **(vi)** new entrants may find it challenging to compete in terms of brand visibility and recognition, as larger companies can afford extensive advertising campaigns and marketing strategies that facilitate the establishment and maintenance of robust brands.

All together, these attributes contribute to economies of scale functioning as barriers to entry, creating challenges for new firms to effectively compete with incumbent counterparts that have already gained efficiencies by expanding their production. This dynamic can lead to market concentration, with a limited number of larger companies dominating the industry.

For further illustration, consider, for example, a hypothetical scenario in which a large firm in the telecommunications industry acquires multiple smaller rivals. Due to its greater scale, the larger company can spread its fixed costs over a greater volume of services, potentially reducing its average cost per unit. This cost advantage could make it difficult for smaller competitors to compete effectively. Consequently, in scenarios where economies of scale play a crucial role and demand substantial production capacity relative to market size, the process of expanding or entering efficiently becomes more is more costly and risky for new entrants. For this reason, the presence of economies of scale means that small companies tend to be inefficient, often leading them to exit the market over time or be absorbed by larger entities.

In these cases, competition authorities are called upon to examine whether the dominant company is leveraging its economies of scale to engage in anti-competitive behavior, such as setting predatory prices to force smaller competitors out of the market or engaging in practices that hinder free economic competition. The enforcement of regulations safeguarding free competition aims to ensure that economies of scale do not lead to the creation of monopolies or the abuse of market power to the detriment of consumers and other stakeholders in the market. In simpler terms, competition law aims to control the use of significant market power and should be able to differentiate between the legitimate use of it and assertive business practices that contribute to social welfare, by applying economic principles to individual cases.

The presence of economies of scale can discourage market entry, even in the absence of strategic behaviors that can be classified as an abuse of a dominant position, particularly when they imply that entry into the market requires substantial sunk costs and could cause tougher price competition.

However, encouraging economies of scale enhances overall social welfare. For that reason, courts and competition authorities should rely on the expertise of economists to recognize and permit the achievement of scale economies. As the determiners of what qualifies as favorable economic conduct, courts and competition authorities bear the responsibility to make such determinations.

Economies of scale are also associated with so-called network effects, where, as the number of network users increases, for example in the telecommunications industry, the average cost decreases and the company increases its profits. Given the above, companies that have been in the market longer and have managed to attract a large number of users have lower costs and higher profits, which give them a comparative advantage over new entrants. The latter not only bear the initial sunk costs but also operate at a less efficient production level. The implications of economies of scale suggest that established companies offering various services to a large user base can significantly reduce costs and disproportionately increase profits compared to newcomers who have not yet entered the business.

Bibliography

Laudati, L. L., Note: Economies of Scale: Weighing Operating Efficiency when Enforcing Antitrust Law, 49 *Fordham L. Rev.* 771 (1981). Available at: https://ir.lawnet.fordham.edu/flr/vol49/iss5/13

OECD. Potential Competition and Antitrust Analysis – Note by Steven C. Salop. *Roundtable on the Concept of Potential Competition*. 10 June 2021

See also

Barriers to entry, Economic analysis, Economic efficiency, Specialization agreement, Online platforms, Network effect, Variable costs

E

ECOSYSTEM FAILURES

Carmelo CENNAMO
Copenhagen Business School

Definition

"Ecosystem failures" are situations in which individual actions of a platform ecosystem's members undermine the effectiveness or functioning of the entire ecosystem. *Functional* failures occur when ecosystem members fail to create and deliver joint value to the final customer. Given the capabilities and resources available among the ecosystem actors, less joint value and/or an inferior joint (system-level) innovation or solution is created than otherwise could be. Distributional failures are associated with participants' inability to capture value proportional to their contribution. *Distributional* failures occur either when the platform ecosystem design allows some members to abuse the system to capture disproportionate value, or when the ecosystem orchestrators abuse their dominance.

Commentary

Ecosystem failures capture new inefficiencies related to competitive *and* cooperative dynamics that are distinct from the competitive behaviour in the subject of competition law. These consist of instances where an inferior product is supplied due to a misalignment in the incentives of ecosystem participants or when the value generated is distributed in a way that fails to sufficiently compensate one or many ecosystem participants. Analysis of such ecosystem failures takes an ecosystem-wide approach and considers the aggregate of the various complementary products and associated firms as the relevant domain of competition analysis; it incorporates the analysis of complementarities between interconnected products rather than just focusing on product substitution; it integrates the impact of interdependencies across markets rather than concentrate on a single "relevant" product market. Although the recent Digital Markets Act by the EU regulating digital platforms does not explicitly refer to ecosystem failures, it includes several pointers throughout the text to new types of ecosystem harms. To the extent that these introduce inefficiencies, they refer to situations that could be assimilated to ecosystem failure problems. The DMA refers, for instance, to "control over whole platform ecosystems" (a gatekeeping position) as a possibly inefficient structural barrier to entry for other players; or the ability of gatekeepers to leverage their dominant position in the ecosystem to create unequal and possibly inefficient conditions of access for some third-party members of the ecosystem to the core and ancillary platform services. More specifically, Articles 5 and 6 of the DMA identify potentially harmful conduct of the gatekeeper, thus imposing obligations to gatekeepers to refrain from these activities or remove such obstacles. To the extent that the gatekeeper's conduct leads to a distortion of business users' incentives or ability to contribute to the ecosystem and to the extent that such distortion decreases the overall value provided by the ecosystem, identified conduct could represent an ecosystem failure.

In the *Google Android* case (2018), the *EU Commission* established that Google abused its dominant position in the worldwide market for Android app stores by, among other things, "making the licensing of the Play Store and the Google Search app conditional on the anti-fragmentation obligations in the anti-fragmentation agreements." The Commission referred to potential issues of distributional failures by arguing that Google exploited is in a dominant position over the Android ecosystem to its own advantage and to the detriment of other members of the ecosystem. The theory of ecosystem failures points to ecosystem fragmention, including forking and incompatibility, as potential issues leading to functional failures. Google submitted that "anti-fragmentation obligations are necessary to protect the Android ecosystem," [...] "to ensure the interoperability of the Android ecosystem," [...] and "to prevent fragmentation that would be detrimental to the Android ecosystem." The Commission, however, concluded that Google did not provide evidence in support of those arguments.

In the *AGCM vs Amazon Italia case* (2021), the Italian Antitrust authority fined Amazon Italia €1.13bn for treating preferentially Amazon Marketplace third-party sellers who used its logistics and delivery services, FBA (Fulfilled by Amazon) – i.e., "Prime" affiliated sellers, at the detriment of "non-prime" sellers. The AGCM argued that Amazon Italia applied more stringent rules to "non-prime" sellers. This made it more difficult and costly for them to comply with the quality standards related to delivery and, as a result, less likely for their products to be displayed among the top choices in customer searches compared to products by "prime" sellers, independently of product or seller quality differences. The AGCM argued that "Prime" sellers were more discoverable and so more likely to secure demand from customers, benefiting systematically from a competitive advantage compared to non-prime sellers. This competitive advantage was artificially created by Amazon Italia's differential treatment. The AGCM did not take issue with the fact that Amazon Italia had a business model built around a "complete ecosystem" integrating multiple services, whereby Amazon plays multiple roles. However, the AGCM argued that Amazon Italia had "artificially tied two separate services", Prime Seller benefits and FBA service, to "create an illegitimate incentive" to buy FBA services. This strategy was deemed to "falsify" competition between Amazon Italia's logistics service and its competitors. While the AGCM did not provide systematic empirical evidence of this issue, under an ecosystem failures framework, this logic would refer primarily to preferential treatment of "Prime" sellers as a possible manifestation of distributional ecosystem failures ("Prime" sellers capturing higher value (compared to "non-Prime" sellers) as result of the platform ecosystem design). Ultimately this would lead to functional ecosystem failures to the extent that this preferential treatment was leading to reduced participation of sellers, as well as a reduced variety and quality of offerings and higher price of offerings for customers.

In the recent decision by the EU Commission to block the proposed acquisition of Flugo Group *Holdings AB ("'eTraveli') by Booking Holdings ("'Booking')* (2023), the Commission referred to the strengthening of Booking's "travel services ecosystem" as problematic. Albeit not explicit in the motivation, the Commission pointed to possible ecosystem failures, both functional and distributional. Post-merger, Booking would enjoy an increased bargaining position in the ecosystem towards hotels (in this case, the ecosystem complementors), which it could exploit to possibly divert demand from cheaper sales channels to Booking and charge higher commission fees to hotels (a distributional failure), eventually leading to higher prices for customers or reduced booking options (a functional failure). However, the Commission did not point to specific conditions of the post-merger ecosystem structure that would cause an ecosystem failure, referring instead more generically to network effects and customer inertia as factors reinforcing, in fact, the enlarged ecosystem of Booking, making it harder for rival platforms to compete. Hence, it seems that the Commission considered the merger problematic because it created greater ecosystem efficiencies (rather than failures).

In the CMA's final report (2023) on the proposed acquisition of *Activision by Microsoft*, the agency contended that, "Microsoft has a multi-product ecosystem that places it in a very strong position relative to most or all rivals in the growing market for cloud gaming services", which Microsoft could leverage "to engage in a foreclosure strategy using Activision's content". Thus, the CMA's logic identified possible risks of functional failures of the emerging cloud gaming services ecosystem due to the incentives that the post-merger ecosystem structure would grant to Microsoft to abuse its central position in its ecosystem and extract rents from ecosystem participants (while potentially excluding rivals from participanting). It is interesting to note that, in its response, Microsoft submitted an opposite view: that the current ecosystem design, centered around the mobile OS ecosystem, was undermining the effectiveness of the cloud gaming services by limiting customer experience and "discoverability on mobile due to app store restrictions." Microsoft thus saw the merger as a way to change the design of the existing ecosystem and address these shortcomings to facilitate the growth of cloud gaming services.

Overall, the agencies tend to be concerned more with potential distributional failures that might originate from ecosystem orchestrators abusing their central position in the ecosystem and less with other potential inefficiencies leading to functional failures. As the analytical tools and knowledge for assessing these ecosystem-wide issues improve, we might expect agencies to consider these broader (in)efficiencies in their assessment.

Bibliography

Cennamo, C., Kretschmer, T., Constantinides, P., Alaimo, C., Santaló, J., 2023. Digital platforms regulation: an innovation-centric view of the EU's Digital Market Act. *Journal of European Competition Law & Practice* 14 (1): 44-51

Cennamo, C. 2023. The EU Digital Markets Act: It Is Not About Markets But Ecosystem Failures! *Network Law Review* (July)

Jacobides, MG., Cennamo, C., Gawer, A. 2024. Externalities and complementarities in platforms and ecosystems: From structural solutions to endogenous failures. *Research Policy* 53: 104906

Jacobides, MG., Lianos, I. 2021. Ecosystems and competition law in theory and practice. Industrial and Corporate Change 30 (5): 1199–1229

Zhu, F., Liu, Q., 2018. Competing with complementors: an empirical look at Amazon.com. *Strategic Management Journal* 39 (10): 2618–2642

Acknowledgements: this entry note has benefited highly from valuable feedback from Eliana Garces, Annabelle Gawer, Martina Facino, Daniel Sokol, Jan Krämer, Bruno Carballa Smichowski, Juan Santaló, Thibault Schrepel.

See also

Online platforms, Network effect

E

EFFECT ON TRADE BETWEEN MEMBER STATES

Mercedes PEDRAZ CALVO
La Audiencia Nacional de España

Definition

Articles 101 and 102 of the TFEU apply to horizontal and vertical agreements and practices of undertakings or abuse of dominance which "*may affect trade between Member States*". Effect on trade between Member States is the key jurisdictional criterion for establishing the scope for the application of European Union antitrust law. It also determines the scope of application of Article 3 of Regulation 1/2003 on the joint application of European and national antitrust law. The appreciable effect on trade between Member States attracts the application of European Union law while national law would be applicable in cases were there is not such an effect.

Commentary

The interpretation of articles 101 and 102 of the Treaty has been carried out by the jurisprudence of the Courts of the European Union and the paragraph "*may affect trade between Member States*" also by the Communication of the European Commission on Guidelines concerning the concept of effect on trade (Commission Notice. Guidelines on the effect on trade concept contained in articles 81 and 82 of the Treaty. 2004/C 101/07).

This Communication systematizes the indications resulting from the Judgments of the European Union Courts and points out the elements to be taken into consideration when assessing whether there is an "*effect on trade between Member States*", although not exhaustively.

In Brasserie de Haecht, the Court already said that "*it is only to the extent to which agreements, decisions or practices are capable of affecting trade between Member States that the alteration of competition comes under Community prohibitions.*"

Three elements must be considered when applying the "*effect on trade*" test: the concept of "*trade between Member States*", what "*may affect*" means and the concept of "*appreciability*"

"*Trade between Member States*": according to the Guidelines (n. 19) this is a wide concept, covering not only exchanges of goods and services across borders, but also any other cross-border economic activity, including establishment. The European Courts have also considered whether the agreement or practice affects the structure of competition.

The concept of "*trade*" refers to all kinds of economic activity, not only the exchange of goods, but also the activities of production, distribution, and provision of services.

Trade "*between Member States*" means that the economic activity takes place between undertakings of different countries or has effects in other Member States. (n. 22 of the Guidelines). Trade between Member States may be affected also in cases where the relevant market is national or sub-national.

It is not necessary that the commercial activity considered is exclusively European Community activity, as it is considered that a commercial transaction between an EU undertaking and a foreign one may also have an effect on trade between Member States.

"*May affect*": according to the Guidelines (n. 23) this notion implies that it must be possible to foresee that the agreement or practice may have a direct or indirect, actual, or potential influence on the "*trade between Member States*". This notion of "*may affect*" implies that it must be possible to foresee with a sufficient degree of probability, on the basis of a group of objective factors of law or fact, that the agreement or practice may have an influence, direct or indirect, actual or potential, in trade flows between Member States.

The term "*affects*" has been interpreted by the European Union Courts as having a negative effect contrary to the objectives of the Treaty.

"*Appreciability*": agreements and practices will not be penalized when they affect the market only to a negligible extent (n. 44 of the Guidelines). It is a settled case-law that an agreement of undertakings falls outside the prohibition of article 101 (1) of the Treaty if it has only an insignificant effect on the market.

Appreciability can thus be measured both in absolute and relative terms by comparing the position of the undertaking or undertakings concerned with that of other operators on the market. This analysis is consistent with the element "*may affect*", and therefore the assessment must consider the ability of the agreement or practice to affect trade between Member States.

It is considered that agreements which simultaneously comply with certain conditions would not, in principle, have an appreciable effect on European Union trade. These conditions are: (a) the parties' combined share of less than 5% in any relevant market; and (b) a total annual turnover in the European Union of the undertakings concerned or of the supplier of the products of less than EUR 40 million. (n.52 of the Guidelines).

The Guidelines establish a quantification criterion intended to provide greater legal certainty. This is known as the "no appreciable effect on trade" rule. This rule shares common grounds with the De Minimis rule as both contribute to the non-application of Article 101 TFEU, and both use the concept of "market share" to define an area where European antitrust law is not applicable. (Communication from the European Commission. Notice on agreements of minor importance which do not appreciably restrict competition under Article 101(1) of the Treaty on the Functioning of the European Union De Minimis Notice 2014/C 291/01).

The 8 November 2022 the European Commission launched a public consultation inviting all interested parties to comment on the draft revised Market Definition Notice (Commission Notice on the definition of relevant market for the purposes of Community competition law 97/C 372/03). Its main objective is to offer more guidance, *transparency*, and legal certainty for businesses to facilitate compliance, and to contribute to a more efficient enforcement by the Commission and National Competition Authorities.

Articles 101 and 102, while applicable, according to the case-law of the Court of Justice, to certain mergers between undertakings, have been considered not sufficient to control all concentrations of undertakings which may prove to be incompatible with the system of undistorted competition envisaged in the Treaty. The EC Merger Regulation (Council Regulation (EC) No 139/2004 of 20 January 2004) statutes the provisions applicable "*to significant structural changes, the impact of which on the market goes beyond the national borders of any one Member State. Such concentrations should, as a general rule, be reviewed exclusively at Community level, in application of a 'one-stop shop' system and in compliance with the principle of subsidiarity.*"

In this field of Mergers, the Commission and the Member States do not have concurrent competences. The Merger Regulation establishes a clear division of competences, and Mergers which exceed the turnover thresholds laid down in Article 1 of the Merger Regulation, fall within the exclusive competence of the Commission. Concentrations which do not reach these thresholds fall within the competence of the Member States.

Bibliography

BARNARD, C., *The Substantive Law of the EU: The Four Freedoms* 7th Edition. August 2022. Oxford

BELLAMY, R., CHILD G., BAILEY, D. , JOHN L. E., *Bellamy & Child European Union Law of Competition*, 8th Edition. December 2018 Oxford

IBÁÑEZ COLOMO, P. and LAMADRID DE PABLO, A., On the notion of restriction of competition: what we know and what we don't know we know.

JOIRE, B., "Orange Caraïbe case: The appreciable effect on trade between Member States reframed by the highest French Court". *Competition Forum*. French Insights, 2022

JONES, A., SUFRIN, B., *EU Competition Law*, Oxford University Press, Oxford, 2016

See also

Applicable law, Parallel imports (parallel trade)

E

EFFECTIVE JUDICIAL PROTECTION

Ian FORRESTER
Ian Forrester Consulting

Definition

Competition laws around the world generally prohibit anti-competitive agreements and abuses of monopoly power. Public enforcement of the competition rules refers to prosecutorial action by an enforcement agency, subject to review an appeal. Private enforcement refers to civil litigation before national courts. In both cases, the role of the judge is to supervise the sound application of the law. When the court is reviewing the actions of the competition authority, a degree of deference to the policy choices of the authority is expected. In both cases, judicial oversight is necessary. It is not uncommon for courts to be more conservative in approaching novel doctrines advanced by private litigants than by competition authorities.

Commentary

The decision of a competition authority stands between economic regulation of the marketplace and punishment for infringing the competition rules. Judicial control of the adequacy of the decision is an essential element of its democratic legitimacy. Without effective judicial oversight, public enforcement would risk appearing (or being) arbitrary, discriminatory, unfair, or illegitimate. Thus, the principle of effective judicial oversight as quality control and as a democratic necessity cannot be doubted. However, the nature and intensity of appropriate judicial review in competition cases have been much debated. Administrative law inevitably involves according a margin of discretion to the public authority.

The European approach to the review judicially of competition decisions, has fluctuated over the years. The

Treaty of Rome established two bases of jurisdiction for the Court: review of legality (Arts 263 TFEU, ex 230 TEC, ex 169 Treaty of Rome) according to enumerated criteria (formal propriety rather than merits) and full jurisdiction (Art 261 TFEU, ex 229 TEC, ex 172, Treaty of Rome) where penalties were imposed. While that approach was neither surprising nor controversial where the European institutions were regulating the agricultural market or organizing production levels of coal and steel, it came under strain in cases where the manufacturer was being accused of cartel activity to the prejudice of consumers, or of hindering cross boarder trade to the prejudice of the internal market. During the 1980s there was a degree of dissatisfaction with the intensity of judicial review concerning antidumping measures and, to a degree, competition decisions. The creation in 1989 of the Court of First Instance, the future General Court of the European Union, was a response to the concerns of industry and of practitioners, (not close enough scrutiny, not enough review of complex facts), balanced against the ever-growing case load of the Court of Justice (too many cases, perfection means delay). The reconciliation of the need for quality control, the independence of the competition authority, reasonable speed, and procedural transparency is a perpetual judicial challenge.

In the classic competition case of *Grundig/Consten* in 1966 and as repeated in *Remia/Nutricia* in 1984, the European Court said that the Court must limit its review to verifying whether the relevant procedural rules have been complied with, whether the reasoning is adequate, and whether there has been any manifest error of appreciation. While this approach was understandable and appropriate in a regulatory context, it appeared less convincing in the context of the imposition of a severe penalty pursuant to an administrative procedure.

During the 1990s, the intensity of the judicial review of Commission decision – making in competition matters sharply intensified but softened somewhat from the enlargement of the EU in 2004. The familiar language of "light judicial review" was used frequently, even in cases where large penalties had been imposed. The highwatermark of this tendency was arguably *Microsoft*, where the General Court ascribed deference to Commission findings on technical matters as well as complex economic ones.

The long-running debate about what judicial review of competition decisions must mean is completely understandable. How far should courts trust the specialised agency to make a fair appraisal and a sound conclusion? Even today the courts are somewhat inconsistent in their description of their task when examining the decision of a competition law authority. For example, how sure should the authority be when finding that its intervention was necessary? Thus, in June 2022 in the case of *Tussencoop T584/19*, the test was "plausible likelihood of harm", whereas in *CK Telecoms T399/16*, May 2020, the test in a merger case was "particularly high likelihood of harm", and the latest iteration in that case suggests a different approach, more respectful to the assessment of the competition authority.

The obligations of the courts confronting the need to make judicial review of a competition authority's decision have been clarified, maybe codified, in the ECtHR case of *Menarini* and the CJEU case of *Halcor/Chalkor*. In essence, the action of the authority must be subject to not merely a review of legality but to a thorough review of facts and law, in principle complete. That does not completely clarify the duty of the Court in all circumstances. Sometimes, there will be a simple argument as to whether Mr. Dupont was present in the Hilton hotel at a meeting on the 13th January. That is a factual controversy, to be settled by examining tickets, receipts and other evidence. There is no room for deference to the authority's conclusion. Does the evidence say yes or no? By contrast, there may be areas where for example the duration of a non-compete clause may be viewed as intrinsically involving the prudent assessment by an expert agency of how long the seller of a business must stay out of the market after the sale. There is no single obviously correct answer. Likewise, an anti-competitive practice which is justified by the needs of health and safety involves a degree of assessment: it could involve reviewing whether internal documents confirm that the reason for the prohibition on attaching products from rivals was due to public policy or a wish to exclude the rivals. Once again, the conclusions of the authority should be examined carefully, without deference, in light of the evidence.

An even more delicate question would be whether the settlement of a patent litigation with a licence for a limited territory is to be regarded as the welcome ending of a costly dispute or the objectionable dividing of the marketplace along national lines. When an online search engine gives prominence to its own advertisers as opposed to neutrally presenting all candidates, is this to be condemned as a gross infringement or is the authority making a normative choice as to how the market ought to work?

The intensity of the judicial review should be more severe in the case of heavy penalties or sanctions. Where the underlying administrative procedures in the authority are rigorous and "contradictoire", greater credibility should be attached to the decision. In short therefore, the question of judicial review is to be approached with an eye to the issue of whether the condemnation under appeal was an act of fact finding or an act of discretionary regulation. Courts ought not to assume that the authority was correct without establishing confidently that the facts underlying the decision were soundly established and that the administrative process was fairly handled.

Judicial protection is thus most obviously necessary as a check upon administrative authority in the case of decisions by public authorities. But it is supplemented and reinforced when judges decide civil cases, so-called private enforcement, in which novel (or well-established) principles are under debate.

Nevertheless, there will remain situations where the crucial issue is arguably a choice between rival policies or norms. Should the authority favour intellectual property or consumer choice? Lower prices for generic pharmaceuticals or higher prices which favour research? There is no single consistent answer as to what line the courts should follow in these circumstances: the best approach (though not dispositive) is a thorough review of acts and law, in principle complete.

Bibliography

Edward, D. and Lane, R., *Edward and Lane on European Union Law*, Edward Elgar, 2013

Forrester, I., « A Bush in need of Pruning: The Luxuriant Growth of "Light Judicial Review », in *European Competition Law Annual: The evaluation of Evidence and its Judicial Review in Competition cases*, Ehlermann and Marquis, European University Institute, Florence 2009

Lenaerts, K., Bray, R., Arts, D. and Maselis, I., *Procedural Law of the European Union*, Sweet & Maxwell 1999

See also

Burden of proof, Judicial review

E

EFFECTS DOCTRINE

Marek MARTYNISZYN
Queen's University Belfast

Definition

The effects doctrine is a principle enabling a forum to assert jurisdiction over parties not present within a state but whose conduct outside the state's territory affects the local market. The effects doctrine is frequently mistakenly equated with extraterritoriality. However, extraterritoriality is a wider concept. It also includes situations when part of the conduct in question occurred within its territory or when piercing of the corporate veil enables to assert jurisdiction over a foreign parent due to the local presence of a subsidiary.

Commentary

The effects doctrine constitutes a significant paradigm shift – from relying on in-country conduct or presence to assert jurisdiction to relying on in-country economic effects of foreign conduct. This now quite common approach to cross-border jurisdiction originated in competition, or antitrust, law.

Historically, states asserted jurisdiction only over their nationals and conduct within their borders. Cross-border scenarios did not fit into this framework. States began to reach beyond their borders when part of the conduct in question took place within their territory. The so-called principle of objective territoriality has been developed and this is how extraterritoriality started to develop. Also, when dealing with larger corporate structures states started to pierce the corporate veil and assume jurisdiction over a foreign parent when they controlled a local subsidiary. While helpful, both approaches do not allow for cases where there is no conduct in the state's territory. That is, cases where competitive harm in the given market is caused by foreign conduct. The effects doctrine addresses such scenarios.

When first coined it was controversial, departing, as it did, from then-established principles of international law. For decades it has been used exclusively by the United States, where it originated, due to judicial interpretation in Alcoa. Initially it met with opposition from other states, sometimes leading to their introduction of domestic blocking legislation to prevent effective extraterritorial application of U.S. antitrust rules. However, the effects doctrine slowly became accepted, internalised and eventually used by other systems. Now, it is ubiquitous and it constitutes a separate, distinct basis for asserting jurisdiction. Recent research demonstrates it is recognised and provided for also in competition laws in over 30 developing countries.

The effects doctrine is typically relied on in the prescriptive (subject-matter, legislative) sense. Asserting extraterritorial enforcement jurisdiction on its basis is impermissible under international law. This includes, for example, imposition of remedies on foreign firms that would relate to their conduct and their assets abroad. Hence, most competition agencies are very careful to use domestic-only remedies.

The effects doctrine has been applied broadly. It has been used in all areas of competition law to deal with international cartels, harmful conduct by dominant foreign firms and foreign-to-foreign (offshore) mergers.

The specific formulations of the effects doctrine differ between countries. For example, two tests exist in the U.S. context. Firstly, in cases involving imports, U.S. rules apply when "foreign conduct … was meant to produce and did in fact produce some substantial effect in the United States" – per holding of the U.S. Supreme Court in Hartford Fire. Secondly, in all other cases U.S. rules apply when there are direct, substantial and reasonably foreseeable effects of the conduct in question on U.S. commerce, per the 1982 Foreign Trade Antitrust Improvements Act (FTAIA). Similarly in the European Union two tests coexist. Firstly, EU competition laws apply when foreign anticompetitive arrangements were implemented in the EU, as framed by the Court of Justice of the European nion in Wood Pulp. Seconply whenever foreign conduct has foreseeable, immediate and substantial effect in the EU, as initially recognised by the then Court of First Instance in Gencor, and endorsed more recently by the Court of Justice in Intel.

As the U.S. and EU experience shows, the effects doctrine came into being through judicial interpretation. Indeed, in the EU it continues not to have any statutory basis. However, in competition laws of various systems it has been codified. For example, per Art. 2 of Brazilian Competition Law (Law n° 12.529 of 30 Nov 2011) rules apply to foreign conduct that "produce or may produce effects" in Brazil. Per Art. 2 of the Chinese Anti-Monopoly Law of 24 June 2022 – rules apply "to monopolistic conducts outside the territory of the People's Republic of China, which serve to eliminate or restrict competition on the domestic market of China." Under Art. 3 of the Icelandic Competition Law (No 44/2005), the Act applies "to agreements, terms and actions with effect, or intended effect, in Iceland."

The effects doctrine has been widely adopted. Controversies arise in relation to its specific applications and ultimate reach. These concern the types of economic effects that permit reliance on the doctrine. That is, what sort of effects are sufficient to use it. For example, the EU's Intel case was the first instance of relying on the effects doctrine in a scenario where there were no direct dealings between a foreign violator and EU customers. In that case the foreign violator incentivised third parties outside the EU not to use inputs of a competing non-EU firm in final products that were sold globally. Similarly, with time it is likely that the relative importance of the competitive harm in question will be tested.

Even as it addresses cross-border situations, the effects doctrine remains unilateral in nature. However, it is a necessary response to the lack of international rules and institutions dealing with anticompetitive conduct that crosses borders. Attempts to incorporate formal rules in the framework of World Trade Organization did not secure necessary support and were abandoned. Therefore the unilateral application of domestic competition law, with the help of the effects doctrine remains essential.

Availability of the effects doctrine in pursuing antitrust violations does not mean bringing such cases is straightforward. These continue to be particularly challenging due to various inadequacies of related rules, especially concerning service of process abroad and collection and use of evidence. Cooperative instruments and platforms enable agencies to overcome some of these obstacles.

Bibliography

Martyniszyn, M., "Competitive Harm Crossing Borders: Regulatory Gaps And A Way Forward", 17(3) *Journal of Competition Law & Economics* 686 (2021)

Martyniszyn, M., Developing Countries' Experience with Extraterritoriality in Competition Law, Report of the United Nations Conference on Trade and Development, UNCTAD/DITC/CPLP/2021/3 (2021)

Martyniszyn, M., "Extraterritoriality in Competition Law: Changing Frictions" in A Parrish and C Ryngaert (eds), *Research Handbook on Extraterritoriality in International Law* (Edward Elgar, 2023)

Martyniszyn, M., "Extraterritoriality in EU Competition Law" in Nuno Cunha Rodrigues (ed), *Extraterritoriality of EU Economic Law* (Springer, 2021)

Martyniszyn, M., "Legislation Blocking Antitrust Investigations and the September 2012 Russian Executive Order", 37(1) *World Competition* 103 (2014)

See also

Applicable law, Extraterritoriality

E

EFTA SURVEILLANCE AUTHORITY (ESA) & COURT

Carl BAUDENBACHER
London School of Economics and Political Science

Definition

The EEA Agreement is a multilateral treaty based on a two pillar model concluded by the EU and its Member States and the EFTA States Iceland, Norway and Liechtenstein. The EFTA Surveillance Authority ("ESA") and the European Commission apply EEA competition law. In state aid law, the ESA has sole jurisdiction in the EFTA pillar. The EFTA Court hears nullity actions against decisions of the ESA and renders preliminary rulings on references from national courts. The EFTA Court is the only court of general jurisdiction which has been referred to by the ECJ when interpreting EU law.

Commentary

General

The EEA Agreement's goal is to extend the EU single market to the participating EFTA States. The treaty is based on a two pillar model. Originally planned for seven EFTA States, the EFTA pillar has since 1 May 1995 consisted of Iceland, Liechtenstein and Norway.

EEA law originates in the EU pillar and is incorporated by way of decision of the EEA Joint Committee. The EEA/EFTA States have no right of co-decision, but a right of co-determination (Art. 99 et seq. EEA). Importantly, they have their own independent Surveillance Authority, the ESA, which operates in parallel to the European Commission; they also have their own independent Court which acts in parallel to the Court of Justice of the European Union ("ECJ"). There is no EFTA Court of First Instance; thus the EFTA Court is also a court of fact.

The types of procedure in the EFTA pillar are essentially identical in substance to the ones in the EU pillar with certain differences in the preliminary ruling procedure (no written obligation on courts of last resort to refer; rulings are of sui generis character). The Commission and ESA have the right to participate in proceedings before each other's courts.

The first basic principle of the EEA Agreement is homogeneity which comes in several forms. Written rules oblige the EFTA Court to follow relevant ECJ case law which predates the signature of the EEA Agreement (2 May 1992) and to take into account relevant subsequent ECJ case law. However, this does not exclude a certain degree of systemic competition. The EFTA Court has upheld liberal EFTA values even in cases where ECJ case law was to the contrary. Moreover, it has had to resolve novel legal questions in the majority of its cases. The dispute settlement mechanism (Article 105 EEA) has never been applied. In practice, conflicts are resolved through judicial dialogue (AG Trstenjak, C-300/10 Marques Almeida, fn. 25). In this process, both courts have occasionally given way.

The second basic principle of the EEA Agreement is reciprocity. The EEA States in both pillars must grant citizens and economic operators the same rights to do business. However, reciprocity also has a procedural dimension. It gives citizens and economic operators in both EEA pillars rights which can be enforced in court (AG Kokott in C-431/11 UK v Council, pt. 42). The EFTA Court has recognised general principles, i.a. State liability and conform interpretation, but not direct effect or primacy. It has also acknowledged fundamental rights. The ECHR and the case law of the European Court of Human Rights are relevant in the latter regard (E-15/10 Posten Norge, para. 100; E-14/15 Holship, paras. 88-91). The ECtHR has for its part made reference to EFTA Court case law (Ástráðsson v. Iceland, no. 26374/18, paras. 75, 80, 140 et seq.).

Written competition law

Articles 53 and 54 EEA reproduce the cartel prohibition and the abuse prohibition of Articles 101 and 102 TFEU. As stated in Article 55 EEA, Articles 53 and 54 EEA are enforced by the Commission and ESA. According to the allocation of competences in Article 56 EEA, the Commission is responsible in most cases. Article 57 EEA gives the competence to control mergers, basically to the Commission. In Articles 61 to 64 EEA, the State aid rules of EU law have been taken over. In cases concerning the EEA/EFTA States, ESA is competent.

Competition practice and case law

In 26 years, ESA has issued three decisions imposing fines for violation of Article 54 EEA. (1) In Norway Post, the fine for abuse of a dominant position in the business-to-consumer parcel delivery market in Norway was reduced by the EFTA Court from EUR 12.89 million to EUR 11.11 million due to the excessive length of the administrative procedure. (2) In Color Line, which concerned the operation of a long-term exclusive harbour agreement concluded with a Municipality, the fine of EUR 18.81 million was not challenged. (3) In Telenor, ESA on 30 June 2020 imposed a fine of EUR 112 million for abuse of a dominant position by a pricing strategy that resulted in rivals making a loss when selling residential mobile broadband services on tablets and laptops. The case is currently pending before the EFTA Court (E-12/20).

The most significant competition law judgment is E-15/10 Norway Post where the EFTA Court held that ESA could not be granted a margin of discretion regarding complex economic appraisals and that competition law decisions that impose fines must be subject to full judicial review. In E-3/16 Ski taxi, the Court, unlike the ECJ in C-67/13 P Cartes Bancaires, adopted AG Wahl's proposition that only conduct whose harmful nature is proven and easily identifiable, in the light of experience and economics, should be regarded as a restriction of competition by object (para. 61, see AG Wahl, pt. 56). In E-29/15 Sorpa, the Court found that municipal bodies are capable of abuse of dominance within the meaning of Article 54 EEA.

In C-67/96 Albany, the ECJ held that collective agreements aimed at improving the working conditions and thus were beyond the scope of European competition law. AG Jacobs had concluded that in virtually all legal systems, including U.S. law, collective agreements were to some extent sheltered from competition law, but that such immunity was not unlimited. The EFTA Court chose to base its E-8/00 LO ruling on AG Jacobs' opinion. It held that provisions of collective agreements prima facie fall outside the scope of Article 53 EEA. If, however, the national court finds that they do not, in fact, pursue the apparent objectives, "they may, in the light of the objectives actually pursued, fall within the scope of Article 53 EEA" (para. 75).

In E-14/15 Holship, the EFTA Court in essence declared dockworkers' priority right to load and unload vessels in Norwegian ports incompatible with EEA competition law and the right of freedom of establishment. The ECtHR has found no violation of Article 11 ECRH (45487/17, Norwegian Confederation of Trade Unions (LO) and Norwegian Transport Workers' Union (NTF) v Norway).

E-18/14 Wow Air was about the interpretation of Regulation EEC 95/93 on common rules for the allocation of slots at EEA airports. The President granted the accelerated preliminary reference procedure stating that "[t]o guarantee fair and effective competition is one of the most important goals of the EEA Agreement. Effective competition benefits both consumers and competitors and contributes to the common good. In the case at hand, Iceland's special geographic situation must be taken into account with Keflavík essentially being the only international airport in the country." (Para. 7.)

In E-8/13 Abelia the EFTA Court held that an in-house counsel cannot generally be denied the right of audience. It must be assessed on a case by case basis whether they are independent or not. In doing so, the EFTA Ct. deliberately deviated from ECJ C-422/11 P and C-423/11 P Prezes. In C-515/17 P and C-561/17 P Uniwersytet Wrocławski, the ECJ's Grand Chamber held on 4 February 2020 that a lecturer who legally represents a university with which he or she is associated is an independent legal counsel.

In E-14/11 DB Schenker I, the Court restricted the presumption underlying the ECJ's case law that access to documents is not to be granted in antitrust, merger and State aid cases, to the latter two. At para. 132, it held that "specific policy considerations arise in requests for access to documents as part of follow-on damages cases brought before national courts concerning Articles 53 and 54 EEA. The private enforcement of these provisions ought to be encouraged, as it can make a significant contribution to the maintenance of effective competition in the EEA [...] While pursuing his private interest, a plaintiff in such proceedings contributes at the same time to the protection of the public interest."

State aid practice and case law

ESA and the EFTA Court have generally followed the Commission's practice and the Union courts' case law Two points may be mentioned:

(1) As regards locus standi of a beneficiary of aid or a competitor of a beneficiary to challenge a State aid decision by ESA, the EFTA Court was quite liberal in the early days (E-2/94 Scottish Salmon Growers). However, in E-2/02 Bellona, the Court deduced from the homogeneity principle that the "Plaumann formula" of the ECJ (25/62) also applied in the EFTA pillar of the EEA and denied Bellona, an environmental foundation, locus standi. The Court stuck to this approach in later cases (E-1/17 Konkurrenten II).

(2) Regarding the substance of State aid law, the EFTA Court held in E-4/97 Husbanken II that the financing of the Norwegian State Housing bank was an undertaking. The EFTA Court basically opted for full review of ESA's decision.

Bibliography

BARBIER DE LA SERRE, E., A lesson on judicial review from the other European Court in Luxembourg, *Kluwer Competition Law Blog* 27 April, 2012

BAUDENBACHER, C., *Judicial Independence. Memoirs of a European Judge*, Springer 2019, Chapters 3, 16, 17, 21

CLIFTON, M.-J., Applying Competition Law and the View Ahead: 25 Years of the EFTA Court, in: Five Years of the Treaty on the Eurasian Economic Union: the role of the Court. *International Conference* (19-20 September 2019, Minsk) A. Bugaeva (Ed.) Minsk, Medison, 2020, 144 et seq

SPEITLER, P., Judicial Homogeneity as a Fundamental Principle of the EEA, in: Carl Baudenbacher, Ed., *The Fundamental Principles of EEA Law: EEA-ities*, Springer, 2017

TEMPLE LANG, J., Competition Law: The Brussels Perspective, in: Baudenbacher, Ed., *The Handbook of EEA Law*, Springer, 2016, 523 et seq

See also

International cooperation, European Competition Network (ECN), International Competition Network (ICN)

E

ENVIRONMENTAL PROTECTION

Simon HOLMES
University of Oxford

■ Definition

"Environmental Protection" is not a term of art in competition (or antitrust) law. In the widest sense it concerns the protection of the natural environment by individuals, organisations and governments. The "environment" means the physical surroundings common to all of us including air, space, water, land, plants, and wildlife – as well as that of future generations. The UN and OECD have defined it as "any activity to maintain or restore the quality of environmental media through preventing the emission of pollutants or reducing the presence of polluting substances in environmental media".

■ Commentary

Although environmental protection ("EP") is not new (the first national parks were established in the 19th century), most laws and agencies to protect the environment date from the 1960s and 70s – with the UN Conference on the Human Environment in 1972 being a particular driver. Since then there have been many international conferences and agreements with an increasing focus on climate change – notably the Kyoto Protocol of 1997 and the Paris Agreement of 2015. The next big milestone is the UN Climate Change Conference of the Parties (COP26) in Glasgow UK, in November, 2021.

From democracies to autocratic regimes (of the left or right) 100s of countries around the world have EP laws. The EU included EP in its founding treaty in 1957 and it is one of the fundamental principles of the Treaty on the Functioning of the EU (TFEU). In particular Article 11 TFEU provides that EP must be "integrated into the definition and implementation of

Union policies and activities" and this is echoed in Article 37 of the EU Charter on Fundamental Rights. Furthermore, the TFEU has a whole chapter on EP (Title XX – Articles 191 to 193). EP is also at the heart of the EU's Green Deal.

The UK has many laws on EP, most notably the Environmental Protection Act of 1974 and its ground breaking Climate Change Act 2008 committing the UK to net-zero emissions by 2050. EP is one area where UK policy may diverge from that of the EU post-Brexit.

The U.S. set up its Environmental Protection Agency (EPA) in 1969 and its National Environmental Policy Act (NEPA) in 1970 (which has served as a model for many EP policies and laws around the world).

At the other end of the political spectrum, China announced in 1983 that EP would be one of its basic national policies and it set up its National Environmental Protection Agency (NEPA) in 1984.

EP is enshrined in the laws and policies of over a hundred countries around the world with some including rights of nature in their laws and even in their constitutions (for example Ecuador, India, Bolivia, Columbia, Mexico, Pakistan, Australia, New Zealand, and several U.S. states).

Environmental Protection and Competition Law

While EP laws are well established around the world, how EP fits into competition law/antitrust is less clear and more controversial. Writers and institutions in Europe have taken the lead in this area building on the requirement in Article 11 TFEU that EP must be taken into account in all EU policies and activities (see above) – with no carve out for competition policy.

The need to combat climate change, and the EU Green Deal, has brought this issue to the top of the competition law agenda. While in many cases regulation or unilateral action by companies will be effective, in many other cases businesses will need to cooperate if the economy is to be transformed at the speed, and on the scale, necessary to meet the existential threat of climate change. In these instances, it is important that businesses can cooperate without undue fear of competition law.

There is also increasing discussion of how EP (and sustainability issues more generally) fit into other areas of competition law (in the widest sense) including abuse of dominance, merger control, state aid and public procurement.

Reflecting this, in September 2020, the European Commission launched a consultation on "Competition Policy supporting the Green Deal" and it is expected that this will lead to amendments to (at least) a number of Commission guidelines on competition policy. The issue is also being considered by international institutions, notably the OECD which held a roundtable on "Sustainability and Competition Policy" in December 2020.

Individual European countries are moving at different speeds on EP and competition law. The Netherlands Authority for Consumers and Markets (ACM) is the leader, publishing Draft guidelines on "Sustainability Agreements" in July 2020 and February 2021. In particular, these provide for more flexible treatment of "Environmental Damage Agreements". Other countries are less advanced with, for example, the UK Competition and Markets Authority (CMA) making climate change and the "transition to a low carbon economy" a "strategic priority" but so far only publishing very general guidelines.

Starting from a more "public interest" perspective several countries have ways to take EP into account in their competition law and enforcement practice. For example, the Australian Competition and Consumer Commission(ACCC) can authorise conduct where the public benefits (which can include EP) outweigh the public detriments. South African competition law and policy expressly take into account social objectives and many believe these (as well as economic objectives) could encompass EP and other sustainability concerns.

The U.S. is less advanced in this area, although it is possible that this may change under the Biden administration (and with the appointment of Lina Khan as chair of the FTC). There are no general guidelines focussing specifically on sustainability agreements but there is extensive case law dealing with many types of cooperation between competitors. This includes cases on standard-setting which can be one of the building blocks for EP. The Department of Justice (DOJ) issues "Business Review" letters to give business guidance on when conduct can fall outside antitrust rules. In principle, these could cover cooperation to fight climate change where regulation and unilateral action will not suffice (the Akutan Catcher Vessel Association letter being an example).

Agreements between competitors on EP issues have been considered by a number of other competition authorities around the world with mixed results (for example, the soya bean moratorium in the Amazon and palm oil deforestation in Indonesia).

Finally, many countries have specific regimes which can take account of EP issues in merger control-either as part of the competition review or outside it. For example, an EU Merger Working Group on "Public Interest Regimes in the EU" in March 2016 found that there were 12 such jurisdictions in the EU. Most of these are capable of taking into account EP issues and some (e.g. Spain) contain express reference to EP. Several recent deals have been cleared in the light of EP considerations despite competition law concerns (e.g. *Miba/Zollern* where the German government approved the deal despite an earlier block by the German Federal Cartel Office (BKA)).

Bibliography

Bell, S., McGillivray, D., Pedersen, O. W., *Environmental Law*, 8th edition, Oxford University Press, 2013.

Holmes, S., Climate Change, "Sustainability and Competition Law', *Oxford Journal of Antitrust Enforcement*, 2020

Kingston, S., *Greening EU Competition Law and Policy*, Cambridge University Press, 2012

Competition policy contributing to the EU Green Deal, Consultation & Conference, DG Competition, European Commission, February 2021

European Green Deal, announced December 2019

OECD Competition Committee Roundtable, Sustainability and Competition, December 2020

See also

Consumer protection, Sustainability

E

ERROR COSTS

Geoffrey MANNE
International Center for Law & Economics

Definition

The objective of the error-cost framework is to ensure that antitrust rules, enforcement decisions, and judicial outcomes minimize the costs of (1) erroneous condemnation and deterrence of beneficial conduct ("false positives," or "Type I errors"); (2) erroneous allowance and under-deterrence of harmful conduct ("false negatives," or "Type II errors"); and (3) the costs of administering the system (including the cost of making and enforcing rules and judicial decisions, the costs of obtaining and evaluating information and evidence relevant to decision-making, and the costs of compliance).

Commentary

Error cost analysis applies a Bayesian decision-theoretic framework designed to address problems of decision-making under uncertainty, which is particularly endemic in antitrust. In antitrust, decision makers are tasked with maximizing consumer welfare. The problem, of course, is that it is never clear in any given case – particularly those that make their way to litigation – what decision will accomplish this objective.

Given this uncertainty, we can recharacterize the effort to maximize consumer welfare in antitrust decision-making as an effort to *minimize* the *loss* of consumer welfare from (inevitably) erroneous decisions. The likelihood of error decreases with additional information, but there is a cost to obtaining new information. Thus, the error-cost framework seeks to minimize error for a given amount of information as well as to determine what amount (and type) of information is optimal.

Antitrust decision-making is inherently uncertain because it is rarely apparent whether any particular challenged conduct is anticompetitive or not. Thus, for example, even conduct that leads to supracompetitive prices in the short run may also attract new entry and incentivize innovation by challengers aimed at capturing those supracompetitive profits. A decision-maker will never know for certain whether the harm to consumers from higher prices in the short term will be outweighed by faster innovation and, ultimately, lower prices and/or higher quality in the long term. The problem is compounded by the need to prescribe rules of broad applicability and by the precedential nature of judicial decisions. "The challenge for an antitrust court lies in stating a general rule for distinguishing between exclusionary acts, which reduce social welfare, and competitive acts, which increase it." *United States v. Microsoft Corp.*, 253 F.3d 34, 58 (D.C. Cir. 2001)

One important example of the implementation of the error-cost framework is found in the imposition of intermediate, simplifying procedures that impose categorization and filters at various stages in the litigation process. Standing rules, for example, are classic error-cost minimization rules. The availability of standing turns on certain indicia that correlate with the expected likelihood that a plaintiff in a given position will have a justiciable case. Where that likelihood is identifiably low, it is more efficient to curtail adjudication before it even begins by denying standing, even though occasionally this will erroneously prevent the adjudication of meritorious cases.

Evidentiary burdens and standards of proof are particularly important implementations of the antitrust error-cost framework. Presumptions and burdens place an evidentiary "thumb on the scale" of antitrust adjudication, ideally in a manner reflecting underlying economic knowledge and its application to the specific facts at hand. A plaintiff need not prove anticompetitive harm with certainty, or "beyond a shadow of doubt": such a standard would, in most circumstances, not reflect the inherent uncertainty of conduct challenged under the antitrust laws. Under a "preponderance of the evidence" standard, by contrast, a plaintiff must adduce evidence sufficient only to demonstrate that challenged conduct is "more likely than not" to have anticompetitive effect. Plaintiffs in most civil litigation in the U.S., including antitrust litigation, are held to this standard. Rebuttable presumptions are sometimes employed as cost-saving substitutes for direct evidence when economic theory predicts a relatively high probability of competitive harm.

The choice between engaging in a full-blown rule of reason analysis and truncating review under the per se standard is one of the most important manifestations of the error cost framework. In simple terms, truncated review costs less. When it is apparent to a court that challenged conduct is almost certainly anticompetitive, the risk of erroneously condemning that conduct under a truncated analysis is low, and the administrative cost savings comparatively high.

The dividing line between per se and rule of reason turns on information: the extent to which a court has knowledge that the type of case presented is always or almost always harmful. Thus the U.S. Supreme Court has noted that the per se rule should be applied "only after courts have had considerable experience with the type of restraint at issue" and "only if courts can predict with confidence that [the restraint] would be invalidated in all or almost all instances under the rule of reason." *Leegin Creative Leather Prod., Inc. v. PSKS, Inc.*, 551 U.S. 877, 886-87 (2007).

Because certain knowledge about the competitive effects of most conduct is not available, condemnation under the per se standard is rarely appropriate. As a result, the error-cost framework leads naturally to a preference for rule of reason analysis for most types of conduct.

Indeed – and not uncontroversially – a commonly understood implication of the error-cost approach is that, all else equal, Type I errors are relatively more costly than Type II errors, and thus decision-makers should be especially cautious of erroneously condemning what may turn out to be procompetitive conduct. For Judge Frank Easterbrook, who pioneered the application of the error-cost framework to antitrust, Type I errors are more costly than Type II errors because self-correction mechanisms mitigate the latter more readily than the former. As a result, writes Easterbrook, "errors on the side of excusing questionable practices are preferable." Frank H. Easterbrook, *The Limits of Antitrust*, 63 Tex. L. Rev. 1, 15 (1984).

Thus, the error-cost approach in antitrust often takes on a more normative objective: a heightened concern with avoiding the over-deterrence of procompetitive activity through the erroneous condemnation of beneficial conduct. Various aspects of antitrust doctrine – ranging from antitrust pleading standards to the market definition exercise to the assignment of evidentiary burdens – have evolved in significant part to constrain the discretion of judges and antitrust enforcers to condemn uncertain, unfamiliar, or nonstandard conduct, lest "uncertain" be erroneously identified as "anticompetitive." As the U.S. Supreme Court has held: "Mistaken inferences and the resulting false condemnations 'are especially costly, because they chill the very conduct the antitrust laws are designed to protect.'" *Verizon Commc'ns Inc. v. Law Offices of Curtis V. Trinko, LLP*, 540 U.S. 398, 414 (2004).

This version of the error-cost framework is not supported by all antitrust scholars, however, and there is a concerted effort today to condemn as too permissive and overly ideological the bias against stringent antitrust enforcement that Judge Easterbrook's error-cost approach counsels. Nevertheless, the legal status of Judge Easterbrook's claim is today well-enshrined in antitrust law, and the Supreme Court has effectively written Judge Easterbrook's principal conclusion about error costs into U.S. antitrust jurisprudence. Error-cost analysis is far less solidified in European law, however, and the European Court of Justice's deferential "manifest error" standard of review for economic decision-making by the Commission (established in its *Holcim* ruling, C-28/03 Holcim (Deutschland) v Commission [2005] ECR II-1357) reflects a distinctly diminished concern with minimizing the costs of false positives.

Bibliography

Ahlborn, C., Evans, D. S. and Padilla, J., The Logic & Limits of the "Exceptional Circumstances Test" in Magill and IMS Health, 28 *Fordham Int'l L. Rev.* 1109 (2004)

Beckner III, C. F. and Salop, S. C., Decision Theory and Antitrust Rules, 67 *Antitrust L.J.* 41 (1999)

Easterbrook, F. H., The Limits of Antitrust, 63 *Tex. L. Rev.* 1 (1984)

Hovenkamp H. J., Antitrust Error Costs, 24 *Univ. Pa. J. Bus. L.* 293 (2022)

Manne, G. A., Error Costs in Digital Markets, in *Global Antitrust Institute Report On The Digital Economy* (Joshua D. Wright & Douglas H. Ginsburg eds., 2020)

See also

Competition policy, Economic analysis

E

ESSENTIAL FACILITY

Inge GRAEF
Tilburg University

Definition

An essential facility is an asset or infrastructure to which a third party needs access to offer its own product or service on a market. A facility is essential if no reasonable alternatives are available and duplication of the facility is not feasible due to legal, economic or technical obstacles. Different assets have been qualified as essential facilities: physical infrastructures like bridges or ports, intellectual property rights and sets of information. Denying access to an essential facility may amount to illegal monopolization (Section 2 of the Sherman Act) or abuse of dominance (Article 102 TFEU) by the undertaking controlling it.

Commentary

The essential facilities doctrine is said to have originated in the judgment of the U.S. Supreme Court in the *Terminal Railroad* case (1912). The U.S. Supreme Court imposed a duty on an association of railroad companies to give competitors access to certain railroad bridges and terminal facilities they had acquired (*Terminal Railroad*, paragraphs 409-411). Without this from of shared access, competitors would not have been able to offer their own railroad service beyond the Mississippi River into and out of Saint Louis. This would have harmed the interests of consumers due to the lack of choice for competing services outside of the control of the owners of the railroad bridges and terminal facilities.

The competition intervention by the Supreme Court in *Terminal Railroad* later became known as the "essential facilities doctrine'. The essential facilities doctrine attacks a form of exclusionary conduct by which an undertaking controls the conditions of access to an asset forming a "bottle-neck" for rivals to compete. Since its inception in U.S. antitrust law, the essential facilities doctrine has been applied in various jurisdictions around the world to assess the legality of refusals to deal under competition law. The finding of a violation of the competition rules in an essential facilities case results into the imposition of a duty to deal as a remedy to address the competitive harm. This is a far-reaching intervention, because it interferes with the generally recognized principles of freedom to contract and freedom of property. The imposition of a duty to deal under competition law is therefore seen as an exception to the rule and requires a careful balancing exercise carrying a high burden of proof.

In its *Trinko* judgment (2004), the U.S. Supreme Court took a restrictive approach towards the essential facilities doctrine by referring to Areeda's seminal article criticizing the doctrine (*Trinko*, paragraph 411). In particular, the Supreme Court stated that the circumstances in which antitrust liability was found for refusals to deal in its 1985 *Aspen Skiing* judgment are "at or near the outer boundary" of liability under Section 2 of the Sherman Act (*Trinko*, paragraph 409). According to the *Trinko* judgment, the Aspen Skiing case constitutes a limited exception to the principle of freedom to contract, which only applies in situations where a monopolist terminates a voluntary and profitable prior course of dealing (*Trinko*, paragraph 409). Following *Trinko*, liability for refusals to deal can be established under U.S. antitrust law if two cumulative conditions are met: (1) the monopolist entered into a pre-existing voluntary course of dealing; and (2) the monopolist is willing to sacrifice short-term profits by refusing to deal in order to achieve an anticompetitive end.

The EU Courts have developed four conditions for the application of the essential facilities doctrine under Article 102 TFEU in cases such as *Magill* (1995), *Bronner* (1998), *IMS Health* (2005) and *Microsoft* (2007). Abuse of dominance only exists in exceptional circumstances, namely if a refusal to deal by a dominant undertaking: (1) relates to an indispensable asset; (2) prevents the emergence of a new product (this condition is only mentioned in cases concerning access to intellectual property-protected assets); (3) excludes effective competition on a downstream market; and (4) has no objective justification.

The standards for applying these conditions vary across cases. On the one hand, the General Court explained in its *Microsoft* judgment regarding the indispensability of access to Microsoft's interoperability information that competitors needed to be able to interoperate with the Windows operating system on an equal footing (*Microsoft*, paragraph 421). On the other hand, the Court of Justice argued in its *Bronner* judgment that access to Mediaprint's nationwide newspaper home-delivery scheme would not be indispensable where alternatives were available to Bronner for distributing its daily newspapers, such as delivery by post and sales in shops, even though these alternatives would be less advantageous (*Bronner*, paragraph 43).

Because the essential facilities doctrine balances the interest in protecting competition with the interest in protecting the incentives of the dominant firm to invest in innovation, the applicable standards may vary depending on the particular circumstances of the case. Calls have been made to lower the standards for applying the essential facilities doctrine in data-driven markets where data is generated as a by-product of providing a service and incentives to produce such data would not be affected by duties to share data.

There is discussion in EU competition law about the role of the requirement of indispensability. In its 2017 *Google Shopping* decision, the European Commission did not apply the indispensability requirement to hold Google's self-preferencing in its general search results abusive. The Commission justified this choice by qualifying the conduct of Google as active behaviour to provide its own comparison shopping service a more favourable position, instead of a passive refusal by Google to give competing comparison shopping services access to a proportion of its general search results pages (*Google Shopping*, paragraph 650). In addition, the Commission considered that Google would not be required to transfer an asset or enter into agreements with competing comparison shopping services to cease its abusive conduct – as is typical for essential facilities cases (*Google Shopping*, paragraph 651).

In its *Slovak Telekom* judgment (2021), the Court of Justice stated that the indispensability of access to Slovak Telekom's local loop did not have to be demonstrated because the case did not concern an outright refusal to deal but instead related to the conditions of access imposed by Slovak Telekom (*Slovak Telekom*, paragraph 50). The Court of Justice thereby applied its reasoning in the *TeliaSonera* judgment (2011) regarding the legal test of price squeezes to non-price based conduct of dominant undertakings. In *TeliaSonera*, the Court of Justice argued that the effectiveness of Article 102 TFEU would be unduly reduced if indispensability had to be established before any conduct of a dominant undertaking in relation to its terms of trade could be regarded as abusive (*TeliaSonera*, paragraph 58). According to the Court of Justice in *Slovak Telekom*, the reference in *TeliaSonera* does not solely concern price squeezes but also other business practices relating to the terms of trade of a dominant undertaking (*Slovak Telekom*, paragraph 53). In its *Lithuanian Railways* judgment (2020), the General Court similarly found that the indispensability requirement was not applicable because sector-specific regulation already imposed a duty to deal on Lithuanian Railways (a factor also considered in *Slovak Telekom*) (*Lithuanian Railways*, paragraph 91). As a result, the necessary balancing of economic incentives, which is normally conducted by applying the conditions of the essential facilities doctrine, had already been carried out by the legislator (*Lithuanian Railways*, paragraph 92).

Bibliography

Areeda, P., "Essential Facilities: An Epithet in Need of Limiting Principles" (1989) 58 *Antitrust Law Journal* 841

Graef, I., *EU Competition Law, Data Protection and Online Platforms: Data as Essential Facility* (Kluwer Law International 2016)

Ibáñez Colomo, P., "Indispensability and Abuse of Dominance: From Commercial Solvents to Slovak Telekom and Google Shopping" (2019) 10 *Journal of European Competition Law & Practice* 532

Richard Whish and David Bailey, *Competition Law* (9th ed., Oxford University Press 2018), Section 4 of Chapter 17

Whish, R. and Bailey, D., "Refusals to Deal" (DAF/COMP(2007)46, September 2009)

See also

Cost-based access, Dominance (notion), Monopoly, Refusal to deal

E

EUROPEAN COMPETITION NETWORK (ECN)

Efstathia PANTOPOULOU
European Commission – DG COMP

Definition

The "European Competition Network" (ECN) is a network formed by the competition authorities of the EU Member States (NCAs) and the European Commission in 2004 at the time of the adoption of Regulation 1/2003. The ECN functions as a forum for discussion and close cooperation in the application and enforcement of Articles 101 and 102 of the Treaty of the Functioning of the European Union (TFEU). The ECN aims at ensuring the coherent application of competition rules across the EU. It also allows the European competition authorities to pool their experience, discuss competition related topics and identify best practices.

Commentary

Regulation 1/2003 introduced a system of parallel competences in which the European Commission and the NCAs have the power to apply Articles 101 and 102 TFEU in full. The same Regulation established the ECN as the new form of close cooperation between the Commission and the NCAs in order to ensure both an effective and consistent application of EU competition rules and an efficient division of work.

The main principles on the functioning of the ECN are set out in the Commission Notice on cooperation within the Network of Competition Authorities (ECN Notice) and the Joint Statement of the Council and the Commission on the Functioning of the Network of Competition Authorities. According to the case law in DHL and in Pfleiderer, the ECN does not adopt legally binding rules for NCAs or national courts.

The ECN is responsible to ensure the efficient division of work on the investigation of cases. The ECN members have agreed on flexible work-sharing mechanisms, including non-binding case allocation rules. The ECN Notice sets out the criteria that indicate when an ECN member is considered well placed to deal with a case. Neither Regulation 1/2003 nor the ECN Notice creates rights or expectations for an undertaking to have its case dealt with by a particular competition authority.

In addition, the NCAs and the Commission cooperate with each other through the ECN by various means, such as by: (i) informing the ECN members of new cases and proposed enforcement decisions; (ii) exchanging evidence and other information; (iii) helping each other with investigations; and (iv) discussing various competition law related issues.

At an early stage of an investigation under Articles 101 and/or Article 102 TFEU, the Commission and the NCAs need to inform each other in accordance with Article 11 of Regulation 1/2003 to ensure an efficient and quick (re-)allocation of cases and avoid multiple procedures.

The NCAs are obliged to inform the Commission of a proposed enforcement decision at least 30 days before its adoption in line with Article 11(4) of Regulation 1/2003. This consultation between the NCAs and the Commission is important to ensure the coherent application of the EU competition rules by all competition enforcers. This consultation is an internal process of the ECN and the exchanges between the Commission and an NCA are treated as "network internal documents" and cannot be shared outside the ECN.

The NCAs and the Commission can also exchange information, including documents and digital information, and use this information in their investigations pursuant to Article 12 of Regulation 1/2003. Finally, an NCA and the Commission may ask another NCA to carry out an inspection or other fact-finding measures (e.g. requests for information or interviews) to collect information on its behalf in the context of the enforcement of EU competition rules.

Over time, the ECN has developed different fora in which its members discuss various issues at different levels, namely the meeting of the heads of the European competition authorities, the so-called DGs' Meeting, the ECN Plenary, the meeting of the working groups of the ECN dealing with horizontal matters of legal, economic or procedural nature, as well as the meeting of the sectoral subgroups dealing with particular sectors. The work in these fora includes fruitful discussions, exchanges of views and the development of common positions and policies.

Since its creation, the ECN has published statements, reports, resolutions, best practices and recommendations on different matters (for example, the Joint statement on application of competition law during the Corona crisis in 2021 and the ECN Model Leniency Programme in 2012). These ECN documents set out the ECN's position and are intended to be used mainly as advocacy tools.

Bibliography

Arsenidou, E., Capiau, J., Sinclair, A. and Stanciute, J., "Cooperation Within the ECN and Strengthening of National Competition Authorities" in E. Rousseva (ed), *EU Antitrust Procedure* (1st edn, Oxford University Press, 2020), Chapter 19

De Smijter, E. and Sinclair, A., "The Enforcement System under Regulation 1/2003, Cooperation between Enforcers" in J. Faull and A. Nikpay (eds), *The EU Law of Competition* (3rd edn, Oxford University Press, 2014), Chapter 2

Rayment, B. and Grubeck, N., "The Enforcement of the Competition Rules by National Competition Authorities, The European Competition Network" in D. Bailey and L. E. John (eds), *Bellamy & Child: European Union Law of Competition* (8th edn, Oxford University Press, 2019), Chapter 15

Whish, R. and Bailey, D., *Competition Law* (10th end, Oxford University Press, 2021), Chapter 7

The views expressed are purely those of the author and may not in any circumstances be regarded as stating an official position of the European Commission.

See also

Cooperation between competition authorities, International cooperation, International Competition Network (ICN)

E

EUROPEAN CONVENTION ON HUMAN RIGHTS (ECHR)

Erik WENNERSTRÖM
European Court of Human Rights

Definition

The ECHR is an international treaty for the protection of human rights and fundamental freedoms in Europe. All 46 member countries of the Council of Europe, 27 of which are EU Member States, have ratified the ECHR and are committed to the regional system of protection that it establishes. It is a system based on subsidiarity, in that it requires the States Parties to the ECHR to apply the convention domestically, while keeping an avenue for individual applications directly to the European Court of Human Rights (the Court) open, for the event that the Convention rights of an individual physical or legal person have been violated and the individual has failed to achieve redress for an alleged violation in spite of having exhausted all domestic remedies. States Parties are bound by the decisions and judgments of the Court. If a violation of the ECHR is found, execution frequently implies payment of *damages* to the victim, and amending the relevant national legislation or its implementation to prevent the violation from recurring.

Commentary

The ECHR has dealt with over one million individual applications since it was established in 1950. (In force since 1953.) Very few of these applications were made by legal persons and most of them have concerned other rights than those normally associated with competition law, i.e. Article 6 (right to a fair trial), Article 13 (right to an effective remedy), as well as Article 1 of the 1st Protocol (protection of property). This is not surprising, considering the ECHR's origins in the will to prevent for the future such atrocities as occurred before and during World War II – i.e. mainly the rights covered by Articles 2 (right to life), 3 (prohibition of torture), 4 (prohibition of slavery and forced labour), and 5 (right to liberty and security) – and the totalitarian regimes associated with them. These origins are manifested in the 1948 Universal Declaration of Human Rights, the principles of which the ECHR implements regionally in Europe.

Although most applications under the ECHR pertain to physical persons, it is nevertheless worth noting that the applicants in several cases of jurisprudential significance are companies or shareholders of companies, that no doubt have had reason to consider not only their own compliance with relevant regulation, but also the compliance of the relevant State and its authorities with international obligations, including the ECHR. In *Dubus S.A. v. France* (5242/04), the applicant was an investment company that was investigated and later disciplinary sanctioned by the French Banking Commission.

The fact that ECHR is applicable also for issues related to the coercive powers of public authority pertaining to competition law, is demonstrated through several instances of the Court's caselaw. The *ratione materiae* relevant to competition law is likely to be linked to national sanctions procedures under competition regulations. The Court has viewed procedures, regardless of how they are categorized under national law, whereby public authorities exercise coercion vis-à-vis individuals (physical or legal) as falling under the first paragraph of Article 6. The right to the peaceful enjoyment of private property, Article 1 of the 1st Protocol, could also be of relevance here.

The ECHR operates through *subsidiarity*, in that it allocates the main responsibility for enforcing the obligations arising from the Convention clearly with its States Parties themselves – it regards the Court as a court of last resort. Only when the States Parties have failed to implement the obligations does the ECHR system and its Court intervene in the process. Subsidiarity presents a procedural aspect, requiring individuals to exhaust domestic remedies before seizing the Court, and a substantive aspect, namely the presumption that States are generally in a better position to assess the necessity and proportionality of acts that may have interfered with specific rights. The execution under the ECHR system portrays a trilateral relationship between the Court, the Council of Europe Committee of Ministers (CM) and national authorities, where execution measures are detailed in the judgment first and the supervision of the execution measures by the national authorities is subsequently carried out by CM.

The text of the Convention has been amended and supplemented over the seven decades of its existence, through 16 different protocols. Throughout this time, the Court has developed the processes and interpretative methods for establishing the standards emerging from the Convention in ways that reflect the societal developments in the States Parties over time. In establishing its living instrument doctrine, the Court stated that the ECHR "must be interpreted in the light of present-day conditions." (*Tyrer v. United Kingdom* (5856/72) § 31.) Another important concept applied in jurisprudence is *European consensus*, which refers to the degree of uniformity in the legal frameworks of the States Parties on a specific issue. The Court engages this concept to justify a wide *margin of appreciation* – another central principle in ECHR jurisprudence – given to States Parties, in the absence of a consensus, and to justify the development of new standards where there is an emerging consensus among States Parties.

As more than half of the States Parties to the ECHR are also EU Member States, the relationship between the two sets of treaty obligations is of paramount importance for several areas of law, including competition law. Significant for this relationship is the jurisprudence evolving from the judgment in *Bosphorus v. Ireland*, (45036/98) where the Court established that ECHR States Parties that also have membership obligations to the EU (or another international organisation) are fully liable under ECHR for "acts and omissions of its organs regardless of whether the act or omission in question was a consequence" of the obligations stemming from, in this case, EU membership. (§ 153) While reiterating full ECHR liability, the Court also stressed the "need to secure the proper functioning of international organisations" (§ 150) and it is the consequence of these two statements (cf. §§ 155 – 156) that has since been referred to as the Bosphorus presumption, an assumption of compliance, when reviewing the way obligations under e.g. EU law, that somehow approaches the rights under ECHR, have been implemented. As with assumptions in general, it remains in place throughout the review, and if nothing in the review suggests otherwise, it will be assumed throughout.

The Court applies a similar approach to the relationship between obligations of States Parties to the ECHR, and their obligations stemming from the UN Charter. In *Al-Jedda v. the United Kingdom* [GC] (27021/08) the Court established the presumption that the United Nations Security Council (UNSC), acting under the UN Charter, would not impose any obligations on UN member states in breach of fundamental principles of human rights. (§ 102) In subsequent cases applying this presumption, the Court has found no normative conflict between UNSC resolutions and the ECHR, while finding a violation of ECHR with the manner in which a State Party was implementing the UNSC measures. (See e.g. *Nada v. Switzerland* [GC] (10593/08), and *Al-Dulimi and Montana Management Inc. v. Switzerland* [GC] (5809/08).)

Bibliography

Forrester, I., "A challenge for Europe's judges: the review of fines in competition cases", *European Law Review*, 2011, 36(2)

Frison-Roche, M.-A. (dir.), La juridictionnalisation de la Compliance, coll."Régulations & Compliance", *Journal of Regulation & Compliance* (JoRC) et Dalloz

Morgan de Rivery, E., Chassaing, E., Competition law and the ECHR: An overview of ECHR and EU case law, 19 April 2016, *e-Competitions ECHR*, Art. N° 79009

Spano, R., "The Future of the European Court of Human Rights – Subsidiarity, Process-Based Review and the Rule of Law" in *Human Rights Law Review*, Volume 18, Issue 3, September 2018

Teleki, C., "Due Process and Fair Trial in EU Competition Law. The Impact of Article 6 of the European Convention on Human Rights", *Nijhoff Studies in European Union Law*, Volume: 18, 2021

See also

Amicus Curiae, Effective Judicial Protection

EXCESSIVE PRICES

David GILO
Tel Aviv University

Definition

Excessive pricing is an antitrust violation that exists in most OECD countries and particularly in EU competition law where a dominant firm charges a price that is excessive relative to an appropriate competitive benchmark in a way that deems it unfair. The violation does not hinge on potential harm to the competitive process, but rather is fulfilled also by mere exploitation of buyers by the dominant firm. The competitive benchmark to which the dominant firm's price is compared includes either an appropriate measure of costs, or a comparison with a lower price charged in a situation comparable to the dominant firm's circumstances.

Commentary

Article 102 TFEU prohibits any abuse by undertakings of a dominant position, and states in sub-section (a) that such abuse may consist in "directly or indirectly imposing unfair purchase or selling prices or other unfair trading conditions." This prohibition has been applied, *inter alia*, to prices that are too high. In particular, the European Court of Justice in *General Motors Continental NV v. Comm'n* (1975) held that a dominant firm's price is unfair if it is "excessive in relation to the economic value of the service provided." The Court of Justice in *United Brands Co. BV v. Comm'n* (1978) clarified the unfairness concept further and held that "[i]t is advisable therefore to ascertain whether the dominant undertaking has made use of the opportunities arising out of its dominant position in such a way as to reap trading benefits which it would not have reaped if there had been normal and sufficiently effective competition. [...] This excess could, inter alia, be determined objectively if it were possible for it to be calculated by making a comparison between the selling price of the product in question and its cost of production [...]." (*United Brands*, paragraphs 249, 251). Hence, the *United Brands* decision discusses a price-cost comparison as a leading competitive benchmark. It holds that when price is excessive relative to cost, the price may be deemed unfair in itself. The economic rationale behind a price-cost comparison used as a competitive benchmark is that the competitive process, which antitrust laws strive for, drives prices toward the cost of production. Of course, costs, in this respect, should include not only variable costs of supplying the product, but also any costs, investments or risks the dominant firm requires in order to supply the product. The UK Court of Appeals in *CMA v. Flynn Pharma Ltd.* (2020, paragraph 97) held that a violation can be based solely on a price-cost comparison.

Instead of using a price-cost comparison, a violation can be shown by using a comparative benchmark. A comparative benchmark sheds light on the excessiveness of the dominant firm's price by comparing it to a lower price taken from a comparable situation. This includes a comparison between the allegedly excessive price and a lower price that the dominant firm charged in a market, segment, or period in which it was subject to stronger competitive pressures, or pressure from price-sensitive consumers, or a regulated price that mimics a competitive price. Another kind of comparative benchmark involves comparison to the lower price charged by other comparable firms that are subject to more intense competition or have less power to raise prices.

The rationale for using comparative benchmarks is that if the benchmark price is indeed comparable, it is reasonable to assume, subject to contrary evidence, that it is an upper bound on the competitive price, which is the price that antitrust laws strive for. In *Bodson v. Pompes Funèbres* (1988), for example, the EU Court of Justice held that the unfairness of an excessive price can be shown by comparing what the dominant firm has charged with lower prices it has charged in markets in which it is subject to more intense competition. In *Latvijas Autoru apvienîba v. Konkurences padome* (2016) the Court of Justice held that if the difference between the price charged by the dominant firm and the comparator price is appreciable, then this is "indicative of abuse of a dominant position and it is for the copyright management organisation holding a dominant position to show that its prices are fair by reference to objective factors that have an impact on management expenses or the remuneration of rightholders." In this case, the comparator used was the price charged by similar firms in two neighboring countries, or by similar firms in a group of other countries.

After establishing the competitive benchmark (cost-based or comparison based) that the dominant firm's price is to be compared to, it needs to be determined whether the difference between the price charged by the dominant firm and this competitive benchmark is so excessive that it is deemed unfair. The degree of excessiveness that amounts to a violation is not made clear in the case law. Some cases held that prices exceeding the competitive benchmark by 25% to 40% were excessive, while other violation decisions concerned much larger gaps. Such ambiguity of legal rules is inherent also to other antitrust violations, and in particular those requiring "substantial harm to competition". "Substantial", like "excessive" or "unfair" is an ambiguous criterion. Some of the academic literature suggests using rebuttable presumptions that a certain gap above the competitive benchmark is excessive, so as to improve the predictability of the prohibition.

Excessive pricing is not recognized as an antitrust violation in all jurisdictions. Under U.S. case law, for example, an excessive price is not considered a violation. Such holdings were based mainly on three grounds. The first is the notion that excessive prices are self-correcting, since they allegedly attract entry of new competitors. The second ground for non-intervention is that excessive prices are necessary to promote pro-consumer investment, and the third is that it is too difficult to assess whether a price was excessive. There is controversy in the academic literature regarding the justifiability of these three grounds for non-intervention. One strand of the literature agrees with these three considerations, and advocates for a general non-interventionist approach, even in jurisdictions in which antitrust law includes the prohibition.

Another strand of the literature questions these grounds for non-intervention and calls for ordinary application of the prohibition on a case-by-case basis. For example, some academic papers show that excessive prices cannot correct themselves. This is because it is the post-entry price that matters for new entrants. If the post-entry price is competitive, this is the price the new entrant will consider before it invests in entry and not the excessive price that prevailed before entry. If the post-entry price is expected to remain excessive, then by definition, entry did not correct it. Similarly, it is claimed that investment considerations can be assessed on a case-by-case basis, rather than constituting an overwhelming justification for non-intervention.

Finally, the literature in favor of intervention shows the resemblance between excessive pricing cases and other complex antitrust litigation based on a rule of reason analysis. The latter too is based on complex economic analysis, coupled with a legal policy determination on a vague standard, such as the requirement that the probable harm be "substantial". Also, many of these other complex antitrust violations also concern pricing, such as predatory pricing, price squeeze, and loyalty discounts, and require assessment of parties' claim that their practice is necessary to stimulate investment.

Bibliography

Ezrachi, A. and Gilo, D., Are excessive prices really self-correcting?, 5(2) *J. Competition L. & Econ.* 249 (2009).

Gilo, D., A Coherent Approach to the Antitrust Prohibition of Excessive Pricing by Dominant Firms, in *Excessive Pricing and Competition Law Enforcement* 99, 107-112 (Yannis Katsoulacos & Frédéric Jenny eds. Springer, 2018)

Jenny, F., Abuse of Dominance by Firms Charging Excessive or Unfair Prices: An Assessment, in *Excessive Pricing and Competition Law Enforcement* (Frédéric Jenny and Yannis Katsoulacos, eds. Springer, 2018)

Kianzad, B. and Minssen, T., How Much is Too Much? Defining the Metes and Bounds of Excessive Pricing in the Pharmaceutical Sector, 2 *Eur. Pharm.L. Rev.* 15 (2018)

See also

Abuse of dominant position, Predatory pricing, Prices

E

EXCHANGES OF INFORMATION

Alden CARIBÉ DE SOUSA, Fernanda GARCIA MACHADO,
Alexandre CORDEIRO MACEDO
Brazilian Administrative Council for Economic Defense (CADE)

■ Definition

Exchanges of information occur when undertakings reciprocally provide or receive fact reports or details about business valuable information. It may be considered an antitrust infringement when it facilitates coordination among competitors, violates ex ante merger control rules or reinforces the effectiveness of anticompetitive agreements in cartel schemes.

■ Commentary

According to OECD, information exchange among competitors falls into three different scenarios under competition rules: (i) as part of a wider price-fixing or market sharing agreement whereby the exchange of information functions as a facilitating factor; (ii) in the context of broader efficiency-enhancing co-operation agreements such as joint venture, standardisation or Research & development agreements; or (iii) as a standalone practice, whereby the exchange of information is the only co-operation among competitors. It is possible to envision a fourth scenario: the information sharing as an executive act of merger before the antitrust agency approval (gun jumping infringement).

In the first scenario, information exchange enables companies to implement or monitor cartels, being a facilitating factor or an ancillary behaviour to a more egregious anticompetitive conduct. To organise a cartel, companies usually share some strategic information such as prices, output, product quality, clients or other commercial variables that otherwise should be independently defined.

The second scenario may occur in the context of a legitimate horizontal co-operation agreement. In these cases, information exchange between firms may lead to economic benefits derived from costs saving, sharing risks and investing in better quality and variety of products and services. The Guidelines on the applicability of Article 101 of the TFEU to horizontal co-operation agreements provide the general principles on the competitive assessment of information exchange. They also establish an analytical framework for the most common types of horizontal co-operation agreements such as Research & development agreements, production agreements, joint purchasing arrangements and commercialisation agreements in a way to provide some guidance on cases which tend to constitute a genuine transaction and those which may impose some potential adverse effects to competition.

The third scenario, the standalone infringement, admits variation of treatment according to jurisdiction. Information exchange is assessed under Article 101 of the TFEU generally as a concerted practice. This conduct is characterised by a form of coordination between undertakings that, without having reached the stage of an agreement, they knowingly substitute practical co-operation between them for the risks of competition (see Case C-8/08 T-Mobile Netherlands BV [2009], parag. 26).

There are circumstances in which an exchange of information is more likely to be considered anticompetitive, notably when the disclosure or exchange of strategic information reduces uncertainty about how companies will operate in a market. Generally, sharing private, disaggregated and confidential information about future prices or output is considered restrictive by object (see Case C-286/13 P – Dole Food Company [2015], para. 128-133, in which companies in the banana sector discussed their own quotation prices and price trends in some meetings).

In the U.S., Section 1 of the Sherman Act outlaws every contract, combination, or conspiracy that restrains trade in interstate commerce or with foreign nations, if it is unreasonable. Agreements with the sole objective of reducing output, fixing prices, allocating markets or rigging bids are always regarded as illegal. These schemes often use information sharing frameworks as an enforcement tool of the conspiracy. In these cases, proof of data exchange will be a surrounding element of the naked agreement and serve as indirect evidence.

For information sharing with no proof of anticompetitive intent (for instance in a standalone exchange of information), the U.S. federal approach assesses the conduct under the rule of reason, with no criminal effects. According to Supreme Court decision in U. S. v. U. S. Gypsum Co., 438 U.S. 422 (1978): "The exchange of price data and other information among competitors does not invariably have anticompetitive effects; indeed such practices can in certain circumstances increase economic efficiency and render markets more, rather than less, competitive. For this reason, we have held that such exchanges of information do not constitute a per se violation of the Sherman Act."

Standalone information exchanges usually raise civil concerns when the private data is about current or future information related to prices, wages, costs, revenues, market-shares, sales volume, output, idle capacity, customers, profit margins and businesses plans (for some of the items, FTC-DoJ Antitrust Guidelines for Collaborations Among Competitors). This information is sensitive because it can dampen rivalry or lead to price uniformity once known by competitors. Under the rule of reason, it tends to be anticompetitive unless shown, by the defendant, to have superior compensatory effects. "Exchanges of current price information, of course, have the greatest potential for generating anticompetitive effects and, although not per se unlawful, have consistently been held to violate the Sherman Act. See American Column & Lumber Co. v. United States, 257 U. S. 377 (1921); United States v. American Linseed Oil Co., 262 U. S. 371 (1923); United States v. Container Corp." (U. S. v. U. S. Gypsum Co., 438 U.S. 422 (1978).

Publicly available information, aggregated and historical information are not generally a matter of concern. The concept of historical data is linked to the time cycles of transactions in a market. Markets with long-run cycles tend to have a succession of contracts with long duration and fewer opportunities for negotiation. Markets with short-run cycles tend to have numerous short term contracts. A piece of information is historical when it is irrelevant to current decisions.

Adopting explicit caution is essential to avoid the anticompetitive effects of standalone information sharing, such as by: (i) using an independent third party to collect the data, (ii) distribution of exclusively historical data in aggregate form. For instance, the FTC/DoJ Statements of Antitrust Enforcement Policy in Healthcare indicates that the third-party must gather the information from a group of at least five players of about the same importance to qualify for be considered aggregate.

The fourth scenario is derived from the prior notification merger control system. To ensure effective antitrust review, applicants are prohibited from integrating assets prior to the approval of mergers. Communicating competitive sensitive information is a violation of this rule. Businesses dealing in this type of information must do so through specially designated people (clean team) and observing precaution protocols for the dissemination of information between the parties.

Bibliography

Canada Competition Bureau Competitor Collaboration Guidelines

Mexican COFECE, Guidelines on information Exchange between Competitors

Netherlands Authority for Consumers and Markets, Guidelines on Collaborations between competitors

OECD, Information Exchanges Between Competitors under Competition Law, 2010

United States FTC-DoJ, Antitrust Guidelines for Collaborations Among Competitors

See also

Anticompetitive practices, Gun jumping, Price signalling

EXCLUSIONARY PRACTICE

Juan David GUTIÉRREZ RODRIGUEZ
Los Andes University

■ Definition

The term "exclusionary practice" refers to a form of anticompetitive conduct that forecloses a market to rivals (leading to their exit) or that deters potential entrants from entering a market. It is considered anticompetitive when it is used to maintain or strengthen market power. Foreclosure is not anticompetitive when it is the result of a firm's superior performance (e.g. greater efficiency). The conduct also encompasses restrictions that do not force rivals to exit the market but that may cause them significant disadvantages, for example, by impeding their expansion.

Synonyms: exclusionary acts, exclusionary behaviour, exclusionary conduct.

■ Commentary

The term "exclusionary practices" is usually not found in competition laws. Instead, the term is used in case law and textbooks to refer to different types of behaviour that forecloses rivals and potential competitors with the objective of maintaining or strengthening a dominant position. Such practices include strategies that force competitors to exit markets, limit their possibility of expansion, and/or that deter new companies from entering a market.

The exclusionary acts may cause horizontal foreclosure (e.g. dominant firm acts against competitors in the market in which it is dominant) and vertical foreclosure (e.g. vertically integrated dominant firm acts against a downstream rival). Exclusionary methods may consist of single-firm behaviour such as the imposition of constraints on rival conduct (e.g. raising rivals' costs), predatory pricing, margin squeezing, tying and bundling, price discrimination, exclusive dealing, fidelity discounts and rebates, refusing to sell or supply, refusing to provide interoperability information and refusing to licence intellectual property rights, among others. Exclusionary practices may also take the form of collective boycotts.

There is a significant variation among jurisdictions on the legality of specific conducts, the elements of each type of exclusionary conduct, the burden of proof, and enforcement practices in general. To illustrate these nuances, the rest of the entry presents leading cases of exclusionary practices from the European Union (EU), United States, and emerging markets. Three types of exclusionary conducts are exemplified through case law: discounts and rebates, refusal to supply (as a horizontal foreclosure), and degrading the quality of an input provided to rivals.

Fidelity discounts. In *British Airways v Commission*, the Court of First Instance (CFI) of the EU confirmed the European Commission's decision, which was that target incentives offered to travel agents by British Airways amounted to an abuse of the company's dominant position. The Commission concluded that the reward schemes implemented by British Airways generated an exclusionary effect due to their "fidelity-building nature." The Commission also found that these fidelity rebates affected competitor airlines and were not based on an economically justified consideration. The CFI judged that "for the purposes of establishing an infringement of Article 82 EC [currently 102] it is not necessary to demonstrate that the abuse in question had a concrete effect on the markets concerned".

Bundled discounts. In *Cascade Health Solutions v PeaceHalth*, the U.S. Court of Appeals for the Ninth Circuit addressed a case between two providers of hospital care in Lane County, Oregon. In the first instance proceedings before the district court, the plaintiff accused the defendant of engaging in "anticompetitive conduct by offering insurers 'bundled' or 'package' discounts." The U.S. Court of Appeals vacated both the district court's summary judgement and the jury's verdict, and "dismissed appeal as moot". The U.S. Court of Appeals summarized its reasoning on bundled discounts and their potential exclusionary effects in the following terms: "the primary anticompetitive danger posed by a multi-product bundled discount is that such a discount can exclude a rival is who is equally efficient at producing the competitive product simply because the rival does not sell as many products as the bundled discounter. Thus, a plaintiff who challenges a package discount as anticompetitive must prove that, when the full amount of the discounts given by the defendant is allocated to the competitive product or products, the resulting *price* of the competitive product or products is below the defendant's incremental cost to produce them. This requirement ensures that the only bundled discounts condemned as exclusionary are those that would exclude an equally efficient producer of the competitive product or products."

Refusal to supply. In *United Brands v Commission*, the Court of Justice of the EU decided a horizontal foreclosure case in which a dominant firm (*United Brands – UBC*) had refused to supply an input (bananas) to a distributor that also sold competitors' products. More specifically, UBC had attempted to punish its distributor for participating in the advertising campaign of one of UBC;'s competitors. The European Commission decided that *UBC* infringed article 102 TFEU through different forms of abuse of its dominant position, including price discrimination, refusal to supply, and imposing excessive prices. The Court of Justice affirmed the Commission's findings with regard to the two first types of conduct and rejected the Commission's conclusion regarding the third. With regard to the unilateral refusal to supply, the Court of Justice held that "an undertaking in a dominant position for the purpose of marketing a product…cannot stop supplying a long standing customer who abides by regular commercial practice, if the orders placed by that customer are in no way out of the ordinary" (paragraph 182). The Court of Justice stated that *UBC* did not "put forward any relevant argument to justify the refusal of supplies". Finally, the Court stated that while dominant firms have the right to take action to protect their commercial interests, such strategy cannot be tolerated when "its actual purpose is to strengthen this dominant position and abuse it" (paragraph 189).

Refusal to supply a key input. In *Aspen Skiing Co. v Aspen Highlands Skiing Corp* thc U.S. Supreme Court decided a case in which a company that owned three mountain facilities for downhill skiing at Aspen was accused by a company that owned another mountain resort of excluding it from the market for downhill skiing services in violation of § 2 of the Sherman Act. The conduct consisted of refraining from cooperating by excluding it from a multi-area ski ticket scheme. The Supreme Court held that while "a firm with monopoly power has no general duty to engage in a joint marketing program with a competitor", but that the "high value that we have placed on the right to refuse to deal with other firms does not mean that the right is unqualified" (page 601). Drawing from previous case law, the Supreme Court argued that refusal to deal is prohibited by the Sherman Act when it is used as a "purposeful means of monopolizing interstate commerce" (page 602). Additionally, the Supreme Court held that to characterize the conduct as "exclusionary" it was not enough to consider its effect on the dominant firm's competitor and that "it is relevant to consider its impact on consumers and whether it has impaired competition in an unnecessarily restrictive way" (page 605).

Degrading the quality of an input provided to rivals. Article 50 (6) of the Colombian competition law (Decree 2153 of 1992) explicitly lists the following exclusionary conduct as a type of abuse of dominant position: "obstructing or impeding third parties from accessing markets or commercialization channels". In the *Bulk Water case* (Resolution 14305/2018), for example, the Colombian competition agency sanctioned Bogota city's water state-owned company for installing a flow restrictor valve and affecting a small company that delivered potable water in the north of the city and nearby towns. The valve reduced the water's pressure by 33%, limiting the capacity of its downstream rival to operate, and negatively impacted the end-users of the small company. The competition agency concluded that the obstruction took place in the bulk water market, in which the state-owned company had a dominant position, but affected the "market for aqueduct services". The agency also found that the state-owned company had explicitly planned the strategy to exclude its rival and that there were no justifications for installing the flow restrictor valve.

Bibliography

BAKER, J., Exclusion as a Core Competition Concern, 78 *Antitrust Law Journal* (2013)

FOX, E. M., "What is harm to competition? Exclusionary practices and anticompetitive effect." *Antitrust Law Journal*, vol. 70, n°. 2, 2002, pp. 371–411

FUMAGALLI, C., MOTTA, M., & CALCAGNO, C. (2018). *Exclusionary Practices: The Economics of Monopolisation and Abuse of Dominance*. Cambridge: Cambridge University Press

POSNER, R. A., "Exclusionary Practices and the Antitrust Laws," 41 *University of Chicago Law Review* 506 (1974)

WHISH, R. and BAILEY, D. (2021). *Competition Law*. 10th edn. Oxford: Oxford University Press

See also

Abuse of dominant position, Anticompetitive practices, Boycott, Bundling, Fidelity rebates, Market power, Margin squeeze, Predatory pricing, Price discrimination, Refusal to deal

E

EXCLUSIVE DISTRIBUTION

Mário MARQUES MENDES
Gómez-Acebo & Pombo

■ Definition

By means of an exclusive distribution agreement a supplier agrees to sell its products to only one distributor, or a limited number of them [as per the draft for a new Vertical Block Exemption Regulation ("VBER")], for resale in a particular territory or to a specific group of customers, or reserves such distribution to itself, while restricting the exclusive distributor from active selling into other territories allocated to the supplier or other exclusive distributors. Passive sales, i.e., answer to unsolicited requests from customers, must, however be permitted, unless exceptional circumstances occur. The current VBER (Regulation 330/2010), currently under review, exempts exclusive distribution agreements from the prohibition laid down in Article 101(1) TFEU where the market share of the supplier and the market share of the distributor do not, individually exceed 30%, as long as there are no "hardcore restrictions" involved. To the extent that an exclusive distribution agreement does not provide for absolute territorial protection – a "hardcore restriction" that would amount to a "by object" violation –, it may not even restrict competition at all. Accordingly, an analysis is required in order to evaluate whether it may restrict competition "by effect".

■ Commentary

The EU

Competition has been an essential instrument in abolishing barriers among Member States and the EC reaffirmed it countless times over the years. The European Court of Justice ("Court" or "ECJ") very early established the same principles in the 1966 landmark judgment in *Consten and Grundig v. Commission:* "*An agreement between producer and distributor that is designed to restore the national partitions in trade between Member States could conflict with the basic objectives of the Community.*" While over time the Commission has evolved to take increasingly into account economic efficiency, the congenital concern over internal market integration remains of paramount importance in the enforcement of competition rules.

Vertical restraints are usually seen as susceptible of contributing to generating efficiencies. The issue is how to balance the negative and the positive effects of vertical restraints.

An agreement through which exclusivity is granted for a specific territory is not, in itself, in violation of article 101(1) TFEU. In *Société Technique Minière v. Maschinenbau Ulm*, which was contemporaneous with the judgment in *Consten*, the Court made clear that in the absence of a *hardcore restriction* – as was the case of the absolute territorial protection found in Consten – "*the consequences of the agreement must then be examined and must justify the conclusion either that the agreement prevents or that it restricts or distorts competition to an appreciable extent*", with special attention given to "*whether the agreement is capable of partitioning the market in certain products between the Member States*". In this case, neither the distributor was prohibited from re-exporting to any other markets of the Community, the same applying to exclusive distributors in other Member States, nor parallel imports were prohibited.

For a long time, the Commission kept a very strict and formalistic approach to vertical agreements, with a permanent and paramount concern regarding market integration going well into the mid and late 1990s. With the gradual completion of the internal market, and with a more efficiency-oriented type of analysis making its way in the case-law of the EU Courts, the Commission came to adopt a more economic and pragmatic approach acknowledging in its analysis the possible existence of efficiencies that could be taken into account. This was notably reflected in its VBERs 2790/99 and 330/2010.

Since Regulation 330/2010, the first step in assessing vertical agreements is the calculation of the market share of the supplier and the buyer on the market where they respectively sell and buy the agreement's goods or services. The 2010 Guidelines (para 153) highlight that "*(t)he market position of the supplier and his competitors is of major importance, as the loss of intra-brand competition can only be problematic if inter-brand competition is limited. The stronger the position of the supplier, the more serious is the loss of intra-brand competition. Above the 30% market share threshold there may be a risk of a significant reduction of intra-brand competition. In order to fulfil the conditions of Article 101(3), the loss of intra-brand competition may need to be balanced with real efficiencies*". Regulation 330/2010 provides for an exemption (article 3) from the application of article 101(1) TFEU where, notably as regards exclusive distribution agreements, "*the market share held by the supplier does not exceed 30% of the relevant market on which it sells the contract goods or services and the market share held by the buyer does not exceed 30 % of the relevant market on which it purchases the contract goods or services*".

However, this so-called safe harbour, shall not apply in case hardcore restrictions (article 4) are involved. If the relevant market share is above 30% as regards the supplier and/or the buyer, then it is necessary to assess whether the agreement violates article 101(1) TFEU and, ultimately, whether it fulfils the prerequisites for an individual exemption under 101(3) TFEU. While hardcore restrictions will hardly benefit from the application of article 101(3) TFEU, paras 60-64 of the 2010 Guidelines give examples of situations in which such an exemption may be considered, *e.g.* where an hardcore restriction may be objectively necessary for reasons of safety or health; where a first sale of a new brand or of an existing brand on a new market requiring substantial investments is at stake, in which case passive sales may also be restricted for a period of up to two years; or in the case of testing of a new product in a limited territory or with a limited customer group which may be coupled with the imposition of restriction of active sales outside the covered area for the period necessary for such testing or introduction of the product.

As regards the assessment of exclusive distribution in cases above the 30% market share threshold, paras 151-167 of the 2010 Guidelines provide valuable guidance. The main risks are reviewed by the Commission which lists notably i) the reduction of intra-brand competition and market partitioning, which may facilitate price discrimination in particular, ii) the softening of competition and facilitation of collusion, both at the suppliers' and the distributors' level, deriving from the fact that most or all of the suppliers apply exclusive distribution and iii) the foreclosure of other distributors and consequent reduction of competition at that level. The Commission notes, in particular, that exclusive distribution may lead to efficiencies "especially where investments by the distributors are required to protect or build up the brand image" and, in general, when the products at stake are new, complex and whose qualities are difficult to assess before, or even after, consumption.

Nevertheless, the Commission is far from abandoning its concern over market integration which continues to be considered an objective which enhances competition in the EU. To this day, it is understood that certain practices are considered restrictive in themselves because they attempt against this objective of market integration, i.e., absolute territorial protection and prohibition or limitation of exports within the EU. But open questions remain, and legal scholars have been debating the relevance and impact of market integration concerns in the analysis of restraints, notably when a territorial restraint may arguably have pro-competitive effects.

The U.S.

The history of American antitrust reveals cyclical debates on what are the main goals of antitrust, *i.e.*, whether antitrust policy promotes, or should promote, any values other than economic efficiency. As Professor L. Sullivan wrote "*[c]hanges in antitrust law and regulatory politics are related to the intellectual history of micro-economic theory. All three are embedded in a common culture*".

The neoclassical, non-interventionist, theories of the 1870s which lasted roughly until the early 1930s were followed by an increasing governmental regulation turned to other economic as well as political and social values, which coincided with the later part of the Court presided over by Chief Justice Warren. Cases such as *Brown Shoe, Philadelphia Bank, Von's Grocery* and *Schwinn* exemplify well this kind of approach, in which antitrust was used to promote a variety of social and political goals, including the protection of dealer independence and the promotion of equity and fairness values in the market.

This blend of economics and populism interventionist approach was slowly replaced by a new emphasis on efficiency concepts, a move somewhat related to the poor performance of the American economy. Efficiency and consumer welfare became the only goals of antitrust, under the inspiration of the Chicago School theorists, who relied on the self-correctness of markets.

This new orthodoxy was gradually received by both the lower federal courts (*e.g. Berkey Photo, Inc.*) and the Supreme Court. The former *per se* rules have been progressively replaced by rule of reason analysis in vertical non-price restraints, with a clear focus on efficiency. The decisions in landmark cases such as *Continental T.V., Inc.* (which overruled *Schwinn*), *National Society of Professional Engineers*, *Gypsum* and *BMI/CBS* illustrate well this new era.

Robert Bork, probably the most influential scholar of this new Supreme Court approach, stated that "*[a]nalysis shows that every vertical restraint should be completely lawful*", which, by the way, he thought should extend to vertical price fixing/resale price maintenance. But only in 2007 was decided, in the *Leegin* judgment, overruling *Dr. Miles*, that vertical price restraints are to be judged by the rule of reason. The Supreme Court, while stating that "*[t]he justifications for vertical price restraints are similar to those for other vertical restraints*", it underlined that "*[n]otwithstanding the risks of unlawful conduct, it cannot be stated with any degree of confidence that retail price maintenance 'always or almost always tend[s] to restrict competition and decrease output*'".

Meanwhile, the 1970s and 1980s Chicago theoretical model came gradually under criticism. In fact, "*the simplicity of the construction may also have been its greater weakness*", as Professor T. Kauper put it. In the 1990s, attacks came not only from those, inside its own ranks, who praising low prices and economic efficiency as an antitrust goal considered that it did not take sufficiently into account realistic analysis of markets, notably the acquisition and results of market power, but also from those who valued the inclusion of social and political values in antitrust enforcement. The cyclical controversy on the goals of antitrust continued over the years following the late 1990s and well into the 21st century, where a common understanding that antitrust enforcement may have been not sufficiently rigorous led to an emphasis, by the Biden Administration, on a stronger antitrust enforcement.

As regards vertical agreements, they resist well U.S. antitrust laws scrutiny. They are in general considered as pro-competitive. The evolution of the case law since the 1977 *Continental T.V., Inc.* allows us to conclude that vertical non-price restrictions, including exclusive distribution, are not per se illegal but can be questioned if anticompetitive effects are shown, notably if interbrand competition is substantially lessened or if market power is found causing a restraint of trade in the relevant market.

Bibliography

Bork, R. H., *The Antitrust Paradox – A Policy at War with Itself*, Basic Books, Inc. 1978

Ibañez Colomo, P., Territorial restrictions in EU competition law: from Consten- Grundig to Ping and Pay-TV, in Adina Claici and Denis Waelbroeck (eds), *Vertical Restraints in The Digital Economy: Vertical Block Exemption Regulation Reform and the Future of Distribution* (Kluwer 2021)

Kauper, T., *The Goals of United States Antitrust Policy – The Current Debate, in Competition Policy: German and American Experience – a Symposium*, 408 (1980)

Solomon, L. M. and Robert D. Joffe, Exclusive Distribution and Antitrust (1984), 53 *Fordham Law Review* 491

Sullivan, L., Antitrust, Microeconomics and Politics: Reflections on Some Recent Relationships, in *The Economics of firm Size, Market Structure and Social Performance*, 9 (1980)

Whish, R. and Bailey, D., *Competition Law* (10th ed., Oxford University Press 2021)

See also

Block exemption (Regulation), Distribution agreement, Hardcore restrictions, Passive sales, Vertical restraints, Selective distribution

E

EXCLUSIVE PURCHASING AGREEMENT

María LUISA ILHARREBORDE ILLANES
University of California, Berkeley

Definition

An exclusive purchasing agreement is a contract through which a buyer – commonly a distributor – promises to buy all or specific goods and services only from a particular seller, being prohibited to buy those products from any other competitor (*inter-brand competition restriction*) during the exclusivity period. Most of these agreements would lead to a "single-branding" strategy, in which a company targets a specific market sector with each of its brands. Antitrust concerns about these vertical agreements are related to the possibility of affecting substantially inter-branding competition in the relevant market.

Commentary

According to TFEU, agreements that have as the object or effect to restrict competition are prohibited. Abuse of a dominant position is also prohibited. The EU case law has developed a doctrine (*Delimitis* test) on abuse of dominant position which started with *Delimitis v Henninger Bräu AG* (1991). In this case, there was a brew supply contract between Henninger Brau AG and Mr. Delimitis, which stipulated that Mr. Delimitis, to maintain the tenure of the tavern, must buy a certain amount of beer and soft drinks each year from the brewery. There was a preliminary request before the ECJ about the interpretation of Art 101 TFEU and its compatibility with the referred agreement. The Court analysis aimed to determine the existence of possible cumulative foreclosure effects, due to the combination of this agreement with others similar in the same relevant market. The Court judgment was based on the consideration of three components: (1) market shares of the contracting parties and proportion of outlets tied to the manufacturer, (2) the duration of the agreement, and (3) other factors related to barriers to entry on the relevant market. The doctrine of *Delimitis* has been applied in several following cases by the CFI (currently, the General Court). In *Langnese* (1995), the Court upheld the decision of the Commission, considering that the agreement between the parties infringed the Article 85(1) of the EEC Treaty, now Art. 101 TFEU, based on the determination of the cumulative effects of the network of similar agreements – for which the CFI considered the rate of outlets tied to the other fundamental ice-cream producer in Germany, which was more than 10% –. Another case that continued the application of the *Delimitis* test was *Van der Bergh Foods* (1998). Through this case, it is possible to point out that when the level of entry barrier is high, the importance of the contract duration is reduced. In other words, when there is a significant participant in the network involved in the agreement, the cumulative effect of the exclusivity contract becomes the main factor to analyze the legality of the agreement.

In general terms, exclusive contracts between manufacturers and suppliers are lawful in the U.S. legal system. Nevertheless, exclusive purchasing agreements have the potential to violate the prescriptions of Section 2 of the U.S. Sherman Act 1980 – which prohibits the acquisition or maintenance of monopoly power or the attempts to monopolize the relevant market through improper ways, such as exclusionary conducts – and Section 5 of the FTC Act – which prohibits "unfair or deceptive acts or practices in or affecting commerce"–, when a monopolist firm through an exclusive contract prevents the entry of new competitors for sales, blocking the smaller rivals. Therefore, to violate Section 2 of the Sherman Act the agreement must harm consumers. For example, in the case *In the Matter of McWane, Inc, and Star Pipe Products, Ltd.*, the FTC actioned against McWane Inc, due to it unlawfully maintained its monopoly in the domestic pipe fittings market by the implementation of an exclusive dealing policy called "Full Support Program", as a response to Star's forthcoming entry in the market. Before Star entered into the market in 2009, McWane was the only manufacturer of domestic fittings and by 2010 Star rapidly gained a 5% market share. The policy implemented by McWane was considered a threat for the distributors who would not be able to buy any more domestic fittings from McWane if they purchased those items from McWane's competitor, Star. As a result of the implementation of the Full Support Program, several distributors decided to cancel orders or to not purchase domestic fittings from Star. The FTC concluded that the Full Support Program harmed competition and lacked offsetting procompetitive benefits for the consumers, violating Section 5 of the FTC Act, based on: (1) McWane possessed monopoly power in the relevant market (ductile iron pipe fittings) and (2) McWane's Full Support Program McWane produced the maintenance of that power illegally. Furthermore, the Commission's Final Order prohibited McWane to require exclusivity from its customers, which was upheld by the Eleventh Circuit. Considering this case, it is possible to conclude that although exclusive purchasing agreements are not unlawful in themselves, in the case of monopolist firms abusing their dominant situation in the market, they can impose obligations and conditions downstream that significantly reduce the competition and prevent the entry of new competitors. The case *United States of America, Appellant, v. Dentsply International, Inc* (2005), contains an interesting analysis in which the U.S. Court of Appeals for the Third Circuit concluded that the monopolist manufacturer-supplier of dental supplies, Dentsply, violated Section 2 of the Sherman Act. Dentsply enjoyed a dominant position in the relevant market of sale of prefabricated artificial teeth in the U.S., with a 75% to 80% market share on a revenue basis. In 1993 this manufacturer adopted an exclusive dealing agreement called Dealer Criterion 6 which the Third Court considered anti-competitive, due to "(…) Dealer Criterion 6 has a significant effect in preserving Dentsply's monopoly. It helps keep sales of competing teeth below the critical level necessary for any rival to pose a real threat to Dentsply's market share. As such, Dealer Criterion 6 is a solid pillar of harm to competition" (399 F.3d at 191). Regarding the legality of exclusive purchasing agreements, the Third Court affirmed that they are not illegal *per se* and the prerequisites that must be met are: (1) "a finding that monopoly power exists" and (2) "the exclusionary conduct must have anti-competitive effect" (399 F.3d at 187). In conclusion, through the application of Dealer Criterion 6, Dentsply was able to exclude rivals from the dealer's network.

The U.S. courts have adopted for the analysis of these cases the effects analysis and the rule of reason. The harm experienced by consumers in the cited cases from the U.S. (the anti-competitive effects) is related to the acquisition or maintenance of monopolist power which impeded and prevented the entry of more competition into the market, through exclusive contracts, excluding the possibility to benefit the society from lower prices and better goods and services.

In conclusion, through the cases previously analysed, it is possible to distinguish a slight difference between the EU and the U.S. regulation of exclusive purchasing agreements to consider them anticompetitive. On the one hand, Article 102 TFEU requires a "dominant position", on the other hand, Section 2 of the Sherman Act refers to the conduct of any competitor who has the effect of "monopolization".

Bibliography

AREEDA, P. and HOVENKAMP, H., *Antitrust Law: An Analysis of Antitrust Principles and their Application*. Tercera. Vol. 3. 14 vols. Nueva York: Wolters Kluwer Law and Business, 2008

BAKER, J., Exclusion as a Core Competition Concern, *Antitrust Law Journal* 78, nº 3 (2013):527-89

ELHAUGE, E., Defining Better Monopolization Standards, *Standford Law Review* 56 (Noviembre 2003): 253-344

INNES, R. and SEXTON, R., Strategic Buyers and Exclusionary Contracts, *The American Economic Review* 84, nº 3 (1994): 566-84

MONTAG, F. and GOYDER, J., Exclusive dealing: Presumptions and bright lines, December 2013, *Concurrences* N° 4-2013, Art. N° 58815

See also

Abuse of dominant position, Distribution agreement, Exclusivity clause, Single branding, Vertical agreement

E

EXCLUSIVE RIGHT (ART. 106 TFEU)

Andreas HEINEMANN
University of Zurich

■ Definition

According to Article 106 TFEU, the Member States of the EU have to respect the treaty rules with respect to *public undertakings* and to undertakings with special or exclusive rights. According to the Transparency Directive 2006/111/EC, the term "exclusive rights" means "rights that are granted by a Member State to one undertaking through any legislative, regulatory or administrative instrument, reserving it the right to provide a service or undertake an activity within a given geographical area". The most prominent example for undertakings with exclusive rights are state monopolies. Thus, Article 106 TFEU is the central norm on the legality of state monopolies in the EU.

■ Commentary

When the European Communities were founded in the 1950s, there were major differences between the six founding countries regarding the role of the state in the economy. The Member States with a modest public sector were afraid that the powerful public undertakings of the more government-oriented countries would crowd out their smaller private enterprises and asked for strict control. The more government-oriented countries, on the other hand, wanted to maintain the operating range of their public undertakings. In the final phase of the treaty negotiations, a compromise was found. A separate article on the public sector (today Article 106 TFEU) contained two messages that accommodated both sides: The first paragraph integrates the public sector in the system of the European treaties by subjecting public undertakings and state monopolies to the competition rules and to all other requirements of the European treaties. The second paragraph, on the other hand, provides an exception for services of general economic interest (SGEI). On an institutional level, the third paragraph grants the European Commission special powers: With respect to the economic activities of the state, the Commission cannot only take decisions but also adopt directives, a competence that is normally reserved for the Council and the Parliament of the EU.

The wording of Article 106 TFEU was deliberately kept obscure to allow both sides to find their point of view. This had an impact on the application of the provision: For a long time, Article 106 TFEU remained dead letter. The numerous state monopolies, for example in energy, transport and telecommunications, were not touched. Starting in the late 1970s, a debate on deregulation and privatization was initiated. The insight gained ground that state monopolies were responsible for high welfare losses. The discussion also left its mark on the law. With respect to Article 106 TFEU, *John Temple Lang* asked the crucial question in 1984: "How Far May a State Establish Monopolies and Privileged Enterprises and Protect Them from Normal Competition?"

Based on these developments, the European Commission launched what has been called the "public turn" of European competition policy (*David J. Gerber*). In the mid-1980s, the European Commission discovered (the precursor provision of) Article 106 TFEU and broke up state monopolies, pioneering in telecommunications. The European Commission started with a small segment, i.e. terminal equipment like for example telephone sets. In a directive from 1988 (Directive 88/301/EEC on competition in the markets in telecommunications terminal equipment), the European Commission obliged the Member States to withdraw all special or exclusive rights granted to certain undertakings for these devices. Until then, consumers in many Member States were limited to buying the telephone sets of the monopolist in their respective country. This excluded competition by domestic firms as well as imports of telephone sets from other Member States. The goal of the European Commission was to allow consumers choosing the equipment best suiting their needs, regardless of its origin. In 1991, the European Court of Justice confirmed the legality of the terminal equipment directive (Case 202/88). The Court found a violation of the rules on the free movement of goods. On the one hand, there is a measure having an effect equivalent to a quantitative restriction because exclusive importing and marketing rights make it impossible for competitors from other Member States to sell their telephones to consumers. On the other hand, a monopolist is not able to offer the entire range of telephones available on the market. All this reduces trade between the Member States, and a justification is not apparent since technical security can be guaranteed in other ways.

The judgment of the European Court of Justice in the terminal equipment case is of paramount importance for exclusive rights in the European Union. The Court has considerably restricted the Member States' discretion to establish state *monopolies*. The fact that Article 106 paragraph 1 mentions "exclusive rights" does not mean that they are necessarily compatible with the European treaties. The question of their legality rather depends on the provisions to which this article refers. On the one hand, the competition rules are expressly mentioned. The European Court of Justice has found an *abuse of a dominant position* if the state monopoly is unable to meet the demand for the monopoly good in terms of quantity, quality or innovation (Cases C-41/90 and C-179/90), or if there is "abusive extension', for example if a monopoly for the telephone network is extended to the market in telecommunications services (Joined Cases C-271/90, C-281/90 and C-289/90). On the other hand, the free movement rules, in particular on goods and services, require the dismantling of state monopolies if no objective justification applies.

On this basis, the European Commission and the European Courts have declared exclusive rights in favour of state monopolies illegal, not only in telecommunications, but also for example in the field of postal services, television, employment services, dockworkers and ambulances. By contrast, with respect to the energy markets, the European Commission has not made use of Article 106 TFEU, but has based its unbundling and liberalization measures on rules involving the Council and the Parliament of the EU (today Article 194 TFEU).

More recently, a swinging back of the pendulum can be observed. Globalization critics and privatization sceptics have stressed the importance of the public sector. Against this backdrop, the original rationale of Article 106 TFEU must be recalled. On the one hand, exclusive rights must not violate competition law and the free movement rules. On the other hand, there is an exception for *services of general economic interest* whose importance is confirmed by other treaty articles (e.g. Article 14 TFEU as well as Article 36 Charter of Fundamental Rights of the European Union) and explained in communications of the European Commission. Thus, European law respects different traditions in the Member States and a diversity of views on public service. However, the granting of exclusive rights is subject to a justification requirement. If state monopolies are established, they must pursue legitimate goals, be capable of fulfilling their task and proportionate. In this sense, Article 106 TFEU is the basic norm for the relationship between the state and the market in the European Union. It differs considerably from the legal situation in the U.S. where antitrust law avoids application to state behaviour ("state action doctrine').

Bibliography

Charbit, N., *Le droit de la concurrence et le secteur public*, Paris 2002

Gerard, D., "EU Competition Policy after Lisbon: Time to Review the 'State Action Doctrine'?" (2010) 1 *Journal of European Competition Law & Practice* 202-210

Gerber, D. J., "The Transformation of European Community Competition Law?" (1994) 35 *Harvard International Law Journal* 97-147

Ibáñez Colomo, P., "Will Article 106 TFEU Case Law Transform EU Competition Law?" (2022) 13 *Journal of European Competition Law & Practice* 385-386

Temple Lang, J., "Community Antitrust Law And Government Measures Relating To Public And Privileged Enterprises: Article 90 EEC Treaty', in: *Annual Proceedings of the Fordham Corporate Law Institute* 1984, New York 1985, 543-581

See also

Monopoly, Public undertaking, Services of general economic interest (SGIE)

E

EXCLUSIVITY CLAUSE

Xolani NYALI
Bowmans

■ Definition

Exclusivity clauses in commercial agreements impose a restraint on a contracting party, limiting that party's freedom to choose the products and/or services it may offer; the customer categories it is permitted to serve; the sales channels to use; or the geographic regions in which it is permitted to operate. Exclusivity agreements are not automatically illegal in South Africa, and where such agreements are proven to have an anti-competitive effect, justifications may be entered proving that technological, efficiency or other pro-competitive gains arising from that agreement outweigh the anti-competitive effects.

■ Commentary

Exclusivity clauses can be assessed either under a per se, effects-based or abuse of dominance framework.

Competition regulators around the world take different approaches to the treatment of exclusivity clauses. In some jurisdictions, exclusivity clauses (also referred to as "exclusive dealing") with the ultimate objective of excluding other sales channels, e.g. online sales, through input foreclosure; and/or, discriminatory practices are per se unlawful. However, other jurisdictions adopt an effects-based approach by assessing whether the impact of the restriction is detrimental on competition using three main theories of harm, viz reducing intra-brand competition; softening inter-brand competition; or foreclosing existing or potential competition. Finally, some jurisdictions also apply the abuse of dominance framework by assessing whether: the one contracting party has market power in the upstream market according to the leveraging theory (i.e. whether manufacturers are leveraging their position in the upstream market to give themselves advantages over their rivals in the downstream market); the intent behind the restriction in the downstream markets; and the effects of the conduct.

In regional trade blocs like the Common Market for Eastern & Southern Africa or the European Union, a fourth theory of harm may be applicable: restrictions may partition national markets according to national borders and frustrate the objective of achieving an integrated single market for the benefit of consumers.

It is typically the case that the jurisdictions with an effects-based framework also assess exclusivity clauses under an abuse of dominance framework, and the theories of harm may be interchangeable.

For example, in South Africa exclusivity clauses are typically assessed in terms of the vertical restraints provisions (section 5(1)) and under the abuse of dominance provisions (sections 8 and 9) of the Competition Act, 89 of 1998 (as amended) (the Competition Act).

Section 5(1) of the Competition Act states that an "agreement between parties in a vertical relationship is prohibited if it has the effect of substantially preventing or lessening competition in a market, unless a party to the agreement can prove that any technological, efficiency or other pro-competitive, gain resulting from that agreement outweighs that effect". This contemplates what is referred to as a "rule-of-reason" or effect-based assessment related to competition effects, rather than a per se consideration. To make a successful claim that a restrictive vertical practice has arisen, the Competition Commission (the Commission) or a complainant (as the case may be) would need to demonstrate that the vertical agreement substantially prevents or lessens competition in a market by foreclosing competition in a significant share of a market and/or by enhancing the market power of the firm in the market. In other words, it would need to be demonstrated that the agreement has a material exclusionary effect. An exclusionary act is viewed as having an anticompetitive effect if it results in actual harm to consumer welfare or if the exclusionary act has potential to limit access significantly or substantially or create barriers to a particular market (Competition Commission v South African Airways). Such an anti-competitive effect, (to the extent that it could be demonstrated), could be countered by showing technological, efficiency or other co-competitive gains that outweigh that effect.

Where either party to an exclusive agreement is dominant in terms of the Competition Act, the abuse of dominance provisions in terms of section 8 of the Competition Act are also relevant. A firm is generally assumed to be dominant when it holds a 35% share of a relevant market. A firm with less than a 35% share can also be dominant but then the Commission or a complainant (whichever applicable) would need to prove that the firm has "market power'. Market power is nebulously defined in the Competition Act as the power of a firm to control prices, to exclude competition or to behave to an appreciable extent independently of its competitors, customers or suppliers. In the context of exclusivity, there are specific statutory abuses of dominance which are potentially relevant, namely, that a dominant firm may not engage in an exclusionary act if the anti-competitive effect of that act outweighs its technological, efficiency or other pro-competitive gain. An exclusionary act is defined as "an act that impedes or prevents a firm from entering into, participating in or expanding within a market". Further, a dominant firm may not require or induce a supplier or customer not to deal with a competitor unless the dominant firm can show technological, efficiency or other pro-competitive gains which outweigh the anti-competitive effects of its act. This also applies in the case of price discrimination (section 9 of the Competition Act).

Therefore, an exclusivity clause that reduces a competitor's ability to sell their goods and service thus causing a reduction of supply and/ or results in an increase in price for a particular product market is anticompetitive. If a firm is accused of engaging in an exclusionary act and the allegation is prima facie established, it bears the onus of proving that such act was efficient in that it benefited the market and/or benefited consumers more than it than harmed them. See Computicket (Pty) Ltd v Competition Commission of South Africa (170/CAC/Feb19) [2019] ZACAC 4.

In Competition Commission of South Africa v Uniplate Group (Pty) Ltd (CR188Nov15), the Competition Tribunal of South Africa (Tribunal) had to determine whether, as alleged by the Commission, an exclusivity clause by a Uniplate (as a dominant firm in the manufacturing of embossing machines and number plate blanks) requiring its customers to purchase all their number plate blank requirements "solely and exclusively" from the firm, irrespective of the type of machine being bought when acquiring a Uniplate embossing machine, was anti-competitive. The Commission alleged that Uniplate's exclusive supply agreements had resulted:

- in the foreclosure of the market to firms competing for the manufacture of number plate blanks. These rivals were unable to sell number plate blanks to embossers who signed Uniplate's exclusive supply agreements; and
- harm to embossers as these exclusive supply agreements deprived them of a choice to purchase their number plate blank requirements from competing manufacturers of blanks often at a cheaper price.

Given that Uniplate is the largest manufacturer of number plate blanks in the country, the Commission was of the view that Uniplate had abused its dominance in the market through the use of these exclusive supply agreements.

In its defense, Uniplate argued that the technological, efficiency and other co-competitive gains of the clause outweighed its anti-competitive effects on the basis that the exclusionary conduct allowed for the products to be sold at a reduced price; prevented free riding; ensured that the products were of requisite quality and adhered to regulations; and enabled Uniplate to offer free servicing and maintenance to its customers. The Tribunal found that the exclusivity clauses foreclosed the market and raised barriers to entry, and that the efficiency arguments did not outweigh the anti-competitive effects of the exclusivity clauses. Uniplate appealed to the Competition Appeal Court, which disagreed with the Tribunal, holding that there was insufficient proof of foreclosure to the market as Uniplate's main rival had grown during this time and competed effectively. Moreover, the available evidence did not prove that smaller firms had been foreclosed by Uniplate's allegedly exclusionary conduct. See Uniplate Group (Pty) Ltd v Competition Commission of South Africa [2020] 1 CPLR 136 (CAC).

It is yet to be determined whether exclusivity clauses in lease agreements wherein a landlord undertakes to not lease property to a competitor of the lessee constitute an "exclusionary act" in terms of either section 5(1) or section 8 the Competition Act, albeit these clauses are frowned upon by South African competition regulators. See Competition Commission v Shoprite Checkers (Pty) Ltd [2020] 2 CPLR 675 (CT).

Bibliography

Sutherland P. and Kemp K., *Competition Law of South Africa*, Issue 13 (2010), LexisNexis

International Competition Network Unilateral Conduct Working Group; Vertical Restraints Multi Year Project, 2016-2019 (April 2019)

The COMESA Guidelines on Restrictive Business Practices, 2019

See also

Abuse of dominant position, Discriminatory practices, Exclusive purchasing agreement

E

EXHAUSTION

Irene CALBOLI
Texas A&M University

■ Definition

The principle of IP exhaustion limits the right of IP holders to control the distribution of their products after their first sale. It allows distributors, retailers, second-hand dealers, and consumers to display, advertise, and resell the products they lawfully purchased without the IP holders' consent. As IP rights in general, exhaustion is based on territoriality and applies to the circulation of products within the national market where they were first sold. On the other hand, there is no international consensus regarding the imports of products lawfully sold in another jurisdiction. These "parallel imports" are treated as either lawful or infringing goods depending on the approach adopted by the importing countries.

■ Commentary

The principle of IP exhaustion was developed in the nineteenth century to limit IP holders from controlling the distribution, and price, of their products after their first lawful sale. To date, the application of this principle is generally straightforward with respect to physical goods sold nationally so long as their quality has not been altered. Less straightforward is the exhaustion of digital goods and self-replicating products (such as plants and seeds), which rely on products' duplication instead of their transfer, and the exhaustion of IP-protected parts and ingredients of complex products. However, a large part of the debate on the topic has focused on parallel imports – unauthorized imports of genuine goods from foreign countries. This short contribution focuses on this debate and refers to the EU and U.S. as examples.

Generally, IP holders oppose parallel imports because of the concerns against the arbitrage of their products from low-cost to high-cost jurisdictions. IP holders are interested in free trade and international IP harmonization to reduce costs as well as simplify IP protection across jurisdictions, but they oppose parallel imports because of the competition these imports create with their own domestic distribution networks. Supporters of parallel imports have noted that the international IP system seeks to eliminate barriers to trade, yet the current system essentially allows IP holders to use IP rights anticompetitively and practice price discrimination across national markets.

A specific mention to the lack of agreement in this respect is included in Article 6 of the Agreement on Trade Related Aspects to Intellectual Property Right (TRIPS Agreement), which states "nothing in this Agreement shall be used to address the issue of the exhaustion of intellectual property rights." Accordingly, the choice of domestic exhaustion regimes depends on desirable economic outcomes based on specific economic and trade-related factors, the size of national markets, and the level of national development.

In particular, countries follow one of three systems today: national, regional, or international exhaustion. Under the principle of *national* exhaustion, IP rights are exhausted after the first sale of the products, but only if this sale occurs in the national territory. This system is the least friendly to international trade and permits IP holders to stop parallel imports at the border or legitimately seize the (genuine) products after importation as infringements. Under the principle of *international* exhaustion, IP holders' right to control the further distribution of the products exhaust after the first sale regardless of the country where this first sale has occurred. Under this system, parallel imports are considered lawful in the country of importation, even though the country from which the goods are imported may apply a different system. Finally, the principle of *regional* exhaustion is a compromise between national and international exhaustion. Under this system, the rights of IP holders are exhausted after the first sale of the products, but only if the sale has occurred in one of the member countries of a regional organizations. Under this system, the import of products originating from countries from outside the region remains unlawful and can be stopped as infringement. Regional exhaustion currently applies in the European Union (EU as extended to the European Economic Area, EEA) and the *Organization Africaine pour la Propriete Intellectuelle* (OAPI).

Notably, since the signing of the EEC Treaty in 1957, the EU's primary objective is the creation of an internal market. Initially, the CJEU turned to Article 81 and 82, the Treaty's competition provisions, and later to Articles 34 and 36, the internal market provisions, to promote the free movement of goods, including IP exhaustion. Today, these provisions apply to the exhaustion of patented goods whereas specific Directives implemented the principle of exhaustion for trademarks and copyrights. In 1989, the Trademark Directive, today Directive 2015/2436, codified the principle of Community-wide exhaustion. In 1994, the Community Trademark Regulation, today replaced by EU Trademark

Regulation 2017/1001, repeated this principle. In the 1990s, the CJEU issues several decisions to confirm that Community/EEA-wide exhaustion was the only system applicable and not a minimum standard. Under EU law, IP holders can still invoke selected "legitimate reasons" as exceptions to trademark exhaustion, notably in instances that could lead to consumer confusion or unfair detriment to the reputation of a mark. Similarly, in 2001, the "InfoSociety Directive" included the principle of Community-wide exhaustion. Directive 2006/115/EC on rental rights, lending rights, and certain rights related to copyright, repeated the same provision with respect to the right of distribution of performers, phonogram producers, producers of the first fixations of films, and broadcasting organisations.

On the other hand, one of the most notable examples of international IP exhaustion today is the U.S. Historically, the U.S. allowed parallel imports of trademarked goods when the marks shared a common business origin. The only exception is when the products "differ materially" from the goods sold domestically, even though the U.S. Customs Service Regulations allows the imports of materially different products so long as importers properly label the goods to avoid confusion. Until recently, however, the U.S. practice national exhaustion for copyrighted and patented products. This changed in the past decade due to two landmark decisions of the Supreme Court. In 2013, *Kirtsaeng v. John Wiley & Sons, Inc.* clarified the language of the 1976 U.S. Copyright Act, which states, on one side, that copyright owners cannot control the transfer of copyrighted works "lawfully made under this title" after their first sale; and on the other side, that "the importation into the United States" of a copyrighted work acquired outside "without the authority of the [copyright] owner" is "an infringement of the exclusive right [of] distribut[ion]." In particular, *Kirtsaeng* clarified that exhaustion applies equally to products "lawfully made" in the U.S. and in foreign countries. Similarly, the position on patent exhaustion was changed in favor of international exhaustion in 2017 by *Impression Products v. Lexmark*. Since the U.S. Patent Act does not elaborate on the geographical extent of the first sale of a patented process, or a product embodying patented process, U.S. courts had adopted the position that the sale of an article in a foreign country did not exhaust the U.S. patent. The Supreme Court reversed this position, even though the Court did not exclude that contractual restrictions could still prevent parallel imports.

In conclusion, the application of the principle of exhaustion continues to vary amongst jurisdictions today, and changes from one system to another are not uncommon both through the implementation of domestic legislation and case law. No less relevant, national positions towards contractual restrictions preventing resale (commonly included in distribution agreements) also vary, which adds uncertainty to the admissibility of parallel imports domestically.

Bibliography

BEIER, F.-K., Industrial Property and the Free Movement of Goods in the Internal European Market, 21(4) *I.I.C.* 131 (1990)

CALBOLI, I., The Intricate Relationship Between Intellectual Property Exhaustion and Free Movement of Goods in Regional Organizations: Comparing the EU/EEA, NAFTA, and ASEAN, 9(1) *Queen Mary J. of Intell. Prop.* 22 (2019)

CHIAPPETTA, V., The Desirability of Agreeing to Disagree: The WTO, TRIPS, International IPR Exhaustion and a Few Other Things, 21 *Mich. J. Int'l L.* 333 (2000)

COTTIER, T., The Exhaustion of Intellectual Property Rights – A Fresh Look, 39(7) *I.I.C.* 755 (2008)

GHOSH, S. and CALBOLI, I., *Exhausting Intellectual Property Rights: A Comparative Law and Policy Analysis* (2018)

See also

Intellectual property right, Parallel imports (parallel trade)

E

EXTRA-TERRITORIALITY

Koren W. WONG-ERVIN
Jones Day

Melanie KISER
LinkedIn

■ Definition

Extraterritorial reach of competition laws refers to the extent to which jurisdictions are permitted to apply their domestic laws to conduct that occurs outside their jurisdiction, including the reach of remedies (i.e., prohibitions or requirements on foreign conduct or with respect to foreign assets).

■ Commentary

Most major jurisdictions apply some sort of effects test comparable to that specified in the U.S. Foreign Trade Antitrust Improvements Act (FTAIA), which provides that foreign conduct is outside the scope of the Sherman Act (which governs monopolization and restraints of trade) unless it: (1) sufficiently affects American commerce, i.e., "has a direct, substantial, and reasonably foreseeable effect" on American domestic, import, or (certain) export commerce; and (2) has an effect of the kind the Sherman Act considers harmful, i.e., the effect must give rise to a Sherman Act claim. Section 5(a)(3) of the Federal Trade Commission (FTC) Act (which governs "unfair methods of competition") closely parallels the FTAIA. Although the FTAIA does not address the reach of the Clayton Act (which primarily governs mergers and acquisitions), the Department of Justice (DOJ) and FTC have said they apply the same principles set forth in the FTAIA and case law interpreting the FTAIA. For a summary of the approaches taken in Brazil, Canada, China, India, Japan, Korea, and Taiwan, see Heimert & Wong-Ervin.

The leading case in the United States is the Supreme Court's 2004 decision in *F. Hoffman-La Roche Ltd. v. Empagran S.A.*, which involved price fixing by vitamin sellers in other countries that led to higher prices both in the United States and, independently, in other countries such as Ecuador and Ukraine. The Court held that a purchaser in the United States could bring a Sherman Act claim under the FTAIA based on domestic injury, but purchasers in other countries could not bring claims based on foreign harm arising from foreign conduct. This decision was reached, in part, because principles of comity recognize that foreign sovereigns have a legitimate interest in regulating their own commercial affairs.

In *Motorola Mobility LLC v. AU Optronics Corp.* (2015), the U.S. Court of Appeals for the Seventh Circuit held that purchases by a U.S. company's foreign subsidiaries of price-fixed goods that were incorporated into products subsequently shipped to the U.S. parent did not give rise to damages claims under the Sherman Act. The court's analysis was largely rooted in the fact that Motorola purposefully established subsidiaries in foreign countries to obtain favorable tax treatment. This tax-driven choice of corporate domicile carried with it access to whatever remedies the foreign countries offered (or did not offer) for supposed wrongs. In addition, although Motorola ultimately received products incorporating the price-fixed goods in the United States, it could not recover on this basis due to the indirect purchaser doctrine, "which forbids a customer of the purchaser who paid a cartel price to sue the cartelist, even if his seller – the direct purchaser from the cartelist – passed on to him some or even all of the cartel's elevated price."

The European Union applies either a "qualified effects" test (reasonably "foreseeable" of having "immediate and substantial" effects in the European Union) or an "implementation" test (focusing on where the conduct is implemented, rather than the location of the undertaking). The Court of Justice of the European Union in its *Intel decision (2017)* clarified that the two tests pursue the "same objective, namely preventing conduct which, while not adopted within the EU, has anticompetitive effects liable to have an impact on the EU market."

In *Intel*, the court upheld jurisdiction of EU institutions over conduct by an American company (Intel) with respect to, *inter alia*, chip sales to a Chinese company (Lenovo) in China, when the conduct was alleged to have harmed another American company (Advanced Micro Devices or AMD). As it concerned sales of chips to Lenovo, only a few thousand of the finished products (computers assembled by Lenovo in China) were implicated (i.e., they allegedly would potentially have included an AMD chip had Intel not induced the breach of contract), and it was unclear if and how many reached the European Economic Area (EEA). In determining whether Intel's conduct was "capable" of having a "substantial, immediate and foreseeable effect" within the EEA, the court held that it was sufficient to consider the "probable effects" of the conduct on competition and that "Intel's conduct vis-à-vis Lenovo formed part of an overall strategy aimed at foreclosing AMD's access to the most important sales channels."

In addition to applying some sort of effects test, most major jurisdictions also take into consideration comity concerns, both in deciding whether to apply domestic laws to foreign conduct and whether to impose extra-jurisdictional remedies. As the DOJ and FTC explained in their 2017 International Guidelines, comity refers to the "broad concept of respect among co-equal sovereign nations and plays a role in determining "the recognition which one nation allows within its territory to the legislative, executive or judicial acts of another nation.'"

The DOJ and FTC assess comity by considering the (1) existence of a purpose to affect or an actual effect on U.S. commerce, (2) significance and foreseeability of the effects on the United States, (3) degree of conflict with the foreign jurisdiction's law or articulated policy, (4) extent to which the enforcement activities or remedies of another jurisdiction may be affected, and (5) effectiveness of foreign enforcement compared to U.S. enforcement. U.S. courts have considered additional factors, including the parties' nationalities or allegiances and principal places of business, the possible effects of extraterritorial jurisdiction upon foreign relations, and whether an order for relief would be acceptable in the United States if the roles were reversed.

With respect to remedies, as the DOJ and FTC explained in a 2017 OECD Note, their "general practice is to seek an effective remedy that is restricted to the United States, which the Agencies believe is the best approach," considering broader remedies "[o]nly when a domestic remedy cannot effectively redress the harm or threatened harm to U.S. commerce or consumers." In cases involving intellectual property, "the Agencies generally rely on a domestic-only licensing remedy because the license can be tailored to permit use of the intellectual property only in the domestic markets affected by the conduct. However, in rare cases, when a broader license may be necessary to provide effective relief, the Antitrust Agencies seek a remedy that is no broader than necessary."

This is consistent with the approaches taken by the European Union and China. For example, in the European Commission's 2014 settlement with Samsung and separate decision against Motorola Mobility , the Commission limited its remedy to conduct occurring in the EEA, and only on patents granted in the EEA. Likewise, China's 2015 penalty decision against Qualcomm was limited to remedies on conduct occurring within China and related to Chinese patents. In contrast, is the highly controversial 2016 decision by the Korea Fair Trade Commission to impose a global licensing remedy on Qualcomm Incorporated. The remedies included prohibitions and requirements on patents not registered or enforceable in Korea.

Bibliography

LIPSKY JR., A. B. and WILMOT, K., The Foreign Trade Antitrust Improvements Act: Did Arbaugh Erase Decades of Consensus Building? (Aug. 2013)

WONG-ERVIN, K. and HEIMERT, A., Extraterritoriality: Approaches Around the World and Model Analysis, *Eleanor Fox Liber Amicorum*, Concurrences 2021

WONG-ERVIN, K., BRUCE H. KOBAYASHI, B. H., WRIGHT, J. D. and GINSBURG, D. H., Extra-Jurisdictional Remedies Involving Patent Licensing (Dec. 14, 2016)

OECD Roundtable on the Extraterritorial Reach of Competition Remedies (Dec. 5, 2017)

U.S. Dep't Of Justice & Fed. Trade Comm'n, Antitrust Guidelines For International Enforcement And Cooperation (Jan. 13, 2017)

See also

Applicable law, Effects doctrine

F

FAILING FIRM DEFENCE

Gwendolyn COOLEY
Wisconsin Department of Justice

Brian YOST
Illinois Attorney General's Office

■ Definition

Under the failing firm defence, a firm may make an otherwise anticompetitive acquisition if financial issues would force the acquiree out of the market and no alternative acquiror exists. The threshold likelihood of (1) business failure, (2) assets exiting a market, and (3) bankruptcy vary by jurisdiction. Essentially, the defence reflects an understanding that a firm's failure and its assets' exit from the market would harm competition more than an ostensibly anticompetitive merger. Both the United States and European Union recognize this defence with substantially similar elements (varying somewhat in application).

■ Commentary

U.S. law prohibits mergers and acquisitions whose effect "may be substantially to lessen competition, or to tend to create a monopoly." Clayton Act Section 7, 15 U.S.C. § 18. But a *prima facie* unlawful merger may occur where (1) the acquiree has "resources so depleted and the prospect of rehabilitation so remote that "it face[s] the grave probability of a business failure,'" there is (2) "'no other prospective purchaser,'" and – in some cases – (3) the firm's "prospects of reorganization" under the bankruptcy laws "would have had to be dim or nonexistent." (*Citizen Pub. Co. v. United States*, 394 U.S. 131, 136-38 (1940) (quoting *Int'l Shoe Co. v. FTC*, 280 U.S. 291, 302-03 (1930))). Some U.S. courts have not required the third element. Compare *U.S. Steel Corp. v. FTC*, 426 F.2d 592, 608-09 (6th Cir. 1970) (concluding that *Citizen* requires reorganization element), with *United States v. Black & Decker Mfg. Co.*, 430 F. Supp. 729, 778 (D. Md. 1976) (concluding the opposite). The burden of proof for this defence rests with the merging parties. (*Citizen*, 394 U.S. 138-39).

The United States' Horizontal Merger Guidelines endorses a less rigorous version of this defence, (1) requiring that the failing firm "be unable to meet its financial obligations in the near future" – unlike the showing of insolvency that many U.S. courts require – and (2) characterizing the lack of an alternative purchase element as met when the firm proves it "made unsuccessful good-faith efforts to elicit reasonable alternative offers" – i.e., offers exceeding the failing firm's liquidation value. (U.S. Dep't of Justice & U.S. Fed. Trade Comm'n, Horizontal Merger Guidelines § 11 (2010)). The doctrine is "a 'lesser of two evils' approach, in which the possible threat to competition resulting from an acquisition is deemed preferable to the adverse impact on competition and other losses if the company goes out of business." (*United States v. Gen. Dynamics Corp.*, 415 U.S. 486, 507 (1974)).

The European Commission also recognizes the failing firm defence. Under the European Council Merger Regulation (Council Regulation (EC) No 139/2004), an "otherwise problematic merger" may proceed if:

- First, the allegedly failing firm would in the near future be forced out of the market because of financial difficulties if not taken over by another undertaking…
- Second, there is no less anti-competitive alternative purchase than the notified merger…
- Third, in the absence of a merger, the assets of the failing firm would inevitably exit the market…

(Commission Decision of October 9, 2013 in Case M.6796 *Aegean/Olympic II*, par. 683 (citing Horizontal Merger Guidelines, (OJ C 31, 5.2.2004, p 5), par. 90).

The third criterion is a "strict" requirement that the firm's production assets could not be purchased by smaller competitors in liquidation or brought back into the market through reorganization. (OECD Competition Committee Meeting of 21 October 2009 Roundtable on Failing Firm Defence Note by the services of the European Commission Directorate-General for Competition, paras. 12, 21 ("EU Roundtable Note")).

The EC views this defence as "a particular application of the general causality test under Article 2 of the Merger Regulation." (Id. par. 15). Accordingly, "even if it cannot be shown that each of these indicative criteria are met, a counterfactual analysis of what would be the development of the market absent the merger could still lead to the conclusion that the deterioration of competition in the market is not a causal effect of the merger." (Id.; see also Commission Decision of May 10, 2007 in Case COMP/M.4381– *JCI/ Fiamm*, paras. 711 & n. 405, 721, 736, 750, 796, 815 (assessing impact of merger as compared to liquidation after concluding the failing firm elements not met)). The merging firms bear the burden of showing that the merger would not cause the deterioration of the market. (Horizontal Merger Guidelines, (OJ C 31, 5.2.2004, p 5), par. 91).

Both the U.S. and the EU recognize the "failing division defence" – a more rigorous off-shoot of the failing firm defence – as well. Under the 2010

U.S. Merger Guidelines, the failing firm defence may apply to a discrete division of a firm facing imminent market exit only if:

1. applying cost allocation rules that reflect true economic costs, the division has a persistently negative cash flow on an operating basis, and such negative cash flow is not economically justified for the firm by benefits such as added sales in complementary markets or enhanced customer goodwill; and
2. the owner of the failing division has made unsuccessful good-faith efforts to elicit reasonable alternative offers that would keep its tangible and intangible assets in the relevant market and pose a less severe danger to competition than does the proposed acquisition.

Unlike a company raising the "failing firm defence," a company raising the "failing division defence" in the EU bears the additional "burden of proving lack of causality between the merger and the creation or strengthening of a dominant position." (Commission Decision of April 2, 2003 in Case COMP/M.2876 – *Newscorp/ Telepiuí*, par. 212). "[T]he Commission's scrutiny will be particularly strict in such cases." (EU Roundtable Note par. 14).

The failing division defence presents special problems: although some commentators contend that "would be unfair to force parent companies to absorb losses that independent companies can avoid," firms may, in some circumstance, manipulate their capital structure to invoke the defence were an attractive acquiror to arise. (Phillip E. Areeda & Herbert Hovenkamp, Antitrust Law: An Analysis of Antitrust Principles and Their Application paras. 953e (5th ed.2022 supp.))

Bibliography

Areeda, P. E. and Hovenkamp, H., *Antitrust Law: An Analysis of Antitrust Principles and Their Application* paras. 951-55 (5th ed. 2022 supp.)

Levy, N. and Cook, C., *European Merger Control Law, Ch. 15* Efficiencies and the Failing Firm Defense, § 15.03 (2022)

Guidelines on the assessment of horizontal mergers under the Council Regulation on the control of concentrations between undertakings, (OJ C 31, 5.2.2004, p 5), paras. 89-91

Horizontal Merger Guidelines, United State Department of Justice & Federal Trade Commission § 11 (Aug. 19, 2010)

OECD Competition Committee Meeting of 21 October 2009 Roundtable on Failing Firm Defence Note by the services of the European Commission Directorate-General for Competition

See also

Burden of proof, Relevant market

F

FIDELITY REBATES

Chris PIKE
Fideres

Definition

Fidelity rebates, or equivalently, loyalty discounts, allow sellers to offer a better price conditional on the buyer demonstrating their loyalty. When loyalty is measured by the share of a buyer's purchases, and the threshold for obtaining the discount is close to 100%, these are exclusivity or "loyalty rebates". When loyalty is measured without reference to a buyer's total purchases, these are "quantity rebates". Rebates can be standardised if the same discount is available to all customers or targeted to an individual. "Retroactive rebates" apply to all units if more than a specified threshold is purchased. In contrast, "incremental rebates" describe discounts paid only on units over and above a threshold.

Commentary

Fidelity rebates can reflect efficiencies, or the kind of competitive behaviour that competition policy seeks to promote. However, they can raise concerns when they induce such loyalty that they effectively become a de-facto exclusive dealing arrangement. In these cases, concerns might include whether the scheme allows the firm to raise its rivals' costs, or apply an effective tax on its rivals' prices. However, in the same way that exclusive dealing by a dominant firm will not always harm consumers, de facto exclusive dealing will not necessarily harm consumers. Instead, if rivals can compete for exclusivity, then the firms can compete for the entirety of a customer's business, rather than competing for each unit purchased. Identifying that a fidelity rebate has "loyalty inducing" effects is therefore, on its own, not sufficient to show an abuse of dominance.

To identify a harmful effect, what is required is some asymmetry between the dominant firm and its rivals in their ability to persuade consumers to purchase exclusively that it did not enjoy when competing for units. This can lead to the competition for customers being less intense than the competition for units was. This asymmetry might include a predatory profit sacrifice (which a price cost test can identify). However, it may also include the ability to raise rivals' costs by denying rivals economies of scale, or access to key input (such as a distribution network). It might also include a willingness and ability to engage in a divide and conquer strategy, or to coordinate with downstream firms to foreclose rivals and increase the retail price of its own product, while splitting the increased profit with the downstream firms so they do not switch to selling a rival's product. Neither a price cost test nor an as-efficient-competitor test would identify such cases and so neither should be used a screening device or safe-harbour. Agencies should therefore be able to demonstrate not only that the scheme creates exclusive relationships, but also explain, with evidence, why rivals are unable to effectively compete for that exclusivity.

In the EU, the courts have distinguished between unproblematic quantity rebates, and "loyalty" rebates that when used by dominant firms were presumptively illegal in the absence of an objective justification (HoffMann-La Roche, paragraph 89) on the erroneous assumptions that their effect is always harmful. In Post Danmark II the courts identified a third type of rebate where an analysis of the likely effects of such rebates on consumers is required. This was a standardised retroactive quantity rebate which did not entail "an obligation for, or promise by, purchasers to obtain all or a given proportion of their supplies from Post Danmark." However, equally it was not considered a quantity rebate, since these are linked solely to the volume of purchasing and are granted in respect of each individual order. For these rebates, the court suggested that the as-efficient-competitor test is one tool for assessing whether there is an abuse of a dominance, however, it noted that there are others, and that the as-efficient-competitor test is not a necessary condition for a finding of abusive.

In *Intel*, the ECJ required the Commission to conduct an "effect analysis" every time that "the undertaking concerned submits, during the administrative procedure, on the basis of supporting evidence, that its conduct was not capable of restricting competition and, in particular, of producing the alleged foreclosure effects." In practice, the Commission will therefore be required to address those arguments. This shift away from allowing "loyalty" rebates only where objective justification is demonstrated, to instead allowing rebuttal on the grounds that the rebate was not capable of restricting competition, creates a more effects-based approach. It completes the move away from a formalistic approach that, while not a per se prohibition, since it always allowed an objective justification defence, was nevertheless a per se presumption on the capability of the practice to restrict competition. As such, it addresses the problem that there was no opportunity for the defendant to rebut the presumed restrictive effect of a rebate which economic analysis suggests has ambiguous competitive effects. At the same time, placing the burden on the firm to provide evidence to support a rebuttal of the presumed effect allows the Commission to simultaneously guard against the risk of under-enforcement that can arise from an effects-based analysis. As in Post Danmark II, the Intel judgement does not suggest that the Commission should always conduct an as-efficient-competitor test, or prove that prices were negative, each of which would create an under-enforcement risk. Indeed the pro-competitive effects of less efficient rivals were explicitly recognized by the ECJ; "…the presence of a less efficient competitor might contribute to intensifying the competitive pressure on that market and, therefore, to exerting a constraint on the conduct of the dominant undertaking."

In the U.S., there is no question that fidelity rebates require an effects-based analysis. Instead, the key area of debate is whether fidelity rebates are a pricing exclusion or an exclusivity exclusion and hence which analytical tests are relevant. For example, in 2012 the U.S. Court of Appeals affirmed a district court finding that Eaton's conduct in the heavy-duty truck transmission market violated the Sherman and the Clayton Act. The Appeal Court ruled against Eaton despite evidence that its prices had remained above cost. The reason, the Court explained, is that in this case price was not the clearly predominant mechanism of exclusion. The exclusionary effect reflected a range of factors in addition to prices such as Eaton's position as a necessary trading partner, the long duration of the contract, and the existence of high barriers to entry in the market. The court ruled that these practices as a whole resulted in de facto partial exclusive dealing. The decision was criticised in a dissenting opinion, which said that the plaintiff's failure to show that price was below cost should have been sufficient to dismiss the case, however, the Supreme Court declined to hear the appeal.

Indeed, the Court of Appeals emphasised that it was not necessary to show that price was below cost when it corrected the District Courts findings on *Eisai/Sanofi*. In particular, it ruled that exclusivity was the predominant mechanism of exclusion, and not price, and so a price-cost test was not required. This was material to the case, as it was clear that even after rebates were applied, Sanofi did not sell its product Lovenox to hospitals at a price that was below its incremental cost. Nevertheless, the Appeals court agreed that Eisai had failed to show either substantial foreclosure of the market, nor any anti-competitive effect such as increased prices.

Bibliography

Geradin, D. (2015). Loyalty Rebates after Intel: Time for the European Court of Justice to Overrule Hoffman-La Roche. *Journal of Competition Law & Economics*, 11(3), 579–615

Pike, C. and Carovano, G. (2019), *Competition Law Under Fire: Responding to Competing Demands for Change in the case of Price Parity Clauses and Loyalty Rebates*

ICN (2009), Report on the analysis of loyalty discounts and rebates under unilateral conduct laws

OECD (2016), Fidelity Rebates – Background Note by the Secretariat

U.S. FTC/DOJ (2014), Conditional Pricing Practices: Public Workshop. Washington DC, 23 June 2014

See also

Abuse of dominant position, Exclusionary practice

F

FINE

John M. CONNOR
Purdue University

Robert H. LANDE
University of Baltimore

■ Definition

A fine is a mandatory monetary penalty that is imposed by a court, commission, or other government authority and is paid to a public treasury. The primary purpose of fines is to deter antitrust or competition law violations. The great majority of antitrust and competition law fines are imposed on companies to deter price fixing, bid rigging, and other illegal collusive conduct. Some jurisdictions impose fines for other offenses, such as illegal dominant firm behavior or failure to report mergers and acquisitions. Fines are imposed by the European Union, the United States, and by most other nations that enforce competition or antitrust laws.

■ Commentary

Not all monetary payments made as a result of antitrust or competition law violations are fines. In most jurisdictions cartelists and other violators can be sued in court to pay damages to buyers that incurred supra-competitive overcharges or, in some cases, to suppliers that received sub-competitive prices. Damages payments are principally from settlements. Governments can themselves be the victim of bid rigging and other illegal activity, and governments usually can act as plaintiffs and collect antitrust damages. Occasionally, courts order both fines and mandatory compensation to victims; the latter is not a fine, but a form of restitution. Similarly, sometimes violators are required to disgorge their illegal profits, and these also are not fines.

In addition to fines for violating antitrust or competition laws, in most jurisdictions courts can impose fines on a company that fails to follow various procedural or reporting rules, such as partially or completely consummating a merger in the absence of final government approval ("gun-jumping") or failing to give advanced notice of transactions to the authority. While a few jurisdictions mention punishment or compensation as the purpose of fines, contemporary surveys of antitrust authorities tend to confirm that deterrence is their primary or sole aim. Most regimes seek general deterrence rather than specific deterrence. Many enforcement authorities follow published fining guidelines intended to deter cartel formation optimally and treat offenders in a proportional and transparent manner. These fines frequently are increased if the violator is a recidivist, and they are decreased for defendants granted leniency. Although payments of fines are mandatory, in most jurisdictions they can be appealed. Parallel non-monetary sanctions may include conduct restrictions, structural orders, and imprisonment.

In the United States, overt price fixing, bid rigging, dividing territorial markets, allocating customers, and similar collusive business conduct can give rise to antitrust fines as can various reporting violations. The companies involved, or the individuals involved, or both, can be fined. Individual fines are far less than corporate fines. Although fines in the United States can only be imposed by courts, as a practical matter the maximum and minimum cartel fine ranges are determined by recommendations of prosecutors justified by the U.S. Sentencing Guidelines (USSGs). In practice, prosecutors have wide discretion to depart from the USSGs' range because they can interpret culpability factors, negotiate the amount of affected commerce, and offer large discounts for defendants' cooperation during prosecution. The maximum corporate fine since 2004 is $100 million (or alternatively double the economic harm); the maximum for individuals is $5 million. As a practical matter, however, the enforcers have a variety of techniques they can use to raise the effective maximum fines to much higher levels.

In the European Union, fines for illegal price fixing and related cartel activity closely follow the EC's Fining Guidelines. Although prosecutors must adhere to this document's numerical ranges, they also have significant interpretive discretion. There is no maximum euro fine for competition law violations, but they are limited to 10% of the violator's ultimate parent company's global sales in all lines of business in the year prior to the Decision. This limit is rarely binding, however, and the actual levels of fines imposed are usually much lower. However, unlike the U.S. approach, the EC Fining Guidelines apply to all types of competition law violations. For example, Google has been fined on multiple occasions a total of nearly the equivalent of $10 billion for abuse of dominance involving the Internet search market. The National Competition Authorities (NCAs) of the EU's Member States employ EU competition law and the EC Fining Guidelines to determine their levels of fines for the competition law violations they prosecute. Neither the EU nor the NCAs imposes fines on the responsible individuals. EC competition law fines are often appealed to European courts, and a high proportion of these appeals result in small downward adjustments in fines, mostly because of procedural errors. In recent years EU fines have been larger than U.S. fines. However, the sum of U.S. fines and private damages actions have been more than the corresponding EU totals.

Most of the world's remaining competition or antitrust enforcement authorities have a fining regime closer to the EC approach than to the U.S. approach. A few jurisdictions (e.g., South Africa) have hybrid anti-cartel laws.

Bibliography

CONNOR, J. M. and LANDE, R. H., "Cartels As Rational Business Strategy: Crime Pays, 34 *Cardozo Law Review* 427 (2012)

CONNOR, J. M. and ROBERT H. LANDE, "Cartel Overcharges and Optimal Cartel Fines,"

CONNOR, J. M., Cartels Portrayed, A 21-Year Perspective: U.S. vs. EC: Who's Winning the Prosecution Race? *AAI Working Paper* No. 11-03 (posted 8/2/2011)

International Competition Network. Building Blocks for Effective Anti-Cartel Regimes: Vol. 1. Bonn, Germany: ICN Working Group on Cartels. (June 2005): p. 52-53

See also

Anticompetitive practices, Damages, Judicial review

F

FINTECH

Tudor N. PANA, Margaux SEAGER
Concurrences

■ Definition

Fintech, a portmanteau for "financial technology", is the rapidly evolving intersection between innovative technologies and the financial sector, blurring and extending the boundaries of the latter. A few fintech examples include mobile banking, blockchain, personal finance management, peer-to-peer lending and robo-advisors (i.e., automated financial guidance and services). In such a movable environment, competition law plays a crucial role in safeguarding fair and open markets, preventing the emergence of monopolies, and promoting innovation. The goal is to establish a level playing field, ensuring that consumers reap the benefits of a vibrant fintech ecosystem without experiencing undue market concentration or anti-competitive practices.

■ Commentary

The swift expansion of fintech has initiated a convergence of competition law and financial regulation, creating an unprecedented landscape. Rising fintech companies are challenging the established dominance of traditional banks and other financial institutions by introducing groundbreaking and often more streamlined financial services. These new facets of the financial sector pose challenges for the authorities, requiring a balancing act of opposing interests. On one hand, there is the fear of legislative fragmentation and over complexity, and on the other, there is the necessity to ensure that laws keep pace with innovation.

The issue of regulatory compliance in the context of excessive and developing legislation is a significant barrier to entry, especially for startups with limited resources. As F. Bostoen points out in his thesis "Abuse of Platform Power" (published by Concurrences), compliance gives large firms a cost advantage over smaller ones due to the growing complexity of regulation. Therefore, until we achieve technology-neutral regulation, which is not in itself a certainty, there is a manifest need for a framework that is capable of adapting to technological progress without hindering it. Before we explore some of the main current and future focal points in the fintech realm, a brief overview of the relevant legislation is required.

Legislation

In the EU, along with the TFEU, there is the 2023 Digital Markets Act (DMA), a tool that complements European and national law, and is recognised as the most comprehensive to date. In the UK, the Digital Markets Unit (DMU) has been established to oversee and enforce the 2020 mandatory Digital Code, which governs the behaviour of tech giants.

In the U.S., home to the majority of fintech companies, there is a relative lack of legislation. The ecosystem is largely shaped by existing antitrust laws, consumer protection regulations, and sector-specific oversight bodies. Policymakers are currently debating the need for more tailored laws to address the unique challenges posed by the rapid evolution of fintech.

Another notable jurisdiction in terms of the fintech prevalence is Singapore. With a proactive regulatory approach, the Monetary Authority of Singapore (MAS) has introduced frameworks such as the Payments Services Act 2019, encouraging innovation while ensuring financial stability, consumer protection, but also addressing competition law issues. This has positioned Singapore as a fintech hub in the Asia-Pacific region.

In addition, the European Parliament published a comprehensive report in 2018 on competition issues in the fintech sector, examining various anticipated challenges in the sector – providing valuable support for future legislative proposals.

Financial stability

In the fintech sector, the interplay between competition and financial stability is becoming increasingly apparent. Finding the equilibrium between fostering innovation, ensuring market integrity, safeguarding investor interests, and fortifying the stability of established financial systems is a crucial exercise.

The announcement of Meta's (formerly, Facebook) Libra cryptocurrency project raised concerns, with regulators worldwide expressing apprehension, highlighting the fine line between fostering fintech innovation and safeguarding established financial systems, eventually leading to the abandonment of the project. Similarly, when Meta attempted to launch WhatsApp Pay in Brazil, it faced opposition from the competition authority and intervention from the central bank. The latter brought forward concerns related to financial stability, given the significant user base of WhatsApp and the serious potential impact on the country's payment system. Eventually, approval was received but only after the Central Bank had developed its own instant payment system (Pix), as a basis for any future payment platforms being developed or used within the country.

Mergers & acquisitions

Analysing mergers in the fintech sector, such as the blocked Visa and Plaid deal worth $5.3 billion, is essential to grasping how competition law safeguards fair markets and prevents monopolies. The U.S. DoJ opposed the merger, suggesting that Plaid, another fintech, could have efficiently challenged Visa's dominant position, and this was nothing but an attempt by Visa to maintain its market power. Interestingly, the UK's CMA did not block the deal, underlining occasional divergences in regulatory opinions.

In the EU, the Commission's thorough supervisory role is visible in the case of Vipps and Mobile Pay. The agreement involved initially the collaboration of Danish, Norwegian and Finnish banks. Under the agreement, MobilePay, Vipps and Pivo were to merge to form a single payment application for consumers in these countries. However, approval of the deal was made conditional on the withdrawal of the Finnish party (Pivo), in order to avoid monopolistic tendencies and protect consumers.

The importance of compliance with merger control is further emphasised in the Illumina / Grail case, where, while the Commission's assessment was still underway, Illumina proceeded with the public announcement of the acquisition, resulting in a fine of 432 million euros and a first-of-its-kind EU order of divestment. In the words of the European Commission: "It is a cornerstone of the European merger control system, that enables the Commission to carry-out its role before structural changes modify the competitive landscape." Fintech companies, like all entities engaging in mergers and acquisitions within the EU that meet certain turnover thresholds, are subject to the same merger control regulations enforced by the European Commission.

Access to data and open banking

As fintech continues to redesign the financial sector, the synergy with competition law extends beyond traditional structures, requiring a nuanced understanding of data privacy regulations. Open banking involves granting third-party providers access to consumer financial data held by banks and other financial institutions, with the explicit consent of the account holder. The collection of large amounts of consumer data raises concerns about anti-competitive behaviour, such as data exclusivity agreements, discriminatory pricing, abuse of market power, algorithmic collusion, or data monopoly.

Without any major fintech related cases to date, fintech companies must look at other jurisprudence in this field, such as Google Spain v. Agencia Española de Protección de Datos (2014), often referred to as the "Right to be Forgotten" case. This decision emphasised the global implications of EU data protection laws, serving as a model for fintech companies handling and transferring customer data across borders. Another example on the usage of customer data stems from the Microsoft v U.S. (2018) case where the court examined the reach of U.S. law enforcement over data stored on foreign servers by American companies. This highlighted the necessity for fintech firms to not only comply with stringent data protection laws but also to navigate the intricate web of international regulations affecting data sovereignty.

Competition law has become a central force shaping the trajectory of financial technology. As the fintech sector continues its rapid innovation and expansion, maintaining fair competition becomes paramount to prevent monopolistic tendencies and encourage market diversity. Going forward, competition policy will continue to shape the industry – dictating the terms of business acquisitions, customer interactions, competitive agreements and access to data.

To sum up, fintech brings a wealth of benefits, such as broadening access to financial services, enhancing financial inclusion, and driving efficiency in transactions. Its innovative applications promise to streamline financial processes, making them more user-friendly and accessible to a wider audience. As such, fintech also plays a crucial role in promoting sustainability through the framework of competition law. By enabling better reporting, monitoring, data collection, and supply chain transparency, a competitive fintech market would be able to support genuine sustainable financing, preventing greenwashing, and working towards democratising sustainable finance.

Bibliography

Bostoen, F. (2023). *Abuse of Platform Power – Leveraging Conduct in Digital Markets under EU Competition Law and Beyond* – Concurrences

Menezes, F. Z., & Ferraz, A. (2023). Tech roundup: WhatsApp v. PIX is not a thing. *The Brazilian Report*

Stylianou, K., Iacovides, M., & Lundqvist, B. (2023). *Fintech Competition*. Bloomsbury Publishing

Competition issues in the Area of Financial technology (FinTech). (2018) (European Parliament 2023)

Examining Facebook's Proposed Digital Currency and Data Privacy Considerations: Hearing Before the S. Comm. on Banking, Hous., & Urban Affairs, 116th Cong. (2019) (statement of David Marcus, Head of Calibra/Novi, Facebook

Facebook cryptocurrency investigated by EU. (2019). Financial Times

Fintech and Competition Law. (2023), Clifford Chance

Fintech Developments and Antitrust Considerations in Payments, Antitrust, Vol. 35, No. 2, Spring 2021. © 2021 by the American Bar Association

See also

Artificial intelligence, AI Collusion (algorithm), Digital Markets Act (DMA), Environmental protection, Market power, Merger, Online platforms, Sustainability

F

FORECLOSURE

Hwang LEE
Korea University

■ Definition

"Foreclosure" refers to the practices that prevent rivals from accessing markets and thereby shutting them out of competition. While "exclusion" tends to imply an active effort to drive competitors out through strategies like predatory pricing, "foreclosure" leans more towards vertical blocking of access to markets through actions like exclusive dealing. However, the distinction is subtle and might vary based on jurisdiction and context. For example, in its Article 102 Guidance, the European Commission uses the term "foreclosure" in the predation context as well. The following commentary focuses on market foreclosure in a vertical sense to distinguish it from exclusion of competitors, as accepted more in the U.S.

■ Commentary

Anticompetitive Foreclosure

In general terms, foreclosure tends to be considered anticompetitive when a significant portion of a market is effectively foreclosed by unilateral or concerted actions. Unlike in the past, however, modern competition law does not perceive foreclosure as intrinsically anticompetitive. Particularly, the foreclosure resulting from vertical arrangements or vertical integration is often deemed competitively neutral or even procompetitive, as it may enhance efficiency by reducing costs without harming consumers. In the case of vertical integration, for example, the elimination of double marginalization might incentivize the merged firm to set lower downstream prices. To condemn foreclosure, several market circumstances including the market coverage and duration of the foreclosure in question must be carefully considered and its adverse effects need to be proven to outweigh the benefits, such as efficiency improvements.

The foreclosure concern is closely related to that of entry barriers. If a market is foreclosed but still has low barriers, then the foreclosure is less likely to be seen as anticompetitive. Nevertheless, it is worth noting that high barriers to entry by themselves do not necessarily indicate unlawful market foreclosure. Indeed, efficiency can itself serve as a barrier to market entry that does not deserve competition condemnation. Thus, a nuanced understanding of the specific market dynamics is essential when establishing anticompetitive foreclosure.

Foreclosure Resulted from Vertical Integration

Practically speaking, the "foreclosure" theory of harm is frequently invoked in cases of vertical integration. Suppose, for example, that a dominant or monopolistic firm supplies an important manufacturing input and seeks to acquire a manufacturer at a downstream level. Competition authorities might express concerns about such an acquisition, fearing the supplier could insulate a significant part, or even the entirety, of the upstream market by limiting rivals' access post-acquisition. Furthermore, the acquisition could heighten concerns about entry barriers, as the subsequent refusal might force new entrants to enter at multiple levels of the supply chain. This form of foreclosure, known as "input foreclosure" (meanwhile, when a vertical merger restricts upstream rivals access to the downstream, it is termed "customer (or output) foreclosure") could be assessed as anticompetitive, prompting intervention from competition authorities. Exceptions might arise if the relevant markets are deemed to remain competitive, entry is still easy, and/or efficiency gains from the acquisition are perceived as substantial.

The U.S. antitrust agencies' 2020 Vertical Merger Guidelines (now, rescinded) describe foreclosure, alongside raising rivals' costs, as a unilateral effect arising from vertical mergers. The guidelines state that when a vertical merger enhances the merged firm's ability and incentive to affect rivals' sales or competitiveness, the merger can raise competitive concerns and warrant antitrust scrutiny. Meanwhile, the EU's non-horizontal merger guidelines (2008/C 265/07) express the same concern as a non-coordinated effect. The EU's guidelines describe "foreclosure" as a situation "where actual or potential rivals' access to supplies or markets is hampered or eliminated as a result of the merger, thereby reducing these companies" ability and/or incentive to compete."

Foreclosure by Vertical Restrictions, e.g., Tie-ins and Exclusive Dealing

The foreclosure offence can also be invoked to challenge vertical contracting arrangements or condemn some business practices, such as tying and exclusive dealing.

Regarding tie-ins, whether implemented unilaterally or through an arrangement between firms, it is widely recognized that a business practice requiring buyers of one product to purchase a different product can raise foreclosure concerns. This is because competitors may face challenges reaching their customers, to the extent of the market presence of the tying and tied products. In other words, for a tie and its foreclosure to be deemed anticompetitive, they should foreclose a significant percentage of the market(s). Not to mention that to be anticompetitive, entering the market(s) should pose significant challenges and there should be no valid justification for the tie.

One of the most notable cases related to tying and its potential for market foreclosure involves Microsoft. In the late 1990s and early 2000s, Microsoft encountered significant antitrust scrutiny in various jurisdictions, including the U.S., the EU, and South Korea. While specific details varied across these jurisdictions, the core allegations remained consistent: Microsoft engaged in anticompetitive practices, inter alia, by technologically tying its products, such as the Internet Explorer web browser (U.S.), Windows Media Player (EU), and Windows Media Service and internet messenger (South Korea), into its dominant PC operating system, Windows, thereby limiting the market access of competing products.

Like tying, exclusive dealing – a contractual arrangement that obliges a buyer to purchase its requirements exclusively from a particular seller – is also frequently condemned based on the foreclosure theory of harm. While in tying cases, the condemnation primarily revolves around the foreclosure that prevents rivals from supplying complementary products to purchasers, in exclusive dealing cases, it centers on the foreclosure that restricts rivals from accessing a purchaser's entire business. In general terms, the intensity of foreclosure is greater in exclusive dealing cases because such deals leave no room for purchasers to buy and use other products. Nevertheless, the fundamental approach to analyzing the anticompetitiveness of foreclosure in both scenarios does not differ significantly (Hovenkamp, 2021, p. 560 and p. 567). In exclusive dealing cases as well, various factors including the arrangement's market coverage, duration, potential for new entrants, and other justifications, are taken into account to establish anticompetitive foreclosure.

The legal standard for exclusive dealing may vary based on time, context, and jurisdiction. One can take a prima facia illegality approach, while another can prefer a thorough analysis. However, it has now become common for major jurisdictions to carefully examine the actual or probable impact on competition rather than determining its illegality based solely on the degree of market foreclosure. In the U.S., for example, the Supreme Court in Tampa Electric clarified that, factors such as the contract's impact on competition, the parties' relative strength, the volume of commerce involved, and the effects of market share pre-emption should be considered when determining the substantiality of foreclosure (at 329). This approach has been subsequently followed by lower courts. Similarly, in Intel, the European Court of Justice refined the Hoffmann-La Roche decision (para 89) and emphasized the importance of a thorough assessment of the capability to restrict competition and produce anticompetitive effects in abuse cases, including exclusive dealing (para 138 et seq).

Meanwhile, when neither of the parties involved in exclusive arrangements holds a dominant position, market foreclosure coverage below 30% is generally not condemned under competition law nowadays, as observed in the U.S. Jefferson Parish case (at 1575) (see also, Article 3(1) of the EU's Vertical Block Exemption Regulation). As a result, 30% market foreclosure may function as a safe harbor in practice.

Bibliography

HOVENKAMP, H., *Federal Antitrust Policy - The Law of Competition and Its Practice* (6th edn. 2021)

WHISH, R. and BAILEY, D., *Competition Law* (10th edn. 2021)

European Commission, Communication from the Commission - Commission Notice - Guidelines on vertical restraints (2022/C 248/01)

European Commission, Communication from the Commission - Guidance on the Commission's enforcement priorities in applying Article 82 of the EC Treaty to abusive exclusionary conduct by dominant undertakings (2009/C 45/02)

European Commission, Guidelines on the assessment of non-horizontal mergers under the Council Regulation on the control of concentrations between undertakings (2008/C 265/07)

U.S. Department of Justice and Federal Trade Commission, Vertical Merger Guidelines (2020)

See also

Abuse of dominant position, Anticompetitive practices, Merger, Vertical agreement, Vertical restraints (or restrictions)

F

FOREIGN DIRECT INVESTMENT (FDI)

Peter D. CAMESASCA
Peter Camesasca Advocaat

Katherine KINGSBURY
Cooley

■ Definition

Foreign Direct Investment (FDI) regulation concerns the review of transactions based on national security or public order considerations. FDI regulation increasingly gives rise to *ex ante* filing obligations but regulators may also have powers to initiate *ex officio* proceedings before, or even after, a transaction is implemented. The focus of FDI regulation varies by jurisdiction, reflecting that FDI regimes are underpinned by political objectives specific to each jurisdiction. The powers available to FDI regulators are typically broad, allowing regulators to assess, investigate, authorize, condition, prohibit or unwind transactions to address national security and other public policy concerns.

■ Commentary

FDI regulation is a matter of national competence, including within the European Union (EU), and, accordingly, there is no universal definition of FDI. In common, however, FDI screening powers are typically targeted towards investments that create a lasting interest between a foreign investor and an asset or economic activity in the host country and through which the investor gains, directly or indirectly, rights to participate in the management or control of the asset. Relevant interests may arise at low-levels, such as the acquisition of 10% interest in shares or voting rights of an entity, and sometimes as low as 3% or 5% interests, including if combined with other management rights or special economic rights. Some FDI regimes apply other criteria in connection with the application of FDI rules and filing requirements – such as thresholds based on turnover or investment value – to exclude *de-minimis* investments from regulatory scrutiny. However, in most regimes, a broad scope of regulatory oversight is maintained on the basis that national security (and other) risks may arise from a range of assets and activities, regardless of their value or scale.

Whether an investor is classified as "foreign" may be a fairly self-evident matter in many jurisdictions. Generally, ultimate beneficial ownership tests apply, but these tests may have differ in scope and application and some jurisdictions also take account of the place of registration of intermediate entities in the chain of control. A handful of FDI measures apply exemptions (full or partial) for investors from certain countries – for example, Poland exempts investors from within the OECD (for some aspects of its FDI laws), Canada raises the financial threshold for WTO investors and the Committee on Foreign Investments in the United States ("CFIUS") grants country-specific exemptions from time to time. The EU FDI Regulation refers to "third countries" and treats investors from non-EU/non-EEA/non-EFTA countries as foreign. However, investments into the most sensitive sectors, such as defense, can often trigger an FDI review for all non-national (and even national) investors. In addition, countries such as France and Italy have extended the application of their FDI regimes to all non-national investors acquiring control of assets in certain sectors.

It is more unusual for FDI laws to target only particular groups of investors. One example is the, so-called, "Press Note 3" regulation introduced by India in 2020, pursuant to which FDI filings are required by all investors from countries bordering India and regardless of the sector of investment. In some other jurisdictions, FDI filing requirements apply on a stricter basis for state-backed investors, including state-owned enterprises, sovereign wealth funds and state pension funds. In accordance with Article 4(2) of the EU FDI Regulation, most EU Member States assess whether an investor is controlled by a foreign government or has been involved in activities detrimental to national security during the substantive review process.

The vulnerabilities of a target company and its specific activities are key factors within the substantive assessment of foreign investments. Most FDI regimes, in some manner, identify those activities or sectors that are regarded as most susceptible to foreign investment risks. For example, Article 4(1) of the EU FDI Regulation provides a non-exhaustive list of sensitive sectors that are prone to trigger FDI review. Most EU Member States incorporate some or all of the sectors mentioned into their own FDI laws, although national definitions of the sectors frequently diverge. Member States may also supplement the list of sectors based on domestic risks and preferences. Typical activities subject to review across all FDI regimes, globally, include military and dual-use goods, critical infrastructure (such as, energy, water, telecommunications, health, transport), critical technologies (such as, artificial intelligence, advanced materials, cyber security, biotechnology), critical inputs and raw materials (such as food), data processing (particularly relating to personal or sensitive data), and media or media plurality. FDI regulators may also have ex officio powers to screen transactions occurring in any sector, for example, in the UK and Germany.

The purpose of FDI regulation also varies by jurisdiction. A number of FDI regimes emerged to address primarily economic concerns – most notably, in Australia, New Zealand and Canada. These regimes apply general "net-benefit" requirements and other investment controls to protect specified domestic industries (e.g. agriculture in Australia), and have introduced screening powers on national security grounds more recently. Other FDI regulators, such as the CFIUS, were empowered with a national security focus from the outset. The UK National Security and Investment Act 2021 is intended to focus on national security, and not other economic, risks. Within the EU, any restriction of the freedom of establishment of capital must be justified under EU law by overriding reasons in the general interest. The European Court of Justice has traditionally applied high standards in this regard, requiring a genuine and sufficiently serious threat to a fundamental interest of society.

Given that FDI proceedings concern national security issues, they are typically confidential. There are few publicly reported cases and even fewer court decisions testing the boundaries of application for FDI laws. However, in October 2021, the European Commission opened an investigation to determine whether Hungary had breached the EU Merger Regulation by blocking the acquisition of sole control over the Dutch Insurer Aegon by Vienna Insurance Group. The transaction was blocked by Hungary based on emergency amendments to its FDI screening regulation, after the European Commission had granted clearance for the transaction pursuant to EU merger control rules. Following its investigation, the European Commission indicated that national security and public policy considerations must be carefully circumscribed and remain compatible with the EU Merger Regulation, particularly where freedom of movement of capital within the EU is at stake.

In another case, in Italy, investors are challenging whether a prohibition decision issued by the FDI authority was a proportionate response to an acknowledged national security risk in circumstance where extensive undertakings were offered.

In terms of process, it is increasingly common for FDI filings to be submitted to a dedicated FDI regulator (sometimes established within a government ministry). In a smaller number of jurisdictions, FDI review remains sectoral and is managed as a component of other regulatory approvals. To the extent that FDI notification requirements remain broad, it is evident that the actual substantive national security and public policy interest is narrower and the overwhelming majority of transactions that are filed under FDI regulations are cleared without intervention by FDI authorities – more than 80% in the EU. In those cases where mitigation is required, regulators frequently favour behavioural remedies (including commitments to maintain a national presence or certain activities/facilities, information barriers or restrictions on the transfer of intellectual property and know-how to other jurisdictions). The blocking of transactions on national security grounds is rare, although the deterrent effect of FDI regulations remains difficult to measure.

Bibliography

Camesasca, P., Henschen, H. and Juhasz, M., Foreign Direct Investment screening in Europe: A comparative perspective on differences and commonalities within Europe, [6 November 2020], *Concurrences No 4-2020*

Regulation (EU) 2019/452 of the European Parliament and of the Council of 19 March 2019 establishing a framework for the screening of foreign direct investments into the Union

Report from the Commission to the European Parliament and the Council: First Annual Report on the screening of foreign direct investments into the Union, COM (2021) 714 final

See also

Foreign Subsidies Regulation (FSR), Competition policy, Industrial policy

F

FOREIGN SUBSIDIES REGULATION (FSR)

Lise DAMELET
FTPA

■ Definition

On 5 May 2021, the European Commission (the "Commission") published a proposal for a Regulation on foreign subsidies distorting the internal market (the "Proposed Regulation"). On 30 June 2022, the Commission and the European Parliament reached a political agreement on the Proposed Regulation. The final Regulation will enter into force once it has been formally adopted by the Council and the European Parliament. This definition is current as of 22 July 2022 and will be updated in the online version of the dictionary once a final version of the Regulation has been adopted. The Proposed Regulation establishes a legal framework to regulate the granting of foreign subsidies by non-EU countries to companies carrying out an economic activity within the EU's single market, regardless of nationality. The Proposed Regulation aims to remedy the distortions created by subsidies granted by non-EU countries and to ensure equal competition in the EU. While the proposed scheme concerns all economic activities, the Proposed Regulation pays particular attention to the impact of such subsidies in the context of mergers or public procurement procedures.

■ Commentary

The Proposed Regulation aims to remedy the distortions created by subsidies granted by non-EU countries and to ensure equal competition in the EU.

This legal framework is intended to fill a long-standing legal gap, which has been discussed for a long time and that could not be addressed by existing European regulations, namely (i) state aid control, (ii) merger control, (iii) public procurement or (iv) foreign investment contrat at EU country level.

Until this Proposed Regulation, only Member States had to comply with State aid rules, as opposed to non-Member States. The assessment of the qualification of foreign subsidies granted by non-Member States borrows its structure to State aid control. The procedural aspects of the regulation are, for their part, inspired by merger control (filing required if certain thresholds are exceeded – in terms of turnover or value, behavioural and structural remedies).

While the Proposed Regulation applies to all economic activities, its content pays particular attention to the impact of such subsidies in the context of mergers or public procurement procedures.

More broadly, this Proposed Regulation introduces several control tools entrusted to the exclusive competence of the Commission. These tools are intended to provide broad oversight of foreign subsidies while allowing the Commission to identify the most critical foreign financial contributions:

- mandatory *ex ante* notification of the most significant foreign subsidies in the context of mergers and large-scale public procurement;
- *ex officio* investigations by the Commission for all other market situations, including smaller mergers and public procurement procedures.

The Proposed Regulation confers broad powers of investigation and sanction to the Commission, which may:

- adopt provisional measures;
- carry out requests for information or investigations within the European Union or in a non-EU country;
- take sanctioning measures in cases of non-cooperation, including fines and penalty payments;

The 4-step analytical approach of anti-competitive foreign subsidies is largely inspired by the State aid control regulation.

Characterization of a foreign subsidy conferring a selective benefit to the recipient

A foreign subsidy is deemed to exist where three cumulative criteria are met:

- a public financial contribution: the financial contribution must be granted, directly or indirectly, by the public authorities of a non-EU country, whether through public or private entities
  - The forms that these foreign subsidies can take are, by analogy, those retained for State aid analysis.
  - In the same way as what prevails in terms of State aid, the financial contributions granted by the non-EU country include both financial contributions granted by (i) the government central and governmental authorities, (ii) foreign public entities, or (iii) any private entity whose acts can be attributed to the relevant non-EU country.
- an economic activity: the financial contribution must grant an advantage to an undertaking carrying out an economic activity within the EU market. Within the meaning of the Proposed Regulation, an undertaking which merges with an undertaking established in the EU,

or which acquires control, or an undertaking that participates in a public procurement procedure, is considered to be carrying out an economic activity within the EU market;
- a selective advantage: the advantage granted to the beneficiary by the public authorities of a non-EU country may be conferred on a particular firm or industry or several firms or industries.

Characterization of a distortion of competition

Foreign subsidies are not prohibited *per se*.

The Proposed Regulation provides that a distortion of the EU market is deemed to exist where (i) the subsidy is such as to strengthen the competitive position of the undertaking concerned and (ii) the subsidy has or is likely to have an adverse effect on competition within the EU market.

The effect of the subsidy is assessed based on indicators provided for in the Proposed Regulation (amount, nature, market situation, level of the beneficiary's economic activity within the internal market, etc.) and in particular the objectives pursued by the subsidy and the conditions under which it was granted. This last criteria differs from the traditional analysis of State aid since the TFEU does not distinguish between the causes or objectives of the interventions in question but defines them in terms of their effects.

The Proposed Regulation focuses, through the *ex-ante* notification mechanism, on mergers and the most critical public procurement:
- in the context of a merger: any public contribution from a non-EU country, where the turnover generated within the EU market by the target company or at least one of the parties to the merger is equal to or greater than EUR 500 million and the foreign financial contribution is at least EUR 50 million. In contrast to the prevailing merger control thresholds, the Proposed Regulation does not provide for a worldwide turnover threshold.
- in the context of public procurement: any bid submitted involving a public financial contribution from a non-EU country, where the estimated value of the public procurement is equal to or greater than €250 million. *In contrast* to the notification mechanism provided for mergers, in the case of a public procurement contract, notification is required where the estimated value of the contract is equal to or greater than €50 million.

The Proposed Regulation also introduces a general *de minimis* threshold, set at EUR 5,000,000 (total amount over three consecutive financial years.).

Balancing the negative and positive effects of the subsidy

Where the Commission characterizes a distortion of competition generated by a foreign subsidy, it balances the negative effects of the subsidy within the EU market with its positive effects on the development of the relevant economic activity.

Some uncertainties will need to be clarified in practice and, possibly by future case law, it will be necessary to better determine how the Commission will balance the distortive effect of the subsidy measure and its positive effects on the economic activity. In particular, it remains to be seen whether these justifications will be assessed using a framework similar to State aid control or whether another test will apply. The Commission has indeed adopted a number of texts specifying the conditions under which categories of State aid may be found compatible under Article 107(3) TFEU. Although these texts do not apply to foreign subsidies, the Commission may be able to replicate them in relation to foreign subsidies.

Commitment and remedial measures

If the Commission considers that the foreign subsidy creates an actual or potential distortion in the EU market, it may impose remedies to address the situation. The undertaking concerned may also submit commitments (behavioral or structural) to the Commission to counterbalance the competitive distortion.

Bibliography

Alexis, A., Foreign subsidy controls: the new European Commission proposal, *Concurrences N° 4-2021*, Art. N° 102820, pp. 210-218

Gordley, C., The EU Commission unveils its proposed regulation on foreign subsidies, 5 May 2021, *e-Competitions May 2021*, Art. N° 101255

Labrousse, F., Amory, B., Antonini, R., de Navacelle, C., Eichhorn, K. H., Monard, E., The EU Commission adopts a proposal for a regulation on foreign subsidies that might be distorting the internal market, 5 May 2021, *e-Competitions May 2021*, Art. N° 100983

Rimsa, A., Laprévote, F.-C., D'Andrea, G., Siragusa, M., Comino, A., The EU Commission proposes a far-reaching regulation to tackle foreign subsidies, 5 May 2021, *e-Competitions May 2021*, Art. N° 101054

Council press release of 30 June, 2022

Council negotiation mandate of 4 May, 2022

Position of the European Parliament on the proposal for a regulation of the European Parliament and of the Council on foreign subsidies distorting the internal market of 4 May 2022

Proposal for a Regulation of the European Parliament and of the Council on foreign subsidies distorting the internal market, published by the Commission on 5 May 2021

See also

Foreign Direct Investment (FDI), Competition policy, Industrial policy

F

FORM CO (EU)

David VIROS
European Commission

Definition

The European Commission must review and clear, before their implementation, mergers, acquisitions of control and certain types of newly formed joint-ventures ("concentrations") that meet the turnover thresholds set out in Regulation No 139/2004 ("the Merger Regulation"). The so-called Form CO, appended to Regulation No 802/2004 implementing the Merger Regulation ("the Implementing Regulation"), sets out the information that must be submitted to the Commission upon notification of such a proposed concentration as well as the structure and order of presentation the notifying parties must follow when furnishing the said information. The information pertains to the transaction, the parties thereto, the markets on which they operate and their specificities as well as alleged efficiencies. The prescribed time limits for the Commission's review only begin to run once the information required by the Form CO is deemed complete.

Commentary

In line with most jurisdictions throughout the world in which a merger control regime exists (see, in this respect, the ICN's Merger Notification and Procedures Template), the European Union requires the notification of contemplated concentrations that fall under its purview prior to their implementation and sets out a detailed list of compulsory information in this context.

Even if, for the purposes of establishing the Commission's jurisdiction in particularly complex cases, the notification may contain ample developments on the transaction underpinning the change of control (Section 3 of Form CO) or even on the turnover to be taken into account with regard to the applicable jurisdictional thresholds (Section 4), the bulk of the information submitted will normally relate to the markets on which the concentration may have an impact. In this regard, the information sought by the Commission covers both static and dynamic dimensions of competition (see Section 7: market size, market shares of parties to the concentration and competitors, capacities; Section 8: structure of supply and demand, product differentiation and closeness of competition, market entry and exit, R&D, cooperative agreements).

Qualification of the relevant market as an "affected" market triggers the obligation to submit the information prescribed under Sections 7 and 8. The thresholds for qualifying as an affected market were revisited by the Commission as part of a simplification package, which entered into force on 1 January 2014. The combined market share threshold of the parties post-transaction on the same relevant market (horizontal overlap) increased from 15% to 20%, whereas, in case of vertical relationships, the combined market share threshold in any of the upstream or downstream markets increased from 25% to 30%. These market share thresholds are, broadly speaking, reflected in Member States' own merger control regimes (see the EU Merger Working Group's Report on Merger Information Requirements, table B – part 3) and recent changes brought at national level have sought, where applicable, to close the gap with the Commission's own requirements as reflected in Form CO (see, e.g., in France Decree n° 2019-339 of 18 April 2019 which raises the vertical threshold from 25% to 30%). Form CO also contemplates the provision of the information prescribed under Sections 7 and 8 in relation to "other markets" where, in the absence of overlaps, other concerns may be flagged in relation to potential competition or conglomeral effects (see Section 6.4).

In keeping with the objective of avoiding undue administrative burdens on notifying parties and seeking information only to the extent necessary to address material competitive concerns (see, in this regard, ICN Recommended Practices for Merger Notification and Procedures, part V), the Commission employs a number of tools to mitigate, where appropriate, the obligations weighing on notifying parties. Thus, on the one hand, it may waive the obligation to provide a number of information otherwise prescribed by the Form CO. Interestingly, the scope of potential waivers appears to be relatively large and includes the obligation to provide internal documents prepared for assessing the rationale of the concentration or competitive conditions on the affected markets – even as, arguably, the provision of the said documents entails, on the part of the parties, no drafting efforts and comparatively limited investigatory efforts. On the other hand, provided certain conditions are fulfilled, notifying parties may only have to provide the more limited information required under the so-called Short Form CO, also appended to the Implementing Regulation. Eligibility conditions vary in nature (see para. 5 of the Commission Notice on a Simplified Procedure) and relate (i) to the absence of horizontal and vertical relationships with regard to any markets on which the parties are present, (ii) their limited combined market share on markets thus concerned, (iii) the acquisition of sole control of an undertaking by a party which already exerts joint control over the former or (iv) the acquisition of a joint venture with negligible activities within the EEA.

The simplification package adjusted the market share thresholds applicable under (ii) in a manner consistent with those applicable to "affected markets" under Form CO (see above) while introducing a new category whereby parties in a horizontal relationship with a combined market share not exceeding 50% and a Herfindahl-Hirschman Index increment not exceeding 150 "may" also benefit from the simplified procedure. In other words, in the latter instance, the Commission retains greater discretion to award the benefit of the simplified procedure, to be discussed with parties at the informal pre-notification stage.

Variations in scope of the simplified procedure witnessed in different jurisdictions may reflect competition authorities' different sensitivities to specific theories of harm. For instance, in France until 2020, a change from joint to sole control exerted by the same undertaking did not render the transaction eligible to a simplified procedure, and has even attracted in-depth investigations and the imposition of substantial remedies (see *Decision 13-DCC-90, Casino/Monoprix*).

Further avenues for simplification, such as exempting certain categories of cases from notification or providing for a self-assessment system combined with voluntary notification (such as exists, for instance, in the United Kingdom), were considered by the Commission in a 2014 White paper and then again in the context of a public consultation in 2017 but have been shelved, at least for the time being, due to somewhat lackluster response (see Commission SWD Evaluation of procedural and jurisdictional aspects of EU Merger control, March 2021). Finally, the omission to notify a concentration, whether through a Form CO or a Short Form, or failure to provide complete information, entails significant legal consequences. Indeed, the Commission has been keen in recent years to ramp its use of fines for procedural infringements, in keeping with Article 14 of the Merger Regulation. The Altice/PT and Canon/Toshiba decisions thus take issue with the fact that the concerned concentrations were implemented in breach of the standstill clause (Article 7 of the Merger Regulation) as well as, at least in part, before notification. The *Facebook/Whatsapp* and *GE/LM Wind Power Holding* fine the notifying parties for providing incorrect information in their notification, respectively 110 and 52 million Euros.

Bibliography

ANDERSON, D., CULLIFORD, P., "Surveying the surveys – The drive for implementation of the ICN's recommended practices for merger notification and review procedures", *Concurrences N° 3-2020*, Art. N° 95408

BAILLY, M., MALAMATARIS, C. Procedural developments in EU merger control. *ERA Forum* 21, 251–265 (2020)

See also

Merger control procedure, Notification

F

FRAND

Kirti GUPTA
Cornerstone Research

■ Definition

The acronym FRAND – which stands for fair, reasonable, and nondiscriminatory – is often used in relation to technical standards that are developed through an open, consensus-based, and industry-led standardization process. Companies that participate in the standard development may commit to offer a license on FRAND terms to patents that are or may become essential to a standard. In that context, the so-called FRAND commitment is a *voluntary* agreement between the patent holder and the standards development organization ("SDO") regarding the licensing conditions for essential technologies. However, FRAND terms have been used also in other contexts, such as telecom regulation and, more recently, in relation to regulation of digital platforms.

■ Commentary

FRAND terms are often discussed in relation to a commitment that a patent owner makes to an SDO. When discussing a standard, SDOs typically require members to publicly declare patents that are potentially essential for that standard – these patents are referred to as standard essential patents ("SEPs") – and clarify whether they are willing to offer a license to SEPs on FRAND terms. The exact scope of the FRAND commitment is defined in the SDO's bylaws and may differ across organizations.

For most SDOs, a patent holder can freely decide whether to make a FRAND commitment or not. Put differently, a commitment to offer a license on FRAND terms is a *voluntary* agreement between the patent holder and the SDO. If the SDO's licensing requirements are too onerous, the patent holder might decline a FRAND commitment. That is why SDOs seek to define a FRAND commitment in a way that balances between the need to ensure access to essential technologies while also allowing patent owners to be adequately compensated for their R&D investments and contributions they make to the standard.

The specific terms of a license for SEPs are ultimately negotiated between the patent holder and an implementer – that is, a company that offers products or services that use the standard. If the parties are unable to reach an agreement on the FRAND terms, they may seek to resolve their dispute in court. Most courtshave found a FRAND commitment to be an enforceable contract. In the United States, for example, several courts have found that implementers of industry standards are the intended third-party beneficiaries of the FRAND commitment, and as such, have the right to enforce the patent holder's contractual obligations in court (*Microsoft Corp. v. Motorola Inc.*).

In the last few years, courts have provided important guidance for resolving FRAND related disputes. For example, the U.S. Court of Appeals for the Federal Circuit said that the analysis of comparable licenses provides a reliable methodology for determining a reasonable royalty for FRAND-encumbered patents (*Ericsson Inc. v. D Link Sys., Inc.*). Similarly, the UK Supreme Court and the Federal Court of Germany said that comparable licenses provide reliable evidence for determining FRAND royalties as well as other terms and conditions of a license (*Sisvel v. Haier; Unwired Planet v. Huawei*). Based on the analysis of comparable licenses, both courts determined that when the implementer sells its products worldwide, a FRAND license is global in scope rather than limited to an individual jurisdiction (*Unwired Planet v. Huawei; Sisvel v. Haier*).

In addition, courts have provided guidance regarding the remedies that a patent owner may seek against an infringer of FRAND committed patents. In 2014, the Court of Justice of the European Union ("CJEU") issued a seminal opinion addressing the allegations that a patent holder's request for an injunction would violate EU competition law. The CJEU did not categorically exclude an antitrust liability but said that if a patent owner takes specific steps (such as notifying the implementer about the infringement and extending an offer that complies with the FRAND obligation), a request for an injunction will raise no concerns under competition law. National courts of the European Union and United Kingdom subsequently confirmed that, depending on the circumstances of the case, a patent owner may be entitled to request and obtain an injunction (*Sisvel v. Haier; Unwired Planet v. Huawei*). In the United States, the Federal Circuit also said there is no "per se rule" against injunctions for SEPs", although a FRAND commitment is a relevant criterium in determining the entitlement to such a remedy.

FRAND commitments have also been discussed in the context of antitrust. Some commentators have argued that a patent holder's breach of the obligations arising from a FRAND commitment should be considered a violation of antitrust law. In the United States, courts have rejected that argument (*FTC v. Qualcomm*). For example, in *FTC v. Qualcomm*, the Ninth Circuit said that establishing an antitrust violation would require evidence of harm to competition, rather than merely evidence that the patent holder breached its contractual duties. In other words, the Ninth Court said that a breach of a FRAND commitment, without more, is not an antitrust violation.

Bibliography

Contreras, J. L., *The Cambridge Handbook of Technical Standardization Law: Competition, Antitrust, and Patents* (2018)

Galetovic, A. and Haber, S., SEP Royalties: What Theory of Value and Distribution Should Courts Apply, 17.2 *OHIO ST. TECH. L.J.* 189 (2021)

Gupta, K. and Petrovèiè, U. , Standards, Patents, and Antitrust Policy: The Road Ahead, *Competition Policy International* (2019)

Sidak, J. G., The FRAND Contract, 3 *The Criterion J. On Innovation* (2018)

See also

Compulsory license, Licensing, Patents, Standard-Essential Patent (SEP)

F

FREE RIDING

Jonathan M. BARNETT
USC Gould School of Law

Definition

Free riding arises in circumstances in which certain entities incur costs to secure a certain benefit while other entities enjoy that benefit without incurring those costs. Certain restraints (principally, vertical restraints) are sometimes deemed to be efficient mechanisms to counteract free-riding that may otherwise deter the provision of services (especially, pre-sale services by distributors) that benefit consumers and enhance competition in the relevant product market.

Commentary

There are three principal types of restraints (which are principally characterized as vertical restraints) that are sometimes deemed to be efficient responses to free-riding. The legal treatment of each restraint under competition law typically involves a trade-off between effects on interbrand and intrabrand competition. When applicable law permits a balancing analysis (under the "rule of reason" in U.S. antitrust law and "effects analysis" under EU competition law), courts or regulators may determine that a particular restraint enhances interbrand competition by discouraging free-riding that would otherwise discourage the provision of promotional and other pre-sale services. Those favorable effects on interbrand competition may outweigh adverse effects on intrabrand competition attributable to any such restraint.

Exclusive Dealing

Exclusive dealing arrangements encompass contractual agreements and other vertical restraints through which a producer or supplier elects to distribute its product through a single distributor or limited number of distributors (which may be situated at the retail or wholesale level). These practices inherently raise concerns about potential harms to intrabrand competition. In certain circumstances, however, exclusive dealing arrangements may yield competitive gains by counteracting free-riding that could have adverse effects on Interbrand competition.

For example, when a producer commits to sell exclusively through a single retailer, it shields the retailer to a certain extent from intrabrand competition and, as a result, enhances the retailer's incentives to invest in efforts to promote the producer's brand or provide other pre-sale services to consumers. This may be especially important in the case of luxury brands, new products and services, or complex products and services that are difficult for customers to evaluate without the provision of technical or other information by the distributor. Absent an exclusive dealing arrangement, retailers would curtail these pre-sale efforts, the producer's brand goodwill would be diminished, and interbrand competition would decline.

Resale Price Maintenance

Resale Price Maintenance (RPM) encompasses contractual provisions or other vertical restraints through which a producer or supplier specifies a fixed price (typically, a minimum price) or price range at which wholesalers or retailers must distribute its products. As a direct intervention in pricing, this practice raises strong concerns over anticompetitive effects. However, RPM may have procompetitive effects if it yields a pricing premium that implicitly compensates distributors for the costs incurred to promote a producer's brand through marketing and other pre-sale services. Absent an RPM clause, any individual distributor would elect to free ride off the pre-sale efforts undertaken by other distributors. For example, "discount" retailers could offer a lower price for the same product to consumers who had been elicited by "full-service" retailers who had incurred costs to provide marketing, display, and informational services. In anticipation of this outcome, no distributor would have a rational incentive to invest in providing these pre-sale services, the producer's brand goodwill may be impaired, and interbrand competition would suffer as a result.

Under EU competition law, RPM is a "hardcore" restriction under Article 4 of Commission Regulation (EU) 2022/720 and a "restriction by object" under Article 101(1) of the Treaty on the Functioning of the European Union (TFEU), which would exclude an efficiency defense based on free-riding considerations. However, the Commission's Guidelines on Vertical Restraints (both as issued in 2010 and updated in 2022) provide that an RPM restraint may nonetheless qualify for an efficiency defense in individual cases under Article 101(3) of the Treaty and specifically address the free-riding considerations that may justify use of an RPM restraint, "in particular where it is supplier driven."

Territorial Allocation

Territorial allocation encompasses agreements or other practices through which exclusive geographic areas are reserved for certain distributors of a particular product. This type of restraint generally raises strong concerns since, depending on competitive conditions, it may confer pricing power on the firm that is allocated each territory. In certain circumstances, however, territorial allocation may encourage distributors to invest in pre-sale efforts that enhance a producer's brand goodwill, elicit consumer interest, and, as a result, enhance interbrand competition. Absent territorial allocation, each distributor would have reduced incentives to invest in promoting the producer's brand since other distributors could free-ride off those services and, not having incurred any or comparable pre-sale costs, offer the same product at a lower price. Territorial allocation enables a producer or supplier to preclude this adverse competitive outcome by enabling each distributor to capture any increase in sales attributable to its pre-sale efforts. When that is the case, territorial allocation can enhance brand goodwill, intensify customer acquisition efforts, and increase interbrand competition, which may outweigh any harms to intrabrand competition within each allocated territory.

Under U.S. antitrust law, any territorial allocation characterized as a horizontal restraint is per se illegal under *U.S. v. Topco Associates*, 405 U.S. 596 (1972), and any favorable effects on interbrand competition as a result of free-riding considerations would then be ignored. However, if a territorial allocation can be reasonably characterized as a vertical restraint, then some form of the rule of reason standard would apply. Under that standard, courts undertake a balancing analysis that (among other considerations) weighs likely harms to intrabrand competition against likely benefits to interbrand competition. Even if a court finds that territorial allocation efficiently deters free-riding and induces pre-sale efforts by distributors, it may still consider whether free-riding could be reasonably addressed through a "less restrictive" alternative that would cause less harm to intrabrand competition.

Under EU competition law, the legal relevance of free-riding considerations in the context of territorial allocation is treated similarly. Restraints on resales by territory presumptively constitute "hardcore" restrictions under Article 4(b) of the Block Exemption Regulation, which would preclude any efficiency defense based on free-riding considerations. However, any such restraint may qualify for one of the exceptions set forth in Article 4(b), in which case an effects analysis would apply. As provided in the Guidelines on Vertical Restraints, the effects analysis may take into account the extent to which territorial exclusivity may promote interbrand competition by inducing pre-sale efforts that would otherwise be discouraged due to free-riding, offset against adverse impacts on intrabrand competition and taking into account less restrictive alternatives.

Considerations relating to free-riding have also emerged in the still-developing treatment under antitrust law of certain practices in multi-sided platform markets. In particular, the U.S. Supreme Court's decision in *Ohio et al. v. American Express Co.*, 138 S. Ct. 355 (2017), concerned a practice in which a credit card issuer contractually barred merchants from "steering" consumers to use competitors' credit cards (which would result in a lower fee for the merchant). The court's decision upholding this restraint relied substantially on the finding that this practice was necessary to prevent merchants (and, indirectly, other credit card issuers) from free riding on the issuer's investments in marketing, rewards programs, and other customer services designed to attract higher-income consumers who tend to make larger expenditures. Without the anti-steering restraint, the card issuer's revenues from merchant fees might decline and it would be compelled to reduce these investments, which the court found had enhanced the quantity and quality of interbrand competition in the relevant market.

Bibliography

GERADIN, D., LAYNE-FARRAR, A. and PETIT, N., *EU Competition Law and Economics* (2012). Oxford University Press

KLEIN, B. and LERNER, A. V., The Expanded Economics of Free-Riding: How Exclusive Dealing Prevents Free-Riding and Creates Undivided Loyalty, 72 *Antitrust Law Journal* 473 (2007)

TESLER, L. G., Why Should Manufacturers Want Free Trade?, 3 *Journal of Law & Economics* 86 (1960)

European Commission, Guidelines on Vertical Restraints, 2022/C 248/01 (2022)

European Commission, Guidelines on Vertical Restraints, OJ C 130 (2010)

See also

Block exemption (Regulation), Vertical restraints (restrictions), Resale price maintenance (RPM), Rule of reason

GEOGRAPHIC MARKET

João AZEVEDO
European Commission – DG COMP

Jani RINGBORG
European Commission – Legal Service

Definition

The area relevant to the assessment of the conduct constitutes the geographic dimension of a relevant antitrust market. Under EU competition law, the relevant geographic market comprises the area in which the undertakings concerned are involved in the supply and demand of products or services, in which the conditions of competition are sufficiently homogeneous and which can be distinguished from neighbouring areas because the conditions of competition are appreciably different in those areas. While the exact definition of a geographic market shows some variation between jurisdictions, many systems of competition law use the concept to identify the geographic boundaries of competition.

Commentary

A relevant market is typically defined in terms of both a product and geographic dimension. The geographic dimension concerns the geographic or territorial boundaries of the market. Its purpose is to identify the geographic boundaries of competition, in other words to identify the suppliers of a given product or service that are capable of constraining the market behaviour of a given company and to whom customers of that product or service can turn.

The European Courts of Justice have long held that a relevant market has a geographic dimension, the definition of which must be based on appropriate evidence. From the early case Europemballage Corporation and Continental Can Company v Commission (1973), the Court of Justice considered it necessary to take account of the geographic dimension of the relevant market. The case concerned an attempt by the Commission to prohibit a concentration under what is today Art 102 TFEU at a time when no specific merger control regulation existed in Community competition law. The Court annulled the Commission's decision for lack of reasoning. The Court explained that the Commission was under an obligation to state legally sufficient reasons or, at least, to prove that the remaining competitors could no longer constrain the merged entity (Continental Can, paragraph 29). In this context, and while the Court approached the question of relevant market primarily from the product market perspective, it explained that "[t]he argument… that the plants of certain manufacturers… were located too far away from most… consumers to enable the latter to decide to use them as a permanent source of supply, has not been substantiated", thus acknowledging that the relevant market had a geographic dimension (Continental Can, paragraph 35). A few years later, in United Brands v Commission (1978, paragraph 10), the Court of Justice stated this explicitly.

Since Continental Can and United Brands, the European Courts of Justice have discussed geographic market definition many times. The long history of case law is enshrined in the EU Market Definition Notice (1997), which describes the European Commission's approach to market definition, including to relevant geographic market. The Notice explains that a relevant market includes a geographic dimension, and that such relevant geographic market comprises the area in which the undertakings concerned are involved in the supply and demand of products or services, in which the conditions of competition are sufficiently homogeneous and which can be distinguished from neighbouring areas because the conditions of competition are appreciably different in those areas (EU Market Definition Notice, paragraph 8). A similar definition is found in Article 9(7) of the EU Merger Regulation, called the "geographic reference market".

The idea of a systematically defined geographic market is widely recognised outside the EU. For example, in the U.S., Section 7 of the Clayton Act prohibits mergers that substantially lessen competition or tend to create a monopoly in any line of commerce "in any section of the country". Ruling on a case under the Clayton Act, the U.S. Supreme Court explained in Brown Shoe Co., Inc. v. United States (1962) that the area of effective competition must be determined by reference to "a geographic market (the 'section of the country')" (Brown Shoe, paragraph 324). The Court further instructed that the definition of such market required "a pragmatic, factual approach" and that the market must "correspond to the commercial realities" of the industry (Brown Shoe, paragraph 336). It follows that the U.S. Horizontal Merger Guidelines (2010) note that the "arena of competition affected by the merger may be geographically bounded if geography limits some customers" willingness or ability to substitute to some products, or some suppliers' willingness or ability to serve some customers' (U.S. Horizontal Merger Guidelines, section 4.2).

The analytical approach to defining a geographic market is largely similar to defining the product market. In the context of a geographic market, demand substitution refers to the possibility of customers in a given area turning to suppliers outside that area. At the same time, supply substitution refers to the possibility of suppliers located outside a given area starting to supply customers inside that area. In this context, it is interesting to observe that different jurisdictions take different approaches to these competitive constraints. In particular, while demand substitution is generally accepted as the main competitive constraint, approach to supply substitution shows some variation. Overall, supply substitution is considered less often than demand substitution and, for example, the U.S. Horizontal Merger Guidelines explicitly state that market definition focuses solely on demand substitution, leaving supply substitution to be considered in the competitive assessment (U.S. Horizontal Merger Guidelines, section 4). In contrast, while demand substitution is typically considered the most effective and immediate constraint under the EU competition law (easyJet, paragraph 99), the EU Market Definition Notice accepts that supply substitution "may" be taken into account, including for the definition of a geographic market, if its effects are equivalent to those of demand substitution in terms of effectiveness and immediacy (EU Market Definition Notice, paragraphs 20 and 21).

The factors considered in the definition of a geographic market may be different from those for a product market. The OECD has observed (OECD 2016, paragraph 44) that, with regard to geographic markets, transport costs are one of the most frequently cited, and potentially determinative, factors. They increase the relative price of imports (or lower their quality) and, if sufficiently high, effectively close a market to foreign producers and support a narrower market definition. Transport costs are nonetheless not the only factor, and the OECD has further observed that product characteristics, regulatory and trade barriers, consumer preferences and characteristics as well as market dynamics and commercial relationships are commonly considered (OECD 2016, sections 3.3.2 – 3.3.5). It could be noted that at least some of these factors appear capable of having an impact on both demand and – where considered – supply substitution: For example transport costs, trade barriers or the perishable nature of a product may have an impact on both demand and supply substitution. In the definition of a geographic market, the practical impact on market definition of demand and supply substitution may thus be close to each other in some respects and cases, or at least closer than in product market definition.

Bibliography

Bailey, D. and John, L. E. (eds.), *Bellamy and Child: European Union Law of Competition* (8th edn, Oxford University Press 2018)

Faull, J. and Nikpay, A. (eds.), *The EU Law of Competition* (3rd edn, Oxford University Press 2014)

Commission Notice on the definition of the relevant market for the purposes of Community competition law, OJ C 372, 9.12.1997, p. 5 ("EU Market Definition Notice")

OECD Secretariat Background Paper, Defining geographic markets across national borders, 28-29 November 2016 ("OECD 2016")

U.S. Department of Justice and the Federal Trade Commission, Horizontal Merger Guidelines (2010) ("U.S. Horizontal Merger Guidelines")

The information and views set out in this text are those of the author(s) and do not necessarily reflect the official opinion of the European Commission.

See also

Dominance (notion), Relevant market

G

GROUP PURCHASING ORGANIZATION

Quentin B. SCHÄFER
University of Strathclyde

Definition

Group purchasing organisations ("GPOs") are organisations that negotiate and jointly purchase inputs from sellers on behalf of a group of buyers. Joint purchasing can take place through jointly controlled or owned companies, cooperatives, contract, or informal arrangements. Other terms for arrangements identical or similar to GPOs include "joint purchasing organisations", "joint purchasing joint ventures", "purchasing alliances", and "joint purchasing agreements". Whereas GPOs are commonly pro-competitive, they must be distinguished from anti-competitive buyer cartels. Their anti-competitive effects and pro-competitive efficiencies, as well as their organisation, determine the legality of GPOs.

Commentary

Joint purchasing arrangements are potentially problematic for two reasons: First, they can create or enhance monopsony power in the upstream buying market. Second, they may enable anti-competitive collusion in the downstream selling market by homogenising cost structures, allowing information exchange, and providing a forum for cartelisation.

GPOs, by placing negotiations and purchases at arms-length and making it transparent that the members are negotiating jointly through the GPO, ameliorate those concerns. Like other cooperation agreements, GPOs may entail other fact-specific efficiency gains, such as cost reductions, economies of scale, or innovation. Market power on the buyers' side may also countervail market power in the upstream selling market.

U.S.

Joint purchasing is potentially suspect under §1 of the Sherman Act as an instance of collusive monopsony. Pure buyer cartels are subject to the Sherman Act's per se prohibition, *Mandeville Island Farms v. American Crystal Sugar*, 334 U.S. 219 (1948), on the basis that cartelisation of buying markets is almost never pro-competitive, whereas joint purchasing arrangements including GPOs are subject to the rule of reason standard because they generally create legitimate efficiencies, *Northwest Wholesale Stationers, Inc. v Pacific Stationery & Printing Co.*, 472 U.S. 284 (1985).

According to the Competitor Collaboration Guidelines, the DoJ and FTC will not normally challenge a joint purchasing arrangement if it accounts for less than 20% of any affected market. The decisional practice of the agencies reveals four factors that are crucial in addition to case-specific efficiencies, see e.g. U.S. Dept. of Justice Business Review Letter to The American Optometric Association and the AOAExcel GPO, LLC (Jan. 15, 2020): First, if members can opt-out of GPO commitments, collusion is disincentivised. Second, membership caps can limit monopsony power. Third, allowing non-members to participate in certain GPO activities decreases market power vis-à-vis other buyers. Fourth, structuring the GPO such that it does not share information between competitors, e.g. employing independent negotiators and ensuring confidentiality, will decrease the risk of collusion.

In the U.S., GPOs are particularly prevalent in the healthcare sector. The Health Care Statements had set out a more lenient approach than the Competitor Collaboration Guidelines, providing a soft safe harbour where the joint purchases (a) account for less than 35% of a seller's total sales of the purchased good or service in the relevant market, and (b) cost less than 20% of the total revenues from all goods and services sold downstream by any competing participant in the GPO. In 2023, the DoJ and FTC withdrew the Health Care Statements. Before their withdrawal, the DoJ had also applied this more lenient standard in other areas. The rationale of the '35-20' soft safe harbour was that the first condition prevents the accumulation of monopsony power and the second condition reduces the likelihood of collusion through commonality of costs.

Given the withdrawal of the Health Care statements, the further application of the "35-20" soft safe harbour is unlikely. The DoJ's statement accompanying their withdrawal notes that the statements were "overly permissive on certain subjects, such as information sharing". The statements also included three further factors outside the safe harbour that reduce scrutiny: non-exclusivity; independent program administrators; and confidentiality between the GPO and individual members. Given that these factors are similar to the decisional practice of the DoJ, they are likely to continue to play a role, though are less likely to absolve agreements that exceed the old or even the new safe harbour.

Yet, it is worth noting that some commentators have doubted whether these factors are effective screens to recognise anti-competitive joint purchasing arrangements.

EU

"Joint purchasing" is potentially suspect under Article 101(1) TFEU. As highlighted in Case C-67/13 P *Groupement des Cartes Bancaires* ECLI:EU:C:2014:2204 and Case C-211/22 *Super Bock* ECLI:EU:C:2023:529, the line between "by object" and "by effect" restrictions is context sensitive. Nonetheless, joint purchasing will generally be assessed "by effect". Yet, when a joint purchasing agreement facilitates cartelisation, including but not limited to "hardcore" restrictions, it will be assessed "by object". Pure buyer cartels are treated as "by object" restrictions "since they involve direct interference with the essential parameters of competition on the relevant market", Case T-29/05 *Deltafina* EU:T:2010:355, para 239. The distinction between joint purchasing arrangements and buyer cartels (outside the inclusion of hardcore restraints) is dependent on whether there are legitimate efficiencies and whether a transparently distinct organisation conducts the joint purchasing instead of competitors coordinating cartel members' actions behind the scenes. This is so even though the term "GPO" is not in use in Europe.

There is no block exemption applicable to joint purchasing arrangements. Nonetheless, the Commission's Guidelines on horizontal co-operation agreements set out a "soft safe harbour": If the undertakings' market share is no more than 15% on the upstream selling market as well as no more than 15% of the downstream buying market, challenges are unlikely.

If found to contravene Article 101(1) TFEU, joint purchasing arrangements can be justified through Article 101(3) TFEU. As a general matter, joint purchasing agreements produce efficiencies, but the efficiencies must be indispensable and passed on to consumers to be recognised under Article 101(3) TFEU. In particular, the Guidelines require that lower purchasing costs achieved through joint purchasing must be passed on to consumers in the form of lower prices, the likelihood of which depends on the undertakings' downstream market power and whether the joint purchasing arrangement is exclusive. The Court of Justice has also emphasised that "in a market where product prices vary according to the volume of orders, the activities of cooperative purchasing associations may, depending on the size of their membership, constitute a significant counterweight to the contractual power of large producers and make way for more effective competition", Case C-250/92 *Gøttrup-Klim* ECLI:EU:C:1994:413, para 32.

Compared to U.S. antitrust law, it remains less clear in how far the organisation of joint purchasing determines its legality. Nonetheless, the organisation of a joint purchasing arrangement is likely to be taken into account when assessing the agreement's categorisation, its effects, and/or pro-competitive benefits under Article 101(3) TFEU; the more independent a joint purchasing arrangement is, the less likely it will give rise to collusion.

In the EU, joint purchasing enforcement has focused on food, retail, agriculture, and commodities. Prominent enforcement actions in relation to buyer cartels were taken in relation to tobacco, retail, and commodities. Meanwhile, prominent enforcement actions in relation to joint purchasing arrangements have been located mainly in the retail sector. Buyer cartels have generally been subject to fines whereas GPOs are generally subject to commitments.

Bibliography

Blair, R. D. and Durrance C. P., "Group Purchasing Organizations, Monopsony, and Antitrust Policy" (2013) 35(7) *Managerial and Decision Economics* 433

Blair, R. D. and Harrison, J. L., "Cooperative Buying, Monopsony Power, and Antitrust Policy" (1991) 86 *Northwestern University Law Review* 331

Blair, R. D. and Herndon, J. B., "An Economic Analysis of the Joint Purchasing Safety Zone" (1995) 23 *Journal of Law, Medicine and Ethics* 177

Gam, L., "European Competition Law Scrutiny of Purchasing Alliances" (June 2021) *CPI Antitrust Chronicle*

Jacobson, J. M. and Dorman G. J., "Joint Purchasing, Monopsony and Antitrust" (1991) 36 *The Antitrust Bulletin* 1

DoJ/FTC, Statements of Antitrust Enforcement Policy in Health Care (August 1996)

DoJ/FTC, Antitrust Guidelines for Collaborations Among Competitors (April 2000)

Guidelines on the applicability of Article 101 of the Treaty on the Functioning of the European Union to horizontal co-operation agreements (2023/C 259/01)

See also

Collective dominance

G

GUIDELINES

Adriana HERNANDEZ PEREZ
Department of Economics, Fundação Getúlio Vargas, Brazil

Gabriel DE ABREU MADEIRA
Department of Economics, Universidade de São Paulo, Brazil

■ Definition

In competition policy, guidelines offer principles for addressing competition cases such as mergers between companies or anticompetitive behaviors like price-fixing and foreclosure. These publications are crafted to reflect sound economic theory and assist members of competition authorities, market agents, and other analysts on how to handle cases and procedures. Guidelines are soft law documents because they provide recommendations that are not legally binding. They are purported to complement the application of the national competition law. Guidelines are also adopted to support practitioners with respect to the institutional procedures of competition agencies. For instance, there are specific guidelines on evidence submissions for companies participating in cartel leniency program and on penalty calculations for antitrust violations.

■ Commentary

Based on best practices and/or well-founded theory, guidelines serve as an essential working tool across various fields, including medicine, engineering, and education. In medicine, guidelines propose protocols for clinical practice, ensuring consistency and adherence to best practices in patient care. In engineering, guidelines promote safety standards, reliability, and efficiency in designing and constructing infrastructure projects. In education, guidelines assist in the development of curricula, teaching methods, and assessment standards.

Competition agencies adopt guidelines of analysis because of their convenience. By providing a roadmap for competition analysis, a guide facilitates the work of members of competition authorities, market agents, and other analysts. However, its contribution extends far beyond this didactic effect. By establishing clear parameters for procedural analysis, guidelines increase predictability regarding the procedural analyses that lead to decisions by competition authorities and, to some extent, to its conclusion.

All competition analyses are grounded on well-established economic theories that identify the conditions under which certain strategies (conducts or market concentration operations) can artificially increase companies' market power without offering benefits to consumers. These theories assist in evaluating the plausibility of potential anticompetitive conducts and/or mergers, informing about the economic conditions and incentives required for their practice, as well as assessing their effects on competition and/or welfare. Moreover, it is essential to analyze robust and reliable empirical evidence related to these anticompetitive actions.

A guide clarifies and makes these elements transparent by structuring and organizing how they should be presented in a case. Often, thorough evaluations can be conducted by following standardized procedures. In such cases, a clear outline of steps for the competition authority is essential. Which types of conduct warrant examination? What evidence is required to substantiate these examinations? Which methodologies are appropriate for analysis? Addressing these questions ensures a comprehensive understanding of the competitive landscape in typical scenarios.

A well-established framework brings predictability and legal certainty. Additionally, the standardization and clarity of the evaluation criteria reduce the likelihood of political or economic influence on decisions. It becomes more challenging to make a favorable decision for a well-connected (and/or well-advised) agent if clear parameters indicate an opposing decision. Additionally, in this context, guidelines can protect competition agency's staff from undue pressure by interest groups.

Moreover, with well-established criteria and parameters, companies are discouraged from engaging in practices that clearly violate competition principles. This is beneficial not only for its deterrent effect but also because it reduces the number of cases reaching antitrust authorities. One important consequence is that it frees up scarce public resources and allows antitrust agencies to focus on more complex cases that require specialized attention.

Despite the clear advantages of having guidelines to perform these analyses, it is important to note that antitrust activity requires some degree of discretion. In complex cases, the formulation of hypotheses and the collection and analysis of evidence demand skilled and less standardized work. Certain indicators, such as a specific level of market concentration, might be concerning in some market contexts (e.g., where capacity constraints are relevant) but may not raise competitive concerns in others.

Additionally, markets are dynamic and evolve over time, leading to shifts in competitive concerns and the development of new theories. For example, digital platform markets, which have recently become a significant focus of competition authorities' attention, involve multiple parties and often create interdependencies between various markets. Consequently, defining the relevant market, a key step in traditional antitrust analysis, becomes more challenging and sometimes less clear-cut and less relevant, as the focus shifts from a single market to its interconnections within the ecosystem.

Therefore, it is helpful when a competition analysis guide delineates the scope for discretion, specifying which factors justify analyzing a case in a traditional manner, based on jurisprudence, and which factors could be evaluated on a case-by-case basis, incorporating new theories of harm and analytical criteria, such as those for digital markets. Additionally, guidelines are updated over time.

Competition analysis guidelines typically share a common structure, with at least three sections. The introductory section describes its scope, overall mission, and main principles. A second section presents the procedures to be followed by the analyst, which, frequently, follow a specific sequence. A third section describes the most important theories of harm that should be investigated. This section aims to connect the well-stablished economic theories to the procedures of analysis by suggesting the type of evidence and factors to investigate when testing a given theory.

Guidelines differ on how didactic they are when discussing procedures and concepts. Historically, competition guidelines have provided the main theoretical references that fundament the concepts and reasonings underpinning the directives. Some guidelines present simple theoretical examples to clarify a concept, others refer to the related jurisprudence and/or other documents published by the competition authority. Finally, there can be guidelines on how to handle more complex sectors, like energy or digital platforms.

The scope of guidelines or recommended practices is extensive. In addition to merger analysis guidelines, competition authorities produce guidelines on market analysis and the assessment of significant market power, guidelines for cartel leniency programs, guidelines for calculating fines, and more.

The most recent American merger guidelines to date was launched in 2023, benefiting from the intense public debate carried over the last years on how to improve antitrust enforcement in the challenging digital landscape. The guidelines refer profusely on the county's jurisprudence to clarify the adopted concepts and the new anticompetitive concerns.

It proposes 11 analysis directives. The first four focus on direct competition between companies (horizontal mergers), while the next two address mergers between companies in related markets (non-horizontal mergers). Together, these six directives help agencies identify whether a merger raises initial competition concerns.

The remaining directives, from 7 to 11, explain how to apply the first six frameworks in specific situations, such as in digital platform markets, consolidating markets, serial mergers, mergers involving rival buyers, and those impacting labor and supplier markets, as well as partial acquisitions.

The Brazilian non-horizontal merger guidelines, launched in 2024, highlights foreclosure theories, and concerns with raising rival's costs and sharing of commercially sensitive information, besides considering coordinated effects. The guidelines mention new concerns, such as evading regulation and discriminatory access to ecosystems.

The European non-horizontal merger guidelines, launched in 2008, emphasize the theories of input and output foreclosure and coordinated effects. They also address concerns regarding the information sharing among companies. Notably, the European jurisprudence evolved to include new theories of harm since the guidelines' publication, as the European Commission's assessments of the Google/FitBit (2020) and NVIDIA/Arm (2022) cases have shown. Also, new regulations, such as the Digital Market Act (2022), have been enacted to tackle anticompetitive behavior in the digital economy considering the new theoretical developments in the field.

References

Sean Sullivan (2024), *The 2023 U.S. Merger Guidelines: a review*, Concurrences.

Brazil, Conselho de Administração de Defesa da Concorrência (2024), Guia de Análise de Fusões Não Horizontais.

European Commission (2022), Guidelines on Vertical Restrains.

European Commission (2008), Guidelines on the assessment of non-horizontal mergers under the Council Regulation on the control of concentrations between undertakings.

OECD (2019) Recommendations and Best Practices on Competition Law and Policy.

U.S., Department of Justice and Federal Trade Commission (2023), Merger Guidelines.

See also

Commission (EU) communication, Relevant market

G

GUN JUMPING

Rafael ALLENDESALAZAR
MLAB Abogados

■ Definition

Most jurisdictions have adopted *ex-ante* merger control regimes, providing for mandatory pre-notification of concentrations above certain thresholds, together with an obligation not to implement them until the competent competition authority has cleared the transaction ("standstill obligation"). Gun-jumping encompasses any behaviour that infringes these closely related obligations by implementing the transaction either before its notification ("procedural gun-jumping") or its approval ("substantive gun-jumping"). The term gun-jumping originated in sports and refers to athletes starting the race before the starting gun is fired. Gun-jumping has lately hit the headlines in the EU as some competition authorities have adopted stricter interpretations of those obligations and imposed staggering fines.

■ Commentary

The concept of gun-jumping is not defined in EU competition Law. It refers to two related infringements of the EUMR: (i) the obligation to notify to the European Commission concentrations having an EU dimension prior to their implementation (Article 4(1)); and (ii) the obligation not to implement such concentrations until they have been approved (Article 7(1)); the Commission has granted a derogation from the standstill obligation (Article 7(3)); or the prescribed time limits have expired, and no decision has been issued (Article 10(6)).

While most jurisdictions have adopted mandatory pre-notification and standstill obligations, some have mandatory pre-merger notification but no standstill obligations (Italy, Latvia) and others have systems of purely voluntary notification (UK, Australia and New Zealand). In these jurisdictions, no sanctions for closing can apply, unless the authorities have previously issued a hold-separate interim order.

Gun-jumping has become a hot topic in the EU, as the Commission has adopted an increasingly stringent and formalistic interpretation of the EUMR, and fines that were not imposed in early cases and then were initially relatively low (€33,000 in *Samsung/AST (1998)* and €229,000 in *A.P. Møller (1999)*, skyrocketed to €20 million in *Electrabel (2009)* and *Marine Harvest (2014)*; €28 million in *Canon (2019)* and €124.5 million in *Altice (2018)*. NCAs normally impose substantially lower fines, although the French Competition Authority slapped Altice with an €80 million fine (2016), and the Slovenian authority fined Agrokor with €54 million (2019).

Procedural gun-jumping may occur primarily in three scenarios. First, it may result from an erroneous application of the notification thresholds. The risk of such infringements is greater in jurisdictions that use thresholds requiring subjective evaluation by the merging firms, as is the case in Spain with the market share threshold. But it may also occur with more objective thresholds such as turnover, as in *A.P. Møller (1999)*. Second, when there are disputes on whether there is a "concentration". Such disputes can occur as most jurisdictions, instead of defining mergers based on objective facts such as requiring a minimum stockholding, apply a definition leaving ample room for interpretation: the "change of control on a lasting basis" (Article 3(1) EUMR) which occurs when an undertaking can influence strategic decisions of another undertaking. The risk of gun-jumping has significantly increased as competition authorities have interpreted that change of control may occur on a purely de facto basis and that it does not require the acquirer to exercise such control; the mere "*possibility*" of exercising decisive influence suffices *(Electrabel; Marine Harvest; Marine Harvest, T-704/14, para. 58)*. Thirdly, lack of notification may be intentional, to avoid delaying the implementation of the merger, as could have occurred in *Canon (2019)*, where the parties agreed to a "warehousing" two-step transaction structure to ensure that the seller could secure full consideration for its subsidiary by a certain date, while Canon would not formally acquire it before obtaining clearance. The Commission, however, concluded the merger occurred already with the first step. The parties may also want to avoid competition scrutiny; a risky strategy as, even though the infringement for not notifying is instantaneous and has a three-year limitation period, the standstill obligations is continuous and lasts until the transaction is cleared *(Marine Harvest, T-704/14, paras. 304 and 355)* or control is abandoned *(Electrabel T-332/09, para. 212)*. For instance, even though its infringement for not notifying was time barred, Electrabel was nevertheless fined €20 million for breaching its standstill obligation.

Substantive gun-jumping can occur as the scope of the standstill obligation remains nebulous. There is no legal definition of "implementation" and the Court had never addressed this question until its *EY* ruling. The Court concluded that Article 7 only prohibits transactions "which, in whole or in part, in fact or in law, contribute[s] to the change in control of the target undertaking", whereas transactions that do not present "a direct functional link" with the implementation of a concentration, even if they are ancillary or preparatory to the merger, do not fall within the scope of that provision (paras. 49 and 59). The Court added that having effects on the market is in itself insufficient to apply Article 7, but measures having no effect might nevertheless contribute to the change in control (paras. 50-51). Finally, the Court rejected the Commission's view that Article 7 and Article 101 TFEU apply in parallel; the former should not apply to measures that give rise to coordination between undertakings if they do not contribute to the implementation of a concentration, as it would unduly extend the scope of Article 7 and reduce that of Regulation 1/2003 and Article 101 TFEU.

The risk of incurring fines in substantive gun-jumping has significantly increased following the Commission's *Altice* decision. This decision has created great turmoil amongst practitioners, as practices that so far were common in M&A, such as including pre-closing covenants in the SPAs requiring the seller to obtain the buyer's consent on certain transactions, and post-merger implementation planning discussions and information exchange, were deemed contrary to Article 7. The appeal that is pending should clarify how to distinguish practices ancillary or preparatory to the concentration form its implementation.

The eye-watering fines totalling €124.5 million imposed on *Altice* also highlight a singularity in the Commission's gun-jumping fining policy, which is reflected in the table of decisions attached hereunder: except in *Electrabel*, where the infringement of Article 4 was time-barred, the Commission imposes in each case not one but two fines, in most cases identical, for one and the same infringement: implementing the concentration before it has been notified and cleared. Since the current EUMR removed the obligation to notify within a specific deadline, any infringement of Article 4 automatically results in an infringement of Article 7. In *Marine Harvest*, the AG concluded that the latter infringement subsumes the former and proposed to annul the Article 4 fine. The CJEU however confirmed both fines based on a formalistic interpretation of the principle of *ne bis in idem* and arguing that the obligation to notify is positive, whereas the standstill obligation is negative. The appellant had not raised the validity of Article 4 EUMR in those proceedings. The legality of such "*unusual*" legal framework (*Marine Harvest T-704/14, p. 306)* will again be examined by the General Court in the pending appeal against the *Altice* Decision. It will have to rule on an objection of illegality and on the proportionality of two fines that are identical notwithstanding the duration of the alleged infringements being radically different: the infringement of Article 4 is instantaneous and lasts the day the transaction is closed, whereas the infringement of

Article 7 is continuous and lasts until the concentration is cleared.

In the U.S., Section 7A of the Hart-Scott-Rodino Act (HSR Act) requires parties to mergers exceeding certain thresholds to notify the FTC and the DOJ before closing. The acquirer must not exercise "substantial operational control" over the target prior to the expiration of the waiting period, which is typically 30 days but can be extended if the agencies issue a "Second Request".

Gun-jumping infringements can be brought under both Section 7A HSR and Section 1 of the Sherman Act, and may result in civil fines, injunctive relief, and disgorgement of illegally obtained profits. Cases are often settled.

Bibliography

Hatton, C., Comtois, Y. and Hamilton, A. (eds.) *Gun Jumping in Merger Control: A Jurisdictional Guide*, Concurrences, International Bar Association, 2019

Modrall, J. and Bourt, V., Gun jumping: An overview of EU and national case law, 20 April 2020, *e-Competitions Gun jumping*, Art. N° 92519

Suspensory Effects of Merger Notifications and Gun Jumping, OECD – Background Note by the Secretariat, 27-28 November 2018, DAF/COMP(2018)11

See also

Exchanges of information, Notification

HARDCORE RESTRICTIONS

Natasha TARDIF, Marc LÉVY, Audrey AUGUSTO
Reed Smith

■ Definition

The concept of "hardcore restrictions" is relevant for the purpose of the application of block exemption regulations implementing Article 101(3) TFEU. It refers to severe restrictions, which are likely to restrict competition and harm consumers or are not indispensable to the attainment of efficiency-enhancing effects. Agreements containing hardcore restrictions are excluded from the benefit of the block exemption, irrespective of the parties' market shares. Examples of hardcore restrictions include the imposition of fixed or minimum resale prices or certain territorial or customer sales restrictions in vertical agreements and market allocations, quantity restrictions or price fixing in horizontal agreements.

■ Commentary

Each block exemption regulation includes a closed list of hardcore restrictions. This list provides some legal certainty to undertakings, which as part of the self-assessment of their agreements, can identify measures likely to raise concerns regarding their compatibility with Article 101 TFEU.

Hardcore restrictions can be direct, for instance through an express contractual provision, or result from indirect measures aimed at inducing the other party to comply with a certain restriction, such as threats of contract termination or financial incentives made conditional upon the other party's compliance with a certain obligation. Hardcore restrictions can be adopted in isolation or in combination with other factors under the control of the parties.

The inclusion of a hardcore restriction in an agreement entails the loss of the benefit of the block exemption for the whole agreement. This means that undertakings would have to carry out a thorough self-examination of both the hardcore restriction and all other restrictions that may be included in their agreement, to try to demonstrate that their agreement complies with Article 101 TFEU.

In addition, agreements containing restrictions listed as hardcore restrictions in block exemption regulations cannot benefit from the safe harbour set out in the De Minimis Notice for agreements between undertakings which the European Commission considers to have non-appreciable effects on competition.

Despite the above, an agreement containing a hardcore restriction does not necessarily infringe Article 101 TFEU. More specifically, a hardcore restriction does not necessarily amount to a restriction by object under Article 101 TFEU. In *Coty*, Advocate General Wahl emphasized that the concept of "hardcore restriction" should be distinguished from the concept of "restrictions of competition by object", although they both refer to restrictions presumed to be particularly harmful for competition.

Undertakings can hence try to demonstrate that a given hardcore restriction, examined in its economic and legal context, is objectively justified and does not fall within the prohibition laid down in Article 101(1) TFEU. This will however be a very difficult endeavor in practice.

In the European Commission's view, hardcore restrictions generally constitute restrictions by object when assessed individually and, as a matter of fact, the hardcore restrictions listed in the various block exemption regulations usually correspond to restrictions which were identified in past decisions as restrictions by object in the category of agreements covered by each regulation. The Commission further considers that there is a presumption that an agreement containing a hardcore restriction has actual or likely negative effects and falls within Article 101(1) TFEU.

This presumption has however been called into question. In *Pedro IV Servicios*, the Court of Justice clarified that, where an agreement does not meet all the conditions provided for by a block exemption regulation, it will be caught by the prohibition laid down in Article 101(1) TFEU only if its object or effect is perceptibly to restrict competition within the internal market and it is capable of affecting trade between Member States. Building on this decision, Advocate General Mazák stated, in his Opinion delivered in *Pierre Fabre*, that, in his view, there was no "legal presumption" that an agreement including an hardcore restriction infringes Article 101(1) TFEU. He added that an individual examination is therefore required in order to assess whether an agreement has an anticompetitive object, even where it contains a hardcore restriction and is ineligible for a block exemption.

The Vertical Guidelines also acknowledge that, in exceptional cases, hardcore restrictions may be objectively necessary for the existence of an agreement of a particular type or nature and fall outside Article 101(1)

TFEU. The Vertical Guidelines give the examples of hardcore sales restrictions necessary to ensure public safety or health, to encourage investments undertaken to develop a new market or to test or introduce a new product.

As another defense, undertakings can argue that a specific agreement containing a hardcore restriction should benefit from an individual exemption under Article 101(3). In *Pierre Fabre*, the Court of Justice held that an undertaking has the option, in all circumstances, to assert, on an individual basis, the applicability of the exception provided for in Article 101(3) TFEU.

The Commission considers that there is a presumption that agreements containing a hardcore restriction are unlikely to fulfill the conditions of Article 101(3), which is why they do not benefit from the block exemption. This presumption is rebuttable and undertakings may demonstrate that likely efficiencies result from including the hardcore restriction in the agreement and that all the conditions of Article 101(3) are fulfilled. However, this has proven to be very difficult in practice, with some commentaries indicating that for the past fifteen years, no undertaking has successfully invoked Article 101(3) TFEU in cases in which the European Commission had significant competition concerns.

Bibliography

BAILEY, D. and JOHN, L. E., *Bellamy & Child European: Union Law of Competition* Oxford University Press, 2018, 8th Edition

FAULL, J. and NIKPAY, A., Faull & Nikpay: *The EU Law of Competition*, Oxford Competition law, 2014, 3rd Edition

GONZAGA, P. and ERDEI-GONZAGA, G., Vertical Restrictions & e-Commerce: An overview of EU and national case law, 14 April 2021, *e-Competitions Vertical Restrictions & E-commerce*, Art. N° 99276

PEEPERKORN, L., Defining restrictions "by object", September 2015, *Concurrences N° 3-2015*, Art. N° 74812, pp. 40-50

TUYTSCHAEVER, F., and WIJCKMANS, F., *Vertical Agreements in EU Competition Law*, 3rd Edition, Oxford University Press, 2018

WHISH, R. and BAILEY, D., *Competition Law*, Oxford University Press, 2018

WITT, A. C., Selective Distribution in the Age of E-Commerce: An overview of EU and national developments, 24 March 2021, *e-Competitions Selective Distribution*, Art. N° 99224

ZUKAKISHVILI, K., Luxury (by) object and the effects of silence of the Court of Justice in *Coty*, 2018

Commission Staff Working Document on the Evaluation of the Vertical Block Exemption Regulation, SWD(2020) 172 final

Guidance on restrictions of competition "by object" for the purpose of defining which agreements may benefit from the De Minimis Notice

Guidelines on the application of Article 81(3) of the Treaty (2004/C 101/08)

Notice on agreements of minor importance which do not appreciably restrict competition under Article 101(1) of the Treaty on the Functioning of the European Union (De Minimis Notice)

See also

Exclusive distribution, Freeriding, White clause, Passive sales

H

HART-SCOTT-RODINO FILING

Martin D'HALLUIN
News Corp

Definition

The Hart-Scott-Rodino Filing (merger) is a premerger notification that parties to certain large transactions must submit to the FTC and DOJ under the Hart-Scott-Rodino Antitrust Improvements Act of 1976, as amended (HSR Act). Premerger notification involves each person completing an HSR Form, also called a "Notification and Report Form for Certain Mergers and Acquisitions," with information about the transaction, information about the business (such as annual revenues broken down by industry, subsidiaries, shareholders, and regulatory filings), and certain documents prepared for the transaction. The HSR Act provides a 30-calendar day waiting period that must elapse before the reported transaction is consummated. The FTC and DOJ can stay that period until the companies provide additional information. At any time, either the FTC or DOJ can challenge the transaction in court if it believes that the proposed transaction would substantially lessen competition in violation of Section 7 of the Clayton Act.

Commentary

The United States was a pioneer among global competition law regimes in requiring parties to large transactions to submit filings before closing. The recent discussion on the costs and benefits of ex-post enforcement of monopolization cases highlights the originality of having the parties to large transactions give agencies a chance to intervene before the parties consummate mergers.

Filing event. Contrary to most jurisdictions, a definitive agreement is not needed to file the HSR Form and trigger the review period. Each party must submit an affidavit with their filings, attesting to the fact that a contract, an agreement in principle, or a letter of intent has been executed and that each person has a good faith intention of completing the transaction.

Filing obligation. The HSR Filing includes two separate forms submitted to the Federal Trade Commission (FTC) and the Antitrust Division of the U.S. Department of Justice (DOJ): one for the acquired person and one for the acquiring person. The acquiring person is the ultimate parent entity of the buyer, defined as the entity that controls the buyer, but is not controlled by any other entity. The acquiring person is the ultimate parent entity of the target. Control for HSR purposes means holding (i) 50% or more of the outstanding voting securities or having the right to 50% or more of the profits/ 50% or more of the assets in the event of dissolution of an unincorporated entity or (ii) having the contractual power presently to designate 50% or more of the directors (separate rules apply to trusts).

The HSR Act requires the acquired and acquiring persons to file notifications if the following thresholds are met (for transactions completed on or after February 23, 2022; amounts adjusted annually):

1. One person has net sales (all sales are for the most recent fiscal year) or total assets (all assets include assumed liabilities) of $20.2 million or more; the other person has net sales or total assets of $202 million or more; and as a result of the transaction, the acquiring person will hold stock and/or assets of the acquired person valued at more than $101 million; or
2. As a result of the transaction, the acquiring person will hold stock and/or assets of the acquired person valued at more than $403.9 million, regardless of the sales or assets of the acquiring and acquired persons.

Certain assets, such as cash or cash equivalent, are not included in the size of transaction test. Filing obligations need to be assessed by professionals on a case-by-case basis.

The parties can consummate a transaction once the initial (30-calendar day) or extended review period expires without challenge from the agencies. No formal approval is needed to close.

Exempt transactions. Certain exemptions apply even when the size of person and size of transaction tests are met. For example, certain acquisitions of assets in the ordinary course of business are exempt, such as acquisitions of new goods and current supplies (e.g., an airline purchases new jets from a manufacturer or a supermarket purchases its inventory from a wholesale distributor). The acquisition of certain types of real property is also exempt, including certain new and used facilities, unproductive real property (e.g., raw land), office and residential buildings, hotels, recreational land, agricultural land and retail rental space/ warehouses. Finally, the acquisition of non-U.S. assets is exempt where the sales within or into the U.S. attributable to those assets are $101 million (as adjusted) or less. This list is not comprehensive and exemptions need to be assessed on a case-by-case basis.

HSR Form. Each reporting entity (which is either the reporting person or an entity within the reporting person) must identify the acquiring and acquired persons involved and the structure of the transaction. Unless specified, a reporting person includes the ultimate parent entity and its controlled entities. The reporting person must provide certain balance sheets and other financial data as well as copies of certain documents that have been filed with the Securities and Exchange Commission. The reporting person must also submit certain planning and evaluation documents reviewed by officers or directors that pertain to the proposed transaction. The HSR Form also requires the reporting party to disclose whether the acquiring person or acquired entity currently derives revenue from businesses that fall within any of the same industry and product North American Industry Classification System ("NAICS") codes, and, if so, in which geographic areas they operate. Identification of overlapping codes may indicate whether the acquiring person and acquired entity engage in similar lines of business. Acquiring persons must describe certain previous acquisitions in the last five years of corporations or assets engaged in businesses in any of the overlapping codes identified. Special rules apply to joint-venture filings.

HSR fees. Each transaction (as opposed to each form) reported under the HSR Act is subject to the following fees: $45,000 for transactions valued at less than $202 million, $125,000 for transactions valued at $202 million or more and less than $919.9 million, and $280,000 for transactions valued at $1.0098 billion or more. The U.S. Senate passed the Merger Filing Fee Modernization Act of 2021 in June 2021. The bill, which remains subject to passage in the House of Representatives and being signed into law, would amend the HSR Act to (1) replace this framework with a six-tiered regime; (2) significantly increase fees for transactions valued at more than $1 billion (up to 7 times current levels); and (3) decrease fees to $30,000 for transactions valued at less than $161.5 million.

Confidentiality. Neither the information submitted nor the fact that a notification has been filed is made public by the agencies except as part of a legal or administrative action in which one of the agencies is a party or in other narrowly defined circumstances permitted by the HSR Act. The fact that a transaction is under investigation may become apparent if the agencies interview third-parties during their investigation.

Failure to file. Companies or individuals that fail to comply with the reporting requirements of the HSR Act are subject to steep civil penalties – up to $46,517 per day as of January 10, 2022 – until a corrective filing is made with the agencies, irrespective of whether the underlying transaction raises antitrust concerns. In a recent December 22, 2021 decision, the FTC settled charges in two separate matters for repeated violations of the HSR Act and imposed fines totaling nearly $2 million.

Possible changes. In September 2020, the agencies proposed two changes to the existing rules. The first change would require filers to disclose additional information about their associates and to aggregate acquisitions by the same issuer across those entities. The second proposed change is a rule that would exempt the acquisition of 10 percent or less of an issuer's voting securities unless the acquiring person has a competitively significant relationship with the issuer.

Bibliography

Acquisitions Under the Hart-Scott-Rodino Antitrust Improvements Act (Third Edition), by S. Axinn

Antitrust Improvements Act Notification and Report Form for Certain Mergers and Acquisitions Instructions OMB: 3084-0005

Premerger Notification Guide I – What is the Premerger Notification Program? An Overview, Federal Trade Commission

Premerger Notification Practice Manual (Fifth Edition)

U.S. Senate Judiciary Committee, Grassley, Klobuchar Bill to Ensure Antitrust Authorities Have Resources to Protect Consumers Unanimously Passes out of Committee, Press Release, 13 May 2021

See also

Notification

HEARING OFFICER

Clara CALINI
Italian Competition Authority

■ Definition

The Hearing Officer is an independent arbiter in disputes on procedural issues that arise when the European Commission applies EU competition law. Domestic systems of competition law that make use of the "adminisrative" systme of law enforcement may make use of the EU's model of the Hearing Officer as a means of enhancing the procedural legality of the decisions of administrative agencies.

■ Commentary

The Hearing Officer in EU competition law is an independent arbiter in disputes on procedural issues arising between case handlers and defendants/interested parties in the context of competition and merger proceedings. The enforcement of competition law may either be carried out by the courts of a state, where the national competition authority – NCA – investigates and then challenges the case before courts, or may be administrative, where the NCA is the prosecutor but also adopts the decision, which is then subject to judicial review if appealed by interested parties. The role of the Hearing Officer in the EU was conceived in the context of the Commission's administrative system of competition law enforcement in order to ensure an independent review of any issues regarding the effective exercise of procedural rights throughout the proceedings, as a means of enhancing the procedural legality of the decisions of administrative agencies.

The EU model of a Hearing Officerhas been adopted by some NCAs in the EU, e.g. the Conseilleur Auditeur in France) and elsewhere (e.g., the Procedural Officer in the UK). Hearing officers act independently in performing their duties and are generally attached to the President/ Commissioners directly; depending on the jurisdiction, the Hearing Officer may have autonomous decisional power (as in the case of the EU or, with a narrower scope, in the UK) or may report on the matter to the College of Commissioners or the President (as in France).

The role and tasks of the European Commission's Hearing Officer are currently defined by decision n. 2011/695 of the President of the European Commission, to which we refer for a comprehensive description of its functions and decisional powers. A first main task of the European Commission's Hearing Officer is that of ensuring the respect of the right to be heard, with a specific role in the organisation of oral hearings that includes the adoption of all preparatory measures to make sure that the parties develop their arguments effectively (such as circulating in advance questions to the addressees of a statement of objections). The preparation of the oral hearing by the Hearing Officer seems an increasingly important procedural safeguard, given the growing complexities of competition and merger cases and the multiplicity of issues arising with respect to an increasing number of sectors (e.g., digital markets). The Hearing Officer has also the specific task of deciding whether third parties are to be heard, when applicants show a sufficient interest in the hearing.

More generally, parties involved in the proceedings may now refer all issues relating to legal professional privilege, the privilege against self-incrimination, the right of access to the investigation file (including confidentiality claims) or deadlines for replying to decisions requiring information: while initially the role of the Hearing Officer was restricted to the state of the procedure following the issue of a statement of objections, the revised mandate adopted in 2011 extends its function to the initial investigative phase, identifying the Hearing Officer as the parties' interlocutor on all the issues listed above. Similarly, defendants can call upon the Hearing Officer to ensure the effective exercise of their procedural rights in the context of commitment or settlement procedures. Depending on the situation, the Hearing Officer has decisional powers, may issue a recommendation or report the matter to the Competition Commissioner/College of Commissioners.

Prior to the adoption of a decision, the Hearing Officer is then attributed the specific task of preparing a final report confirming that the draft decision deals only with objections in respect of which the parties have been given the opportunity of making known their views.

Going forward, the Hearing Officer is expected to continue playing a crucial role in ensuring procedural fairness of administrative decision making: since competition and merger proceedings are becoming increasingly complex in terms of issues as well as significant when looking at fines and remedies, ensuring fairness of the procedure by which a decision is made not only reduces unnecessary litigation but also contributes to reinforcing the legality of its outcome based on the input and effective interaction of all interested parties. European Courts are pushing in this direction with a number of important judgements, such as Intel and Qualcomm (both on the failure to record interviews), or UPS (on disclosure of econometric models prior to a decision) and Unilever (on the obligation to examine the evidence submitted), which make a common point on the importance to have due regard for the defendants' rights of defence throughout the administrative proceedings. The Hearing Officer may thus contribute to verifying ex ante that the parties are put in a position to effectively defend themselves in each specific case, thereby also enhancing the impartiality and quality of the final decision.

Bibliography

CALVANI, T. and LEAHY, J., "A Larger Role for the Hearing Officer: a Modest Proposal" (2018) 6 *Journal of Antitrust Enforcement* 2

PRETE, L., DEKEYSER, K. et al. (eds.), *Regulation 1/2003 and EU Antitrust Enforcement: A Systematic Guide* (1st edn, Kluwer Law International 2022), Chapter 4

WILS, W. P. J., "The Role of the Hearing Officer in Competition Proceedings before the European Commission" (2012) 35 *World Competition Law and Economics Review* 3

See also

Akzo procedure, Independence and impartiality

H

HORIZONTAL COOPERATION AGREEMENT

Sara CAPOZZI, Stefano FIRPO
Assonime

■ Definition

The term horizontal agreement refers to an agreement concluded between undertakings operating at the same level of the production or distribution chain. Since they involve competing companies, horizontal agreements are considered more problematic than vertical agreements from a competition law perspective. Agreements designed to eliminate competition among competitors, like cartel arrangements to jointly fix prices, restrict output or partition markets, are a key concern of most systems of competition law. However, competitors may enter into agreements with one another with the aim of cooperating in certain areas, such as research and development (R&D), production, commercialization or standardisation. Unlike cartels, such cooperation agreements are not necessarily anti-competitive. On the contrary, by allowing companies to join efforts and resources and integrate economic activities, they may be efficiency-enhancing and procompetitive.

■ Commentary

In the EU Article 101 (1) TFEU prohibits agreements that restrict competition, unless they satisfy the criteria in Article 101(3) which allows for weighing the restrictive effects against the efficiencies created by the agreement.

Horizontal cooperation can bring about significant efficiencies and economic benefits to consumers, by enabling firms to share risk, pool know-how, activities and skills, save costs, achieve economies of scale or scope and, thus, for example, develop and market new products or technology, penetrate new markets or address shortages and disruptions in supply chains.

Moreover, especially for small and medium-sized firms, cooperation can be an important means to adapt to changing market dynamics and compete more effectively. On the other hand, horizontal cooperation agreements can also raise competition concerns, in particular where they increase the market power held by the parties to an extent that enables them to charge higher prices or negatively affect other parameters of competition (output, variety, innovation). They may also lead to a collusive outcome by facilitating coordination outside the field of cooperation, for instance as a result of the disclosure of commercially sensitive information or the achievement of a significant commonality of costs. Moreover, some agreements, such as production and standardisation agreements, may lead to anticompetitive foreclosure of competitors, for example by denying effective access to an important input or excluding innovative technologies.

The EU Commission's recently revised framework to evaluate the compatibility of horizontal cooperation agreements with Article 101 TFEU consists of two block exemption regulations ("HBERs") covering R&D and specialisation agreements, regulation 2023/1066 and regulation 2023/1067 respectively, which entered into force on 1 July 2023, and a set of Guidelines on the applicability of Article 101 TFEU to horizontal cooperation agreements ("Horizontal Guidelines"). According to the Commission, the new texts update and further clarify the application of competition rules in this area, so that companies are not discouraged from collaborating in ways which are economically desirable, with a view, for example, to supporting the green and digital transitions, promoting the resilience of the internal market and achieving other key policy objectives of the EU industrial strategy.

The HBERs create a safe harbour for certain categories of R&D and specialisation agreements which are exempted from the Article 101(1) prohibition, on the assumption that they satisfy the conditions set out in Article 101(3). For the safe harbour to apply, the combined market share of the parties to the agreement must not exceed specified thresholds (25% for R&D and 20% for specialisation agreements). Moreover, the block exemption only applies as far as the agreement does not contain any of the hardcore restrictions listed in the HBERs and other specific conditions are satisfied. The Horizontal Guidelines set out the analytical framework for the competitive assessment of horizontal cooperation agreements and provide specific guidance in relation to the most common types of horizontal cooperation in areas such as R&D, production, joint purchasing, commercialisation, standardisation and information exchange. Importantly, the revised Guidelines now contain a new chapter aimed to clarify how cooperation agreements will be assessed when they pursue sustainability objectives.

The Commission's framework covers only "horizontal" cooperation, that is, agreements entered into between actual or potential competitors. In this perspective, a fundamental question is whether the parties can be deemed to be at least potential competitors, otherwise the agreement is not a horizontal one and usually less likely to be caught by the Article 101 (1) prohibition. According to the Guidelines, an undertaking is considered a potential competitor if, in the absence of the agreement, it is likely that, within a short period of time, it would undertake the investments, including the switching costs, needed to enter the relevant market. As clarified, this assessment should be based on realistic ground as a mere theoretical possibility to enter a market is not sufficient (HGL § 16). Further considerations stemming from the latest case law of the EU Court of Justice (e.g. absence of insurmountable barriers to entry, perception of an established operator in the market) may also be taken into account (see, for example, Generics (UK), C- 307/18, paragraphs 36-58; Lundbeck, C-591/16 P, paragraphs 38 and 58-59).

For cooperation agreements falling into the scope of Article 101 (1) TFEU, the first step is to determine whether they have as their object or effect an appreciable restriction of competition. The approach adopted by the Commission is that in principle cooperation agreements will only restrict competition by object if they do not genuinely concern, for example, R&D, production or joint purchasing, but serve simply as a tool to engage in a disguised cartel. This also reflects the ECJ's case law, whereby the notion of restriction of competition by object is to be interpreted strictly and only refers to certain types of cooperation that are by their very nature so harmful to competition that it is not necessary to examine their impact on the market (see, for example, Cartes Bancaires, C-67/13 P, paragraphs 49-51; Budapest Bank, C-228/18, paragraphs 35-37).

Accordingly, in any other case a closer examination of the actual or potential effects is required. The Commission will assess case by case whether cooperation agreements have or are likely to have a negative impact on one or more competitive parameters (price, output, quality, variety or innovation) against the "counterfactual" scenario (i.e. competition that would have existed in the absence of the agreement). Consideration needs to be given to the actual economic context in which the cooperation occurs, including the market structure and the parties' market power (HGL § 30). Cooperation agreements are indeed less likely to give rise to competition concerns when the parties have a low combined market share. In this respect, for some types of agreements the Guidelines provide safe harbour thresholds (20% for production agreements; 15% for joint purchasing and commercialization agreements). Apart from safe harbours, they indicate that cooperation agreements generally fall outside the scope of Article 101(1) where the parties to the agreement would not be able to independently enter a market or carry out the project or the activity covered by the cooperation (HGL § 33).

When a cooperation agreement is found to restrict competition, it is for the parties to demonstrate, in the context of Article 101(3), that it creates efficiency gains sufficient to offset the negative impact on competition. As emphasised in the Guidelines, the analysis of the efficiency gains largely focuses on identifying the complementary resources, skills and assets (e.g. capital, technology, logistic or distribution networks) that each of the parties brings to the cooperation and evaluating whether the resulting efficiencies are such that all four conditions of Article 101(3) are fulfilled (HGL §§ 37-38).

In the U.S. the competitive analysis of agreements between competitors is conducted under Section 1 of the Sherman Act 1890 and the approach adopted by U.S. Antitrust Agencies is to a large extent consistent with that of the EU Commission. While hardcore cartels are generally treated as criminal offences and per se infringements of the Sherman Act, all other cooperation agreements are analysed under the rule of reason to determine their overall competitive effect (see Antitrust Guidelines for collaborations among competitors, issued by the Federal Trade Commission and the U.S. Department of Justice, April 2000).

Bibliography

JONES, A., SUFRIN, B. and DUNNE, N., *Jones & Sufrin's EU Competition Law: Text, Cases and Materials*, Oxford University Press, 6th edition, 2019, Chapters 9 and 10

WHISH, R. and BAILEY, D., *Competition Law*, Oxford University Press, 10th edition, chapter 15

Antitrust Guidelines for collaborations among competitors, issued by the Federal Trade Commission and the U.S. Department of Justice, April 2000

Communication from the Commission - Guidelines on the applicability of Article 101 of the Treaty on the Functioning of the European Union to horizontal cooperation agreements, 2023/C 259/01

Commission Regulation (EU) 2023/1066 of 1 June 2023 on the application of Article 101(3) of the Treaty on the Functioning of the European Union to certain categories of research and development agreements

Commission Regulation (UE) 2023/1067 of 1 June 2023 on the application of Article 101(3) of the Treaty on the Functioning of the European Union to certain categories of specialisation agreements

See also

Consortium, Distribution agreement, Vertical agreement

I

INDEPENDENCE AND IMPARTIALITY

Peter FREEMAN
Competition Appeal Tribunal

■ Definition

Independence and impartiality are related aspects of the wider principle of justice, but are subtly different in their scope and, in the competition law context, their application.For judges (and courts) the United Nations Basic Principles on the Independence of the Judiciary provide:

1. *The independence of the judiciary shall be guaranteed by the State and enshrined in the constitution or the law of the country. It is the duty of all governmental and other institutions to respect and observe the independence of the judiciary.*

2. *The judiciary shall decide matters before them impartially, on the basis of facts and in accordance with the law, without any restrictions, improper influences, inducements, pressures, threats or interferences, direct or indirect, from any quarter or for any reason.*

Competition authorities are not independent in the same sense as courts but enjoy varying degrees of operational independence. The principle of impartiality can apply to authorities when taking decisions.

■ Commentary

The principle of judicial independence is acknowledged by most countries in the world, and certainly by those with a recognisable system of competition law. In the UK, the principle was recognised in the Act of Settlement 1701, which confirmed that judges no longer held office at the sovereign's pleasure. In the European Union, the independence of the General Court and the Court of Justice are guaranteed by the Treaties (Articles 19 of the Treaty on the European Union and 251-254 of the Treaty on the Functioning of the European Union – TFEU) and their independence is a fundamental principle of EU law. In the United States of America, the principle of judicial independence is enshrined in the Constitution (Article III section 1).

Behind the principle, however, lie some important issues. Independence means being free from the interests of the state, that is the executive and the legislature, and from the parties in any dispute.

Freedom from state interest is illustrated in the United Kingdom by a 1770 case in which Lord Mansfield gave judgment against the background of a baying mob outside the court. He said:

"Reasons of policy are urged, from danger to the kingdom, by commotions and general confusion... The constitution does not allow reasons of State to influence our judgments: God forbid it should!"

In considering whether judges (and hence courts) are independent, relevant factors include the manner of the judge's appointment, the duration of their term of office, guarantees against outside pressures and the appearance of independence. Within a judicial system there are further nuances, for example how to prevent junior judges from deferring to more senior colleagues in the hope of career advancement. These matters are dealt with by different regimes in different ways. All contribute in greater or lesser measure to the extent of actual judicial independence, i.e., the freedom of a judge to decide the case at hand freely and fairly.

Impartiality is closely linked to independence. Again, it is fundamental that a judge must decide a case on the evidence available, free from influence, bias or prejudice, whether actual or apparent. Judges generally swear an oath on accepting office. In the UK this is to administer justice "without fear or favour, affection or ill-will".

There are subjective criteria (arising from the prejudice or bias of a particular judge) and objective criteria (whether the composition of the court offers sufficient guarantee of impartiality) for assessing impartiality. These approaches can merge in a given case.

An example of this was the *Pinochet* case in the UK, where the House of Lords set aside a decision it had given on the grounds that one of the judges involved had a connection with a campaigning organisation such that apparently compromised his independence. It follows that judges must disclose any personal interest in and, if necessary, recuse themselves from, any case in which their impartiality might be in doubt.

In relation to competition authorities, different issues arise. The so called "independent agency model" under which many competition authorities have been established as separate "arm's length" bodies, often with decision-making power, involves a degree of operational independence.

There should be a secure legal basis for the authority's remit (although not normally with the same constitutional status as the courts) and the same issues of appointment, term, remuneration, discipline, behaviour and removal from office apply. Each system deals with these matters in its own way.

In the EU, the enforcement of competition policy is entrusted to the Commission by the Treaties (Article 245 TFEU). The Commission is free, during its term of office, to use its decision-making power to enforce the law as it wishes, answerable to the European Parliament and the EU Courts, but not to the member states. In the USA, the Department of Justice, part of the executive, enforces antitrust law primarily through the courts. The terms of its independence are set by its statutory powers but its activities may be influenced, through the system of appointments, by the policies of the current administration. Similarly, the Federal Trade Commission, established by Act of Congress, has substantial freedom of action within its jurisdiction, but its activities may be influenced by the policy of the administration. In the UK, the Competition and Markets Authority (CMA) is established by statute with substantial operational freedom, accountable for its actions to parliament (and to the courts). The government controls its membership, terms of remuneration and budget. The government's policy preferences are expressed through an (annual) communication to the CMA.

The principle of impartiality can also apply to authorities. Where an authority has a decision-making function, it must act fairly and impartially, at risk of appeal. Thus, in 2009, the UK Competition Commission's decision in BAA Airports was quashed by the Competition Appeal Tribunal (CAT) on the grounds that one member of the deciding panel had connections that gave an appearance of bias. This finding was reversed on appeal but the principle that authority decisions should be free from actual or apparent bias was reaffirmed.

The case of *Menarini*, in the European Court of Human Rights (ECHR), illustrates how these principles apply differently to authorities and to courts. Article 6 (1) of the European Convention on Human Rights provides:

"In the determination of his civil rights and obligations or of any criminal charge against him, everyone is entitled to a fair and public hearing... by an independent and impartial tribunal established by law."

The ECHR examined whether the Italian competition authority's processes met these requirements and found that they did not; but the majority decided that judicial review by the administrative courts was sufficient to satisfy Article 6. One judge (Pinto de Alberquerque J.) disagreed that the administrative courts' review was sufficient. The majority approach has since been endorsed and followed by the Court of Justice of the EU and Article 47 of the Charter of Fundamental Rights reflects the wording of Article 6(1) of the European Convention.

This broadly reflects the position in the UK. A competition authority must seek to act fairly, but, because of its investigative and enforcement role, cannot necessarily give an impartial decision; it is for the courts to remedy any deficiency, normally by an appeal on the merits to the CAT.

Bibliography

Charter of Fundamental Rights of the European Union [2000] OJ C 364/1

European Convention on Human Rights (Convention for the Protection of Human Rights and Fundamental Freedoms) 1950, as amended by Protocols Nos 11 and 14 and supplemented by Protocols Nos 1,4,6,7,12,13 and 16 (European Court of Human Rights, Council of Europe, F-67075 Strasbourg cedex)

Guide on Article 6 of the European Convention of Human Rights (European Court of Human Rights, Strasbourg, updated to 31st August 2021)

Judicial Independence - Lecture to the Commonwealth Law Conference, Kenya, given by Lord Phillips (Lord Chief Justice) September 2007

United Nations Basic Principles on the Independence of the Judiciary (adopted 26th August - 6th September 1985 and endorsed by General Assembly Resolutions 40/32 of 29th November 1985 and 40/146 of 13th December 1985)

See also

Competition policy, Hearing Officer

I

INDIVIDUAL EXEMPTION

Ryan STONES
City University of London

■ Definition

Agreements that restrict competition by object or effect contrary to Article 101(1) TFEU may nevertheless be deemed compatible with EU competition law if they meet the cumulative requirements for individual exemption set out in Article 101(3) TFEU. Exemption is given for otherwise prohibited agreements that produce an economic benefit where consumers receive a fair share, but without resorting to unnecessary restrictions for achieving the benefit and without substantially eliminating competition. Comparable two-step analysis of prohibition and then exemption of agreements is common in many competition regimes worldwide. In contrast, analysis pursuant to section 1 of the U.S. Sherman Act does not share this bifurcated form.

■ Commentary

An agreement (or other coordination) that restricts competition by object or effect within the meaning of the Article 101(1) TFEU prohibition is not necessarily illegal. It is still possible that the Commission, EU Courts, or equivalent Member State authorities applying EU law will find the arrangement lawful through meeting the conditions set out in Article 101(3) TFEU. The analytical logic of Article 101 TFEU is for a two-step review of agreements for restrictions under paragraph 1 and then exemption under paragraph 3. Similar bifurcation can be found in Member State equivalents to Article 101 TFEU and competition regimes beyond the EU (e.g. Pakistan, Turkey, UK).

Four conditions must be satisfied for a finding of legality pursuant to Article 101(3) TFEU. These conditions are cumulative (Matra Hachette, paragraph 104) and are explained in the Commission's 2004 *Guidelines on the application of Article 101(3) TFEU.* The first condition is that the restriction of competition is counterbalanced by some improvement in production or distribution of the goods or promotion of technical or economic progress. Benefits must be objective and sufficiently substantiated with verifiable evidence (*Guidelines*, paragraphs 49, 55-57). The *Guidelines* reflect a narrow focus upon efficiencies as possible benefits, primarily through reduced costs (e.g. economies of scale and scope, new production methods, synergies from integration of assets), quality improvements, technological advancements, and new products (*Guidelines*, paragraphs 59, 64-72). The second requirement is that consumers receive a fair share of the claimed benefit. "Consumers" is interpreted broadly to include customers of the parties and any subsequent purchasers (including final consumers) (Guidelines, paragraph 84). A fair share requires that the claimed benefits of the restrictive agreement compensate consumers for any negative impact (*Guidelines*, paragraph 85). Third, the agreement itself and its restrictions must be indispensable for achieving the claimed benefit. The Commission will not be satisfied of this where it considers there to be realistic alternatives that are less restrictive of competition than the overall agreement and each individual restriction (*Guidelines*, paragraphs 75-76). Fourth and finally, the agreement should not eliminate competition for a substantial part of the market(s) affected. This reflects caution about exempting agreements that leave competition in the relevant markets insufficiently robust, despite their potential benefits.

According to Article 2 of Regulation 1/2003, the burden of proof is on the parties seeking the exemption who must raise "convincing arguments and evidence" (GSK, paragraph 235). When the parties have raised proof, the Commission must subject it to a proper examination and adequately substantiate any disagreement (GSK, paragraph 303). In MasterCard the General Court rejected the common claim that the Commission has imposed an excessively high burden of proof on undertakings for satisfying the requirements of Article 101(3) TFEU (paragraphs 194-237).

Article 101(3) TFEU is an example of analytical divergence between EU competition law (and comparable regimes) and U.S. antitrust pursuant to section 1 of the Sherman Act. First, it is possible for the parties to seek exemption pursuant to Article 101(3) TFEU for any restrictions of competition, including those by object (Matra Hachette, paragraph 85). As a result, EU competition law does not have practices prohibited per se as in U.S. antitrust; conduct presumed illegal by object under Article 101(1) TFEU, including price-fixing cartels, may be granted an Article 101(3) TFEU exemption, although it is highly unlikely that it will satisfy the conditions (*Guidelines*, paragraph 46). Second, the balancing of anticompetitive and procompetitive consequences of an agreement akin to the U.S. rule of reason standard only occurs in the context of Article 101(3), not in the analysis of whether a restriction by object or effect exists under Article 101(1) TFEU (MasterCard, paragraph 80). The Court of Justice has however made the divide between paragraphs 1 and 3 of Article 101 less stark by ruling that presumptions of restrictions of competition by object should not be applied if relevant and significant pro-competitive effects are demonstrated (Generics, paragraphs 103-110).

While the language of an "individual exemption" is still useful to distinguish agreements deemed legal by direct application of Article 101(3) TFEU from those falling within the conditions of a block exemption regulation (themselves applications of paragraph 3 by proxies), this is an evolution from when "individual exemption" had a specific meaning. Prior to Articles 5 and 6 of Regulation 1/2003 giving Member State courts and competition authorities the power to apply all parts of Article 101 TFEU, the Commission had the sole power (subject to judicial oversight) to find agreements that breached the Article 101(1) prohibition nevertheless lawful pursuant to Article 101(3). Parties to agreements within the scope of Article 101(1) had to notify the Commission to receive an individual exemption. Especially when combined with the then expansive approach to the meaning of Article 101(1), the Commission could not cope with formally granting individual exemption under Article 101(3) to all notified agreements, often resorting to informal "comfort letters". Following decentralisation via Regulation 1/2003, Article 101(3) is primarily intended to be assessed by the parties to agreements, though with national courts, competition authorities, the Commission, and EU Courts having the ability to accept or reject their analysis in any subsequent investigation or adjudication. At EU level, formal decisions on the application of Article 101(3) have been few and far between since 2004.

Regulation 1/2003 also marked a shift in the substantive application of Article 101(3) TFEU, at least from the Commission's perspective. Its *Guidelines* limit the acceptable benefits that can be raised by the parties to economic efficiencies (e.g. cost and price reductions, new products). The fear was that a broader category of acceptable benefits would lead to the inconsistent application of Article 101(3) by national authorities throughout the EU. But when the Commission alone could grant an individual exemption it was less narrow in focus, with several instances of Article 101(3) being granted based on the restrictive agreement contributing to regional development, environmental protection, employment, and even arrangements reducing market output in a gentle manner (essentially crisis cartels). Indeed, the General Court gave some support to taking into account "considerations connected with the pursuit of the public interest" when deciding upon individual exemption (Métropole, paragraph 118). Although the Commission has since shifted emphasis in its (non-binding) 2004 *Guidelines*, the application of Article 101(3) by some Member State authorities remains more expansive, particularly in the Netherlands and Greece. Whether the Commission will stick with its narrow focus on efficiencies when (rarely) applying paragraph 3 is unclear; it may be swayed by growing calls for competition enforcement to promote environmental sustainability.

Bibliography

Bailey, D., "Reinvigorating the Role of Article 101(3) under Regulation 1/2003" (2016-2017) 81(1) *Antitrust Law Journal* 111-144

Brook, O., "Struggling with Article 101(3) TFEU: Diverging Approaches of the Commission, EU Courts, and Five Competition Authorities" (2019) 56(1) *Common Market Law Review* 121-156

Jones, A., Sufrin, B. and Dunne, N., *EU Competition Law: Text, Cases, and Materials* (8th edn, Oxford University Press 2023), Chapter 5

Whish, R. and Bailey, D., *Competition Law* (10th edn, Oxford University Press 2021), Chapter 4

Communication from the Commission – Notice – Guidelines on the Application of Article [101](3) of the Treaty [2004] C 101/97 ("Guidelines")

See also

Block exemption (Regulation), Negative clearance

I

INDUSTRIAL POLICY

Margarida MATOS ROSA
Former President of the Portuguese Competition Authority

■ Definition

In a broad sense, industrial policy refers to State intervention aiming at improving the prospects for industrial competitiveness and economic growth. It may involve supporting specific firms or industries ("vertical" policies) or deploying across-the-board investment, targeting for example infrastructure or skills ("horizontal" policies). Its instruments range from subsidies and tax breaks to trade protection and intellectual property rights, as well as competition policy.

■ Commentary

A conventional rationale behind industrial policy is that it remedies market failures such as for example in providing public goods or subsidizing activities which would otherwise not attract sufficient private investment.

Earlier examples of well-known industrial policy efforts include the Pentagon's Defense Advanced Research Projects Agency, created in 1958 following the Soviet Union's launch of Sputnik, the first artificial satellite, and which has been credited with paving the way for the modern internet and the Global Positioning System (GPS). In Europe, the aerospace operator Airbus, a consortium formed in 1970, is the result of a collaborative effort by the British, French, German and Spanish governments to challenge American companies such as Boeing.

While the 1980s saw a turn against heavy state involvement, there has been a renewed debate about the role of industrial policy in the context of recent challenges such as the 2008 financial crisis, the digital transition, climate change, the rise of China, the COVID-19 pandemic, and global chain disruptions.

Some of these challenges have led to the latest examples of industry policy efforts in the EU and U.S., such as the

EU's *Important Projects of Common European Interest* (IPCEI), Europe's state aid tool of choice to support the European Commission's industrial goals, including on semiconductors and hydrogen, and the U.S.' Inflation Reduction Act, which for example promotes investment in domestic clean energy.

While competition and industrial policy are sometimes portrayed as foes, they can be complementary given the role of competition as a driver for growth, innovation and productivity. Industrial policies stand to gain from embedding competition principles, in particular in times of economic distress. Competition policy can act as a catalyst for countries' efforts, contributing to an inclusive recovery by delivering prices that are more competitive and enhancing new employment creation. However, this position has not always gathered support.

In the U.S., the National Industrial Recovery Act of 1933 was enacted as a response to the Great Depression. This policy measure allowed firms to agree on prices and quantities in certain sectors, as long as companies raised wages above market-clearing levels. Economists have argued that this approach may have aggravated the impact of the Great Depression, rather than contributing to the economic recovery.

More recently, in 2019, the proposed merger of the railway operations of the German conglomerate Siemens and French company Alstom was at the heart of the EU's industrial policy debate. The discussion focused on how the EU should support its economy, and whether it should promote so-called *European champions* in order for its industry to compete against China's state-backed firms. The European Commission reviewed the merger under the EU Merger Control regime and eventually blocked the deal in February 2019, arguing that it would have left consumers in the EU worse-off, by significantly impeding competition in the markets for rail signaling systems and very high-speed trains.

In the aftermath of the Siemens/Alstom case, the EU issued *A New Industrial Strategy for Europe* (2020), where it upheld an independent EU competition policy, while simultaneously turning its attention to trade defense mechanisms and paving the way for the Foreign subsidies Regulation (2022). The latter intends to address distortions in the Internal Market caused by foreign subsidies.

If governments are to engage in industrial policy, they should adopt a competitively neutral policy. This is one of the eight key recommendations highlighted by Tirole (2017) for industrial policy design.

In this respect, competition authorities may play an important role in informing governments and policymakers to ensure that industrial policy initiatives do not negatively impact competition. This is particularly important when governments prepare responses to economic shocks.

For example, in 2021 the Portuguese Competition Authority (AdC) published a report on "*The role of competition implementing the economic recovery strategy*", highlighting a set of principles to promote competition, efficiency and innovation to strengthen the path to an inclusive and sustainable economic growth. The Portuguese economic recovery strategy aimed at restoring the ability of firms to resume their activity, defining a set of investments to mitigate the business-financing gap, given solvency issues. In particular, the strategy foresaw direct and debt financing to firms. The AdC's report emphasized the need to promote competition and efficiency when deploying State support, recommending that the latter should be proportionate, well targeted, and should not result in adverse effects on competition. The AdC highlighted that State support should be based on objective criteria and, if possible, applicable to all firms in a given sector. This is desirable in order to ensure competitive neutrality and minimize distortions between competing firms in the market. In addition, State support for specific firms should be limited in duration, and an effective exit strategy for public financing should be put in place to avoid a negative impact on the incentives to compete and innovate in the market.

Bibliography

AGHION, P., CAI, J., DEWATRIPONT, M., DU, L., HARRISON, A. and LEGROS, P., "Industrial Policy and Competition", 2015, *American Economic Journal: Macroeconomics*, 7 (4): 1-32

TIROLE, J., "Competition and the industrial challenge for the digital age?", *IFS Deaton Review of Inequalities*, 2022

WARWICK, K., "Beyond Industrial Policy: Emerging Issues and New Trends", *OECD Science, Technology and Industry Policy Papers*, No. 2, OECD Publishing, Paris, 2013

Autoridade da Concorrência, "The Role of Competition in Implementing the Economic Recovery Strategy", 2021

European Commission, European Political Strategy Centre, "EU industrial policy after Siemens-Alstom: finding a new balance between openness and protection", Publications Office, 2019

See also

Competition policy, Foreign Direct Investment (FDI), Foreign Subsidies Regulation (FSR)

I

INTELLECTUAL PROPERTY RIGHT

Michael A. CARRIER
Rutgers University

■ Definition

The intersection of intellectual property (IP) and competition presents critical issues. The centerpiece of IP is the right to exclude, which is designed to encourage the creation of new products that benefit society. But if IP-related conduct harms rivals or consumers, competition law can punish that very exclusion. The most challenging issues at the intersection of IP and competition are presented by patents. And the two leading settings in which patent-based issues have arisen are pharmaceuticals and standards.

■ Commentary

Pharmaceuticals

The importance of patents in fostering innovation varies between industries. The pharmaceutical industry, in which it is difficult and expensive to reach the market, is one in which patents are crucial. The industry also is marked by complex regulatory regimes that promote not just innovation but also competition. The Hatch-Waxman Act in the U.S. provides 180 days of exclusivity to the first generic to challenge a brand firm's patents. And substitution laws in the U.S. and EU allow or require pharmacists to substitute a generic when a doctor prescribes the brand version of a drug.

The pharmaceutical industry also is characterized by a pivotal moment: the time when generics enter the market, dramatically lowering price. It is no surprise, then, that brand firms have engaged in an array of conduct to delay this moment as long as possible. Across the world, they have used a variety of strategies to do this: "pay for delay" settlements involving payments to generics to settle patent litigation; "product hopping", consisting of switches from one version of a drug to another; citizen petitions filed with regulatory agencies; and denials of samples that generics need to enter the market.

Just to pick one example, pay-for-delay settlements involve brand firms colluding with generics to delay entry. In 2013, the U.S. Supreme Court in FTC v. Actavis held that these agreements could have significant anticompetitive effects and violate antitrust law. The Supreme Court held that antitrust law (and not just patent law) plays an important role in determining a settlement's competitive effects. The Court also held that a policy favoring settlements was not dispositive and instructed courts to determine patent strength by analyzing not the patent but whether the brand made a large and unjustified payment to the generic.

Europe also has targeted settlements. One example is the EC's 2014 € 427 million fine levied on Servier and generic rivals for settlements that delayed generic entry. The Commission concluded that "Servier sought protection against generic entry by concluding five patent settlement agreements with the (most) advanced generic contenders" that "consisted of significant payments, or other inducements, to the generic companies, and the obligation for them not to challenge Servier's patents and not to enter the market (directly or indirectly) for a number of years." The Commission also revealed factors for determining whether a settlement falls under the category of restriction by object (which punishes conduct without analyzing its economic effects): (1) whether the brand and generic "were at least potential competitors"; (2) whether the generic "committed itself in the agreement to limit, for the duration of the agreement, its independent efforts to enter one or more EU markets with a generic product"; and (3) whether there was a "transfer of value… as a significant inducement which substantially reduced the incentives of the generic undertaking to independently pursue its efforts to enter one or more EU markets with the generic product."

In short, pay-for-delay settlements reveal how competition law can play an important role even where the brand company has an issued patent.

Standards

A second setting involving patents and competition is presented by standards, which are common platforms that allow products to work together. Standards provide the certainty for consumers to know that their plugs will fit into outlets and their phones will connect to wireless networks. But some companies owning patents needed to use a standard, after promising to license the patent on reasonable terms, seek to block the product or charge an exorbitant price.

In such a case, the users of the standard are stuck. They have invested in technologies based on the standard. And they may be forced to pay a price reflecting not the added value of the technology but the costs of switching to a new technology. In other words, they are subject to "patent holdup."

For years, the concerns threatened by patent holdup were consistently acknowledged by U.S. officials. A unanimously adopted 2007 report of the antitrust agencies (at 35-36) explained the difference between a patentee's power ex ante (when "multiple technologies may compete to be incorporated into the standard") and ex post (when "the chosen technology may lack effective substitutes," which lets patentees "extract higher royalties"). Similarly, the Federal Trade Commission (FTC) unanimously endorsed a 2011 report that highlighted (at 234) how "an entire industry" could be "susceptible" to the "particularly acute" concern of holdup, which can result in "higher prices" and "discourage standard setting activities and collaboration, which can delay innovation."

That all changed, however, during the Trump Administration, as the head of the Antitrust Division, Makan Delrahim, staked out an aggressively pro-patent position. Delrahim asserted that patents present a type of absolute property for which owners are entitled to a right to exclude and automatic injunction. And he claimed that patent holdup is not an antitrust problem. These positions were far outside the antitrust mainstream and should be reversed.

The EU has offered a more nuanced position. In Huawei v. ZTE, the European Court of Justice (at ¶¶ 61-71) set forth a framework by which the parties had shifting responsibilities, with the patentee notifying the defendant of infringement, the defendant showing its willingness to license, the patentee making a written offer including the royalty, and the defendant (who is able to challenge patent validity or essentiality) accepting the offer or making a counteroffer.

In addition, a 2017 EC Communication (at 6) made clear that licensing terms must have "a clear relationship to the economic value of the patented technology" that "focus[es] on the technology itself" and does not "include any element resulting from the decision to include the technology in the standard." The Communication also (at 7) sought to "avoid royalty stacking" as the parties "need to take into account a reasonable aggregate rate for the standard."

In short, competition plays a crucial role in analyzing how patents are used in the standards context, as recognized by Europe and (other than during the Trump Administration) United States.

As the pharmaceutical and standards examples show, the intersection of patents and competition presents crucial issues.

Bibliography

FTC, The Evolving IP Marketplace: Aligning Patent Notice and Remedies with Competition (2011)

U.S. Dept. of Justice & FTC, Antitrust Enforcement and Intellectual Property Rights: Promoting Innovation and Competition (2007)

See also

Copyright, Collecting society, Compulsory license, Exhaustion, Know-how, Patents, Trademark

I

INTERIM MEASURES

Mel MARQUIS
Monash Law School

■ Definition

Interim measures may be prohibitory or mandatory and may be granted by a court or a public authority to preserve or restore the status quo, or otherwise provide temporary relief pending resolution of the merits of a case. This powerful instrument ideally ensures that the effectiveness of any remedy finally adopted in the main action will not be jeopardized. The grant of interim measures is typically conditioned on a demonstration that (i) the prima facie elements of an infringement appear to be satisfied or (in some jurisdictions) there is a serious question to be tried, and (ii) the measures are justified by the risk of serious, irreparable harm (absent the requested measures) that monetary damages would fail to rectify. In some countries, such measures will be granted only if supported by a balancing of the interests of the parties and third parties (often referred to as the "balance of convenience"). The public interest or public policy may also be relevant. An important practical point is that some of these conditions may be applied according to a sliding scale: e.g., if the demonstration of a prima facie case is particularly strong, the requirement of irreparable harm may liberally construed. Some competition authorities and at least one legislature (the German Parliament in the 10th amendment of the GWB, January 2021) have respectively embraced, and lowered the threshold requirements for, interim measures as a rapid response tool for the digital sector, where empire-building commercial strategies by incumbents can outpace conventional instruments of enforcement. The need for such a tool may be mitigated, but not eliminated, by a shift toward more *ex ante* regulation of so-called "gatekeepers" in this sector. In the gaps that such regulation leaves unaddressed, the extent to which Courts will embrace a greater use of interim measures to meet the digital challenge remains to be seen.

▪ Commentary

Interim measures may be requested in the context of public as well as private enforcement. Taking the EU as an example of the former, the Commission may impose interim measures on an undertaking, or an undertaking may seek to suspend operation of a Commission decision by applying to the (President of) the General Court. In most jurisdictions, interim measures may also be requested in the context of private disputes, whether in B-2-B or consumer litigation. Due to space constraints the emphasis here will be on public enforcement.

Use or non-use of interim measures may create error costs. Such measures are potent and should generally be granted only on an exceptional basis. Where they are imposed by or requested by a competition authority, an inappropriately low standard of proof could cause serious disruption of business operations based on a relatively cursory investigation. However, the arguments supporting an increased use of interim measures as a rapid response tool are strong.

European Union

The ECJ ruled in 1980 that the Commission had the implied power to adopt interim measures, and Regulation 1/2003 made that power explicit. Article 8 provides that in cases of "urgency" due to the risk of "serious and irreparable damage to competition", and on the basis of a *prima facie* finding of infringement, the Commission may order interim measures. The Commission's assessment of "urgency" must take into account the effects of the alleged conduct and of the interim measures on the undertakings concerned as well as third parties such as consumers. Interim measures can be adopted only where there is danger of harm to competition, not to particular competitors. The case law requires that such measures must comply with proportionality, the same standard that applies to remedies in Article 7 infringement cases. Before being subject to interim measures, the undertaking concerned must have an opportunity to contest the Commission's objections in writing and in an oral hearing if it so requests.

Interim measures have become a "hot topic" in the EU. Unlike some national authorities (notably the Autorité de la concurrence in France–where the legal standards are more permissive), the Commission had let its interim measures power "fade into oblivion" since 2001, mainly due to: (i) the restrictive wording of Article 8 of Regulation 1/2003, (ii) the exacting standards of the EU Courts, (iii) the frequent use of the Article 9 commitment procedure, and possibly (iv) the risk of type I errors. However, the Commission in 2019 adopted interim measures under Regulation 1 for the first time, and this could conceivably lead to more frequent use of the instrument, in particular where there is a danger of market tipping.

Motivated by a desire for more discretion in adopting interim measures, the Commission – in a Declaration accompanying EU Directive 2019/1 – states: "With a view to enabling competition authorities to deal more effectively with developments in fast-moving markets, the Commission commits that it will undertake an analysis of whether there are means to simplify the adoption of interim measures within the European Competition Network within two years from the date of transposition of this Directive [i.e. within two years of 4 February 2021]. The results of this will be presented to the European Parliament and the Council."

United States

The preliminary injunction requirements are established in 15 USC § 26 (private injunctions) and 15 USC § 25 (public injunctions). The former, § 26, is more restrictive in that it refers to "threatened loss or damage" and imposes a causation requirement. The detailed application of the rules on injunctions varies from Circuit to Circuit. However, U.S. Courts generally consider: (i) the applicant's likelihood of success on the merits; (ii) the likelihood that the applicant will suffer irreparable harm if an injunction is denied; (iii) the balancing of hardships or "equities" resulting from the grant/denial of a request; and, where appropriate, (iv) the effect of the grant/denial on the public interest. Where the applicant is a private party, a Court may choose – based on principles of equity such as "unclean hands" – to reject the request for preliminary relief. Where the plaintiff is the Government, and where a reasonable likelihood of success on the merits is established, Courts assume that the risk of irreparable harm is likewise established. If granted, a preliminary injunction may be of indefinite duration and it is immediately appealable. While U.S. Courts do not typically speak of "proportionality", there are functionally equivalent principles, and if a proposed remedy has no reasonable relationship with an alleged antitrust infringement, it will be denied.

The party opposing the motion for a preliminary injunction must be given a fair opportunity to be heard. However, exigent and specific facts can justify a temporary restraining order (TRO), a short-term and generally unappealable measure that a court may adopt in *ex parte*proceedings (Rule 65(b) FRCP). Such exigency may arise in particular where the DOJ or FTC seeks to stop a merger.

Challenging a merger under Section 7 of the Clayton Act is indeed the main (albeit not the only) scenario where the federal agencies may request a preliminary injunction or TRO. Where the DOJ handles the case, it will simultaneously seek from the Court both a permanent injunction and a preliminary injunction/TRO. When the Court balances the equities (criterion iii above), it will attach more weight to the Government's interest than it will to the private interests of the parties to the proposed merger. Compared to the procedure governing DOJ actions, the procedure that applies to the FTC has special features. Section 13(b) of the FTC Act authorizes the FTC to file suit seeking a preliminary injunction/TRO when it has cause to believe that an entity "is violating, or is about to violate" any provision of law enforced by the FTC. Unlike the

DOJ, the FTC does not seek a permanent injunction from the District Court. Instead, if the Court grants the temporary relief, the FTC then files an administrative complaint and the merits are adjudicated in-house in an administrative procedure under Part 3 of the FTC's Rules of Practice. The FTC thus becomes the first-instance decision maker. With regard to the FTC's request for temporary relief, the Courts interpret the legislative intent of the FTC Act as supporting broad access to injunctive relief – a deviation from the more demanding traditional principles of equity. This idiosyncratic feature was criticized by the Antitrust Modernization Commission in 2007, as the DOJ does not benefit from quite the same generous treatment, leading to at least the perception of uneven enforcement.

Bibliography

CAMINADE J., CHAPSAL, A. and PENGLASE, J., "Interim Measures in Antitrust Investigations: An Economic Discussion" (2021) 17 *Journal of Competition Law and Economics* 437-457

DENLOW, M., "The Motion for a Preliminary Injunction: Time for a Uniform Federal Standard" (2003) 22 *Review of Litigation* 495-539

GÁL, G. and STROUVALI, K., "Interim Measures", in Ekaterina Rousseva (ed.), *EU Antitrust Procedure* (Oxford: Oxford University Press, 2020) 289-304

IDOT, L., "Urgence et concurrences : Mesures provisoires, référés-suspension... Toujours trop tard ?", *Concurrences No 3-2018*, 17-19

MANTZARI, D., "Interim Measures in EU Competition Cases: Origins, Evolution, and Implications for Digital Markets" (2020) 11 *Journal of European Competition Law & Practice* 487-498

MUSCATO, A., "The Preliminary Injunction in Business Litigation" (2007) 3 *New York University Journal of Law & Business* 649-674

RUIZ FEASES, A., "Sharpening the European Commission's tools: interim measures" (2020) 16 *European Competition Journal* 404-430

European Competition Network, Recommendation on the power to adopt interim measures

European Union, Directive (EU) 2019/1 of the European Parliament and of the Council of 11 December 2018 to empower the competition authorities of the Member States to be more effective enforcers and to ensure the proper functioning of the internal market, [2019] OJ L 11/3, recital 38 and Article 11

See also

Error costs

I

INTERNATIONAL COOPERATION

Elizabeth KRAUS
Walmart

■ Definition

With the globalization of business and competition law, competition agencies should, where possible, work together to promote policy coherence and consistent case enforcement. They do so through International Cooperation – a loose term encompassing policy and enforcement cooperation, sometimes used to refer solely to enforcement cooperation. Through enforcement cooperation, competition agencies investigating the same matter coordinate to improve their analyses and learning, avoid inconsistent outcomes, and enhance investigational efficiency. Through policy cooperation, competition agencies rely on bilateral relations and engagement in regional and multilateral fora to promote understanding and convergence toward sound competition policy and practice across jurisdictions. The policy and enforcement prongs of international cooperation are intertwined and mutually supportive.

■ Commentary

Over 130 jurisdictions have competition laws and agencies. While these competition laws often are premised on the same objectives, the distinct legal structure, economic development, and history of each jurisdiction has resulted in differences among competition laws, tools, and enforcement practices. As business activities continue to expand internationally and competition agencies from multiple jurisdictions increasingly assess the same conduct or merger, the development of coherent competition approaches and consistent enforcement outcomes is desirable. Through international cooperation, both policy and enforcement cooperation, competition agencies voluntarily work with one another to exchange learning and experience to better understand these differences, promote substantive and procedural convergence toward best practice, and to avoid conflicting enforcement outcomes. These efforts are often facilitated by private parties and practitioners.

Through policy cooperation, competition agencies build trust and understanding via the development of bilateral relations and the exchange of experience in regional and multilateral fora. This can range from capacity building to detailed discussions of procedural and substantive approaches and novel enforcement issues. Through this engagement, the international competition community has identified consensual international approaches to competition policy and practice and developed and adopted important guidance and international best practice recommendations on substantive antitrust and procedural fairness in multilateral fora such as the Organisation for Economic Co-operation and Development ("OECD") and the International Competition Network ("ICN"). These efforts serve as the foundation for international convergence toward sound competition law and enforcement. Such consistent approaches to competition law, policy and procedures across jurisdictions facilitates enforcement cooperation among competition authorities. As agencies develop similar analytical and procedural approaches, the potential for conflicting enforcement outcomes narrows. Moreover, efforts to forge policy convergence foster improved relations among agencies that are instrumental to enforcement cooperation.

Enforcement cooperation has transformed since its inception almost sixty years ago. Initially used primarily to manage conflicts that arose from the extraterritorial impact of antitrust enforcement by one agency in the jurisdiction of another, enforcement cooperation continues to mature and develop as competition agencies and laws increasingly focus on common objectives. Modern enforcement cooperation aims to allow agencies reviewing the same matters to identify issues of common interest, streamline investigations, improve their analyses, and avoid inconsistent outcomes. Enforcement cooperation is a key means for improving the effectiveness of individual agency investigations and producing consistent outcomes in similar circumstances, reducing the burden, for the business community and the enforcement agencies alike. As business transactions and conduct continue to transcend national borders and the number of competition agencies assessing the same conduct and transactions expands, the need for enforcement cooperation intensifies. A recent OECD/ICN joint report on cooperation identified a continued trend toward increasing enforcement cooperation among competition agencies in all enforcement areas – mergers, cartels and unilateral conduct. (Joint Report at Chapter 12)

Competition agencies enter into enforcement cooperation agreements voluntarily, with the nature of such cooperation dependent on the needs of the individual case: for example, whether the investigations raise similar competitive overlaps or cross-border concerns, or a remedy considered by one agency may impact another. Enforcement cooperation may range from merely informing cooperating authorities of the stages of the investigation, to engaging in regular, detailed discussion of substantive issues, to coordinating "dawn raids," to exchanging information and conducting joint interviews, to coordinating remedy design and implementation and may even include investigative assistance (U.S. International Guidelines at Chapter 5). Similarly, if multiple agencies are cooperating on a matter, the cooperation may be differentiated among the agencies, depending on the competitive impact and intensity of the investigation in each jurisdiction.

Any enforcement cooperation undertaken by agencies must be consistent with their domestic rules, notably as concerns confidentiality and privilege. Prior to engaging in such cooperation, the agencies will have a common understanding regarding confidentiality protection of information shared. This can be based on formal agreements or less formal arrangements such as memoranda of understanding, the OECD Cooperation Recommendation and the ICN Framework for Merger Review Cooperation.

With a common understanding in place, the agencies will frequently exchange publicly available information as well as "agency confidential" information, which is information that the agencies are not statutorily prohibited from disclosing, but normally treat as non-public, e.g., the fact that the agencies have opened an investigation and how the staff analyzes the case, including product and geographic market definition, assessment of competitive effects, as well as potential remedies, as relevant. For some matters, the exchange of this information is sufficient to meet the agencies' cooperation needs. For matters requiring deeper cooperation, the agencies may seek to exchange confidential business information, i.e., information received from parties or third parties the confidentiality of which is protected by statute. However, agencies can exchange such information only pursuant to a waiver of confidentiality (an instrument provided voluntarily by a party or third party that enables two or more investigating agencies to share the party's confidential business information as related to the investigation), or through a provision in the law or a mutual assistance agreement that allows confidential business information to be shared without consent. Some regional enforcement network agreements also provide for this type of information sharing, such as the European Competition Network in the application of European Union competition rules. (Council Regulation 1/2003 at Art. 12)

Practically, enforcement cooperation is most effective when the cooperating agencies' investigative timetables allow staff to engage on substantive issues at key stages of their respective investigations. This can be facilitated through early communication, including with parties, who may be able to time notification submissions to optimize such coordination. Early communication and coordination is also critical to cooperation on remedies, and may result in the development of a remedial package that comprehensively addresses the concerns of multiple authorities, or even in one authority's forgoing its remedy by taking into account and informally deferring to a cooperating agency's remedy. Agencies have set out core approaches to cooperation in important practical tools, training materials and best practices developed bilaterally and in the context of multilateral organizations, such as the ICN, OECD and UNCTAD. (See e.g., U.S.-EU Merger Cooperation Best Practices, ICN Leniency Cooperation Guidance, and UNCTAD Cooperation Guiding Policies). Agencies also continue to seek to improve cooperation tools to allow for cooperation among a broader range of agencies and to deepen cooperation among key partners to foster increased opportunities to request investigative assistance and the exchange of confidential materials. These issues are addressed through policy dialogue and in the context of enforcement cooperation and demonstrate the mutually supportive nature of both prongs of international cooperation.

Bibliography

Antitrust Guidelines for International Enforcement and Cooperation, issued by the U.S. Department of Justice and the Federal Trade Commission, 2017

Council Regulation 1/2003 of 16 December 2002 on the implementation of the rules on competition laid down in Articles [101] and [102] of the Treaty (Official Journal L 1, 04.01.2003, p.1-25)

ICN Framework for Merger Review Cooperation, 2012

ICN Guidance on Enhancing Cross-Border Leniency Cooperation (2020)

Recommendations and Best Practices on Competition: ICN and OECD

OECD/ICN Joint Report on International Co-Operation in Competition Enforcement 2021

Recommendation of the OECD Council concerning International Co-operation on Competition Investigations and Proceedings, 2014

U.S.-EU Merger Working Group Best Practices on Cooperation in Merger Investigations, 2011

Multilateral Mutual Assistance and Cooperation Framework for Competition Authorities, 2020, Memorandum of Understanding among the Australian Competition and Consumer Commission; the Competition Bureau of the Government of Canada; the New Zealand Commerce Commission; the United Kingdom Competition and Markets Authority; the United States Department of Justice; and the United States Federal Trade Commission

United Nations Conference on Trade and Development Guiding Policies and Procedures under section F of the Set of Multilaterally Agreed Equitable Principles and Rules for the Control of Restrictive Business Practices, UNCTAD/DITC/CPLP/MISC/2021/2, 2020

See also

Competition policy, Cooperation between competition authorities, EFTA Surveillance Authority (ESA) & Court, European Competition Network (ECN), International Competition Network (ICN)

I

INTERNATIONAL COMPETITION NETWORK (ICN)

Andreas MUNDT
German Competition Authority

Definition

The ICN is a global network of competition agencies dedicated to competition policy and law with the mission to advance procedural and substantive convergence and facilitate cooperation. The members of the ICN represent national and multinational competition authorities. The ICN member agencies produce work products based on consensus in project orientated working groups which are open to the participation of representatives from the business sector, consumer groups, academics, and the legal and economic professions as non-governmental advisers (NGAs). Members and NGAs convene at annual conferences, workshops and virtual events. The ICN was founded in October 2001 and currently comprises 140 member agencies from 130 jurisdictions.

Commentary

The International Competition Network, ICN, is a global, specialized, and informal network of competition agencies. It is dedicated to competition policy and law. Its mission is to advocate the adoption of superior standards and procedures in competition policy around the world, formulate proposals for procedural and substantive convergence, and seek to facilitate effective international cooperation for the benefit of member agencies, consumers and economies worldwide.

The ICN was launched on 25 October 2001 by antitrust officials from 14 jurisdictions – Australia, Canada, the EU, France, Germany, Israel, Italy, Japan, Korea, Mexico, South Africa, the UK, the U.S., and Zambia. Recognizing the implications of increasing economic globalization, the concept of the ICN came from discussions and recommendations in particular in North America and Europe to facilitate meaningful international cooperation for competition law and policy.

The ICN takes a welcoming approach to new members: Membership is open to all national or multinational competition agencies entrusted with the enforcement of competition law. To foster the engagement of younger agencies the ICN conducts outreach programs. The network is not an intergovernmental organisation and agency representatives act as experts, not as country representatives. NGAs are directly involved and interaction is not mediated through a committee or the like. To promote NGA involvement, the ICN has established a dedicated ICN/NGA liaison.

The ICN is a virtual organisation without headquarters or staff. The work takes place in results-based, project-oriented, and specialised Working Groups operating by consensus. Initially focused on issues such as multi-jurisdictional merger review, the ICN currently has five Working Groups: Advocacy, Agency Effectiveness, Cartel, Merger and Unilateral Conduct.

Each Working Group is led by three co-chairs from different jurisdictions serving staggered three-year terms. The Working Groups have created a growing encyclopaedia of best practices, practical recommendations, and other tools, including among others Recommended Practices for Investigative Process, the Anti-Cartel Enforcement Manual, Guidance on Enhancing Cross-Border Leniency Cooperation, Recommended Practices for Merger Notification and Review Procedures, Recommended Practices for Merger Analysis, Guiding Principles for Merger Notification and Review Procedure, Recommended Practices on Dominance/Substantial Market Power Analysis, Recommended Practices on State-Created Monopolies Analysis Pursuant to Unilateral Conduct Laws, and Recommended Practices on Predatory Pricing Analysis. All ICN work is publicly available to interested agencies and experts via the ICN website.

ICN members and NGAs convene at annual conferences, workshops and virtual events such as webinars hosted by ICN members. The first ICN Annual Conference took place in 2002 in Naples, Italy, followed by conferences in Merida, Seoul, Bonn, Cape Town, Moscow, Kyoto, Zurich, Istanbul, The Hague, Rio de Janeiro, Warsaw, Marrakesh, Sydney, Singapore, Porto, New Delhi, Cartagena, and two virtual events hosted by the U.S. agencies and the Hungarian competition authority. The 21st ICN Annual Conference will take place in May 2022 in Berlin.

The ICN is guided by a Steering Group that consists of selected representatives of competition agencies and ex officio members and is chaired by one SG member elected for a renewable two-year term. The Steering Group ensures that the ICN focuses on topics that are relevant for its members and takes the needs of its diverse membership into account. In addition to the Working Groups, the Steering Group also leads projects, e.g. on the Intersection of Competition, Consumer Protection, & Privacy (initiated in 2019). The Steering Group publishes Statements such as the Statement on Competition during and after the COVID-19 Pandemic (2020).

The Steering Group and the Working Groups are supported by the ICN Secretariat, the Horizontal Coordinator, and two Vice Chairs. The ICN closely cooperates on antitrust issues with other international bodies working in the same field primarily via liaisons, notably the Organisation for Economic Co-operation and Development and the United Nations Conference on Trade and Development. Together with the World Bank Group, the ICN organizes a yearly advocacy contest.

The ICN has established frameworks to facilitate cooperation in the field of merger control and cartel enforcement, as well as the ICN Framework for Competition Agency Procedures (ICN CAP), an opt-in framework which combines a catalogue of principles for fair and effective agency procedures and implementation instruments.

The ICN follows a soft-law approach, that is, the work products aren't legally binding in a court of law. It does not exercise any rule-making function and ICN work products are not mandatory. Where the ICN reaches consensus, individual competition authorities decide whether and how to implement the recommendations, or use them as an advocacy tool vis a vis the legislator. This allows the ICN to follow ambitious, future oriented projects which are not restricted by the current practice of the agencies involved. At the same time, ICN recommendations serve as international gold standards and the Network's inclusive bottom-up approach and a certain level of peer-pressure ensure that members feel committed to putting the work products into practice.

Bibliography

Mundt, A., The ICN at twenty, Who is global if not the ICN? ICN milestones and the future of the agencies' network, in *The International Competition Network at Twenty, Origins, Accomplishments and Aspirations* (P. Lugard and D. Anderson (Eds.), Concurrences (2022)

Mundt, A., Development of Multilateral Cooperation from a National Competition Authority's Point of View, in *Frédéric Jenny Liber Amicorum, Standing Up for Convergence and Relevance in Antitrust, Volume I*, Concurrences (2018)

Mundt, A., Globalisation of Competition Law and Policy – Multilateral cooperation in the context of International Organisations, in: *Special edition of the Competition Mirror on the occasion of the 25th anniversary celebration of the Gazdasági Versenyhivatal*, GVH, Hungary (2015)

See also

Competition policy, Cooperation between competition authorities, European Competition Network (ECN), International cooperation

I

INVESTIGATIONS/INQUIRIES

Irma URMONAITĖ
Lithuanian Competition Authority

Definition

An investigation is an evidence gathering and assessment process conducted by competition authorities for the purpose of ascertaining whether specific undertakings have infringed competition law. Competition authorities use both proactive and reactive methods to detect possible competition law infringements and subsequently launch an investigation. Evidence gathering powers differ depending on the jurisdiction and the enforcement regime in place, but typically include powers to request information, inspect business premises and conduct interviews. If sufficient evidence is uncovered, an investigation might result in sanctions and/or other remedies being imposed on infringing undertakings.

Commentary

Investigation is an evidence gathering and assessment tool used by competition authorities in order to uncover competition law infringements. By collecting, interpreting and assessing the evidence, competition authorities are required to prove the facts constituting an infringement, its scope, the involvement of different undertakings, the continuation and duration of the illegal conduct.

The illegal conduct under investigation and the evidence gathering methods directly depends on the powers granted to competition authorities.

In the EU, the principal competition law enforcement agency is the European Commission (EC). The investigative powers are provided by Regulation 1/2003 of 16 December 2002 on the implementation of the rules on competition laid down in Articles 101 and 102 of the TFEU. The EC performs activities of fact-finding and has the power to make determination on liability. In the U.S., both the Federal

Trade Commission (FTC) and the U.S. Department of Justice (DOJ) Antitrust Division enforce the U.S. antitrust laws. By enforcing Federal Trade Commission Act, FTC is primarily responsible for civil violations of antitrust laws and can initiate proceedings in court or adjudicate them administratively. By enforcing the Sherman Act, the DOJ is also empowered to bring civil cases, but it has the exclusive competence to prosecute criminal antitrust law violations. However, the DOJ must seek criminal enforcement actions exclusively in federal courts. In the UK, the Competition and Markets Authority (CMA) has competition law powers which apply across the whole economy, while sectoral regulators may exercise competition law powers concurrently with the CMA in those sectors for which they have responsibility. The CMA uses its powers to investigate suspected infringements of competition law and impose sanctions under Chapters I and II of the Competition Act 1998, as well as under the Enterprise Act 2002.

Usually, the focus of investigations is undertakings but, in some jurisdictions, including the UK and the U.S., competition authorities also have the power to investigate individuals in case of the most serious competition law infringements.

Investigations may originate in different ways. For example, competition authorities may react and launch investigation after receiving complaints made by a third party, information provided by individuals ("whistleblowers"), leniency applications from one of the participants to a cartel and information received from other governmental bodies, or alternatively, they may take proactive steps to identify potential competition law infringements and gather information on their own initiative. The combined effects of emerging digital economy and lowering numbers of leniency applications are the main drivers beyond the decisions by several competition authorities to establish dedicated intelligence and data units. The use of the IT tools such as data engineering, artificial intelligence and machine learning could help the authorities to analyse digital markets and large sets of data more easily, thereby increasing the number of ex officio investigations.

Several types of evidence can be used to prove competition law infringements. The U.S. legislation provides a broad definition where antitrust evidence means "information, testimony, statement, documents, or other things that are obtained in anticipation of, or during the course of, an investigation or proceeding under any of the Federal antitrust laws or any of the foreign antitrust laws" (15 USC 6211(1)). Competition authorities rely on both direct evidence, such as documents, written or oral statements that directly embodies or describe an infringement, and circumstantial evidence which can come in different forms, including communication evidence between undertakings (e.g. records of telephone conversations, minutes or notes) and economic evidence (OECD, 2006).

In the EU, the EC is empowered to require undertakings and associations of undertakings to provide all information necessary for an investigation, inspect business and private premises in order to examine their records and potentially seize relevant evidence, and interview any natural or representatives of legal person who consents to be interviewed. With respect to the criterion that requires information to be necessary, EU courts have ruled that EC enjoys a considerable margin of appreciation (*Qualcom*, paragraph 69). Further, the EC does not have to follow any specific sequence when it chooses among investigative tools. For example, the fact that inspections have already taken place cannot diminish powers to request information and *vice versa* (*Orkem*, paragraph 14). With a view to empower the competition authorities of the EU Member States to be more effective enforcers and to harmonise the enforcement rules, in 2019 EU legislators adopted the ECN+ Directive which aligns enforcement powers of national competition authorities with those held by the Commission. In the U.S., FTC and DOJ can gather information by issuing a subpoena or by civil investigative demands requesting testimony, documents, written reports, and written answers. In criminal investigations, DOJ may also use searches of business and private premises supported by the FBI investigators. In jurisdictions where some competition infringements are prosecuted as criminal offenses (for example, in the U.S., UK, Denmark, Canada, Brazil and Israel), the authorities are also empowered to exercise additional criminal investigation powers to detect cartels (e.g using wiretaps or undercover agents). All the investigative powers intervene with the private spheres of companies and individuals concerned and must therefore be exercised in line with due process. The European Court of Justice (ECJ) repeatedly ruled that the EC must respect the rights of defense which are fundamental rights forming an integral part of the general principles of law (*Aalborg Portland*, paragraph 64). The need to separate investigatory and adjudicatory functions and to ensure judicial review which are essential to ensuring fairness to parties has been also extensively discussed in the courts' decision both in the U.S. and EU. In Wong Yang Sung v. McGrath, at paragraph 41, the U.S. Supreme Court emphasised the need to "curtail and change the practice of embodying in one person or agency the duties of prosecutor and judge". Similarly, the ECJ recognised "the need for protection against arbitrary or disproportionate intervention by public authorities" (*Roquette Frerres*, paragraph 27). The OECD conducted a number of roundtables on procedural fairness and transparency while the International Competition Network (ICN) adopted its Recommended Practices on Investigative Process as well as the ICN Framework for Competition Agency Procedures, both designed to strengthen procedural fairness in competition law enforcement.

If sufficient evidence has been gathered by competition authorities to prove an infringement, an investigation might lead to an infringement decision with sanctions (both fines and/or remedies) being imposed on infringing undertakings as well as on individuals in certain cases. Some investigations might be terminated by settlement or commitments decisions.

Bibliography

BRODER, D. F., *U.S. Antitrust Law and Enforcement, A Practice Introduction*, 2016

ORTIZ BLANC, L., *EU Competition Procedure*, 4th edition, Oxford University Press, 2022

DOJ Civil Antitrust Practice and Procedure Manual, Second Edition Paperback – January 1, 2018, Section of Antitrust Law

OECD Policy Roundtables. Prosecuting Cartels without Direct Evidence, 2006

See also

ECHR, Legal privilege, Sector inquiry

J

JUDICIAL REVIEW

Giovanni PITRUZZELLA
Italian Constitutional Court

Definition

In the EU it is possible to bring an action before the General Court (the Judge of first instance) and ultimately, on points of law, before the Court of Justice, against a decision adopted by the European Commission (hereinafter, the "Commission") in competition matters. In the U.S., although the decision about whether or not to take enforcement action is committed to agency discretion, the Antitrust Division of the U.S. Department of Justice (hereinafter, the "DOJ") is a law enforcement agency that has no adjudicative power of its own. Thus, in order to enforce the federal antitrust statutes under its purview, the DOJ, like a State or private enforcer, must file an action in a federal district court. In addition, courts review cases that the Federal Trade Commission (the "FTC") decides through its internal adjudicative process.

Commentary

The anticompetitive conduct is ascertained by the Commission, who can order the parties to end the infraction and impose penalties and remedies, while the European courts review the legality of the administrative decision. Under Article 265 TFEU, it is possible to bring an action against the Commission where, in infringement of the Treaty, it has failed to act. Under Article 263 TFEU, it is possible to bring an action to have various acts of the Commission annulled. Apart from Member States and the Council, Article 263(4) TFEU provides that any undertaking may challenge a decision addressed to it or to another person if it is of "direct and individual concern to it". The Commission's decision may be challenged on grounds of lack of competence, infringement of an essential procedural requirement, infringement of the Treaties or of any rule of law relating to their application, or misuse of powers. The review of legality is supplemented by the "unlimited jurisdiction" which Article 31 of Regulation 1/2003 vests in the EU Courts in accordance with Article 261 TFEU. "Unlimited jurisdiction" empowers the Courts, in addition to carrying out a mere review of lawfulness of the penalty, to substitute their own appraisal for that of the Commission and consequently to cancel, reduce or increase the fine or penalty payment imposed.

It is useful to distinguish the "standard of proof" and the "standard of judicial review". The standard of proof determines the degree of likelihood that must be established in relation to factual findings when the primary decision-maker makes its initial decision. It has to be distinguished from the standard of judicial review, which is the standard that courts must apply in deciding whether the primary decision-maker has met the standard of proof required. It is the latter that tells us how far the reviewing court should reassess findings of fact made by the primary decision-maker to decide whether the standard of proof for the initial decision has been attained or not. The case law on judicial review of fact reveals low-, high- and medium-intensity review.

In the U.S. system, the court is the arbiter of whether the law has been violated and, if so, it orders appropriate remedies. Regardless of whether a case is initiated by one of the federal enforcers, a State enforcer or a private citizen, the process is adversarial: the parties submit their evidence and arguments regarding the relevant facts to a judge (or a jury in criminal cases). Based on the parties' submissions, the judge determines the ultimate facts and the court decides the case in accordance with the controlling law and precedent. Due process protection is provided to the defendant before liability can be imposed. In presence of a FTC Administrative process, the final decision of the FTC is directly appealable to any federal circuit court in whose jurisdictional region the defendant does business. The case then proceeds from that point along the same path as cases originally filed in the district courts. The appellate court reviews questions of law de novo, but generally will not alter the factual determinations found by the FTC that are supported by substantial evidence.

In the context of competition, the approach initially followed by the Court of Justice was very careful as regards the scope and the intensity of its own review of the Commission's decisions, as shown in the leading case Consten and Grundig. This jurisprudential line has been progressively replaced by a more intense scrutiny in competition cases (such as in the Intel case). Three main factors influenced this evolution. The first one was the jurisprudence of the European Court of Human Rights concerning Article 6 of the Convention, that provides the guarantee of fair trial, which encompasses the provision of "full jurisdiction", in the presence of an infringement of criminal nature. In the seminal ruling Engel, the Court of Human Rights stated that the criminal nature of the infringement is affirmed if the sanction is severe and has deterrence as function. This is the case of the sanction provided by competition law, as affirmed in another landmark decision, in the Menarini case. As a consequence, the judicial review of competition decisions should be extended to all the questions of facts and laws concerning the administrative decision. The second factor was the Charter of Fundamental Rights of the European Union which, after the Treaty of Lisbon (2009), has the same legal value of the Treaties. Competition decisions should comply with the Charter and, in particular, with the presumption of innocence, the right to fair proceedings and the right to effective judicial remedy. Finally, there was the adoption of a "more economic approach" by the Commission in the 2000s, that involved a shift from a formal qualification of the conduct of undertakings to a more comprehensive analysis of the economic and legal context of the behaviour in question. As a consequence of all these factors, the judicial review in competition matters has become high-intensive.

It is for the Commission to set out in a clear and unequivocal fashion its reasoning, to enable the persons concerned to ascertain the grounds for the measure and the competent Court to exercise its power of review. It is for the Applicant to identify the impugned elements of the contested decision, to formulate grounds of challenge in that regard and to adduce corresponding evidence showing that the reasons relied on by the Commission do not support to the requisite legal standard the conclusion endorsed in the contested act. The EU judicature not only establishes whether the evidence put forward by the Commission "is factually accurate, reliable and consistent, but must also determine whether that evidence contains all the relevant data that must be taken into consideration in appraising a complex situation and whether it is capable of substantiating the conclusions drawn from it" (Chalkor v. Commission). As concern the appeal before the Court of Justice, it is limited to points of law (Article 256 TFEU and Article 58 of its Statute). Assessment of the facts does not constitute a question of law submitted as such for review by the Court of Justice save where there have been distortion of the facts or evidence.

The models of antitrust enforcement are quite different in the EU and in the U.S., but in both systems the role of courts is very relevant, due process is observed and the rights of private undertakings safeguarded. It is noteworthy that many competition cases decided by the EU Courts concern the respect of fundamental rights, including the right to privacy, the right to be heard, the duty to state reasons, the right to good administration and the duty of impartiality.

The text expresses the personal opinion of the Author and in no way commits the institution to which he belongs.

Bibliography

Craig, P., *EU Administrative Law*, third Edition, Oxford University Press, 2018

Da Cruz Vilaça, J. L., The intensity of judicial review in complex economic matters - recent competition law judgements of the Court of Justice of the EU, *in Journal of Antitrust Enforcement*, 2018, 6, 173 ss

Gryllos, G., *Discretion and judicial review in EU competition law: A technical analysis on sources of discretion, judicial review and implications for the litigants*

Jourdan, J., Competition Law and Fundamental Rights, *in Journal of European Competition Law and Practice*, 2018, 9, 666 ss

OECD, The standard of review by courts in competition cases - Note by the United States, 4 June 2019

See also

Effective judicial protection, ECHR

K

KNOW-HOW

Jorge L. CONTRERAS
University of Utah

Definition

Know-how refers to designs, plans, lists, techniques, processes, methods, skills and other information that is useful for some purpose. Know-how may be conveyed through the exchange of documents and physical artifacts, as well as through demonstration, instruction and training (sometimes referred to as "show-how"). Though some definitions of know-how require an element of secrecy, many definitions, particularly in private agreements, do not require that know-how satisfy the legal definition of trade secrecy. Likewise, know-how may involve the use or manufacture of patented articles or the performance of patented processes, but may itself be unpatented.

Commentary

Because know-how is not a formally recognized type of IP right, it owes its legal existence largely to private licensing agreements among parties. Licenses of know-how have been granted across industries since at least the early twentieth century, either in stand-alone transactions or, more commonly, as components of patent licenses. Studies of the prevalence of know-how licenses in various contexts are summarized in Chien (2016, 1689-90).

Knowledge Transfer. There are two principal functions that know-how plays in IP licenses. First, if the licensor provides training, support, consultation, expertise or some other technical assistance to the licensee, then the information and skills conveyed through those services may be "licensed" as know-how.

In many cases, however, no such knowledge transfer is contemplated, yet the agreement (usually a patent license agreement) still contains a license of know-how. In these cases, the know-how license may be included as a means by which the licensor may continue to collect royalties after the relevant patents expire, given that it is considered patent "misuse" under U.S. law for a patent licensor to collect royalties after the licensed patent has expired (*Kimble*(2015)). To get around this limitation, patent holders can license patents and know-how together, so that even after the patents expire, there is still a valuable asset to support the payment of royalties (often at a reduced level). The same logic applies to patents that are invalidated after being licensed, and to sales of products in countries where patent protection does not exist. In all of these cases, royalties can be collected with respect to know-how, even though no enforceable patents are licensed (Gilbert & Shapiro (1997, 322-23); Contreras (2022, 139)).

Beginning in 2020, know-how attracted significant global attention in the debate over manufacturing technology for COVID-19 vaccines. Commentators observed that, even without patent barriers, the manufacture of advanced biological products is not feasible without significant transfers of know-how by current producers (Price II et al. (2020)). These observations have led to calls for governmental intervention and potential compulsory disclosures of manufacturing know-how (ibid.).

Antitrust and Competition Law. In the 1950s and 1960s, there was significant concern among scholars and policy makers that the licensing of vaguely defined know-how might run afoul of the antitrust laws. Several of these concerns arose from the malleable nature of the know-how concept: unlike patents or copyrights, know-how never expires, leading to the potential for perpetual arrangements; unlike trade secrets, which are destroyed upon public disclosure, know-how need not remain secret in order to support a royalty payment, thereby creating a virtually indestructible, perpetual source for ongoing royalties and associated restraints on conduct. As a result, early observers viewed know-how licenses as potential pretexts for market and territorial allocation schemes and other illegal restraints.

In 1970, the U.S. Department of Justice (DOJ) Antitrust Division laid out "Nine No-Nos" of patent and know-how licensing – practices that were virtually guaranteed to violate the antitrust laws through "attempts by patent holders to extend their patent monopolies to unpatented supplies, to gain control over improvements of their innovations, to determine prices for resale of their patented products, or to engage in market allocations" (Gilbert & Shapiro (1997, 285). Know-how licensing was seen to facilitate several of these illegal practices. But the DOJ's suspicion of IP arrangements began to wane by the 1980s, and in 1995 the DOJ and Federal Trade Commission jointly released *Antitrust Guidelines for the Licensing of Intellectual Property* (updated in 2017). The *Guidelines* recognized the generally pro-competitive nature of IP licensing arrangements and endorsed their analysis under the "rule of reason", which continues to be applied today.

In the EU, know-how licenses are addressed by the European Commission's Technology Transfer Block Exemption Regulation (TTBER) (Reg. 316/2014), which exempts such licenses from liability under Article 101 of the TFEU if they fall within permitted market share limits and are free of any enumerated "hardcore" restrictions.

Know-How and Trade Secrecy. The potential for anticompetitive abuse through know-how licensing led some early commentators to argue that in order to be licensed, know-how must meet the requirements of trade secrecy, a conclusion supported by a U.S. district court in *Mycalex* (1946). This reasoning, however, leads to incongruous results. Take, for example, the case of a new, unpatented device that is disclosed and licensed to a manufacturer, who then sells it to the public. Were the licensed know-how supporting the agreement required to be a trade secret, then the licensed asset would evaporate upon the first sale of a product to the public. The U.S. Supreme Court confirmed in *Aronson* (1979) that the disclosure of an unpatented and non-secret invention could support a royalty agreement indefinitely.

While know-how licenses around the world often define know-how as encompassing both secret and non-secret information, the TTBER exemption only covers know-how while it remains secret (TTBER, Arts. 1(1)(i)), 2(2)), irrespective of how it may be defined in the underlying agreement. This seeming discrepancy appears to exist because the term "know-how" functions in the TTBER as a stand-in for the term "trade secret" (Sousa e Silva (2014, 924)), a form of IP that was not generally recognized under this name in the EU until the adoption in 2016 of the European Trade Secrecy Directive, No. 2016/943. As a result, licenses of non-secret know-how under Article 101 do not appear to benefit from the TTBER exemption and would be analysed directly under Article 101.

Bibliography

CHIEN, C. V., "Software Patents as a Currency, Not Tax, On Innovation" (2016) 31 *Berkeley Technology Law Journal* 1669

CONTRERAS, J. L., *Intellectual Property Licensing and Transactions: Theory and Practice* (Cambridge Univ Press 2022), § 6.1.3

GILBERT, R. and SHAPIRO, C., "Antitrust Issues in the Licensing of Intellectual Property: The Nine No-No's Meet the Nineties" (1997) *Brookings Papers on Economic Activity. Microeconomics*, 283

NICHOLSON PRICE II, W., RAI, A. K. and MINSSEN, T., "Knowledge Transfer for Large-Scale Vaccine Manufacturing" (2020) 369 *Science* 912

SOUSA E SILVA, N., "What exactly is a trade secret under the proposed directive?" (2014) 9 *Journal of Intellectual Property Law & Practice* 923

See also

Ancillary restraints, Intellectual property right

L

LEGAL PRIVILEGE

Jacques BUHART
McDermott Will & Emery

Definition

Legal professional privilege ("LPP") is the possibility for a client to refuse to produce, during court proceedings or investigations, documents containing legal advice received from a lawyer. In common law countries, LPP applies to communications with external lawyers or in-house lawyers. At EU level, the LPP does not extend to communications with in-house lawyers. The purpose of LPP is to ensure confidentiality of the attorney-client relationship and to encourage the complete disclosure of the facts to lawyers without the fear that any disclosure of those communications may prejudice the client in the future.

Commentary

In the EU, neither Regulation 1/2003 nor its predecessor Regulation 17 contain a provision dealing with LPP. However, in *AM&S Ltd v Commission* the CJEU provided for such protection and defined the conditions under which it is available. These conditions have been further developed in subsequent judgments.

According to settled case law, LPP only applies where the communication involves an external lawyer entitled to practice the legal profession in one of the EU Member States. (*AM&S*, paragraphs 20 to 24). As such, LPP does not apply to communication between the company and an in-house lawyer. The EU courts revisited the question of LPP in *Hilti*. It found that LPP still applies where internal communications simply report the content of legal advice received from external legal advisers (*Hilti*, paragraph 18).

LPP was also considered in *Akzo*. In particular, Akzo sought protection for documents that were prepared for the purposes of seeking legal advice from a lawyer, in the exercise of the rights of defence. These documents were not themselves communications with a lawyer. They were not created for the purpose of being sent physically to a lawyer (as in *AM&S*), nor did they report the contents of communications with a lawyer (as in *Hilti*). The General Court held that LPP should in principle attach to such "preparatory documents", but it did not accept Akzo's claim for LPP concerning the particular documents in question (*Akzo* paragraph 123). Akzo appealed this judgment to the Court of Justice on a separate issue, namely whether LPP could attach to communications with in-house counsel. The Court of Justice rejected Akzo's appeal, relying on the proposition that a lawyer is not independent if bound to his or her client by a relationship of employment (*Akzo*, Court of Justice Judgment, paragraphs 40 to 51). This is the case even if the lawyer is enrolled with a Bar and thus subject to certain professional and ethical obligations.

In her opinion on the *Akzo* case, Advocate General Kokott provided some elements, which were generally endorsed by the Court of Justice, to conclude that in-house lawyers bound by a relationship of employment cannot be deemed to be "independent lawyers". First, the in-house counsel is economically dependent on their employer, who provides most of the counsel's income in the form of salary, even if there is a protection against dismissal. Second, in-house counsel cannot ignore the company's commercial strategy. This affects the counsels' ability to exercise professional independence. Third, in-house lawyers are "structurally, hierarchically and functionally" dependent and integrated to their employer. Finally, in-house lawyers may be required to carry out other tasks for the company, reinforcing the close ties with the company (*Akzo* Opinion, paragraphs 61 to 71).

In November 2018, the Organisation for Economic Co-operation and Development ("OECD") held a discussion on the treatment of privileged information in competition proceedings. In its position paper, the European Commission clarified that in practice it may extend LPP to communications with independent lawyers qualified in jurisdictions other than the EU upon the request of a company.

LPP is more broad in the USA than in the EU. First, the USA has a more liberal conception of attorney-client privilege, as it may also cover communication with in-house lawyers who are active members of a national bar. It is necessary to fulfil the following four conditions for the privilege to apply: the party asserting LPP must be a client; the communication must include advice of a lawyer; the communication must be intended to be confidential; and the communication must be made to seek or provide legal advice. Second, the U.S. also includes work product privilege, which originated in the 1947 Supreme Court case, *Hickman v. Taylor*. Accordingly, a party cannot be compelled to disclose written or oral materials prepared by or for an attorney in anticipation of litigation or in preparation for trial (*Hickman v. Taylor*, paragraphs 510 to 511).

In the USA, different courts rely on differing standards as regards the application of LPP to foreign lawyers. For example, a Federal Court recognised the privilege for a French in-house lawyer, based on a "functional equivalence" standard. However, other courts have rejected this approach. Perhaps as a result of this lack of clarity, the U.S. federal competition agencies do not tend to challenge LPP based solely on the fact that the communication comes from a foreign lawyer or foreign in-house counsel. However, they scrutinise whether the other conditions of LPP are fulfilled.

National competition authorities do not need to follow the principle of LPP as developed at EU level. Indeed, the Court of Justice confirmed that this rule applies only to competition proceedings run by the European Commission under Regulation 1/2003 (*Akzo*, paragraphs 102 and 105). Therefore, national LPP rules will continue to apply where investigations are undertaken by national competition authorities themselves. The LPP framework has changed over the last decade, at the national level. For example, in July 2021, a Spanish regulation entered into force that expressly recognizes LPP for in-house lawyers. Belgium has granted LPP to in-house counsel even when they are not enrolled at the Bar, but subject to their membership of the Belgian Association of Corporate Counsel. Similar development has occurred in other Member States such as The Netherlands, Hungary, Portugal, and Finland. At EEA level (including the UK under the Withdrawal Agreement), 16 Member States provide LPP for in-house counsel, while 14 refuse it.

Bibliography

Etsuko, K., *Legal Professional Privilege in EU Competition Investigations*, Kameoko Etsuko, Edward Elgar Publishing, 2013

Giraud, A. and Estrade, A., The rise of in-house counsel privilege: Time has come to revisit Akzo, March 2024, *Concurrences N° 1-2024*, Art. N° 116769

Ortiz Blanco, L. (ed.), *EU Competition Law and Procedure* (4th edn., Oxford University Press, 2021), Chapter 5

See also

Investigation/inquiries, Judicial Review

L

LENIENCY

Johan YSEWYN
Covington & Burling

Definition

Leniency is the total or partial reduction of fines or other penalties granted by competition authorities to companies involved in cartels in exchange for disclosing the existence of the cartel agreement or for their cooperation during the authorities' investigation by bringing forward evidence. This tool helps detect secret cartels, and also to deter companies from entering into cartel agreements. It is based on the prisoner's dilemma: its objective is to create distrust amongst cartel participants, as there is a constant threat that one of them may report the cartel to the authorities. Therefore, in combination with severe penalties, leniency programmes maintain constant pressure on companies to cooperate with competition authorities.

Commentary

Companies involved in cartels can receive severe penalties: a leniency system means that the company disclosing the existence of the cartel can receive full immunity, and companies not benefitting from full immunity can receive fine reductions by disclosing insider evidence of the cartel infringement, if that evidence represents significant added value in the authorities' task to prove the infringement. Experience shows that leniency programmes by competition authorities are a crucial tool in uncovering cartels, both in the EU and in the U.S.

As described in further detail here, these leniency programmes not only aim to detect secret cartels but also to deter companies from entering into such agreements. Leniency programmes typically only apply to hard-core secret cartels involving direct competitors, but some jurisdictions make leniency available for hub-and-spoke cartels (involving both horizontal and vertical features), and for resale price maintenance (RPM). In the EU and the U.S., horizontal agreements covered by these leniency programmes generally involve price fixing among competitors, bid rigging, capacity restrictions, or market, customer, sale or production allocation. These anticompetitive agreements are considered per se or hardcore infringements, meaning that competition authorities do not need to prove the anticompetitive effects stemming from them. Purely vertical agreements are much less often included in the scope of leniency programmes: when leniency programmes include vertical agreements, the scope is generally limited to the most severe vertical infringements such as RPM.

However, not all undertakings involved in the cartel may be entitled to benefit from these programmes. For instance, under the ECN Model Leniency Programme ("MLP") and the Commission's 2006 Notice or the U.S. DOJ Leniency Program, immunity or leniency is not available to undertakings which have taken steps to coerce others to participate in the cartel. Some EU jurisdictions even take a stricter approach and exclude the initiator or the sole ringleader from immunity. In addition, some competition authorities extend leniency programmes to individuals for two main reasons. First, this allows individuals involved in the cartel to be protected against criminal or financial penalties for their involvement in the cartel when they blow the whistle. Second, it increases incentives for managers and employees to blow the whistle. Some jurisdictions go still further in having incentives for individuals by financially rewarding whistleblowers. Immunity protection for individuals is increasingly popular, because competition authorities consider this as a very important tool to tackle decreasing leniency applications. It is important to note that in many jurisdictions, leniency programmes cover criminal sanctions and fines, but not other administrative penalties to which an individual can be exposed or civil procedures. For instance, in some EU jurisdictions and in the U.S., a third party can bring action for follow-on damage against the leniency applicant. But damage claims against leniency applicants in the U.S. are limited to single damages, not the treble damages that are generally available to claimants.

On the procedural side, the timing of a leniency application and the quality and nature of the evidence provided are essential elements. First, the timeliness of the application will define whether an undertaking obtains full immunity or a partial reduction of the fine (if any). Mere minutes can make the difference here. Second, when assessing the quality and nature of the evidence, competition authorities will consider whether the information is sufficient to allow them to launch an investigation or to prove the existence of a cartel infringement (in case the authority has sufficient information to launch an investigation). Competition authorities will then grant leniency when the evidence provides "significant added value" which reinforces its cartel case.

In Europe, the Model Leniency Programme lists several requirements for an applicant to benefit from immunity or leniency. First, the applicant must cooperate fully, genuinely, expeditiously, on a continuous basis and in a sincere spirit of cooperation. Second, it must terminate its participation in the infringement as of the date of the application. Third, the applicant must ensure that no evidence is destroyed. Finally, the applicant cannot reveal the existence of the leniency application.

In the U.S., the DOJ Leniency Program requires that the leniency applicant terminates its part in the activity, cooperates with the DOJ's investigation, confesses to the wrongdoing and provides restitution to parties injured by its involvement in the cartel. In addition, in cases in which the DOJ already has knowledge of the relevant conduct, the DOJ will determine if leniency would be unfair to others, considering several elements, such as the applicant's role in the cartel, the nature of the cartel and the applicant's timing when revealing the cartel.

Bibliography

Ysewyn, J. and Boudet, J., Leniency and competition law: An overview of EU and national case law, 2 August 2018, *e-Competitions Leniency*, Art. N° 72355

Amendments to the Commission Notice on Immunity from fines and reduction of fines in cartel cases, *Official Journal* C 256, 5.8.2015, p. 1

Commission Notice on Immunity from fines and reduction of fines in cartel cases, Official Journal C 298, 8.12.2006, p. 17

Leniency and competition law: an overview of EU and national case law

U.S. Department of Justice Leniency Program

See also

Cartel, Fine

L

LERNER INDEX

Daniel L. RUBINFELD
NYU School of Law

Definition

The Lerner index, measured as the percentage markup of price above marginal cost, (P-MC)/P, has often been used as a measure of a firm's market power. The Lerner index always has a value between zero and one. For a textbook-perfectly competitive firm, P=MC so that L=0. The larger is L, the greater is the degree of market power.

Commentary

The Lerner index was first developed in Abba Lerner's 1934 paper, *The Concept of Monopoly and the Measurement of Monopoly Power*. Elzinga and Mills (2011) offer a historical overview and update. Perhaps the most useful adaption of the Lerner Index comes from the fact that a profit-maximizing firm will price its product inversely to the elasticity of demand facing the firm, L = -1/Ed. Unfortunately, determining a firm-related demand elasticity is much more difficult than determining a market demand elasticity, since a firm must consider how its competitors will react to price changes.

There is a significant limitation to the Lerner Index that has particular relevance in today's technology-driven world. A firm may price substantially above its marginal cost (at its average rather than marginal cost). The reason: the firm needs to cover its fixed costs (moreover, if those expenditures pay for assets that are not redeployable elsewhere, they create a barrier to entry).

The most common source of the price-cost divergence arises when there are scale economies and the firm prices based on marginal cost. The computer software and pharmaceuticals industries are illustrative. For most software or pharmaceutical companies, marginal cost will be close to zero. Therefore, the presence of substantial fixed costs will lead to a Lerner Index slightly below 1.0, whether the software company is big, small or otherwise, and whether the market is highly competitive or monopolistic.

The Lerner Index has not been used extensively in antitrust enforcement. The primary reason is that market power requires the presence of meaningful barriers to entry, whether structural (e.g., substantial scale economies) or behavioural (e.g., substantial brand equity). For antitrust enforcement, the primary focus is on barriers to entry and the secondary focus is on substantial, sustainable high market shares (which are estimated, for example, through the use of the Herfindahl-Hirschman index (HHI).

In the U.S., the Lerner Index received quite a bit of attention in the 1995 monopolization case brought by the Department of Justice (DOJ) against Eastman Kodak. The DOJ's expert used an estimated demand elasticity of 2 to infer a high Lerner Index (.5) and substantial market power. The court correctly rejected this view, citing among other things the presence of substantial fixed costs (p. 109).

In the decades following the *Kodak* opinion, U.S. courts have continued to be critical of reliance on the Lerner Index to prove market power, while not ruling out the possibility that it may nevertheless be informative. In *Dial Corp. v. News Corp (2016)*, for example, the court held that the plaintiff's expert's use of the Lerner Index in a critical loss analysis of market definition could not be excluded, noting that the Second Circuit's *Eastman Kodak* decision did not prohibit use of the Lerner Index in all circumstances (pp. 41-42).

Furthermore, in *In re Solodyn (Minocycline Hydrochloride) Antitrust Litigation, (2018 U.S. Dist. LEXIS 11921)* the court found that the presence of high sunk costs does not rule out the price of a branded drug being anti-competitive. The Court noted that high margins indicated by a Lerner Index calculation, without more, are insufficient to demonstrate supra-competitive pricing. A similar conclusion was reached by the court in *In re Intuniv Antitrust Litigation 2020 U.S. Dist. LEXIS 187579 (D. Mass. Sep. 21, 2020)*, with the Court noting that high margins indicated by a Lerner Index calculation, without more, are insufficient to demonstrate supracompetitive pricing.

Explicit use of the Lerner Index in the UK and the European Union has been even less common than in the U.S. Two telecom cases are worth noting. First, the European court found Slovak Telekom in violation of Article 102 *(Council Regulation (EC) 1/2003 on Case AT.39523 – Re Slovak Telekom, 2014 O.J. (C 7465))*, but also found the use of the Lerner Index to calculate a market demand elasticity (not an individual demand) to be highly implausible as the basis of a relevant market analysis. Along similar lines, the UK Competition Appeals Tribunal agreed with the lower court in *British Telecommunications Plc v. Office of Communications (British Telecommunications Plc, Everything Everywhere*

Ltd. v. Office of Communications, (U.K. Competition Appeal Tribunal (Aug. 1, 2011)) that the Lerner Index is likely to suggest overly elastic demand when products included in Lerner Index are complements.

Bibliography

ELZINGA, K. G. and MILLS, D. E., "The Lerner Index of Monopoly Power: Origins and Uses," *American Economic Review: Papers & Proceedings*, 2011. 101:3, 558-564 ;

LERNER, A. P., "The Concept of Monopoly and the Measurement of Monopoly," *Review of Economic Studies*, 1: 157-75

PINDYCK, R. S. and RUBINFELD D. L., *Microeconomics*, 9th Edition, Pearson, 2019 ;

See also

Market power, Marginal costs, Monopoly

L

LETTER OF FORMAL NOTICE

Leo FLYNN
European Commission – Legal Service

Definition

The letter of formal notice is the first step of the infringement procedure under Article 258 TFEU, a breach of European Union law. The letter must indicate the violation with sufficient precision to the Member State. In that way, the Member State can resolve the problem or, if it disagrees with the evaluation of the Commission, defend itself against the complaint. The letter of formal notice serves to delineate the scope of the action before the Court. It is an essential procedural requirement and the lack of a proper letter of formal notice means that the infringement action is inadmissible.

Commentary

Article 258 TFEU allows the Commission to bring a Member State before the Court of Justice alleging its failure to comply with its obligations under Union law only "after giving the State concerned the opportunity to submit its observations". The Commission does so by sending a letter of formal notice ("LFN") to the Member State, and that pre-litigation step has a threefold function in the infringement procedure. It allows the Member State to bring the alleged infringement to an end, it allows the Member State to exercise its rights of defence, and it determines the ambit of the litigation in the event that the Court is seized of the matter.

As a result, the LFN establishes the scope of the infringement procedure, and the litigation which follows must relate to the complaints set out. While the Commission is free to drop grievances raised in the initial LFN, if the Commission wishes to adapt the procedure by enlarging it to take account of new elements identified or arising, it should send the Member State a supplementary LFN. An infringement action will be inadmissible to the extent that the Commission includes in its application before the Court allegations that the Member State breached provisions of Union law which did not feature in the LFN and were invoked only in the reasoned opinion.

By contrast, there need not be a perfect overlap between the LFN, the reasoned opinion and the application before the Court, since in the latter the Commission can detail complaints that it had set out in a more general way in the LFN. Given the preliminary role of the LFN in the pre-litigation procedure, the Court accepts that in drawing up the LFN the Commission is not required to be as precise as it must be at the stage of drafting the reasoned opinion, since the LFN is necessarily a first, succinct, summary of the complaints.

By way of example of how those principles play out, in Case C-522/09 the Commission applied to the Court for a declaration that Romania had not classified a sufficient number of special protection areas under the Wild Birds Directive. The Court found the infringement action inadmissible because the LFN complained of a failure to designate such areas (i.e., lack of any transposition of the relevant provisions of the Directive) while in light of the application the litigation turned on whether there had been enough classification decisions (i.e., incomplete or incorrect transposition of those provisions).

Without the proper exposition in the LFN of the complaints pursued under Article 258 TFEU, the Member State cannot meaningfully provide observations to the Commission on the alleged breaches of Union law. In essence, the LFN will be compliant with the requirements flowing from its threefold purpose if the Member State is put into a situation where it has all relevant information for its defence. A further operational consequence of that test for the LFN is that the Member State must have a reasonable time to reply to the Commission, with the notion of "reasonableness" to be evaluated in light of all of the circumstances of the case. Such factors would include the urgency of the case (although the Commission can justify a short reaction time by claims of urgency where the institution could have started the pre-litigation dialogue earlier and was inactive) and whether the Member State is fully informed of the definitive views of the Commission before it received the LFN. In general, the Commission allows Member States two months to reply to a LFN, and it frequently extends the deadline in response to a request from the Member State concerned.

Because the LFN is the first step in the pre-litigation phase of an infringement procedure, it must relate to an alleged infringement of Union law by the Member State concerned rather than identifying a prospective breach. The existence of a draft measure of national law that would be non-compliant if adopted when the Commission sends the LFN is insufficient to ground a subsequent infringement action.

Bibliography

Lenaerts, K., Maselis, I. and Gutman, K., *EU Procedural Law* (OUP, 2014), chapter 5

Prete, L., *Infringement Proceedings in EU Law* (Kluwer, 2017)

Prete, L. and Smulders, B., The Age of Maturity of Infringement Proceedings (2021) 58 *CMLRev* 285-232

See also

Anticompetitive practices, Complaint

L

LICENSING

Gail ELIZABETH EVANS
Queen Mary University of London

Definition

The licensing of intellectual property (notably, patents, copyright, and trademarks) may incur liability under European competition law when either the exercise of the intellectual property rights or the restrictive terms of the contract are considered to have an adverse impact on trade. To this end, the competition law of the European Union (EU) prohibits licensing agreements which may affect trade between Member States and which have as their object or effect the prevention or restriction of competition (Arts. 101 and 102 Treaty on the Functioning of the European Union (TFEU); c.f. sections 1 and 2 of the Sherman Act).

Commentary

Where the effect of an agreement is to obtain absolute territorial protection for the licensee by preventing parallel imports, there will generally be a breach of competition law (*Consten and Grundig v Commission*), the Court of Justice held that absolute territorial protection granted to a licensee in order to enable parallel imports to be controlled and prevented results in the artificial maintenance of separate national markets, contrary to the Treaty.

However, in *Nungesser KG v Commission* an exclusive licence of plant variety rights (Regulation 2100/94 on Community plant variety rights, 1994) that granted the licensee rights to market over hybrid maize seeds throughout the territory of Germany was saved by the exemption within the TFEU as serving to promote technical progress, while also allowing consumers a fair share of the benefits (Article 101(3) TFEU).

Alternatively, a selective distribution network within a licensing agreements would not incur liability under competition law, where the manufacturer supplies only selected distributors or retailers who meet certain qualitative criteria, and who in turn are not to sell outside the authorised network (*Copad SA v Christian Dior couture SA*); regarding online distribution: (*Coty Germany GmbH v Parfümerie Akzente GmbH*). Nevertheless, where licensing agreements seek to restrict not only active but also unsolicited cross-border sales of licensed products, it will breach EU competition law (*Nike v Commission*).

Secondly, certain kinds of clauses in patent licences are considered more likely to adversely affect inter-technology competition, in particular non-challenge clauses that attempt to prohibit the licensee from challenging the validity of the licensed patent. Historically, the Court of Justice has sought to promote competition by taking a restrictive approach to no-challenge clauses (*Windsurfing International Inc. v Commission*), an approach that is now reflected in the Technology Transfer Block Exemption Regulation (TTBER, Regulation 316/2014), whereby a clause preventing the licensee from challenging the validity of the licensed intellectual property, will only be exempted from liability under competition law if the clause is included in an exclusive licensing agreement. Similarly, the TTBER takes a stringent approach to exclusive grant backs to the licensor of improvements to the patented technology. While requiring the licensee to grant back to the licensor improvements on a non-exclusive basis, a clause requiring the licensee to exclusively license all improvements to the licensor would breach competition law. (Art. 101; TTBER, Art.5(1)(a)).

In the event the holder of intellectual property acquires a dominant position in the technology or product market, there is no general obligation to grant a licence (*Volvo v Veng*). While EU Competition law prohibits any abuse by one or more undertakings of a dominant position within the internal market "as incompatible with the internal market in so far as it may affect trade between Member States", there must be evidence that a firm has leveraged its dominance in the market enabling it to behave to an appreciable extent independently of its competitors and customers (*Hoffmann-La Roche v Commission*). For example, Microsoft abused its dominant position in the personal computer market by refusing to provide its competitors with interoperability information that would have enabled the development of competing products in the operating system market (*Microsoft Corp. v European Commission*).

Nevertheless, in the case of standards for mobile telecommunications industry (such as 4G or 5G telephony), holders of standard essential patents (SEPs) essential to the technology's operation, are required to allow implementers of that standard to obtain a licence to use the relevant patents on fair, reasonable and non-discriminatory (FRAND) terms. It may breach competition law if the holder of a SEP brings suit for patent infringement against a prospective licensee (a) without notice; and (b) assuming the infringer is willing to negotiate, without having offered a licence on FRAND terms (*Huawei Technologies v ZTE Corp.*; *Unwired Planet v Huawei*).

Bibliography

Evans, G. E., "Negotiating FRAND Encumbered Patent Licences" *Oxford Journal of Intellectual Property Law & Practice*, Volume 16, Issue 10, October 2021, Pages 1091–1108

Evans, G. E., "Strategic Patent Licensing for Public Research Organizations: Deploying Restriction and Reservation Clauses to Promote Medical R&D in Developing Countries" (2008) 43:2-3 *American Journal of Law and Medicine* pp.175-223

Davis, R., St Quintin, T. and Tritton, G., Tritton on *Intellectual Property in Europe* (5th Edition Sweet & Maxwell 2020) Chapter 9

Whish, R. and Bailey, D., *Competition Law* (10th edition OUP Oxford 2021) Chapter 19

See also

Compulsory licensing, FRAND, Patents

L

LIMITATION PERIOD

Tania ZÚÑIGA
Pontificia Universidad Católica del Perú

Definition

Limitation period is a limitation on the punitive power (ius puniendi) of the authority competent to impose or enforce sanctions, and has the effect of extinguishing the liability derived from the administrative infringement or sanction, but it does not necessarily imply that the fact that the infringement has been committed (that it has not been sanctioned) or that a sanction has been imposed (that it has not been executed) disappears. Limitation period applies to the exercise of the punitive power because it is not extinguished. The authority does not lose punitive power. The application of this legal institution depends exclusively on the presence of the objective elements of the passing of the legally established time limit or the interruption of the procedure independently of any reference to the procedural conduct of the holder of the action for which the penalty is imposed. The limitation period has been set differently across jurisdictions globally, ranging from two to six years.

Commentary

Limitation period is not merely a legal procedural limit to the power of the authority but extinguishes the administrative sanctioning liability of the individual, in other words, setting limitation period safeguards the principle of due process by establishing a time limit on the exercise of the power to impose or enforce penalties.

The relevance of setting the limitation period is based on the principle of legal certainty.

The authority (public administration, court) is subject to the law and to the order. The existence of a time limit is essential in order to guarantee this legal certainty adequately.

The imprescriptibility of the exercise of authority in terms of sanctioning power, without any time limit, would be inadmissible. The statute of limitations for punitive prosecution is of constitutional relevance, since it is linked to the content of the right to a reasonable time limit for the proceedings, which is part of the fundamental right to due process.

Limitation period has a double dimension, on the one hand, this legal institution consists of a limitation to the manifestation of the sanctioning power of the public body; on the other hand, it must also be considered as a right, since it is part of the right to due process.

From the procedural perspective, the statute of limitations is a restrictive conception, based on reasons of legal certainty and not of intrinsic justice, whose application may depend on the concurrence of the subjective element of abandonment or neglect in the exercise of the action itself, on the contrary, limitation period depends exclusively on the presence of the objective elements related to the reasonable time limit, in order to prevent untimely or extemporaneous action.

Limitation period may be also conceived as an institution of a substantive or material nature as a cause of the material extinction of the liability which is based on principles of public order, general interest or criminal policy, which are brought back to the principle of the necessity of punishment, inserted in the broader principle of minimum intervention by the State in the exercise of ius puniendi.

Limitation period as an integral part of the right to due process, can be considered prima facie as a fundamental right of legal configuration, since it is up to the legislator to configure the elements (types, time limits, exceptions, conditions, etc.) that must be fulfilled for it to operate, as well as to prefigure the procedure that must be followed for it to do so.

The minimum conditions that must be regulated to limitation period in any administrative sanctioning procedure are: (i) the length of the limitation period; (ii) the beginning of the computation of the limitation period according to the type of infringement; (iii) the normative assumptions (scenarios) to the interruption of the limitation period; (iv) the computation of the period will be resumed in the event the procedure is interrupted under certain conditions.

In the case of Peru, the Constitutional Court has emphatically recognised that the right to prescription exists as a fundamental right. On the other hand, the General Administrative Procedure Law, Law N° 27444, applicable to all types of administrative procedures, recognises the statute of limitations not only as a defence mechanism, and establishes a clear obligation of the Administration to declare, ex officio, the statute of limitations, when appropriate. In the case of Peru, the aforementioned law establishes that sectoral laws, such as the Competition Law approved by Legislative Decree N° 1034, should not establish less favourable conditions, especially in the area of the administrative sanctioning procedure.

In the European Union, according to Article 25, the powers conferred on the Commission by Articles 23 (fines) and 24 (periodic penalty payments) of the Council Regulation (EC) N° 1/2003 shall be subject to the following limitation periods: (a) three years in the case of infringements of provisions concerning requests for information or the conduct of inspections; (b) five years in the case of all other infringements. The computation of the time shall begin to run on the day on which the infringement is committed. However, in the case of continuing or repeated infringements, time shall begin to run on the day on which the infringement ceases. Article 26 provides that the power of the Commission to enforce decisions taken pursuant to Articles 23 and 24 shall be subject to a limitation period of five years. In the same line, the power of the Commission to enforce decisions taken pursuant to Articles 23 and 24 shall be subject to a limitation period of five years. Time shall begin to run on the day on which the decision becomes final.

An instantaneous offence is one that is committed at a given moment, whereas a continuous offence is one in which there are several actions that constitute the offence and in respect of which there is a relationship of continuity, as opposed to what occurs with permanent offences where such continuity is maintained over time. This distinction is relevant in order to be able to distinguish the types of infringements and the differences that exist, the computation of the statute of limitations in each of them.

An overview of the provisions on the application of the statute of limitations at the global level shows, for the most part of jurisdictions, the establishment of five years as the limitation period, as is the case in Argentina, Austria, Belgium, Chile, Colombia, France, Germany, Hong Kong, Hungary, Italy, Mexico, The Netherlands, Peru, Philippines, Poland, Spain, Sweden, four years in Japan and the Unites States of America, six years in Australia, United Kingdom and eight years, Ecuador. But, on the other hand, shorter periods are observed in some jurisdictions such as Brazil, India, Poland, Russia and Switzerland for three years and two years in Canada, China, Singapore and Turkey. In the Andean Community, the limitation period has been regulated for the application of the sanction to three years in accordance with Article 43 of Decision N° 608 on competition infringements, i.e. cartels and abuse of dominant position.

One of the relevant aspects to consider is the difference between interruption and suspension of the limitation period. In the EU, any action taken by the Commission or by the competition authority of a Member State for the purpose of the investigation or proceedings in respect of an infringement shall interrupt the limitation period for the imposition of fines or periodic penalty payments. The limitation period shall be interrupted with effect from the date on which the action is notified to at least one undertaking or association of undertakings which has participated in the infringement. Actions which interrupt the running of the period shall include in particular the following: (a) written requests for information by the Commission or by the competition authority of a Member State; (b) written authorisations to conduct inspections issued to its officials by the Commission or by the competition authority of a Member State; (c) the initiation of proceedings by the Commission or by the competition authority of a Member State; (d) notification of the statement of objections of the Commission or of the competition authority of a Member State. The limitation period for the imposition of fines or periodic penalty payments shall be suspended for as long as the decision of the Commission is the subject of proceedings pending before the Court of Justice.

Another relevant aspect, is the computation issue of the infringement. An instantaneous offence is one that is committed at a given moment, whereas a continuous offence is one in which there are several actions that constitute the offence and in respect of which there is a relationship of continuity, as opposed to what occurs with permanent offences where such continuity is maintained over time. This distinction is relevant in order to be able to distinguish the types of infringements and the differences that exist, the computation of limitation period in each of them.

The European doctrinal construction regarding the assessment of collusive practices under the concept of single and continuous infringement (SCI) to resolve complex collusion cases, however, has not been free from criticism. Several agreements are understood to constitute a single infringement, even if there are interruptions. This has direct consequences on the computation of the institution of limitation period, since in the case of the application of SCI to collusion scenarios, the consideration of several agreements adopted over several years as a single infringement would lead to the rejection of the statute of limitations in respect of the oldest collusive agreements.

See also

Damages

M

MARGIN SQUEEZE

David FRUITMAN
DFDL

Definition

A margin squeeze refers to circumstances where a vertically-integrated enterprise, which is dominant in an upstream market ("Dominant Market"), prices its products or services in the Dominant Market into the vertically-related downstream market in which it is not dominant at a level such that equally efficient competitors in that market are unable to earn sufficient margins to compete effectively.

Commentary

U.S. – Section 2 of the Sherman Act makes it unlawful for any person to "monopolize, or attempt to monopolize, or combine or conspire with any other person or persons, to monopolize any part of the trade or commerce among the several States, or with foreign nations…." The treatment of margin squeezes under Section 2 of the Serman Act was explicitly addressed by the U.S. Supreme Court decision in Pacific Bell Tel. Co. v. LinkLine, 555 U.S. 438 (2009) ("Linkline"). Effectively relying on Verizon v. Trinko, 540 U.S. 398, the court in Linkline found that without a duty to deal, there is no obligation to deal under terms and conditions favorable to competitors. On this basis, at writing, there is no independent antitrust prohibition on margin squeezes under the Sherman Act absent any duty to deal or predatory pricing claim.

EU – Article 102 TFEU prohibits the abuse of a dominant position. The Court of Justice's judgments in and Telefónica SA and Telefónica de España SAU v European Commission (Case C-295/12 P, 10 July 2014) ("Telefonica"), Deutsche Telekom AG v Commission (Case C-152/19 P, 25 March 2021) ("Deutsche") and Slovak Telekom, a.s. v European Commission (Case C-165/19 P, March 25, 2021) ("Slovak") are recent leading authorities on margin squeezes. In Telefonica, the ECJ rejected an appeal against the judgment of the General Court (Case T-336/07, 29 March 2012) which had affirmed the original Commission decision finding a violation of Article 102. In its judgment, the ECJ confirmed that a margin squeeze is an independent form of abuse distinct from refusal to supply and that the essential nature of the input is not a pre-requisite in margin squeeze cases (para 96). Further details on margin squeezes were set out by the judgment of the General Court which, among other things, held that:

- a margin squeeze is "the result of the spread between the prices for wholesale services and those for retail services and not of the level of those prices as such." (para 187); and
- that the test to assess the margin squeeze is the potential impact on an equally efficient competitor as the dominant enterprise (para 194).

In Deutsche and Slovak the ECJ rejected appeals against the judgments of the General Court, largely affirming the underlying Commission finding that Slovak had committed a margin squeeze in relation to the provision of broadband internet access services. In particular, the ECJ:

- reaffirmed the distinction between refusal to supply cases which are guided by Bronner and abuses such as margin squeezes where the Bronner criteria such as indispensability are not a requirement; (see Slovak, paras 59 and 60);
- reaffirmed the Commission's application of the equally efficient competitor test for margin squeeze cases (see Slovak, paras 114-120).

In 2023, the European Commission amended its priorities in applying Article [102] of the TFEU to abusive exclusionary conduct by dominant undertakings to add a new paragraph 90 specifically addressing margin squeezes as follows:

A dominant undertaking may charge a price for the product on the upstream market which, compared to the price it charges on the downstream market(3), does not allow even an equally efficient competitor to trade profitably in the downstream market on a lasting basis (a so-called "margin squeeze")(4). In margin squeeze cases the benchmark which the Commission will generally rely on to determine the costs of an equally efficient competitor are the LRAIC of the downstream division of the integrated dominant undertaking(5).

(3) This includes a situation in which an integrated undertaking that sells a "system" of complementary products sells one of the complementary products on an unbundled basis to a competitor that produces the other complementary product.

(4) This conduct constitutes an independent form of abuse distinct from that of refusal to supply, judgment of 17 February 2011, TeliaSonera Sverige, C-52/09, EU:C:2011:83, paragraph 56.

(5) In some cases, however, the LRAIC of a non-integrated competitor downstream might be used as the benchmark, for example when it is not possible to clearly allocate the dominant undertaking's costs to downstream and upstream operations.'

ASEAN – a Proposed Decision of the Malaysia Competition Commission ("MyCC") dated 30 October 2013 was issued in relation to the alleged

Infringement of Section 10(1) of the Competition Act 2010 by Megasteel Sdn. Bhd. ("Megasteel") in which the MyCC concluded that Megasteel was dominant in the Hot Rolled Coil ("HRC") market and also competed in the downstream Cold Rolled Coil ("CRC") market. In the Proposed Decision, the MyCC determined that Megasteel had engaged in a margin squeeze by pricing HRC at a level that constrained, or potentially could constrain, reasonably efficient competitors in the CRC market from realizing sufficient margins. Of interest, the MyCC noted that HRC was an essential input into CRC and that the squeeze was based on the price of CRC which Megasteel was pricing at a level which did not allow it to recover the full costs of transforming HRC into CRC. In its Final Decision dated 15 April 2016, the MyCC determined, after additional information was provided, that no such margin squeeze had occurred as Megasteel had not been inappropriately pricing its CRC.

The Competition and Consumer Commission of Singapore's Guidelines on the Section 47 Prohibition address margin squeezes as follows:

11.18 A vertically integrated undertaking may be dominant in the supply of an important input for a downstream market in which it also operates. In such a case, the vertically integrated undertaking could potentially harm competition by setting such a low margin between its input price (e.g. wholesale price) and the price it sets in the downstream market (e.g. retail price) such that an equally efficient downstream competitor is forced to exit the market or is unable to compete effectively. This is known as a "margin squeeze", and is likely to constitute an abuse of a dominant position where it harms (or is likely to harm) competition.

11.19 In testing for a margin squeeze, CCCS will generally determine whether an efficient downstream competitor would earn (at least) a normal profit when paying input prices set by the vertically integrated undertaking. The test is typically applied to the downstream arm of the vertically integrated undertaking. The test asks whether the integrated undertaking's downstream business would make (at least) a normal profit if it paid the same input price that it charged its competitors, given its revenues at the time of the alleged margin squeeze.

Bibliography

BERGQVIST, C. and TOWNSEND J., *Abusive margin squeeze: The Franken-stein monster of Article 102 TFEU?*, 2021

VELJANOVSKI, C., Margin squeeze and competition law: An overview of EU and national case law, 5 June 2012, *e-Competitions Margin squeeze*, Art. N° 46442

YANELIS, D., Margin Squeeze in the U.S. and the EU, *European Scientific Journal* November 2015 /SPECIAL/ edition, 495

OECD Policy Roundtables: Margin Squeeze, 2009

See also

Abuse of dominant position, Economic analysis, Exclusionary practice

M

MARGINAL COSTS

John M. YUN
George Mason University

Definition

Marginal cost is the additional cost that a supplier incurs from producing an incremental unit of output. Alternatively, marginal cost can be framed as the cost that is saved when one less unit of output is produced. Marginal cost need not be restricted to changes in one unit, however, and can also be used for any incremental change in output. For instance, a supplier may wish to know the additional cost from producing the next 100 units.

Commentary

Marginal cost can be best understood in relation to all the other various types of "cost." To that end, the relevant starting point is the concept of total cost, which is the sum of all the opportunity costs involved in the production of a good or service at a given level of output. Total cost can be further decomposed into variable costs and fixed costs. Variable costs represent those costs that change when output changes, such as, the costs associated with hiring more labor to run an additional shift at a plant. In contrast, fixed costs are costs that, at least for a period of time and range of output, do not vary as output changes, such as, the cost of municipal permits to operate a plant or the expenses required to develop patents used in the production process. Consequently, if production is stopped, then the fixed costs are not saved. Within this context, marginal cost represents the change in variable costs when there is an incremental change in output, which obviously does not include fixed costs. Alternatively, variable costs represent the sum of all the prior marginal costs of production. For example, suppose marginal cost is $10 per unit. If so, the variable cost to produce three units of output is $30, which is simply $10 plus $10 plus $10.

As output levels increase, marginal cost can increase, stay the same, or even decrease. For instance, a firm approaching capacity of its various fixed, capital inputs (e.g., factories, machinery) may experience increasing marginal costs as labor experiences diminishing returns. Alternatively, if additional units of labor allow a firm to better organize and specialize the production process, then the marginal cost of production may actually decrease – at least for a range of output. Generally, however, economists tend to assume that marginal cost is constant or increasing.

Ultimately, firms care about marginal cost because it helps answer the question of how much to make and what price to charge. When expanding output, firms will consider both the marginal benefit of production (that is, the marginal revenue) and the marginal cost of that production. These considerations will lead to a result that will maximize the profit of the firm. This is the textbook treatment of profit maximization. That being said, the reality is that firms may view cost more broadly without necessarily delineating fixed and variable costs into identifiable categories – given that all costs are variable at some point and, relatedly, the line between fixed and variable costs is not always clear.

Within antitrust, marginal cost can be relevant in various contexts. For instance, an enduring argument is that the degree to which price exceeds marginal cost is a measure of a firm's market power. This idea is formalized in the Lerner Index, which is the ratio of (a) the firm's price minus its marginal cost to (b) the firm's price. Thus, as the Lerner Index approaches one, then this could indicate greater market power. While such a proxy for market power may be appropriate in markets with low fixed costs, the problem is when fixed costs are significant such as industries with large overhead or R&D expenditures. In those cases, pricing above marginal cost does not necessarily correspond to market power or supra-competitive profits. Rather, the pricing practice could simply represent the margin necessary to recoup the investments in fixed costs or the risks associated with product development and production.

Relatedly, marginal cost can be used as a key input in the calculation of critical loss, which is a tool to delineate relevant markets. Critical loss is a formula involving a small, but significant and non-transitory increase in price (SSNIP) and the price-cost margin (i.e., the Lerner Index). The relevant measure of cost in this context is the cost that is saved if output is reduced due to a price increase. Marginal cost naturally fits this profile; although, other measures of cost may be used such as average variable cost (AVC), which is simply variable cost divided by the amount of production.

Marginal cost reductions are also considered an efficiency in merger analysis, such as, when the combination of two companies with complementary production facilities results in lower transportation costs. Reductions in marginal cost are part of the paradigm established by the economist Oliver Williamson to highlight the potential trade-offs from a merger. Specifically, a merger can create both an upward pressure on the post-merger price due to a loss of competition and a downward pressure on price due to merger-specific savings in marginal cost.

Marginal cost can also be invoked when considering theories of harm that involve pricing below cost, such as, predatory pricing. For predatory pricing cases, measuring marginal cost for litigation may prove challenging and, thus, courts tend to favor other measures of costs including average variable cost. Whether AVC represent a reasonable proxy for marginal cost, however, will depend on the particular cost structure that a firm faces. Further, whether one would conceptually prefer marginal cost or AVC as a measure of below-cost pricing is still a point of contention.

Ultimately, understanding marginal cost is often central to antitrust analyses because the concept captures a firm's opportunity cost of production at a particular point in time for a particular change in output. Given that antitrust law is concerned with understanding business conduct, this task cannot be accomplished without understanding marginal cost. The difficulty is often in estimating marginal cost for analyses such as critical loss, efficiencies, and predatory pricing – as marginal cost is not necessarily something that all firms track or even know.

Bibliography

BAUMOL, W. J., Predation and the Logic of the Average Variable Cost Test, 39 *J.L. & ECON.* 49 (1996)

COATE, M. B., ULRICK, S. W. and YUN, J. M., Critical Loss in Market Definition: Methods and Court Decisions, 10 *J. Antitrust Enforcement* 419 (2022)

LANDES, W. M. and POSNER, R. A., Market Power in Antitrust Cases, 94 *Harv. L. Rev.* 937 (1981)

LERNER, A., The Concept of Monopoly and the Measurement of Monopoly Power, 1 *Rev. Econ. Stud.* 157 (1934)

MANKIW, N. G., *Principles of Microeconomics*, 6th edition, South-western, Cengage learning (2012)

O'BRIEN, D. P. and WICKELGREN, A. L., A Critical Analysis of Critical Loss Analysis, 71 *ANTITRUST L.J.* 16 (2003)

PITTMAN, R., Who are You Calling Irrational? Marginal Costs, Variable Costs, and the Pricing Practices of Firms, Economic Analysis Group Discussion Paper, EAG 09-3, July 2009

WILLIAMSON, O. E., economies as an anti-trust defense: the welfare tradeoffs, in *Readings in Industrial Economics*: Volume two: Private Enterprise and State Intervention (1972)

Department of Justice & Federal Trade Commission, 2010 Horizontal Merger Guidelines (2010)

See also

Economic analysis, Lerner index, Variable costs

M

MARKET ECONOMY INVESTOR

Dimitrios KYRIAZIS
National and Kapodistrian University of Athens

■ Definition

Article 107(1) TFEU prohibits the grant of state aid from Member States to undertakings. For a measure to be state aid, six cumulative conditions need to be fulfilled, i.e. the conferral of an advantage to the undertaking(s) through the state measure, said measure must be imputable to the State, State resources must be employed, the measure needs to be selective, and it must also (at the very least) threaten to distort competition and affect inter-State trade. The Market Economy Operator Principle ("MEOP") mandates that transactions carried out by Member States do not confer an advantage on undertakings, and therefore do not constitute state aid, if they are carried out in line with normal market conditions.

■ Commentary

The MEOP, and its corresponding test, the MEOT (Market Economy Operator Test), are essentially a way of identifying whether an advantage has been conferred in the context of a transaction between a Member State (or public body, or public undertakings) and an undertaking. An advantage is defined, in settled CJEU case law, as an economic benefit – of any form whatsoever – that the recipient undertaking would not have obtained under normal market conditions. In order to ascertain whether the recipient undertaking would have obtained it under normal market conditions, one needs to compare and contrast the actions of the State (the alleged aid measure) with those that a market economy operator would have made in a similar situation. If a market economy operator would have acted in a similar manner, no advantage has been conferred. If not, and the action or its conditions or terms, is any way different from that which would have been agreed on by a market economy operator, and they are, also, more favourable to the recipient undertaking, an advantage has been conferred. If all other state aid conditions are also fulfilled, state aid has been granted.

The MEOP is the main point of entry of economic analysis in state aid law. Contrary to the rest of competition law, economic analysis does not play any real role in the definition of market shares or the distortion of competition and effect on trade conditions. However, it features prominently in the MEOP analysis. The reason is evident: one needs to employ economic tools in order to determine whether a market economy operator (also sometimes called a "private" operator) would have taken the same route with regard to a certain transaction. For example: would a private bank have granted a loan to this undertaking under the same terms as the loan issued by the State? Would a private proprietor have sold a particular building for the price it was sold at by the State, or would they have asked for more? To answer these questions, economic analysis is indispensable.

What is irrelevant, in principle, are considerations that a market economy operator would not take into account, thus not including them in their decision-making process. For instance, a private economy investor would, in principle, not make an investment that would be loss-making, simply because the investment would benefit the local economy and/or the environment, or boost employment. On the contrary, they would focus on the profitability of the future investment and take into account factors that would influence it. There are various versions/iterations of the market economy operator principle, depending on the capacity in which the Member State is acting and the kind of transaction it is engaged in. For example, building on the previous example, to establish whether a State's investment State aid, it is necessary to determine whether a private investor of a comparable size operating in normal market economy conditions would have made the investment in question. When the State grants a loan, the comparison will be with a private creditor (usually a commercial bank). When the State makes a sale, the comparison will be with a private vendor, and the test will examine whether a private vendor might have gotten the same or better price under normal market conditions. A similar test would apply to the acquisition of assets or any other transaction that could be undertaken by a private party, e.g. a lease.

The considerations that need to be taken into account are those existing at the time of the transaction and not later on (*ex ante* assessment). For instance, if, with the available data at hand, a certain investment made business sense, the measure will not confer an advantage, even if it later proves to be a disastrous investment. However, the opposite is also true. An investment, by the State, in a certain company that made no business sense and would not have been undertaken by a private investor, will still qualify as state aid, even if, by chance, it ended up being highly profitable. Therefore, it is important for a Member State to carry out its own ex *ante* assessment of financial prospects of a project (e.g.

a business plan), and not rely on *ex post* expert reports. Finally, it is worth noting that the fact that the measure was a fiscal (tax) measure does not rule out the possibility of it complying with the MEOP.

Bibliography

Hancher, L., Ottervanger, T. and Slot, P. J., *EU State Aids* (6th edn, Sweet and Maxwell 2021), Chapter 1

Quigley QC, C., *European State Aid Law and Policy (and UK Subsidy Control)*, (4th edn, Hart Publishing 2022), Chapter 4

Commission Notice on the notion of State aid as referred to in Article 107(1) of the Treaty on the Functioning of the European Union (2016/C 262/01), section 4.2

See also

Economic analysis, Public undertaking, Privatization, State measure, State aid

M

MARKET POWER

Adriana HERNANDEZ PEREZ
Fundação Getúlio Varga

Aldo GONZALEZ
University of Chile

Definition

Market power refers to the ability of a company or a group of companies to establish their policies such as their prices, product quality and investments in innovation, to a significant extent without a severe competitive constraint from competitors, customers or consumers. When a company, whether a buyer or seller, has market power, it can influence market outcomes such as prices, quality, the volume of output or contractual conditions. In antitrust analysis, the concept is used to identify whether a company would have the ability to act anticompetitively in a given market.

Commentary

In economic theory, the term market power is originally associated with the ability of a company to set prices above its marginal cost and be profitable in economic terms. The concept of market power is not a zero-one state, but a continuum. A monopoly represents the highest level of market power, whereas a "price-taker" company, positioned at the opposite end of the spectrum, lacks the ability to deviate from prevailing market outcomes determined by the interplay of supply and demand forces, thus having no market power. Companies seek market power because they reach maximum economic profitability under conditions of monopoly, whereas they obtain zero profit if they find themselves in the role of a "price-taker", where they have to accept the prevailing market price.

It is important to recognise that having market power is not inherently problematic. A company's market power may stem from barriers to entry, related to past investments, as well as brand reputation, exogenous regulation, economies of scale, network effects, intellectual property or any other factor that differentiates it from its competitors. The issue for competition law is how market power is employed within the market. For example, a company may exploit its dominant position to unjustly eliminate competitors, an action that raises concerns from a competition standpoint.

As an illustration, consider a vertically-integrated company, i.e. a company that operates at different stages of the production or distribution chain of a finished product or service. If the entity holds market power on the production of a vital input, it may have the capacity to foreclose its downstream rivals. By denying them access to the essential input, the new entity has the ability to keep competitors from entering the market or forcing them to leave it, leading to potential concerns about market concentration and reduced competition.

In standard competition analysis, the substitutability of the different services and products offered by a company is an important step to assess its market power. The concept is also related to the company's demand price elasticity. The lower the (absolute) price elasticity, the higher the company's market power and vice-versa. Also, a company with market power must be able to sustain above-normal profits in the long run. Therefore, any antitrust analysis on the matter must consider both static and dynamic elements.

Following the insights oligopoly theory, market shares are commonly adopted as a proxy of a company's market power once the relevant market is defined. In some jurisdictions, certain market shares trigger a presumption of dominance in the market. For example, the European Commission's Guidelines for evaluating horizontal mergers regard mergers that yield market shares of 40% to 50%, and in some instances even below 40%, as potentially leading to the establishment or reinforcement of a dominant position.

Evaluating market power using market-share analysis often involves considering other elements that signal a company's influence, including product differentiation, brand loyalty, exclusive contracts, exclusive access to vital inputs or customer bases, economies of scale and scope, barriers to entry, network effects, intellectual property and regulatory and technological change.

The significance of each factor varies according to the industry's dynamics. In markets that are more contestable with low entry barriers, a company with a high market share is unlikely to sustain above-normal profits, as it can attract new competitors and, once these new players become active in the market, they may pressure price downwards through increased competition. In these circumstances, possessing a high market share does not necessarily equate to having market power that enables it to sustain elevated profits. Therefore, other factors besides market shares have to be included in the analysis.

The assessment of market power in the context of digital multisided platforms has renewed the discussion on the use of alternative mechanisms to demonstrate market power. In this respect, Franck and

Peitz (2019) suggested a careful analysis of platform profitability – as low profits or losses do not necessarily imply a lack of market power –, the absence of new entry in the market, the deliberate reduction of quality of services and the presence of (positive) network benefits on one side of the platform.

In Europe, the term market power is associated with the concept of dominant position in Article 102 of the Treaty and is applied to monitor abusive conduct by companies that have a dominant position on a particular market.

In the U.S., the 2023 Merger guidelines, while not formally defining market power, outline various strategies that can lessen competition or tend to create a monopoly increase, extend, or entrench market power, depriving the public from the benefits of competition. For example, a company may "diminish competitive constraints, reduce the number or attractiveness of alternatives available to trading partners, or reduce the intensity with which market participants compete."

The Brazilian antitrust authority, Conselho Administrativo de Defesa da Concorrência (Cade), outlines in its guidelines that market power refers to the ability of a company of a group of companies to set its prices systematically above the competitive prices without losing most of its customers. In its assessments, market shares have an important role, but are considered together with other variables such as the existence of barriers to entry, the possibility of imports or the rivalry between the company that has a dominant position and its competitors.

Bibliography

Cabral, L. M., *Introduction to industrial organization*, 2nd edition, MIT Press, 2017

Franck, J. U. and Peitz, M., Market definition and market power in the platform economy, in *Centre on Regulation in Europe asbl*, 2019

Jullien, B. and Sand-Zantman, W., The economics of platforms: A theory guide for competition policy, in *Information Economics and Policy*, no 54-2021, p. 100880

Conselho Administrativo de Defesa da Concorrência (Cade), Cartilha do Cade, 2016

Federal Trade Commission and Department of Justice (DoJ), Merger Guidelines, 2023

See also

Barriers to entry, Buyer power, Concentration indexes, Dominance (notion), Economic analysis, Fintech, Market share, Mobility barriers

M

MARKET SHARE

Julia SUDEROW, Alejandro MARTÍNEZ LUNA
Suderow Fernandez

Definition

Market shares enable to calculate not just the share, but the total market size. It is crucial to determine whether an undertaking has a dominant position (sine qua non condition to abusing such position) or even, as in the case of Spain, to determine the legality of a concentration (30% threshold). It also determines whether the de minimis rule applies, whether a block exemption is granted, or whether a concentration can have an effect on trade and must undergo examination. As the United Nations have noted, despite its usefulness, market shares can be very complex indicators and must be used cautiously.

Commentary

The literature has focused heavily on how market shares are calculated, taking for granted what is meant by "market share". Why market share plays such an important role is a less addressed question.

Market share is just a tool, a measure for an otherwise unquantifiable trait: market power. Law resorted to economic analysis to identify anti-competitive conducts, and the selected proxy for this task was market share.

The European Commission, in its draft revised Commission Notice, reckoned that market shares are not the sole indicator of an undertaking's strength in the market, and that other factors, such as the degree of substitutability may also be relevant (e.g. the Ryanair case before the CJEU (T-342/07) par. 42). The Commission may also use market shares as a first screening tool to assess whether competition concers may arise.

Inaccuracy would be the first criticism to the term, which assumes that high shares equal bestowing market power, but in reality, it does not purely resemble it. Market share is a static concept that must be complemented with elements about the dynamics of an industry, such as innovation.

Secondly, despite being "flawed" by default (as market power cannot be genuinely measured), actually calculating the share of a company's share is very complex. Its results rely heavily on economic and market assumptions.

And the third problem added to the equation is that market share is, in itself, a byproduct of the relevant market. The judgment of the Court of Justice of the European Union (CJEU) dated 16 June 2011 (T-209/08 – Stichting) expressly stated that "in order to calculate a market share, it is necessary first to determine that market" (par. 108). The 2004 European Commission Guidelines on the effect on trade concept also point in the same direction (par. 55). As a consequence, an incorrect market definition will, almost inevitably, lead to unreliable market shares. Likewise, market shares depend heavily on a correct geographic scope of the affected market.

Then, it is no surprise that lawyers often try to fight the relevant market definition to tackle high market shares.

Some authors like KAPLOW argue that market shares can be misleading and should be adjusted in light of economic reality to not render the market definition moot.

To sum up the above: (i) market share is not the same as market power, (ii) market share cannot give exact results on the influence of an undertaking in a given market, and; (iii) the relevant market is to be correctly defined from the start for market shares to have a meaningful sense.

Each relevant market needs a different approach to calculating market shares. Dividing the company's sales by the industry's total sales does not suffice. In fact, market share is more studied in economic forums than in legal ones. However, there are alternative approaches. For instance, the Spanish Competition Authority (CNMC) determined market share in the railroad sector based on non-economic terms and focused only on the number of passengers transported.

The 2024 Commission Notice on the definition of the relevant market also pays attention to other forms of calculating market share involving non-economic metrics, such as capacity or production volumes, number of suppliers, number of tenders awarded, reserves held, or even expenditure and investment in R&D (par. 108).

Economists also consider market asymmetry, marketing efforts, demand elasticity, customer attraction, or purchase frequency. Despite criticism to economic models, there are well-elaborated formulas that truly grasp the insights of the market.

As the European Commission has admitted (2022 Guidelines on vertical restraints, par. 175), market share is a moldable concept that adapts its criteria and methodology on a case-by-case basis. There is not a single parameter in the market share formula that cannot be subject to change.

Nevertheless, a rigorous analysis is not always needed. Market share criteria have proven to be flexible. Vague market shares often suffice (e.g. approximate percentages). The CJEU, in its 11 July 2013 judgement (C-439/11 Ziegler), accepted that despite not having the relevant market well defined, a "sufficiently detailed description of the relevant sector" (par. 73) was enough to determine whether the specific threshold was met.

Spanish case law has also faced situations where market shares were calculated counterintuitively. The Supreme Court judgment dated 24 February 2009 dealt with a case to determine whether a dominant telecommunications service provider had suffered a competitive disadvantage. Interestingly, the Court calculated the market share of the dominant company based on a relevant market that was much larger than the market where their competitors operated.

In conclusion, market shares as indicators are not free of criticism, though it has become a central player in competition law procedures. Some countries like Spain are loyal supporters of this system. In contrast, others like Türkiye or Brasil decided to erase It from their legal systems (Russia, for instance, kept it only for dominant position presumptions). As such, it is a concept with great potential, but experience has shown that it can also be risky.

Bibliography

Barnard, C., & Peers, S. (Eds.). (2020). *European Union law*. Oxford University Press

Cooper, L. G. (1993). Market-share models. Handbooks in *operations research and management science*, 5, 259-314

Gasull, A. et al. (2015). *Problemas prácticos y actualidad del Derecho de la Competencia* [Anuario 2015]. Thomson Reuters. Civitas

Kaplow, L. (2013). Market definition: Impossible and counterproductive. *Antitrust LJ*, 79, 361

Whish, R., & Bailey, D. (2021). *Competition law*. Oxford University Press

See also

Concentration indexes, Market power, Mobility barriers, Notification

M

MEDIA PLURALISM

Christina ETTELDORF
Institute of European Media Law

■ Definition

Media pluralism describes a state where, independent of the form of a medium offer, a free and democratic public opinion-forming process is enabled by a diversity of media providers (external media pluralism) or a diversity of opinion-forming media content within a medium (internal media pluralism) or a combination thereof.

■ Commentary

A globally accepted definition of media pluralism does not exist. Rather, both concept and demand for media pluralism are shaped by the constitutional law of each state and originate essentially in the fundamental rights of freedom of the media, expression and information. The concept developed significantly after World War II in the field of broadcasting to avoid dominance of media content by states or other actors, striving for access to diverse, free and independent information for citizens. At the time, the global broadcasting landscape was still dominated by state-owned public broadcasters and the global West began to shift towards an independent and internally pluralistic organisation of public service broadcasters – in Europe driven by models from the UK, France and Western Germany which had been modelled by influences from the U.S. With the emergence of commercial broadcasting, *dual systems* began to evolve, combining the existing idea of internal pluralism with an external plurality of the media landscape. Today, the notion of media pluralism is increasingly understood in a "media-neutral" way, embracing a number of aspects such as a diversity of ownership, views and information sources available, and focusing on content rather than the category of media.

Media pluralism is a fundamental rights value under Art. 10 European

Convention on Human Rights which follows a protection goal-oriented approach. As the European Court of Human Rights emphasised in *Informationsverein Lentia* (paragraph 38), the press can only successfully fulfil its essential function as a public watchdog within a democratic society, i.e. provide the public with information of general interest, if this is based on the principle of pluralism. In this context, the state is seen as the "ultimate guarantor" of pluralism adding a dimension to the fundamental right beyond a mere defensive position against state interference. Traditionally, the press and audiovisual media have been accorded particular importance but recent judgments have also emphasised the relevance of communication processes on the internet and citizen journalism in shaping public opinion.

Unlike many other constitutional texts, Article 11(2) of the Charter of Fundamental Rights of the European Union explicitly states that "pluralism of the media shall be respected". The case law of the Court of Justice of the European Union (ECJ) regularly focuses on the relevance of media pluralism in relation to other fundamental rights and freedoms. Confirming its previous case law, the ECJ emphasised in *Fussl Modestraße Mayr* (paragraphs 54, 55) that the preservation of a pluralistic media offer "unquestionably constitutes a legitimate aim in the general interest, the importance of which in a democratic and pluralistic society must be stressed in particular" and which is capable of justifying a restriction of fundamental freedoms provided for in the Treaty on the Functioning of the European Union (TFEU).

In the U.S., media pluralism is not included as clearly as in Europe within the constitutional framework. In the context of the protection of free speech under the First Amendment the U.S. Supreme Court has in certain cases pointed out that media pluralism is a value included in the scope. In *Turner Broadcasting* (paragraph 663), for example, a case involving traditional broadcasting, it acknowledged that assuring public access to a multiplicity of information sources is a governmental purpose of the highest order. Such public access promotes central values and it has long been a basic tenet of national communications policy to ensure the widest possible dissemination of information from diverse and contrasting sources because this is essential to public welfare. Nonetheless, this is a relatively narrow application of the principle in fundamental rights terms.

Besides the fundamental rights dimension, in competition law safeguarding media pluralism has several points of reference.

At EU level, this includes Article 106(2) TFEU, which allows exemptions from the competition rules for 'undertakings entrusted with the operation of services of general economic interest' insofar as their application would obstruct the performance of the tasks of such undertakings. This allows state financing of public service media to safeguard pluralism, which would otherwise be prohibited under state aid rules. However, additional conditions were explicitly laid down for the broadcasting sector in the Communication from the Commission on the application of State aid rules to public service broadcasting setting out conditions on the scope of entrustment, monitoring and transparency of state or state initiated funding.

The legal implication of media pluralism is even more obvious in the field of anti-trust law. Media concentration rules describe special measures that take into account the fact that the media industry is different from other industries due to their importance not only from an economic but a cultural perspective. While ordinary concentration law aims at preventing dominant market power of single entities and thereby relies solely on economic market assessment criteria, special rules under media concentration law aim at preventing dominant opinion power of single entities and assess the effects of mergers or the change of shareholding structures (also) in relation to the preservation of a pluralistic information and media landscape. In order to prevent individual actors from exerting a dominant and thus unilateral influence on the information and media landscape in a particular reception area, such rules, for example, set limits to ownership of media companies, often in a cross-ownership dimension covering different type of media.

In the EU, merger control of a Union-wide dimension is the exclusive responsibility of the European Commission. This extends to mergers of media companies. Although the control of market dominance can have an indirect effect on ensuring pluralism, because power over markets can also mean power over opinions, perpetuation of media pluralism is yet not an assessment criterion for the Commission. Rather, it is a matter of economic assessment based on criteria of competition and consumer protection. However, Article 21(4) of the Council Regulation (EC) No 139/2004 of 20 January 2004 on the control of concentrations between undertakings provides that Member States may take appropriate measures to protect legitimate interests, one of them being the plurality of the media, which can then supplement the applicable competition law assessment.

A majority of EU Member States have implemented rules on media concentration that impose limits on media ownership, but these vary significantly. There are limitations of audience reach, restrictions on market shares and cross-media ownership limitations, some of them being tied to licensing obligations in broadcasting law or addressed in national competition law with special rules for the press.

However, EU Member States are not completely free when establishing media concentration rules. As the ECJ highlighted in *Vivendi* (paragraphs 57 et seq.) in light of an Italian rule on revenue limits in the electronic communications sector, Member States are bound to the principle of proportionality when taking measures to reach the legitimate aim of safeguarding media pluralism, i.e. national legislation has to be appropriate and necessary in order to achieve this objective and the aim must not be able to be achieved by a measure that is less intrusive or limits fundamental freedoms to a lesser extent.

In the U.S., mergers of media companies are examined under the Sherman Antitrust Act of 1890 and the Clayton Antitrust Act of 1914 which do not constitute limitations of the First Amendment protection, but are rather protecting the marketplace of ideas, as underlined by the U.S. Supreme Court in *Associated Press* (paragraph 326 et seq.). Furthermore, there are specific rules on media ownership concentration limiting merger possibilities for example under the Newspaper Preservation Act of 1970 or Section 7 of the Clayton Act. The FCC sets limits on the number of broadcast stations one entity can own. The former cross-ownership ban hindering companies from owning a daily newspaper and a broadcasting station in the same market were, however, revoked in 2017.

Although media content on the internet is considered relevant for opinion-forming from a constitutional perspective and intermediaries such as social media are an important source of information for large parts of the population in today's media environment, media concentration rules still regularly cover only traditional providers such as television, radio and press and do not (yet) extend to the online context, which many voices see as highly problematic against the background of a continued relevance of media pluralism.

Bibliography

Bania, K., *The Role of Media Pluralism in the Enforcement of EU Competition Law*, Concurrences, 2019

Cole, M., Jörg Ukrow and Christina Etteldorf, *On the Allocation of Competences between the European Union and its Member States in the Media Sector – An Analysis with particular Consideration of Measures concerning Media Pluralism* (Nomos, 2020)

Fisch, W. B., "Plurality of Political Opinion and the Concentration of Media in the United States" (2010), *American Journal of Comparative Law* 58

Valcke, P., Sükösd, M. and Picard, R. G. (eds.), *Media Pluralism and Diversity – Concepts, Risks and Global Trends* (Palgrave Macmillan UK, 2015)

European Commission, Directorate-General for Communications Networks, Content and Technology, Pier Luigi Parcu, Elda Brogi, Sofia Verza, et al., *Study on media plurality and diversity online: final report* (Publications Office of the European Union, 2022)

See also

Consumer protection, Principle of proportionality, Services of general economic interest (SGIE)

M

MERGER (NOTION)

Willard MWEMBA
COMESA

Definition

A merger occurs when one or more undertakings acquires direct or indirect control of one or more other undertakings. The control acquired should be on a lasting basis. Such acquisition of control may include through: the acquisition of shares, the acquisition of assets, the lease of assets, by contract, joint ventures between two or more independent enterprises. Post-merger the acquiring undertaking/s assumes influence on the target undertaking or undertakings' commercial strategy or policy direction in the market.

Commentary

The term chosen to describe the merger depends on the purpose of the business transaction and the competitive relationship between the merging parties. Generally, competition laws have categorised mergers into three types. These are horizontal, conglomerate and vertical mergers. Some mergers may have two or all the aspects of the three types of mergers.

Horizontal mergers are those that involve actual or potential competitors. They are most likely to raise competition concerns than other types of mergers because they directly reduce number of competitors in the market. Vertical mergers are not mergers among competitors but between firms situated at different levels of the value chain e.g. supplier of a computer software and manufacturer of computers. They usually result in efficiency enhancing gains. Nevertheless, they may also raise competition concerns especially through foreclosure effects. On the other hand, Conglomerate mergers involve transactions where the merging parties are not in direct actual or potential competition and they are not in the same value chain e.g. cement company and supplier of livestock. They rarely raise competition concerns. However, competition concerns may arise if the merged entity engages in mixed bundling.

Mergers are an important area of corporate restructuring, an avenue for growth and for consolidation. This allows firms to acquire market share, expand into new territories, add to their product range and to meet global demand among others. However, sometimes firms may merge with the anticompetitive motives, such as to eliminate effective competition that threatens their own survival in the market.

Though the term merger is defined in most competition laws, its application to transactions has not been free from dispute and controversy between competition authorities on the one hand and the merging parties on the other.

In the European Union, problems in establishing the existence of a merger situation have arisen with regard to sole control and minority rights acquisition. Some minority rights acquisitions may confer sole control. The minority rights acquisition may be so large compared to the other right holders that it may be able to exert significant influence in shareholder meetings for example. This is supported by the decision in the *Electrabel/Compagnie Nationale du Rhone (CNR)* merger, where the European Commission determined that Electrabel had acquired sole control over CNR despite being a minority shareholder, on the basis of a number of different considerations, including that it was assured of a de-facto majority at CNR's General Meeting. This position was affirmed by the General Court and the Court of Justice on appeal.

Another controversy over the notion of merger was highlighted in the United Kingdom in the decision *Société Coopérative de Production Seafrance SA v Competition and Markets Authority and anor*. *SeaFrance*, a cross-channel ferry operator, had gone into liquidation and could not be sold as going concern. Eurotunnel proposed to operate as a cross-channel ferry business and in partnership with another party bought three ferries and various other assets from SeaFrance. The UK Competition Commission concluded that there was a "relevant merger situation" for the purpose of the merger control provisions of the Enterprise Act. The UK's Competition Commission considered that the collection of assets bought by Eurotunnel amounted to an enterprise.

An appeal against the decision of the Competition Commission was brought before the Court of Appeal which ruled that an enterprise required the transfer of both vessels and crew and given that the crew had been terminated when they were acquired, there was no relevant merger situation to which the Enterprise Act should have been applied.

In December 2015, the Supreme Court, unanimously overturned the decision of the Court of Appeal. It was highlighted that the underlying principle was to distinguish bare asset acquisitions – assets that could have been acquired on the open market – from acquisitions where the purchaser also acquired something over and above what might have been so acquired and which was attributable to the fact that those assets had previously been used in the activities of the target enterprise. It ruled that the test to establish what constitutes an enterprise is an economic one and requires carrying out a wide economic analysis of the operation. In this sense, even when an entity has been dissolved, if the means to continue its activity live on, an enterprise may be found to exist.

Finally, in the *Common Market for Eastern and Southern Africa (COMESA), CFAO and Compagnie Financière Michelin SCMA ("Michelin")* announced on March 21 2018, the conclusion of an agreement for the distribution and retail of multi-brand tyres, tyre-related accessories and providing tyre-related services (the JV Business) in Kenya and Uganda, through a joint venture company. The transaction was not notified to the COMESA Competition Commission (the CCC) and the parties contended that:

- the joint venture (JV) did not involve the integration of parts of the business of the undertakings to the joint venture as neither Michelin nor CFAO undertook the JV Business in Kenya and Uganda and as a result there was no reduction or elimination of competition between the parties to the JV;
- the JV Business was auxiliary to the principal business activities of Michelin and CFAO;
- the JV's commercial policy (the business plan and budget) was based and represented the commercial aspirations of Michelin and CFAO;
- the JV Business largely relied on distribution of its shareholders products and service network/outlets;
- the JV's existence relied heavily on involvement of a management team granted to the JV by its shareholders which would typically run the JV Company's day-to-day operations within Kenya and Uganda; and
- the JV agreement was for a five (5) year period and was to be automatically renewed for another successive five (5) year period.

The COMESA Merger Assessment Guidelines provides that for a joint venture to constitute a "merger" within the meaning of Article 23(1) of the Regulations, it must be a "full-function" joint venture, i.e. it must perform, for a long duration (typically 5 or more years) all the functions of an autonomous economic entity, including: (a) operating on a market and performing the functions normally carried out by undertakings operating on the same market; and (b) having a management dedicated to its day-to-day operations and access to sufficient resources including finance, staff and assets (tangible and intangible) in order to conduct for a long duration its business activities within the area provided for in the joint-venture agreement.

The CCC observed that the joint venture company would have its own management, operationally independent from that of the parent companies, and the joint venture agreement provided that administrative services provided by a parent company to the JV Company would be conducted at arm's length, on the basis of normal commercial conditions.

In assessing the full-function character of the JV, the CCC also had regard, to the extent of commercial relationship between the joint venture and its parents. In the case at hand, the CCC observed that the JV was expected to market both Michelin Group brands and non-Michelin Group brands and would thus be sourcing supplies not only from Michelin but also from competing manufacturers or distributors. Further, while the JV Company would have access to CFAO's distribution channels in Kenya and Uganda, it was intended for the JV Company to also market its products through other channels including. The CCC further noted that there was a specific market for the distribution of tyres, as tyre manufacturers often appoint independent distributors or agents to carry out this function. The JV Company would compete in this market with other full-function entities.

The CCC was satisfied that the JV Company met the requirements of a full-function joint venture having regard to the fact that the JV Company would have the financial and other resources to perform its activities as an autonomous economic entity on the market on a lasting basis (minimum 5 years), and therefore constituted a "merger" within the meaning of Article 23 of the Regulations. The CCC rejected the parties' justifications that the joint venture did not amount to a merger. The transaction was subsequently notified on 11th July 2019.

Bibliography

Marco Colino, S., *Competition Law of the EU and UK*, 8th Edition, Oxford University Press, 208, p. 472

COMESA Competition Regulations, December 2004

COMESA Merger Assessment Guidelines, October 2014

Council Regulation (EC) No 139/2004 of 20 January 2004 on the control of concentrations between undertakings (the EC Merger Regulation)

Guidelines on the assessment of horizontal mergers under the Council Regulation on the control of concentrations between undertakings (2004/C 31/03)

The United Kingdom Enterprise Act 2002

United Kingdom Merger Assessment Guidelines, Revised 2021 (CMA129)

See also

Ancillary restraints, Control (notion), Gun jumping, Economic analysis, Merger (Article 11 Letter), Merger (clearance phase II), Merger control procedure, Merger (coordinated effects), Merger (non-horizontal), Merger (prohibition), Merger (referral), Merger (remedies), Merger (sole control) Merger (test SIEC), Merger (test SLC), Merger (trustee), Merger (turnover threshold), Merger (withdrawal), Minority shareholdings, Notification

M

MERGER (ARTICLE 11 LETTER)

Philipp GIRARDET, Rahul SAHA, Kyle LE CROY
Willkie Farr & Gallagher

Definition

Requests for information under Article 11 of the EU Merger Regulation are issued by the European Commission, in connection with its merger control procedures, to the parties to the merger and other potentially impacted market participants. Such requests may take the form of "simple requests" or "formal decisions" which require the addressee to provide the information and/or documents requested. Formal decisions are also notified by the European Commission to the competition authorities of the relevant EU Member States. Responses which are incomplete or misleading, as well as the failure to reply to a formal decision within the specified time limit, are punishable by fines.

Commentary

Article 11(1) of the EU Merger Regulation ("EUMR") empowers the European Commission ("Commission") to require persons controlling undertakings, as well as undertakings and associations of undertakings, to provide "all necessary information" in order for the Commission to carry out its duties under the EUMR (principally, the determination of a concentration's compatibility with the EU's internal market). While Article 11(7) EUMR also empowers the Commission to interview natural and legal persons, the focus of this note will be the use of requests to obtain written information and documentation from the parties to a merger and from other market participants.

The Commission's discretion to issue requests is wide. In *Omya* (2009), the General Court held that the "necessity" of the information must be assessed by reference to the view that the Commission could reasonably have held at the time the request was made, rather than any actual need for the information in the subsequent procedure (paragraph 30). This discretion also extends to the time limit fixed for a response. In *Schneider Electric* (2002) the General Court considered as reasonable a request for information which contained 322 questions and concerned 300,000 pieces of information to be gathered in only five working days, on the basis of the "requirement for speed" which characterises the EU merger regime (paragraphs 79 and 94-100).

While the Commission often makes informal requests for information from the merger parties during the pre-notification phase, the Commission will make a formal request ordinarily only after the date of the official merger notification, in accordance with its Best Practice Guidelines (paragraphs 26-28). Such formal requests may take the form of "simple requests" or "formal decisions" which can be enforced with fines and periodic penalty payments. Requests must state their legal basis, specify what information is required, fix a time limit for the response, and indicate the penalties for the provision of incorrect or misleading information. Requests made by formal decision must also inform the addressee of its right to judicial review before the Court of Justice of the EU.

Unlike the U.S. merger control procedures, requests for information in the EU are not confined to in-depth Phase II investigations, but instead are investigative tools frequently used when reviewing mergers in Phase I. Such requests historically only called for written submissions and data concerning, for example, closeness of competition, sales, pricing, or tenders. However, in more recent years the volume of requests for documents has grown significantly, principally due to reforms introduced after a trio of watershed judgments criticising the Commission's use of the available evidence. Alongside econometric analysis, documents now play an important role in the Commission's assessment of a merger's competitive effects, an approach which the EU Courts have endorsed (Ryanair, paragraph 138). This trend is clearest in complex merger cases in which the Commission's requests for documents can span multiple custodians, time periods, and issues. As recent examples, market participants have received extensive requests in connection with mergers in industries which the Commission has considered to be characterised by innovation-driven competition (e.g., pharmaceuticals, chemicals) and high concentration (e.g., telecoms, online platforms).

Few formal requirements apply to requests for documents (discussed above), though guidance is expected to be issued during the current Commission's term (2019-2024). In practice, even extensive requests for documents contain three principal sections: (i) definitions and scope, (ii) documents, and (iii) instructions. "Document" typically includes any electronically stored information (e.g., e-mails, presentations, reports, spreadsheets) within the addressee's possession, custody, or control (produced internally or by a third party). The scope of the custodians whose documents are to be searched varies, but typically includes senior managers, salespersons, and in-house legal counsel (whose communications, unlike those of external legal counsel, do not enjoy legal professional privilege in their own right under EU law). For documents within scope, date ranges of three to five years before the proposed merger are not uncommon. The second section of the request specifies the contents of the documents which concern the merger parties' competitively related activities (e.g., in relation to overlaps in their commercial activities, such as e-mails, business plans, board minutes, investment strategies, competitive assessments). In complex cases, the Commission has developed a practice of sharing a draft of the request with the intended addressees for discussion, including agreeing any keywords to which electronic searches might be limited. The final section of the request specifies the format in which the documents must be produced (ordinarily, in native format and formatted for optical character recognition after removal of any passwords). Additional instructions may require the addressee to produce a methodology report and a legal privilege log. To date, no formal requirement for translation of documents exists.

The production of incorrect, incomplete, or misleading information in response to a simple request or formal decision, or the failure to supply the information required by a formal decision within the time limit fixed by the Commission, can entail fines and periodic penalty payments for a request's addressee, including third parties (*Mitsubishi Heavy Industries*), even if the Commission considers that the breach had no impact on the outcome of its investigation (*Facebook/WhatsApp*, paragraph 100). It may also lead the Commission to "stop the clock" in an ongoing merger review, *i.e.*, the suspension of the review timetable set out in the EUMR.

Decisions regarding the exclusion of information or documents on grounds of the request's proportionality or legal professional privilege, should be taken with care. Although the Commission's power to issue requests is subject to the principle of proportionality (*Omya*, paragraph 34), as discussed above, the EU Courts have accepted that the "requirement for speed", and the duty to assess the issue of proportionality at the time the request is made, may permit wide requests within a short period of time. That said, as regards the reliance on legal professional privilege over communications from in-house counsel located outside the EU in a jurisdiction where there is privilege protection for in-house counsel advice (such as in the U.S.), to the authors' knowledge the Commission has to date not sought to enforce the production of such documents.

Finally, in multi-jurisdictional merger reviews, the decision of an addressee regarding the scope of its response to a request or approach to legal professional privilege, in a given jurisdiction, may produce effects in multiple others. Articles 11(5)-(6) EUMR establish cooperation mechanisms within the EU, but the Commission also regularly coordinates with other leading competition authorities whose administrative timetables, or rules of legal professional privilege or data protection, may differ from its own. Addressees of requests should consider such potential effects, including in relation to any merger to which the addressee may be party in future, in consultation with external counsel.

Bibliography

HOLIAN, J., CRUISE, J., PARKER, J., and MOTTA, R., "Three Key Issues for Managing Discovery in Global Merger Investigations. Coordinating Multijurisdictional Antitrust Reviews in Light of New Developments in UK and EU Merger Control Investigations" (2019) 10(3) *Journal of European Competition Law and Practice* 131-140

LEVY, N. and KARADAKOVA, V., "The EC's increasing reliance on internal documents under the EU Merger Regulation: issues and implications" (2018) 31(1) *European Competition Law Review* 12-23

MARK POWELL, M. and CZAPRACKA, K., "The Shifting Sands of EU Merger Control – Un, Deux, Trois, Piano" (2017) 3(4) *Competition Law & Policy Debate* 41-53

VAN GERVEN, G. and GOTLIEB, M., "Data Gathering and Analysis: The Anatomy of a Merger Investigation in Europe" (2015) 39(1) *Fordham International Law Journal* 1-24

WILSON, T., "Document requests in complex EU merger cases" (2017) 15(2) *Zeitschrift für Wettbewerbsrecht* 146-165

See also

Merger, Merger control procedure

M

MERGER (CLEARANCE PHASE II)

Hemangini DADWAL, Rishabh JAIN
AZB & Partners

■ Definition

An ex-ante merger clearance provided by competition authorities across the globe after a detailed investigation or "market testing" the likely effects of the proposed transaction is termed as a Phase II merger clearance. Since the transactions that enter into a detailed investigation are likely to raise anti-competitive concerns in the proposed form, such clearances often involve modifications to the transaction in the form of either "structural" remedies, i.e., divestiture of business or assets or "behavioral" remedies, i.e., an undertaking to modify certain business practices (example, not implement price changes, exclusivity) or both. Phase II clearances are time-consuming and entail significant production of information.

■ Commentary

India, the European Union (EU), and the United States (U.S.) have a mandatory, suspensory merger control regime. This means that any transaction, that meets the notification requirements, must be notified to the antitrust agency before it is consummated. Failure to do this can result in significant fines, post-review, remedies, and potential unraveling of the transaction, as a notifiable transaction is deemed "void" if consummated without approval from the Indian competition authority, the Competition Commission of India (CCI). Merger review is an ex-ante review process; transactions are reviewed to test if their consummation is likely to adversely affect competition in the market with the primary aim of preventing consolidation.

Merger reviews typically take place in two phases. In the first phase, antitrust authorities screen problematic transactions based on a preliminary review of the transaction. Where the evidence suggests that the transaction is unlikely to raise any anti-competitive concerns, the transaction is cleared in the first phase. Otherwise, the transaction moves to a Phase II review in the EU and India. In the U.S., Phase II review is termed as a "second request", post the issuance of which, the Federal Trade Commission (FTC) and the Department of Justice (DoJ) undertake an in-depth analysis. A majority of transactions are cleared at the Phase I stage.

Initiation of a Phase II investigation is burdensome and costly for parties. Authorities seek extensive information from parties to conduct a detailed investigation into the effects of the transaction. In India, only 8 out of around 1050 notified transactions, i.e., less than 1% of cases have received a Phase II merger clearance. These usually involve competitor-to-competitor transactions where the combined market share of the parties in a concentrated market is more than 50%. Similarly, in the EU, less than 4% of all transactions move to Phase II.

Typically, after a Phase II investigation, the competition authorities have three options: (a) unconditionally approve the transaction which is rare; (b) approve it with modifications, most likely; or (c) prohibit/ block the transaction (in cases where the authority does not believe any kind of remedy would address potential competition risks from the transaction).

Remedies. As mentioned above, transactions that have been escalated to a Phase II investigation usually will receive "conditional" approval, i.e., the transaction will be approved by the authority if certain modifications (structural, behavioral, or both) to the transaction are implemented. In India, of the eight Phase II merger clearances, the CCI has granted Phase II clearance in 7 cases, only after directing structural remedies or a combination of structural and behavioral remedies. In one case, the CCI approved the transaction after directing behavioral remedies, alone. The DoJ and the FTC have also exhibited skepticism over the effectiveness of behavioral remedies. Neither agency has accepted a purely behavioral remedy since 2019 for granting a Phase II clearance.

Article 69 of the European Commission's (EC) notice on remedies prescribes that the EC will examine behavioural remedies, only in exceptional circumstances, such as in competition concerns arising in conglomerate structures. Commitments concerning interoperability, access to key infrastructure and networks, or concerns relating to exclusivity in long-term contracts may also be accepted. As such, structural solutions are often preferred, particularly in traditional markets, as they do not require the agency to invest in continuous monitoring. Structural modifications typically involve divesting an overlapping business or asset to an independent third party with insignificant market shares to maintain competitive alternatives.

Economic tools. Economic tools used by competition authorities around the world are typically (i) combined market shares of the parties; (ii) the Herfindahl–Hirschman index (i.e., an index that measures the market concentration of an industry), (iii) the number of competitors in the market, (iv) concentration ratios (i.e., a sum of the percentage of market share taken up by the largest firms in the market), and (v) the number of competitors in the market to order a remedy (post negotiation) in its decision.

Theories of harm. The theories of harm for examining transactions are the same as for ex-post review, i.e., checking whether the transaction is likely to exhibit anti-competitive: (i) unilateral effects, i.e., exploitative or exclusionary effects that may be caused when parties engaged in the same business with high combined market shares (typically, more than 40%) enter into a transaction through which they can unilaterally effect the market, (ii) coordinated effects, i.e., anti-competitive effects arising out of common ownership of a company in two competing business undertakings, and (iii) portfolio effects, i.e., anti-competitive effects arising out of transacting entities having complementary or overlapping products/services that may incentivize bundling as well as creating an enhanced market position of the ultimate surviving entity. The CCI has addressed concerns about unilateral effects in Holcim/Lafarge and portfolio effects in L&T/Schneider. The EC goes one step ahead and also considers whether the transaction limits the incentives of the players to innovate in the innovation spaces (see Dow/DuPont). In the U.S., the draft merger guidelines of the FTC and the DoJ require agencies to consider the impact of the transaction on labour markets also.

Market testing. During a Phase II investigation, antitrust regulators solicit objections/ comments on the structure of the transaction from the public/ third parties on the transaction. These are accounted for when reaching a decision on the order, including devising the type of remedies.

Timelines. There is typically an outer limit for the authorities to arrive at a decision post a Phase II investigation. In the EU, the EC has 90 working days from the initiation of a Phase II investigation to pass an order. In the U.S., to pass an order, the agencies get around 30 days (or 10 days in the case of a cash tender offer or bankruptcy filing) from the date on which the parties have substantially complied with the second request for information. On the other hand, in India, the agency has 210 days to clear or block a transaction.

Bibliography

Elliott, P. and Gordley, C., Merger Control 2023, EU Chapter, in *Chambers Global Practice Guides*

Justus, B., Dunlop, L., Walden, M. and Jowdy, J., Merger Control 2023, USA Chapter, in *Chambers Global Practice Guides*

Commission notice on remedies acceptable under Council Regulation (EC) No 139/2004 and under Commission Regulation (EC) No 802/2004, October 2008

Draft Merger Guidelines U.S. Department of Justice and the Federal Trade Commission 2023

Merger Control 2023 | EU, June 2023

Merger Control 2023 | USA, June 2023

See also

Merger, Merger (remedies)

M

MERGER CONTROL PROCEDURE

Felipe IRARRÁZABAL PHILIPPI
CentroCompetencia

■ Definition

A merger control procedure is the formal channel through which a competition authority reviews mergers within its jurisdiction. Since not every transaction is relevant from a competition policy perspective, and time is of the essence for the undertakings involved, merger control procedures typically include rules to screen transactions and time periods to limit the length of investigations. The procedure normally starts with notification from the merging parties and ends when competition authorities reach a decision on whether the merger may be regarded as unproblematic, unproblematic conditional upon remedies, or prohibited, depending on the substantive assessment.

■ Commentary

Although the main features of merger control procedures differ among jurisdictions, every system seeks a balance between effective scrutiny of competition and avoiding unnecessary costs for the merging and third parties. Triggering events and thresholds, jurisdiction provisions, notification mechanisms, information requirements, deadlines, burden and standard of proof, rules for access to the file and judicial review are all procedural institutions aimed at achieving that balance.

A first question that a merger control procedure must address is which specific transactions are subject to it. Two or more previously independent undertakings merging into a single one is the most common triggering event (or "concentration"), but there are other possible combinations that may be covered by merger control and further criteria may be needed – e.g. joint ventures, acquisition of minority shareholdings or the purchase of securities or assets. These requirements are usually complemented by rules establishing an appropriate nexus between the merger and the jurisdiction. For example, in the European regime these aspects are dealt with in the Commission's Jurisdictional Notice, which specifies the meaning of "concentration" and provides guidance on when a concentration has a Union dimension following the provisions of the EU Regulation No. 139/2004 (EUMR).

Another key element at the beginning of any merger control procedure is notification. In a mandatory pre-notification regime, undertakings must inform competition agencies of their transaction prior to its completion. However, even when notification is compulsory, thresholds apply as a proxy to filter mergers that are more prone to raise competition concern. These thresholds aim to follow objective and measurable criteria. The most common thresholds are set according to the parties' turnover, the value of the transaction and/or market shares. For instance, in the United States (U.S.) the thresholds are updated annually and are based on the value of the transaction and the size of the merging parties.

Closely related with mandatory pre-merger notification is the usual standstill obligation which affects notifying parties. As a general rule, after filing the transaction with the authority the parties must not implement the concentration without clearance from the authority. In Europe, the EUMR article 7 (1) establishes that a concentration "shall not be implemented either before its notification or until it has been declared compatible with the common market". In the case of the U.S., according to the Hart-Scott-Rodino Act of 1976 (HSR Act) –the first legislation enacting a mandatory regime in the world– the parties should not close their deal until the waiting period has passed, or the agency has granted early termination of the waiting period. In both jurisdictions, relevant and relatively recent case-law has further specified what type of conduct may be deemed as failure to notify and standstill obligation infringements, a subject labelled " gun jumping" in competition law (See M.7993 *Altice/PT Portugal* 2018, and *U.S. v. Flakeboard and SierraPine*, 2014).

While mandatory pre-notification systems have become the standard as competition policy has developed globally, there are still many jurisdictions where notification is voluntary (e.g. Australia, New Zealand, Singapore or the UK).

In mandatory pre-notification regimes, parties may normally notify the authority any time prior to the implementation of the merger, but submitting notifications may be time-consuming and a major hurdle in certain cases. Normally, regulations specify the content for notifications. Especially for systems with strict deadlines, the idea of these initial requirements is to provide the authority with basic and valuable information at initial stages of merger investigations (e.g., a description of the transaction, details of the parties, balance sheets and financial data, supporting documentation, information on market definitions and affected markets). Competition authorities typically provide additional guidelines and encourage early informal contacts between parties and officials or formal pre-notification procedures to solve issues related to the notification process.

In the European system, the notification requirements are set out within the Commission Regulation No. 802/2004 (Implementing Regulation), and its annexes establish how the information should be presented – Form CO and Short Form CO (for simplified merger notifications). In the U.S., premerger filings under the HSR Act must be submitted to the FTC or the DOJ by completing a "Notification and Report Form for Certain Mergers and Acquisitions" or HSR Form. Following their initial review of this Form, both U.S. authorities may issue a "Request for Additional Information and Documentary" (informally known as "Second Request") if they have reason to believe that the proposed transaction is likely to raise competition concerns.

One of the most salient differences between merger investigations and other antitrust probes is time. Business dynamics typically require a prompt official response in order to have legal certainty and be able to move forward. Accordingly, after notification, merger control procedures are usually limited by deadlines and authorities find themselves running against the clock. In Europe, for example, a generally rigid timetable applies. Once the notification is declared complete, the Commission must take a decision generally within 25 working days (Phase I Investigation). This period could be extended to 35 working days if parties present commitments. Where the Commission has serious doubts regarding a merger's compatibility with the internal market, a second period starts, of an additional 90 working days, that may be extended to 105 working days if undertakings offer commitments. Importantly, where the Commission has not taken a decision within these time limits, the concentration "shall be deemed to have been declared compatible with the common market" (See article 10.6 EUMR).

The outcome of a merger control procedure typically may involve three alternatives: the merger is unconditionally cleared, cleared subject to remedies, or prohibited. Systems may differ on how these decisions are taken. For example, in the U.S., after a review of the premerger filing, authorities may grant early termination or let the initial waiting period expire. This would mean that the merger remains unchallenged. After the parties submit the Second Request, the DOJ or the FTC may still close the investigation and clear the deal, enter into negotiated consent agreements with companies or seek to block the transaction through a preliminary injunction in federal court. In Europe, the Commission may declare the concentration to be compatible with the common market, may accept commitments from the parties as a condition to declare the merger compatible with the common market, or declare it incompatible with the common market.

When conducting investigations, authorities may require information from the notifying parties or third parties. The European Commission has power to impose fines when undertakings intentionally or negligently failing to respond to a request, or supply incorrect or misleading information. For example, in *Facebook/Whatsapp* (2017), the Commission imposed fines for €110 million for providing misleading information.

Best practice mandates procedural fairness for merging parties (See, for example OECD Recommendation on Merger Review, 2005). This includes the opportunity for merging parties to access the case file and obtain information about competitive concerns, a meaningful opportunity to confront such concerns, and the right to seek review by a separate body. Indeed, a final dimension worthy of mention is judicial review. The U.S. system is based on judicial review and administrative bodies are unable to prohibit a merger without a court ruling. In the case of Europe, the Commission's decisions may be appealed to the General Court, but the competition agency has the "first say". As it is well known in competition law, the type of court (administrative courts, general jurisdiction courts or specialized courts) and the scope of revision influence decisions of competition authorities.

Today most of the countries that have competition regimes in place have some form of merger control procedure. Consequently, mergers that involve multinational companies with worldwide activities are usually reviewed by more than one jurisdiction. To be aware of their procedural differences and practical aspects may be challenging for practitioners and authorities and increases the need for intense international communication and collaboration. At the same time, the international trend today of multi-jurisdictional mergers has led to increased harmonization of procedures across systems, fostered by organizations such as the International Competition Network or the OECD.

Bibliography

Jones, A., Sufrin, B. and Dunne, N., *EU Competition Law*, Seventh Edition (2019), OUP pp. 1058-1107

Whish, R. and Bailey, D., *Competition Law*, Ninth Edition (2018), OUP, pp. 827-931

Federal Trade Commission, HSR Resources

See also

Merger, Merger (Article 11 Letter), Form CO (EU), Gun jumping, Hart-Scott-Rodino Filing (US), Notification, Merger (withdrawal)

M

MERGER (COORDINATED EFFECTS)

Jeffrey PRINCE
Kelley School of Business, Indiana University

■ Definition

The coordinated effects of a merger are harms from incremental collusive behavior by a subset of post-merger firms. In contrast to unilateral effects, which result from the profitable exercise of market power by the merged firm alone, the collusive behavior that gives rise to coordinated effects relies for its success on the accommodating reactions of other firms in the market. Coordinated effects may arise from express or tacit collusion that may or may not be inherently unlawful, and may or may not involve the merged firm.

■ Commentary

The analysis of coordinated effects of a merger typically answers two questions: First, what is the harm of coordination in the post-merger world? Second, what is the probability that firms will choose to coordinate? Coordinated and unilateral effects analysis both generally predict market outcomes under scenarios of greater concentration and/or collusive pricing. Coordinated effects analysis faces the additional challenge of assessing the post-merger incremental risk associated with each possible coordinated outcome.

The central economic theory underlying coordinated effects in antitrust enforcement comes from Stigler (1964). Stigler's contribution was to establish a list of practical obstacles to coordination with broad applicability across schemes and markets. He enumerated the necessary elements of coordination: agreement on an outcome (price or market shares) and the detection and punishment of deviations. These elements are more likely to be sustained under certain market conditions, such as homogeneous products, small buyers making frequent purchases, and common knowledge of the prices sellers offer to buyers. Stigler's analysis applies to differentiated products markets and procurement markets and to a broad range of coordinated behavior, including explicit, unlawful collusion and "conscious parallelism" expected to arise under oligopolistic competition (Chamberlin, 1933).

The U.S. Horizontal Merger Guidelines ("Guidelines") gradually incorporated Stigler's ideas, focusing on the incremental risk of collusive behavior when considering coordinated effects. The 1984 Guidelines were the first to acknowledge coordinated effects in line with Stigler's theory, highlighting the conditions that allow firms to "quickly detect and retaliate against deviations from the agreed prices..." The 1992 Guidelines flag "the nature of the procurement process" as potentially relevant. The 2010 Guidelines define coordination to include "parallel accommodating conduct... not motivated by retaliation or deterrence nor intended to sustain an agreed-upon market outcome..." In any case, the risk of coordination depends on, "the strength and predictability of rivals' responses to a price change or other competitive initiative." The Guidelines' emphasis on risk encompasses future coordination that might not be readily detected or fall foul of the Sherman Act (Hovenkamp, 2018).

The agencies and courts assess the risk of post-merger coordination using qualitative and quantitative analysis. Qualitative analyses speak to how coordination would be carried out in the post-merger world. Agency challenges and court rulings highlight risk factors for coordination in line with Stigler's theory. For example: (1) Markets are more susceptible to coordinated effects when products are more homogeneous. Archer-Daniels-Midland was allowed to lease additional capacity for the production of high fructose corn syrup (HFCS) on the grounds that "significant differences in costs and product mix among firms in the HFCS industry" made future coordination unlikely. (2) The risk of coordination is greater when the market consists of small buyers. In *FTC v. University Health*, the merging hospitals argued that their customers were large insurance companies who would block any attempted price increase. However, the court reasoned that the relevant buyers were individual patients who have no purchasing power. (3) Coordination is more likely when demand is stable because deviations from the coordinated policy are easier to detect. On the other hand, demand fluctuations may hinder the government's ability to detect collusion in historical data, as in *FTC v. Arch Coal*. (4) A merger is more likely to produce coordinated effects when the target firm is a "maverick" with a history of deviating from the pricing behavior of its competitors. The role of Northwest Airlines as a maverick was pivotal in blocking its acquisition by Continental Airlines. (5) Finally, the Agencies look out for a history of coordination (explicit or tacit), as in *U.S. v. Premdor, Inc., et al.*, where the government's complaint noted that Premdor's subsidiaries had previously pled guilty to price-fixing.

Quantitative models provide methods for quantifying the outcomes (e.g., prices, profits) of collusive arrangements (including no collusion) as well as the risk of these arrangements occurring. In principle, both can be measured using some of the same merger simulation models applied to unilateral effects. However, in the context of coordinated effects, the modeler generally specifies which firms will collude and to what extent, and assigns a probability to each possible combination pre- and post-merger. Quantitative tools can accommodate less-than-perfect collusion and conscious parallelism: for example, Miller, Sheu, and Weinberg (2021) study a quantitative price leadership game in a retrospective analysis of the Miller/Coors merger, complementing an earlier study that estimates a conduct parameter that captures varying degrees of collusion. As for the probability of collusion, Kovacic et al. (2009) propose to measure the risk of coordinated effects based on the incremental profitability of collusion for subsets of firms in the post-merger world. Research on methods for quantitative assessment of coordinated effects is ongoing.

Bibliography

Chamberlin, E. H. (1933). *The Theory of Monopolistic Competition*. Harvard University Press

Hovenkamp, H. (2018). "Prophylactic Merger Policy," *Hastings Law Journal*, 70, pp. 45-74

Kovacic, W. E., Marshall, R., Marx, L. M. and Schulenberg, S. P. (2009). Quantitative Analysis of Coordinated Effects. *Antitrust Law Journal*, 76(2), pp. 397-430

Miller, N. H., Sheu, G. and Weinberg, M. C. (2021). Oligopolistic Price Leadership and Mergers: The United States Beer Industry, *American Economic Review*, 111(10), pp. 3123-59

Stigler, G. J. (1964). "A Theory of Oligopoly," *The Journal of Political Economy*, 72(1), pp. 44-61

See also

Merger, Economic analysis

M

MERGERS (NON-HORIZONTAL)

Caio MARIO DA SILVA PEREIRA NETO,
Ricardo FERREIRA PASTORE, Daniel DOUEK
Pereira Neto, Macedo, Rocco Advogados

■ Definition

Non-horizontal mergers (NHMs) are forms of concentration (i.e., combination of two or more firms) that involve parties actually or potentially active in different relevant markets, which do not exert direct competitive pressure on one another. Such mergers do not increase market concentration in any given relevant market. The literature discusses two known types of non-horizontal mergers. Vertical mergers involve parties operating in vertically related markets, i.e., in different stages of the same supply chain. Conglomerate mergers take place when there are no horizontal or vertical relations between parties, although there may be some degree of complementarity between their products or services.

■ Commentary

NHMs typically implicate complementary lines of business – often vertically linked in the same supply chain (e.g., mergers between supplier/customer or manufacturer/distributor) –, which is why they tend to generate noticeable efficiencies. NHMs are deemed to be mostly pro-competitive. Under certain circumstances, however, scholars and competition authorities note that such transactions may pose concerns to competition.

In the U.S., NHMs have been subject to merger control since the 1950 Clayton Act amendments to Section 7. Upon reviewing the legislative history of such amendments, the Supreme Court concluded that "§ 7 applie[s] not only to mergers between actual competitors, but also to vertical and conglomerate mergers whose effect may tend to lessen competition (…)" – *Brown Shoe Co., Inc. v. United States, 370 U.S. 294, 317 (1962).*

The focus on the consumer welfare standard since the 1970s placed an emphasis on the desirable efficiencies commonly arising from NHMs. Over the following decade, economic scholarship consistently advocated a more favourable substantive assessment of such transactions. The 1984 U.S. DOJ *Non-Horizontal Merger Guidelines*' language translated this stance vis-à-vis vertical mergers: "*Although non-horizontal mergers are less likely than horizontal mergers to create competitive problems, they are not invariably innocuous*".

Since the 1990s, the assessment of NHMs has become more nuanced, with the development and application of more sophisticated theories of harm, especially those related to the raising of rivals' costs, exclusion, entry deterrence, and market foreclosure. For a recent example, see the FTC's attempt to block AT&T/Time Warner, a rare example of vertical merger enforcement in the U.S. and the first trial in over 40 years (*United States v. AT&T Inc., 310 F. Supp. 3d 161 D.D.C. 2018*).

In Europe, the general principles on the assessment of NHMs can be traced back to the 2004 Commission v. Tetra Laval judgment by the the European Court of Justice ("ECJ"). The ECJ established that, for the European Commission ("Commission") to oppose a vertical or conglomerate merger, it must provide strong evidence that a significant damage to competition is likely to occur. One year later (2005), the then Court of First Instance ("CFI") ruling on *General Electric v. Commission* made these principles operational by setting out three steps for the Commission to follow in its analyses.

These steps were incorporated to the Commission's 2008 *Guidelines on the assessment of non-horizontal mergers*, which also outlined the theories of harm and countervailing efficiencies that ought to be assessed in the merger control of NHMs. Essentially, the Commission must present proof of (i) ability to foreclose a relevant market (that the merged firm would have market power and be positioned to limit competitors' access to a certain stage of the production chain, such as inputs, distribution channels or customer bases, in a way that negatively affects the vertically related markets in terms of price and quality), (ii) likelihood and incentive to implement a foreclosure strategy (e.g., that the merged firm would have the incentive to do so, usually by an assessment of the extent to which it would be more profitable to obtain higher profit gain expanding sales downstream in comparison to the profit loss upstream by restricting access of input to competitors), and, finally, (iii) whether a foreclosure strategy would create or strengthen a dominant position (harming competition up- or downstream). Therefore, assessing the unilateral effects of vertical mergers usually requires demonstrating that the merged entity would have an incentive and capacity to foreclose, leading to exclusionary effects on competition.

Besides unilateral effects, NHMs may also raise concerns regarding coordinated effects. In this realm, authorities' main concern is that NHMs may alter market structures in ways that make them more conducive to collusion. A merger may facilitate coordination when it increases the level of market transparency and makes monitoring easier for a cartel to be implemented. For example, vertical integration between producers and distributors, may facilitate monitoring prices in a market prone to collusive arrangements.

In contrast to the negative effects, there is a broad consensus that vertical mergers often bring about relevant efficiencies. It is worth mentioning a few: economies of scope, reduced (transaction) costs, improved product quality resulting from the transfer of knowledge or coordination in production and distribution (optimized value chain in the design of goods, customer experience or logistics), higher responsivity to fluctuations in demand, internalized double mark-ups (generating incentives to decrease prices and increase output), facilitated one-stop-shopping, among others.

Conglomerate mergers, which occur between parties active in closely but not vertically related markets (e.g. complementary products), have attracted increasing attention over the last few years, after a period of complete oblivion. Indeed, NHMs in digital markets mergers led to the development of novel theories of harm concerned with conglomerate effects (e.g., *Google/Fitbit* in 2020, *Meta/Within* in 2023). Although there is still a general perception of limited harm and potential efficiencies generated in conglomerate mergers, authorities are more attentive to some potential negative effects coming from these transactions.

In a similar way to the assessment of vertical mergers, theories of harm commonly associated with conglomerate effects concern unilateral (e.g. market foreclosure) and coordinated effects but would point out tying and bundling as aspects of potential concern in discussions of foreclosure. In the digital sector, mergers are often used as a strategy for expansion and product development, through which the parties seek combination of complementary products, interoperability and/or innovation. The elimination of actual or potential emerging competition is also a growing concern among authorities, as conglomerate mergers may strengthen a platform's (or ecosystem's) dominance by facilitating a combination (e.g. envelopment) of adjacent markets. Conglomerate transactions may also involve the acquisition of valuable, irreplicable data, providing the acquiring firm a competitive advantage.

In sum, authorities' overall focus on NHMs has been growing since the late 2010's. Among other reasons, there is a perception that NHMs cleared in several jurisdictions led to consolidation of the digital industries, with entrenchment of market power. In light of this perception, merger control notification thresholds and intervention standards are being called into question, with a growing call to fine-tune current rules to avoid underenforcement (Type 2 errors) in such mergers. Consequently, mergers that used to be cleared with little or no scrutiny are now under significantly more detailed analysis. Nascent firm acquisitions and the specific dynamics of conglomerate effects in data- and innovation-driven businesses are salient topics that will deserve attention in years to come.

Bibliography

Bourreau, M. and De Streel, A.. "Digital conglomerates and EU competition policy" (2019)

Hovenkamp, H., "Competitive Harm from Vertical Mergers" (2020). Faculty Scholarship at Penn Carey Law. 2218

Riordan, M. H. and Salop, S. C., 1995. "Evaluating Vertical Mergers: A post-Chicago Approach." *Antitrust Law Journal* 63: 513-568

Scheffman, D. T. and Higgins, R. S. "Vertical mergers: Theory and policy." *Geo. Mason L. Rev. 12* (2003): 967

Whish, R. and Bailey, D., *Competition Law* (10th end, Oxford University Press 2021), Chapter 20

See also

Merger, Economic analysis

M

MERGER (PROHIBITION)

Aurélien PORTUESE
George Washington University – School of Law

■ Definition

Under competition law, a merger is any commercial operation that results in the common ownership or control of previously independent companies or assets. Competition authorities or courts may prohibit mergers which gives rise to competition concerns. In the U.S. Section 1 of the Sherman Act (1890) was ineffective as a tool of merger control. Congress therefore passed the Clayton Act in 1914. Section 7 prohibits mergers where the effect "may be substantially to lessen competition, or to tend to create a monopoly." A conglomerate merger, where there is no horizontal or vertical relationship between the parties, may be covered by Section 5 of the Federal Trade Commission Act 1914, which forbids "unfair methods of competition." In the European Union (EU) mergers that would significantly impede effective competition may be prohibited under the EU Merger Control Regulation which was originally adopted in 1989 and revised by Regulation 139/2004. Most jurisdictions with competition laws have a prohibition on mergers or consolidations which adversely affect competition.

■ Commentary

Merger prohibition is not and should not be the first tool to prevent illegal mergers. Merger remedies such as structural remedies (i.e., divestitures) or behavioral remedies (i.e., commitments as to future behaviour) are antitrust authorities' primary tools to address the potential harm derived from mergers. Consequently, a merger prohibition is a relative rarity, to be deployed when there are no adequate merger remedies. In its 2020 Merger Remedies Manual, the U.S. Department of Justice clarified that "if the Division is not satisfied that the parties have addressed the risk of a failed remedy, a more appropriate course may be to sue to block the transaction." Thus, seeking to block a merger is appropriate only after remedies have failed or are likely to fail.

Consequently, merger prohibition is a solution of last resort: the regulator must demonstrate the inadequacy of the possible remedies.

Merger prohibition starts with a prima facie case made by the antitrust agencies of the anticompetitive effects of the envisaged merger. A prima facie case (or "quick look") necessitates the presence of initial evidence to demonstrate a reasonable likelihood that the merger in question could adversely affect competitive conditions within the relevant market. This constitutes the preliminary burden of proof requisite for the instigation of comprehensive investigative proceedings.

For instance, in the U.S., it suffices for the plaintiff to demonstrate that the merger's consummation "may be substantially to lessen competition," or might lead towards the establishment of a monopoly. The defendant can rebut the presumption (established by United States v. Phila. Nat'l Bank, 374 U.S. 321, 363, 1963) with a "clear showing" that the merger is procompetitive. But "the more compelling the prima facie case, the more evidence the defendant must present to rebut it successfully" as the court found in United States v. Baker Hughes Inc. (908 F.2d 981, 991, D.C. Cir. 1990). The robustness of the prima facie case thereby significantly burdens the defendant with the obligation to furnish compelling evidence in rebuttal, thereby contesting the assertions of anticompetitive repercussions effectively.

Merger prohibition can also result from violating the remedies that allowed the merger to be cleared in the first place. However, it is rare for antitrust authorities to seek to unwind a consummated merger following a breach of commitment remedies. In the EU, this situation occurred for the first time in 2019 when the European Commission issued a statement of objections to Telefonica Deutschland alleging that the company violated the commitments that led to the acquisition of E-Plus in 2014 for 8.5 billion euros. If the breach is confirmed, the European Commission could impose a fine of up to 10 percent of Telefonica Deutschland's annual world turnover, or revoke the decision – namely, prohibit a posteriori the merger and require the transaction to be unwound. Articles 14(2)(d) and 15(1)(c) of the EUMR enable the Commission to impose fines and periodic penalty payments in case of breach of remedies, respectively. However, Article 8(6)(d) of the EUMR enables the Commission to revoke the clearance decision, thereby prohibiting the merger after consummation.

In the U.S., there has recently been a return to a greater use of merger prohibitions rather than accepting remedies for problematic mergers. The FTC and DOJ have stepped up their efforts to block mergers, influenced by a revival of strict enforcement philosophies exemplified by historical cases like Brown Shoe Co. vs. United States (1962). This change reflects a broader movement towards stricter merger regulations, underscoring a significant shift towards more aggressive antitrust enforcement.

For instance, in the merger case of Meta/Within, challenged by the Federal Trade Commission (FTC), the judge acknowledged the FTC's significant reliance on the practical indicia established in the Brown Shoe case. These indicia were utilized not only to define markets but also to evaluate the existence of potential and emerging competition. The case of FTC v Meta, which took place in the Northern District of California in 2023, is illustrative of an enforcement policy aimed at prohibiting mergers by reviving old cases such as Brown Shoe.

The Brown Shoe decision, originating from an era 60 years ago marked by particularly stringent antitrust enforcement, is now considered by some to represent an excessively aggressive stance on merger prohibitions. This perspective has been underscored in the antitrust agencies' recent draft Merger Guidelines, which cite the Brown Shoe case as a precedent, suggesting a move towards a more restrictive approach to merger approvals, reflective of a bygone era's rigorous regulatory framework. The proposed Guidelines, particularly Guideline 6, demonstrate the antitrust agencies' renewed inclination to ban vertical mergers. Such ban includes not only those mergers that involve companies representing 50% of market shares since such mergers undermine the competitive market structure, but also vertical mergers involving companies with less than 50% market shares following the Brown Shoe judgement.

The revived desire of antitrust agencies to ban mergers using novel theories of harms experience some setbacks but also few successes. For instance, a federal court blocked the Penguin Random House acquisitions of Simon and Schuster due to the threat of monopolization of the market for U.S. publishing rights to anticipated top-selling books.

In statistics, merger prohibitions are often associated with merger abandonment: anticipating a protracted challenge before agencies and courts, merging companies may abandon transactions. Blocked and abandoned mergers account for approximately 21 percent of notified mergers in the EU, whereas they account for 37 percent of notified mergers in the U.S. It is likely that these numbers, both in the EU and in the U.S., will increase over the next few years since merger prohibition – rather than merger remedies – have recently become a major enforcement priority.

Bibliography

Dechert, "DAMITT 2021 Report: Merger Investigation Activity Sinks More Deals", January 31, 2022

Department of Justice, "Merger Remedies Manual," Antitrust Division U.S. Department of Justice, September 2020

See also

Merger, Merger (withdrawal)

M

MERGER (REFERRAL)

Gintarė SURBLYTĖ-NAMAVIČIENĖ
Vilnius University

Definition

In the European Union (EU), a referral of a concentration is part of a merger review re-allocation mechanism, which redistributes powers between the European Commission and the national competition authorities of the Member States. Whereas concentrations with a Community dimension are, as a rule, examined exlusively by the European Commission, the EU Merger Regulation No 139/2004 (EUMR) provides a possibility to review such mergers nationally. Vice versa, concentrations without a Community dimension may be requested to be examined by the European Commission in case of the likely cross-border effects. Such a reallocation of powers balances between the principle of "one-stop shop" and the most appropriate authority reviewing the merger.

Commentary

In the EU, two types of referrals of a concentration (thereafter used interchangeably with a "merger") are enshrined in the EUMR: a pre-notification and a post-notification referral. The merger referral mechanism is regulated in Articles 4, 9 and 22 EUMR, whereas further guidance is provided by the Commission Notice on Case Referral in respect of concentrations (OJ [2005] C 56/2).

A Member State (upon its own initiative or upon the invitation of the European Commission) may request the European Commission to refer a notified concentration to the national authorities of that Member State if the criteria of Article 9 EUMR are fulfilled, i.e. if "a concentration threatens to affect significantly competition in a market within that Member State, which presents all the characteristics of a distinct market, or a concentration affects competition in a market within that Member State, which presents all the characteristics of a distinct market and which does not constitute a substantial part of the common market" (Article 9(2) letters a) and b) EUMR). In the latter case, the European Commission has to refer the whole or part of the case to the Member State, whereas in the former case it has a power of discretion. For example, in SEB/ Moulinex the European Commission, upon the request of France, referred to the French authorities part of the case that was related to the transaction's potential impact on competition in France. The French authorities cleared the merger for France unconditionally, whereas the European Commission allowed the concentration subject to conditions relating to a number of other European countries. The referral decision was upheld by the EU General Court, which stated that the referral mechanism in Article 9 contains an inherent risk of the fragmented assessment of the concentration that may undermine the "one-stop shop" principle; yet, the legality of the referral must be assessed at the time of its adoption and should not be affected by the analysis of the compatibility of final decisions.

A referral of a merger from the European Commission to the Member States is also regulated in Article 4(4) EUMR, the difference from Article 9 being that a request for a referral has to be submitted before a notification of the concentration with a Community dimension by concerned undertakings. The main requirement is that "the concentration may significantly affect competition in a market within a Member State which presents all the characteristics of a distinct market" (Article 4(4) EUMR). Hence, the likely effect on competition should be in the national, or even narrower, geographic market; however, even in the latter case, not all referrals may be accepted, for example, because of the potential cross-border effects of the concentration or in case of a number of national markets involved. Moreover, the respective Member State(s) has/have to express their (dis) agreement on whether to take over the case; even if the Member State agrees, the European Commission decides whether to refer the whole or part of the concentration.

A post-notification referral mechanism, opposite to the one in Article 9, is provided by Article 22 EUMR. Accordingly, one or several Member States, on their own initiative or upon the invitation of the European Commission, may request the European Commission to examine the concentration (as defined in Article 3 EUMR) that was notified or otherwise made known to them and that does not have a Community dimension, "but affects trade between Member States and threatens to significantly affect competition within the territory of the Member State or States making the request" (Article 22(1) EUMR). After the European Commission informs all the Member States about the referral, any of them may join the initial request. As explained in the ECA's Principles on Articles 4(5) and 22, while considering whether to join the referral, national competition authorities may want to take into account the scope of the potentially affected geographical market (national or wider), the potential difficulties in gathering information (e.g. one of the parties not based in the Member State) or any likely difficulties while enforcing suitable remedies, etc. If the European Commission decides to examine the concentration, it does so on behalf of the requesting Member States, so that any national proceedings in the requesting Member States are terminated, whereas the Member States that did not join the referral may still apply their national laws while examining the concentration.

Although, originally (Merger Regulation No 4064/89), Article 22 was meant to capture mergers where national merger control regimes were missing (the so-called "Dutch clause"), the modern industrial context has shed new light on Article 22. According to the European Commission's Guidance on Article 22 (2021), referrals under Article 22 may be particularly suitable for the merger control in the digital economy and pharmaceutical markets, where in the case of technology start-ups or the research and development phase of pharmaceuticals, etc., the company's (mostly, the target's) turnover thresholds may not trigger the duty to notify the concentration, yet the legal requirements set out in Article 22 may nevertheless be fulfilled. An example of the concentration that neither had a Community dimension nor did it have to be notified in any Member State, but, upon the invitation of the European Commission, was referred to it by a number of Member States under Article 22 and was subsequently analysed by the European Commission, is the Illumina/Grail case. In fact, after an in-depth investigation, the implemented concentration was prohibited by the European Commission owing to the fact that the transaction could foreclose Grail's competitors by cutting their access to the Illumina's technology crucial for developing blood-based tests for detecting cancer in early stages. The European Commission's decisions to accept the referrals in this case were upheld by the EU General Court, which stated that any concentration, even if it is not notifiable in a Member State because it falls short of the turnover thresholds or because that Member State lacks any merger control rules, may be referred to the European Commission if it meets the legal requirements under Article 22. The case is yet pending before the European Court of Justice. In this regard, it is also noteworthy that, in order to fill the abovementioned legal gap, some Member States changed their national laws. In 2017, Germany and Austria, in order to capture concentrations that did not reach the existing turnover thresholds for a duty to notify, introduced additional jurisdictional thresholds based on the value of the transaction. Finally, the EU Digital Markets Act (DMA) (Regulation 2022/1925) contains an obligation for the gatekeepers, regardless of whether the concentration is notifiable to the European Commission or in the Member States, to inform the European Commission of any intended concentration (falling under Article 3 EUMR) "where the merging entities or the target of concentration provide core platform services or any other services in the digital sector or enable the collection of data" (Article 14(1)). The European Commission shares such information with the national authorities, which may use it for submitting requests under Article 22 EUMR (Article 14(4), 14(5) DMA).

Finally, pursuant to Article 4(5) EUMR, a concentration (as defined in Article 3 EUMR) without a Community dimension, prior to the notification of such a concentration, may be requested by undertakings to be examined by the European Commission, if it "is capable of being reviewed under the national competition laws of at least three Member States". If none of the competent national authorities disagrees with the referral, the merger will be deemed to have a Community dimension and would thus be examined exclusively by the European Commission. Article 4(5) was, for example, applied in the review of the acquisition of DoubleClick by Google and in the Facebook/WhatsApp merger.

Bibliography

EZRACHI, A., *EU Competition Law: An Analytical Guide to the Leading Cases*, 7th ed., Hart Publishing 2021, Chapter 9

JONES, A., SUFRIN, B., DUNNE N., *Jones & Suffrin's EU Competition Law: Text, Cases, and Materials*, 7th ed., Oxford University Press 2019, Chapter 15

MESTMÄCKER, E.-J., SCHWEITZER, H., Europäisches Wettbewerbsrecht, 3. Auflage, C.H.Beck 2014, 6. Kapitel

RICHTER, H., Prospects of Merger Review in the Digital Age: A Critical Look at the EU, the United States, and Germany, IIC – *International Review of Intellectual Property and Competition Law*, Vol. 52, Issue 2, pp. 223 – 267

WHISH, R., BAILEY D., *Competition Law*, 10th ed., Oxford University Press 2021, Chapter 21

See also

Merger, Applicable law

M

MERGER (REMEDIES)

Pablo TREVISÁN
Instituto de Derecho de la Competencia

Definition

Merger remedies are used by competition authorities to maintain or restore competition in the market, by resolving and preventing the harm to the competitive process that may result as a consequence of a merger. By eliminating the harm that a given transaction may cause to competition, remedies allow for the approval of mergers that would otherwise be challenged or prohibited. They are generally classified as structural, if they require the divestiture of a business, an asset or other rights, or behavioural, if they impose an obligation to engage, modify or constrain the future conduct of the merging firms.

Commentary

The Notice on Remedies (2008) acknowledges that the Commission shall not impose unilaterally conditions on the clearance of a merger. The parties shall offer the commitments to the Commission (*EDP v Commission*). The Commission tests the commitments submitted by taking them to the market, transparency must be maintained and Member States and interested third parties should be consulted.

In practice, a structural solution might be preferable since the commitment may prevent significant impediment to effective competition and it does not require monitoring measures (*Praxair/Linde*). In AB InBev/SAB Miller (2016), the Commission stated that the most effective means of restoring effective competition is through divestiture of a subsidiary or production facilities and the creation of a new competitive entity or the strengthening of existing competitors. Divestitures might also be used to remove links between the parties and competitors where these links contribute to competitive concerns raised by the merger (*Time Warner/AOL (2000)*).

Divested activities must consist of a viable business that, if operated by a suitable purchaser, can compete effectively with the merged entity on a lasting basis. There is skepticism about the divestiture of assets such as brands that have not been a uniform and viable business in the past.

The business must be transferred to a suitable purchaser, meaning a purchaser who is independent of the parties, who has the financial resources, expertise, incentive, and ability to maintain and develop the divested business, and who will be in a position to acquire the business without regulatory problems.

Competition authorities may require the business to be divested within a fixed time after the conditional decision, or to identify an "up-front" buyer before the transaction can be completed, or accept a "fix-it-first" solution where a specific purchaser is identified during the investigation itself and the parties enter into a legally-binding agreement to sell. A behavioural solution might be difficult to control and enforce. In *GE/Honeywell* (2001) the parties offered commitments to abstain from certain commercial behaviour to deal with the Commission's concerns.

Access remedies and change of long-term exclusive contracts might also be accepted as remedies. Commitments giving access to infrastructure or key technology might open the market to competitors. Enforcement authorities might exceptionally modify or waive commitments attached to a clearance decision or charge a company for breaching a commitment.

Monitoring or divestiture trustees roles are, among others, to ensure that the business to be divested is not degraded during the interim period; to monitor the splitting of assets and the allocation of personnel between the divested and retained businesses; to oversee the parties' efforts to find a potential purchaser and to transfer the business; to report on these issues to the authority in periodic compliance reports.

Remedy-setting sometimes involves extensive cooperation between competition authorities in various jurisdictions, which might include the signing of a Memorandum of Understanding between the respective authorities.

Sometimes no remedy may be adequate to deal with the adverse effects identified or may be so complex that the competition authority cannot determine with the required degree of certainty that effective competition will be restored.

Bibliography

Ezrachi, A., Behavioural Remedies in EC Merger Control – Scope and Limitations, (2006), 29 *World Competition* 459

Jones, A., Sufrin, B. and Dunne, N., *EU Competition Law*, Seventh Edition (2019), OUP, pp. 1174-1179

Trevisán, P., Argentina, in *Merger Remedies Guide*, Second Edition (2019), GCR, pp. 181-189

Whish, R. and Bailey, D., *Competition Law*, Ninth Edition (2018), OUP, pp. 907-913

See also

Divestiture, Merger, Merger (clearance phase II), Merger (trustee)

M

MERGER (SOLE CONTROL)

Piero FATTORI
Gianni & Origoni

Definition

According to the Commission's Consolidated Jurisdictional Notice, sole control is acquired – either on a legal or a de facto basis – if one person or an undertaking alone can exercise a decisive influence over another undertaking. Decisive influence can be exercised either through the power to determine the strategic commercial decisions of the controlled undertaking (so-called positive sole control, usually achieved by the acquisition of a majority of voting rights), or through the power of vetoing them (so-called negative sole control). In this scenario, the veto power allows the shareholder to threaten the creation of a deadlock situation to determine the strategic behaviour of the controlled undertaking.

Commentary

Control (sole) occurs in two general situations, which are referred to as "positive" sole control and "negative" sole control. In the first scenario, only one person or undertaking is in the position to actively make decisions on another undertaking's business strategy. When no one can single handedly adopt those kinds of resolutions and only one person or undertaking has the power of blocking the strategic decisions of the controlled undertaking, a situation of negative sole control arises. This was the situation examined by the Commission in Case M.2777 Cinven Limited/Angel Street Holdings (2002) where, despite the fact that Cinven could not "impose its will", it was deemed able to exert decisive influence over the target "by virtue of its sole veto right over a range of strategic decisions, […] being alone able to create a deadlock situation by blocking key decisions".

Control (sole) may be enjoyed on a legal ("de jure") or a factual ("de facto") basis.

De jure sole control arises, in the simplest of cases, when an undertaking acquires the majority of the share capital of another undertaking, and symmetrically the majority of the voting rights and the majority in the board of directors. This form of control can also occur when an undertaking does not have the majority of voting shares, if a minority shareholder has preferential shares related to strategic commercial decisions, or the power to determine the company's business strategy according to its organizational structure. In other words, de jure sole control may derive from: (i) the acquisition of a majority of the voting rights in an undertaking; (ii) the acquisition of a minority shareholding with specific rights attached; or (iii) the attainment of the right to manage the activities of the undertaking and to determine its business policy on the basis of its organizational structure.

De facto sole control is acquired when a minority shareholder is highly likely to achieve a majority at the shareholder's meetings. Its evaluation is rather complex and requires a case-by-case prospective analysis, based on the voting pattern of previous shareholders' meetings. This type of evaluation allows the Commission to take into account the foreseeable changes in the structure of shareholders' meetings, and especially whether it is likely that the voting rights of the minority shareholders are sufficient to meet the majorities required for strategic decisions.

The relevant criteria in the assessment of de facto sole control have been progressively elaborated in the Commission's practice. In its decision in case M.025 Arjomari/Wiggins Teape (1990), for example, the Commission took into account the dispersion of capital as a factor to determine the likelihood of a minority shareholder to reach the majority, while in case M.343 Société Générale de Belgique/Générale de Banque (1993), the Commission analyzed the attendance rate in shareholders' meetings in previous years. Indeed, where, on the basis of the number of shareholders attending the shareholders' meetings (preferably regular and not extraordinary ones), a minority shareholder has a stable majority of the votes in this meeting, then the large minority shareholder is considered to have sole control.

Nevertheless, historic voting patterns at the shareholders' meetings may not always provide a sufficiently reliable basis to assess the existence of de facto control, and it may therefore become necessary to also consider other elements in order to verify whether a minority shareholder has acquired the ability to exercise decisive influence over strategic decisions of an undertaking. To this end, the Commission's decision in in case M.8465 Vivendi/ Telecom Italia (2017) provides examples of the factual elements that may be assessed to ascertain whether a minority shareholder exerts control over an undertaking in the absence of legal means to exercise such control or an informative voting pattern at the shareholders' meetings.

Indeed, the Commission established that Vivendi had acquired de facto sole control of Telecom because, "even though it did not achieve a majority of votes at the shareholders" meeting of 4 May 2017, Vivendi was still in a position to appoint the majority of the board of directors, which is in charge of taking TIM's strategic decisions". Indeed, the specific rules governing the appointment of the members of Telecom Italia's board of directors allowed the shareholder with the highest number of votes cast to appoint the majority of these members, and at that time Vivendi was the largest, and the only industrial, shareholder of Telecom Italia (holding 23.93% of the voting rights, with no other shareholder holding more than 5% of the shares).

Conversely, in the same decision, the Commission found that Vivendi, which held 28.80% of the share capital and 29.94% of the voting rights in Mediaset, did not jointly or solely control Mediaset. This was essentially due to the fact that: (i) another industrial shareholder (Fininvest) historically held the largest share of Mediaset's share capital (at that time amounting to 39.53% of the ordinary share capital and 41.09% of the voting share capital) and that it had obtained the majority of the voting rights in the previous six shareholders' meetings and appointed the majority of the board in the previous two terms; (ii) Vivendi had not been able to appoint any members of the board of directors and did not enjoy any specific information or other rights, which materially differed from those of any other minority shareholder; and (iii) Vivendi and Mediaset were engaged in ongoing litigation following the breakdown of the negotiations for the acquisition of Mediaset Premium by Vivendi, which thus seemed to exclude the existence of a commonality of interests between Vivendi and Fininvest.

Lastly, as clarified by the General Court in Air France v. Commission (1994), an option to purchase or convert shares does not constitute a sufficient element to establish sole control. The grant of an option may be relevant if it is clear that the option will be exercised soon on the basis of legally binding agreements, in which case it may exceptionally lead to an assessment of control. Otherwise, it might be taken into consideration, alongside other circumstances, to infer a situation of de facto sole control.

Bibliography

Bailey, D. and John, L. E. (eds.), *Bellamy and Child: European Union Law of Competition* (8th edn, Oxford University Press 2018), Chapter 8

Faull, J. and Nikpay, A. (eds.), *The EU Law of Competition* (3rd edn, Oxford University Press 2014), Chapter 5

Whish, R. and Bailey, D., *Competition Law* (10th end, Oxford University Press 2021), Chapter 21

Commission Consolidated Jurisdictional Notice under Council Regulation (EC) No 139/2004 on the control of concentrations between undertakings (2008/C 95/01)

See also

Control (notion), Merger, Merger control procedure

M

MERGER (TEST SIEC)

Hanna STAKHEYEVA
Boğaziçi University

Definition

The SIEC test is the cornerstone of the concentration control, since a decision of a competition authority of whether a transaction should or not be cleared derives from an economic assessment structured on the substantive test. Mergers that lead to a significant impediment of effective competition in the relevant market or a substantial part of it are prohibited under the EU Merger Regulation as well as respective laws of other jurisdictions beyond the EU (e.g. the USA, Canada, Turkey, Ukraine). The SIEC test enables a more effects-based approach when assessing concentrations.

Commentary

The SIEC test is a substantive test that the competition authorities apply in the course of the merger review. Merger controls of various jurisdictions vary with respect to the test for compatibility of the proposed concentration with the competition in the market with the SIEC and dominance tests being the most commonly used ones.

Article 2 of the EU Merger Regulation sets forth the SIEC test as the basic rule for appraising the concentrations with the EU dimension with a view to establishing whether they are compatible with the internal market. For that purpose, the European Commission must assess whether a concentration would significantly impede effective competition, in particular as a result of the creation or strengthening of a dominant position in the market or a substantial part of it. Concentrations will be allowed unless they lead to a significant impediment of competition.

The SIEC test goes beyond the concept of dominance. The SIEC test captures transactions that do not necessarily create or strengthen a dominant position but still cause an impediment to competition (i.e. where the merging firms are able to raise prices, and thus exercise market power, without coordination and without holding the largest market share in the market). As practice shows dominance is viewed as a leading (although not the only) factor that may cause the SIEC. The creation and strengthening of a dominant position is no longer a prerequisite for prohibiting the transactions as long as a healthy post-merger competitive environment exists. In order to assess whether or not a healthy competitive environment exists or will exist after the concentration, in the first stage, it is assessed whether or not the entity to be formed as a result of concentration shall be able to impede effective competition in the market. Creation or strengthening of a dominant position is cited as a major factor causing such an effect.

When assessing whether a concentration significantly impedes competition the competition authorities would look at the structure of all related markets, actual and potential competitors, market shares of undertakings party to the concentration, convenience of access to market and inputs by these undertakings, availability of product/service alternatives to the products/services of the undertakings which are part of the concentration, supply and demand trends related to these products/services, legal and/or other barriers to entrance to the market, benefits to intermediaries and consumers and finally contribution to economic and technical development.

The competitive conditions existing at the time of the merger constitute the relevant comparison for evaluating the effects of a merger in most cases. In some circumstances, the future changes to the market that can reasonably be predicted may be considered. In particular, the likely entry or exit of firms absent the merger may be taken into account. For example, in *Essilor/Luxottica* the European Commission concluded that Luxottica's current and planned activities in ophthalmic lenses would be insufficient to allow it to exert a strong competitive constraint on Essilor as an existing or potential competitor.

Dominance is considered as part of the economic analysis while applying the SIEC test. For instance, in *EssilorLuxottica/Grandvision* the Turkish Competition Authority assessed the company's dominant position within the framework of factors such as market shares, market entry conditions and buyer power. It stated that concentrations could significantly impede competition in two ways, including by: (i) creating or strengthening a dominant position as a result of the transaction, and (ii) cooperating with undertakings with which there was no coordination prior to the transaction. It was concluded that in the retail market where horizontal overlap was observed, the product and customer portfolios of the undertakings differed to a large extent and their market shares did not reach a level that would raise competitive concerns, so that a situation that would significantly impede competition would not arise. The remarkable point in the decision in terms of the SIEC test is the parties' submission of commitments regarding vertical markets, even though the dominant position was not determined. While the dominant position test was insufficient to go beyond the dominance evaluation, together with the economic evaluations made within the scope of the SIEC test, competitive concerns that can be observed even in the absence of determination of a dominant position were put forward and the transaction was cleared conditionally.

The *Migros/Carrefour* can be cited as another example of the SIEC test in practice. The TCA evaluated the transaction regarding the acquisition of the tenancy right of 34 stores of Carrefour by Migros. Here, the TCA's assessment was not limited to market shares and dominant position analysis. It looked into the possibility of the new entries to the market, obstacle for competitors to increase capacity, market foreclosure etc. Based on these considerations, the TCA concluded that there would be no significant impediment of effective competition and granted clearance to the transaction. Although it was determined that a dominant position would not be created as a result of the transaction, the examination was not limited to this.

The main difference between the SIEC test and the dominance test may be seen in terms of the transactions that do not create a dominant position or strengthen an existing dominant position, but the ones in which the undertakings can increase the price unilaterally after the transaction. The *Marport*, the first case that was blocked by the TCA due to the application of the SIEC test, emphasizes that the SIEC test may prohibit the transactions that significantly impede competition, within the evaluation of theories of harm, in addition to the transactions that result in the creation of a dominant position or the strengthening of the current dominant position.

All in all, the SIEC test shows less reliance placed on market share indicators, but with greater emphasis to assessing the competitive characteristics of the relevant market, the dynamics of competition between the concentration parties and the effects of notified transactions.

Bibliography

Röller, L.-H. De La Mano, M., The Impact of The New Substantive Test In European Merger Control, *European Competition Journal*, 2006, Vol. 2 No. 1, pp. 9-28

Toksoy, F., Balki, B., Stakheyeva, H., *Merger Control in the EU and Turkey: A Comparative Guide*, 2019, Wolters Kluwer, Book – International Competition Law Series

Council Regulation (EC) No 139/2004 of 20 January 2004 On the Control of Concentrations Between Undertakings, L 24/1

The Output, Quarterly Bulletin, ACTECON, 2020

See also

Economic analysis, Merger, Merger (test SLC)

MERGER (TEST SLC)

Lazar RADIC
International Center for Law & Economics

Definition

The substantial lessening of competition or "SLC" test is a standard that regulatory authorities use to assess the legality of proposed mergers and acquisitions. The SLC test examines whether a prospective merger is likely to substantially lessen competition in a given market. Its purpose is to prevent mergers that increase prices, reduce output, limit consumer choice, or stifle innovation as a result of a decrease in competition. Mergers that substantially lessen competition are prohibited under the laws of the jurisdictions that utilize this test, such as the USA, EU, Canada, the United Kingdom, Australia and Nigeria, amongst others.

Commentary

The SLC test is one of the two major tests deployed by competition authorities to determine whether a merger is anticompetitive, the other being the dominance test. Today, most merger control regimes use the SLC test. There are two main reasons for this: the difficulty of assessing coordinated effects and non-horizontal mergers under a dominance test and the increased rigor of effects-based economic analysis allowed by the SLC test (OECD, Standard for Merger Review, page 6).

The SLC test examines likely coordinated and non-coordinated effects in all three types of mergers: horizontal, vertical, and conglomerate. Horizontal mergers may substantially lessen competition by eliminating a significant competitive constraint on one or more firms or by changing the nature of competition so that firms that have not been coordinating their behaviour will be more likely to do so. Vertical and conglomerate mergers tend to pose less of a risk to competition (EU Commission, Guidelines on Non-Horizontal Mergers, paras. 11-13). Still, there are facts and circumstances under which they can substantially lessen competition by, for example, foreclosing rivals from necessary inputs, supplies, or markets.

The SLC test is necessarily forward-looking. Unlike the dominance test, which focuses on the threshold structural issues such as market shares, the SLC test adopts a more effects-based approach. An assessment under the SLC test focuses on whether prices are likely to rise or fall or whether innovation is likely to be diminished post-merger. Despite the SLC test's focus on effects, market concentration can be significant, and it is often used to gauge the potential impact on competition. A significant increase in market concentration may thus signal a risk of competitive harm and warrant a closer examination of likely effects.

To satisfy the SLC test, what is required is neither a showing of certainty nor mere possibilities but rather a reasonable probability of harm to competition (*Brown Shoe*, 323). In the U.S., the SLC test requires a showing that the effects of an acquisition *may be* to substantially lessen competition, in line with Section 7 of the Clayton Act. In *Hospital Corporation of America v Federal Trade Commission* (1389), the U.S. Court of Appeals for the Seventh Circuit held that, under Section 7, it is not necessary to demonstrate that a merger or acquisition immediately resulted in increased prices within the affected market. Instead, the question is whether the merger could lead to a noticeable risk of such price changes in the future. The court emphasized that decisions about future outcomes require predictive judgment, inherently based on probabilities and judgment calls rather than demonstrable evidence. However, this does not mean that "anything goes". The word "may" in Section 7 should not be taken to suggest that the mere possibility of harm renders a merger (consummated or proposed) unlawful; otherwise, authorities would deem every acquisition unlawful (*FTC v. Elders Grain, Inc.*, 906). Instead, there must be a demonstrable link between a merger and the likelihood of an anticompetitive outcome. As the U.S. Supreme Court has said, Section 7 "deals in "probabilities," not "ephemeral possibilities."" The standard articulated by the U.S. Courts is similar to the approach in other jurisdictions, such as the EU. In *European Commission* v. *CJ Telecoms UK Investment Ltd*, for example, the ECJ held that the European Commission is required to show a balance of probabilities on the existence of a significant impediment to effective competition. According to the Court, the harm to competition must be "more likely than not" *CJ Telecoms UK Investment Ltd*, paras 87-8.

The factors that are typically taken into account when assessing a merger under the SLC test include the structure of related markets, the merger's underlying economic rationale, market accessibility for potential entrants, market shares of undertakings involved, whether the market is capacity constrained, the presence of competitors (existing and potential), consumer behaviour (willingness and ability of consumers to switch to alternative products), the likely effect on consumers, the financial investment required for market entry, and the market share necessary for a buyer or seller to achieve profitability or economies of scale. In making its assessment based on these factors, it is generally not sufficient for the competent authority to show that a merger might lessen competition. It must show that the merger is likely to do so *substantially* (*UnitedHealth, 132-133*). A merger that is found to substantially lessen competition may nevertheless be exempted if it gives rise to countervailing merger-specific efficiencies that benefit consumers.

Since the elements of the SLC test are not self-evident, competition authorities have typically set out detailed guidelines which provide frameworks for assessing and evaluating mergers. In December 2023, the U.S. Federal Trade Commission and Department of Justice issued new Horizontal Merger Guidelines, which might have implications for the SLC test. The guidelines suggest an overall scepticism to mergers and an approach to merger control similar to the dominance test, with its emphasis on strong structural presumptions. However, it is important to note that while the guidelines reflect current agencies' views about the law, they do not have any legal force on their own, and courts are not required to follow them.

In conclusion, the SLC test stands as a linchpin in merger evaluation. Its emphasis on foreseeing future outcomes, assessing competitive harm, and balancing economic efficiencies is what defines its role in modern antitrust regimes.

Bibliography

U.S. Department of Justice and Federal Trade Commission Merger Guidelines (2023)

OECD, "OECD Policy Roundtable – Standard for Merger Review" (2009)

EU Commission, Guidelines on the assessment of non-horizontal mergers under the Council Regulation on the control of concentrations between undertakings (2008/C 265/07)

See also

Economic analysis, Merger, Merger (test SIEC)

M

MERGER (TRUSTEE)

Ayberk KURT
ACTECON

Definition

In the context of mergers, a trustee refers to an appointed independent third party (natural or legal) to monitor and ensure compliance with remedies or conditions imposed as a part of the merger clearance process. The appointment process can differ among the jurisdictions however it is always subject to competition authorities' approval. The trustee ensures that the merger's conditions are met impartially, reporting to the regulatory authority and taking corrective actions if necessary. Trustee appointments are a regulatory tool to safeguard competition while allowing mergers to proceed under specified behavioural or/and structural conditions.

Commentary

In the EU, if the Commission conditionally clears a merger, depending on the conditions, the merging parties may be required to submit one or more candidate trustees to the Commission, along with comprehensive details regarding the trustee's scope of power and a work plan outline. The Commission holds the authority to approve both the trustee's appointment and the terms of its mandate. The Commission has the discretion to select the trustee and will evaluate the candidate's suitability for the specific tasks involved. The appointed trustee must maintain independence from the merging parties, possess the requisite qualifications for fulfilling their mandate, and avoid any conflicts of interest. The Commission has a standard model for trustee mandates in divestiture commitments which sets out the role and functions of the trustee in order to guide the merging parties.

A trustee in a merger case may be a monitoring trustee or a divestiture trustee. When the Commission clears a merger with a divestiture remedy, the parties have to propose the appointment of a monitoring trustee and a divestiture trustee. Depending on the commitments, the monitoring trustee may be the same person as the divestiture trustee subject to the Commission's approval and their services are paid for by the parties (Bellamy & Child, para. 8.189).

The monitoring trustee is considered as the Commission's "eyes and ears" (Remedies Notice, para. 118). It is the guardian ensuring that the business is managed and maintained on a stand-alone basis in the interim period and divestiture process. If the merging parties cannot find a suitable purchaser within the first divestiture period, then in the trustee divestiture period, the divestiture trustee will hold sole responsibility for selling the divestment business without a specified minimum price requirement to a suitable purchaser.

The obligations of the monitoring trustee will normally start immediately after the adoption of the Commission decision and last until the legal and actual transfer of the business to the approved purchaser. The Remedies Notice lists five main and non-exhaustive tasks for the monitoring trustee: (i) shall supervise the protective measures for the business to be divested during the interim period, (ii) in carve out cases, shall monitor the separation of divested business from the retained business, (iii) shall oversee the parties' efforts to find a potential suitable purchaser, (iv) shall act as a contact point for third parties about commitments and (v) shall submit periodic reports on compliance to the Commission.

Almost 40% of the conditionally cleared mergers globally include behavioural remedies (Allen & Overy). Due to the extended timeframes and complex nature of behavioural commitments, they typically require significant monitoring efforts to enable the Commission to effectively assess their successful implementation. Therefore, the Commission seeks the appointment of a monitoring trustee in order to ensure effective monitoring of the commitments.

In certain merger clearances, the monitoring trustee has unconventional responsibilities in monitoring the compliance of complex and long term remedies. In the Google/Fitbit Decision, the Commission pointed out that the monitoring trustee "will have far-reaching competences, including access to Google's records, personnel, facilities or technical information" in order to monitor the implementation of the commitments for 10 years. The reporting obligation of the trustee also included reporting to the Irish Data Protection Commission as well as the Commission. The monitoring trustee also played a proactive role and had assistance with technical issues from other firms.

In the UK, similarly to the EU, trustee candidates are remunerated by the merging parties and approved by the CMA. Independence from the parties, having capability and suitable qualifications and being conflict free are also sought as the characteristics of the trustee. The CMA also mentions that trustees may be part of an accounting firm, management consultancy or other professional organisation. The role of a divestiture trustee and a monitoring trustee differs; however the two roles may be performed by the same person.

In the UK merger control regime, the CMA may adopt interim measures until it ends its investigation of a proposed merger. In this case, a monitoring trustee may be required by the CMA to monitor and report on the merging parties' compliance with the interim measures and it may act as a hold-separate manager, if applicable.

There might be significant consequences for the merging parties if they do not comply with the interim measures. In 2021, the CMA imposed a fine of £50.5 million on Facebook for its failure to comply with the initial enforcement order (hold separate order) during the acquisition period of Giphy. In the decision, the CMA stated that Facebook had not fully cooperated with the monitoring trustee in full in compliance with the interim measures (Facebook/Giphy para. 318).

In the U.S., an independent trustee is appointed by the U.S. regulatory authorities, rather than by the parties. The appointment of a monitoring trustee is not always required. If the technical expertise of the agency is not sufficient or the monitoring compliance would create a high burden on the agencies, the appointment of a monitoring trustee by the parties may be sought (DOJ Merger Remedies Manual, p. 30).

In terms of divestiture remedies, the U.S. Agencies must have the ability to seek the appointment of a trustee to sell the assets if the parties are unable to complete the ordered sale within the period prescribed by the decree (DOJ Merger Remedies Manual, p. 29).

Similarly to the Commission, the FTC stated that the trustee serves as the "eyes and ears" of the FTC and the staff and therefore FTC is looking for someone who – in addition to having no conflict – has experience divesting assets in the affected industry (FTC – Competition Guidance – Negotiating Merger Remedies).

Bibliography

Bailey, D. and John, L. E. (eds.), *Bellamy and Child: European Union Law of Competition* (8th edn, Oxford University Press 2018)

Hoehn, T., Trustees in Mergers: An overview of EU and national case law, 19 August 2021, *e-Competitions Trustees in Mergers*, Art. N° 101466

Allen Overy's Global trends in merger control enforcement

Antitrust Division U.S. Department of Justice Merger Remedies Manual (September 2020)

Commission Notice on remedies acceptable under Council Regulation (EC) No 139/2004 and under Commission Regulation (EC) No 802/2004

FTC – Competition Guidance – Negotiating Merger Remedies

See also

Merger, Merger (remedies)

M

MERGER (TURNOVER THRESHOLD)

Damiano CANAPA
University of Lausanne

Definition

In the context of mergers, turnover thresholds are criteria allocating competence for the administrative control of a concentration. Under EU law and Swiss law, certain turnover thresholds must be reached to trigger the obligation to notify a "concentration" to the European Commission (Article 3 EUMR), or the Swiss Competition Commission ([COMCO], Article 9 Swiss Cartel Act [CartA]) respectively; under U.S. law, a "combination" is subject to premerger notification depending on the turnover thresholds if the transaction reaches a certain size (Brown Shoe, para. 44). Turnover thresholds refers to the aggregate turnover of the preceding financial year, comprising the amounts derived "from the sale of products and the provision of services falling within the undertakings' ordinary activities after deduction of sales rebates and of value added tax and other taxes directly related to turnover" (Article 5[1] EUMR, see also Article 4 Swiss Merger Control Ordinance; "annual net sales", 15 USC 18a [a]).

Commentary

The turnover threshold which must be reached to trigger the review of a concentration by competition authorities is a purely quantitative criterion indicating the size of the parties to the concentration; they govern jurisdiction and provide legal certainty through a simple and objective test. Turnover thresholds determine whether a concentration has a "Union dimension" under EU law, while under Swiss and U.S. law whether it must be notified premerger; they do not "assess the market position of the parties to the concentration nor the impact of the operation" (Jurisdictional Notice, para. 127). However, if the parties have high turnovers, this element tends to indicate a significant change in the market that could reduce competition significantly. Turnover thresholds are thus used as a proxy to measure those economic resources that are aggregated, and reflect the geographic distribution of those resources (Jurisdictional Notice, para. 124). To calculate turnover thresholds, the main field of activity of the undertakings concerned is irrelevant: the undertakings or parts thereof that are party to the concentration must have activities in the EU (EU law), worldwide (U.S. law) or at national level (Switzerland). Neither the seat of the undertakings concerned, nor the transaction, need to be located in a given country.

In the EU, a concentration falls under the exclusive competence of the Commission (based on the one-stop-shop principle) when it has a Union dimension. This happens, if (1) the combined aggregate worldwide turnover of all the undertakings concerned exceeds EUR 5,000 million and, (2) the aggregate Union-wide turnover of each of at least two of the undertakings concerned is more than EUR 250 million (Article 1[2] EUMR). The purpose is to reflect, on a worldwide basis, the overall size of the undertakings concerned to ascertain a minimum level of activity within the EU and to exclude from the EU jurisdiction transactions that are purely domestic (Jurisdictional Notice, para. 125). On the other hand, a concentration has a Union dimension if it has a substantial impact on competition in at least three Member States (Jurisdictional Notice, para. 126). This is the case if (1) the combined aggregate worldwide turnover of all the undertakings concerned is more than EUR 2,500 million, where, in each of at least three Member States, (2) the combined aggregate turnover of all the undertakings concerned is more than EUR 100 million and that (3) the aggregate turnover of each of at least two of these undertakings is more than EUR 25 million. Finally, (4) the aggregate Union-wide turnover of each of at least two of the undertakings concerned must exceed EUR 100 million (Article 1[3] EUMR). However, a concentration has no Union dimension despite fulfilling one of these two alternatives if each of the undertakings concerned achieves more than two-thirds of its turnover within one and the same Member State.

In Switzerland, a planned concentration must be notified to COMCO if, on the one hand, the undertakings concerned together reported a turnover of at least 2 billion Swiss francs, or a turnover in Switzerland of at least 500 million Swiss francs, and that, on the other hand, at least two of the undertakings concerned each reported a turnover in Switzerland of at least 100 million Swiss francs (Article 9[1] CartA). When an insurance company is involved, "turnover" is replaced by "annual gross insurance premium income", and when a bank or a financial intermediary that is subject to the accounting regulations set out in the Swiss Banking Act of 8 November 1934 is involved, turnover is replaced by "gross income" (Article 9[3] CartA). However, if one of the undertakings concerned has been previously held – in a final decision – to be dominant in a market in Switzerland, any concentration that takes place in that market, in an adjacent market, or in a market upstream or downstream thereof must be notified (Article 9[4] CartA).

In the U.S., a merger is subject to premerger notification where the size of the transaction (i.e., the value of stocks and assets the acquiring firm will hold after the transaction, including the value of previously acquired stocks) is above $50 million but not more than $200 million (below $50 million, the transaction is not reportable and over $200 million, the transaction must be reported), where (1) the acquiring firm has assets or annual net sales more than $100 million and the acquired firm has (i) assets or annual net sales of $10 million or more if the acquired firm is engaged in manufacturing, or (ii) assets of $10 million or more if the acquired firm is not engaged in manufacturing; and (2) where the acquiring firm acquires at least 15 % of the stocks or assets of the firm or an aggregate total amount of the stocks or assets of the firm over $15 million (15 USC 18a [a], Amendment 2000).

Where a concentration consists in the acquisition of a part of one undertaking, such as an IP right, only the turnover relating to this part must thus be taken into account with regard to the seller (Otto/Primondo Assets, paras 9 f.; Jurisdictional Notice, 136). If a joint venture is created (Article 3[4] EUMR), the turnovers of each of the undertakings founding the joint venture are relevant, and if the undertakings acquire joint control of an existing undertaking or parts thereof, the turnovers of the undertakings acquiring control and of the acquired undertaking are considered (Jurisdictional Notice, para. 140).

Turnover thresholds have been criticized for not being able to assess in a satisfactory way so-called "killer acquisitions" (e.g., the Facebook/Whatsapp merger [paras 9 ff.] was reviewed by the Commission, because it was notified under Article 4 (5) EUMR; the EUMR turnover thresholds were not met); turnover thresholds are then not met even though an undertaking or parts thereof is acquired for a large sum of money, thereby allowing the acquirer to prevent the development of potential competitors on a given market. Such operations typically involve "start-up" companies in digital markets, or pharmaceutical companies that have developed a new drug with great potential (despite the fact that they have not yet received marketing authorization). Other criteria have thus been considered to determine jurisdiction. Certain countries, such as Germany and Austria, have introduced additional thresholds based on the value of the transaction.

Others, such as Spain or the UK, foresee a share of supply test that allows competition authorities to address operations where a company with a certain market share acquires a nascent competitor. Finally, certain jurisdictions, such as the U.S., but also the UK, Hungary, Canada, Japan, Mexico or Brazil, foresee ex-post reviews of mergers as a complementary instrument. Another way to proceed could be to consider that the turnover thresholds are met at the moment of the concentration if they would be reached with certainty within three years (fiction of reaching a given turnover). A similar rule exists in the EU for the calculation of the internal turnover of an outsourcing activity, where the previous internal turnover does not correspond to a market valuation of the activities and where the forecast revenues to be received on the basis of an agreement with the former parent may be a suitable proxy.

In the EU, as a complement to the above, the General Court has confirmed that another possibility for the Commission to assess a killer acquisition is provided by the fact that one or more Member States – after a notification has been made to their national competition authority – can request the Commission to examine a concentration which would affect trade between Member States and threaten to significantly affect competition within the territory of the Member State or States making the request (Article 22[1] EUMR) despite having no Union dimension (Notice on Case Referral, para. 42 ff.). This rule also applies if the referring authority would have no jurisdiction under national law, because the national turnover thresholds would not be met (Illumina Grail, paras 85 ff., and already Procter & Gamble/Sara Lee Air care, para. 7). It must be underscored, however, that an appeal against the judgment of the General Court is currently pending before the Court of Justice of the European Union. Depending on the outcome of this case, this practice could be abandoned.

Bibliography

Areeda, P. E. and Hovenkamp, H., *Antitrust law: An analysis of antitrust principles and their application: Volume 4* (4th ed., Wolters Kluwer 1998);

Broberg, M., Improving the EU Merger Regulation's Delimitation of Jurisdiction: Re-defining the Notion of Union Dimension, (2014) 5(5) *Journal of European Competition Law and Practice* 261;

Whish, R. and Bailey, D., *Competition Law* (10th ed., Oxford University Press 2021), Chapter 21;

European Commission, Commission Consolidated Jurisdictional Notice under Council Regulation (EC) No. 139/2004 on the control of concentration between undertakings of 16 April 2008, [2004] O.J. C 95/1;

European Commission, Commission Notice on Case Referral in respect of concentration of 5 March 2005, [2005] O.J. C56/2

See also

Form CO (EU), Merger, Merger Control Procedure, Hart-Scott-Rodino Filing (US)

M

MERGER (WITHDRAWAL)

David READER
University of Glasgow

Definition

At any stage prior to a final decision being tabled in a merger control investigation, the merging parties have the prerogative to withdraw the original notification and, in doing so, signal their intentions to re-notify a restructured transaction or abandon the merger in its entirety. Once the parties have provided the competition authority with satisfactory assurances that their merger has been abandoned, it follows that the transaction is no longer subject to merger control laws, meaning the competition authority will typically cancel its investigation of the transaction, including suspending any information requests or plans to issue a decision.

Commentary

Reasons for withdrawing notifications are numerous. Where a competition authority indicates that it is likely to issue a Phase II referral, table a prohibition decision, or request significant undertakings/remedies, the merging parties may decide to abandon their transaction to avoid incurring further delays, administrative fees and shareholder uncertainty. Parties may also abandon a merger when extraneous factors result in a loss of public appetite for the merger (e.g. NewsCorp/BSkyB), or if the completion of a merger is conditional on the transaction not being referred to Phase II. Alternatively, the parties may have reason to restructure their transaction and withdraw their notification in anticipation of re-notifying a revised deal at a later date.

While merger withdrawals bring about an end to formal investigation proceedings, they nonetheless stand to have significant implications in practice. A withdrawn case deprives the authority of an opportunity to table a full decision or present its line of reasoning and theories of harm before a court. It also restricts the potential for subsequent appeals or judicial review proceedings. A formal notification of withdrawal, however, enables authorities to efficiently reallocate resources once it becomes clear that the merging parties no longer intend to proceed with their deal.

After the European Commission has initiated Phase II proceedings under the EU Merger Regulation (EUMR), the Commission may only close those proceedings by way of adopting a formal decision (under EUMR, art 8), or where "the undertakings concerned have demonstrated to the satisfaction of the Commission that they have abandoned the concentration" (EUMR, art 6(1)(c)). The Commission's Consolidated Jurisdictional Notice provides clarification on the types of evidence that parties are required to present in order to adequately demonstrate that their merger has been abandoned. It is clear that the mere withdrawal of notification – or minor modifications to a merger "which do not affect the change in control or the quality of that change", e.g. timing of completion, slight adjustments to shareholding allocations, etc – are insufficient proof that a merger has been abandoned (Jurisdictional Notice, para 120). Rather, the parties must demonstrate that they have taken proportionate steps to reverse, inter alia, the legal form, format and intensity of the arrangements that have been put in place to facilitate the merger, namely: a binding agreement, a good faith intention to conclude an agreement, a public announcement of (an intention to make) a public bid, or an implemented merger (paras 119-120). In the latter case, where a merger has already been implemented, the parties may only demonstrate abandonment having first taken steps to unwind integration between the firms, such that there is proof that the parties have re-established the status quo ante conditions prevailing before the merger was implemented.

Following an adequate demonstration of withdrawal by the merging parties, the Commission ceases to have competence to adopt a decision under Article 8 EUMR in respect of that transaction. Doing so is likely to result in annulment of the decision on appeal, including in instances where the Commission has omitted to inform the merging parties that their notice of withdrawal is deemed inadequate (MCI v Commission (2004)). However, the Courts have clarified that the Commission retains its competence to examine a merger until such time that complete abandonment is established; where merging parties offer commitments that would restructure the transaction below the EUMR turnover thresholds, the Commission retains its competence over the merger, unless it considers the restructuring to be so substantial that it appears likely the original notified merger has been abandoned (Cementbouw (2007)).

In the United States, under the Hart-Scott-Rodino Antitrust Improvements Act of 1976 (HSR Act), amendments were introduced in 2013 to formalise a longstanding "withdraw and refile notification" procedure intended to facilitate more efficient use of scarce agency resources in the event of a merger withdrawal or abandonment. The procedure affords additional time for the authorities to review a transaction during the initial HSR waiting period, allowing ample opportunity for the merging parties to notify a withdrawal where they perceive a risk of a costly Second Request. Three main parts of 16 CFR §803.12 establish the relevant rules and procedures. Firstly, either one of the merging parties may voluntarily withdraw its HSR notification at any time (§803.12(a)), which may be conveyed in writing to the FTC and the Antitrust Division of the Department of Justice (DOJ), resulting in the nullification of the filing and termination of any Second Request for additional information. Secondly, an HSR notification is automatically deemed to have been withdrawn if either merging party makes a filing with the U.S. Securities and Exchange Commission (SEC) that "publicly announces the expiration, termination or withdrawal of a tender offer or the termination of an agreement or letter of intent" (§803.12(b)). In such cases, the party that files with the SEC is under an obligation to notify the FTC and DOJ in writing. Thirdly, where the acquiring party has withdrawn its HSR notification by virtue of §803.12(a) or (b), that party may resubmit its notification of the transaction without incurring a new filing fee, subject to certain conditions related to, inter alia, timings and the merger not changing in any material way (§803.12(c)).

In a similar vein to the U.S., amendments to the merger control rules of the United Kingdom under the Enterprise and Regulatory Reform Act 2013 can be seen to aid the competition authority's ability to allocate resources effectively by factoring in the prospect of a merger being withdrawn. The Competition and Markets Authority (CMA) may suspend the start of a Phase II investigation by up to three weeks, if the merging parties request this (Enterprise Act 2002, §39(8A)(a)) and the CMA is of a reasonable belief that the parties will abandon the merger imminently (§39(8A)(b)). Given that a significant number of mergers are abandoned following a Phase II reference, the temporary suspension procedure is intended to prevent important resources being wasted where a Phase II investigation is opened swiftly, only for the parties to withdraw a short time later.

Bibliography

Bernhardt, L., "Withdrawn and Prohibited Merger Cases in the EU" (2022) 13(4) *Journal of European Competition Law & Practice* 296

Jones, A., Sufrin, B. and Dunne, N., *Jones & Sufrin's EU Competition Law: Text, Cases, and Materials* (8th edn, OUP 2023)

Van Bael, I., *Due Process in EU Competition Proceedings* (Kluwer 2011)

Whish, R. and Bailey, D., *Competition Law* (10th edn, OUP 2021)

See also

Merger, Merger (prohibition)

M

MINORITY SHAREHOLDINGS

Anna TZANAKI
University of Leeds

Definition

Minority shareholdings are situations whereby a shareholder acquires and holds less than 50% of the share capital or voting rights of a company. Minority shareholdings may either confer "control" or "influence" upon the acquirer, or they may qualify as "non-controlling" (also known as "structural links"). Economic theory suggests that all types of minority shareholdings in competitors may give rise to anticompetitive concerns of different nature and degree depending on the circumstances. However, the extent to which key competition law regimes in Europe and the U.S. can capture and remedy potentially anticompetitive "non-controlling" minority shareholdings under their merger control or antitrust rules varies.

Commentary

EU antitrust law, and laws based in EU law, prohibit anticompetitive agreements between *separate* competing undertakings (Article 101 TFEU) and abuse of a dominant position by a single firm or a group of separate undertakings that are connected by either legal, economic or structural links (Article 102 TFEU). Merger laws target mergers or acquisitions where two competitors come under (full or partial) *common* ownership and control – they become a single undertaking and therefore cease to compete in the market. Under the EU Merger Regulation (EUMR), partial acquisitions are subject to *ex ante* review if they entail a "lasting change of control" of the undertakings concerned. Minority shareholding acquisitions that confer "control" – defined as "*decisive* influence" pursuant to Article 3 of the EUMR – either on a *de jure* or a *de facto* basis on the acquirer may trigger merger scrutiny in the EU. Minority shareholdings that are considered "non-controlling" fall outside the scope of the EU merger regime. Yet, other jurisdictions in Europe rely on broader jurisdictional tests to bring partial ownership acquisitions within their merger control rules. For instance, the UK employs a "*material* influence" threshold and Germany a "competitively significant influence" threshold that allows them to scrutinise minority shareholdings that escape EU scrutiny.

U.S. merger control (Section 7 of the Clayton Act) is even broader than any of these regimes. Its substantive prohibition relies on an "effects-based" test: any merger that leads to *likely anticompetitive* effects (i.e. "may be substantially to lessen competition") is unlawful. According to U.S. case law, "control" is not a necessary or decisive factor for finding that an acquisition violates Section 7 of the Clayton Act (*Denver & Rio Grande*, 501). Therefore, any potentially harmful minority shareholdings may in principle run afoul U.S. merger rules. The Horizontal Merger Guidelines (§13) reiterate this principle: the antitrust agencies will review "partial acquisitions that do not result in effective control" for "any way" they may affect or lessen competition, focusing in particular on (i) the acquirer's *ability to influence* the competitive conduct of the target; (ii) a reduction in the acquirer's *incentive to compete*; (iii) *access to* non-public, competitively sensitive *information* of the target (or acquiring) firm. There is however a "solely for investment" exemption for substantive (and filing) purposes under U.S. merger law, which applies under strict requirements and allows for more lenient treatment of *actually* "non-controlling" or "passive" minority shareholdings. These may be subject to review and liability if antitrust agencies can show "actual" anticompetitive effects, rather than "likely" effects as in other merger cases. Further, "passive" minority shareholdings are liable under U.S. merger law at "any time" – not only at the time of their acquisition, when they may be considered lawful, but also later when they may face *ex post* scrutiny because "subsequent use of the stock" makes it anticompetitive (*du Pont*, 597-598, 607).

In addition, minority shareholdings that do not bring about a change of ownership and control between the interlinked undertakings, or otherwise fall outside merger control, may still be captured by antitrust rules. Longstanding EU case law that precedes the adoption of the EU-wide system of merger control had crystalised this principle. Pursuant to *Philip Morris*, Article 101 TFEU may apply to agreements between undertakings based on which a minority shareholding is acquired when it is shown that in light of its economic and legal context, such agreement has "the object or effect of influencing the competitive behaviour of the companies on the relevant market" (para 45). The European Court of Justice further clarified in this case that "the acquisition by one company of an equity interest in a competitor does not in itself constitute conduct restricting competition" but it "may nevertheless serve as an *instrument for influencing* the commercial conduct of the companies in question so as to restrict or distort competition on the market on which they carry on business" (para 37). That is, shareholding acquisitions are not a "by object" restriction but need to be evaluated based on their effects. Accordingly, a minority shareholding may be found to be restrictive of competition if it gives rise to either *coordination* or exchange of commercially sensitive information, or to effective *control*, at present or in the future, or some degree of *influence*over the competitor's commercial conduct (paras 38-40). It is debatable whether the scope of the "influence" standard under Article 101, which is lower than "decisive" influence under the EUMR, is flexible enough to address seemingly passive minority shareholdings that merely give rise to unilateral anticompetitive effects. The main limitation of Article 101 is that it requires a finding of "agreement" or at least "concerted practice" (i.e. some element of reciprocity rather than a unilateral act) between "undertakings" (rather than an undertaking and an individual with no independent economic activity) for a potentially anticompetitive minority shareholding to come within its ambit.

Article 102 TFEU may on the other hand cover *unilateral* acquisitions of a minority shareholding by undertakings in a dominant position if found to be abusive. In this context, *Philip Morris* established that abuse under Article 102 "can only arise where the shareholding in question results in effective control of the other company or at least in *some influence* on its commercial policy" (para 65). The Commission's decision in *Gillette* later confirmed that even an indirect, non-voting minority interest in a competitor in connection with other special factors (financial loan arrangements and other agreements) could be found to violate Article 102. This case made clear that the "influence" standard under Article 102 is even lower and more malleable than the one under Article 101. As such, Article 102 may tackle further instances of potentially anticompetitive minority shareholdings that are otherwise hard to reach under EU competition law. Specifically, it was considered that the creation of the link(s) between the acquirer and its main competitor had changed the structure of the market with adverse effects on competition (i.e. its behaviour "influenced" market conditions), which a dominant undertaking has a "special responsibility" not to impair in the common market (para 23). *Gillette* is important because it is the only antitrust case where disposal of the equity interest and its interest as creditor has been ordered by the Commission (para 42). The drawback of Article 102 is that it requires a finding of "dominance" besides abuse to apply.

These antitrust rules have been sparingly applied after the coming into force of the EUMR in 1990 and have fallen to complete disuse after the modernisation of the EU antitrust enforcement system and its decentralisation in 2003. Recent EU jurisprudence has reaffirmed however that Articles 101 and 102 TFEU can scrutinise and remedy anticompetitive conduct arising out of "non-controlling" minority shareholdings, which escape *ex ante* merger scrutiny, *following* their acquisition (Order of the President of the

Court of First Instance in *Aer Lingus*, para 103). Articles 101 and 102 have national equivalents in EU Member States and similar antitrust provisions exist in the United Kingdom and in the United States that may address minority shareholdings that raise competition concerns. U.S. antitrust law (Sections 1 and 2 of the Sherman Act) is more encompassing as its application is not restricted to "undertakings" but applies to anticompetitive practices of any "persons" including natural ones. Accordingly, an acquisition of a minority shareholding by an individual shareholder in a business entity could be liable under U.S. antitrust law.

Bibliography

Areeda, P. E. and Hovenkamp, H., *Antitrust Law: An Analysis of Antitrust Principles and Their Application*, vol 5 (3rd ed., Aspen Publishers 2009) ¶1203-¶1205

Burnside, A. J., "Minority Shareholdings: An Overview of EU and National Case Law" (2013) *e-Competitions Bulletin* N° 56676

Tzanaki, A., "Common Ownership and Minority Shareholding at the Intersection of Competition and Corporate Law: Looking Through the Past to Return to the Future?" in Marco Corradi and Julian Nowag (eds.), *The Intersections between Antitrust and Corporate Law*, Cambridge University Press, 2023

Annex I "Economic Literature on Non-Controlling Minority Shareholdings ("Structural links")" to Commission Staff Working Document, "Towards More Effective EU Merger Control" SWD(2013) 239 final

OECD, "Antitrust Issues Involving Minority Shareholdings and Interlocking Directorates" (2009) DAF/COMP(2008)30

See also

Anticompetitive object or effect, Control (notion), Control (change), Merger

M

MISINFORMATION

Seth B. SACHER
U.S. Federal Trade Commission (FTC)

■ Definition

Misinformation is defined as false or inaccurate information that may or may not be meant to intentionally mislead. It differs from propaganda in that it always refers to something which is not true. Disinformation can be viewed as a subset of misinformation that is deliberately intended to mislead. There have been longstanding concerns in antitrust regarding the provision of disinformation meant to affect the structure of the marketplace. More recently, some antitrust observers have raised concerns that lax antitrust enforcement can lead to the provision of misinformation.

■ Commentary

Antitrust is typically considered a remedy for market failures associated with market power. Market failures associated with distortions of information generally come under the rubric of various consumer protection statutes. However, at times, the provision of misinformation, particularly misinformation which is deliberately intended to mislead, also known as disinformation, has been found to conflict with antitrust and competition law statutes. More recently, in addition to concerns that disinformation can hinder the competitive process, some observers have raised concerns that market power and a lack of competition may lead to the marketplace providing information that is distorted. These observers contend that such situations should also be a matter for antitrust enforcement.

Averitt and Lande (1997) provide a taxonomy for distinguishing when disinformation comes under the rubric of consumer protection and when it constitutes an antitrust violation. When the manipulation of information interferes with the ability of consumers to choose effectively among options available in the marketplace, consumer protection laws are implicated. Provisions of disinformation that affect the structure of the marketplace itself should be analyzed under the rubric of antitrust.

The provision of disinformation as it relates to hindering the competitive process can raise concerns in a number of contexts. Thus, violations have been found when the disinformation is provided on a unilateral as well as a coordinated basis. Disinformation can be a violation when it is provided to competitors, customers and other market participants, such as regulatory agencies, standard-setting organizations (SSOs) and market intermediaries. It can apply to the active provision of disinformation but can also include actions to withhold or thwart the provision of useful or timely information.

Many prominent cases involve misrepresentations to regulatory agencies, especially misrepresentations meant to obtain or extend the life of intellectual property protections. In the United States, in addition to violating the patent statutes, in *Walker Process* (1965) the Supreme Court held enforcement of a patent through knowing and willful fraud may also constitute a monopolization offense (Arquit (1990)). Hence, the provision of disinformation on a unilateral basis can constitute an antitrust violation. The *Hoffman-LaRoche* matter (2018) decided by the European Court of Justice involved findings that two pharmaceutical companies disseminated misleading safety claims on a coordinated basis for the purpose of allocating markets. Further, the disinformation was directed not only at the drug safety regulator, but also toward physicians and consumers.

As noted above, the withholding of relevant information can be seen as an antitrust violation. A number of matters pertaining to the practices of various professional associations fall into this category. These cases generally involved coordinated actions to interfere with the flow of information to consumers or various market intermediaries. For example, in *Detroit Auto Dealers' Association* matter (1985), the USFTC found that a group of more than ninety auto dealers agreed to keep their showrooms closed on Saturdays and on three weekday evenings. The restrictions on shopping times made it more difficult for consumers to compare prices, quality, variety, and features of cars. This had the indirect effect of diminishing price competition in the market.

Another area involving the provision of disinformation concern standard setting organizations (SSOs). The Rambus matter, investigated by both the USFTC and European Commission, is an example. This matter involved unilateral action regarding the withholding of relevant information for yet to be adopted technologies from competitors. Rambus, a developer of chip technologies took part in an SSO engaged in the development of a type of computer memory named "dynamic random access memory" (DRAM). Rambus was accused of hiding from other SSO participants that it owned some blocking patents needed to practice the new standard. After that standard was adopted, Rambus left the organization and filed infringement actions. Rambus was able to obtain high royalties by licensing the blocking patents. The FTC contended this deception was an exclusionary action that amounted to unlawful monopolization. The DC circuit court rejected the FTC's claims, based, in part, on the argument that there was insufficient evidence the SSO would have adopted a different standard but for Rambus' actions. European regulators focused on the high royalties Rambus was able to charge in finding an abuse of dominance.

More recently, some commentators have argued that a lack of competition can lead to the provision of misinformation. These observers argue that such concerns should fall under the purview of antitrust. Many of these contentions pertain to concerns over the power held by the so-called "tech giants," especially various social media platforms. For example, Hubbard (2017) contends Facebook's market power incentivizes it to disseminate fake news articles because this increases users' time on-site, thereby allowing it to sell more ads. Hubbard argues if Facebook faced more competition there would be greater financial consequences for providing such misinformation.

Others have raised both factual and theoretical questions regarding these contentions. For example, Sacher & Yun (2019) note that more competition (perhaps through "breaking up" the tech giants) could increase rather than ameliorate any such putative problems. Consider the dissemination of fake news on social media sites. In addition to a fake news article, a consumer has an array of options – other choices may include legitimate news articles, other activities on the social media site or within the internet more broadly, or even activities off the internet. Assuming the consumer chooses to engage with the fake news article means the fake news item was better at gaining the reader's attention relative to the alternatives. Given that the very essence of media competition is to gain the consumer's attention, increased competition may very well lead to more fake news dissemination, not less. Such reasoning would appear to hold regarding other arguments that a lack of competition can lead to the dissemination of misinformation, such as contentions that a lack of competition facilitates the ability of various online shopping entities to "manipulate" customers and get them to purchase things they otherwise wouldn't buy.

In sum, while a finding of an antitrust offense, as in any other context, is a fact specific endeavor, the theoretical basis for the contention that the provision of disinformation can adversely affect the competitive process appears sound. Such concerns have formed the basis for antitrust enforcement actions in a number of contexts, although they have been rejected by adjudicators on a factual basis in some instances. In contrast, the contention that a lack of competition can lead to the provision of misinformation generally, and whether this should be of antitrust concern, is currently subject to greater debate.

Bibliography

ARQUIT, K., Patent Abuse and the Antitrust Laws, 59 *Antitrust Law Journal* 739 (1990)

AVERITT, N. and LANDE, R., Consumer Sovereignty: A United Theory of Antitrust and Consumer Protection Law, 65 *Antitrust Law Journal* 713 (1997)

HUBBARD, S., (January 10, 2017), Why Fake News is an Antitrust Problem, Forbes.com

SACHER, S. B. and YUN, J. M., Fake News is Not an Antitrust Problem, *CPI Antitrust Chron.* (Dec. 2017)

SACHER, S. B. and YUN, J. M., Twelve Fallacies of the "Neo-Antitrust" Movement, 26 *Geo. Mason L. Rev.* 1491 (2019)

See also

Antitrust, Competition Policy, Consumer protection, Market power

M

MOBILITY BARRIERS

Liana JAPARIDZE
University of Sussex

■ Definition

The term "mobility barriers" can be defined in several ways. The narrowest definition denotes the factors preventing competitors from upward mobility – i.e., gaining market share. In this sense, "mobility barriers" are synonymous with "barriers to (market) expansion". The broadest definition refers to the factors that deter firms from switching or expanding to other markets. In this sense, "mobility barriers" is a generic term encompassing entry/exit barriers and barriers to moving within the industry for firms already active in at least one market.

■ Commentary

Originating in industrial organisation economics, the term "mobility barriers" was proposed to evolve the definition of "entry barriers". In his seminal work, Joe Bain referred to "entry barriers" as the extent of competitors' capability to raise their prices above costs without prompting potential competitors to enter the market (absolute cost advantage). This definition of entry barriers assumed that potential entrants were starting their market activities from scratch (see Caves and Porter, 1977). Hence, the concept overlooked at least two real-life market issues.

First, firms already active in one market could enter another by switching or expanding business activities. As a result, not every potential entrant started production from zero. Second, markets frequently involved groups of firms with significantly different capabilities (e.g. different market shares) – referred to as "strategic groups". Hence, established market participants attempting to switch from one strategic group to another (e.g. by increasing their market shares) could face constraints similar to those encountered by new market entrants. The concept of "mobility barriers"/"barriers to mobility" was proposed to remedy these gaps.

Mobility barriers can be defined in several ways. The narrowest definition addresses only the second gap highlighted in the previous paragraph (switching between strategic groups). This definition differentiates "entry" from "mobility" based on whether the firm is in or outside the market. In this way, barriers to entry concern the factors that deter firms from entering markets altogether, while mobility barriers refer to the obstacles that prevent already established market players from upward mobility – i.e., from increasing their market presence. If defined this way, mobility barriers become synonymous with "barriers to (market) expansion" – a concept that is frequently used by competition enforcers worldwide (alongside the concept of market entry) as one of the factors to assess the market power of existing market competitors (see the notion of "barriers to entry").

Other literature defines mobility barriers that address only the first gap identified above. For example, when discussing the mobility barriers in the European Civil Aviation Market, Pitelis (2022) clarifies that "[a] barrier to mobility is regarded as a characteristic of an airline market that prevents [an established] carrier from entering a new route". This definition focuses on the barriers that deter the entry of experienced firms but overlooks the barriers to expansion.

Finally, most of the literature uses the notion of mobility barriers that addresses both above-mentioned issues. Namely, in addition to the upward mobility obstacles, this term refers to the factors that obstruct players of one market from entering another, either by switching markets or by expanding/diversifying their business portfolio. This overarching definition looks at the advantages of incumbent firms (i.e. firms already operating in a particular market) as opposed to firms that want to move to or scale up in the same market. Gilbert's (1989) definitions of "barriers to entry" and "barriers to mobility (of capital)" reflect this well. Here, barriers to entry refer to benefits derived from the first mover advantage – i.e. "additional profit that a firm can earn as a sole consequence of being established in an industry". However, when discussing mobility barriers, Gilbert discusses the importance of assessing the obstacles of both entry and exit that could complicate the movement of capital from one market to another. Similarly, when Olusoga, Mokwa and Noble (1995) discuss various definitions of mobility barriers, they broadly refer to two main scenarios: a) costs incurred by entrants that were already established in another industry to move to a new industry or a new segment of the same industry; b) costs incurred by market participants to switch from one strategic group to another to increase their market presence.

While widely used in industrial literature, the term "mobility barriers" is rarely (if at all) seen in legal literature and case law. One reason for this is that, in a vast majority of instances, the analysis of mobility barriers can be covered by the analysis of barriers to entry/expansion and exit. To note:

factors such as sunk costs, economies of scale, reputation of the actual competitors, and structural characteristics of the market can be considered as both entry and mobility barriers.

Therefore, if a particular market power analysis requires assessing these factors, this can be done under the "barriers to entry" concept already well-established in the law. For example, the EU Commission recently assessed whether high investment costs were barriers to entry in the *Amazon case* (para 65). Considering the substantial amount of investment required to enter the relevant market in this case, one could say that high investment costs could have also been barriers to mobility – i.e. they could deter both the firms established in other markets, as well as competitors (if any) desiring to expand their market shares.

A similar assumption could be made about some of the entry deterrent factors that have emerged with the uprise of the digital economy. For example, in the EU Commission's *Google Shopping case*, potential competitors noted needing a large quantity of data to develop an alternative search engine that could compete with Google (paras 286-289). Here, Google had the first-move advantage in the relevant market. Consequently, neither potential competitors that already operated in other digital markets (i.e. had prior experience in the industry) nor the existing competitors in the relevant market of search engines could scale up to match the strength and efficiency of the market leader – Google – in terms of the search engine functions. This example shows that possessing a large amount of data could be both barriers to entry and mobility in the digital economy.

Bibliography

Ade Olusoga, S., Mokwa, M. R. and Noble, C. H., 'Strategic Groups, Mobility Barriers, and Competitive Advantage: An Empirical Investigation' (1995) *Journal of Business Research* 33, 153-164

Caves, R. E. and Porter, M. E., 'From Entry Barriers to Mobility Barriers: Conjectural Decisions and Contrived Deterrence to New Competition' (1977) 91 *The Quarterly Journal of Economics* 2, 241-262

Gilbert, R., 'Mobility Barriers and the Value of Incumbency' in Richard Schmalensee and Robert Willig (eds) *Handbook of Industrial Organization* (1989) Chapter 8

Jones, A., Sufrin, B. and Dunne, N., *Competition Law: Text, Cases and Materials* (8th edition, Oxford University Press, 2023), Chapter 2, 143-151

Pitelis, C., 'Barriers to Mobility in Europe's Civil Aviation Markets: Theory and New Evidence (2002) 20 *Review of Industrial Organization* 2, 127-150

See also

Barriers to entry, Market power, Market share, Relevant market

M

MONOPOLY

David H. REICHENBERG, Stephen D. LIBOWSKY
Manatt, Phelps & Phillips

Definition

Section 2 of the Sherman Act in the United States and the analogous provisions around the world prohibit "monopolization" or "attempted monopolization." The possession of a monopoly is not illegal in and of itself. How one obtained and how one allegedly uses monopoly power is crucial to whether a Section 2 claim exists. A monopolist has "the power to control prices or exclude competition." A monopoly is generally defined with relation to a specific Relevant Product Market and Relevant Geographic Market. Other relevant factors considered as to whether a monopoly in a given market exists includes market shares, barriers to entry and expansion, market structure, and market performance over time.

Commentary

The power to control price or exclude competition are factors that are intertwined and generally refer to the phenomenon that when an alleged monopolist is threatened by a competitor, the monopolist has the unilateral ability to exclude that competitor, and/or has the ability to maintain its prices and market shares in face of competitive forces. While not the subject of this entry, the second element of monopolization – the "wilful acquisition or maintenance of [monopoly] power as distinguished from growth or development as a consequence of a superior product, [legal rights such as a patent,] business acumen, or historic accident" – is applicable to an entity that allegedly has the ability to accomplish this end given the market structure and other factors.

Monopoly power can be shown through direct or indirect evidence, with the former being evidence illustrating control over price and/or the exclusion of competition from the relevant market at issue. Indirect evidence usually starts with a defendant's share of a relevant market and the alleged existence of barriers to entry or expansion.

Courts generally accept market shares higher than 70% as an indication of monopoly power if pared with significant barriers to entry or expansion. Market shares between 50 and 70 percent have been considered supportive of monopoly power in similar circumstances, upon illustration of other factors regarding the size and ability of competitors to penetrate the market. While for a long time market shares below 50% were not considered prima facie evidence of monopoly power, in the Department of Justice's latest antitrust case against American Express, the lower court found that AmEx's 26% share of the general purpose card market was supportive of monopoly power given the alleged sustained ability to raise price without competitive consequence. The Second Circuit and Supreme Court reversed and the Judgment against AmEx respectively, based on the finding that the relevant market was improperly defined, but the Second Circuit did not directly overturn the lower court's finding of monopoly power in a single-sided market (should it have found to been appropriate).

Barriers to entry and expansion play a significant role in determining monopoly power, because if meaningful entry or expansion can occur in response to a small, but significant price increase, that will likely defeat the ability to raise or maintain such prices for a sustained period of time. Courts have considered the context, success, frequency, and magnitude of entry and expansion to determine the ability to control price or exclude competition.

Market structure and competitor performance can also be relevant to a determination of monopoly power. While each market should be assessed on its own merits, the characteristics of competitors can be relevant, such as their size and strength over time, their production capacity, and their ability to price discriminate against certain purchasers. Overall market factors such as the likely development of the industry, the elasticity of consumer demand, potential substitution from outside the relevant market, and the pace of technological advances can also be considered as relevant to a market power inquiry.

The FTC's case against Qualcomm highlights that definition of the relevant market for alleged monopoly power can be a critical determinant in whether an alleged practice can be found liable for monopolization. In *Qualcomm*, the FTC accused Qualcomm of monopolization by utilizing a "no license, no chips" policy with OEMs, in which Qualcomm allegedly would not sell critical chipsets for which it was a monopolist unless OEMs capitulated to certain royalty rates it requested for standard essential patents. After the lower court found for the FTC, the Ninth Circuit criticized the lower court for "fail[ing] to distinguish between Qualcomm's licensing practices (which primarily impacted OEMs) and its practices relating to modem chip sales (the relevant antitrust market). This was, no doubt, intentional: the district court characterized Qualcomm's various business practices as "interrelated" and mutually reinforcing, and it described their anticompetitive effects as "compounding" and "cyclical." But even if Qualcomm's practices are interrelated, actual or alleged harms to customers and consumers outside the relevant markets are beyond the scope of antitrust law." In other words, only relevant markets in which there is an alleged monopoly can be used to determine if there has been an anticompetitive effect resulting from the accused conduct.

While the term monopoly has both legal and economic implications, as a practical matter the determination is whether a firm's conduct has the capacity to have market-wide consequences for a given consumer population. The Supreme Court's opinion in *AmEx* found that the lower court had not correctly defined the relevant market to include both consumers of credit cards and the merchants who were accepting them, and thus the trial court's analysis of competitive effects was misguided. This confirms that the market in which alleged monopolist has power is an important step in any inquiry.

Recent commentary and current U.S. agency enforcement efforts are suggesting that monopoly power should be defined as something broader than that the ability to control price or exclude competition. By referencing allegedly critical data that may not have a direct price component, courts will likely have to find a suitable and reliable proxy for these standard inquiries to fit the realities of present day technology and other markets. The upcoming updated merger guidelines will likely provide insight as to how the government is considering other non-price factors to be relevant to an analysis of market power.

See also

Collective dominance, Dominance (notion), Essential facility, Exclusive right (Art. 106 TFEU), Market power, Oligopoly, Relevant market, Single branding

N

NE BIS IN IDEM

Enrique VERGARA VIAL
Court for the Defense of Free Competition

■ Definition

The *ne bis in idem* is a criminal law principle under which a person cannot be punished and be subject to several procedures twice for the same facts. In simple terms, the principle pursues to avoid double prosecutions and double punishments.

■ Commentary

As we can see, there are two dimensions of *ne bis in idem*. On the one hand, we can find the so-called objective or substantive phase, that is to say, a person cannot be judged and punished twice for the same facts. On the other hand, there is the procedural aspect, which pursues to prevent that a person be subject to several procedures for the same facts.

In competition law, this principle may be applicable when criminal and administrative prosecution coexist (cartel cases). In fact, most of the authorities in charge of the prosecution, investigation and punishment of anticompetitive conducts are administrative bodies not criminal prosecutors or judges, except in cartel cases where there is some intersection between both institutions. The problem arises from the fact that administrative and criminal law authorities may prosecute, investigate and, eventually, decide upon the same facts or the same persons. Therefore, as an expression of administrative law proceedings, the principles of criminal law – being one of them the ne bis in idem – must be applied for establishing these responsibilities.

Nonetheless, it is very infrequent to find cases where prosecutions are considered unlawful on the basis of this principle. Anyway, this dilemma may also be resolved in two ways. The first one is practical: in most cartel cases the economic agent that is condemned differs in the administrative and criminal procedures and thus, the condition called "unity of offender", required by the *ne bis in idem* principle, is not fulfilled. Indeed, generally the corporate entity (undertaking) is fined by the competition authority (administrative procedure), whereas the executives or representatives involved in the cartel are accused by criminal prosecutors. The second approach is appealing to the principle under which different liabilities can coexist for the same fact if the assertion of those liabilities responds to different objectives or legal interests protected. In other words, if the punitive ground is different, there is not a violation of *ne bis in idem*. However, this distinction is not totally clear in the prosecution of cartels. In fact, while competition law pursues the protection of the competitive process and consumer welfare, criminal law pursues a similar objective, that is, to protect the economic order, in a broader sense.

Bibliography

Caravaca, C., "Derecho Antitrust Europeo", Tomo I, Parte General, *La Competencia*, Ed. Colex, 2009, p. 620-621

De La Cuesta, J. L., "Les compétences criminelles concurrentes nationales et internationales et le principe 'ne bis in idem'". Rapport général. Dans *Revue internationale de droit pénal* 2002/3-4 (Vol. 73), pages 673 à 705

Gomez, F., "El non bis in idem en el derecho administrativo sancionador. Revisión de sus alcances en la jurisprudencia administrativa" *Revista de Derecho de la Pontificia Universidad Católica de Valparaíso*, XLIX, 2017, p. 101-13

Mañalich, J. P., "El principio ne bis in idem frente a la superposición del derecho penal y el derecho administrativo sancionatorio". *Polít. crim.* Vol. 9, N° 18 (Diciembre 2014), Art. 8, pp. 543-563

See also

Judicial review, Effective judicial protection, Criminal sanctions, Cartel, ECHR

N

NEGATIVE CLEARANCE

Athanassios SKOURTIS
Nottingham Law School

Stefanos MERIKAS
University of Reading

■ Definition

Historically, a negative clearance was one way undertakings could avoid the application of EU competition rules. A negative clearance, as determined by the provision of Art. 2 Reg. 17/62, was an official European Commission decision issued upon application submitted to the Commission by undertakings or associations of undertakings, to the effect that, on the basis of the facts available to the Commission, there were no grounds under Art. 101 or 102 TFEU (pursuant to current numbering) for the practice in question to be considered an infringement of EU competition rules.

■ Commentary

The option to apply for negative clearance was available to interested undertakings from 1962, when Council Regulation 17/62/EEC: First Regulation implementing Articles 85 and 86 [subsequently numbered Articles 81 and 82 respectively and from 2009 onwards Articles 101 and 102] of the Treaty was enacted, until the coming into force of Reg. 1/2003. The European Commission had sole competence to issue a decision. In the course of the procedure, before the decision was adopted, interested undertakings had the right to be heard on the matters to which the Commission had taken objection pursuant to Reg. 17/62. Being one of the types of official Commission decisions, negative clearance decisions had to be published to series L of the Official Journal.

The procedure for negative clearance consisted of three stages. At the initial stage, concerned undertakings applied to the Commission notifying their agreement and seeking to obtain negative clearance. If the Commission intended to grant a negative clearance according to Art. 19(3) Reg. 17/62, it published a summary of the relevant application and invited all interested third parties to submit their comments and observations within a fixed time limit which could not be shorter than a month. Publication of the summary took into consideration the protection of the business secrets of the undertakings involved, and this principle also applied to the published decision if applicable.

Negative clearance resembled individual exemptions and shared common characteristics. First, the Commission alone had the exclusive powers to enforce Art. 101(3) by granting an individual exemption or issuing a negative clearance. Both were types of formal decisions publishable in the Official Journal. Second, forms A/B prescribed by Regulation 3385/94 were used not only for applications for formal decisions of exemptions, but for negative clearance as well. Nonetheless, two characteristics differentiated negative clearances from individual exemptions. First, an individual exemption was granted when an agreement or a concerted practice was caught by paragraph 1 of Art. 101 TFEU but satisfied the cumulative criteria of paragraph 3. A negative clearance meant that the practice did not come within the ambit of paragraph 1 in the first place and therefore did not infringe competition rules. Second, although individual exemptions were issued in cases involving Art.101, a negative clearance, at least theoretically, could be issued for Art. 102 cases.

Whilst negative clearance decisions were useful and of assistance to the parties seeking them, they nevertheless did not provide complete certainty for two reasons. First, the issuance of a negative clearance decision did not preclude the Commission from holding at a later point in time that the conduct could be held to violate competition rules in the event of alteration of circumstances. An example of a subsequent change of circumstances could lie in the discrepancy between the notified agreement which may have been granted negative clearance and its actual implementation, such as in case IV/28.748 – AEG-Telefunken. Second, it was well established that the workload of the Commission was one of the main reasons why the notification system was abolished. It is nevertheless necessary to specify that negative clearance decisions constituted only a small percentage of the overall number of formal decisions adopted annually by the Commission. The Commission's aim was to use negative clearance to serve as a roadmap to undertakings on whether their business practices in significant cases amounted to an infringement of competition rules in order to clarify the key features of competition rules.

It could be argued that a negative clearance was not applied by the Commission as a tool to delineate competition rules. Only a couple of negative clearances were issued annually. The explanation for this was twofold: on the one hand, concerned undertakings would choose to avoid this time consuming non-binding option and would instead seek a comfort letter, which would have similar results and the same level of protection to a negative clearance; on the other hand, the Commission's view was that soft law such as notices and guidelines served the same purpose but avoided the time consuming process of negative clearance.

On 1 May 2004 Council Regulation 1/2003, the so-called "Modernisation Regulation", replaced its predecessor, Council Regulation 17/62, bringing about a substantial overhaul of the framework governing the application of EU competition law rules. The Commission's exclusive competence to grant individual exemptions through ex-post monitoring or "negative clearances" was abandoned and the "self-assessment era" of continuous compliance obligation of undertakings was introduced. More than twenty years later, one could argue that the change shifted enforcement in the right direction, and that the limited overall number of negative clearance decisions over the forty-two years it was available reflects the limited extent of its functionality.

Bibliography

Ehlermann, C. D., The Modernization of EC Antitrust Policy. A Legal and Cultural Revolution, *EUI Working Paper, Robert Schuman Centre for Advanced Studies*, RSC No. 2000/17 (2000)

McCullough J. T. IV, Continuing Search for Greater Certainty: Suggestions for Improving U.S. and EEC Antitrust Clearance Procedures, 6 *Nw. J. Int'l L. & Bus.* 803 (1984-1985)

Montag, F., The Case for a Reform of Regulation 17/62: Problems and Possible Solutions from a Practitioner's Point of View, *Fordham International Law Review* 1998, Vol. 22 Issue 3, p. 819-852

Whish, R., & Sufrin, B. (1993). *Whish: Competition Law* 3rd Edition. Butterworths

Commission Regulation (EC) No 3385/94 of 21 December 1994 on the form, content and other details of applications and notifications provided for in Council Regulation No 17, OJ L 377, 31.12.1994, p. 28–58

EEC Council: Regulation No 17: First Regulation implementing Articles 85 and 86 of the Treaty, OJ 13, 21.2.1962, p. 204–211

82/267/EEC: Commission Decision of 6 January 1982 relating to a proceeding under Article 85 of the EEC Treaty (IV/28.748 – AEG-Telefunken) OJ L 117, 30.4.1982, p. 15–28

See also

Agreement (notion)

N

NETWORK EFFECT

Christopher YOO
University of Pennsylvania Law School

■ Definition

A network effect exists when the value of a product or service increases as the number of other people using the same product or service increases. It has emerged as one of the primary sources of value in the digital economy and the leading theoretical basis for the competition law cases against large tech firms, beginning with the cases against Microsoft.

■ Commentary

Although the concept was invoked as far back as the Annual Reports AT&T issued for 1901 and 1908, the modern study of network effects began with Jeffrey Rohlfs's 1974 article in the *Bell Journal of Economics and Management Science*. The literature expanded greatly during the 1980s after a seminal series of publications by Joseph Farrell and Garth Saloner and Michael Katz and Carl Shapiro. It is also deeply linked to the literature on path dependence pioneered by W. Brian Arthur and Paul David. Networks effects are often theoretically grounded in Metcalfe's Law, which recognizes that the number of pairwise connections increases quadratically with the number of nodes. Network effects also formed the basis for the government's landmark cases against Microsoft resolved by the courts in 1998 and 2001.

Network effects may be direct or indirect. Direct network effects arise when the value is determined by the number of people using the same product. Indirect effects arise when two or more groups of people use the network to exchange value.

Network effects are often said to give rise to two types of market failure. First, the fact that a consumer's decision to join a network increases the value of those who are already part of the network is sometimes said to create a positive network externality that creates benefits for other consumers who have already joined the network that the adopter does not internalize. This can cause consumers faced with a choice between two network technologies to postpone choosing between them until other consumers have acted, which can cause a delay in the adoption of a superior technology until the market reaches critical mass. Even after a technology has passed this tipping point, the inability to internalize all of the benefits of an adoption decision may lead marginal consumers to decline to adopt the technology even when doing so would be socially beneficially.

Second, networks that have passed this tipping point can become locked in even after a superior alternative has emerged until adoption of that new technology passes its own tipping point. The greater value enjoyed by the largest network can theoretically become a source of market power. In the limit, network effects can create a winner-take-all dynamic in which the higher value associated with the largest firm allows it to capture the entire market. These concerns have led some to invoke antitrust or regulation to impose some form of mandatory interoperability.

A close reading of this literature reveals that these inferences are too simplistic. The seminal analysis by Joseph Farrell and Garth Saloner points out that the decision to adopt a new network technology creates two separate externalities pushing in opposite directions. At the same time an adoption decision increases the value of the new network, it simultaneously decreases the value of the old network that is being abandoned. This means that whether a market with network effects will exhibit *excess friction* or *excess momentum* depends on which of these externalities dominates and cannot be determined a priori.

The theoretical ambiguity has prompted the creation of an empirical literature attempting to identify examples of markets subject to network effects. Prominent examples of supposedly inferior technologies that have become locked in include the QWERTY keyboard and the VHS videotape format, among others. A vibrant literature has arisen challenging each of these examples.

In addition, a number of common market features can solve many of these supposed problems associated with network effects. For example, giving discounts to newcomers can allow them to internalize the benefits that they provide to existing members of a network. Heterogeneity of preferences can also eliminate any tendency for everyone to join a single network, as those confronted with a choice between being part of a larger network built around a disfavoured standard may choose to join a smaller network built around the standard they prefer more. In addition, markets undergoing rapid growth are not susceptible to lock in, because the number of customers currently controlled by any one actor matters little when there are even more new customers joining the market for whose business other actors can compete. For similar reasons, a large customer can unstick a tipped market by allowing a new technology to achieve critical mass. Network effects also lead to market failure only under certain market structures: in markets with at least three nondominant players, the equilibrium outcome is for all of the networks to interconnect. Furthermore, as Jeffrey Rohlfs has noted, diminishing marginal returns to scale are inevitable. Lastly, the existence of gateways between networks or technologies that allow consumers to join multiple networks simultaneously (known as *multihoming*) eliminate the winner-take-all aspects of network effects by allowing consumers to be members of multiple networks simultaneously.

One particularly interesting application of network effects arises when a network consists of two different types of actors and the value to one type of actor is determined by the number of the other type. This can create two-sided markets, in which the price charged to one type of actor is determined by the revenue generated by the other type. In extreme cases, it can be both profitable and efficient for one side to subsidize the other side. Economic theory concludes that proper analyses of two-sided markets require taking both sides of the market into account, a conclusion that the Supreme Court of the U.S. adopted in *Ohio v. American Express Co.*

The complexity of the issues surrounding network effects reveals the truth of the *Microsoft* court's observation that "[s]imply invoking the phrase "network effects" without pointing to more evidence does not suffice to carry plaintiffs' burden." A proper determination of the impact of network effects requires an empirical evaluation of each particular circumstance in which problems are asserted to arise.

Bibliography

Farrell, J. and Saloner, G., "Installed Base and Compatibility: Innovation, Product Preannouncements, and Predation" (1986) 76 *American Economic Review* 940

Katz, M. L. and Shapiro, C., "Product Introduction with Network Externalities" (1992) 40 *Journal of Industrial Economics* 55

Metcalfe, B., "Metcalfe's Law: A Network Becomes More Valuable as It Reaches More Users" (1995) *InfoWorld*, Oct. 2, p. 53

Rohlfs, J. H., *Bandwagon Effects in High-Technology Industries* (MIT Press 2001)

Yoo, C. S., "Network Effects in Action", in Douglas H. Ginsburg and Joshua D. Wright (eds.), *GAI Report on the Digital Economy* 159–191 (Global Antitrust Institute 2020)

See also

Economies of scale, Ecosystem failures, Online platforms, Tipping

N

NON-COMPETE OBLIGATION

Geoffrey MANNE
International Center for Law & Economics

■ Definition

A non-compete obligation is a contractual promise by one party to refrain from conducting business of a similar nature to that of the other party. Non-compete obligations are encountered principally in contracts for the sale of a business and contracts of employment. In general (although with localized exceptions, e.g., regarding employment in the State of California), such agreements are enforceable provided they are reasonable and limited in scope, territory, and duration. In addition, employment non-compete obligations typically must be supported by adequate consideration. Non-compete obligations may be anticompetitive if they amount to a naked division of territory or customers among the parties or are collusively deployed among competing firms (i.e., "no poach agreements").

■ Commentary

A non-compete obligation is a contractual promise by one party to refrain from conducting business of a similar nature to that of the other party. Non-compete obligations are encountered in many circumstances, but principally in contracts for the sale of a business or contracts of employment.

The U.S. Supreme Court in United States v. Addyston Pipe & Steel Co. concluded that it would be impossible for the Sherman Act to prohibit every restraint of trade because virtually every contract, including those that include non-compete obligations, involves some restraint of trade. Following common law precedent, the court ruled that reasonable restraints were permitted, but only if the restraint was ancillary to the main purpose of the agreement and necessary to protect the enjoyment of legitimate fruits of the contract or protect from the danger of unjust use of those fruits by the other party.

Business-to-business non-compete obligations

In the United States, courts are generally more deferential to non-compete obligations associated with the sale of a business than those regarding employment. In particular, courts note that a non-compete obligation reduces the risk that the seller will diminish the goodwill acquired by the buyer by re-entering the market to compete against the buyer. See, e.g., Shearson v. Schmertzler ("[C]ovenants not to compete incident to the sale of a business are more liberally enforced "on the premise that a buyer of a business should be permitted to restrict his seller's freedom of trade so as to prevent the latter from recapturing and utilizing, by his competition, the good will of the very business which he transferred for value.'").

A non-compete obligation is generally enforceable provided it is reasonable and limited as to time and territory. See United States v. Addyston Pipe & Steel Co. (a "reasonable" contract in restraint of trade was enforceable provided that it was made for "good and adequate consideration" and imposed a restraint which was "particular" rather than "general").

Despite the deference generally accorded to non-compete obligations associated with the sale of a business, courts have scrutinized contracts that amount to a de facto market allocation agreement. In In re Wholesale Grocery Prods. Antitrust Litig., an asset-exchange agreement between two grocery wholesalers included an agreement not to compete for each other's former customers. The court opined that, while the agreement pertained only to former customers, there was evidence that the wholesalers may have had a tacit agreement not to compete for current and future customers ("[T]he written non-compete agreement applied to former customers, theoretically permitting the wholesalers to compete for the existing and future customers. But this is not a contracts case in which the scope of the alleged anticompetitive agreement is cabined by the four corners of the written document. [Plaintiff] could use all manner of extrinsic evidence to persuade a jury that what the wholesalers actually agreed to was a naked division of territory and customers.").

In Europe, article 1(d) of EU Regulation 330/2010 (Vertical Block Exemption Regulation, VBER) defines a "non-compete obligation" as any contractual "obligation causing the buyer not to manufacture, purchase, sell or resell goods or services which compete with the contract goods or services." This also includes any agreement in which 80% or more of a buyer's total purchases in the relevant market are provided by the contracted supplier or its designee.

VBER Article 2(1) exempts non-compete obligations from TFEU Article 101(1) prohibitions if several conditions are fulfilled. In particular, the market share of each buyer and seller cannot exceed 30% (Article 3) and the duration of the non-compete obligation cannot exceed five years or be indefinite (Article 5(1)(a)). A non-compete obligation that is tacitly renewable beyond a period of five years is deemed to have an indefinite duration (Article 5(1)).

Post-term non-compete obligations are generally excluded from the exemption provided by the VBER (Article 5(1)(b)) unless the restriction is indispensable to protect seller know-how and narrowly limited both geographically and temporally (Article 5(2)). Nor do the VBER exemptions generally apply to vertical agreements entered into by competing companies, except in the case of non-reciprocal vertical agreements (Article 2(4)).

Employee non-compete obligations

While employment non-compete obligations may appear to be clear restraints of trade that impair an employee's job mobility, they can also serve legitimate economic interests, such as the protection of trade secrets, customer lists, and business methods specific to a particular employer. Unique qualifications of an employee also have been held to constitute legitimate interest for protection by covenants not to compete. See United States v. Addyston Pipe & Steel Co. (employers "would naturally be reluctant" to train employees unless the employees were "able to bind themselves not to set up a rival business in the vicinity after learning the details and secrets of the business of their employers"); Ticor Title Ins. Co. v. Cohen ("Unique services have been found in various categories of employment where the services are dependent on an employee's special talents; such categories include musicians, professional athletes, actors and the like."). But see Vencor, Inc. v. Webb (refusing to enforce a non-compete where the information to which the employee had access was confidential but "not unique or proprietary").

U.S. courts that have evaluated the legality of employment non-compete clauses under the Sherman Act have applied the rule of reason, rather than subjecting the agreements to per se treatment. See Bradford v. N.Y. Times Co. ("Although employee restraints have been known to the common law since the 15th century, their evolving history illustrates that rule of reason considerations continue to apply… There is therefore not enough here to justify… classify[ing] such a restraint as a per se violation of the Sherman Act."). Courts will thus generally enforce employment non-compete clauses under the antitrust laws when it is part of a valid agreement supported by consideration, is reasonable in time and scope, and serves to protect the employer's legitimate economic interests.

Employment non-compete obligations are more likely to violate U.S. antitrust law if they stem from naked horizontal agreements among competitors to allocate employees. For example, "no-poach agreements" among competitors have been subject to intense scrutiny from U.S. competition agencies and from private plaintiffs. The most well-known instance is United States. v. Adobe Systems Inc., et al., in which the U.S. Department of Justice alleged several tech firms had violated Section 1 of the Sherman Act by entering into a series of bilateral "No Cold Call" agreements to prevent recruitment of their employees. The case was settled before trial. This was followed by a class action lawsuit, In re High-Tech Employee Antitrust Litigation, filed on behalf of the firms' employees, who claimed that their wages were suppressed due to the alleged agreements. This case also settled.

In Europe, Article 15 of the European Charter of Fundamental Rights establishes a freedom to choose an occupation and the right to engage in work, which may be infringed by a non-compete obligation that is arbitrary or excessive. Even so, employment non-compete obligations are not specifically governed by EU competition law.

Bibliography

Bishara, N. D. and Starr, E., The Incomplete Noncompete Picture, 20 *Lewis & Clark L. Rev.* 497 (2016)

Kobayashi, B. H., Antitrust, Non-Competition, and No-Poach Agreements in Digital Industries, in *Global Antitrust Institute Report on the Digital Economy* (Joshua D. Wright & Douglas H. Ginsburg eds., 2020) 707

McAdams, J. M., Non-Compete Agreements: A Review of the Literature, *Federal Trade Commission Working Paper* (Dec. 31, 2019)

Antitrust Section of the American Bar Association, Comments Submitted in Connection with the Federal Trade Commission Workshop on "Non-Competes in the Workplace: Examining Antitrust and Consumer Protection Issues", FTC Comment ID FTC-2019-0093-0329 (Apr. 24, 2020)

OECD, Competition Concerns in Labour Markets – Background Note by the Secretariat (Jun. 5, 2019)

See also

Ancillary restraints, Rule of reason

N

NOTIFICATION

Dario DA SILVA OLIVEIRA NETO
Global Antitrust Institute (GAI)

■ Definition

The legal rule (mandatory or voluntary) that determines that a merger or an acquisition (hereinafter "merger") must be submitted, prior to or after the consummation of the merger, to a public authority's review. In most jurisdictions, notification is not required of all mergers but only those that fulfill the notification thresholds prescribed by law. The most common notification criteria include turnover, assets, market share, and transaction value. The act of notifying a merger usually involves the submission of a completed form to the Authority, together with certain documents related to the merger, and paying a filing fee in the jurisdictions where is required.

■ Commentary

Merger notification is one of the most important tools of a merger control regime. It enables the competition authority (or any other authority responsible for Antitrust) to review if a transaction would have any adverse effects on competition.

The Hart-Scott-Rodino Antitrust Improvements Act of 1976 (the HSR Act) amended the Clayton Act of 1914, establishing a mandatory premerger notification regime for all mergers that meet certain statutory thresholds. Premerger notifications must be submitted to both U.S. Federal Antitrust Agencies, the Federal Trade Commission (FTC) and the Antitrust Division of the Department of Justice (DOJ). In addition to the mandatory notification, the HSR Act prohibits the merging parties from consummating the deal during a waiting period of 30 days from the filling of the completed notification, unless the agencies grant "early termination" for the transaction. Should the agencies issue a so-called "Second Request" for additional documents and information needed to evaluate the transaction, the parties are further prohibited from consummating the deal until 30 days following substantial compliance with the request. The statute allows the agencies to analyze the merger before the integration of assets by the merging firms, solving the problem known as “unscrambling the eggs”. Before 1976, it sometimes occurred that mergers were often consummated before agency analysis could be completed – hindering the probability of a divestiture or other remedy. The HSR Act ended this problem for merges subject to notification, since consummation of the transaction before termination of the waiting period is considered an infringement – the gun jumping violation. The failure to notify a transaction that reaches the notification thresholds is usually defined as procedural gun jumping.

In the U.S., the notification criteria are based on two main tests: “Size of Transaction” and “Size of Person”. While the first is grounded in the value of the transaction, the second deals with the size of the parties’ assets or annual sales. One important feature of the U.S. notification thresholds is that the values specified for the Size of Transaction and the Size of Person Tests are adjusted every year to reflect the change (upward or downward) in GDP. Notification of a merger is completed by filing the HSR Form (which, on June 27, 2023, FTC and DOJ proposed to change the Notification form, substantially increasing the notification requirements) and by paying a filing fee based on transaction size (also adjusted annually).

In the European Union, the merger control regime is established by the European Union Merger Regulation (EUMR, Council Regulation (EC) No 139/2004). The EU also employs a mandatory premerger notification regime for certain changes in the control of business entities (“undertakings”) that have a Community dimension according to Article 1(2) and 1(3). Differently from the U.S., the EUMR established a notification criterion based on turnover rather than value of the transaction or assets.

One important aspect of the EU merger control system is that Article 21 establishes a one-stop rule for mergers with Community dimension. Hence, if a merger satisfies the thresholds of Article 1 (2) or 1 (3), the merging parties do not need to notify the merger to the National Competition Authorities (competition agencies of the EU Member States). However, the contrary may not be true. A merger that does not fulfill the notification thresholds of the EUMR may fulfill the thresholds established by the Member States’ merger rules. Besides that, EUMR rules permit case referrals to or from the Commission if special conditions are satisfied. The notification of a merger is completed with the filling of Form CO and there is no filing fee in the EU.

The two jurisdictions briefly analyzed above have, as internationally classified by the Antitrust literature, an ex-ante and mandatory merger control regime. A system that prohibits consummation before clearance by the authorities is classified as an ex-ante system – in contrast to an ex-post system, which permits consummation prior to clearance or approval by the Competition Authority. In an ex-post regime, the parties may have to break up the company through divestiture to reestablish that status quo ante situation if the Antitrust Authority rejects the merger. In Brazil, the most important modification by the current Brazilian Competition Law (Federal Law No. 12.529 from 2011), if compared to the old Brazilian Competition Law (Federal Law No. 8.884 from 1994), is the change from an ex-post to an ex-ante merger control regime.

The notification system can also be classified as mandatory or voluntary. A mandatory notification system requires the parties to submit the merger to the Competition Authority's analysis if the thresholds are fulfilled, while a voluntary system does not have this same rule. Instead, in a voluntary system, it is the parties' decision whether to notify the merger to the Authority (normally based on a risk assessment). The UK and Australia are examples of countries that employ a voluntary notification regime.

Jurisdictions usually adopt one or more of the following notification criteria: turnover, assets, market share, or transaction value. According to the OECD (2021), the turnover criterion is by far the most used one (51 out of 54 countries). The same survey found that the mandatory and pre-merger regimes (46 of 54), the existence of filling fees (35 of 54), the use of a simplified merger regime for cases with low likelihood of competition concerns (41 of 54), and the use of two-phase approach to merger analysis (47 of 54) are the most common practices adopted by countries.

Big international mergers may require notification in several dozen countries. For example, the Bayer and Monsanto merger was notified in 29 countries and the Microsoft-Activision merger was notified in 16 countries. This high number of notifications and analyses creates the potential for international disputes. There is a tradeoff between achieving convergent decisions by the different Competition Authorities and respecting the sovereignty of the countries to produce their own merger decisions.

One hot topic in terms of notification is the possible weakness of the turnover notification criterion, the most commonly used criterion worldwide, to establish competence in merger cases involving digital markets. Since start-up digital companies normally must create and build big data and user bases before starting to monetize their business, these companies, in their initial years, may have substantial market value, but with limited turnover. In countries where notification is based solely on turnover, the Competition Authority commonly lacks jurisdiction to analyze the case because the acquired company has a low or zero value on turnover, although the transaction value could be very substantial. In order to address this jurisdictional problem, Germany and Austria , for example, amended their competition laws to add a subsidiary transaction value threshold. This is an attempt to require notification for mergers that would not have met turnover criteria.

Bibliography

AXINN, S. M.; FOGG, B. V.; STOLL, N. R.; PRAGER, B. J., NISA, J. P. Acquisitions under the Hart-Scott-Rodino Antitrust Improvements *Act. Law Journal Press*, 3rd Edition, 2010

GAVIL, A. I.; KOVACI, W. E.; BAKER, J. B.; WRIGHT, J. D. *Antitrust Law in Perspective: cases, concepts and problems in competition policy*. West Academic Publishing, 4th Edition, 2022, ch 5

WHISH, R. and BAILEY, D., *Competition Law*, Oxford University Press, 9th Edition, 2018, ch 21 and 22

ABA Section of Antitrust Law. The Merger Review Process: a step-by-step guide to Federal Merger Review. ABA Publishing. 3rd Edition, 2006

OECD (Organisation for Economic Co-operation and Development). Global Merger Control. OEDC Competition Trends, Volume II. 2021

See also

Form CO (EU), Gun jumping, Hart-Scott-Rodino Filing (US), Merger control procedure

N

NULLITY

Andreas STEPHAN
University of East Anglia

Definition

Under laws that prohibit agreements between competing businesses that restrict competition, the obligations created by a contract are automatically null and void, to the extent that the contract (or part of the contract) constitutes a breach of competition law. Nullity will not generally occur where the agreement benefits from a defence or exemption, such as the conditions laid down in Article 101(3) TFEU, or in relation to terms that are severable from the prohibited conduct.

Commentary

The principle of nullity prevents parties from enforcing a contract that amounts to a breach of competition law. This is consistent with the general principle of contract law that when a contract cannot be performed without engaging in something illegal, it is void. In many jurisdictions, nullity is explicitly set out in the prohibition of anti-competitive agreements and applies regardless of whether the competition authority has delivered a prior decision relating to that agreement. For example, Article 101(2) TFEU states, "Any agreements or decisions prohibited pursuant to this Article shall be automatically void". In the EU case of *Courage v Crehan*, the Court of Justice of the European Union established that any contracting party can invoke nullity in relation to a contract that breaches Article 101(1) TFEU. Nullity brought about by a breach of competition law does not necessarily render the contract void in its entirety. In *Société Technique Minière* it was held that nullity affects only the clauses in the agreement that are prohibited. The contract will only therefore be void as a whole if the remaining terms cannot be executed without the prohibited clauses, or if the two sets of terms are not severable.

This is generally the approach in competition law regimes around the world.

The principle of severance is considered important because it means that an illegality affecting only a small or secondary obligation within the contract, does not result in the uncertainty and cost of complete contractual voidness. In Australia, severability is set out in the Competition and Consumer Act, s.4L, which *requires* remaining terms to be valid and enforceable to the greatest extent possible. This goes further than the common law severance principles that would otherwise apply and which simply *permit* severance.

How the principle of severability works in practice varies considerably between jurisdictions and is a question for national courts within the EU. Courts must decide, not only whether any parts of the agreement can be saved, but also any effect on closely related contracts that do not fall foul of competition law but whose function relies on the prohibited clauses (e.g. contracts between a business and its customers). Lamadrid de Pablo and L Oritz Blanco's study *Nullity/Voidness*, found substantial divergence in how national courts within the EU implement severability, due to diverging approaches and the discretion enjoyed by the courts.

For example, UK courts tend to be quite permissive of severing remaining terms. In the case of *Passmore v Morland* (1999) it was held that nullity of contract under competition law was a transient principle, meaning that where a contract breached competition law when it was created but no longer does so (in this case, because a new landlord's operations had no effect on trade within the EU), the contract was held to be valid and enforceable. Contrast this with the German Civil Code, s.139, which provides for a presumption of complete nullity unless the parties would have agreed to the contract without the prohibited clauses. The courts in the Netherlands also take a conservative approach when the anticompetitive clauses are core to the overall agreement.

When it comes to contracts that are related to the anti-competitive conduct but do not amount to an infringement in themselves, courts will generally not interfere without good justification. In U.S. Antitrust Law, for example, there is a reluctance to allow businesses to use the Sherman Act as a shield against contractual obligations, where they cannot be said to enforce the violation of the Act itself. Thus, in *Kelly v Kosuga* (1959), a completed purchase for 50 cars of onions between two parties to a cartel was not ruled null and void, despite the transaction being an instrument of a conspiracy to suppress their supply and drive-up prices. The court's rationale for this approach was that the transaction amounted to "a completed sale of onions at a fair price", that the contract itself did not breach the Sherman Act and that nullifying the agreement could encourage opportunistic behaviour that could allow parties to get "other people's property for nothing when they purport to be buying it".

Nullity can have a similar effect in relation to abuse of dominance for example in rendering null and void terms that have an exclusionary effect, or in relation to an essential facility. However, it is not explicitly set out in prohibitions like Article 102 TFEU and its effect is not generally automatic, but will arise as part of a decision of the competition authority or court. In the UK case of *English Welsh & Scottish Railway Ltd v E.On* (2007) the English High Court ruled that the rules of severability for Article 101 applied equally to Article 102 TFEU for these purposes.

Bibliography

BENOHR, I., "The Impact of Competition Law on the Private Law Concepts of Nullity and Damages" in H-W Micklitz and C Sieburgh (eds.) *Primary EU Law and Private Law Concepts* (Intersentia: Cambridge 2018, pp. 133-164

CAUFFMAN, C., "Nullity/Voidness: An Overview of EU and National case Law" (2019) *e-Competitions Special Issue: Nullity / Voidness*

LEONHARD, C., "Illegal Agreements and the Lesser Evil Principle" (2015) 64 *Catholic University Law Review* 4, pp. 833-866

DE PABLO, A.-L. and BLANCO, L. O., "Nullity/Voidness: An Overview of EU and National Case Law" *e-Competitions*

SOBEL, L. S., "Antitrust Defenses to Contract Actions: A Question of Policy Priorities", (1971) 16 *Antitrust Bulletin* 455

See also

Anticompetitive practices, Abuse of dominant position

OLIGOPOLY

Evgeny KHOKHLOV
Antitrust Advisory

Definition

An oligopoly (from Ancient Greek "few" and "I sell, or I trade") is a market structure in which market power (ability to raise prices above the competitive level and/or restrict competition otherwise) belongs to several undertakings. An oligopoly is one of the models of imperfect competition. In an oligopoly, undertakings can act as a "collective subject" being independent of each other. However, this happens not as a result of collusion but because of a peculiar market structure (primarily as a result of informational transparency). It is the market structure that allows oligopolists to foresee each other's behaviour and repeat it (e.g. by simultaneously raising prices).

Commentary

In economics, an oligopoly is described as a special market structure and a subtype of the model of imperfect competition. It includes a small number of operating undertakings. Although they are institutionally independent of each other, they can act in a coordinated manner without directly colluding with each other. As a rule, undertakings in oligopolistic markets are about the same size (i.e. they have comparable market shares), and none of them has market power individually.

The key difference between an oligopoly and a monopoly is that active competition is possible in the case of an oligopoly. However, such competition is usually qualitative rather than price related. Price competition, as a rule, is not an oligopoly's feature, because it is not profitable for any of the oligopolists to decrease their prices. If one decreases the price, the other(-s) would also have to do the same in order not to lose volumes. This would in turn result in the overall reduction in prices and profits for all the market participants.

Since undertakings' market shares are comparable, the oligopolists' most rational behaviour is to repeat each other's behaviour. As soon as one starts deviating from the "mainstream" behaviour (e.g. by decreasing prices), the other oligopolist(-s) could apply collective "punishment" measures (in particular, by decreasing prices to even a more significant degree, thus poaching customers). Ultimately, the deviant behaviour benefits none of the oligopolists, which is the reason why they tend to act on each other's expected behaviour.

But coordination between oligopolists might not be perfect as different undertakings have different cost structures and production and sales efficiency. Besides, non-price (qualitative) competition adds to the difference. Therefore, oligopolists, in addition to qualitative competition, may also try to compete by "hidden" price solutions (e.g. by granting discounts to certain customers or by providing special commercial terms that can be quantified, such as a deferred payment or additional service support). However, such deviations would most likely be relatively insignificant, and the oligopolists' prices would still differ from the competitive price level.

An oligopoly is not equal to a highly concentrated market (i.e. a market in which several undertakings have significant market shares). For an oligopoly structure to be present, informational transparency is of fundamental importance, that is a relatively free access to information regarding the competitors' sales volumes and/or prices. In the absence of informational transparency, undertakings will likely not be able to predict each other's behaviour. Accordingly, there will be no mechanism allowing them to act in a coordinated manner, in which case coordination would only be possible through plain collusion.

In addition, facilitating practices could be used allowing oligopolists to increase informational transparency in the market. These include regular exchange of information (e.g. through customers or trade associations), a price leader model (when an undertaking raises prices and others follow that), and product standardisation. These practices could also be applied in non-oligopolistic markets, but their presence (in addition to a high market concentration) will likely indicate the presence of an oligopoly.

Other parameters indicating market power are also relevant, i.e. absence of product substitutes, significant barriers to entry, absence of large buyers, etc. In fact, these are the same factors that apply to cases where market power belongs to a single undertaking (i.e. individual dominance).

Most economic models of oligopoly applied in practice are based on two basic models: the Bertrand model and the Cournot model. Their fundamental difference is that the Bertrand model shows that companies in an oligopolistic market may lack market power, while market participants have market power in the Cournot model even in the absence of collusion (but it is less significant than in case of a monopoly).

In order to model the undertakings' behaviour in oligopolistic markets, game theory is also used. It allows predicting possible outcomes of the market participants' interaction on the assumption of their rationality, primarily regarding pricing strategics.

Finally, products offered by different undertakings may in reality differ significantly both in quality and in terms of consumer preferences, which also affects the undertakings' market power. Therefore, other economic models could be used to analyse oligopoly (e.g. the Hotelling product differentiation model).

While the concept of an oligopoly is described in economics as a special interaction of the market participants, competition law uses various legal concepts to describe an oligopoly. The notion of oligopolistic interaction could be applied in the context of an abuse of a dominant position, collusion and merger control. An oligopoly could also be identified as part the market analysis outside the context of a specific infringement.

Collective dominance is the closest legal concept to the notion of an oligopoly. It exists in competition law of the EU and a number of other jurisdictions, but it has no direct equivalent in U.S. antitrust law. The criteria of collective dominance essentially match that of the oligopolistic market. This concept is applied both for the purposes of ex-post control (i.e. abuse of a dominant position) and ex-ante control (i.e. merger control). The modern definitions of collective dominance were formulated in the judgements in *Compagnie Maritime Belge* (for the purposes of the abuse of a dominant position) and *Airtours* (for the purposes of merger control).
In addition to collective dominance, oligopolistic interaction could be embodied in the concepts describing collusion between competitors. In the case of an oligopoly, explicit collusion is unlikely because undertakings are already able to coordinate their behaviour by virtue of the market structure. Therefore, an oligopoly is typically viewed as tacit collusion. This is what violations in oligopolistic markets are usually considered to be in U.S. antitrust law (see, e.g., *United States v. American Airlines* 743 F.2d 1114 (5th Cir. 1984)).

Concerted actions (a concept existing in EU competition law but absent in U.S. antitrust law) could hardly be deemed a manifestation of an oligopoly. From the economic point of view, it does not matter how the oligopolists' parallel behaviour is qualified: as collective dominance or concerted actions. But from the legal point of view, concerted actions cannot take place to the extent the parallelism is explained by rational behaviour. This is the case of an oligopoly, which allows undertakings to act in a coordinated manner by virtue of the market structure. EU competition law drew exactly this divide between an oligopoly and concerted actions in the *Woodpulp* case.

With respect to merger control, the concept of "coordinated effects" is often used in addition to collective dominance. In EU competition law, these are defined as follows: changing the nature of competition in such a way that firms that previously were not coordinating their behaviour, are now significantly more likely to coordinate and raise prices or otherwise harm effective competition (rf. Guidelines on the assessment of horizontal mergers under the Council Regulation on the control of concentrations between undertakings (2004/C 31/03), para 22).

Bibliography

BISHOP, S. and WALKER, M., *The Economics of EC Competition Law: Concepts, Application and Measurement*, Sweet& Maxwell, 2010

WHISH, R. and BAILEY, D., *Competition Law* (10th ed.), Oxford University Press, 2021

Guidelines on the assessment of horizontal mergers under the Council Regulation on the control of concentrations between undertakings (2004/C 31/03)

OECD Policy Roundtable on Oligopoly (1999)

See also

Bertrand (Nash) equilibrium, Cournot (Nash) equilibrium, Collective dominance, Dominance (notion), Market power, Monopoly, Price leadership, Single branding

O

ONLINE PLATFORMS

Bahadýr BALKÝ
ACTECON

■ Definition

An online platform is a digital service connecting two or more interrelated sets of customers on different sides of the market; these sets of customers may be businesses and/or individuals and the platform may creating commercial and/or social networking opportunities. Online platforms can bring about numerous efficiencies due to their unprecedented ability to grow and expand, facilitate trade and create new opportunities to the benefit of the economic activities of businesses and the individuals that use them. Nevertheless, online platforms may also pose certain challenges to the regulators and policy makers, including the competition authorities in various jurisdictions; this has led to numerous legal developments throughout the world. As far as competition is concerned, some online platforms may come to occupy a particularly dominant role in relation to a range of services, giving rise to competition concerns: they may have a "*gatekeeper*" role which is suggested by European jurisdictions to necessitate close scrutiny by competition authorities, or even the adoption of bespoke regulatory rules. On the other hand, firms operating in multi-sided markets must often consider the effects of their pricing and output decisions to both sets of customers, as well as the interrelationship among the customers on each side. These complex dynamics mean that conduct that might appear anticompetitive when only one set of customers is considered may in fact be entirely consistent with and actually promote – healthy competition when competition on both sides is considered.

■ Commentary

Online platforms are a key part of the business environment that has emerged with the development of the internet, information technology and e-commerce. They cover various activities, for example marketplaces, app stores, price comparison websites, search engines, booking platforms, social media, accommodation-sharing platforms etc. Several models of online platform services may be distinguished, such as business-to-consumer (B2C), consumer-to-consumer (C2C), business-to-business (B2B), business to government (B2G), and consumer to government (C2G). The most common ones are B2C and C2C. They mediate the realization of transactions by bringing together the sellers/service providers and consumers registered on their online media in relation to a wide range of activities, such as social networking, online search engines, online marketplaces, software application stores, price comparison, cloud computing services, advertising, video-sharing platform service, etc.

Online platforms are a major driver of innovation. They challenge traditional market players to improve and innovate. While creating a range of efficiencies and benefits to the economy, such as consumer choice, competitiveness of industry, consumer welfare, access to information, online platforms are also a target of allegations in terms of competition restrictions and unfair trade practices, the imposition of unfair terms and conditions, refusals of market access, the unfair promotion of their own services to the disadvantage of other suppliers, parity clauses, as well as lack of transparency in relation to their fees and search results. Such allegations may be particularly serious in the case of "*gatekeepers*" that achieve market power in their spheres of operation. According to the EU Digital Markets Act of 2022, gatekeepers are online platforms that have a significant impact on the market, operate one or more important gateways to customers and (are expected to) enjoy an established and solid position in their operations; qualitative and/or quantitative criteria determine which gatekeepers are to be "designated" under the DMA and subjected to ex ante rules. Other jurisdictions are exploring similar rules but how the EU will implement the DMA bears the upmost importance for these jurisdictions; frontrunning the main regulatory initiative by these jurisdictions would bear the risk of creating additional and unnecessary regulatory burdens.

Yet the regulators and competition policy enforcers must not forget that the overall landscape is defined by disruptive innovation. Thanks to the current ecosystem a good idea combined with a small investment and a small team (thanks to diminishing economies of scale and thus reduced cost) can easily find its way into the market and grow massively in terms of both sides of its platform. By the same token, regulators failing to understand the competitive dynamics that impact all sides of a multi-sided firm, raises the risk of enforcers and courts condemning pro-competitive conduct that benefits consumers, potentially stifling innovation.

The regulatory authorities of various jurisdictions have been working on assessing public and private interests and ensuring better compliance with the regulatory standards to respond effectively to the challenges posed by online platforms and to ensure fair competition and respect for fundamental right online for all. For instance, under the Digital Markets Act, once an online platform is designated as a gatekeeper, it is subjected to various prohibitions and obligations, which vary and are often based on practices such as MFN clauses, tying, self-preferencing, interoperability restrictions, etc. There is also a new information requirement for gatekeepers. They are obliged to inform the European Commission of any contemplated concentrations with a party that is also providing core platform services or any other services in the digital sector. Additionally, the gatekeeper is required to report within six months after its designation as a gatekeeper on the measures taken to implement the obligations imposed by the Digital Markets Act. It is noteworthy that the DMA does not take into account the differences between gatekeepers, their business models and their unique characteristics and all obligations are automatically levied over all gatekeepers' Core Platform Services.

As far as competition law is concerned, market definition is complex in the case of online platforms markets; the interrelationship between the different sides of the market needs to be taken into account. Multi sided firms create value by bringing market participants together. They help reduce practical barriers and transaction costs. But because many multi-sided firms work by facilitating interactions among diverse customer sets, the demand for the services that such a firm offers to each of its "sides" depends on the demand for the services it offers to its other sides. This interrelated demand has significant consequences for antitrust analysis. It may lead multi-sided firms to set prices in ways that bear little resemblance to pricing by single-sided firms. And it means that seemingly small changes in demand on any side of the market could be amplified by corresponding changes on the other sides. The fact that services/products may be "free" on one side of the market is an additional problem, that cannot be addressed through the application of the "SSNIP" test that looks at markets through the prism of increases in price. Platforms are constrained by the availability of substitute products, but they may also face the additional constraint of interrelated demand from multiple sets of customers. One effect of such interrelated demand is to limit a multi-sided firm's ability to unilaterally raise prices or reduce output. If the tests of market definition and market power fail to account for these additional constraints, they may cause multi-sided firms to appear to enjoy power over price and output when they are, in fact, engaged in vigorous competition. U.S. and EU courts have confirmed that market definitions should take into account the dynamic nature of digital platform markets.

As regards the merger control involving online platforms, there are suggestions to amend the notification thresholds by providing jurisdiction over certain mergers based, for example, on the value of the acquisition, or the market shares of the undertakings involved or the characteristics of the acquirer. In cases where the turnover thresholds are not met, the competition authority could be given power to look at the economic value of the transaction as an indicator of its importance for the parties and of high market potential of the target company, if the price of the transaction is high enough. While the German and Austrian merger control regimes have introduced value of transaction thresholds in addition to the turnover threshold to achieve similar goals, in Turkey, for instance, the turnover thresholds were amended in 2022 and an exception was added for transactions involving acquisitions of "*technology undertakings*", i.e. undertakings or related assets operating in the fields of digital platforms, software and gaming software, financial technologies, biotechnology, pharmacology, agrochemicals and health technology. In the acquisitions of technology undertakings that are active or have R&D activities in the Turkish geographic market or that provide services to customers in Turkey, threshold that is needed to be satisfied by the Target is not applicable. It is in any event safe to assume that online platforms fall into the category of "*technology undertakings*" as the definition itself contains the "*digital platforms*". The aim is to catch start-up acquisitions of undertakings that engage in the development of valuable products but do not yet have significant turnover.

Bibliography

Ballon, P. and Van Heesvelde, E., "ICT platforms and regulatory concerns in Europe" [2011] *Telecommunications Policy*, Vol. 35 No.8, pp. 702–708

Krämer, J. (ed.), *Digital markets and Online Platforms: New Perspectives on Regulation and Competition Law, Center on Regulation in Europe*

Toksoy F., Balki, B. and Stakheyeva, H., *Merger Control in the EU and Turkey: A Comparative Guide*, Second edition, 2022, Wolters Kluwer, Book – International Competition Law Series

An Introduction to Online Platforms and Their Role in the Digital Transformation, 2019, OECD Publishing, Paris

Regulation (EU) 2022/1925 of the European Parliament and of the Council of 14 September 2022 on contestable and fair markets in the digital sector and amending Directives (EU) 2019/1937 and (EU) 2020/1828 (Digital Markets Act), PE/17/2022/REV/1, OJ L 265, 12.10.2022, p. 1–66

See also

Economies of scale, Ecosystem failures, Fintech, Network effect, Self-preference, Tipping

PARALLEL IMPORTS (PARALLEL TRADE)

Laurent CENATIEMPO
European Brands Association – AIM

■ Definition

In the EU context, parallel trade refers to the practice of importing genuine products from a low-price Member State and exporting them to a high-price Member State through channels other than those established by the manufacturer of the products, usually by independent parallel importers/exporters seeking arbitrage profits. While parallel trade can promote EU market integration and benefit consumers by increasing competition and lowering prices, it can also undermine manufacturers' incentives to develop distribution channels in both high-price and low-price Member States, and to innovate and invest in research and development, as well as distributors' own incentives. Outside of the EU, several jurisdictions, such as Australia, New Zealand and South Korea, treat parallel trade as a means of promoting competition and consumer choice and have established legal frameworks that allow for parallel imports under certain conditions.

■ Commentary

Articles 101(1) and 102 TFEU respectively prohibit concerted and abusive practices that restrict competition and "may affect trade between Member States", making restrictions on cross-border trade within the EU prima facie unlawful, regardless of their effects. "Agreements aimed at partitioning national markets according to national borders or making the interpenetration of national markets more difficult, in particular those aimed at preventing or restricting parallel exports" must be considered restrictive by object because they "frustrate the Treaty's objective of achieving the integration of national markets through the establishment of a single market" (Consten, p. 340; Sot. Lélos, § 65; GlaxoSmithKline, § 61).

According to Article 4 of the Vertical Block Exemption Regulation (VBER) 2022/720, vertical agreements having as their object "the restriction of the territory into which [the distributor(s)] may actively or passively sell the contract goods or services" are presumed to restrict competition and are therefore excluded from the VBER safe harbour unless one of the exceptions listed in paragraphs 202-244 of the European Commission (EC) 2022 Guidelines on Vertical Restraints applies. In such a case, a manufacturer may legitimately restrict parallel trade, for example to protect the integrity of a selective or exclusive distribution system against unauthorised distributors free-riding on its investments or those of its authorised resellers.

While unilateral measures restricting parallel trade may infringe Article 102 TFEU if implemented by a dominant undertaking, they are not agreements and therefore cannot infringe Article 101(1) TFEU. However, the threshold for finding an "agreement" or "concerted practice" under this provision is rather low.

In its Bayer judgment subsequently upheld by the Court of Justice (ECJ), the General Court (formerly the Court of First Instance (CFI)) found that there was no "agreement" between Bayer and its distributors. After recalling that a manufacturer's unilateral decision "escapes the prohibition" of Article 101(1) TFEU (§ 66), the CFI held that the existence of an agreement can only be established where undertakings "have expressed their joint intention to conduct themselves on the market in a specific way" (§ 67), regardless of "the form in which [their concurrence of wills] is manifested (...) so long as it constitutes the faithful expression of the parties' intention" (§ 69). The CFI explained that "measures adopted or imposed in an apparently unilateral manner by a manufacturer in the context of his continuing relations with his distributors [may be] regarded as constituting an agreement" if they are not "genuinely unilateral" and "receive at least the tacit acquiescence of those dealers" (§§ 70-71).

Since the wholesalers did not acquiesce in Bayer's policy of restricting exports in view of their "conduct demonstrating a firm and persistent intention to react against a policy that was fundamentally contrary to their interests" (§ 129), the CFI concluded that "provided he does so without abusing a dominant position, and there is no concurrence of wills between him and his wholesalers, a manufacturer may adopt the supply policy which he considers necessary, even if, by the very nature of its aim, for example, to hinder parallel imports, the implementation of that policy may entail restrictions on competition and affect trade between Member States" (§ 176).

This important judgment highlights the risks for manufacturers of unilaterally announcing supply reductions in order to prevent parallel trade, as the mere acquiescence of their distributors to such a unilateral announcement (by reducing orders or ceasing parallel trade) may be sufficient to constitute an agreement or concerted practice. The CFI noted that tacit acquiescence may be inferred from coercive measures such as "systematic monitoring of the actual final destination" of the product(s) whose distribution is restricted, implementing "a policy of threats and sanctions against exporting wholesalers" or making the supply of the product(s) "conditional on compliance with the alleged export ban" (§ 109).

Balancing the benefits and drawbacks of parallel trade, Articles 101(3) and 102 TFEU recognise that restrictions on parallel trade resulting from concerted practices or abusive exclusionary conduct, while in principle illegal, may be compensated or justified in certain circumstances. However, in practice, European and national courts have rarely accepted them. In any event, the assessment of objective justifications and efficiencies that may outweigh anti-competitive effects must be based on the specific circumstances of each case, including the nature of the agreement and/or practice, the relevant market(s), and the competitive environment.

The EC 2004 Guidelines on criteria for exemption under Article 101(3) TFEU from the prohibition under Article 101(1) TFEU state that four cumulative conditions must be fulfilled: (i) the claimed efficiencies must generate benefits, whether direct or indirect, economic or non-economic, (ii) of which consumers receive a fair share, (iii) without imposing restrictions that are not indispensable to obtain those benefits, and (iv) without eliminating competition in respect of a substantial part of the products whose distribution is restricted. To meet these conditions, the claims must, inter alia, be based on "objective factors" (§§ 18 and 31), be "substantiated so that they can be verified" (§§ 51 and 55) and have "a sufficient causal link" to the restrictive agreement (§§ 53-54).

Paragraph 181 of the EC 2022 Guidelines on Vertical Restraints adds that "an undertaking may demonstrate pro-competitive effects" by showing that "efficiencies are likely and (...) likely to result from including the hardcore restriction in the agreement" and by "demonstrating that the other conditions of Article 101(3) of the Treaty are fulfilled."

In GlaxoSmithKline, the ECJ clarified that efficiency arguments under Article 101(3) TFEU must also be properly assessed in cases involving hardcore restrictions of parallel trade. To determine whether a restrictive agreement may "contribute to improving the production or distribution of goods or to promoting technical or economic progress (...) with appreciable objective advantages of such a kind as to compensate for the resulting disadvantages for competition" (§§ 92 and 102; see also Consten pp. 348-349), it is necessary to ascertain "whether, in the light of the factual arguments and the evidence provided, it seems more likely [than not] that the agreement in question must make it possible to obtain appreciable advantages" (§§ 94 and 102). The required "prospective analysis" (§ 105) must aim at balancing the negative effects of the restriction on parallel trade and intra-brand competition on consumer choice against its positive effects on R&D funding and inter-brand competition.

Pursuant to paragraphs 28-31 of the EC 2009 Guidance on its enforcement priorities in applying Article 102 TFEU, a dominant undertaking may be able to legitimise a restriction on parallel trade by providing an "objective justification" for the need for the restriction or by satisfying four conditions (similar to those in Article 101(3) TFEU) to demonstrate "substantial efficiencies which outweigh any anti-competitive effects on consumers".

In Sot. Lelos, the ECJ held that a dominant company's refusal to meet orders in full in order to restrict parallel trade is not per se abusive. Although a dominant undertaking may not refuse to fulfil ordinary orders from an existing customer simply because some of those orders are likely to be resold in another EU Member State, it is entitled "to counter in a reasonable and proportionate way the threat to its own commercial interests potentially posed by" orders of "significant quantities of products that are essentially destined for parallel export" (§ 71). The ECJ clarified that whether orders "are out of the ordinary in terms of quantity" (§ 76) depends on "the size of those orders in relation to the requirements of the market (…) and the previous business relations between [the supplier] and the wholesalers" (§ 77).

Bibliography

Ibáñez Colomo, P., "Territorial restrictions in EU competition law: from Consten-Grundig to Ping and Pay-TV" (February 10, 2021)

Petit, N., "The Economics of Parallel Trade – Iconoclast Views on a Dogma of EU Competition Law" (August 19, 2010)

Stothers, C., *Parallel Trade in Europe: Intellectual Property, Competition and Regulatory Law* Hart Publishing (2007)

See also

Concerted practices, Consumer protection, Effect on trade between Member States, Exhaustion

P

PASSING-ON

Till SCHREIBER, Carsten KRÜGER, Martin SEEGERS
CDC Cartel Damage Claims

Definition

Passing on, a concept well-accepted in economic theory, refers to the situation where an injured party passes on its actual loss resulting from an antitrust infringement ("overcharge") to the next level of the supply chain, by increasing the price of its products or services sold to its own customers at the downstream market-level ("indirect purchasers"). Therefore, pass-on can serve as a "sword", where an indirect purchaser alleges that the overcharge has caused it harm because of upstream pass-on. It can also be used as a "shield", where an infringer invokes as a defence that downstream pass-on by the claimant had reduced the actual harm the latter has suffered.

Commentary

Any person harmed by an antitrust infringement (e.g. price fixing cartel, abuse of a dominant market position) may claim full compensation for its harm. Regarding passing on, three legal and economical elements of that harm are relevant: firstly, actual loss occurred due to an overcharge resulting from the price difference between the actual transaction price and the "but-for" price in the absence of the infringement; secondly, the passing-on effect by which the claimant may have, fully or partially, passed on this overcharge to its own customers, by adjusting its own prices to the cost increase; thirdly, the compensation for lost profits which the direct purchaser may claim if, due to the price increase to its own customers, it has suffered a reduction in sales volumes ("volume effect").

The compensatory principle requires that direct as well as indirect purchasers are put in the situation they would have been in but for the infringement, to avoid both over- and under-compensation, and to ensure that the infringer does not pay damages for the same wrong twice. It is therefore appropriate that the indirect purchaser to whom the overcharge is passed on is entitled to claim compensation from the infringer ("sword" scenario), while the infringer may rely on passing-on to object to a damage claim brought by the direct or any other upstream purchaser ("shield" scenario). The burden of proof lies with the party that relies on the passing-on argument, i.e. the claimant in the "sword" scenario and the defendant in the "shield" scenario.

According to economic theory, the existence and the scope of passing-on effects, i.e. the associated price and volume effects, are determined by a large range of factors, including: the nature and intensity of competition in the markets where the direct or indirect purchasers are active (e.g., imperfect competition and differentiated goods are supposed to result in lower pass-on rates for industrywide overcharges), the nature of input costs subject to an overcharge (whether these costs are fixed or variable, whether the overcharge is industrywide or firm-specific), the nature of the product demand that the direct or indirect purchasers face (especially the link between the demand and price level), other elements, such as price adjustment costs, the proportion of a firm's costs affected by the overcharge, buyer power, vertical integration of direct and indirect purchasers, price regulation or the timing of the pricing decisions undertaken at the various levels of the supply chain. The impact of these factors is case-specific, and the results may be mixed. In addition, in the legal assessment of damages, any benefit taken into account must bear some relation to the damage suffered by the claimant as a result of the infringement (causation).

Due to the difficulty of determining pass-on effects, the U.S. Supreme Court rejected the passing-on defence and allowed the claimant to use the full overcharge as the basis of its claim (Hanover Shoe). It further held that only direct purchasers may sue for damages under federal law to prevent the risk of multiple liability for the antitrust infringement (Illinois Brick). Both rulings are highly controversial. They also compete with many state antitrust laws in the U.S. that allow indirect, as well as direct, purchasers to recover damages.

For an infringement of competition law in the EU, in contrast, both the standing of indirect purchasers and the passing-on defence is recognised, at least since the implementation of Directive 2014/104/EU (Chapter IV), in some member states even before (e.g., for Germany, the pre-Brexit UK and the Netherlands, see *ORWI*, *Sainsbury's* and *TenneT v ABB*). The scope of the passing-on defence is generally interpreted narrowly. The infringer bears the burden to plead and prove the existence and extent of the passing-on of overcharges. It cannot rely on any legal presumption in this regard. It remains open yet whether the infringer even must show the non-existence of the volume effect for a successful passing-on defence, or whether that effect is exclusively to be substantiated by the claimant. The infringer bearing the burden of proof of the passing-on defence has a right to disclosure of evidence, also against third parties. In case of a damage action by an indirect purchaser the Directive provides a (rebuttable) presumption of the existence of pass-on to the benefit of the indirect purchaser. Further, the courts are empowered to estimate all passing-on effects, on prices and volumes, in both shield and sword scenarios, based on the information reasonably available.

The non-binding COM Guidelines provide courts and other stakeholders in damages actions for infringements of EU competition law with practical guidance on how to estimate passing-on effects. They describe the theoretical concepts underlying passing-on and set out the factors that can have an impact on it. It also becomes clear that there are different approaches and methods to quantify the overcharge (e.g. by comparator-based methods), the scope of passing-on related price effects (either directly by employing comparator-based methods or indirectly by estimating the rate at which the increase in the affected input cost should have been passed on) and the volume effect. The COM Guidelines also help to determine the sources of relevant (qualitative and quantitative) evidence, whether a disclosure request is proportionate, and assessing the statements of the parties on passing-on and any economic expert opinion that may be presented to the court.

The courts in Europe also consider that the legal concept of damage is distinct from its economic concept. In particular, the passing-on defence has been refused in cases where there is no risk of multiple liability, but rather a risk of absence of liability, because the next market level is characterised by a large number of customers with small-value and dispersed claims. In such a scenario there is little interest in bringing a damage action, so that the infringers would de facto retain the fruits of their illegal activity. This is especially relevant in case of damages of end-consumers. In the interest of an effective competition law, the goal to avoid absence of liability of infringers shall outweigh the potential overcompensation of the claimant.

If, however, several purchasers along the supply chain bring parallel actions for damages relating to the same overcharge, the Directive provides that the courts shall consider, in the interest of compensation and consistency between judgments, all appropriate procedural and substantive means available under EU or national law (e.g. joinder of claims, estimation, staying of proceedings). Direct and indirect purchasers may also assign their respective damages claims to a single plaintiff, for example, so that any passing-on among them does not concern the enforcement of the bundled claims against the infringer but is left to internal agreements between those purchasers.

Bibliography

CARO DE SOUSA, P., 'EU and national approaches to passing on and causation in competition damages cases: A doctrine in search of balance' (2018) 55 *Common Market Law Review* 1751

Centre for European Policy Studies, Erasmus University Rotterdam and Luis Guido Carlo, Study on making antitrust damages actions more effective in the EU: welfare impact and potential scenarios (2007), Part II, Chapter 5

Communication from the European Commission, Guidelines for national courts on how to estimate the share of overcharge which was passed on to the indirect purchaser ('COM Guidelines'), OJ [2019] C267/4

RBB Economics and Cuartrecasas, Gonçalves Pereira, Study on the Passing-on of Overcharges (2016)

U.S. Antitrust Modernization Commission, Report and Recommendations (2007), Chapter III.B

See also

Collective redress (class action), Economic analysis, Damages, Private enforcement

P

PASSIVE SALES

Ercüment ERDEM
Erdem & Erdem

Definition

Passive sales are sales made to customers who have not been actively targeted by a seller. Any advertising activity, promotions made through media, online sales, use of search engine optimization tools and techniques intended to improve the visibility or ranking of the online store in search engine results, are considered to be passive sales – provided that they enable potential customers to reach the seller. Unless it is requested by the customers, sending e-mails and catalogues to a customer group or territory exclusively allocated to a particular reseller is not considered passive sales. The restriction on passive sales is considered to be a hard-core restriction under European Union (EU) competition law and many other systems of competition law and therefore, preventing passive sales cannot benefit from the protective cloak of the block exemption regime related to distribution systems.

Commentary

The exemption regime provided under Article 4 of the Commission Regulation (EU) 2022/720 distinguishes between restrictions of active sales and restrictions of passive sales by the supplier in the context of distribution systems. In general, in an exclusive distribution system, the supplier is allowed to prohibit active sales of the selected distributors. This includes approaching customers by direct mail, visits or advertisements that specifically target customers in a region or customer group assigned to another distributor. On the other hand, in any type of distribution system (e.g. exclusive or selective distribution) the supplier is generally banned from prohibiting a distributor's passive sales. These are sales made in response to unsolicited orders, including delivery of the products. This distinction between active sales and passive sales is important especially considering the application of the block exemption regime in the online context. For instance, online advertisements specifically addressed to certain customers are considered active sales, whereas general advertising such as sponsored content on the website of a local or national newspaper that may be accessed by any visitor to that website, or the use of price comparison services with generic and non-country-specific domain names, are considered passive sales.

The reason that passive sales are considered a hardcore restriction within the EU regime is associated with the strong and long-standing objection to the compartmentalization of the single market. In contrast, United States antitrust law does not make a distinction between active and passive sales in the context of vertical restraints. Since passive sales are not considered by object restrictions in United States antitrust law, restrictions on online sales call for a case-specific analysis.

Conversely, the European Commission, in its newly introduced Guidelines on Vertical Restraints (Vertical Guidelines) expressed that "*to prevent market partitioning, passive sales into [exclusively allocated] territories or customer groups may not be restricted.*" The idea is that passive sales enhance stronger price competition and a wider choice of products for the consumer and, therefore, should not be prevented. Given that passive sales are viewed as a powerful tool to meet potential customers, online sales are generally considered as part of passive sales and in this regard restrictions on online sales are also generally seen as hardcore violations.

There are important decisions of the European Court of Justice (ECJ) and other jurisdictions as well as local competition authorities on passive sales. For instance, in 2011, the ECJ, in the Pierre Fabre case, held that absolute prohibition imposed on distributors to sell their goods online restrict competition. The ECJ classified the ban of online sales as a by object restriction, unless the qualifications of the product can be presented as an objective justification.

On the other hand, the position as per the prohibition of online marketplaces was not clear until the ECJ's *Coty* decision of 2017 that relates to a restriction preventing luxury products being sold on third-party online platforms. In *Coty*, the ECJ ruled that although it is possible to impose a platform ban for luxury products under certain conditions, such ban cannot be applicable to all branded products and cannot go beyond what is necessary in order to preserve the luxury image of those goods. The *Coty* decision states that all restrictions with regard to online sales are not considered as a restriction of passive sales to end users by object and therefore, there are other factors which may justify these restrictions on condition that it is laid down uniformly and not applied in a discriminatory fashion, and that it is proportionate in the light of the objective pursued.

In line with the *Coty* decision, in the *Guess* decision the European Commission ruled that Guess imposed different anti-competitive restrictions on its authorized distributors. These restrictions included not using the Guess brand names and trademarks for the purposes of online search advertising as well as not selling online without first obtaining a specific authorization from Guess. The European Commission concluded that the ban was not justified under EU trademark law or by Guess' legitimate objective to protect its brand image. Therefore, the European Commission ruled that the restrictions imposed by Guess restricted competition by object and reduced the ability of authorized retailers to advertise and sell the contract products to customers.

Additionally, there are a variety of decisions where the Turkish Competition Board (Board) has condemned undertakings due to restrictions of passive sales. The Board's attitude towards passive sales prohibitions was relatively lenient compared to other vertical restraints until the developments in online sales. With the increase in online sales, the Board adopted a stricter approach towards the restriction of passive sales compared to the European Commission. Despite being inspired by the EU's approach, Turkish competition law envisaged an absolute ban for the restriction of passive sales while the EU has adopted a more permissive approach towards the ban of sales on online marketplaces.

The Board's recent *BSH* decision is noteworthy as it indicates that the Board does not exempt practices that entirely restrict the sales of dealers through online platforms. The decision relates to a negative clearance and individual exemption application made by a manufacturer of household appliances, namely BSH, for its vertical agreements with authorized resellers, including an absolute ban on sales through online marketplaces. The Board rejected the application and held that the agreement cannot benefit from the block exemption regime. The decision clearly demonstrates that the Board's approach differs from European Commission's approach as projected in the *Coty* decision and the European Commission's new Vertical Block Exemption Regulation entered into force in 2022, which confirm that the ban of sales made by authorized dealers over e-commerce platforms in selective distribution systems can meet the exemption conditions. There are two main reasons why the Board distinguished BSH's application from the *Coty* decision. Firstly, the Board determined that the EU approach set forth in *Coty* could only be applied to luxury products, not the sort of household appliances manufactured by BSH. Secondly, the significance of marketplaces in Turkey is high among consumers' online shopping choices. For these reasons, the Board decided to adopt a strict position. Nonetheless, the Board's approach may vary according to sector.

Bibliography

BRENNING-LOUKO, M., GRUIN, A. PEEPERKORN, L. and VIERTIÖN K., *Vertical Agreements: New Competition Rules for the Next Decade* (2nd edn, Competition Policy Newsletter 2010)

WHISH, R. and BAILEY, D., *Competition Law* (7th Edition, Oxford University Press 2012), p. 640

European Commission, *Guidelines on Vertical Restraints* (Commission Notice 2022/C 248/01, 30.06.2022), p. 212

OECD, *Policy Roundtables on Vertical Restraints for On-line Sales* (2013) p.25

Turkish Competition Authority, Block Exemption Communiqué on Vertical Agreements (Communiqué No. 2002/2) and Guidelines on Vertical Agreements

See also

Exclusive distribution, Hardcore restrictions, Selective distribution

P

PATENTS

Reiko AOKI
Japan Fair Trade Commission

Definition

A patent is a right to exclude others from using an invention for a given length of time in exchange for making the invention public. In the U.S. Patent Code, conditions for patentability are (1) patentable subject matter (technology): machine, manufactured product, composition made from two or more substances, process for manufacturing objects; (2) utility: some positive benefit to society; invention must be "enabling" and "reduced to practice" (3) novelty and non obviousness: not trivial, no prior art; not obvious to someone "trained in the art". Patent laws are country specific but patentability requirements are similar and length of protection is 20 years from the date of patent application filing in most countries. EU member countries have respective patent laws but the application and various administration process are coordinated by the European Patent Office (EPO).

Commentary

In most countries, scientific theories, laws of nature, mathematical methods, plant or animal varieties, natural substances, commercial methods, methods for medical treatment (as opposed to medical products) or computer programs are generally not patentable and often have separate laws of intellectual property. Patentable subject matter can change as technology and economies evolve. Pharmaceutical products (new chemical entities) became patentable in Japan in 1976 and in India in 1995. Some software and "business methods" were ruled patentable in the U.S. ("State Street" 1998) and the USPTO granted the "one-click" patent, an on-line transaction method, patent to Amazon.com Inc in 1999.

The goal of patent system is to promote innovation, including implementation of new technologies. Patent is an intellectual property balancing two trade-offs, 1) exclusive use of invention and public availability of the invention, and 2) short-run inefficiency from monopoly and long-run efficiency from innovation. Patent laws often state goal 1) while goal 2) is an interpretation of the law which is in line with antitrust framework. Patent does not equal monopoly or market power because it is only a right to exclude others from using the technology. Patent owner may choose not to exercise it and even if the right is exercised, extent of market power depends on availability of substitute technology or products ("Illinois", 2006). Using a patent to exclude others for purposes that do not promote innovation would be an abuse of the right. Such use would also be anticompetitive because competitive environment such as free entry is necessary for innovation and innovation process itself is competitive. Using a patent to control rivals resulting in foreclosure and other unfair competition would be violation of Sections 1 and 2 of the Sherman Act, Section 3 of the Clayton Act, and Section 5 of the Federal Trade Commission (FTC) Act. In the EU, Articles 101 and 102 of the Treaty on the Functioning of the European Union (TFEU) as well as Merger Regulation rules apply to exercising patent rights. Patent transfer or licensing are used in merger remedies to address competition concerns of innovation and future product markets ("Bayer" 2019). Licensing multiple patents of multiple owners together such as patent pools, can control price and outputs in the final product market like a cartel and are subject to antitrust laws.

In Japan, Article 21 of the Japanese Antimonopoly Act (AMA) states that "the provisions of the Act shall not apply to such act recognizable as the exercise of rights under the Copyright Act, the Patent Act, the Utility Model Act, the Design Act, or the Trademark Act." Article 10 of Intellectual Property Basic Act states that "In promoting measures for the creation, protection and exploitation of intellectual property, consideration is to be paid to secure the fair exploitation of intellectual property and public interests and to promote fair and free competition." Thus any action which may appear to be exercise of rights cannot be recognizable as "the exercise of rights" prescribed by AMA Article 21, if it deviates from or runs counter to the intent and objectives of the patent and other IPs, which is to motivate companies to actualize their creative efforts and make use of technology, i.e, promote innovation and its implementation.

The Tokyo District Court rejected Ricoh Co. Ltd's injunction request against DS Japan Inc. et al (recycling companies) for infringing ink jet printer ink cartridge patent because using patents to exclude non-genuine cartridges interfered with trade between recycling companies and final users and impeded fair competition ("Ricoh" 2021). Ricoh's exercise of patent rights thus ran counter to the intent and objectives of the patents and violated AMA Article 19 and Article 2, Paragraph 9, Item 6 and Paragraph 14 of the Designation of Unfair Trade Practices. The court cited JFTC statement (October 21, 2006) regarding investigation of Canon Inc. Canon had refused to provide IC tag information to a recycling company preventing the recycling company from recreating the laser printer toner cartridge's user interface which could be an AMA Article 19 violation. JFTC terminated the investigation after Canon provided the necessary information to the recycling company and JFTC verified that the company was producing and selling toner cartridges for Canon laser printers.

Relationship between patent and market power, and competitive effects of patent pool are more pronounced, in case of standard essential patents (SEPs). There are no substitutes for SEPs by definition implying patent equals market power. On the other hand, all SEPs for one standard are complimentary implying licensing as a bundle is procompetitive. While there is less concern for anticompetitive effect of patent pools of SEPs than other patents, market power of SEPs requires antitrust attention.

A pharmaceutical product is defined by one patent for chemical structure usually with no substitutes and thus substantial market power. In case of pharmaceuticals, competition in the innovation stage is important and patent function to promote such competition should be respected. On the other hand, competition in the product market stage between original product and generics is in price. In order for a generic manufacturer to take advantage of patent expiration, it is necessary to start before the patent expiration date. However there is no need for a licensing agreement to prepare for introduction of generics because U.S. Patent Code Section 27 provides exemption for such research by generic manufacturers for the purpose of obtaining FDA approval ("Merck" 2005). Agreements between drug manufacturer and generics would have some other motive, such as pay for delay ("Actavis" 2013). In general, non-commercial research using patented technology does not infringe. Academic research is protected by this "research exemption" but the interpretation has been narrowed when Duke University was found to infringe on a patent owned by former employee John Mandey because Duke University the research was done "in furtherance of the alleged infringer's legitimate business." Research exemptions, as well as service inventions would be relevant for mobility of researchers.

Patent related practices such as tying, grant-backs and non-assertion agreements have attracted antitrust scrutiny in the past but since there are procompetitive or innovation promoting effects, they require case by case examination. For instance, tying of two patented products can be welfare enhancing if they are complementary. A single patent could be tied to foreclose that market although incentive to do so and effectiveness is questionable. The strongest argument for this would be when patents are SEPs

("Qualcomm", 2019, 2020). Grant-backs and non-assertion can internalize investment externalities.

International coordination has a very long history, starting with the Paris

Convention (1898) that guarantees national treatment (no residency requirement) and priority rules (which determines starting of protection). 179 nations are members of the Convention as of 2022. Patent protection is valid only in the country it is granted but prior art can be from anywhere in the world. Priority rules guarantee that patent application in one country will not compromise non-obviousness and novelty in another. Patent Cooperation Treaty (PCT) was completed in 1970 making it possible to file to multiple countries simultaneously. The treaty also provides common classification technology and patents and has 157 members. Further streamlining and harmonization of filing and examination procedures was achieved among 43 signatories of Patent Law Treaty in 2000 including the European Patent Office.

Bibliography

Aoki, R. (ed.), *Topics in Economics of Intellectual Property and Innovation* (Maruzen Co., 2009)

Scotchmer, S., *Innovation and Incentives* (MIT Press, 2006), Chapter 3

Federal Trade Commission, "To Promote Innovation: The Proper Balance of Competition and Patent Law and Policy", October 2003

OECD Competition Committee, "Licensing of IP rights and competition law – Note by the EU", June 2019

OECD Competition Committee, "Licensing of IP rights and competition law – Note by the Secreteriat", June 2019

See also

FRAND, Intellectual property rights, Licensing, Pay-for-delay, Standard-Essential Patent (SEP)

P

PAY-FOR-DELAY

Noah Joshua PHILLIPS
Cravath Swaine & Moore

■ Definition

Pay-for-delay occurs when a patentee agrees to compensate a potential or alleged patent infringer to refrain from competing against the patentee for some period of time. These agreements are also called "reverse-payments", because the payments flow in the "wrong" direction, from patentee to infringer (that is, plaintiff to defendant), rather than from infringer to patentee, as is the norm. Pay-for-delay occurs most frequently, if not exclusively, in the pharmaceutical industry, when an originator of a branded drug agrees to pay a generic producer to settle or avoid litigation that may invalidate the originator's patent(s), in exchange for the generic's commitment not to compete with originator's drug for a period of time. Both EU and U.S. competition law are concerned about pay-for-delay agreements because they can allow patentees to avoid competition and maintain supracompetitive prices by sharing their monopoly rents with would-be competitors, to the detriment of consumers.

■ Commentary

European Commission

Pay-for-delay agreements can violate Article 101 of the TFEU. Most recently, in Lundbeck v. Commission (2021), the European Court of Justice (E.C.J.) held that the pay-for-delay agreements at issue constituted restrictions of competition by object under Article 101(1). These agreements between Lundbeck and four generic suppliers concerned Lundbeck's antidepressant citalopram (sold under different brand names in different member states). The generic suppliers committed not to produce or sell generic citalopram or transfer their existing marketing authorizations to any third party, and to sell all existing citalopram inventory to Lundbeck. In exchange, Lundbeck agreed to provide the generic suppliers with significant cash payments and guaranteed profits via distribution agreements, with the amounts based on the profits the generics would have earned had they entered the market. When the parties executed these agreements, Lundbeck's citalopram patent had already expired, but Lundbeck still held patents on some methods of making citalopram (i.e., process patents). The European Commission (E.C.) determined these agreements restricted competition by object and fined the parties € 146 million in June 2013. The European Union General Court (G.C.) affirmed in September 2016. The parties then appealed to the E.C.J.

In affirming the G.C.'s decision, the E.C.J. made several key points relevant to future pay-for-delay cases. First, as to whether the generics were potential competitors to Lundbeck under Article 101, it was not necessary to assess the strength and likely validity of Lundbeck's remaining patents, to prove definitively that the generics' products would not have infringed them, or to demonstrate with certainty that generics would have entered the market and succeeded. The generics' intention and ability to enter the market, and the fact that they had taken affirmative steps to do so, were sufficient. Second, as to whether the agreements were restrictions by object, that concept "must be interpreted strictly and can be applied only to some agreements". Nevertheless, by-object treatment is not only appropriate, but necessary when "it is plain from the examination of the [reverse-payment] settlement agreement concerned that the transfers of value... cannot have any explanation other than the commercial interest of both the holder of the patent at issue and the party allegedly infringing the patent not to engage in competition on the merits". Such agreements "can clearly be characterised as "restrictions by object" because they involve "competitors deliberately substitut[ing] practical cooperation between them for the risks of competition". Determining whether a particular pay-for-delay agreement fits this description requires a case-by-case assessment of whether the transfer of value from the originator to the generic was sufficiently large to incentivize the generic not to enter and compete on the merits. Turning the agreements at issue, the Court rejected Lundbeck's argument that they merely secured protection within the scope of the process patents, in part because the Court found no basis to assume that those patents were valid and would have been infringed. Consequently, the G.C.'s finding that Lundbeck's payments under these agreements completely extinguished the generics' incentives to challenge Lundbeck's patents was sufficient to establish a restriction by object.

The E.C.'s assessments of pay-for-delay agreements in other cases have been more expansive than Lundbeck. In Servier (2014) and Cephalon (2020), the E.C. found that the patent litigation settlement agreements at issue violated Article 101(1) not only by object, but by effect as well. According to the Servier decision, the E.C. conducted a by-effect analysis "for the sake of completeness". (Unlike the Lundbeck agreements, the Servier and Cephalon agreements settled active patent litigation.) The Servier decision also applied Article 102, concluding that Servier had abused its dominance in a perindopril-only product market. In Servier v. Commission (2018), the G.C. affirmed the E.C.'s by-object and by-effect determinations for all agreements except the license agreement between Servier and Krka, a generic manufacturer. The E.C. had treated that agreement as part of the reverse-payment settlement between Servier and Krka, and thus as part of a single violation of Article 101(1). But the G.C., noting that licensure may be a legitimate way to settle patent dispute, analyzed the license agreement separately and found the E.C. had met neither its by-object nor its by-effect burdens. The G.C. also rejected the E.C.'s abuse-of-dominance determination after finding the E.C.'s market definition too narrow. Servier and Cephalon are pending on appeal before the E.C.J and G.C., respectively.

United States

Pay-for-delay agreements can violate Section 1 of the Sherman Act and, in suits brought by the Federal Trade Commission (F.T.C.), the Section 5 of the F.T.C. Act (which reaches practices that violate the Sherman Act and other antitrust laws). The key pay-for-delay case in the U.S. is F.T.C. v. Actavis (2013), in which the Supreme Court held that pay-for-delay agreements that permit entry within the patent term may be subject to rule-of-reason analysis. The agreements at issue concerned Solvay's patent on Androgel. Pursuant to the process for generic entry established under U.S. law by the Hatch-Waxman Act, Actavis and Paddock alleged that Solvay's patent was invalid and not infringed by the generic testosterone gels they planned to introduce, and Solvay responded by suing both for patent infringement. (The Supreme Court's opinion details the Hatch-Waxman process.) To settle the litigation, Actavis and Paddock agreed to delay the launch of their products for approximately nine years and to help market Androgel in the meantime. In return, Solvay agreed to pay the generics hundreds of millions of dollars. The case reached the Supreme Court on appeal from the U.S. Court of Appeals for the Eleventh Circuit, which had dismissed the F.T.C.'s complaint based on the scope-of-the-patent test – i.e., antitrust generally does not condemn a pay-for-delay settlement if it does not limit competition more than the exclusionary potential of the patent. The Eleventh Circuit concluded that these settlements satisfied the test – and were thus not subject to antitrust scrutiny – because the generics' commitment not to enter the market was set to expire before Sovlay's patent. In reversing, the Supreme Court rejected the scope-of-the-patent test, explaining that it requires an assumption that the patents are valid and infringed, which is the very thing the settled litigation called into question and left unresolved. Indeed, pay-for-delay agreements can cause anticompetitive harm because they eliminate the risk of competition posed by meritorious patent disputes.

The Court also provided guidance on what the rule-of-reason analysis should consider. Although the scope-of-the-patent test is inappropriate, courts need not go to other extreme of evaluating in detail a patent's validity. Instead, courts often may infer from a large and unjustified reverse payment that the patent holder "has serious doubts about the patent's survival" and that "the payment's objective is to maintain supracompetitive prices to be shared among the patentee and the challenger rather than face what might have been a competitive market." At the same time, a reverse-payment settlement can have "offsetting or redeeming virtues" and does not raise the same antitrust concerns if it "reflects traditional settlement considerations, such as avoided litigation costs or fair value for services". Thus, factors to consider when deciding whether a reverse payment is likely anticompetitive include "its size, its scale in relation to the payor's anticipated future litigation costs, its independence from other services for which it might represent payment, and the lack of any other convincing justification." Actavis remains the controlling authority and starting point when applying U.S. antitrust law to pay-for-delay settlements.

In Impax Laboratories (2019), the F.T.C. decided its first pay-for-delay case after Actavis. Sitting as an adjudicative body, the five-member Commission unanimously held that the F.T.C.'s prosecuting attorneys had proven that the agreement violated Section 5 of the F.T.C. Act. Impax appealed to the U.S. Court of Appeals for the Fifth Circuit, which affirmed the Commission's decision, in Impax Laboratories v. F.T.C. (2021). The offending agreement involved Endo compensating generic supplier Impax to abandon its Hatch-Waxman challenge of Endo's patent and to delay launching a generic version of Endo's branded opioid Opana ER for two-and-a-half years. The court agreed with the Commission's application of "the burden-shifting analysis that courts have used in other rule of reason cases, as informed by the Supreme Court's reasoning in Actavis." At the first step, it required and found proof of "a large, unjustified payment… made in exchange for deferring entry into the market or for abandoning a patent suit, plus the existence of market power." To calculate the size of the payment, the Commission (consistent with other courts) "consider[ed] all value – cash and otherwise – that the branded drug manufacturer transfer[ed] to the generic through the settlement (including any side agreements that contemporaneous timing or other circumstances indicate should be considered part of the same transaction)." Endo's commitments that could be attributed to the reverse payment were enough to constitute a large, unjustified payment to Impax, as their value "exceeded the payor's [Endo's] anticipated saved litigation costs plus the value to be rendered under the agreement[,] and… no other clear justification present[ed] itself." The Fifth Circuit likewise found the payment large, "comparable to other cases where courts have inferred anticompetitive effect", and not otherwise justified. Both the Commission and the court also found this payment restrained trade. The required showing is not that generic competition was certain, or even probable, absent the payment, but that there was a risk or "a real threat" of such competition. Proceeding to the second step, the settlement's alleged procompetitive benefits, the Commission found that they were not adequately linked to the reverse payment to delay Imapx's entry, and that they could have been achieved without the challenged restraint. The Fifth Circuit reached no conclusion on the former finding, but determined that the latter was supported by the evidence and sufficient to conclude the court's review in the Commission's favor.

Bibliography

Barazza, S., Pay-for-Delay Agreements in the EU Pharmaceutical Industry: Patent Law and Competition Law in Light of *Lundbeck*, 1 *EPLR* 3 (2017)

Chaiehloudj, W., *Les accords de report d'entrée: Contribution à l'étude de la relation du droit de la concurrence et du droit des brevets*, Concurrences, 2019

Edlin, A., Hemphill, S., Hovenkamp, H. and Shapiro, C., The *Actavis* Inference: Theory and Practice, 67 *Rutgers U. L. Rev.* 585 (2015)

Gallasch, S., Activating *Actavis* in Europe – The Proposal of a Structured Effects-Based Analysis for Pay-for-Delay Settlements, 36 *Legal Stud.* 683 (2016)

Kobayashi, B. H., Wright, J. D., Ginsburg, D. H. and Tsai, J., *Actavis* and Multiple ANDA Entrants: Beyond the Temporary Duopoly, 29 *Antitrust* 89 (2015)

Korah, V. (ed.), *Competition Law of the European Union* § 9.04 (2nd ed., Matthew Bender & Company, Inc. 2020)

See also

Intellectual property rights, Patents, Rule of reason

P

PERIODIC PENALTY PAYMENT

Okeoghene ODUDU
University of Cambridge

■ Definition

A periodic penalty is a sum imposed to provide an incentive for undertakings to comply with a decision in a timely manner. Gleiss distinguishes periodic penalties from fines as the later are imposed to punish past violations, while the former are designed to prevent future offences (*Alfred Gleiss and Martin Hirsch Common Market Cartel Law, 3rd American ed. Bureau of National Affairs, 1981, 547-548*). The decision to be complied with may be substantive, such as to bring an infringement to an end, or procedural, such as to supply information or to submit to an investigation. A daily amount is fixed and accrues for each day that the undertaking fails to comply with the decision. The final penalty is the product of the fixed amount multiplied by the number of days of non-compliance. The periodic penalty is separate from any penalty imposed in the decision it is seeking to secure compliance with.

■ Commentary

Article 24 of Regulation 1/2003 (as did Article 16 of Regulation No 17) and Article 16 of Directive (EU) 2019/1 respectively allow the EU Commission and the competition authorities of EU member states to impose periodic penalties to re-enforce compliance with a number of their decisions. Penalties may be imposed to compel compliance with a decision to bring an infringement to an end; a decision ordering interim measures; a decision accepting binding commitments; a decision to supply complete and correct information; and a decision to submit to an inspection (*Article 24(1) of Regulation 1/2003*). Initially the maximum daily fine was in the order of $1000 USD (*Christopher Bellamy and Graham D Child Common Market Law of Competition, Sweet and Maxwell, 1973, para. 1219 and Frederick Honig Cartel Law of the European Economic Community, Butterworths, 1963, 71-73*). The maximum daily penalty has increased over time and currently stands at 5% of world-wide turnover.

As is made clear in the Commission's Antitrust Manual of Procedures from March 2012, Article 24 of the Regulation sets out a two stage process. In the first stage there is a threat to impose the penalty (*See for example Commission Decision of 19 December 2007 in Cases Comp/34.579, Comp/36.518 and Comp/38.580 MasterCard, para 774*). In the second stage the actual penalty is imposed. Ordinarily, the mere threat that the penalty will be imposed is sufficient to secure compliance with the decision. As such, reaching the second stage of the process, and taking a decision to actually impose the threatened penalty is rare. This occurred for the first time in Microsoft, when the Commission threatened to impose a periodic penalty of €1.5 million for each day that Microsoft failed to bring an infringement to an end. The infringement continued and for the period between 16 December 2005 and 20 June 2006 a fine of €280.5 was fixed (*IP/06/979: Commission imposes penalty payment of €280.5 million on Microsoft for continued non-compliance with March 2004 Decision, 12th July 2006*). The Commission took a further decision threating that if Microsoft failed to bring the infringement to an end the periodic penalty would increase to up to €2 million per day and further increase to up to €3 million per day if the infringement had not been brought to an end within six months (*MEMO/06/430: Competition: state of play on Microsoft's compliance with March 2004 Decision, 15th November 2006*). On 27 February 2008, the European Commission announced that it has imposed a penalty payment of €899 million on the basis that Microsoft had not complied with the infringement decision until 22 October 2007 (*IP/08/318, SPEECH/08/105 and MEMO/08/125*). The penalty was reviewed by the General Court and reduced from €899 million to €860 million (*Case T-167/08, Microsoft v Commission, ECLI:EU:T:2012:323*).

Periodic penalties have more often been used in response to failures to supply information and so encourage provision of information in a timely manner (*See Baccarat OJ 1991 L79/16 and Commission Decisions of 8 February 2010 in Case COMP/39.523 and 3 September 2009 in Case Comp/39.523 Slovak Telecom*). Article 15 of Regulation 139/2004 (on merger control) allows the EU Commission to impose periodic penalty payments of up to 5% of aggregate daily worldwide turnover in order to reinforce compliance with a decision under Article 11(3) to supply complete and correct information; a decision under Article 13(4) to submit to an inspection; a decision under Article 6(1)(b), Article 7(3) or Article 8(2) to comply with an obligation; and a decision under Article 8(4) or 8(5) to comply with a measure. This power has been used against undertakings that are not party to the merger transaction for failing to supply accurate information.

Bibliography

Commission's Explanatory memorandum to its proposal for Regulation 1/2003 COM (2000) 582 final

Council Regulation (EC) No 1/2003

European Commission Antitrust Manual of Procedures: Internal DG Competition working documents on procedures for the application of Articles 101 and 102 TFEU (March 2012)

See also

Fine

P

POTENTIAL COMPETITION

Paul CSISZAR
European Commission – DG COMP

■ Definition

The elimination or substantial reduction of potential competition can be as harmful as the elimination of already existing, actual competition between rivals. Agreements not only between actual competitors but also between potential competitors that restrict competition are generally prohibited by antitrust laws, and the unilateral conduct of firms with significant market power that forecloses potential rivals may also be deemed anticompetitive similarly to the foreclosure or raising costs of actual rivals. Additionally, a merger with a potential competitor, or a merger that makes potential competitors' expansion more difficult, can have anticompetitive effects similarly to mergers between direct competitors who are already active on the same market.

■ Commentary

A potential competitor, although not yet actively in the relevant market, may already exert some competitive constraint or it will likely do so in the foreseeable future, and the loss of such constraint could lead to anticompetitive effects. The question whether there is potential competition that should be preserved in a given case is often a difficult one, and it should always be examined in light of the structure of the specific market, and the economic and legal context within which it operates. (See, for example, *Case C-307/18 Generics (UK) and others v CMA (Paroxetine)*, 2020).

The loss of potential competition presupposes that the parties to an agreement or merger are at least potential competitors. The European Court of Justice stated in Paroxetine that in order to be deemed a potential competitor, the firm cannot face any insurmountable barriers to entry, it has to have real and concrete possibilities of joining the relevant market and competing with one or more of the firms already competing in that market. (*Generics (UK)* above. pp 44, 45) The perception of the established operator in a market is also among the relevant factors to consider. If another firm is perceived as a potential entrant by such an operator, then this fact in itself may, by reason that such perception exists, already give rise to competitive pressure on the operator who is established in that market. (*Generics (UK)* above, p 42).

In *Paroxetine*, the ECJ held that under Article 101(1) TFEU an originator pharmaceutical company who is the holder of a manufacturing process patent for an active ingredient that is already in the public domain, on the one hand, and the manufacturers of generic medicines who are preparing to enter the market of the medicine containing that active ingredient, on the other hand, and who are in dispute as to whether that patent is valid or whether the generic medicines concerned infringe that patent, are potential competitors for the purposes of Art 101 TFEU, provided that the generic manufacturer has in fact a firm intention and an inherent ability to enter the market and it does not face insurmountable barriers to entry. The Court further noted that the existence of the manufacturing process patent of the active ingredient cannot, as such, be regarded as an insurmountable barrier to entry, and the genuineness of the parties' patent dispute, particularly when it is the subject of court proceedings, is evidence of an already existing potential competitive relationship between them. (*Generics (U)* above, pp 46 and 52)

Similar tests for identifying potential competitors are found in the soft laws of several competition authorities. In the context of collaborations among competitors, for example, the FTC and the DOJ consider a firm a potential competitor, and consequently treat it the same as an actual competitor for the purposes of assessing collaborations among them, if there is evidence that entry by that firm is reasonably probable in the absence of the collaborative agreement in question, or that competitively significant decisions by actual competitors are constrained by concerns that anticompetitive conduct likely would induce the firm to enter.

DG Comp, in the context technology transfer agreements, considers a firm a potential competitor (and treats it as an actual competitor) if it is likely, in the absence of the technology transfer agreement, that the firm would undertake the necessary additional investments to enter the relevant market in response to a small but permanent increase in product prices. Such entry is more likely if the licensee possesses assets that can easily be used to enter the market without incurring significant sunk costs or if it has already developed plans, or otherwise started to invest, to enter the market.

In merger review, a merger with a potential competitor could be problematic if the potential competitor possesses such assets or where the merging partner is very likely to incur the necessary sunk costs to enter the market in a relatively short period of time after which this company would constrain the behaviour of the firms currently active in the market. To assess the degree of the anticompetitive effects of the merger, all potential competitors in addition to the actual competitors should be identified. For a merger with a potential competitor to have significant anti-competitive effects, two basic conditions must be fulfilled under the EC horizontal guidelines: (i) the potential competitor must already exert a significant constraining influence or there must be a significant likelihood that it would grow into an effective competitive force, and (ii) there must not be a sufficient number of other potential competitors, which could maintain sufficient competitive pressure after the merger.

The potential competition doctrine is traced back to the Clayton Act and said to be fallen on hard times in the past decades due to rigorous economic scrutiny and high evidentiary standards set by some courts. Today, however, when faced with oligopolistic markets with high barriers to entry, it is important to focus more on preserving dynamic competition through safeguarding potential competition, innovation competition and other aspects of future competition. The importance of the potential competition doctrine is also increasing as competition authorities are encouraged to scrutinize more the so-called "killer acquisitions" by big tech and pharma companies.

Bibliography

Cunningham, C., Ederer, F. and Ma, S., Killer Acquisitions, *Journal of Political Economy*, 2021

Glick, M. and Ruetschlin, C., Big Tech Acquisitions and the Potential Competition Doctrine: The Case of Facebook, Working Paper No. 104 October 2019;

Sullivan, L., Grimes, W. and Sagers, C., *The Law of Antitrust, An Integrated Handbook*, 3rd Edition, 2016

Antitrust Guidelines for Collaborations Among Competitors, issued by the Federal Trade Commission and the U.S. Department of Justice, April 2000

Big Tech Acquisitions and the Potential Competition Doctrine: The Case of Facebook Mark Glick and Catherine Ruetschlin, Working Paper No. 104 October 2019; *see also The Law of Antitrust, An Integrated Handbook*, by Sullivan, Grimes and Sagers, 3rd Edition, 2016

Guidelines on the application of Article 101 of the Treaty on the Functioning of the European Union to technology transfer agreements (2014/C 89/03), para 31

Guidelines on the assessment of horizontal mergers under the Council Regulation on the control of concentrations between undertakings (2004/C 31/03), para 58-60

Horizontal Merger Guidelines, U.S. Department of Justice and the Federal Trade Commission Issued April 2, 1992, revised April 8, 1997, Para 1.32

See also

Actual competitor, Barriers to entry, Merger, Relevant market

P

PREDATORY PRICING

Gönenç GÜRKAYNAK, O. Onur ÖZGÜMÜŞ
ELIG Gürkaynak Attorneys-at-Law

Definition

The concept of predatory pricing comes into play when a dominant undertaking deliberately reduces its prices to a loss-making level for a short-term to discipline its existing competitors or foreclose the market to new entrants with a view to strengthening or maintaining its market power later on by way of the foreclosing effect of such predation. To that end, in broad terms, predatory pricing could be defined as the setting of prices at an unreasonably low level (below a cost parameter) to induce a competitor to exit the market or to deter its entry or expansion.

Commentary

In general, the starting point of the analysis is to assess whether the dominant undertaking incurred or is incurring avoidable losses for the relevant time period (i.e. whether the conduct entails a deliberate sacrifice). For such analysis, various cost parameters (in line with the competitive landscape/characteristics of the relevant market) could be taken into account in conjunction with direct evidence (e.g. documents that show a predatory strategy), if any. If sufficient reliable data are available, the equally efficient competitor analysis could also be applied to determine whether the conduct is capable of harming consumers. In general, it is considered unlikely that predatory conduct will create efficiencies.

From EU perspective, predatory pricing falls within the scope of Article 102 of the Treaty on the Functioning of the European Union ("TFEU"). The Guidance on the Commission's enforcement priorities in applying Article 82 of the EC Treaty to abusive exclusionary conduct by dominant undertakings ("Commission's Guidelines") provides two elements for predatory pricing: (i) sacrifice and (ii) anti-competitive foreclosure. In terms of the sacrifice element, European Commission ("Commission") will assess whether by charging a lower price for its output or by expanding its output over the relevant time period, the dominant undertaking incurred or is incurring losses that could have been avoided. Average avoidable cost ("AAC") is taken into account as a starting point in determining whether sacrifice occurred and if a dominant undertaking charges a price below AAC, this is viewed in most cases as a clear indication of sacrifice. However, if the Commission establishes that an alleged conduct led to net revenues lower than could have been expected from a reasonable alternative in the short term, or in other words, that the dominant undertaking incurred a loss that could have avoided, this may also indicate predatory strategy. Accordingly, predatory intent should be proven to establish the existence of predatory conduct if the dominant undertaking sets prices higher than AAC.

In terms of anti-competitive foreclosure, the Commission will apply the equally efficient competitor analysis to determine whether the conduct is capable of harming consumers. The Commission acknowledges that, normally, only pricing below long-run average incremental cost ("LRAIC") is capable of foreclosing as efficient competitors from the market. The Commission is not required to demonstrate that competitors have exited the market in order to prove anti-competitive foreclosure. The Commission's Guidelines indicate that consumers are likely to be harmed if the dominant undertaking – after the predatory conduct comes to an end – can reasonably expect its market power to be greater than it would have been had the undertaking not engaged in that conduct in the first place. That being said, it also clarifies that this does not mean that the Commission would only intervene if the dominant undertaking would be likely to be able to increase its prices above the level existing before the conduct and proof of overall profits is not required for identifying consumer harm.

The European Court of Justice ("ECJ") assessed predatory pricing for the first time in Akzo case. According to the ECJ, prices below average variable cost ("AVC") by a dominant undertaking will be presumed abusive; while prices below average total cost ("ATC") but above AVC will be regarded as abusive if they are part of a plan to eliminate competitors. The ECJ further developed its case law in Tetra Pak II and France Télécom v Commission. In Tetra Pak II, where anti-competitive intention of Tetra Pak was particularly clear, as manifested in a series of abusive acts, the ECJ indicated that "in circumstances of the present case" it is not required to show the dominant undertaking had a "realistic chance of recouping its losses". Additionally, in France Télécom v Commission, the ECJ held that the case law of the Court did not require proving the possibility of recoupment of losses as a necessary precondition to establishing that such a pricing policy is abusive. It further noted that the Commission could still consider the possibility of recoupment a relevant factor for predatory pricing analysis.

In the U.S., a predatory pricing case may be brought under Section 2 of the Sherman Act of 1890 or the Robinson-Patman Act of 1936. While the essence of the predatory pricing claim is the same under either statute, the standard of proof differs. Sherman Act requires proof of a "dangerous probability" of monopolization, while the Robinson-Patman Act requires only a "reasonable possibility" of substantial injury to competition. One of the most important differences between the EU and U.S. approaches regarding predatory pricing is the recoupment requirement. U.S. competition law condemns prices below cost, but only where there is a showing of potential recoupment of those costs in the future. Meanwhile, the EU has a stricter test that condemns below-cost prices without a showing of potential recoupment. The U.S. Supreme Court established a new framework for predatory pricing analysis in the *Brooke* decision. First, predatory pricing required proof of below-cost pricing, second, predatory pricing required proof of recoupment. Proof of recoupment requires not only that the below-cost price exclude or discipline the predatory victim, but also proof that the predator will be able to raise prices above the competitive level sufficient to compensate the predator for its predatory investment.

Under Turkish competition law, given that Article 6 of Law No. 4054 on the Protection of Competition ("Law No. 4054") and the Turkish Competition Authority's ("Authority") Guidelines on the Assessment of Exclusionary Abusive Conduct by Dominant Undertakings ("Authority's Guidelines") are closely modelled after Article 102 of TFEU and the Commission's Guidelines, the Turkish Competition Board's ("Board") analysis in terms of predatory pricing is generally in line with the EU approach. In fact, there are numerous cases where the Board applied the test utilized in Akzo case. In its U.N. RO-RO decision, the Board based its analysis upon three elements; (i) the proof of below-cost pricing, (ii) the existence of intention of elimination and (iii) anti-competitive foreclosure. Although U.N. RO-RO's prices were below its AAC, the Board nevertheless focused on the existence of predatory intention in order to demonstrate that the only plausible explanation of the undertaking's pricing strategy was to eliminate its competitor. To that end, the Board also highlighted that U.N. RO-RO also had the possibility to recoup its losses, while indicating that this was not a precondition for finding predatory pricing.

Bibliography

BAILEY, D. and JOHN, L. E. (eds.), *Bellamy and Child: European Union Law of Competition* (8th edn, Oxford University Press 2018)

BOLTON, P., BRODLEY, J. F. and RIORDAN, M. H. (2000), Predatory Policy: Strategic Theory and Legal Policy, *The Georgetown Law Journal*, pp: 2239-2330

HAWK, B. E., (2020), *Antitrust and Competition Laws*, Juris Publishing, Inc

JONES, A. and SUFRIN, B., (2016), *EU Competition Law, Text, Cases and Materials* Oxford University Press, 6th Edition

LESLIE, C. R., (2013), Predatory Pricing And Recoupment, *Columbia Law Review*, Vol. 113, No. 7 (November 2013), pp. 1695-1771

See also

Abuse of dominant position, Excessive prices, Exclusionary practice, Resale below cost

P

PRELIMINARY RULING (ART. 267 TFEU)

José LUÍS DA CRUZ VILAÇA
Cruz Vilaça Advogados

Definition

The preliminary ruling procedure is a mechanism of cooperation between the Court of Justice and the national courts of Member States which aims to ensure the effective and uniform application of EU law. Article 267 TFEU empowers the Court of Justice to give preliminary rulings on the interpretation of EU law and on the validity of acts of the institutions and other bodies of the Union. It plays an important role in the application of competition law, thanks to the direct effect granted to Articles 101 and 102 TFEU and the power conferred on national competition authorities and national courts to apply those rules at national level.

Commentary

General considerations

The preliminary ruling mechanism is generally considered the veritable keystone of the EU legal and judicial system.

The Court of Justice has held (*van Gend & Loos*, 1963; *Costa*, 1964; *Opinion* 2/13, 2014) that the founding EU Treaties established a new legal order for the benefit of which the Member States have limited their sovereign rights.

To ensure that the specific characteristics and the autonomy of that legal order are preserved, the Treaties have established a judicial system designed to secure consistency and uniformity in the interpretation of EU law. It is for the national courts and tribunals and for the Court of Justice to ensure full application of EU law and to provide legal certainty and judicial protection for individuals under that law (*Opinion*2/13).

The preliminary reference procedure is governed by Article 267 TFEU (ex-Article 177 EEC and ex-Article 234 EC). It sets up a dialogue between the Court of Justice and the courts and tribunals of Member States, which is crucial to achieving the Treaties' objectives and ultimately to furthering the integration process.

The EU judicial system is therefore not a pure federal system as conceived in other countries such as Germany or the USA. There is no hierarchy between national courts and the Court of Justice (but rather a relation of judicial cooperation) and there are no EU courts in charge of applying EU law in the Member States.

The latter task falls to the national courts by virtue of the direct effect recognised to EU law provisions, such as Articles 101 and 102 TFEU (Article 6 of Regulation 1/2003), in cooperation with the Court of Justice. The preliminary ruling procedure is the privileged instrument of such cooperation.

To that effect, Article 267 TFEU empowers the Court of Justice to give preliminary rulings on the interpretation of EU law and on the validity of acts of the institutions, bodies, offices, and agencies of the Union. Any court or tribunal of a Member State is entitled to refer questions for preliminary ruling to the Court of Justice. However, if an issue concerning the validity or the interpretation of EU law is raised before a court or tribunal against whose decisions there is no judicial remedy under national law, that court or tribunal must bring the matter before the Court of Justice. The Court's case-law (*Foto-Frost*, 1987) has extended that obligation to any court or tribunal whenever it has doubts as to the validity of an act of the institutions: it may not make a finding of invalidity itself, but musk seek a preliminary ruling thereon from the Court of Justice.

Difficulties of application

In competition matters, Regulation 1/2003 lays down rules (Articles 3, 11-16) applicable to the relationship between Articles 101 and 102 TFEU and national competition laws, as well as to cooperation between the Commission, national authorities, and national courts.

The EU Courts case-law offers examples of doubts and difficulties that may arise in the functioning of such a complex system.

First, it is not impossible for the same situation to fall within the scope of both Community and national competition law, even if they consider restrictive practices from different points of view.

In those circumstances, the fact that a national court is dealing with a dispute under national competition law should not prevent it from making a reference to the Court on the interpretation of EU law, when it considers that a conflict between Community law and national law can arise (*Oscar Bronner*, 1998).

Secondly, as stated in recital 22 of Regulation 1/2003, in a system of parallel powers, conflicting decisions must be avoided. In this regard, the

Court of Justice held (*Delimitis*, 1991; *Masterfoods*) that national courts shall avoid taking decisions which conflict with those taken or envisaged by the Commission in the application of Articles 101 and 102 TFEU. The Court stated (*Commission v BASF*, 1994; *Masterfoods*) that acts of the EU institutions are presumed to be lawful until such time they are annulled (by the competent EU Courts, either the Court of Justice or the General Court) or withdrawn.

Consequently, when the outcome of a dispute before a national court depends on the validity of a Commission decision that has been challenged before the EU courts, it follows from the obligation of sincere cooperation under Article 4(3) TEU that the national court must stay proceedings pending final judgment in the action for annulment, unless it considers that a question to the Court of Justice on the validity of the Commission decision is warranted.

Thirdly, a similar (but somehow more complex) situation may happen within the field of State aid, when both the Member State which granted the aid, and the aid recipient may challenge before the EU courts the legality of a Commission decision declaring the aid incompatible with the internal market. However, unlike the Member State concerned, the aid recipient may bring such an action only when it meets the admissibility criteria under Article 263(4) TFEU.

In that case, it follows from the Court's case-law in *TWD* (1994) and *Georgsmarienhütte* (2018) that the beneficiary of the aid cannot rely on the invalidity of the Commission decision in an action before a national court for annulment of a decision of national authorities implementing that Commission decision, unless it has challenged that decision directly before the EU courts within the prescribed period, failing which the Court of Justice will declare inadmissible any question concerning the validity of the Commission's decision.

In fact, the preliminary ruling procedure is not the suitable framework to engage in full judicial review of EU acts, particularly in technical and complex fields such as State aid (*Georgsmarienhütte*). Unlike the action for annulment, the preliminary ruling procedure is not adversarial and does not allow private parties other than the parties to the main proceedings to intervene.

Who can refer a question for a preliminary ruling?

Only a court or tribunal of a Member State can refer a question for preliminary ruling to the Court of Justice. In order to determine whether a body making a reference is a court or tribunal for the purposes of Article 267 TFEU, the Court takes account of a number of factors, such as whether (i) the body is established by law, (ii) it is permanent, (iii) its jurisdiction is compulsory, (iv) its procedure is *inter partes*, (v) it applies rules of law, (vi) it is independent and whether (vii) it is called upon to give judgment in proceedings intended to lead to a decision of a judicial nature.

It has been debated whether certain national competition authorities satisfied those conditions. In *Dirección General de Defensa de la Competencia/ Asociación Española de Banca Privada* (1992), the Court of Justice accepted a reference for a preliminary ruling on the interpretation of Article 214 EEC and Regulation No 17 from the Tribunal de Defensa de la Competencia (*Tribunal for the Defence of Competition*) without even questioning the latter's quality to do so.

Conversely, in *Syfait* a.o. (2005), the Court refused to recognize that quality to the Epitropi Antagonismou (*Greek Competition Commission*) for not satisfying the requested criteria.

Importance in competition matters

Notwithstanding the abovementioned shortcomings, important issues of competition law have been clarified (or caused controversy…) through preliminary rulings. Classic or modern cases include, in addition to those already cited, *Pronuptia* (1986), *Corbeau*(1993); *Almelo* (1994); *IMS Health* (2004); *Courage v Crehan* (2001); *Post Danmark I*(2012) and *II* (2015); *Budapest Bank* (2020).

Bibliography

BROBERG, M. and FENGER, N., *Broberg and Fenger on Preliminary References to the European Court of Justice*, 3rd Edition, Oxford University Press, 2021

EZRACHI, A., *EU Competition Law: An Analytical Guide to the Leading Cases*, 6th Edition, Hart Publishing, 2018

LENAERTS, K., MASELIS, I. and GUTMAN, K., Ignace Maselis and Kathleen Gutman, *EU Procedural Law*, Oxford University Press, 2014

See also

Direct effect, Effective judicial protection, International cooperation, Judicial review

P

PRICE

Yongama NJISANE
South African Competition Commission

■ Definition

Price is the amount of money or other consideration that is required and paid in exchange for a good or service. Economic literature identifies price as one of the outcomes of both market structures and the nature or extent of competitive rivalry in markets. For this reason price competition is one of the most direct considerations when assessing the competitive effects of both prohibited firm conduct and firm consolidation. In South Africa, abusive pricing practices are prohibited under sections eight and nine of the Competition Act while in the European Union similar prohibitions fall under Article 102 TFEU. Notably, for most other jurisdictions these prohibitions are similarly formulated.

■ Commentary

The concept of price in competition enforcement is inclusive of base prices, discounts and rebates granted to customers or consumers. Under a Bertrand (Nash) equilibrium, where firms are of equal or similar size, face identical and constant costs, and produce homogenous products, prices are independently set at marginal cost. However, prices may rise above marginal cost where products are differentiated (Khemani, 1993, p.15). Neoclassical price theory establishes that in competitive markets, rivalry between firms yields an equilibrium of competitive prices, output and trading terms which increase welfare in society (Straddler, 2015, p13). From this perspective, mergers and acquisitions, single firm conduct and agreements between competitors which limit competition and thus result in prices that deviate durably from the "competitive" level (i.e., increases in prices), are generally considered anticompetitive if there are no compelling efficiency, technological or other procompetitive justifications that outweigh the arising harm.

Price can and is used by firms in markets in an exploitative or exclusionary manner. The exploitative use of price typically manifests itself in the context of excessive pricing which can give rise to customer and/or consumer harm. The exclusionary context in which prices can be used includes various pricing strategies such as predatory pricing, conditional rebates, bundling and tying of products and services, margin squeeze, price discrimination and price fixing, all of which can be used to exclude rivals in markets. These abusive price practices fall under unilateral firm conduct and are assessed based on their economic effect in markets. In other instances, competitors agree on the price to be charged (and its components such as discounts etc.) as a means to avoid competition and jointly maximise profit. This is an outright prohibited price practice referred to as price fixing.

For the sake of brevity, the discussion below will focus on two price strategies (excessive pricing and predatory pricing) that give rise to consumer harm (in the form of high prices) and foreclosure of new entry and expansion by rivals in markets. Two principles are critical when evaluating abusive price conduct, (i) the determination of the dominant firm's costs (allowing for normal economic profit) relative to the price charged and (ii) competitive rivalry will lead to removal of less efficient firms, leaving only those competitors who are as efficient as the dominant firm in the market. This view finds credence in the *Intel v EU Commission* and *Commission v Mittal* cases and is also affirmed by the European Commission's Enforcement Priorities in Applying Article [102 TFEU] to Abusive Exclusionary Conduct by Dominant Undertakings.

While abusive price practices are uniformly prohibited across jurisdictions, differences of opinion remain in respect of excessive prices. While the EU, South Africa and China, for example, prohibit the charging of excessive prices, the U.S. does not expressly outlaw this practice. The charging of excessively high prices (referred to as unfair purchase or selling prices) raises interesting questions for competition enforcement. The key challenge relates to the determination of "excessiveness" and the levels at which such excessiveness can be deemed abusive. The South African Competition Act 89 of 1998 (as amended) defines an excessive price as one that "bears no reasonable relation to the economic value of that good or service; and higher than the value referred to..." The approach taken by the South African competition authorities follows that adopted in *United Brands vs Commission* and *General Motors vs Commission*. In *Commission vs Mittal*, the Competition Appeal Court (CAC) set out a four-step test for determining whether a price is excessive which was later applied in Commission vs Sasol Chemical Industries. The steps include (1) the determination of the actual price charged; (2) the economic value of the good or service must be ascertained; (3) if the actual price exceeds the economic value, it must be determined whether the difference between them is unreasonable; and (4) if so, it must be determined if the charging of the excessive price is to the detriment of consumers.

The determination of economic value remains a challenging task facing competition authorities and litigants alike. *United Brands* gives guidance on this, indicating that economic value can be determined on the basis of the dominant firm's production costs or other benchmarks such as the prices of competing products. In *Mittal*, the CAC defined economic value as the notional price that would be charged in circumstances of long-run competitive equilibrium. The CAC indicated that prices ordinarily charged in other markets by the same or cost-comparable firms may serve as a measure of economic value if the other markets are characterised by effective competition in the long run. Calcagno et al (2019, 169), citing the findings of the Organisation for Economic Cooperation and Development, note that global best practice is to compare the prices charged for the same product or service in different geographic markets, time periods, or prices charged for similar products by other firms. There is also a view that the determination of economic value must expand beyond price and cost and take into account the value derived by customers, for example, elements such as convenience and willingness to pay. In *Scandlines*, the European Commission ("EC") found that convenience was an important consideration while the Court of Appeal for England and Wales, in the *British Horseracing Board* case, found that willingness to pay was a relevant factor in deriving economic value.

The charging of predatory prices is another example of a prohibited price strategy where a dominant firm engages in below cost pricing in order to undermine or foreclose rivals. Whish (2018) describes the conduct as a deliberate strategy in which a dominant player charges loss-making prices in response to competition from an existing competitor(s) or new entrant(s), with a view to disciplining existing players or foreclosing an entrant. Once the discipline or foreclosure is achieved, the dominant firm raises its prices in order to recoup its losses, thereby causing consumer harm. This type of price conduct is also fraught with challenges relating to the determination of the appropriate cost standard to be applied. The *Commission vs Media24* case affirmed marginal or average variable costs as the appropriate cost standards in South Africa. Amendments to the Competition Act have since introduced average avoidable costs as an additional standard that can be used.

Bibliography

Calcagno, C., Chapsal, A. and White, J., 2019. Economics of excessive pricing: an application to the pharmaceutical industry. *Journal of European Competition Law & Practice*, 10(3), pp.166-171

Khemani, R.S., 1993. Glossary of industrial organisation economics and competition law. Organisation for Economic Co-operation and Development; Washington, DC: *OECD Publications and Information Centre*

Meese, A.J., 2003. Price Theory, Competition, and the Rule of Reason. U. *Ill. L. Rev.*, p.77. Meese, Alan J., "Price Theory, Competition, and the Rule of Reason" (2003). Faculty Publications. 553

Strader, J.M., 2015. *The impact of neoclassical price theory on monopolization law: a transatlantic perspective* (Doctoral dissertation, UCL (University College London))

See also

Administered prices, Bertrand (Nash) equilibrium, Cost-based access, Cross subsidisation, Excessive prices, Price discrimination, Price-fixing agreement, Price signalling, Predatory pricing, Resale below cost

P

PRICE DISCRIMINATION

Richard STEPPE
KU Leuven

Friso BOSTOEN
University of Tilburg

■ Definition

Price discrimination takes place when a firm sells identical or similar goods or services at different prices, such differences in price not motivated by different costs. From an economic perspective, price discrimination requires some degree of market power, arbitrage control, differing price sensitivities across buyers or units and an ability to link these sensitivities to the appropriate buyers. From a legal perspective, price discrimination is targeted by various legal provisions including Articles 101–102 TFEU in the European Union and §§1–2 of the Sherman Act in the United States. As a wide variety of practices involve price discrimination, enforcement standards differ depending on the exact nature of the conduct.

■ Commentary

Price discrimination occurs when the same undertaking sells identical or similar goods or services at different prices and these differences cannot be motivated by different cost structures.

From an economic point of view, price discrimination can only take place if certain feasibility conditions are fulfilled. First, a price-discriminating firm should have some degree of market power. Second, the firm should be able to control arbitrage of its products. This condition implies that firms should be able to limit both (i) the ability of buyers to resell the firm's products at prices below those charged by the firm ("transferability of the commodity") and (ii) the ability of buyers to purchase products targeted at other buyers ("transferability of demand"). Third, price sensitivities should differ across buyers or units. Finally, firms must be able to link those price sensitivities to the corresponding buyers.

Firms may base their price discrimination strategies on a wide variety of criteria, including quantity, buyer characteristics (e.g. age or employee status), time (e.g. off-peak and peak periods) or geography (e.g. nationality or location).

To categorise different types of price discrimination, economists have conceived various taxonomies. The most widespread taxonomy was coined by Pigou, distinguishing between price discrimination of the first degree (where each buyer is charged their reservation price), second degree (where pricing depends on the sold number of units) and third degree (where each buyer group is charged differently).

Price discrimination could enhance or decrease social welfare, depending among other variables on the form of consumer heterogeneity, the products for sale and the available instruments for price discrimination. For instance, total welfare could expand under certain conditions if price discrimination enables undertakings to serve markets that would otherwise not be served. However, increased output by one firm does not necessarily expand total output as other firms may exit the market as a result. The welfare effects of price discrimination and any related policy recommendations therefore call for a casuistic approach.

Various legal areas are applicable to price discrimination, including legislation on consumer protection and commercial practices, EU free movement provisions, anti-discrimination laws, geo-blocking regulations, and competition law.

In the EU, Article 102 TFEU precludes abusive conduct by undertakings holding a dominant position on a relevant market. Subparagraph (c) of that provision explicitly prohibits firms from applying dissimilar conditions to equivalent transactions with trading parties if the latter are placed at a competitive disadvantage. While price discrimination can be exploitative, the wording of Article 102(c) TFEU suggests a focus on cases of secondary-line injury where exclusionary effects are felt by co-contractors of the dominant firm (C-82/01 P *Aéroports de Paris*; C-525/16 *MEO*). That said, firms generally have no incentive to distort competition between their trading partners. This is different when a dominant firm integrates vertically and thus competes with its own trading partners but, despite case law to that effect (C-242/95 *GT-Link*), it is debated whether Article 102(c) TFEU offers a solid legal basis for such cases.

Indeed, most price discrimination cases under Article 102 TFEU target primary-line injury where the dominant firm inflicts exclusionary effects on its competitors.

For example, extensive case law exists around rebates, discounts and bonuses. Quantity rebates – linked solely to the volume of purchases – are presumptively legal under certain conditions (C-23/14 *Post Danmark II*). By contrast, exclusivity rebates – conditional on the customer obtaining (almost) all requirements from the dominant firm – are presumptively illegal when preventing purchasers from dealing with competitors of the dominant undertaking (85/76 *Hoffmann-La Roche*). Nevertheless, when a dominant firm submits evidence that its rebates are incapable of restricting competition, the Commission must analyse the foreclosure effects in depth (C-413/14 P Intel). A third category of rebates, neither based solely on volume nor conditioned on exclusivity, may be abusive in case of fidelity-building effects (C-95/04 P *British Airways*; C-23/14 *Post Danmark II*). All circumstances are taken into account for the above assessments, including the retroactivity of rebates, the length of the rebate's reference period or their market coverage.

Many other forms of abuse may also imply price discrimination and vice versa. For example, selective price cuts have been assessed with regard to average total costs (C-209/10 *Post Danmark I*) in a manner comparable to predatory pricing cases (C-62/86 Akzo). Vertically-integrated firms may charge downstream competitors more than their own downstream operations, though the assessment of such "margin squeeze" conduct has centred around the as-efficient-competitor test and, as part of that analysis, the spread between wholesale and retail prices (C-52/09 *TeliaSonera*). Discriminatory prices can also be abusive when excessive in nature (2001/892/EC *Deutsche Post*). Finally, multi-product rebates or bundled discounts, where the sum of the prices of the separate products is higher than the bundled price, may be anticompetitive by excluding competitors who sell only some components of the bundle (Commission Guidance Paper 2009, para. 59).

Given its unique market integration objective, EU competition law has also been used to combat geographic price discrimination. For instance, Article 102 TFEU has targeted practices that artificially partition national markets (27/76 *United Brands*) and that impede parallel imports through dissuasive rebates (T-65/89 *British Gypsum*) or excessive pricing (226/84 *British Leyland*). Similarly, the EU's ban on restrictive agreements and concerted practices, contained in Article 101 TFEU, precludes differential pricing practices which make it economically uninteresting for market operators to engage in parallel trade (80/789/EEC *Distillers*; IV/36.957/F3 *Glaxo Wellcome*). In addition, Article 101 TFEU prohibits deals between competing suppliers to price discriminate jointly against buyers by using the same methodology (74/431/EEC *Papiers peints de Belgique*) and restricts efforts by intermediaries to coordinate discounts charged by competitors (C-74/14 *Eturas*). EU competition law hence not only targets discriminatory prices directly but also affects the feasibility conditions for charging such prices (e.g. control of arbitrage).

In the U.S., the 1913 Robinson-Patman Act – as an amendment to the Clayton Act – specifically prohibits certain unjustified forms of price discrimination that injure competition. Even though this prohibition was enforced in the past (*Morton Salt*, 334 U.S. 37), it has now fallen into disuse as a potential result of its protectionist origins, complexity and narrow scope. That said, price discrimination – and rebates in particular – may still be captured by §§1–2 of the Sherman Act. The Supreme Court has held that volume rebates, or even cases of primary-line injury more generally, should be assessed in line with the price–cost test adopted in predatory pricing cases (*Brooke Group*, 509 U.S. 209). With respect to loyalty and bundled rebates, however, lower courts disagree on the preferred approach as some opt for a rule-of-reason-type analysis (*Le Page*, 324 F.3d 141 (3d Cir. 2003)) while others focus on price–cost comparisons (*Peacehealth*, 515 F.3d 883 (9th Cir. 2007)).

Bibliography

GERADIN, D. and PETIT, N., "Price Discrimination under EC Competition Law: Another Antitrust Doctrine in Search of Limiting Principles?" (2006) 2(3) *Journal of Competition Law and Economics* 479

GIFFORD, D. and KUDRLE, R., "The Law and Economics of Price Discrimination in Modern Economies: Time for Reconciliation?" (2010) 43 *UC Davis Law Review* 1235

IBÁÑEZ COLOMO, P., "Exclusionary Discrimination under Article 102 TFEU" (2014) 51(1) *Common Market Law Review* 141

STEPPE, R., *Algorithmic Pricing and Tacit Collusion: Perspectives from EU Competition Law* (Harvard Law School 2018) 136 pp

VARIAN, H. R., "Price Discrimination" in Richard Schmalensee and Robert Willig (eds), *Handbook of industrial organization* – Volume I (Elsevier 1989) 597

See also

Abuse of dominant position, Abuse of economic dependence, Discriminatory practices, Excessive prices, Exclusionary practice, Prices, Predatory pricing, Principle of equal treatment

P

PRICE LEADERSHIP

James HARVEY
Economic Insight

Definition

Price leadership occurs when one firm in a market (the leader) sets its price level or price change, and the other firms in the market (the followers) adopt the same or similar price level or price change. Seaton and Waterson (2013) provide a narrower definition of price leadership so that, under their definition, the existence or otherwise of price leadership can be tested empirically: "*Price leadership occurs when one firm makes a change in a price (or set of prices) that is followed within a predetermined short period by the other (more generally, another) firm making a price change of exactly the same monetary amount in the same direction on the same product(s), and doing so significantly more often than would be expected by chance.*"

Commentary

Price leadership is a form of strategic interdependence between firms in oligopolistic markets. The idea of strategic interdependence is that firms in oligopolistic markets will recognise that the prices they set will influence the prices that other firms set. The typical competition concern is that through repeated interaction, the firms will learn that it is in their self-interest to coordinate with one another to set higher prices than they would in a more competitive market, to the detriment of consumers. Such coordination does not necessarily require explicit communication or agreement between firms and so is often referred to by economists as "tacit collusion" (or "tacit coordination" or "conscious parallelism").

One way that firms could coordinate is for one firm to play the role of leader (perhaps a dominant or the largest firm) and the other firms to be followers. The leader increases its prices and then the followers increase their prices because they conclude that it is more profitable to do so than not.

In effect, the leader creates a rising tide which lifts all of the ships. Price leadership could therefore be viewed as a way of facilitating tacit collusion and/or a symptom of it.

However, without evidence of explicit communication or agreement, distinguishing between potentially harmful leader-follower behaviour of this type and "normal" competitive behaviour is difficult. For example, one might observe that one firm increased its prices and so did other firms at a similar time. But this would not by itself constitute evidence of harmful leader-follower behaviour because all of the firms may simply be responding to a common increase in the cost of their materials or other inputs.

Therefore, a coherent theory of harm based on the apparent presence of "price leadership" must be capable of answering several difficult questions, including:

- Why would a firm want to be a leader rather than a follower?
- How would other firms know who the leader is?
- Why would the other firms want to follow the leader?

After all, a would-be leader faces the risk of being undercut by any rivals that do not follow its lead. Likewise, if it is more profitable to take up the mantle of being a leader, why would any firm prefer to be a follower? Put simply, one needs to explain why and how price leadership could displace normal competition.

There is a rich body of economic literature that has sought to answer these questions and, more generally, the circumstances under which this type of coordinated behaviour is likely to arise. One theme that emerges from the literature is that firms involved in such coordinated behaviour must be able to detect and punish departures from it (for example, by instigating a price war). If the cost of punishment is high enough, followers would have an incentive to follow the leader rather than undercut it, and in doing so price leadership could displace competition.

The economic literature has also considered other forms of strategic interdependence and leader-follower behaviour that could result in supra-competitive prices, but which differ from price leadership. One example is when a leader "overinvests" in its own capacity to discourage followers to invest in their own. This type of behaviour could increase scarcity and therefore market prices.

Bibliography

MOTTA, M., *Competition Policy Theory and Practice* (Cambridge University Press 2004), Chapter 4

SEATON, J. S. and WATERSON, M., Identifying and characterising price leadership in British supermarkets (*International Journal of Industrial Organization*, September 2013), Pages 392-403

TIROLE, J., *The Theory of Industrial Organization* (The MIT Press 1988), Chapter 6

WHISH, R. and BAILEY, D., *Competition Law* (Oxford University Press Tenth Edition 2021), Chapter 14

European Commission, *Guidelines on the assessment of horizontal mergers under the Council Regulation on the control of concentrations between undertakings* (2004), Section 4

See also

Abuse of dominant position, Abuse of economic dependence, Oligopoly, Prices

PRICE SIGNALLING

Martin ANDREAS GRAVENGAARD
Danish Competition and Consumer Authority

■ Definition

The notion "price signalling" is generally understood as the unilateral, public exchange of information concerning the future market behaviour of an undertaking that depending on the facts at hand may lead to illegal coordination between competitors. "Signalling" is not a legal notion and should be understood broadly to comprise not only unilateral, public exchange of information concerning the future intended or binding prices of an undertaking but also, e.g., exchange of information on future output and commercial strategy. In contrast to a private exchange of information – in this context exchange of information taking place directly between competitors – pure price signalling concerns only public or indirect exchange of information through publicly available means where the exchanged information is equally accessible to all competitors and customers. Typical examples are posts on publically available websites, press releases, newsletters, statements made during the earnings calls of public companies, on conventions or in public media such as TV, radio, newspapers, trade journals etc.

■ Commentary

Whether and when price signalling may be anti-competitive is a controversial and highly debated topic. Price signalling has therefore been characterized as "perhaps the most elusive infringement that lurks in the antitrust jungle" or "a trophy for the agency that already has everything" (Henry Vane, GCR, 2015).

Price signalling is not defined in legislation or case law, and a clear legal test as to when it constitutes an infringement of competition or antitrust rules does not appear to exist in any jurisdiction in spite of increased enforcement efforts in recent years, particularly within the EU. Across jurisdictions price signalling is a grey area and finding an actual infringement is a highly fact-specific exercise that will depend on the entire body of evidence available.

In each EU case involving price signalling practices the EU Commission or European National Competition Authorities ("NCA's") have investigated whether these involved the exchange of strategic or commercially sensitive information and could be a "concerted practice" (and not an "agreement") under Article 101(1) TFEU and/or the equivalent national provisions. A price signalling infringement within the EU should therefore for all practical purposes meet the requirements for establishing a concerted practice that can be inferred from EU case law including "concertation" which requires the existence of direct – or indirect – reciprocal contact between competitors.

The EU Commission's *Horizontal Guidelines* (2023) provide some guidance. Para. 398 states that "The fact that an undertaking discloses commercially sensitive information through a public announcement [...] does not in itself exclude the possibility that the announcement may constitute a concerted practice within the meaning of Article 101(1). Indeed, public disclosure may in some cases form part of a communication channel between competitors to signal future intentions to behave on the market in a specific way, or to provide a focal point for coordination between competitors and thereby fall within Article 101(1)."

The *Horizontal Guidelines* further state in para. 416 that "Depending on the legal and economic context and on the objectives an undertaking seeks to attain, a public disclosure that signals the undertaking's future intentions on key competition parameters, for instance, prices or quantities, may [also] be considered a restriction by object. Similarly, a public disclosure that does not clearly benefit customers but does signal to competitors how they should act, or the consequences of acting or failing to act in a certain way, or how the undertaking will react to competitors' conduct, will be considered a restriction by object".

These statements have been further elaborated upon in examples which the EU Commission has set out in para. 431, 432 and 435 of its *Horizontal Guidelines*.

Even if price signaling practices have been investigated several times and increasingly by the EU Commission and NCA's in the recent years, the first administrative prohibition decision actually establishing an infringement – and which has also been upheld on appeal – remains to be seen.

In *Wood Pulp* where the EU Commission found that wood pulp manufacturers had actually concerted on prices through inter alia quarterly public announcements of future, binding maximum prices for wood pulp, the EU Court (1993) annulled the EU Commission's prohibition decision.

Since then, every administrative decision by the EU Commission or the NCA's involving pure price signaling practices has been a commitment decision where no infringement of article 101(1) TFEU and/or the equivalent national provisions has been established or admitted. Among the most recent and notable decisions are *Dutch Mobile Operators*(2014), *Container Shipping* (2016), *Norwegian Retail Fuel* (2020), *Irish Private Motor Insurance* (2022).

Although no clear legal test exists as to when price signaling or public price announcements constitutes an infringement of Art. 101(1) TEUF, it is – on the basis of inter alia the above mentioned decisions and the EU Commission's *Horizontal Guidelines* (2023) – possible to derive a practical checklist over factual circumstances (not all being conditions as such), which may increase the likelihood of establishing an infringement. This non-exhaustive, practical checklist includes the below factual circumstances.

Practical checklist:

The public price announcements:

1. concern future, intended prices (as opposed to binding/committal fixed or maximum prices), which the suppliers may adjust before the intended implementation date.
2. have actually been adjusted and (if relevant) in addition been (systematically) aligned with subsequent price announcements ("responses") of competitors, without any plausible commercial reason for such adjustment.
3. are (almost) parallel regarding inter alia announcement date, intended implementation date, size of the price/price change, products/countries concerned and/or are made often, regularly and/or over a long period of time.
4. are not required in order to meet legal requirements in other areas of law such as Security Trading Acts, sector specific rules etc.
5. are of none or low user-value/benefit/relevance for customers in making their purchase decisions (e.g. future prices that are not binding/committal, transparent and timely).
6. are sufficiently clear and specific to serve as a focal point for coordination between competitors (regarding inter alia size of the price/price change, timing and scope).
7. are made (well) earlier than the point in time where (most) customers (typically) decide to purchase the product and/or are made (sufficiently) early before the intended implementation date allowing to "test" the viability of a price change with competitors and to adjust or cancel an intended price change.
8. are – according to internal company documents – used intentionally for signalling purposes and as a means for coordination.
9. contain an outright invitation to collude and/or are made dependent/contingent on the reactions of competitors or "the market".
10. are introduced on the supplier-side's own initiative (as opposed to being a response to requests from the customer-side).
11. are difficult to explain in the light of the current conditions of supply and demand (e.g. price increases in times where demand decreases).

12. only relate to price increases (as opposed to decreases) and/or do not appear as a suitable means to attract customers.
13. are made by minimum two competitors prior to the implementation date.
14. are made in markets characterised by being highly concentrated, transparent, stable, having high barriers to entry, homogeneous products and/or undertakings.
15. lack any commercial rationale or plausible explanation other than being used for signalling purposes and as a coordination means.

In addition to a relatively high number of EU Commission and NCA cases within the EU, price signalling practices have also been investigated by competition authorities in other jurisdictions. Most frequently in the U.S. but it has also been investigated, for example, in Australia, Taiwan, Russia and South Africa.

With respect to U.S. antitrust law, unilateral price announcements may violate Section 1 of the Sherman Act, which prohibits "every contract, combination, or conspiracy in restraint of trade", provided there is proof of concerted behaviour such as an actual agreement among competitors to fix prices, which in practice is a high evidentiary threshold to meet.

Even without proof of an actual agreement, the Federal Trade Commission's ("FTC") enforcement practice shows that the FTC considers, that mere attempts or "invitations to collude" inter alia on prices violates Section 5 of the FTC Act, which prohibits "unfair methods of competition in or affecting commerce". The cases brought by the FTC under Section 5 have not been prosecuted criminally but have been settled by consent agreements. In general the cases have concerned private invitations to collude, but the – until then unprecedented – Valassis Settlement (2006) shows that, in the opinion of the FTC, also purely public invitations to collude, in this case on an earnings call open to the public via telephone and the internet, violate Section 5 of the FTC Act.

Bibliography

BAILEY, D. and JOHN, L. E. (eds.), *Bellamy and Child: European Union Law of Competition* (8th edition, Oxford University Press 2018), Chapter 5, p. 362-363 and p. 397-324

DE CONINCK, R., *Information Exchanges and Price Signaling: An Economic Perspective*, Charles River Associates, 2016

GORECKI, P., *Price Signalling and Private Motor Insurance in Ireland: A Breach of Competition Law?* Munich Personal RePEc Archive Paper No. 115473, 2022

HALL, M., *Recent Developments in Price Signalling in the EU*, McGuireWoods LLP, 2015

JONES, A., SUFRIN, B. and DUNNE, N., *Jones & Sufrin, EU Competition Law, Text, Cases and Materials* (7th edition, Oxford University Press 2019), Chapter 9, p. 662-688)

MAROSI, Z. and SOARES, M. (eds.), *Information Exchange and related Risks. A Jurisdictional Guide*, (Concurrences and International Bar Association 2022), p. 1-457

RABINOVICI, I., Public Exchange of Information After Container Shipping, *Journal of European Competition Law and Practice*, 2017, Vol. 8, no. 3

VAN BAEL & BELLIS, *Competition Law of the European Union* (6th edition, Wolters Kluwer 2021), Chapter 4, p. 408-423

WHISH, R. and BAILEY, D., *Competition Law* (10th edition, Oxford University Press 2021), Chapter 14, p. 596-602

See also

Agreement (notion), Concerted practice, Exchanges of information, Predatory pricing, Prices, Undertaking (notion)

P

PRICE-FIXING AGREEMENT

Ioannis KOKKORIS
Queen Mary University of London

Claudia LEMUS
The Office of Gas and Electricity Markets (OFGEM)

Definition

Price-fixing is an anticompetitive agreement between competitors to fix prices. In the United States this type of agreement is classified as "illegal per se." Agreements that are illegal per se are not subject to a rule of reason. Under the rule of reason an investigation is undertaken to determine whether the pro-competitive aspects of the agreement offset its anticompetitive aspects. In the European Union price-fixing is restrictive by object. An agreement is deemed restrictive by object where it is presumed to have a net negative impact on competition making it unnecessary to assess its effects. This presumption can be rebutted if certain requirements for justification are met.

Commentary

In the United States, anticompetitive agreements violate Section 1 of the Sherman Act that prohibits "restraints of trade." In a landmark U.S. court decision, the *Standard Oil Co*case, the per se rule was established. According to this rule, it is possible to classify certain conducts that are intrinsically anticompetitive given their "nature and character" and forbid them in a summary manner. In a subsequent decision, the *U.S. v Socony*, price-fixing was classified as a *per se* agreement. The adoption and development of the *per se* rule of illegality by the courts facilitates the enforcement of fix-pricing agreements because no further litigation is required. Price-fixing agreements, also known as "naked agreements," are considered to deserve immediate censure as their consequences are presumed to be harmful. The *per se* illegality of price-fixing agreements makes irrelevant rule of reason analysis. Under rule of reason analysis, it is possible to assess efficiency claims.

In the European Union, Article 101(1) of the Treaty on the Functioning of the European Union (TFEU) prohibits agreements which significantly restrict competition by object or effect. The EU courts have stated that an agreement is restrictive of competition by object if there are no credible pro-competitive reasons for its implementation. A price-fixing agreement is deemed anticompetitive as its object reveals itself to have a sufficient degree of harm to competition. The European Court of Justice has indicated that whether an agreement has the object of restricting competition must be established by studying its content, purpose, and the economic context in which it is to be applied. The content and purpose of a price-fixing agreement will often be to eliminate the competition between the parties with the aim of increasing prices. The likelihood that a price-fixing agreement brings negative effects on competition makes it unnecessary to prove their actual effects.

There is a difference between the "*per se* rule of illegality" applied in the United States and the prohibition contained in Article 101(1) TFEU. In the former, agreements that violate section 1 of the Sherman Act are irrefutably deemed anticompetitive and there is no need to balance the anticompetitive aspects of the agreement against its possible procompetitive aspects. In the latter, an agreement that has the object of restricting competition, such as price fixing, can nevertheless be saved by the provision contained in Article 101(3). This provision indicates that the Article 101(1) prohibition can be declared inapplicable to any agreement that satisfies the following four conditions: (i) it achieves objective economic benefits; (ii) it benefits consumers; (iii) it does not contain indispensable restraints; and (iv) it does not eliminate competition in respect of a substantial part of the products in question. Regulation 1/2003 allocates the burden to prove the Article 101(3) justifications to the defendant. Unlike the United States, in the European Union there are no absolute rules of per se illegality, even in cases where anticompetitive effects are assumed, harmful agreements can always be justified.

Although the European Union allows justifications for anticompetitive agreements, it is very unlikely that a price-fixing agreement (a hardcore cartel) will meet the requirements for justification. In general, this type of agreement fails to create objective economic advantages, does not benefit consumers, it is uncertain whether it is indispensable to the attainment of any efficiencies created by the agreement and has the potential to remove competitive forces from the market (a price-fixing agreement can plausibly harm firms' ability and incentive to compete). It is with difficulty that the parties involved in a price-fixing agreement can overcome the strong presumption of illegality that surrounds this conduct. It is also unclear how parties involved in a hardcore cartel like price-fixing can establish that demonstrated beneficial effects offset anticompetitive effects.

Both the U.S. and the EU rely heavily on presumptions about the impact of price-fixing agreements considered to be naked agreements or hardcore cartels. Yet even if in theory there is a difference between the "*per se* rule of illegality" applied in the United

States and the approach applied in the European Union, in practice the difference is not significant. The European Commission has set out a high standard of proof for the efficiency defence, its enforcement decisions almost exclusively cover conducts that are restrictive by object, and it is unlikely that an Article 101(3) defence can be successful. Article 101(3) efficiency-based justifications are a theoretical rather than a practical option.

Bibliography

Ibáñez Colomo, P. and Lamadrid de Pablo, A., On the Notion of Restriction of Competition: What we Know and what we don't know we know. In Gerard, Damien, Merola, Massimo and Meyring, Bernd, (eds) *The Notion of Restriction of Competition: Revisiting the Foundations of Antitrust Enforcement in Europe* (Bruylant 2017)

Jones, A. and Kovacic, W. E., Identifying Anticompetitive Agreements in the United States and the European Union: Developing a Coherent Antitrust Analytical Framework, 62 *Antitrust BULL.* 254 (2017)

Witt, A., The Enforcement of Article 101 TFEU – What has happened to the Effects Analysis?, *Common Market Law Review*, Volume 55, Issue 2 (2018)

See also

Bid-rigging, Cartel, Prices, Rule of reason

P

PRINCIPLE OF EQUAL TREATMENT

Alessandro SIA, Ramin SILVAN GOHARI
Swiss Competition Commission

■ Definition

The principle of equal treatment (principle of non-discrimination) requires that comparable situations must not be treated differently and that different situations must not be treated in the same way, unless such treatment is objectively justified (*Akzo Nobel Chemicals and Akcros Chemicals*, para 55 and the case-law cited). A breach of the principle of equal treatment presumes that the situations concerned are comparable, having regard to all the elements which characterise them. The comparability must in particular be determined and assessed in the light of the subject matter and purpose of the EU act which makes the distinction (*Team Relocations*, para 187 and the case-law cited). A difference in treatment is justified if it is based on an objective and reasonable criterion, that is to say, if it is related to a legitimate aim pursued by the legislation in question and that difference is proportionate to the aim pursued by the treatment in question (*Herbert Schaible*, para 77 and the case-law cited).

■ Commentary

Within the framework of competition law, the principle of equal treatment has gained relevance in particular (1) as a general principle and fundamental right that the European Commission and the courts must respect in the exercise of their activities (standard for authority conduct), and, more recently, (2) as a factor in the substantive analysis of abusive behaviour (standard for dominant undertaking conduct).

(1) The principle of equal treatment is a general principle of European Union law, enshrined in Articles 20 and 21 of the Charter of Fundamental Rights of the European Union (*Akzo Nobel*

Chemicals and Akcros Chemicals, para 54).

Where the European Commission enjoys discretionary powers, it must have due regard to the fundamental rights guaranteed by the European Union, in particular the principle of equal treatment (*Schenker*, para. 48). The principle of equal treatment must also be observed by the European courts (*Erste Group Bank*, para. 166).

The European courts have regularly applied the principle of equal treatment in the context of the review of the setting of the fine and have held, in particular, the following:

- The European Commission enjoys a wide discretion in setting the amount of fines and is not bound by assessments made by it in the past. Its practice in previous decisions can nonetheless give an indication for the purpose of determining whether there is discrimination (*Erste Group Bank*, paras 123 and 233 and the case-law cited).
- When the amount of the fine is determined, there cannot, by the application of different methods of calculation, be any discrimination between the undertakings which have participated in an agreement or a concerted practice contrary to Article 101(1) TFEU (*Ziegler*, para 133 and the case-law cited).
- When calculating the overall turnover used to determine the fine, no distinction should be made between sales made to entities belonging to the same undertaking (internal sales) and sales made with independent third parties (external sales). Excluding internal sales from the calculation of the fine would give an unjustified advantage to vertically integrated undertakings over non-integrated ones by allowing them to avoid the imposition of a fine proportionate to their importance on the product market to which the infringement relates (*Guardian Industries and Guardian*, para 59 and the case-law cited).
- A distinction in the calculation of the fine may be justified, for example, in the case of an undertaking applying for immunity under the leniency programme and an undertaking cooperating during the investigation, their situations with regard to the reduction of the fine being not the same (*Schenker*, paras 74–75).
- Applying the same reduction of the fine to two undertakings participating in a cartel despite their different situations (e.g., a more limited role in the cartel and lower turnover) must be justified by objective reasons (*Pometon,* paras 150–152).
- The European Commission infringes the principle of equal treatment by failing to take into consideration, when calculating the amount of the fines, the fact that an undertaking has participated in only one branch of a cartel, unlike other members of that cartel, and by therefore treating different situations in an identical manner, without such treatment being objectively justified (*Chalkor AE Epexergasias Metallon*, para 104).

The principle of equal treatment has also been applied in the context of the attorney-client privilege (legal professional privilege), where it has been held that since in-house lawyers do not enjoy a level of professional independence equal to that of external lawyers they are in a fundamentally different position from external lawyers so that their respective circumstances are not comparable for the purposes of the principle of equal treatment (*Akzo Nobel Chemicals and Akcros Chemicals*, paras 54–59).

The principle of legality, according to which a person may not rely in support of their claim on an unlawful act committed in favour of a third party, leads to a limitation of the principle of equal treatment (no equal treatment in the event of breaches of the law; *Printeos and Others v. Commission*, para 144). In particular, an undertaking on which a fine has been imposed for its participation in a cartel in breach of the competition rules, cannot request the annulment or reduction of that fine, on the ground that another participant in the same cartel was not penalized in respect of a part, or all, of its participation in that cartel (*Samsung SDI and Samsung SDI (Malaysia)*, paras 37–38 and the case-law cited).

(2) In *Google Shopping*, the General Court referred to the principle of equal treatment in the context of the analysis of abusive conduct (Google Shopping, para 155). Google had been accused of abusing its dominant position on the market for general search services by favouring its own comparison shopping service over competing comparison shopping services (*Google Shopping*, paras 167ff). The General Court held that, given in particular the universal vocation of Google's general search engine, such self-preferencing constituted an abnormality and that certain differences in treatment could be considered contrary to Article 102 TFEU when what was at issue were favouring practices established by operators in a dominant position in the internet sector (*Google Shopping*, paras 176ff). The relationship of *Google Shopping* in particular to the traditional discrimination case-law and the *Bronner* case-law is currently debated. Traditional discrimination case-law is not commonly discussed in the context of the principle of equal treatment in the above-mentioned sense. While also based on a logic of equal treatment, it focuses on unequal treatment distorting the competitive process in a manner relevant under substantive competition law. In this vein, according to Article 102(2)(c) TFEU, the application, by a dominant undertaking, of dissimilar conditions to equivalent transactions with other trading parties may constitute prohibited abusive conduct if the latter are thereby placed at a competitive disadvantage. For example, in the context of a price discrimination case, it was held that for the conditions of this article to be met, there must be a finding, not only that the behaviour of an undertaking in a dominant market position is discriminatory, but also that it tends to distort that competitive relationship (*MEO – Serviços de Comunicações e Multimédia*, para 25).

Bibliography

AHLBORN, C., VAN GERVEN, G. and LESLIE, W. , Bronner revisited: Google Shopping and the Resurrection of Discrimination Under Article 102 TFEU, *Journal of European Competition Law & Practice*, 2022, vol 13(2), 87–98

EZRACHI, A., EU Competition Law, *An analytical guide to the leading cases*, 7th edn, Hart Publishing, 2021

FRESE, M., *Sanctions in EU Competition Law: Principles and Practice*, Hart Publishing, 2016

MUIR, E., The Essence of the Fundamental Right to Equal Treatment: Back to the Origins, *German Law Journal*, 2019, vol 20(6), 817-839

ORTIZ BLANCO, L. (ed.), *EU Competition Procedure*, 4th edn, Oxford University Press, 2021

PEERS, S. *et al* (eds.), *The EU Charter of Fundamental Rights, A Commentary*, 2nd edn, Hart Publishing, 2021

ROUSSEVA, E. (ed), *EU Antitrust Procedure*, Oxford University Press, 2020

SIMONATI, A., The Principles of Administrative Procedure and the EU Courts: an Evolution in Progress?, *Review of European Administrative Law*, 2011, vol 4(1), 45–81

VAN BAEL & BELLIS (ed), *Competition Law of the European Union*, 6th edn, Kluwer Law International, 2021

See also

Principle of proportionality, Price discrimination, Principle of equivalence

P

PRINCIPLE OF EQUIVALENCE

Diana-Urania GALETTA
University of Milan

Definition

Although it has evolved significantly in the ECJ case law, especially in the 1990s, the principle of equivalence in the context of EU law is still based on the fundamental idea – put forward in the *Rewe* decision of 1976 – that the protection within a national legal system of EU-law-based rights must not be less favourable than in the case of individual rights based on national law. The principle is closely related to the general principle of equal treatment and the prohibition of discrimination from which it is derived. It is also a well-known international law principle which, together with the principle of mutual recognition, serves as a cooperation-promoting instrument.

Commentary

In order to promote cooperation at the international level in the best possible way, harmonization of national legislation would probably be the best instrument to be used, also within the framework of international trade organizations. The aim of harmonization is to standardize legislation on an international basis. Nevertheless, full harmonization may not be achievable in practice or even desirable for legitimate reasons. Thus, in international law, the principles of mutual recognition and equivalence are normally used as cooperation-promoting instruments. This applies also within the framework of the World Trade Organization. An important threshold for achieving equivalence in this context is to define the regulatory objectives and, on this basis, to determine the level (such as the minimum level of protection) that national legislation/measures must achieve. This is the case also in the context of European Union (EU) law and the specific reason why the Court of Justice of the European Union (ECJ) has, from the outset, referred together to the two criteria of equivalence and effectiveness.

More specifically, in the context of EU Law, the principle of equivalence requires Member States not to treat matters under EU law less favorably than purely domestic matters. This legal principle was developed by the ECJ when it became clear – especially in *Comet* (1976) – that there was an important first obstacle to the proper implementation of substantive (directly applicable) Community law: discrimination of Community law issues against similar, purely domestic issues as a consequence of the application of national (procedural law) regulations. Therefore, already in *Rewe* (1976) the ECJ clarified that similar situations may not be treated differently unless this unequal treatment is objectively justified, including when it is for the domestic legal system of Member States to identify the competent Courts and/or to determine the procedural conditions governing actions at law intended to ensure the protection of the rights which citizens have from the direct effect of Community law. Such "conditions", even if determined by national law of Member States, cannot be less favorable than those relating to similar actions of a "domestic nature" (*Rewe*, paragraphs 5-6). In EU Law, the principle of equivalence is thus closely linked to the general principle of equal treatment and the prohibition of discrimination derived therefrom.

The principle of equivalence is based on the key idea – set out in the *Rewe* decision (1976) – that the "instruments" (access to Courts and procedural conditions governing actions at law) for protecting the rights which individuals have as a consequence of the direct effect of EU law must not be "designed" less favorably than in the case of "domestic rights" provided for by national law. The difficulties involved, however, have less to do with direct discrimination. The cases dealt with in ECJ case-law are mostly of indirect discrimination where, for example, there are different procedural arrangements in national law, depending on whether national or Union law matters are affected.

On the basis of the original "*Rewe*-formula", the content and meaning of the principle of equivalence have been progressively clarified in the ECJ case-law. The most important period in its development was during the Nineties. In the *Levez* case (1998) the ECJ set out a kind of decalogue on how national courts should apply the principle of equivalence by stating that:

- The principle of equivalence requires that the rule at issue be applied without distinction, whether the infringement alleged is of EU law or national law, where the purpose and cause of action are similar (*Levez*, paragraph 41).
- The principle of equivalence is not to be interpreted as requiring Member States to extend their most favorable rules to all actions brought in a certain field of law (Levez, paragraph 42). This means, as it is clearly stated for example in *Târşia* (2005), that it does not require equivalence of national procedural rules applicable to different types of proceedings such as – as in the dispute in the main proceedings in *Târşia* – civil proceedings

on the one hand and administrative proceedings on the other (*Târşia*, paragraph 34).

- In order to determine whether the principle of equivalence has been complied with, the national court – which alone has direct knowledge of the procedural rules governing actions in the different national law fields – must consider both the purpose and the essential characteristics of allegedly similar domestic actions (*Levez*, paragraph 43).
- Whenever it falls to be determined whether a procedural rule of national law is less favorable than those governing similar domestic actions, the national court must take into account the role played by that provision in the procedure as a whole, as well as the operation and any special features of that procedure before the different national courts (*Levez*, paragraph 44). In this respect, the ECJ later pointed out that the national court must also verify this "objectively, in the abstract" (*Preston*, 2000, paragraph 63).

To conclude, in the context of what has been identified as a kind of "EU judicial federalism" (Wells, 2017), the principle of equivalence is much more about how and to what extent the national and the EU level, via their courts, succeed in working together in a cooperative relationship. For this reason, the ECJ explicitly referred to the principle of sincere cooperation laid down in article 5 EEC (now art. 4, paragraph 3, TEU) already in its *Rewe* decision (paragraph 5).

The situation is different in the United States' context where the kind of "judicial federalism" in which most issues of EU law are adjudicated in the Member State courts does not exist. In the U.S., there is an identified "a network of lower federal courts" (Wells, 2017) adjudicating many federal law issues. More importantly, the U.S. Supreme Court may review both federal and state decisions referring to federal law. That appears to be the reason whya principle of equivalence has not been developed in the USA. Perhaps if U.S. state courts were the only courts dealing with these issues apart from the U.S. Supreme Court and the lower federal courts did not exist, there would be more room for the principle.

Bibliography

GALETTA, D.-U., 'Äquivalenz und Effektivität', Wolfang Kahl, Markus Ludwigs (eds.), *Handbuch des Verwaltungsrechts*, Vol. 2 (Heidelberg, 2021), chapter 46, 625-658

LENAERTS, K., "National Remedies for Private Parties in the Light of the EU Law Principles of Equivalence and Effectiveness" (2011) 46 *The Irish Jurist* 13

LENAERTS, K., "The Decentralised Enforcement of EU Law: the Principle of Equivalence and Effectiveness", *Scritti in onore di Giuseppe Tesauro*, Vol. II, (Editoriale Scientifica 2014), 1057–1085

WELLS, M. L., "Judicial Federalism in the European Union" (2017) 54 *Hous L Rev* 697

ZÚÑIGA SCHRODER, H., *Harmonization, Equivalence and Mutual Recognition of Standards in WTO Law* (Wolters Kluwer 2011)

See also

Principle of equal treatment, Principle of proportionality

P

PRINCIPLE OF PROPORTIONALITY

Eda ŞAHIN-ŞENGÜL
Boğaziçi University

■ Definition

The principle of proportionality as one of the general principles of European Law is well-established in the European Union (EU) legal order. The principle of proportionality works along with the principle of subsidiarity to oversee the use of the powers conferred by the member states to the EU, and thereby applies to all actions performed by the EU institutions. The principle of proportionality necessitates acceptable measures to be taken and determines whether there are more appropriate or less restrictive measures available. By doing so, this principle requires the actions of the EU institutions to be within the limits of what is necessary to achieve the desired goal by the measure taken.

■ Commentary

The concern that the EU intervention should not be unnecessary and unwarranted has led to the adoption of the principle of proportionality for the first time in the European Council Conclusions in 1992. As the guidelines developed by the Conclusions referred to the jurisprudence, the Court of Justice had reflected on the principle of proportionality in its earlier cases. Although implicit the Court in its judgment of *Federation Charbonnière de Belgique v High Authority of the European Coal and Steel Community* in 1956 stated that "In accordance with a generally accepted rule of law an indirect reaction by the High Authority to illegal action on the part of undertakings must be in proportion to the scale of that action." This case was followed by another judgment in 1970 (Case 11/70 *Internationale Handelsgesellschaft*) where the defendants challenged the validity of a Regulation on the grounds of, inter alia, the principle of proportionality.

Despite the AG's explicit reference to this principle, the Court used the principle without mentioning its name in its assessment and stated that "[a] method [should be] both necessary and appropriate to enable the competent authorities to determine in the most effective manner their interventions on the marke[t]." Finally in 1983 the Court explicitly reviewed the facts of the case on the basis of the principle of proportionality and declared that this principle referred to "[t]he power of the member states to prohibit imports of the products in question from other member states should be restricted to what is necessary to attain the legitimate aim of protecting health."

The legal basis of the principle of proportionality was for the first time found in the Maastricht Treaty and currently is laid down in the article 5 of the Treaty on European Union (TEU) and in the Protocol (No 2) on the Application of the Principles of Subsidiarity and Proportionality (Protocol (No 2)). According to the article 5 of the TEU, the principle of conferral, principles of subsidiarity and proportionality determine the competences of the EU. After defining other principles, the article 5 of the TEU states that "Under the principle of proportionality, the content and form of Union action shall not exceed what is necessary to achieve the objectives of the Treaties." Protocol (No 1) on the Role of National Parliaments in the European Union states in article 3 that "National Parliaments may send to the Presidents of the European Parliament, the Council and the Commission a reasoned opinion on whether a draft legislative act complies with the principle of subsidiarity, in accordance with the procedure laid down in the Protocol on the application of the principles of subsidiarity and proportionality." After drawing attention to the necessity of complete compliance with the principles of subsidiarity and proportionality by each institution in the article 1 of the Protocol (No 2), the article 5 of the Protocol (No 2) laid down the way of realising this necessity. It is required that all draft legislative acts should have a detailed analysis to show that they are in line with the principles of subsidiarity and proportionality. This analysis is comprised of the proposal's financial impact and, if it is a directive, of its implications for the Member States. The article 5 of the Protocol (No 2) states that qualitative and, if possible, quantitative statistics should be used to demonstrate a Union objective is better achieved at Union level.

The application of the principle of proportionality can thus be found in various areas of EU competition law. Firstly, the "Council Regulation (EC) No 1/2003 of 16 December 2002 on the implementation of the rules on competition laid down in Articles 81 and 82 of the Treaty" brought about a decentralised network of National Competition Authorities to enforce EU competition rules through the European Competition Network. The Regulation refers to the principle of proportionality when establishing the EU Commission's power to impose behavioural or structural remedies where it is required to effectively end the infringement, meaning that the Commission should inflict a more appropriate or less restrictive available remedy to the case. The need for a Regulation is indicated with respect to the principle of proportionality, stating that the introduction of a Regulation is necessary to achieve the objective of the effective application of EU competition rules. Secondly, the "Directive 2014/104/EU of the European Parliament and of the Council of 26 November 2014 on certain rules governing actions for damages under national law for infringements of the competition law provisions of the Member States and of the European Union" seeks to ensure the effective application of Articles 101 and 102 of the Treaty on the Functioning of the European Union (TFEU) throughout the EU in order to safeguard the undistorted competition in the internal market. It contains rules concerning right to full compensation, disclosure of evidence, effect of national decisions, limitation periods, joint and several liability, the passing-on of overcharges, quantification of harm and consensual dispute resolution. The Directive declares that it is fully in accordance with the principle of proportionality and does not go beyond what is necessary in order to realise its objective as the full effect of Articles 101 and 102 TFEU cannot be satisfactorily ensured by the Member States but better be ensured at the EU level. Thirdly, the "Directive (EU) 2019/1 of the European Parliament and of the Council of 11 December 2018 to empower the competition authorities of the Member States to be more effective enforcers and to ensure the proper functioning of the internal market" aims to guarantee national competition authorities independence, resources, enforcement and fining powers required for the effective application of Articles 101 and 102 TFEU and of national competition law in parallel to Articles 101 and 102 TFEU. According to the Directive, realising this aim would result in ensuring the effective functioning of the internal market and the European Competition Network. Therefore, the Directive states that it respects the principle of proportionality and does not go beyond what is necessary to attain its aim, because for the reasons of the requisite effectiveness and uniformity in the application of Articles 101 and 102 TFEU this aim can adequately be achieved at Union level rather than by the Member States.

Bibliography

ASHTON, D., *Competition Damages Actions in the EU: Law and Practice*, Second Edition, Edward Elgar 2018

LENAERTS, K., Keynote Speech: "Proportionality as a matrix principle promoting the effectiveness of EU law and the legitimacy of EU action" (ECB Legal Conference 2021 Continuity and change – how the challenges of today prepare the ground for tomorrow)

RODGER, B. J. and MACCULLOCH, A., *Competition Law and Policy in the EU and UK*, Sixth Edition, Routledge 2022

SCACCIA, G., "Proportionality and the Balancing of Rights in the Case-law of European Courts" (2019) federalismi.it

STEENBERGEN, J., "Proportionality in Competition Law and Policy" (2008) 35 *Legal Issues of Economic Integration* pp. 259-268

See also

Principle of equal treatment, Media pluralism

P

PRIVACY AND DATA PROTECTION

Claudia BERG
Information Commissioner's Office

Definition

There is no singular, agreed definition of "privacy". This is partly because the approach to privacy differs between countries as well as between individuals. Broadly speaking, privacy is rooted in human dignity and liberty. It is often regarded as encompassing the right to be free from interference and intrusion, and to have control over information about yourself. Data protection originates from the right to privacy, and supports the broader objective of preserving the fundamental right to privacy in the context of personal data.

Commentary

The terms "privacy" and "data protection" are often used interchangeably, but are not identical in their meaning or scope. Data protection legislation originates from the right to privacy, and sets out specific rules to ensure that personal data is processed in a way that protects individuals' fundamental rights.

Privacy as a Fundamental Right

In the EU and UK, the protection of privacy is a fundamental right. The European Convention on Human Rights ("ECHR"), adopted by the Council of Europe in 1950, gave legal effect to certain rights set out in the Universal Declaration of Human Rights 1948, including the right to privacy. Article 8 ECHR protects individuals against interference with private, family life, home and correspondence. Over time, this has developed to include the protection of personal data, which the European Court of Human Rights has stated "is of fundamental importance to a person's enjoyment of his or her right to respect for private and family life".

As technology developed further, the Council of Europe adopted Convention

108 for the Protection of Individuals with regard to Automatic Processing of Personal Data in 1981 (updated in 2018, and referred to as Convention 108+). More recently, in 2009, the Charter of Fundamental Rights of the EU codified the fundamental rights protected under EU law, including a specific right to the protection of personal data (Article 8).

In contrast to the EU, there is no explicit reference to privacy in the U.S. Constitution. However, the concept of privacy in U.S. law arguably dates back to an article entitled "The Right to Privacy" in 1890 by Samuel Warren and Louis Brandeis. This article is often considered to be the first publication in the U.S. to advocate for a right to privacy, particularly "the right to be let alone".

Data Protection Legislation

Following earlier data protection legislation, the current General Data Protection Regulation (GDPR) came into force in the EU on 25 May 2018 and provides a consistent set of data protection rules across all EU Member States. Following Brexit, the UK retained the GDPR in domestic legislation (referred to as UK GDPR).

The GDPR recognises that everyone has the right to the protection of their personal data and adopts a principles and rights-based approach. Seven key principles lie at the heart of the GDPR. These include that personal data shall be processed lawfully, fairly and transparently and only used for specified, explicit purposes. Under the GDPR, individuals are empowered with specific rights in respect of their personal data, for example, the right to access their personal data. In the EU, the GDPR is enforced by national data protection authorities, which cooperate through the European Data Protection Board , and in the UK the UK GDPR is enforced by the Information Commissioner. The U.S. currently does not have a single, comprehensive federal law that addresses data protection, although there are a number of consumer protection laws that relate to data privacy enforced by the Federal Trade Commission (such as the Fair Credit Reporting Act). However individual states, including California, are beginning to implement their own data privacy legislation.

There are now more than 130 data protection and privacy authorities globally. While there are variations between jurisdictions, data privacy legislation often follows common themes: increased privacy rights for individuals, enforcement powers for regulators, and stricter compliance obligations for businesses.

Privacy and Competition

The interaction between competition law and privacy/data protection law is increasingly a focus for law-makers and regulators because of the importance of personal data in today's digital economy. While some regard the two areas of law as being in tension, there are also significant synergies in their aims. For example, data protection law ensures that individuals have appropriate control over their personal data and can make meaningful choices about whether and for what purposes it is processed. Effective data protection can therefore support healthy competition, as rival companies compete to build trust and consumers can make informed decisions.

In antitrust and merger control cases, privacy has typically been considered as an aspect of quality. In Microsoft/LinkedIn, the European Commission concluded that data privacy was an important parameter of competition that could have been negatively affected by the transaction. By contrast, potential privacy-related concerns about increased concentration of data as a result of mergers have generally been left to data protection regulation, as was the case in Facebook/Whatsapp.

More recently, regulators have been addressing other aspects of the interaction between privacy and competition, particularly in relation to the market power of "big tech" firms. For example, in 2019 the German Federal Cartel Office found that Facebook had infringed competition law by using its dominant position to impose terms and conditions on users that compelled excessive disclosure of personal data, which was itself also a breach of the GDPR. In addition, in 2022, the UK Competition and Markets Authority accepted commitments from Google in relation to its Privacy Sandbox proposals to remove third-party cookies from its Chrome browser, working closely with the UK Information Commissioner's Office to ensure that privacy issues were properly addressed.

Finally, privacy and data protection is an important consideration in the development of new digital markets regulation. For example, the EU's Digital Markets Act contains specific obligations on gatekeepers to ensure the protection of personal data of end users and prevent the combination or cross-use of personal data without consent (Article 5(2)).

Bibliography

WARREN, S. D. and BRANDEIS, L. D., (1890) The Right to Privacy, *Harvard Law Review* 4(5), 193-220

CMA, "Decision to accept commitments offered by Google in relation to its Privacy Sandbox Proposals" Case number 50972, 11 February 2022

CMA/ICO, "Competition and data protection in digital markets: a joint statement between the CMA and ICO", 19 May 2021

DOUGLAS, E. M., "Digital Crossroads: The intersection of competition law and data privacy", July 2021 (Annexed to Global Privacy Assembly, Digital Citizen and Consumer Working Group, Report, August 2021)

European Data Protection Supervisor, Preliminary Opinion on "Privacy and competitiveness in the age of big data: the interplay between data protection, competition law and consumer protection in the Digital Economy", 26 March 2014

OECD, "Consumer data rights and competition", June 2020

"Stigler Committee on Digital Platforms", Final Report, 2019

See also

Market Power, European Convention on Human Rights (ECHR), Competition policy, Consumer protection

P

PRIVATE ENFORCEMENT

Michael D. HAUSFELD
Hausfeld

Definition

Many countries authorize private suits challenging conduct claimed to violate their competition laws. In some jurisdictions such suits are limited to cases that "follow-on" a successful government suit, but "stand alone" suits are permitted in the U.S., many EU Member States, and the UK. Suits generally may be instituted by competitors, suppliers, and customers. Such suits usually seek damages compensating plaintiffs for injury caused by the anticompetitive conduct and/or injunctive relief to force its discontinuance. The U.S. is unique in requiring treble damages to be awarded to successful plaintiffs. U.S. federal antitrust law generally disallows suits by indirect purchasers claiming damages passed on to them, but many other jurisdictions allow such suits.

Commentary

Private enforcement of competition laws is permitted in many countries. While some jurisdictions limit private enforcement to cases that "follow-on" from a successful government enforcement action, "stand-alone" private suits also are permitted in the United States (U.S.), European Union (EU), and the United Kingdom (UK). As summarized below, the policies of all three jurisdictions provide for private enforcement in order to ensure that those injured by antitrust violations are fully compensated, but private enforcement is also intended to deter antitrust violations.

Jury trials are authorized for antitrust private damages suits in the U.S. but are not authorized in the EU or UK. There is a four-year statute of limitations in the U.S., between one and five years in the EU (depending on the Member State), and six years in the UK for claims in the English High Court. The period is tolled in the U.S. and certain EU Member States while governmental proceedings are pending and for a short time period thereafter.

The Competition Appeal Tribunal (CAT) is a specialized competition court in the UK that hears both standalone and follow-on damage claims. There is a "fast track" procedure available before the CAT pursuant to which hearings are to be held within six months for small or medium firms if the hearing can be concluded within three days and will not involve complex or novel issues. Different limitation periods also apply to CAT claims.

In the U.S., liability findings against a defendant in a federal government antitrust case are admissible in a follow-on private antitrust suit as prima facie evidence of a violation. In the EU on the other hand, the finding of a violation by the European Commission is binding in a follow-on private action in the national court of Member States that have adopted the 2014 EU Damages Directive. Post-Brexit, European Commission decisions are not binding in the UK, but infringement decisions issued by the UK's Competition and Markets Authority remain binding on defendants in follow-on private suits.

Most jurisdictions, including the UK and EU Member States, provide for single damages. The U.S. is the only major jurisdiction providing a mandatory treble damage remedy to private enforcers of the Sherman Act. Additionally, a successful private plaintiff in the U.S. recovers its attorneys' fees from the defendant. In the UK the same rule applies although only part of the successful plaintiff's fees normally is recovered. Most EU Member States only allow successful parties to recover a relatively small portion of their cost, but mandatory interest is assessed from the inception of the wrongdoing in the UK and some EU Member States.

In the U.S., only direct customers generally have standing to sue cartel members or monopolists engaged in abusive conduct for overcharges under the Sherman Act. The impact of this judicially established federal rule has been somewhat muted, however, by the large number of states that permit indirect purchasers to recover under their state antitrust laws, which are not preempted by the federal antitrust laws. In UK and EU Member States that have adopted the EU Damages Directive, indirect customers of wrongdoers can bring claims but must prove that losses were "passed on" to them by direct purchasers. In 2019 the European Commission issued non-binding guidelines to national courts on how to estimate the overcharge that that was passed-on to indirect purchasers.

In the U.S., the determination whether a plaintiff may proceed with an antitrust claim is based on an evaluation of the following factors: (1) the causal connection between the alleged violation and the harm to the plaintiff; (2) the nature of the injury, including whether the plaintiff is a consumer or competitor in the relevant market; (3) the directness of the injury, and whether the damage claim is too speculative; (4) the potential for duplicative damages or complex damages apportionment issues; and (5) the existence of more efficient enforcers. In the UK and most EU Member States there is a proximate cause standard requiring a plaintiff to establish that its injury was caused in whole or substantial part by the alleged violation of the competition laws.

Defendants in cartel suits in all three jurisdictions are subject to joint and several liability. However, in the U.S. there is no right to contribution from co-defendants while in the UK and many EU Member States, infringing companies do have contribution claims against each other. However, in those EU Member States where the EU Damages is followed, small and medium sized companies, as well as companies that have been granted amnesty, are liable only to their own (direct or indirect) customers.

In cartel cases in all three jurisdictions, the amount of damages is based on the amount of overcharge proven by the plaintiff, and in cases involving exclusionary abuses by dominant companies, damages are based on the profit the plaintiff can prove it would have made in a competitive market.

Calculation of damages to injured antitrust plaintiffs in all three jurisdictions need not be precise and can be determined on reasonable estimates based on relevant data. However, damages cannot be calculated by speculation or guesswork. Although specific rules on quantification vary among EU Member States, the European Commission has issued Practical Guides for Quantifying Harm in Actions for Damages.

Private damages claims are regularly filed in all three jurisdictions challenging cartels, but there are fewer private abuse of dominance cases. This is not surprising for three reasons. First, dominance cases are less frequently instituted by government enforcers, particularly in the U.S. Second, such cases require (more) economic analysis, including defining the relevant market, and assessing whether the alleged wrongdoer is dominant in that market. Third, the damage quantification in dominance cases is less straightforward than in cartel cases, where the basic issue is whether the alleged cartel members entered into the unlawful agreement at issue.

Claims for injunctive relief in antitrust suits to remedy actual or threatened harm are permitted in the U.S. and UK, either with or without damage claims.

Bibliography

HOVENKAMP, H., Federal Antitrust Policy, *The Law of Competition and Its Practice*, Ch. 16 (West Academic Publishing, 6th Ed. 2020)

PARCU, P. L., MONTI, G. and BOTTA, M. (eds.), *Private Enforcement of EU Competition Law* (Edward Elgar Publishing 2018)

KELLAWAY, R., THOMPSON, R. and BROWN, C. (eds.), *UK Competition Law: The New Framework*, Ch. 8 (Oxford Univ. Press 2016)

Section of Antitrust Law, *Antitrust Law Developments*, Ch. 9 (ABA Book Publishing, 8th Ed. 2017)

See also

Collective redress (class action), Damages

P

PRIVATIZATION

Tomotake HORIMATSU
Japan Fair Trade Commission

■ Definition

The term privatization refers to transfer of ownership and control of government or state assets, firms and operations to private investors. For instance, state owned airline enterprises, telecommunications and energy have been privatized in many countries. This transfer, in some cases, takes the form of issue and sale or outright distribution of shares to the general public. In addition, and more broadly, this term refers to any shift of the activities or functions from the state to the public sector. Accordingly, privatization includes privatizing the management of state activities through contracts and leases, and the contracting out of activities that were previously done by the state, such as selling railway tickets or managing jails. Privatization can be solely conducted, based on the belief that efficient performance depends on private ownership per se, although privatization is sometimes carried out in combination with liberalization or deregulation, with the idea that competition is the critical spur to efficiency.

■ Commentary

The purpose of privatization includes efficiency, and protection from competition on privatized businesses can reduce such efficiency; thus, vigorous enforcement of competition law against anticompetitive conducts of privatized businesses may be a key to achieving the efficiency attributed to privatization. Accordingly, in several jurisdictions, there are several cases in which privatization itself or privatized businesses got subject to competition law.

The following explores the two stages concerning privatization and what can be problematic or constitute the violation of competition law in each of the stages: the process of privatization itself and the post-privatization stage.

First of all, the process of privatization itself may be subject to competition law in the jurisdiction where state aid regulation is included in the competition law regime as in Europe. In the EU, Article 107 of the Treaty on the Functioning of the European Union prohibits state aid, which includes sale of public assets or privatization entailing selective advantage, distortion of competition and an effect on trade between Member States of EU; simply put, privatization in which any advantage is given to the buyer and/or the sold undertaking may be prohibited as state aid. Whether privatization is regarded as state aid is decided by the so called Market Economy Investor Principle (MEIP) or the Market Economy Vendor Principle test, which MEIP is translated into in a privatization context; according to the test, the state does not give any advantage to the buyer/or the sold undertaking and therefore does not grant to it state aid when the selling authority acts as a private vendor who seeks to maximize the revenue or minimize the loss from the sale.

It should be noted that some preparatory measures for privatization, such as debt write-off, may contain state aid subject to competition law. For the decisions concerning these measures as well MEIP is applied; when the state acts in the capacity of a creditor, the test is called the Market Economy Creditor Principle (MECP). In PZL Hydral (C 40/2008), where it was scrutinized that debts to the Polish state were settled in preparation for privatization, it was found that the settlement had not constitute state aid on the grands that it was performed on market terms; namely, public creditor was better-off in case of the privatization or sale of all the assets than in the counterfactual scenario of ordinary bankruptcy leading to liquidation.

Secondly, after privatization is accomplished, particularly when liberalization is brought about as well, it should be born in mind that privatized enterprises' conducts may be subject to competition law. This point is particularly important in the jurisdiction where publicly owned enterprises are immune to competition law, since compliance to competition law is none of their business before privatization; for instance, in the United States, some federal government entities may be exempted from the competition law (U.S. Postal Service v. Flamingo Industries (USA), Ltd.) unless otherwise stipulated in legislation.

The question is what sort of privatized enterprises' conducts may be subject to competition law. As regards this point, one of their characteristics is worth noting, namely, owning heavily invested facilities. Typically, in the network industry, such as telecommunication, electricity and gas, privatized enterprises have taken over the network which was established when they were state-owned; sometimes supply of the services based on such network is liberalized, hence on the supply side, competition is expected among the privatized enterprises and new entries, when the privatized enterprises are vertically integrated (management of the network, namely, wholesale of the connection to the network, and supply based on the network).

For instance, in Japan, data communication was state-owned and monopolized, and after the privatization and liberalization of the data communication, Nippon Telegraph and Telephone Corporation (NTT) came into born as a successor of the state-owned enterprise. Before privatization, R&D for Fiber To The Home (FTTH) was conducted by the predecessor of NTT; based on this R&D, NTT established the NTTH network throughout Japan. NTT's subsidiary in charge of the east area of Japan, Nippon Telegraph and Telephone East Corporation (NTT East) managed the network in the east area of Japan, and supplied the FTTH service based on the network, which means NTT EAST was vertically integrated; namely, NTT EAST supplied the network connection service to the provider of the NTTH service and competed with these providers in supply of the NTTH service. In this situation, NTT East set the price of the NTTH service to its users below the price of the network connection service to other providers of the NTTH service; this conduct was found for NTT East to exclude its competitors in supply of the NTTH service on the grounds that other NTTH service providers were forced to pay the price of the network connection service necessary to supply the NTTH service in competing with NTT East, whose price of the NTTH service was below that of the network connection service, hence to supply the NTTH service with deficit (Monopolization, NTT East (2009, Administrative, appeal-heard, No. 348)). This case shows that if privatized enterprises are vertically integrated, their conducts may be subject to competition law in the following perspective: predatory pricing in a down-stream market and/or refusal to supply of the service necessary to conduct the business in a down-stream market (reference to the so-called margin squeeze may be helpful for understanding).

Bibliography

NICOLAIDES, P., How EU state aid rules apply to privatisation of public enterprises, January 2015, *Concurrences No 1-2015*, Art. No 69245

SHIRLEY, M. (1988). The Experience with Privatization, Finance & Development, 0025(003), A010. Retrieved Nov 20, 2023

STARR, P., "The Meaning of Privatization," *Yale Law and Policy Review* 6 (1988): 6-41

VOLOKH, A., Privatization and Competition Policy (2014). *Competition and the State* (Thomas K. Cheng, Ioannis Lianos, and D. Daniel Sokol eds., 2014)

Competition Policy Research Center of the Japan Fair Trade Commission, Competition Policy in Network Industries – Comparative Legal Studies across Japan, USA and EU and Economic Analysis – (2012.10.11)

OECD (1993), Glossary of Industrial Organisation Economics and Competition Law, Retrieved Nov 20, 2023

The Guidance Paper SWD (2012) 14 final, 10/2/2012

*The views expressed in this article are solely those of the author and do not necessarily reflect those of the JFTC.

See also

Market economy investor, State aid (notion)

P

PROCEDURAL AUTONOMY

Luca PRETE, Nicolaj KUPLEWATZKY
European Court of Justice

Definition

National procedural autonomy is a principle of European Union ("EU") law. It stipulates that EU Member States are free to establish their own national procedural rules to govern the exercise of EU law. However, those rules must respect the effectiveness and equivalence of EU law. Effectiveness seeks to prevent a situation in which the national procedural rules would make the exercise of EU law based rights impossible or excessively difficult. Equivalence requires that the Member State shall not discriminate between claims based on national law and claims arising out of EU law.

Commentary

The principle of national procedural autonomy was first voiced by the European Court of Justice ("the Court") in its judgment in *Rewe* (33/76, EU:C:1976:188). There, the Court explained that in the absence of EU law provisions, the exercise of EU law on the national level is governed by the institutional and procedural rules of the Member States. The reliance on national procedural rules is, however, made subject to the condition that the effectiveness and equivalence of EU law is upheld. Effectiveness seeks to prevent a situation in which the national procedural rules would make the exercise of EU law-based rights impossible or excessively difficult. Equivalence requires that the Member State shall not discriminate between claims deriving from national law and claims arising out of EU law. The combination of the absence of procedural provisions at the EU law level and the dual requirement of equivalence and effectiveness recognises national diversity, all the while ensuring a degree of surveillance of national remedial rules by EU law.

The judgement in *Courage and Crehan* (C-453/99, EU:C:2001:465) is a prominent example where the Court had to reconcile the effectiveness of what is now Article 101(1) TFEU with national rules on remedies. That case concerned a challenge to the validity of a beer tie agreement and an action for damages for breach of competition law. However, English law did not permit a party to a contract which was liable to restrict or distort competition to claim damages for loss caused by the performance of that contract. The Court held that, since Article 101(1) TFEU conferred an express right for competitors and individuals to claim damages arising from the breach of competition rules directly before the competent courts of the Member States, national rules precluding that right ought to be disapplied for failing to ensure the full effectiveness of Article 101(1) TFEU.

Other instances where the Court found national procedural rules to jeopardise the full effectiveness of EU law arose in *Manfredi* (C-295/04 to C-298/04, EU:C:2006:461) (which concerned national procedural rules on limitation periods; damages claims for breaches of competition law; and the possibility to apply for interest); *Vebic* (C-439/08, EU:C:2010:739) (which dealt with the participation of the Belgian national competition authority in review proceedings against decisions adopted by it); *Pfleiderer*(C-360/09, EU:C:2011:389) (which related to the interplay between public and private enforcement and the granting of access for private claimants to self-incriminating documents retained by the German competition authority); *Otis* (C-199/11, EU:C:2012:684) (which recognised the right to claim damages for the infringement of competition rules also for the European Commission); *Donau-Chemie* (C-536/11, EU:C:2013:366) (which reviewed national law categorically prohibiting access to certain documents); *Kone and Others* (C-557/12, EU:C:2014:1317) (where, under national law, compensatory claims relating to damages arising from "umbrella pricing effects" were prohibited); *Eturas and Others* (C-74/14, EU:C:2016:42) (which dealt with the presumption of innocence and the inference of knowledge of concerted practices); *Skanska* (C-724/17, EU:C:2019:204) (where the Court required the piercing of the corporate veil to ensure effective damages claims); and *Cogeco* (C-637/17, EU:C:2019:263) (which concerned national time limits for bringing cartel damages cases).

Bibliography

Biondi, A. and Gentile, G., "National Procedural Autonomy", *Max Planck Encyclopedias of International Law*. OUP Oxford (4 Sep 2019), p. 1-15

Van Cleynenbruegel, P., "Embedding Procedural Autonomy: The Directive and National Procedural Rules", in *Harmonising EU Competition Litigation: the new directive and beyond* (Eds. Maria Bergström, Marios Iacovides and Magnus Strand) (Bloomsbury, 2016)

See also

Applicable law

P

PROFESSIONAL ASSOCIATION

Sean HEATHER
U.S. Chamber of Commerce

Definition

Professional and trade associations are membership organizations, usually non-profit, that serve the interests of members who share a common field of activity. In general, professional associations consist of individuals of a common profession, whereas trade associations consist of companies in a particular economic sector or across many sectors. Associations advocate for the interests of their members to be reflected in government policy through tools such as lobbying, litigation, business development, and the development of common industry or professional standards. For those associations that develop industry or professional standards, the standards that they create are often recognized by governments through regulation. In these instances, a public-private partnership is effectively created where government regulatory objectives can be best achieved via technical standards that leverage industry's expertise. Most associations are *private law* associations that are formed privately (not under a governmental mandate) as a non-profit association and whose members decide to pay dues and join voluntarily. Although in some countries, there are also *public law associations* that are formed as a branch or under strict control of a government or regulatory agency and whose members often are required to join by law. Finally, in many countries national laws guarantee freedom of association, while internationally, ILO Convention number 87 guarantees such freedom to both employers and employees.

Commentary

Europe

In Europe, associations have formal institutional structures, voluntary membership, independence from the government, and regular activity in the public arena. Most associations carry out their activities in particular regions, though some cross international boundaries.

Given the range of countries across Europe, the influence and specific activities of professional and trade associations vary across the region. In general, and as in other parts of the world, trade and professional associations in Europe gather intelligence, advocate on behalf of their members, share information with their members, and provide a platform for direct engagement with officials.

Across Europe, some of the largest or most prominent associations include BUSINESSEUROPE (which represents national business confederations as well as companies), Digital Europe, the European Association for the Promotion of Cogeneration, Accountancy Europe, Confederation of British Industry, and the Standing Committee of European Doctors.

United States

In the U.S., trade associations advocate for their members' interests in many ways. At both the federal and state levels, trade associations regularly provide information to legislators and regulators through in-person briefings, regulatory filings, and white papers. Association advocacy today also includes grassroots mobilization and communications campaigns. Associations also educate their members about developments that may affect their interests and facilitate their ability to contact policymakers directly. Government officials, in turn, often seek out the views of associations to understand how particular proposals might affect a particular economic sector or the business community as a whole.

These advocacy efforts are protected by the First Amendment to the U.S. Constitution, which protects the right to free speech and right to petition the government. Interpreting the First Amendment, a series of decisions from the U.S. Supreme Court allowed associations to advocate on behalf of their members who, in other contexts, compete vigorously against each other. These court cases created what is now known as the *Noerr-Pennington Doctrine*. Notwithstanding these constitutional protections, trade associations, particularly those that represent individual sectors of the economy, must take care that they do not facilitate cartelization.

Beyond policy work, associations also advocate for their members through the court system. In certain circumstances, an association may have the legal ability to bring a lawsuit on behalf of its members. Through such lawsuits, associations can challenge the legality of statutes and regulations that adversely affect their members. In other cases, associations may file *amicus*, or "friend of the court", briefs, that provide the courts with useful information relevant to a particular legal dispute. The courts, including the U.S. Supreme Court, sometime cite such *amicus* briefs in their written opinions.

In the U.S., some of the largest trade associations include the U.S. Chamber of Commerce, the National Association of Homebuilders; and the American Hospital Association. Large professional associations include the National Association of Realtors, American Bar Association, American Institute of Certified Public Accountants, and American Medical Association.

Bibliography

De Fouloy, C., *Top Industry Associations in the EU*, Association of Accredited Public Policy Advocates to the European Union (2019)

European Commission, *Associations and Foundations*

European Commission, *Communication from the Commission on Promoting the Role of Voluntary Organisations and Foundations in Europe*, Ref. Ares(2014)78436

Federal Trade Commission, *Enforcement Perspectives on the Noerr-Pennington Doctrine*, Federal Trade Commission Staff Report (2006)

Reference for Business Encyclopedia, *Professional and Trade Organizations*

See also

Consumer association, Undertaking (notion)

P

PUBLIC PROCUREMENT

Albert SÁNCHEZ GRAELLS
University of Bristol – Law School

Definition

Public procurement rules govern the award of government or public contracts for the acquisition of supplies, works or services, including the direct provision of public services to citizens. Public procurement rules seek to foster effective competition for public contracts to generate value for money, and to harness competition as an anticorruption tool to ensure integrity and probity in the expenditure of public funds. The main challenges to effective competition in public procurement settings are bid rigging (or collusion among bidders), which risk is heightened by the transparency inherent to procurement processes, and anticompetitive requirements imposed by the public buyer.

Commentary

The effectiveness of public procurement and its ability to deliver value for money depend on the existence of two layers of competition: competition in the market for the goods, works or services to be acquired, and competition within the tender for a specific contract. While most competition analysis focuses on the existence (or absence) of competition within the tender and tends to assimilate this with models of competition for the market, this is a short-sighted approach. Except for very rare public contracts for goods, services or works for which the public buyer is a monopsonist – mainly in sectors such as defence – most public tenders take place in a framework of competition in the market, and one with many private and public buyers seeking to purchase from a range of potential suppliers (for example, tenders for the acquisition of cloud services, general supplies, or school meals). Therefore, it is important not only to ensure that procurement rules and administrative practices prevent distortions of competition within a given tender, but also that they do not generate negative knock-on effects on (dynamic) competition in the relevant market.

The most commonly discussed distortion of competition within a public tender concerns anticompetitive agreements between bidders (bid rigging) that seek to manipulate the competition for the public contract and to extract excessive rents from the public buyer. The mechanics of bid rigging schemes are widely understood, including predominant strategies such as cover bidding, bid suppression, bid rotation and market allocation. However, these anticompetitive practices are also difficult to prevent in oligopolistic or concentrated markets because the transparency inherent to public tenders significantly facilitates monitoring of the cartelists' bidding behaviour, and because the atomisation of public tenders requires a significant investment in market screening tools to spot suspicious patterns across regional markets and over time. Fighting cartels in public procurement settings has become a high priority for most competition authorities in recent years, in part as a result of the OECD's work on this area – see its 2012 Recommendation on *Fighting Bid Rigging in Public Procurement* – as well as the push by the International Competition Network. There is also hope in the development of effective systems of automated screening and red flags where public procurement is conducted electronically (of which there is longstanding experience eg in Korea in relation to its eProcurement platform KONEPS), but these require a solid procurement data architecture which absence has marred recent attempts in jurisdictions such as the UK and its now abandoned "Screening for cartels" tool.

An additional difficulty in ensuring effective competition within a given tender derives from the unclear boundary between anticompetitive practices such as bid rigging and procompetitive cooperation through teaming, joint bidding and subcontracting arrangements between bidders. There is currently significant debate about the limits to cooperation between (potential) competitors in the context of procurement procedures, as well as whether it should be treated as a restriction of competition by object or by effect for the purposes of Article 101 TFEU. The debate is particularly alive in Scandinavian countries, following a 2016 Decision by the EFTA Court in the *Ski* and *Follo Taxi* case, and a more recent 2019 Judgment by the Danish Supreme Court in the *Road Markings* case, which has led to a revision of the Danish Competition and Consumer Authority's guidelines on joint bidding. The main points of contention about the state of the law concern the counterfactual to be used to determine that joint bidders are (potential) competitors, as well as the measurement of any efficiencies passed on to the public buyer.

In order to empower public buyers to self-protect against bid rigging and to strengthen the effectiveness of competition law in public procurement settings, EU procurement rules have created discretionary grounds for the exclusion of bidders "where the contracting authority has sufficiently plausible indications to conclude that the economic operator has entered into agreements with other economic operators aimed at distorting competition", as well as in cases "where the contracting authority can demonstrate by appropriate means that the economic operator is guilty of grave professional misconduct, which renders its integrity questionable" – which the Court of Justice of the EU has interpreted as inclusive of non-procurement related breaches of competition law (*Generali-Providencia Biztosító*). Recent Court of Justice case law has clarified the extent to which these exclusion grounds are applicable where bidders have benefitted from leniency, as well as the intensity of the duty to cooperate incumbent upon bidders seeking to avoid exclusion through self-cleaning measures (*Vossloh Laeis*). In 2021, the European Commission has published a Notice on tools to fight collusion in public procurement and on guidance on how to apply the related exclusion ground that seeks to increase the use of these instruments. The system created under the EU rules is converging with those of other major jurisdictions, such as the U.S., where the Federal Acquisitions Regulations allow for similar approaches to assessing the responsiveness (or reliability) of bidders engaged in anticompetitive practices.

Beyond the above mentioned issues, which are all concerned with bidder behaviour, it is important to stress that competition within a public tender can be restricted through decisions made by the public buyer, such as the imposition of excessive participation requirements, the choice of suppliers in less than fully open procedures or foreclosure through, for example, the use of excessively broad and excessively long framework agreements. Such restrictions of competition can not only generate losses of value for money in the allocation of the specific contract, but also have negative effects on dynamic competition in the relevant market. Unfortunately, the direct application of competition law (ie Article 102 TFEU) to the public buyer has been excluded by the case law of the Court of Justice, except in rather rare situations where the public buyer is engaged in downstream market activities (*FENIN*). However, a principle of competition has been explicitly enshrined in EU public procurement law to prevent public buyers from "artificially narrowing competition", in particular where "the design of the procurement is made with the intention of unduly favouring or disadvantageing certain economic operators". This is a promising tool to prevent publicly-generated restrictions of competition in public procurement settings, although its interpretation generates some difficulties and its application is yet to be tested in the EU Courts.

Bibliography

ANDERSON, R., KOVACIC, W. E. and MÜLLER, A. C., Promoting Competition and Deterring Corruption in *Public Procurement Markets: Synergies with Trade Liberalisation* (2016)

JONES, A., "Spotlight on Cartels: Bid Rigging Affecting Public Procurement" (*Concurrentialiste*, 16 Nov 2020)

KUŸMA, K. and HARTUNG, W. , *Combating Collusion in Public Procurement. Legal Limitations on Joint Bidding* (Edward Elgar 2020)

SANCHEZ-GRAELLS, A., *Public Procurement and the EU Competition Rules* (2nd edn, Hart 2015), Chapter 5

SANCHEZ-GRAELLS, A., "'Screening for Cartels' in Public Procurement: Cheating at Solitaire to Sell Fool's Gold?" (2019) 10(4) *Journal of European Competition Law & Practice* 199-211

See also

Bid rigging

P

PUBLIC UNDERTAKING

Łukasz GRZEJDZIAK
University of Lodz

■ Definition

Article 106 (1) TFEU prohibits Member States from introducing and maintaining, in respect of public undertakings and undertakings to which they grant special or exclusive rights, measures contrary to the provisions of the Treaties. The purpose of Article 106 TFEU is to prevent preferential treatment by the Member States of undertakings listed therein. The notion of public undertaking is defined in the Directive on the transparency of financial relations as any undertaking over which the public authorities may exercise directly or indirectly a dominant influence by virtue of their ownership of it, their financial participation therein, or the rules which govern it.

■ Commentary

Article 106(1) 1 TFEU concretizes the principle of neutrality expressed in Article 345 TFEU, according to which the Treaties shall in no way prejudice the rules in Member States governing the system of property ownership. Thus, although Member States are generally free to choose this system, there should be no unjustified discrimination between public and private undertakings in the application of the rules on competition (Directive 2006/111/EC, recital 4). In particular, Member States must avoid favouring public undertakings by granting State aid, preferences in public procurement, or creating the conditions for exercising exclusive or special rights granted to them in an anti-competitive manner. In GB-INNO-B.M. v. ATAB (1977), the CJEU held that from the principle of sincere cooperation and from Art. 106 TFEU follows that in the case of public undertakings and undertakings to which Member States grant special or exclusive rights, Member States shall neither enact nor maintain in force any measure contrary inter alia to the rules provided for in Articles 101 to 109 TFEU.

The categories of undertakings listed in Article 106 (1) TFEU should be treated separately. In Commission v. DEI (2014), the CJEU held that a public undertaking does not have to be the beneficiary of special or exclusive rights to fall within the scope of this provision.

The decisive criterion for defining a public undertaking is the possibility of exercising direct or indirect influence over an undertaking by public authorities. The transparency directive defines public authorities broadly as to include the State, regional, local, and all other territorial authorities. The dominant influence is presumed when public authorities, directly or indirectly in relation to an undertaking:

(i) hold the major part of the undertaking's subscribed capital; or
(ii) control the majority of the votes attaching to shares issued by the undertakings; or
(iii) can appoint more than half of the members of the undertaking's administrative, managerial or supervisory body;

Article 106 TFEU has no independent effect and must be read in conjunction with the relevant rules of the Treaty (Asemfo v. Trags et al. (2007), paragraph 40). It was applied in conjunction with Article 45 TFEU on the free movement of workers (Merci convenzionali porto di Genova (1991), paragraph 24), Articles 49 and 56 TFEU on freedom of establishment and freedom to provide services (ASM Brescia SpA v. Comune di Rodengo Saiano (2008) paragraph 61) and Article 34 TFEU on the free movement of goods (Inter-Huiles (1983), paragraph. 15).

Most often, however, in accordance with the basic role assigned to it, Article 106 (1) TFEU has been applied in conjunction with competition rules. In GB-INNO-B.M. v. ATAB, the Court held that Article 106 TFEU imposes a duty on Member States not to adopt or maintain in force any measure which could deprive Article 102 TFEU of its effectiveness. [E]ven within the framework of Article 106 TFEU, Article 102 TFEU of the Treaty has direct effect and confers on individuals' rights which the national courts must protect (Carra and others paragraph 17).

The mere exercise of exclusive or special rights is not an infringement of Article 106 (1) TFEU (La Crespelle (1994), paragraphs 18–20; Ambulanz Glöckner (2001), paragraph. 39; Servizi (2006) paragraphs 21–23). In Höfner and Elser v. Macrotron CJEU held that "[A] Member State is in breach of the prohibition contained in those two provisions only if the undertaking in question, merely by exercising the exclusive right granted to it, cannot avoid abusing its dominant position. […] [s]uch an abuse may in particular consist in limiting the provision of a service, to the prejudice of those seeking to avail themselves of it." (see as well Sacchi, (1974), paragraph 14 and RTT v. GB-Inno-BM, (1991) paragraphs 20 and 21; ERT v. DEP, paragraph 38).

On the other hand, in Commission v. DEI (2014), the CJEU ruled that "Infringement of Article 106 TFEU in conjunction with Article 102 TFEU may be established irrespective of whether any abuse actually exists. All that is necessary is for the Commission to identify a potential or actual anti-competitive consequence liable to result from the State measure at issue." Therefore, granting the holder of special or exclusive rights any additional rights enabling her to extend or strengthen her dominant position is a violation of Article 106 (1) of the Treaty (see also Bodson v. Pompes funèbres and RTT v. GB-Inno-BM).

The CJEU also found the following practices to be a violation of Art. 106 (1) in conjunction with Article 102 TFEU: granting exclusive rights resulting in the inability to effectively meet the demand from potential buyers (AG2R Prévoyance (2011), Job Centre coop. arl. (1997); Slovenská Pošta v. Commission (2015)), the creation of conditions enabling price discrimination and excessive pricing (GT-Link v. De Danske Stadbaner (1997) paragraph 46), approval by public authorities of tariffs containing excessively high prices (Corsica Ferries (1994) paragraph 43) and national measures giving rise to a conflict of interests that inevitably led to discrimination or unequal conditions of competition (MOTOE v. Elliniko Dimosio (2008) paragraph 53; Silvano Raso (1998), paragraphs 28–30).

In Corbeau, the Court did not identify a specific state measure constituting a violation of Art. 106 (1) TFEU, thus implying that the maintenance of the Belgian Post's monopoly on courier services was as such an infringement of this provision.

Article 106 (2) TFEU establishes a derogation from the Treaty rules in respect of undertakings entrusted with the operation of services of general economic interest or having the character of a revenue-producing monopoly, in so far as the application of such rules does not obstruct the performance, in law or in fact, of the particular tasks assigned to them. The development of trade must not be affected to such an extent as would be contrary to the interests of the Union. Although Article 106 (2) TFEU is addressed to undertakings, the exemption established therein applies also to measures taken in respect of them by Member States.

Article 106(3) TFEU makes the Commission responsible for ensuring the application of the provisions of Article 106 and contains a delegation for the Commission to issue directives and decisions addressed to Member States for this purpose.

Bibliography

BUENDIA SIERRA, J. L., *Exclusive Rights and State Monopolies in EC Law* (Oxford University Press, 2000)

CREMONA, M. (ed.), *Market Integration and Public Service in the EU* (Oxford University Press, 2011)

HANCHER, L. and SAUTER, W., *EU Competition and Internal Market Law in the Healthcare Sector* (Oxford University Press, 2012)

PROSSER, T., *The Limits of Competition Law* (Oxford University Press, 2005)

SAUTER, W., *Public Services in EU Law* (Cambridge University Press, 2014)

See also

Market economy investor, Undertaking (notion) Exclusive right (Art. 106 TFEU)

R

R&D AGREEMENT

Björn LUNDQVIST
Stockholm University

Definition

An Research & development agreement is a specific type of collaboration that may either fall outside the ambit of Article 101(1) TFEU or be exempted under Article 101(3) TFEU, and where there is a block exemption and guidelines clarifying the definition and the terms of such collaboration. In essence it implies that all collaborative efforts agreeing to pursue activities aimed at acquiring know-how relating to existing or new products, technologies, processes or R&D poles including the carrying out analysis, experimentation, technical testing and experimental production, and the obtaining of intellectual property rights for the results are Research & development agreements.

Commentary

According to the 2010 Horizontal Guidelines, an Research & development agreement can restrict competition in various ways: "*First, it may reduce or slow down innovation, leading to fewer or worse products coming to the market later than they otherwise would. Secondly, on product or technology markets the R&D cooperation may reduce significantly competition between the parties outside the scope of the agreement or it may make anti-competitive coordination on those markets likely, thereby leading to higher prices. A foreclosure problem may arise in the context of cooperation involving at least one player with a significant degree of market power (which does not necessarily amount to dominance) for a key technology and the exclusive exploitation of the results.*"

The new proposed 2023 Horizontal Guidelines state moreover that "agreements relating to R&D restrict competition by object if their main purpose is not R&D, but to serve as a tool to engage in a cartel or in other by object infringements under Article 101(1), such as price fixing, output limitation, market allocation or restrictions of technical development".

An Research & development agreement may restrict technical development when, instead of cooperating for promoting technical and economic progress, the parties use the R&D cooperation to (a) prevent or delay the market entry of products or technologies, (b) coordinate the characteristics of products or technologies which are not covered by the Research & development agreement or (c) limit the potential of a jointly developed product or technology when they bring such a product or technology individually to the market.

A R&D exemption under EU Competition law can be traced back to a notice issued in 1968 where the Commission stated *inter alia* that pure R&D co-operations generally do not restrict competition, on the condition that the parties are free to pursue their own research, and if there is no restriction regarding the use of the R&D results.

It should be stressed that the requirement already mentioned in the 1968 notice that the collaborating parties should be free to pursue their own research, and that there is no restriction regarding the use of the R&D results after the termination of the R&D collaboration is still applicable and unique for the EU. The U.S. Joint R&D exemption does not stipulate a similar requirement. It shows that the EU is concerned with the outcome of the R&D collaboration, and that even though two firms may enter into a Research & development agreement as non-competitors, they will often exit the collaboration as competitors or potential competitors. The spill-over or knowledge leaking a cooperation create between the parties may place them on equal footing in competition in innovation *ex post* the end of the collaboration.

On 29 November 2000, the first "modern" block exemption for the application of Art. 101(3) to Research & development agreements was adopted after the introduction of the so-called more economic approach. This block exemption was just one in a series of new block exemptions published since 1999 until 2004 where the Commission implemented the more economic approach. A major change to the block exemptions under the more economic approach was the introduction of market share ceilings. The 2000 block exemption expired in 2010 and was replaced by the current R&D BER published on 14 December 2010, which was made applicable to parties when their combined market share did not exceed 25% of the relevant product and technology markets.

The new proposed 2023 R&D BER is more detailed than its predecessors, while it still stipulates a markets share ceiling of 25% on the relevant product and technology markets; or in case of an Research & development agreement involving paid-for research and development, the combined market share of the financing party and all the parties with which the financing party has entered into Research & development agreements does not exceed 25% on the relevant product and technology markets. Moreover, where two or more of the parties to the Research & development agreement are undertakings competing in innovation, the exemption shall apply for the duration of the research and development if, at the time the Research & development agreement is entered into, there are three or more competing R&D efforts in addition to and comparable with those of the parties to the Research & development agreement.

For the R&D BER to be applicable there is still conditions for the parties to have access to the final results and pre-existing know-how, and there is a list of hard-core clauses and excluded restrictions.

Taking the requirement that the parties to the Research & development agreement should have access to the result and the pre-existing know-how first: the obligation has several limitations but as a general rule, the parties to the Research & development agreement will often in theory exit the collaboration as at least potential competitors with access to the same R&D result and background know-how.

The hard-core clauses and exempted clauses resemble similar lists in other BERs, while there are some unique features mainly focus on the restriction of the freedom of the parties to carry out research and development independently or in cooperation with third parties.

It should be stressed that Research & development agreements falling outside the R&D BER may still benefit from the application of Article 101(3) TFEU. As depicted the 2023 Horizontal Guidelines, generally, R&D collaborations are generally viewed as benign or procompetitive under Article 101 TFEU.

Bibliography

Fuchs, A., *Kartellrechtliche Grenzen der Forschungskooperation* (Nomos Verlaggesellschaft 1989)

Lundqvist, B., *R&D collaborations under the Competition Rules of the European Union and The Antitrust Laws of the United States* (Edward Elgar 2015)

Silva Morais, L., *Joint ventures and EU competition law* Hart Publishing, 2013

Ullrich, H., *Kooperative Forschung and Kartellrecht* (Verlag Recht und Wirtschaft 1988)

Commission regulation No 2659/2000 29 November 2000 on the application of Art 81(3) of the Treaty to categories of research and development agreements OJ L 304, 05.12.2000, 7 *et seq* (defined earlier as the 2000 R&D BER). The previous R&D BER was enacted in 1985; Commission Regulation (EEC) No. 418/85 of 19 December 1984 on the application of Art 85 (3) of the Treaty to categories of research and development agreements (Hereinafter the 1984 or old block exemption

See also

FRAND

R

REFUSAL TO DEAL

Luis Jose DIEZ CANSECO NÚÑEZ, Robert VENERO PERALTA,
José Carlos GONZÁLES CUCHO
Díez Canseco

Definition

Refuse to deal with customers or suppliers by an undertaking with a dominant position can be considered as act of abuse when it prevents or threaten competitors on the market to enhance or preserve their market power. The rationale to justify this refusal is evaluated in a case-by-case basis.

Commentary

Refuse to deal is not per se illegal since undertakings have in principle the freedom to choose their economic partners. However, under exceptional circumstances, competition laws in the EU and the U.S. (i.e., article 102 TFEU and Section 2 of the Sherman Act) impose undertakings with a dominant position a duty to deal with competitors or customers to preserve competition on the market and avoid act of monopolization that harm consumer welfare.

Under Article 102 of the TFEU, refusal to deal as an act of abuse of a dominance position involves two markets in one of which an undertaking with a dominant position creates or threatens to impose restrictions to competition in the other market unjustifiably. Regarding this conduct, in the United Brands Case (1978), the Court of Justice determined that the justification for the refusal to contract by a company with a dominant position cannot be the mere protection of their own interests when the purpose of the conduct is to reinforce and abuse a dominant position (paragraph 189). Likewise, they pointed out that a dominant supplier cannot stop supplying its long-standing customers without justification (paragraph 182).

In relation to the justifications in the commercial relations between the dominant company and non-competitors, in the BBI / B & H Case (1987), the Commission pointed out that in those cases in which the interests of a dominant company are threatened by the association of a buyer with a competitor or with a potential competitor of said manufacturing company, the latter may take measures commensurate with the threat, but this does not enable the dominant producer to withdraw supplies immediately or to retaliate against the buyer. Thus, the dominant company can even review the commercial relations with the buyer and can terminate their relationship giving adequate notice (paragraph 19).

Regarding the relationships of the dominant company with competitors or potential competitors, in the Commercial Solvents Case (1974), the Court of Justice interpreted Article 102 indicating that the company that has a dominant position in the market of "raw materials" incurs in an abuse of dominance practice when, with the aim of reserving them for its own production of derivative products, it refuses to supply to a buyer who is also a producer of said derivative products, generating the risk of eliminating all competition from this buyer's side. Later, in Telemarketing Case (1985), The Court of Justice pointed out that this rule also applies to a company that occupies a dominant position in the market of an "essential service" for the activities of another company in another market, even when it is different from that of the dominant company (paragraph 26). In these cases, the refusal must also have an objective justification in technical or commercial needs related to the service of the dominant company.

Otherwise, when the reservation is given to eliminate the competition of third parties, such behavior will be prohibited as a practice of abuse of a dominant position by article 86 (currently 102 TFEU).

An important case in which the discussion on the doctrine of "essential facilities" was introduced and from which the criterion of the requisiteness of the means of production was developed in greater depth occurred with the Bronner Case (1998). A first outstanding aspect of this ruling is that the Court of Justice expressly indicates the criteria to be evaluated in order to determine the existence of an abuse of dominance position (paragraph 41): (i) the refusal may eliminate all jurisdiction in the market by the applicant, (ii) there is no objective justification and (iii) indispensable service for the person requesting the dominant company. Likewise, it also points out that the analysis of requisiteness assumes that there is no "real or potential alternative" to the service being requested. Moreover, when analyzing whether the distribution service in question ("national newspaper distribution system") was indispensable, the Court of Justice found that in the case this had not been proven because there were other modalities under which the service could be provided (for example, distribution by mail and sale in shops and kiosks) and there were no technical, financial or legal obstacles to creating a new distribution system alone or in collaboration with other competitors.

Furthermore, the position finally adopted by the Court of Justice was largely based on the Opinion of the

General Counsel Mr. Jacobs who pointed out that the application of the essential facilities doctrine or the refusal to sell goods or services could be justified when a dominant company has complete dominance in the linked market. Therefore, it is not enough that a company's control over a facility gives it a competitive advantage (paragraph 65). Likewise, it pointed out that, although the duplication of the facility can be a barrier to entry, the existence of abuse requires demonstrating that the level of investment required to replicate the distribution system at the national level of the dominant company would be such that it could disincentive to a competing company to enter the market (paragraph 68).

Now, a matter that it is necessary to point out that the Court has specified that the aforementioned "elimination of all competition" as the effect of the refusal constituting an abusive practice is proven once it has demonstrated that in adjacent or downstream markets there are no substitutes for the means of production to which they do not have access. It is not necessary to wait for the effective and total elimination of the competition.

In comparison to U.S. Competition Law, under Art. 102 TFEU, the EU requires a lower standard of liability for a refusal to deal to be considered anticompetitive. On the one hand, in the case of the EU, market power alone may be sufficient to be compelled to contract if competition in the market is excluded. In contrast, under Section 2 of the Sherman Act of the U.S., a higher standard is required. While in the case of the EU, a high market share can be considered evidence of the existence of a dominant position, in the USA other factors are also considered, such as the ease of entry of competitors into the market. Furthermore, regarding the "exclusory effects" of the anticompetitive conduct, in the EU this is related to the "indispensability" of the facility and the effects that the refusal to access to this facility may have on competition. In the case of the U.S., case law has required an unjustified change in a course of dealing and qualified anticompetitive effects of profit sacrifice or clear harm to consumer welfare.

Bibliography

Hou, L., Refusal to Deal within EU Competition Law (June 11, 2010)

International Competition Network (2010). Report on the Analysis of Refusal to Deal with a Rival Under Unilateral Conduct Laws

OCDE (2007). Refusals to deal. DAF/COMP (2007)46

Dario Morales and Camila Chamorro – Díez Canseco associates – have also helped in the preparation of the definition above

See also

Abuse of dominant position, Essential facility, Exclusionary practice, Market Power, Self-preference

R

REGISTRY OF THE GENERAL COURT OF THE EUROPEAN UNION

Emmanuel COULON
Former Registrar of the General Court of the European Union

Definition

Within the Court of Justice of the European Union, which is composed of the Court of Justice and the General Court (GC), the Registry of the GC is the sole department of the GC. As such, its very existence is inherent to the judicial autonomy of the GC. Its essential task is to assist in the efficient administration of Justice, which implies notably to enable Judges to carry out their duties in the best possible conditions and to organise the entire conduct of proceedings, in all its aspects, from the lodging of the application to the publication of the final decision, having regard to all the applicable rules and the objectives pursued by the GC.

Commentary

The Registry is headed by the Registrar, who is elected by the Judges of the GC for a renewable term of six years. Before taking his duties, the Registrar takes the oath, provided for in Article 2 of the Protocol on the Statute of the Court of Justice of the European Union (Statute), before the Judges of the GC.

The Registry contributes fully, in compliance with the provisions of the Rules of Procedure of the GC and the Practice Rules for the Implementation of the Rules of Procedure of the General Court ('PRI'), to the activities of that Court. Its task is not expressly set out in the Statute, the Rules of Procedure or the PRI, but they can be inferred from the responsibilities entrusted to the Registrar, as they are described in the Rules of Procedure and the PRI.

The legal framework for the Registry's activities is laid down in Articles 32 to 39 of the Rules of Procedure. Those articles are supplemented by, inter alia, paragraph 1 of the PRI.

The services provided by the Registry have a twofold purpose: to act as the exclusive interlocutor between the parties (lawyers and agents of the Member States and the institutions) throughout the judicial proceedings, except the hearing (external role), and to provide direct assistance to the 54 Judges of the GC as well as to play an active role in the life of the institution (internal role).

Four main objectives

The Registry's contribution to the efficient administration of Justice can be divided into activities centred around four main objectives:

- *to ensure communication with the parties' representatives and the Judges in judicial proceedings.* The Registry receives, transmits and stores all documents and make the necessary arrangements for service as required by the Rules of Procedure.
- *to ensure the proper conduct of proceedings.* Every procedural document lodged in a case pending before the GC is handled by the Registry (11.729 in 2023, compared with 10.412 in 2022). Such processing involves various actions: review of compliance with formal requirements and other conditions; pre-analysis of the document (1.271 applications in 2023, compared with 904 in 2022), which involves the review of jurisdiction and of certain conditions of admissibility; entry of the documents into the register (62.019 in 2023, compared with 60.691 in 2022); placement on the case file; transmission to the chambers of the judges concerned together with, where appropriate, requests for decisions (in 2023, 14.615 digital transmission sheets were exchanged with the Judges' Chambers in the course of proceedings, compared with 14.631 in 2022); requests for translation and authentication.
- *to provide technical and legal assistance to the Judges of the GC and their staff in different ways.* The Registry helps in ensuring consistency in decision-making in procedural matters, preparing procedural orders and in assisting the Judges during the administrative meetings of chambers (known as "chamber conferences") and during the hearings.
- *to contribute to the administration of the GC under the authority of the President of the GC and with the assistance of the departments of the Court of Justice of the European Union.* To that effect, the Registrar attends the sittings of the GC and is involved in the works of the internal committees. Furthermore, the Registrar and the representatives of the Registry participate in various bodies of the Court of Justice of the European Union.

Parameters

The Registry has no control over the number of cases brought before the GC, the number of cases closed, or the number of procedural documents lodged in pending cases. It is required to deal with all procedural documents itself in any of the 24 official languages of the EU and it interacts with the parties' representatives, both in writing and orally, in the language of the case.

All phases of the proceedings (from the filing of the document initiating proceedings to the service of the final decision, which is signed and stored electronically) have been progressively dematerialised between 2005 and 2022. Written communications between the Registry and the parties' representatives in direct actions have been provided in exclusively electronic format, via the e-Curia application, since December 1, 2018 (1.762.453 pages filed by e-Curia in 2023, compared with 979.676 in 2022). Hearings may be held by videoconference under the conditions set out in the Rules of procedure.

Its involvement must be measured against three benchmarks: time, quality and ethics.

In 2023, the registry had 71 budgetary posts within an institution made up of 2.302 people.

The Registry and Competition law cases

Competition law applicable to undertakings (cartels, abuse of a dominant position or mergers) and State aid law are two of the more than 40 listed matters that the GC and its Registry have to deal with. Cases in these areas are monitored by the Registry teams responsible for the languages in which the cases are lodged. Where related actions (such as cartel cases seeking annulment of the same Commission decision) are brought in different procedural languages, a special system is set up within the Registry to ensure coordinated management.

The managing of confidentiality issues

Proceedings in Competition cases are frequently peppered with confidentiality issues that require particular vigilance on the part of the Registry. These include requests to omit data mentioned in documents and information to which the public has access, requests for confidentiality between main parties (following a measure of inquiry), and requests for confidentiality vis-à-vis an intervener or another party in a joined case. The conditions for implementing the adversarial principle may be agreed upon, for example in the form of a confidentiality agreement.

The Registry manages the exchange of confidential and non-confidential versions of the documents with the parties' representatives and with the Judges of the competent formation (including the decision terminating the proceedings) and ensures that the case file is properly updated.

The organisation of hearings in important cases

The Registry is responsible for summoning the parties' representatives, communicating the hearing report and notifying the questions the GC may have (without prejudice to the measures to be taken in the event of a request for videoconferencing). It assists the Judges during the hearing, draws up the draft minutes of the hearing and serves the minutes.

Special arrangements can be made to optimize the conduct of hearings in large-scale cases or series of cases.

In 2023, 419 cases were pleaded, including 26 Competition cases and 88 State aid cases (compared with 303, including 21 Competition cases and 38 State aid cases, in 2022).

For example, the Registrar assists the Judges when the GC decides to organize a pre-hearing meeting with the parties' representatives to clarify certain points and make the hearing fully interactive. The meeting covers speaking times, the order in which speakers are to take the floor, the issues to be addressed by category of plea, any outstanding procedural incidents, and issues relating to the confidentiality of data that must be preserved in the context of a public debate. Practical issues can also be addressed, such as the secure storage of files for the duration of the hearing, or the provision of premises for representatives.

In addition, the Registry makes special arrangements for coordination with the institution's departments (interpreters, court ushers, security, communications, multimedia) and the judge-rapporteur's chambers to ensure that hearings in certain Competition cases run smoothly [for example, in 2021, the oral hearing in Case T-604/18, *Google and Alphabet v. Commission* (Google Android), took place over five days with 74 participants representing thirteen parties to the proceedings].

Bibliography

Amalfitano (C.), Condinanzi (M.), Iannuccelli (P.), *Le Regole del processo dinanzi al giudice dell'Unione europea*, Editoriale Scientifica, Napoli, 2017

Coulon (E.), « Numérisation du processus judiciaire : un pas de plus avec e-Curia obligatoire devant le Tribunal de l'Union européenne », *L'Observateur de Bruxelles*, n° 117, 2019

Coulon (E.), « Registry: General Court of the European Union », *Max Planck Encyclopedias of International Law*, Module du Max Planck Encyclopedia of International Procedural Law, 2021

Article 254 (4) TFEU

Consolidated version of the Statute of the Court of Justice of the European Union

Consolidated version of the Practice Rules for the Implementation of the Rules of Procedure of the General Court

Consolidated version of the Rules of Procedure of the General Court

Page « Procedure » of the General Court on the website of the Court of Justice of the European Union

Page « Statistics concerning the judicial activity of the General Court » on the website of the Court of Justice of the European Union

See also

Judicial review

R

RELEVANT MARKET

Paulo BURNIER DA SILVEIRA
OECD – Competition Division

Definition

Relevant Market is a set of products or services that are considered substitutes by consumers, both in terms of their characteristics and the geographic area where they are offered. The notion serves to identify the boundaries of the market where companies compete, and to assess market power for competition policy purposes. The test commonly used to identify the relevant market is to examine if consumers would switch to other suppliers in the hypothetical event of small but significant and non-transitory increase in prices of a particular product or service (the so-called SSNIP test).

Commentary

A relevant market is a market that is worth monopolising (Bishop and Darcey, 1995). In this sense, the exercise of monopoly power will not be feasible if buyers can easily switch to other products (demand side substitution), or other companies are able to increase production or easily enter the market (supply side substitution).

The notion of substitutability is core to properly understanding and defining the relevant market. On the demand side, a relevant market includes all products and services that consumers see as interchangeable or substitutable due to their characteristics, their prices, their intended use and the location of those firms involved in the supply of those products or services (EU Commission Notice on the Definition of Relevant Market, 1997). Demand side substitution is particularly important in certain jurisdictions including U.S. and Canada, which focus on demand responses to changes in relative prices after the merger. The ability of a firm or group of firms to raise prices without losing sufficient sales to make the price increase unprofitable ultimately depends on buyers' willingness to pay the higher price (Canada's Merger Enforcement Guidelines, 2011). On the supply side, the market concerns products and services that could readily be put into the market by other suppliers without significant switching costs or by potential competitors at reasonable cost and within a limited timeframe. In these situations, the increased level of supply may render a rise of prices by the hypothetical monopolist unprofitable, and those suppliers should therefore be included in the analysis of the relevant market.

Concerning the geographic dimension, the relevant market includes the area in which the conditions of competition are sufficiently homogenous and which can be distinguished from neighbouring areas based on the conditions for competition. Cases may define a relevant geographic market as local, national, regional, or global for instance. In addition to importation and transportation costs, evidence may include that buyers have shifted purchases between different geographic locations in response to changes in price, as well as the timing and costs of switching suppliers (U.S. Horizontal Merger Guidelines, 2010).

The SSNIP test, also known as Hypothetical Monopolist Test, is the most common tool to define a relevant market. Briefly, a relevant market is found if a "Small but Significant Non-transitory Increase in Price" above the competitive level is profitable and sustainable when exercised by a hypothetical monopolist. In practice, the exercise usually starts from the narrowest possible market definition and asks if a hypothetical monopolist would be able to profitably raise prices beyond the competitive level by a small but significant amount (i.e. 5-10%). If the answer is negative, the exercise continues with a wider market definition until the answer is positive. From the consumers' standpoint, they are asked if they would still buy a given product or service in case of a 10% price increase. If the answer is yes, the market is well defined.

The SSNIP test is a quantitative test and generally applied when sufficient data is available. However, when sufficient or reliable data are not available, a qualitative assessment may gather evidence to help to identify the products and services that provide competitive pressures to one another, and then seek approximate results to the SSNIP test. In addition, other economic techniques may be used to define markets depending on the specificities of the case. They include price correlation, shock analysis, historic events, in addition to economic tests such as Gross Upward Pricing Pressure (GUPPI) and Upward Pricing Pressure (UPP). All of them have advantages and inconveniences, so they are often used in a complementary or alternative way to the SSNIP test, adding to a more robust analysis when the results of one technique confirms the other.

Malcolm Coate and Jeffrey Fischer (2007) provide an interesting study based on 116 market definition decisions issued by the U.S. Federal Trade Commission (FTC). They argue that the demand-side analysis was relatively simple in over half of the reviewed cases. In the remaining cases, other techniques were employed to identify the relevant market. The research also shows a variety in data requirements, sophistication and analytical technique. Supply side considerations affected only a few markets and price discrimination supported more focused analysis in about ten cases.

In digital markets, certain techniques may have to be adapted since these markets are often characterized by zero-price services, which limits the application of the traditional SSNIP test. They are also frequently characterized by two-sided markets, which add particular issues in determining the relevant product market. In the Google Shopping case, the European General Court confirmed the Commission's assessment by reference to consumer demand despite the fact that the services were provided at a price of zero to consumers. The European Commission had concluded that the relevant product markets were the market for online general search services and the market for online comparison shopping services, in which the two-sided business model based on free services was cross-funded by advertising. This approach was replicated by several other jurisdictions concerning this stage of relevant market definition.

The definition of a relevant market allows the calculation of market shares, which can provide a useful initial indication of potential market power. Market share calculation may also serve as safe harbours in certain jurisdictions, below which investigations will not be conducted. Nonetheless, market definition techniques are also subject to critics, for instance when product differentiation is a crucial dimension of competition given that substitution across products might be imperfect. It is also the case when firms compete on other dimensions than price (i.e., quality or innovation).

Finally, it is important to highlight that market definition is not an end in itself but rather a tool to assess market power. As mentioned by Mario Monti, former European Commissioner for Competition: "market definition is a cornerstone of competition policy, but not the entire building" (speech by Commissioner Mario Monti, 2001). Having this main objective in mind helps both enforcers and practitioners to focus on the essential, which is assessing market power and analysing the effects of its exercise. For this reason, the precise relevant market is often left open, namely when it is difficult to establish its precise definition and/or in the context of fast-track merger analysis that require a speedy decision. In these cases, most competition authorities can leave the definition open and indicate alternative plausible market definitions (except to certain jurisdictions including Mexico, where the legal framework requires a precise definition of the relevant market in all analysis).

Bibliography

Bishop, S. and Darcey, M. (1995): *A Relevant Market Is Something Worth Monopolising*. Unpublished Mimeo

Coate, M. and Fischer, J. (2007), "A Practical Guide to the Hypothetical Monopolist Test for Market Definition", *Journal of Competition Law and Economics*

Whish, R. and Bailey, D. (2018), *Competition Law*, 9th ed, Oxford University Press, Chapter 1

ICN Investigative Techniques Handbook for Merger Review (2013), Chapter 4

OECD Policy Roundtable on Market Definition (2012)

The information and views set out in this text are those of the author and do not reflect the official opinion of the OECD or its Member States

See also

Barriers to entry, Mobility barriers, Potential competition

R

REMEDIES (ANTITRUST)

Michal HALPERIN
Harvard University – Harvard Kennedy School

Definition

Remedies are commitments or restrictions that are taken by parties or imposed by an antitrust agency to correct a harm to competition or as a means to eliminate competition concerns. Remedies are usually discussed in the context of mergers. Agencies may allow the parties to the merger to suggest remedies that will eliminate the competition concern in order to avoid total objection to the merger. Remedies are also relevant in cases of infringement of competition law, if they correct the harm to competition or eliminate the concern of harm to competition that was caused by the violating conduct or collaboration. In most infringement cases, remedies will replace enforcement action.

Commentary

Remedies are in most cases an outcome of negotiations between interested parties and a competition agency for the purpose of avoiding the blockage of a merger or enforcement steps following a violation of competition law. Many agencies published guidelines or manuals that specify the principles that guide them in considering remedies. A few key principles in considering remedies are common for many agencies: (1) remedies should be considered only in cases where the agency can establish a concern to competition; (2) the remedies must completely preserve or restore competition; (3) remedies should be the least restrictive means to effectively eliminate competition concerns; (4) the remedies should address only competition concerns and should not be used for industrial planning or other non-competition purposes; and (5) remedies must be implementable within a short period of time and must be enforceable.

Non-compliance of parties with remedies that were imposed on them or taken as a commitment by them is usually considered a violation of competition laws.

There is a distinction between structural remedies and behavioral remedies (sometime called conduct remedies). Structural remedies usually include divestiture of assets while behavioral remedies can include commitments to provide certain services or goods under specified conditions; to deal in a non-discriminatory manner; to avoid bundling of products; or to maintain certain price level. Behavioral remedies are characterized by an ongoing intervention in the market and therefore considered by competition agencies as less desirable. They are also more difficult to enforce. Nevertheless, competition agencies continue to impose behavioral remedies in some cases. For example, in 2020, the European Commission accepted commitments proposed by Google in connection with its acquisition of Fitbit and imposed a series of behavioral remedies as a condition to the approval of the merger. In 2010, the U.S. DOJ reached a consent decree with Ticketmaster and Live Nation which included behavioral remedies and paved the way to the approval of their merger.

Structural remedies are usually considered more effective in correcting the harm to competition and in sustaining long term competition in the markets. They are also considered easier to enforce – mainly due to their characteristic as a onetime intervention in the market. In addition, they are less vulnerable to creative interpretation and creative circumvention by the parties. Nevertheless, the experience of many agencies shows that structural remedies are also difficult to design in a manner that will assure maintenance or restoration of competition. In many cases, for example, parties obligated to divest have difficulties to find an acquirer. In other cases, assets are divested to an acquirer that is not well suited to maintain the previous level of competition. The experience of agencies with enforcing structural remedies is only partially successful.

There are several ways in which competition agencies can improve their rate of success with divestiture. One of the tools is to impose a "fix it first" remedy, which requires the parties to comply fully with their divestiture duties prior to the consummation of the merger transaction.

Another complementary tool is requiring the approval of the agency for the identity of the acquirer. In addition, it is important to pay attention to the scope of the assets that the parties are required to divest. The goal is, on the one hand, to require the divestiture of the least amount of assets required to restore or maintain competition. On the other hand, agencies need to make sure that the divested assets will enable the creation of a stand-alone business and will be divested with the relevant commercial arrangements that will allow the acquirer to compete.

The Israeli experience with remedies is a demonstration of the lessons that can be learned about the imposition of remedies. In the early years of the 21st century close to 20% of mergers were approved subject to remedies imposed on the parties, of those between 40% to 65% were behavioral remedies. In some cases, remedies were imposed to regulate the market in a way that was seen by the Israeli Competition Authority as improving competition and were not necessarily related to the merger at hand. However, growing recognition by the Israeli agency that remedies should be limited to cases where specific competition concern exists, and growing recognition that behavioral remedies are less desirable, brought a substantial decrease in the percentage of remedies that are imposed. Behavioral remedies were abandoned almost completely. In recent years approximately 0.5% to 2.5% of the mergers in Israel were approved subject to any remedies at all, and behavioral remedies are rare. In addition, the Israeli Competition Authority encountered frequent difficulties in enforcing the divestiture duties that it imposed on parties, which in turn evolved to legal dispute or to the need for enforcement steps. In 2017 the Competition Authority changed its policy and started to insist on "fix it first" divestiture as a condition to consummating a merger transaction. This caused a dramatic improvement in the compliance of parties with the imposed remedies and an improvement in their effectiveness.

Bibliography

OECD Competition Commission Policy Roundtable on Remedies in Merger Cases (2011)

The Commission Notice on Remedies Acceptable under Council Regulation (EC) No 139/2004 and under Commission Regulation (EC) No 802/2004 of (2008)

The U.S. Department of Justice Antitrust Division Merger Remedies Manual of September 2020

See also

Divestiture, Merger remedies

R

REQUEST FOR INFORMATION

Catrina LAM
Des Vœux Chambers

Godfrey LAM
The Court of Appeal of Hong Kong

Definition

A request for information is a formal request made by competition authorities to obtain information or documents either from the subjects of their investigation or from other individuals or entities that have relevant materials which may assist with the authorities' investigation. These requests can vary in scope, ranging from a straightforward request for document production to a more complex request for the production of digital data through a virtual data room. Although the purpose of these requests is to facilitate investigations, it is crucial to strike a balance between this objective and considerations such as preserving the investigation target's privilege against self-incrimination and safeguarding data privacy.

Commentary

EU

In the EU, Article 18 of Regulation 1/2003 empowers the Commission to require the provision of "all necessary information" for carrying out the duties assigned to it by Regulation 1/2003. The concept of "necessity" imports a requirement that requests can only be made for information that will enable the Commission to investigate putative infringements or identify conduct which falls foul of the EU competition provisions (see Case T-446/05 *Amann & Söhne v Commission* EU:T:2010:165, para. 333; Rousseva (ed), *EU Antitrust Procedure*, para. 2.19).

Under Article 18, a request for information may take one of two forms: a simple request or a request by decision of the Commission. In either form, the

Commission must state the legal basis and the purpose of the request, specify what information is required, fix the time-limit within which the information is to be provided, and indicate the penalties for supplying incorrect or misleading information under Article 23.

A request by decision is reviewable by the EU Courts and is typically more effective, as failure to supply the requested information within the specified time-limit may lead to the imposition of a daily fine not exceeding 5% of the average daily turnover of the undertaking in the preceding business year under Article 24. However, there is a general duty on the Commission to choose the least onerous investigative measure, meaning that a request by decision can only be adopted if a simple request is unable to achieve the Commission's legitimate objectives (see Rousseva (ed), *EU Antitrust Procedure*, para. 2.19).

Once an undertaking is subject to a request for information, it must comply with the request and cooperate proactively with the Commission (see Case 374/87 *Orkem v Commission* EU:C:1989:387, para. 27). The request may extend to all information concerning an entire undertaking even though it is addressed only to certain entities within the undertaking. The Commission can also require an undertaking to supply information even if it has to be collected from a third party.

An undertaking's obligation to cooperate with the Commission is subject to a limited privilege against self-incrimination. In *Orkem*, it was held that the Commission cannot compel undertakings to directly admit to an infringement, but it can require an undertaking to provide all necessary factual information known to it and disclose documents, even if such documents may later be used to establish a competition infringement against that undertaking.

U.S.

In the U.S., the equivalent of a request for information is known as a civil investigative demand (CID). CIDs are used by competition regulators such as the Federal Trade Commission (FTC) and the Department of Justice Antitrust Division (DOJ) to obtain information relevant to antitrust violations.

The FTC's power to issue CIDs is derived from section 57b-1 of the Federal Trade Commission Act. Under that provision, if the FTC has reasons to believe that any person may be in possession, custody or control of any documentary material, or may have information relevant to antitrust violations, a CID may be issued. The person in question may be required to produce the requested documentary material for inspection or answer questions concerning the relevant information. Persons subject to a CID are obligated to comply, and non-compliance can be enforced through court proceedings.

The DOJ possesses broadly similar powers under section 1312 of the Antitrust Civil Process Act.

Similar to the EU, the obligation to comply with a CID in the U.S. is limited by the privilege against self-incrimination. In the U.S., the privilege against self-incrimination is safeguarded through compelled testimony and use immunity. If a person invokes the privilege against self-incrimination and refuses to answer a CID, their testimony can be compelled after obtaining approval from the Attorney General. However, the compelled testimony cannot be used against the witness in any criminal case, except for cases arising from the falsity of the testimony (e.g. contempt proceedings). In *Kastigar v United States* 406 U.S. 441 (1972), the U.S. Supreme Court held that this combination of compulsion and immunity represented a rational accommodation between the imperatives of the privilege against self-incrimination and the legitimate demands of the government to compel citizens to testify (at 446). Therefore, such a compromise is constitutional. However, compelled testimony can be used against the deponent in proceedings seeking only civil sanctions, including civil penalty proceedings.

Hong Kong

In Hong Kong, the regime for requests for information in competition investigations is similar. Section 41 of the Competition Ordinance (Cap 619) (Ordinance) empowers the Competition Commission (Commission) to require a person to produce documents or provide information relevant to an investigation if there is reasonable cause to suspect that the person has possession or control of such materials. Additionally, under section 42(1) of the Ordinance, a person may be required to attend before the Commission to answer questions relating to any matter it reasonably believes to be relevant to the investigation. Failure to comply with such requests constitutes an offence and may result in a fine or imprisonment under section 52.

The scheme adopted in Hong Kong is to provide for abrogation of the privilege against self-incrimination, to impose restriction on the direct use of the statements obtained, and to be silent on – thereby inferentially permitting – derivative use of statements (see*Competition Commission v. Nutanix Hong Kong Ltd (No 2)* [2017] 5 HKLRD 712 para. 44). Section 45(1) expressly abrogates a person's privilege against self-incrimination, meaning that the privilege is not an excuse for refusing to give an explanation or answer a question. However, section 45(2) provides a "direct use prohibition", specifying that no statement made by a person under compulsion is admissible in criminal proceedings and proceedings for a pecuniary penalty for breach of competition rules under the Ordinance against that person. This restriction on direct use protects the statement-maker. It only benefits the person to whom a notice issued under section 42 is addressed and does not extend to third parties (see *Nutanix*, para. 101), so that if a section 42 notice is addressed to an employee, the employer cannot rely on the direct use prohibition to exclude its employee's compelled answers from being admissible as evidence against itself. Additionally, section 46 specifies that a person is not excused from providing information or documents to the Commission merely because they owe a duty of confidence to any other person.

Bibliography

BAILEY, D. and JOHN, L. E. (eds.), *Bellamy & Child: European Union Law of Competition* (8th edn, Oxford University Press 2018), Chapter 13

KHAN, N. (ed.), *Kerse & Khan on EU Antitrust Procedure* (6th edn, Sweet & Maxwell 2012), Chapter 3

ROUSSEVA, E. (ed.), *EU Antitrust Procedure* (1st edn, Oxford University Press 2020), Chapter 2

SULLIVAN, E. T., HOVENKAMP, H., SHELANSKI, H. A. and LESLIE, C. R., *Antitrust Law, Policy, and Procedure: Cases, Materials, Problems* (8th edn, Carolina Academic Press 2019), Chapter 3

See also

Investigations/Inquiries

R

RESALE BELOW COST

Niccolo CIULLI
EuroCommerce

Definition

"Resale below cost" occurs when a business (e.g. a retailer) purchases a product from a supplier (e.g. a manufacturer) and then resells it (to another business or to end-consumers) at a price which is lower than the price paid to its supplier. A number of jurisdictions around the world impose restrictions or outright prohibitions under competition or commercial law on the possibility for resellers to sell products below cost. Restrictions on customers reselling below cost regulated at national level are distinct from prohibitions of predatory pricing under EU competition law as they may apply regardless of whether the undertaking has a dominant position in the market.

Commentary

Competition law often prohibits suppliers from proscribing the retail price at which their buyers should resell their products or services (see resale price maintenance). However, certain forms of price setting by resellers may be regulated by law, for instance by limiting promotions, discounts or prohibiting reselling below cost.

"Cost" is usually defined as the cost incurred by the buyer when acquiring the product, although certain countries (such as Italy) also prohibit buyers from reselling products below the cost of production incurred by the supplier.

In practice, a reseller may for strategic reasons decide to sell below cost temporarily, for example to attract new customers or to launch a new product. Reselling below cost can then promote competition and lead to better prices for consumers.

However, certain jurisdictions see resale below cost as an anti-competitive strategy used by larger companies to the detriment of smaller companies. Similarly, resellers may increase the prices of some products in their range to keep others artificially low.

Prohibitions around below-cost selling may seek to pursue other policy objectives: in recent years, certain countries (e.g. France) have implemented rules on below-cost selling to improve the negotiating position of primary producers and ensure fair remuneration for farmers. Other policy objectives of such types of restrictions may be for instance related to public health: the United Kingdom has banned below-cost selling of alcohol to limit the availability of alcohol at prices which are too low and prevent the effects that has on health.

The OECD has argued that prohibitions on resale below cost are likely to harm consumers and protect inefficient competitors, fail to account adequately for pro-competitive business justifications for loss leader sales and detract from economic dynamism and growth.

Additionally, in relation to non-competition policy goals pursued by below cost selling (e.g. fair remuneration of suppliers, public health), the OECD notes that there may be other means to achieve the same objectives "*without causing the potential consumer harm associated with*" prohibitions on reselling below cost.

Other antitrust authorities have a similar stance on resale below cost as the OECD. For instance, the United States Federal Trade Commission notes that "*a firm's independent decision to reduce prices to a level below its own costs does not necessarily injure competition, and, in fact, may simply reflect particularly vigorous competition' and that "consumers are harmed only if below-cost pricing allows a dominant competitor to knock its rivals out of the market and then raise prices to above-market levels for a substantial time.*"

Similarly, under article 102 of the Treaty on the Functioning of the European Union, predatory pricing (which may include reselling below cost) is only illegal if it is carried out by one or more undertakings which have a dominant position in a market.

The European Commission's enforcement priorities clarify that the Commission will be to intervene when "*a dominant undertaking engages in predatory conduct by deliberately incurring losses or foregoing profits in the short term* [...] *so as to foreclose or be likely to foreclose one or more of its actual or potential competitors with a view to strengthening or maintaining its market power, thereby causing consumer harm*" [European Commission Guidance on the Commission's enforcement priorities in applying Article 82 of the EC Treaty to abusive exclusionary conduct by dominant undertakings (2009/C 45/02)].

As illustrated by the examples below, there is legislation regulating reselling below cost under commercial or competition law in several countries in Europe, in Japan and at state level in the United States.

Several member states of the European Union (including Belgium, Germany,

Greece, France, Luxembourg, Hungary, Italy, Spain) prohibit below-cost selling, although the nature of legislation varies widely and the general or specific prohibitions are subject to exceptions. For instance, Belgium prohibits traders from selling at a loss, with exceptions for products sold as part of a promotion, in liquidation or at risk of rapid deterioration. Similar exceptions can be found in other jurisdictions.

In Germany, the law differentiates between food products (which may never be sold below cost) and "other products and commercial services" which may "occasionally" be sold below costs (i.e. for a limited time per year). Objective justifications are possible for food products, such as preventing deterioration or the imminent unsaleability of the goods at the retailer's premises through a timely sale, or in equally severe cases.

As noted above, certain jurisdictions may also prohibit buyers from purchasing or reselling a product below the supplier's cost of production (e.g. Italy, Spain) to ensure a fair remuneration of suppliers in the supply chain. However, buyers may encounter practical difficulties with these types of prohibition as they have no means to verify the declaration of costs by producers. In fact, smaller producers may not be aware of their actual costs of production.

In Japan, the Antimonopoly Law prohibits regular below-cost selling without justification as an unfair trading practice.

The United States does not have a federal ban on selling below cost, but there are prohibitions in state law (e.g. California, Minnesota, Arkansas, Wisconsin, Tennessee), usually subject to justifications. For instance, Californian law prohibits selling below cost if it is done "*for the purpose of injuring competitors or destroying competition*" [California Business and Professions Code 17043]. States also allow resellers to argue a "meeting-competition defence", i.e. to justify an infringement of the relevant provisions if it is one in good faith to meet the legal price of a competitor selling the same article or product [California Business and Professions Code 17050(d)].

The European Union legal regime does not prohibit sales below cost throughout the Union, although EU law does not preclude this type of legislation at national level (provided that they are not discriminatory with regard to their application and their legal and factual effect) [C-267/91 and C-268/91 *Keck and Mithouard*].

However, certain general national prohibitions of resale below cost have been held incompatible with EU law in a number of specific cases [C-343/12 *Euronics Belgium*, C-295/16, *Europamur*].

The matter of a prohibition under EU law was raised during the drafting on the Directive (EU) 2019/633 on unfair trading practices ("UTP") in business-to-business relationships in the agricultural and food supply chain, but the stakeholders' consultation by the European Commission did not identify the issue as a priority and the impact assessment noted that "*inflationary effects on consumer prices have however been argued in case of UTP rules prohibiting below-cost sales*" [European Commission Staff Working Document Impact Assessment Initiative to improve the food supply chain (unfair trading practices) SWD/2018/092 final – 2018/082 (COD)].

Bibliography

ALLAIN, M.-L. and CHAMBOLLE, C., Anticompetitive effects of resale-below-cost laws *INSEE Serie des Documents de Travail du Crest* 2007-29

KEIRSBILCK, B., Does EU Economic Law Preclude National Prohibitions of Sales below Cost? *Erasmus Law Review*, Vol. 5, No. 4, 2012

OECD Policy Roundtable *Resale below cost* 2005

OECD Policy Roundtable *Resale below cost* 2005

See also

Abuse of dominant position, Economic analysis, Predatory pricing, Prices

R

RESALE PRICE MAINTENANCE (RPM)

Timo KLEIN
Utrecht University

Definition

Resale Price Maintenance (RPM) is a vertical restraint by an upstream supplier that constrains the resale prices of downstream resellers such as retailers or distributors. Authorities generally view fixed-price or minimum-price RPM with suspicion, as it can reduce or eliminate intra-brand competition between resellers or facilitate inter-brand collusion between suppliers. In some cases, however, it may be an effective tool to avoid harmful free-riding behaviour by resellers and protect investment incentives, or to coordinate brand-level pricing campaigns. RPM in the form of a maximum or recommended price is generally regarded as less problematic, provided that resellers do not use it as an anticompetitive focal point to coordinate on.

Commentary

Resale Price Maintenance (RPM) is a vertical agreement or concerted practice between an upstream supplier and a downstream reseller (such as a retailer or distributor) that constrains or sets the resale price downstream. While RPM can have anticompetitive consequences when it involves a fixed or minimum price, its unclear effects and potential procompetitive justifications make it legally and economically contentious. This commentary summarises the seminal case law in the USA that has driven contemporary legal and economic thinking on fixed and minimum RPM, explains the main economic theories of harm and benefit, and closes off with a brief discussion of maximum, recommended and indirect RPM.

Fixed or minimum RPM was formerly treated with hostility. In its 1911 *Dr Miles* judgment, the U.S. Supreme

Court even imposed a per se prohibition. This case involved a producer of proprietary medicines setting the prices at which pharmacists could resell them. The Supreme Court rejected the defence that eliminating intra-brand competition on these medicines was required to ensure that pharmacists made sufficient profit in return for promoting the products. However, in its 2007 *Leegin*judgment, the U.S. Supreme Court overturned *Dr Miles* and instead imposed a rule of reason approach to RPM. In this case, the Supreme Court accepted the defence that the discounting of certain leather accessories would harm the brand's luxury image and undermine the ability of retailers to offer top-quality customer service. A further discussion on this case, including a link to EU competition law, is provided by Peeperkorn (2008).

In the EU, a fixed or minimum RPM is considered a "hardcore" vertical restriction that does not enjoy a block exemption under the 2010 vertical block exemption regulation (or its 2021 draft update). However, as also clarified in the 2010 vertical guidelines (and their 2021 draft update), RPM may still be exempted under Article 101(3) TFEU.

Several economic theories of harm may justify a suspicious treatment of (fixed or minimum) RPM, depending on the case. First, RPM may benefit resellers by eliminating intra-brand competition (e.g. among competing retailers all selling Coca-Cola). This also means that resellers could advocate for RPM as a means to facilitate "hub-and-spoke" collusion among themselves via a common supplier. This elimination of intra-brand competition may involve immediate harm to consumers through higher prices, but also dynamic harm because of reduced expansion by more efficient resellers (which benefit the most from competition).

At the same time, it is not always clear what the benefit would be to the supplier from an elimination of intra-brand competition: in a pure resell model, suppliers generally benefit from efficient distribution, lower retail prices, and higher output (although this may change when suppliers set two-part tariffs – see Rey and Vergé, 2010). Moreover, it is important to note that the effect on market outcomes from any reduction in intra-brand competition is smaller when there is stronger inter-brand competition (e.g. between Coca-Cola and Pepsi).

Second, RPM may facilitate collusion among competing suppliers by reducing price fluctuations in the downstream market and increasing price transparency (Jullien and Rey, 2007). The importance of monitoring in this coordination theory of harm is also recognised in the 2022 EU vertical guidelines, which point towards an increase in e-commerce price monitoring tools. RPM may also facilitate supplier collusion by reducing the ability for suppliers to profitably deviate through a reduction in wholesale prices – as fixed resale prices limit the subsequent demand increase.

Third, RPM may be used by a dominant supplier to foreclose smaller rivals by enabling higher margins for resellers and hence an incentive to favour the supplier's brand over those of rivals when selling to customers. However, this works only if these rival suppliers do not have alternative routes to market. Moreover, supplier foreclosure may end up harming resellers by limiting their supply options – and hence require some form of retailer coordination failure to implement (Fumagalli, Motta and Calgano, 2018, Section 2.3.2).

Finally, a uniform RPM policy may be used to remove a procompetitive commitment problem on the side of the supplier: by committing to sufficiently high retail margins, the supplier may eliminate its own ability and incentive to attract additional competing resellers – the prospect of which would have resulted in any initial reseller already demanding lower wholesale prices (O'Brien and Shaffer, 1992). However, case law generally appears to sideline this theory of harm.

In parallel to the above theories of harm, there are ways in which restricting downstream price-setting may actually work to enhance inter-brand competition. First, when suppliers cannot enforce resellers' pre-sale services by contract, RPM may be an effective alternative to eliminate the ability of low-cost resellers to free-ride on their competitors' efforts to attract customer interest – enhancing (non-price) inter-brand competition. Second, RPM may increase resellers' investment incentives by increasing their ability to appropriate value. This may be particularly relevant when upfront retailer investment is required – again increasing inter-brand competition. Third, fixed resale prices may be necessary to impose an effective brand-level pricing campaign – which may be procompetitive, provided that it is temporary and aimed at coordinating on low rather than high common prices.

Maximum and recommended RPM are generally regarded as less problematic than fixed and minimum RPM. This is because the above theories of harm do not apply. Moreover, maximum RPM may help to reduce the harm to both consumers and firms from double marginalisation (different levels of the supply chain all imposing a markup); and recommended RPM may help to overcome an informational disadvantage on what an appropriate resale price is. However, maximum or recommended RPM may still fall foul of competition law when it is perceived as fixed RPM or when it provides for an anticompetitive focal point.

Finally, it is worth noting that fixed or minimum RPM does not have to be imposed directly in order to infringe competition law. For example, in 2021 the Netherlands Authority for Consumers and Markets concluded that Samsung exercised "undue influence" on several online retailers of Samsung television sets, despite a claim of price recommendations (and irrespective of any effects analysis). In contrast, in a 2014 decision by the UK Office of Fair Trading (now Competition and Markets Authority), it was concluded that price communication between a supplier of sports bras and major department stores did not infringe competition law, because the parties provided credible alternative explanations for their communications and there was no clear effect on price levels.

Bibliography

FUMAGALLI, C., MOTTA, M. and CALCAGNO, C. (2018), *Exclusionary practices: The economics of monopolisation and abuse of dominance*, Cambridge University Press

JULLIEN, B. and REY, P. (2007), "Resale Price Maintenance and collusion", *The RAND Journal of Economics*, 38(4), pp. 983–1001

O'BRIEN, D.P. and SHAFFER, G. (1992), "Vertical control with bilateral contracts", *The RAND Journal of Economics*, pp. 299–308

PEEPERKORN, L. (2008), "Resale Price Maintenance and its alleged efficiencies", *European Competition Journal*, 4(1), pp. 201–212

REY, P. and VERGÉ, T. (2010), "Resale Price Maintenance and interlocking relationships", *The Journal of Industrial Economics*, 58(4), pp. 928–961

See also

Vertical restraints (or restrictions) Prices, Price fixing-agreement

R

RESTRICTION ON EXPORTATION

Simon J. EVENETT
University of St. Gallen

Definition

Through a variety of means, a state may ban, restrict, or condition the exportation of goods by commercial enterprises. Those means include outright prohibitions of exports, export quotas, export authorization schemes, behind-the-scenes or public exhortation of potential exporters, and state requisition of all goods produced in or shipped through their customs territory. The transparency of state-imposed export restrictions varies considerably. Under certain conditions, some governments grant exemptions from relevant antitrust law so as to allow private sector competitors to collaborate in their sales efforts in foreign markets. In extremis, none of these matters are constrained by existing international agreements.

Commentary

Governments restrain exports for at least four reasons: to depress the domestic price of the good in question to benefit domestic buyers, including downstream corporate customers; to reserve domestically-produced supplies for use within its borders; to raise prices charged to foreign customers; and to prevent goods deemed sensitive from falling into the hands of foreign governments or foreign parties in general.

Examples of export restrictions include the following. The Indian government frequently resorts to export controls on onions so as to lower the price of this staple food to its population. A decade ago, the Chinese government imposed export limits on Rare Earth minerals so as to ensure sufficient supply for downstream industries. During the first half of 2020, according to the Global Trade Alert, no less than 72 governments imposed 159 different types of export controls to ban or limit the cross-border shipment of medical goods (including personal protective equipment, medical equipment, and medicines) to foreign buyers at the start of the COVID-19 pandemic.

Furthermore, governments have also taken steps, individually or in groups, to raise the price of commodities, such as oil and rice. In other cases, governments have regimes to review applications to export dual-use technologies or cutting-edge technologies. As geopolitical rivalry intensifies, the exports of more and more products fall under such export control regimes. As these examples demonstrate, government-imposed export restraints serve multiple public purposes and are frequently deployed.

The last sentence should not be taken to imply that export restraints are the best way to address the public policy goals in question. Indeed, governments often resort to export curbs as an emergency measure when faced with domestic shortages. Too often little thought is given as to why shortages arose in the first place, to why demand surges from time to time, to whether incentives can be supplied to the private sector to scale up production and deliveries when demand expands, and to whether stockpiling and other responses can limit the duration and extent of any shortage.

In the prominent area of public health, the imposition of export curbs is in the power of, or heavily influenced, by public health officials, many of whom lack an understanding of the incentives faced by the private sector and how the latter organize their production, often along extensive cross-border supply chains.

When export transactions touch upon foreign policy and national security concerns, economic and commercial logic is less likely to guide official decision-making. Together these influences can result in abrupt swings in public policy towards export restraints (as evidenced by the swift imposition and removal of many export bans on personal protective equipment in 2020 during the pandemic crisis), less than transparent decision-making, and little or no respect for due process of affected private parties. Any informed assessment of the political risks faced by the private sector ought to take account of these considerations.

Economic analysis of the impact of export restraints on competitive market outcomes highlights the redistributive nature of this form of trade policy. Imposing an export ban or other limit tends to redirect supply to domestic markets, depressing observed prices and increasing the volumes purchased by domestic buyers. Therefore, export curbs raise the welfare of domestic buyers at the expense of affected domestic producers.

Foreign buyers must secure supplies elsewhere, potentially at higher prices if the goods in question are available on world markets, and so are worse off too. To the extent that a government limits but does not ban exports, the higher prices charged to foreign customers represents a terms of trade gain and potentially higher revenues for the exporting nation.

In light of the uncertainty created by export restraints and their largely redistributive effects, one might have thought these policies would be and should be subject to binding international trade obligations. While it would be wrong to argue that there are no multilateral trade rules on the resort to export restraints (see, in particular, Articles XIII and XX of the General Agreement on Tariffs and Trade), in effect those rules have done little to "discipline" government resort to these measures.

To the extent that a government is found to have broken the World Trade Organization's (WTO's) rules, as China was in the Raw Materials case in 2012, then recall that, under the Dispute Settlement Understanding of the WTO, the offending government need only remove the measure in question to come back into compliance. Such a government is under no obligation to offer compensation to harmed third parties.

Given the time-limited or otherwise temporary nature of many state-imposed export restraints, often such curbs lapse before a ruling by a WTO panel or the Appellate Body. Moreover, the reality that, in regional and global emergencies, multiple governments simultaneously impose export restraints tends to diminish the incentive for any one of them to bring a WTO case against another. For all of these reasons, in practice binding WTO rules on export restraints have little bite.

Likewise regional trade agreements, few of which contain obligations on export restraints by governments. Even the Treaty on the Functioning of the European Union includes Article 36 that permits Member State governments to impose export controls "when these are justified by general, non-economic considerations (e.g. public morality, public policy or public security)." Furthermore, while the Group of 20 nations committed at the start of the COVID-19 pandemic to adopt crisis-era trade measures that were "targeted, proportionate, transparent, and temporary, and that they do not create unnecessary barriers to trade or disruption to global supply chains, and are consistent with WTO rules", available suggests this injunction was honored in the breach.

There is one other, distinct, aspect of state-related export restraints. Some governments permit private sector firms that might otherwise compete for the same foreign customers to form marketing and sales organizations. In the United States the Export Trade Act of 1918 (commonly referred to as the Webb-Pomerene Act) allows for an exemption from the cartel provisions of various U.S. antitrust laws under certain conditions for firms that form an "export trade association". Applications to form such associations must be approved by U.S. officials and decisions to approve such associations are made public. Unsurprisingly, to the extent that such associations result in higher prices paid by foreign customers, the trading partners of the United States are unenthusiastic about this legal provision.

Bibliography

EVENETT, S. J., FIORINI, M., FRITZ, J., HOEKMAN, B. M., LUKASZUK, P., ROCHA, N., RUTA, M., SANTI, F. and SHINGAL, A., "Trade Policy Responses to the COVID-19 pandemic crisis: Evidence from a New Dataset." *World Economy*. 2021

European Union. *Consolidated version of the Treaty on the Functioning of the European Union. Document* 12012E/TXT

G20. "G20 Trade and Investment Ministerial Statement." 30 March 2021

United States. Export Trade Act of 1918

World Trade Organization. *The WTO Agreements: The Marrakesh Agreement Establishing the World Trade Organization and its Annexes.* Cambridge University Press. *2018*

See also

Parallel imports (parallel trade)

R

RULE OF REASON

David BAILEY
King's College London

■ Definition

The "rule of reason" requires a court to balance an agreement's pro-and anti-competitive effects under section 1 of the Sherman Act 1890 in the U.S.; where the latter outweigh the former, the agreement will be regarded as an unlawful restraint of trade. EU competition law does not recognise a rule of reason under Article 101(1) TFEU. That is because the structure of Article 101 is different from that of section 1 of the Sherman Act; the pro-and anti-competitive effects of an agreement are weighed under Article 101(3) TFEU.

■ Commentary

Section 1 of the Sherman Act 1890 prohibits "every contract, combination in the form of trust or otherwise, or conspiracy, in restraint of trade or commerce." Taken literally, this wording prohibits every restraint of trade. Since the earliest judgments of the U.S. Supreme Court interpreting this provision in the 20th century, the Court held that it prohibits only unreasonable restraints of trade. Apart from restraints that would always or almost always tend to restrict competition, which are considered "per se" to be in violation of section 1, the U.S. courts apply the "rule of reason" in order to decide whether collusive behaviour constitutes an unreasonable restraint on competition: *Chicago Board of Trade v United States (1918)*. Factors relevant to this case-by-case evaluation include the history of the restraint in question, the purpose sought to be attained and its actual and probable effects: *Continental TV v GTE Sylvania (1977)*. Whether the firms involved have market power is a further, significant consideration: *Leegin Creative Leather Products v PSKS (2007)*.

It is fair to say that, over the last 40 years, the rule of reason standard has become the starting point for determining whether collusive practices restrain trade in violation of section 1. This is not to say that the rule of reason has been immune to criticism. It has been pointed out that the rule of reason is, as often as not, imprecise and unpredictable: *ABA Antitrust Section, Monograph No. 23, The Rule of Reason (1999*). The U.S. Supreme Court has responded to this concern by allowing the courts to create "a litigation structure" that enables the rule of reason to eliminate anticompetitive restraints and to provide more guidance to businesses *(Leegin)*. The judgment of the U.S. Court of Appeals for the D.C. Circuit in *PolyGram v Federal Trade Commission*(2005) is an example of a more structured rule of reason. The Court of Appeals first considered the alleged competitive harm, then examined any legitimate justification for the conduct complained about, and finally assessed the overall effects on consumers and competition.

Much of the commentary in the 1980s and early 1990s was critical of the formalistic and unduly broad application of Article 101(1), in consequence of which, so it was argued, meant many agreements required exemption under Article 101(3) which should have fallen outside of Article 101(1) because they did not restrict competition at all. Many commentators called for the adoption in EU law of a "rule of reason" in the application of Article 101(1). The Court of Justice has consistently resisted this clarion call. In *Consten and Grundig v Commission (1966)*, the Court refused to weigh up the pro- and anti-competitive effects of a distribution agreement conferring "absolute territorial protection" on the distributor; an agreement of that kind prevents parallel trade within the EU and was held to be unlawful under Article 101. In *Generics (UK) v Competition and Markets Authority (2020)*, the Court recently reaffirmed the position: EU competition law does not recognise a rule of reason (paragraph 104).

The General Court's judgment in *Métropole v Commission* (2001) provides a helpful explanation of why there is no rule of reason under Article 101. That case involved the creation of a new channel for pay TV in France, and whether the rule of reason should be applied in order to find that certain restraints in the joint venture agreement were not caught by Article 101(1). The Court emphasised three points.

First, it drew attention to the "bifurcation" of Article 101, which prohibits anti-competitive agreements in Article 101(1) but which provides that this prohibition "may be declared inapplicable" in the case of agreements that satisfy the terms of Article 101(3) (paragraph 73). Article 101 clearly differs from the simpler structure of section 1 of the Sherman Act, which does not have an equivalent of Article 101(3).

Secondly, if a rule of reason approach were adopted under Article 101(1), analysing the pro- and anti-competitive aspects of an agreement at that stage, Article 101(3) would lose much of its effectiveness. Instead, the pro- and anti-competitive effects of a restrictive agreement may only be weighed when considering whether that agreement satisfies Article 101(3) (paragraph 74).

Thirdly, the General Court acknowledged that various judgments of the EU Courts had been "more flexible" in their interpretation of Article 101(1), but pointed out that this did not mean that they entailed (still less required) a rule of reason in the sense of U.S. law (paragraph 75). Rather, what the EU jurisprudence demonstrates is that a restriction of competition cannot be found in the abstract; it generally requires a careful analysis of the relevant factual, legal and economic context on a case-by-case basis (paragraph 76).

It is fair to say that, over the last 25 years, the European Commission has been more willing to conclude that an agreement falls outside Article 101(1) altogether, rather than to find an infringement of Article 101(1) and then to grant an exemption under Article 101(3). This development does not mean that it has applied a rule of reason standard. Rather, the Commission has adopted a more realistic economics-based approach to Article 101(1) than it has done in the past. As a result, agreements that do not have as their object the restriction of competition and do not create or strengthen the parties' market power are unlikely to infringe Article 101(1).

In conclusion, the rule of reason is pivotal to the interpretation and application of section 1 of the Sherman Act in many cases in the U.S. but is not recognised under Article 101(1) TFEU. U.S. and EU competition law are materially different in a number of respects, and one should exercise caution before importing terminology and techniques from one system of competition law into another.

Bibliography

Bailey, D. and John, L. E. (eds.), *Bellamy & Child's European Union Law of Competition*, (Oxford University Press, 8th edn, 2018), ch 2

Forrester, I. and Norall, C. "The Laicization of Community Law: Self-help and the Rule of Reason" (1984), 21 *Common Market Law Review* 11

Hovenkamp, H., "The Rule of Reason" (2018), 70 *Florida Law Review* 81

Stucke, M. "Does the Rule of Reason Violate the Rule of Law?" (2009), 42 *University of California, Davis Law Review* 1375

Whish, R. and Bailey, D., *Competition Law*, (Oxford University Press, 10th ed, 2021), ch 3

See also

Anticompetitive practices, Ancillary restraints, Concerted practices

S

SECTOR INQUIRY

Sean ENNIS
University of East Anglia

Definition

A sector inquiry is an examination into why a particular sector or market may experience restricted or distorted competition – taking into account regulatory and economic factors as well as business and consumer behaviour – and how to reduce such restrictions or distortions.

Commentary

"Sector inquiries" as performed by competition authorities are focused on first, identifying regulatory, behavioural or structural problems in a market that can explain perceived failures of competition and second, suggesting solutions for improving competitive outcomes or processes. This note focuses on sector inquiries (or market studies), in the context of competition.

Most OECD competition authorities have either an informal or legally granted power to prepare and release sector inquiries. These studies are generally performed as an activity that supplements competition law enforcement duties related to mergers, abuse of dominance and cartels. Sector inquiries do not target individual companies nor arise from specific evidence of a cartel, thus distinguishing them from typical competition law enforcement. Such inquiries provide reasoned support for advocacy activities of competition authorities. The advocacy activities flowing from a market study can, for example, focus on changing government behaviour and regulations, changing private sector behaviour, and changing standards. Some market studies conclude that no changes are needed, either because they find that there is no problem with competition or that there is no reasonable solution for a problem that is identified. In some jurisdictions, market studies can at times result in opening of competition law investigations.

Competition authorities such as the U.S. FTC have carried out sector studies for more than 50 years (and have addressed sectors varying from contact lenses to car fuel, for example). Other authorities such as the European Commission, Chilean, French, German, Mexican and UK authorities have performed multiple sector-focused market studies (including for notaries (Chile), payments and insurance (EC), long-distance coach transport, hearing aids, Fintech, food retailing (France), milk, gas transmission, and district heating (Germany), ride-hailing, tortillas (Mexico), airports, classified directories, and groceries (UK)).

The opening of a sector inquiry is often based on "own-initiative" by competition authorities. The opening may also arise from other sources. Governments (e.g., France, Mexico), legislatures (e.g., U.S.) or even specifically identified bodies may have an ability to request a market study (e.g, in France with local authorities, courts, trade unions, professional or consumer associations, or the U.K. with a "super-complaints" process). In Mexico demands by government to open a market examination require substantial reasons including detailed explanation of indicators of the presence of a competitive restraint. Such reasons ensure that externally requested studies are started for reasons clearly related to lack of competition. The existence of a sector inquiry request by external parties does not necessarily guarantee that such an inquiry will be performed, as the competition authority could, in some jurisdictions (e.g., Mexico) determine that the reasons for requesting a study are not sufficient, the remedial actions are unlikely to work or that resources may be better used for other work.

The OECD notes that a high percentage of competition authorities carrying out market studies have powers to request information about the sector in question. Nonetheless, the information gathering powers of authorities for such inquiries are often more constrained than for the most serious competition law investigations. For example, the information gathering powers of a competition authority for market studies would typically not extend to unannounced inspections.

The use of sector inquiries to examine government restrictions on competition can be performed using the OECD's Competition Assessment Toolkit methodology, which is focused on identifying general principles for finding regulatory restrictions that are valid across sectors. These restrictions focus, in particular, on identifying rules and regulations that: (1) create unduly strict entry barriers, (2) limit the actions that businesses take in competition with each other, (3) restrict companies' incentives to compete with each other (all three of these addressing supply side restrictions) and (4) affect consumer information and consumer ability to switch (demand side restrictions). This methodology has been adopted and adapted by many countries and is available in translation in more than fifteen languages. The European Commission used the OECD approach as the basis of its own competition assessment of new regulations, as did Korea. Other jurisdictions, such as ASEAN economies, Brazil, Greece, Iceland, Portugal, the Philippines, Romania and Tunisia have successfully applied this approach to develop sector-specific recommendations for pro-competitive regulatory revisions.

A small number of governments (including France, Iceland, Mexico, and the UK) have supplemented the sector inquiry powers of competition authorities with further powers for competition authorities to perform market investigations. Outcomes of such investigations can include the ability to impose remedies. Remedies in such cases can be behavioural or structural, affecting private actors, or can include obligations on government to change rules and procedures, including to implement price regulation or regulatory oversight of an activity. Behavioural remedies can include, e.g., unbundling, limiting restrictions in agreements, disclosure requirements, measures to improve consumer engagement and switching. In one example of structural remedies, UK airports in London that were commonly owned were separated from each other as a result of a market investigation. Other remedies can include limits on referral incentives, market share limits and market redesign. The possibility for a competition authority to impose remedies in the context of a market investigation is considered a particularly invasive government intervention when applied to the private sector. Consequently, the procedures of competition investigations provide due process opportunities for parties that would be affected by the investigation to access and challenge evidence, enter their own arguments into the process and appeal decisions.

Bibliography

ICN (2016) "Market studies good practice handbook",

OECD (2018) "Market studies guide for competition authorities"

OECD (2015) "Competition assessment toolkit"

See also

Economic analysis, Investigations/inquiries

S

SELECTIVE DISTRIBUTION

Florian WAGNER-VON PAPP
Helmut Schmidt University of the Armed Forces

■ Definition

Selective distribution systems (SDS) consist of vertical agreements between a supplier and one or more distributors that (1) specify selection criteria which have to be met by undertakings/firms before they can be admitted into the SDS as "authorized distributors", and (2) prevent the re-sale of the product to non-authorized distributors. Resale is only permitted to other authorized distributors or end consumers. The selection criteria may pertain purely to quality standards ("qualitative SDS"), but in some cases also limit the number of authorized distributors overall and/or in any given area ("quantitative SDS"). The selectiveness means some intra-brand competition is sacrificed, with a bias in favor of high quality over low prices.

■ Commentary

Where a supplier wishes to establish a distribution system that guarantees customers a certain quality standard for pre-sale services, such as pre-sale advice by trained staff or a luxurious sales environment, such wishes may be undermined by freeriding from discounters. This would lead to underinvestment in pre-sale services by other distributors. SDS impose the quality criteria contractually and close the system against non-autorized distributors to prevent freeriding. Accordingly, SDS restrict intra-brand competition with regard to price, but allow for quality distribution that could otherwise not be realized. Interbrand competition may then fill any remaining demand for no frills, low-cost products. As a form of vertical non-price restraints, SDS are comparatively benign.

In the EU, a legal definition of SDS can be found in Article 1(1)(e) of the Vertical Block Exemption Regulation 330/2010 ("vBER"). Purely qualitative SDS, i.e., those that fulfill the so-called *Metro I* criteria, do not even constitute a restriction of competition in the meaning of Article 101(1) TFEU (*Metro v Commission* (1977)). These criteria are today restated as follows: "[T]he organisation of a selective distribution network is not prohibited by Article 101(1) TFEU, to the extent that resellers are chosen on the basis of objective criteria of a qualitative nature, laid down uniformly for all potential resellers and not applied in a discriminatory fashion, that the characteristics of the product in question necessitate such a network in order to preserve its quality and ensure its proper use and, finally, that the criteria laid down do not go beyond what is necessary [...]." (*Coty Germany v Parfümerie Akzente (2017)* at [24]). The first requirement is that the characteristics (or the "nature") of the product in question requires an SDS. This is typically the case where the restriction is necessary to preserve the quality of the product, to ensure its proper use (especially in the case of technical products), or to preserve the "luxury image" or "prestigious image" of a product. The second *Metro I* criterion is that the selection criteria for distributors must be objective, qualitative and applied in a non-discriminatory manner. The third criterion is that the qualitative criteria must not go beyond that which is necessary. If these criteria are fulfilled, the potential number of distributors is not limited; any undertaking fulfilling the criteria must be admitted into the system. For this reason, such purely qualitative SDS are not even considered to constitute a restriction of competition; while even these SDS limit intra-brand *price* competition to some degree, this is compensated by the fact that the SDS enables competition on the parameter "distribution quality" that would otherwise not be possible.

Where the *Metro I* criteria are not fulfilled – e.g., where the criteria add direct or indirect quantitative selection criteria – the restrictions on distributors constitute (intra-brand) restrictions of competition in the meaning of Article 101(1) TFEU. However, such SDS may still be block exempted by the vBER. This is the case where neither the supplier nor the distributor exceeds 30% market share on their respective markets, and where no "hardcore restriction" is involved. In the case of selective distribution system, the most relevant hardcore restrictions that may make the vBER inapplicable are restrictions on passive sales and restrictions on active cross-sales to other authorized distributors or sales to end consumers.

In recent years one of the most controversial questions in the EU has been to what extent SDS may restrict their distributors from selling online. *Pierre Fabre Dermo-Cosméthique v Président de l'Autorité de la concurrence* (2011) seemed to make two statements: first, that "[t]he aim of maintaining a prestigious image is not a legitimate aim for restricting competition and cannot therefore justify a finding that a contractual clause pursuing such an aim does not fall within Article 101(1) TFEU" (*at* [46]) and secondly, that a de facto prohibition of the use of internet sales by authorized distributors was a restriction by object and a hardcore restriction, thus making the vBER inapplicable. The first statement seemed flatly to contradict case law going back decades. In *Coty v Parfümerie Akzente* (2017), the Court clarified that this was a misunderstanding, and that it is a legitimate use of SDS where it ensures that "the goods are displayed in sales outlets in a manner that enhances their value, contributes to the reputation of the goods at issue and therefore contributes to sustaining the aura of luxury surrounding them". *Coty* therefore sought to restrict *Pierre Fabre* to its facts (*at* [31]). The problem is that *Coty* itself is not entirely clear on the distinguishing factors. *Coty* could be read to make a distinction based on whether the product in question is a "luxury good" (ibid. *at* [32]). However, SDS are not restricted to luxury goods, but can also be used for other branded products. This is a near-logical necessity: whether a product is considered a luxury product depends to a large degree on the "aura of luxury" created by the distribution system; requiring the qualification as a luxury good to be a prerequisite for the introduction of SDS would be putting the cart before the horse. The better interpretation of *Coty* is that *Pierre Fabre* prohibits de facto prohibitions of internet sales as going beyond that which is necessary, while in Coty the clause in question allowed authorized distributors direct online sales via their own website or via third-party websites that were not recognizable as such, and only prohibited sales via third-party platforms such as Amazon or eBay; this latter restriction was considered not to amount to a hardcore restriction. Less than a week after *Coty* was handed down, a German court decided, however, in a case whose facts are located between the goalposts of *Pierre Fabre* on the one hand and *Coty* on the other, that prohibiting distributors from supporting the functionality of price comparison websites and preventing them from advertising on third-party websites amounted to a hardcore restriction under the vBER (*Asics (2017)*).

Where neither the *Metro I* criteria, nor the conditions for the block exemption are met, a selective distribution system may still qualify for exemption under Article 101(3) TFEU.

In the U.S., SDS are not usually treated as a separate antitrust category. As non-price vertical restrictions, they are subject only to a rule of reason, *Continental TV v GTE Sylvania* (1977). Those SDS that are purely qualitative in the EU sense are not usually even called vertical restraints in the U.S., and they are said to be "virtually per se lawful" (Areeda & Hovenkamp 2017 at §1600b in fn 14 and accompanying text). Other SDS, in particular quantitative ones, may, depending on the restrictions agreed in the specific case, raise issues of territorial or customer limitations or single dealer appointments (Areeda & Hovenkamp 2017 at Ch. 16D and 16E).

Bibliography

Areeda, P. E. and Hovenkamp, H., *Antitrust Law - An Analysis of Antitrust Principles and Their Application*, Volume VIII (4th edn Wolters Kluwer 2017) Chapter 16

Bailey, D. and John, L. E. (eds.), *Bellamy and Child: European Union Law of Competition* (8th edn, Oxford University Press 2018), paras 7.094–7.117

Goyder, J., *EU Distribution Law* (5th edn Hart Publishing 2011) Chapter 4

Wijckmans, F. and Tuytschaever, F., *Vertical Agreements in EU Competition Law* (3rd edn, Oxford University Press 2018), paras 9.14–9.48

See also

Brand competition, Distribution agreement, Exclusive distribution, Passive sales, Vertical agreement, Vertical restraints (or restrictions)

S

SELF-PREFERENCE

Roberto RUSTICHELLI
Italian Competition Authority

Definition

Among exclusionary abuses of dominant position, self-preferencing is a conduct that falls under the more general category of abusive leverage, as it assumes an undertaking abusing its dominant position in a given market to extend that position in a closely related market (upstream, downstream or adjacent), to the detriment of competitor on the latter market. In particular, by using its market power on the dominated market the dominant undertaking gives a preferential treatment to its own product on the non-dominated market and this might be capable of having exclusionary effect, absent any objective justification or proof of efficiencies.

Commentary

Self-preferencing is a relatively new type of abusive conduct (at least formally), often associated to the market power held by digital platforms and to risks deriving from their vertical and conglomerate integration.

In fact, its first mentioning derives from the *Google Search (Shopping)* Decision (2017), in which the European Commission held that Google had abused its dominant position in thirteen national markets for general search services, by positioning and displaying more favourably, in its general search results pages, its own comparison shopping service compared to competing comparison shopping services (paragraph 341).

In particular, while competing comparison shopping services could appear only as generic search results and were prone to the ranking of their web pages in generic search results on Google's general search results pages being demoted by certain algorithms, Google's own comparison shopping service was prominently positioned, displayed in rich format and was never demoted by those algorithms (paragraph 344). The conduct decreased traffic from Google's general search results pages to competing comparison shopping services and increased traffic from Google's general search results pages to Google's own comparison shopping service and was capable to have anti-competitive effects in the national markets for comparison shopping services.

The European Commission argued that Article 102 TFEU prohibits abusive leveraging (paragraph 334 of the Decision) but, nonetheless, it did not qualified Google's conduct as any known leveraging practice, rejecting Google's argument that the conduct could have been considered abusive only if the criteria established in the *Bronner case* (Case C-7/97, EU:C:1998:569) were fulfilled.

This conclusion is shared by the General Court in its judgment of November 2021, which confirmed the Commission's Decision. In fact, the General Court noted that leveraging is a generic term in relation to the impact which a practice identified on one market may have on another market, and by this term can be addressed several different practices that are capable of being abusive, such as tying and refusal to deal, letting go without saying that the list might not be exhaustive as it is not the one contained in Article 102 TFEU (paragraph 163).

Given that leveraging practices of a dominant undertaking are not prohibited as such by Article 102 TFEU and that the actual scope of the special responsibility imposed on a dominant undertaking must be considered in the light of the specific circumstances of each case (paragraph 165), practices may be found abusive that are not included among those already assessed in the decisional practice of the European Commission and in the case law of the European Court of Justice.

Based on that, the General Court did not rely on a specific test to find Google's conduct abusive, but let it understand that the analysis of the specific circumstances of the case is fundamental to assess whether the dominant undertaking's conduct deviates from competition on the merits, without any objective justification or proof of efficiencies.

In November 2021, the Italian Competition Authority fined Amazon as it had abusively leveraged its dominant position in the Italian market for intermediation services on marketplaces to favour the adoption of its own logistics service (FBA) by sellers active on Amazon.it to the detriment of the logistics services offered by competing operators, as well as to strengthen its own dominant position.

More specifically, Amazon conditioned sellers' access to a set of exclusive benefits essential for gaining visibility and increasing sales on the platform to buying Amazon's logistics service. Among those benefits, sellers using Amazon's logistics service were not subject to the performance indicators Amazon applied to other sellers, which could even lead to the suspension of non-compliant sellers' account. This in turn, along with FBA-sellers being given access to the Prime badge for their offers, allowed FBA-sellers to get a greater probability of winning the so called Buy Box, which accounts for a very high portion of customer purchase on Amazon.it.

In other words, Amazon gave a preferential treatment to its own logistics service, whose performance was not subject to the metrics used to monitor the performance of competing logistics services (paragraphs 745-749 of the Decision).

Self-preferencing practices are also dealt with by Regulation (EU) 2022/1925 (Digital Markets Act), that imposes on gatekeepers obligations clearly shaped in the wake of European Commission's decisional practice.

Gatekeepers are often vertically integrated (Recital 51) and they "*should not engage in any form of differentiated or preferential treatment in ranking on the core platform service, and related indexing and crawling, whether through legal, commercial or technical means, in favour of products or services it offers itself or through a business user which it controls*" (Recital 52).

Based on that, Article 6, paragraph 5, forbids gatekeepers from "*treat[ing] more favourably, in ranking and related indexing and crawling, services and products offered by the gatekeeper itself than similar services or products of a third party. The gatekeeper shall apply transparent, fair and non-discriminatory conditions to such ranking*".

It is clear that the Digital Markets Act introduces for gatekeepers a *per se* rule for self-preferencing practises, while the antitrust enforcement approach remains based on the principles followed by the European Commission and the General Court as stated in the *Google Search (Shopping)* Decision and the following judgment, according to which self-preferencing is not abusive *per se*, as it might not be capable to have anti-competitive effects and undertakings could always prove an objective justification or efficiencies.

By not giving this opportunity to gatekeepers, the Digital Markets Act does not allow to seize potential pro-competitive features of self-preferencing, according to the specific circumstances of the case. Being the prohibition under Article 6 of the Regulation, it is only possible for the European Commission to further specify the measures that the gatekeeper concerned is to implement in order to effectively comply with the obligation (Article 8, paragraph 2 of the Regulation).

In the United States the Federal Trade Commission and the Department of Justice raised the level of attention towards antitrust risks in digital markets and reoriented their enforcement priority towards discriminatory strategies that digital platforms use to maintain their market power, such as self-preferencing. To tackle anti-competitive practices in digital markets, the United States Congress proposed the American Innovation and Choice

Online Act (S. 2992 – 117th Congress (2021-2022)) which "*prohibits certain large online platforms from engaging in specified acts, including giving preference to their own products on the platform, unfairly limiting the availability on the platform of competing products from another business, or discriminating in the application or enforcement of the platform's terms of service among similarly situated users*".

Bibliography

Ezrachi, A., *An Analytical Guide to the Leading Cases*, Bloomsbury Publishing, 7th Edition, 2021, pp. 315-317

Whish, R. and Bailey, D., *Competition Law*, Oxford University Press, 9th Edition, 2018, ch. 5, 17

See also

Abuse of dominant position, Online platforms, Refusal to deal

S

SERVICES OF GENERAL ECONOMIC INTEREST (SGIE)

Despoina (Deni) MANTZARI
University College London

■ Definition

"Service of general economic interest" (SGEI) is a rather elusive and evolving EU legal category that provides an exception to the Treaty rules on competition in favour of the proportionate pursuit of legitimate public interest goals by private undertakings. At its most basic, a SGEI is service of an economic nature that public authorities identify as being of particular importance to citizens. Examples include energy supply, telecommunications, postal services, transport, water, and waste disposal services. Because these services cannot be supplied by market forces alone, they may need public intervention. On the basis of Article 14 TFEU and Article 4 (2) TEU, Member States enjoy a broad discretion in defining and organizing their SGEI by virtue of their proximity to citizens. This margin is however significantly narrowed whenever sector-specific legislation incorporating SGEI is enacted at the EU level.

■ Commentary

The legal concept of SGEI allows proportionate restrictions on competition to be imposed to the benefit of an undertaking charged with SGEI to the extent necessary to perform their public service tasks. Mindful of the different ways in which Member States may wish to organise their SGEI, it allows legitimate national interests to be taken into account and enables a tailor-made solution for each SGEI by means of a proportional exemption based on A. 106 (2) TFEU. The legal basis is to be found in Articles 14 TFEU, 4 TEU and in Protocol No 26 on Services of General Interest inserted by the Treaty of Lisbon.

To better appreciate the rather elusive and constantly evolving concept of an SGEI, we shall focus on its manifestation in the context of energy supply, which has long been listed by the CJEU as a SGEI [See Case C-393/92, *Municipality of Almelo and Others*, EU:C:1994:171, paras. 46-48 and Case C-159/94, *Commission v France*, EU:C:1997:501, para. 57]. The concept of SGEI, as understood in energy supply, is underpinned by important social solidarity considerations in the form of social and territorial cohesion and by affordability concerns. This is understandable given that the provision of energy supply in a given society is crucial in realizing its territorial cohesion and stability. Energy undertakings carry out activities which are essential for the functioning of the society and on which many other activities depend. They are also important for social cohesion, as being cut off from electricity would amount to social exclusion.

Social solidarity is reflected in the Preamble to the EU Charter of Fundamental Rights as one of the founding values of the "ever closer Union" and in Chapter IV. It further informs the EU energy *acquis* objective of ensuring "high standards of universal and public service" and the protection of "final consumer", especially the "vulnerable" one, in the context of liberalized energy markets, from which stem various instruments for pursuing affordability.

To better appreciate its normative connotations, one should dig into the intellectual roots of the concept, which are to be found in the French legal concept of *service public* (public service) that has in turn profoundly influenced the EU's approach towards services of general economic interest. As developed by the French public law scholar Léon Duguit, the concept of *service public* prescribed that any type of state intervention into society could only be legitimized by its function "to protect the necessary preconditions for social interdependence and interaction", i.e. to serve the needs of society (*service public*). In light of this conceptualization, the notion of service public represents the state's commitment to social solidarity and prescribes the basis and limits of state action. However, the meaning of the service public eventually shifted over time within the French *École de service public* from representing the basis and limits of state's legitimacy to actually making the public interest the binding goal of the state, leading to an expansion of state's activities. The state is defined by its task to represent the public interest; but defining the public interest is within the free discretion of the state.

Understanding the notion of social solidarity as it finds its expression in the continental legal concept of service public is crucial as it underpins other important elements of SGEI, namely Universal Service Obligations (USOs) and Public Service Obligations (PSOs), enshrined in Article 3(1) of the energy liberalization directives 2009/72/EC and 2009/73/EC. USOs intend to guarantee the supply of electricity at "reasonable prices" to those who cannot afford it at the market price. They thus depart from cost-reflective pricing to allow for redistributive pricing. Redistributive pricing is achieved by imposing on one or more firms an obligation to supply energy to all consumers on a non-discriminatory basis, i.e. regardless of any variations in the cost of supplying different groups. Distribution is directed to high-cost service customers who, if market forces alone operated, would simply not be served as it would be uneconomic to do so, let alone at an affordable price. Hence USOs intends to socialize the costs of energy supply that in the era of state-owned monopolies were addressed through cross subsidization in order to promote non-efficiency objectives such as social solidarity and the desire to prevent social exclusion.

USOs should not be conflated with Public Service Obligations (PSO's). The latter are broader in their scope and may involve not only USOs, but also security of supply and environmental objectives and price regulation. As affordable energy supplies are essential to end-uses, the directives allow Member States to depart from the constitutional imperative of "open and undistorted competition" upon which the internal market is premised and impose PSOs on undertakings operating in the energy sector with respect to inter alia the *price* of electricity supply. Such PSOs must be clearly defined, transparent, non-discriminatory and guarantee equality of access for undertakings to national customers. [See Art. 3(2) of Electricity Directive 2009/72 EC and Gas Directive 2009/73/EC].

On the basis of this provision, Member States have sought to regulate retail energy prices so as to address "unreasonable prices" generated by the market mechanism, although in practice justifying this intervention proves to be difficult due to the ECJ's insistence on construing it narrowly. While on the basis of Article 14 TFEU and Article 4 (2) TEU, Member States enjoy a broad discretion in defining and organizing their SGEI by virtue of their proximity to citizens (soft version of proportionality, see e.g. Case C-320/91, Corbeau) this margin is significantly narrowed, whenever sector-specific legislation incorporating SGEI is enacted at the EU level (strict proportionality of the *least restrictive alternative*).

However, experience of the energy sector suggests that EU Member States have considerable freedom to determine the scope and contents of public service obligations and are allowed to take national circumstances and policy objectives into account. In fact, because of the poor clarification of the concept of PSO at the EU level and the lack of EU competence to design social policy in the field of energy, let alone a clear basis for energy until the Treaty of Lisbon (194 TFEU), Member States have been acting as gap-fillers in the EU policy, defining national solutions to counteract the impact of liberalization. The permissive approach is, however, subject to a strict degree of supervision by the European Commission for the possible effects of the measures on national competition. It is also complemented by the duty of the NRAs to monitor the level and effectiveness of market opening and competition at the retail level, including prices for household customers.

Bibliography

Hancher, L. and Larouche, P., "The Coming Age of EU Regulation of Network Industries and Services of General Economic Interest (SGIE)" in Craig and De Burca (Eds.), *The Evolution of EU Law* (OUP 2011)

Mantzari, D., "The Quest for Reasonable Retail Energy Prices in Europe: Positive and Normative Dimensions" (2017) 36 (1) *Yearbook of European Law* 599–627

Micklitz, H., "Universal Services: Nucleus for a Social European Private Law in Cremona (Ed.), *Market Integration and Public Services in the European Union,* (OUP, 2011)

Sauter, W., *Public Services in EU Law* (CUP 2015)

Schweitzer, H., "Services of General Economic Interest (SGIE): European Law's Impact on the Role of Markets and of Member States' in Cremona (Ed.), *Market Integration and Public Services in the European Union* (OUP 2011)

See also

Exclusive right (Art. 106 TFEU), Media pluralism, Universal service

S

SINGLE BRANDING

Isabella CARCIONE
Accademia del Lusso

■ Definition

Single Branding is a strategy based on an agreement whereby a retailer, or wholesaler, is bound to purchase from a supplier in the knowledge that no other distributor will be appointed or receive supplies in particular geographic area.

■ Commentary

Single branding agreements (so called in Europe) are vertical agreements that bind the customer to purchase all or most of a specific type of goods or services only from the dominant supplier (Article 102 TFEU). The term of the exclusivity agreement is applicable to an exclusive supply obligation, where there is a limitation for the supplier to supply to anyone other than the specific downstream customer and the other way around.

It should be noted that the Commission stated in the guidelines on vertical restraints that binding agreements for the purchase of assets of 80% or more, will be taken in line with the meaning of the exclusive deals and could be found to be abusive (*Hoffmann-La Roche v Commission*).

An exclusive purchase agreement is not in itself illegal under Article 102 (*Intel Corp Inc v European Commission*) and can only be considered abusive if it can have a foreclosure effect on equally efficient competitors and does not have a objective justification. Thus, a defense that the client voluntarily entered into an agreement will not be sufficient; the question is whether the deal could horizontally foreclose competitors efficiently (or more) than the dominant company in the market.

Exclusive trade is not inherently or allegedly illegal (Sherman Act, 15 U.S.C. §§ 1-7; Clayton Act, 15 U.S.C. §§ 12-27). Antitrust concerns about exclusivity agreements are based on the possibility that the execution of the agreement precludes competition in substantial proportion of the relevant line of business.

To determine whether a particular exclusivity arrangement operates as an unlawful restriction on trade, courts apply the rule of reason articulated by Judge Brandeis in Board of Trade of City of Chicago v. U.S., 246 U.S. 231 (1918). "*The real test of legality is whether the restriction imposed is such that it merely regulates and perhaps thereby promotes competition or whether it is such as to suppress or even destroy competition.*" To determine this question the court must normally consider the peculiar facts of the activity to which the restriction applies; its condition before and after the restriction was imposed; the nature of the restriction and its actual or probable effect.

Most exclusivity agreements are beneficial because they encourage marketing support for the manufacturer's brand. By becoming an expert in manufacturer's products, the retailer is encouraged to specialize in promoting that manufacturer's brand. This may include offering special services or services that cost money, such as an attractive shop, skilled salespeople, extended business hours, a handy product inventory, or quick warranty service.

Single branding can be seen as a barrier to entry, especially in markets operating under conditions of imperfect competition, monopoly or oligopoly, where there is price and product differentiation, as well as an imbalance of market power between incumbents, competitors and competitors due to the existence of vertical integrations within the market, which lead to market inefficiencies.

The Chicago and TCE accounts of single branding suggest that the "workable competition" account of such agreements and antitrust's resulting hostility toward them is not justified. Of course, this observation still begs the question of what purposes these restraints did serve. TCE fills this gap, providing possible explanations for agreements that seem ill-suited for causing anticompetitive harm.

Indeed, at a more basic level, TCE's recognition that exclusive dealing between separate firms is simply a particular form of nonstandard contracting, analogous to the nonstandard contract known as the firm, should immediately give pause to those who would pursue aggressive policies toward exclusive dealing agreements. One can reject the strong critique offered by Bork and other members of the Chicago school without contradicting their observation that many restraints once deemed unlawful by the courts arose in circumstance in which anticompetitive harm seemed quite unlikely, even during the inhospitality era (*FTC v. Brown Shoe Co.*). Absent some empirical or even theoretical showing, and I know of none, that "concerted" exclusive dealing produces more net harm than exclusivity that takes place "within the firm," pursuant to agreements between various actors, there seems to be no apparent rationale for the inhospitality era's relative hostility toward such agreements. Any policy toward exclusive dealing, then, must rest upon a theoretical apparatus divorced from the workable competition model and its outmoded theory of the firm.

The response of Transaction Cost Economics or TCE sought to undermine price theory itself, or at least its conception of the firm and other non-standard contracts. Unlike the Chicago School, TCE offered to explain how exclusive dealing within and between firms produced benefits. In particular, TCE argued that complete and partial integration was a method of reducing or eliminating the costs of relying upon unbridled markets to conduct economic activity, particularly costs flowing from anticipated opportunism. Exclusive dealing, it was said, was no exception, and economists have identified several beneficial effects that such contracts can create.

Bibliography

Meese, A. J., *Exclusive Dealing, the Theory of the Firm, and Raising Rivals' Costs: Toward a New Synthesis*, William & Mary Law School Faculty Publications (2005)

Posner, R. A., *Antitrust Law* 251-54, The University of Chicago Press (2d ed. 2001)

See also

Exclusive purchasing agreement, Vertical restraints (or restrictions)

S

SPECIALIZATION AGREEMENTS

Mariateresa MAGGIOLINO
Bocconi University

Definition

In a specialization agreement, parties dedicate themselves to manufacturing products where they showcase superior expertise. Unilateral specialization agreements involve one party ceasing or reducing the production of a specific product, while the other party takes over its supply. Reciprocal specialization agreements entail both parties stopping the production of their respective products and relying on each other for procurement. Given the intricate nature of contemporary industrial processes, encompassing multiple stages and resulting in various intermediate and final products, specialization agreements fall under the umbrella of horizontal production agreements. This category also encompasses joint ventures and subcontracting arrangements.

Commentary

Specialization agreements give rise to three primary horizontal anticompetitive effects, as the parties cease competition in the production of one or more products. First, these agreements strip the parties of their autonomy in determining offers, especially in adapting to changes in market demand. Second, they induce cost-sharing among the parties, thereby facilitating price collusion. Notably, the likelihood of collusion increases with the extent of shared costs. Lastly, specialization agreements can serve as veils to conceal explicit agreements to limit output, whereby the parties decide to restrict the quantity of goods produced, subsequently raising market prices.

Moreover, specialization agreements can result in foreclosure effects. If a specialization agreement causes the price of the jointly produced product to rise and if such a product is crucial for the production of downstream firms, then the specialization agreement may lead to the exit of downstream firms from the market when they can no longer afford the higher price.

As is often the case, the significance of these coordinated and unilateral anticompetitive effects increases with higher joint market shares, a higher concentration ratio in the relevant market, market maturity, and static conditions, as well as the production capacity of other firms in the market and the structural bounds among rivals.

On the other hand, specialization agreements can yield procompetitive effects by allowing firms to reduce costs that would otherwise be duplicated. This cost-saving may result from economies of scale, where marginal costs decrease with increased output, or from economies of scope if the agreement enables the parties to diversify the range of products they manufacture. Additionally, specialization agreements have the potential to enhance various aspects: (i) product quality: collaborating firms can improve product quality by leveraging complementary skills and know-how; (ii) product variety: the agreements may lead to an increased product variety that the parties might not have been able to afford or achieve independently; and (iii) technological advancements: collaboration can foster advancements in production technologies or facilitate the launch of new products, endeavors that the parties might not have undertaken individually, possibly due to limited technical capabilities. In essence, specialization agreements offer the potential for positive outcomes, fostering efficiency and innovation in various dimensions.

Hence, under Section 1 of the Sherman Act, specialization agreements do not constitute naked restraints on competition, unless they involve concealing price-fixing agreements. In other words, if they represent genuine (market- or product- division) ancillary restraints, they are subject to the rule of reason analysis; and this clearly necessitates an examination of the power of the parties and the competitive impact of the agreement.

In particular, the Federal Trade Commission and the Department of Justice, in their 2000 Guidelines on Collaboration Agreements, highlighted instances where competitor collaborations, like specialization agreements, could yield effects akin to those of a partial or complete merger and thus should be subject to analysis based on the Horizontal Merger Guidelines. This scenario arises when the agreement extends over several years, featuring an efficiency-driven integration of economic activities and the cessation of competition among the parties.

Similarly, under Article 101 of the Treaty on the Functioning of the European Union, specialization agreements cannot be classified as restrictions by object because they admit various procompetitive justifications. Therefore, unless they are intended to conceal cartels, specialization agreements amount to restrictions by effect that must be prohibited if they entail significant anticompetitive effects without satisfying the four conditions listed in Article 101(3).

In particular, to facilitate the self-assessment of specialization agreements, the European Commission (EC) adopted Regulation (EU) 2023/1067 on June 1, 2023. This regulation outlines the conditions under which specialization agreements are block-exempted from the prohibition included in Article 101(1). For instance, to qualify for the block-exemption, the combined market share of the parties should not exceed 20% on the relevant market(s) to which the specialization products belong, and – clearly enough – the agreement cannot serve to hide any price fixing, output limitation, or allocation of customers and markets.

On the same date, the Commission also issued revised accompanying guidelines on the application of Article 101(3) that clarify how to interpret the block exemption regulations and how to self-assess other specialization agreements between competitors not covered by the block regulation.

Bibliography

Faull, J. and Nikpay, A., *The EU law of competition*, Oxford University Press, 2014, 2nd ed., 941-961

Hovenkamp, H., *Antitrust law*, Aspen Publishers, 2005, 2nd ed., Vol. XIII, 189-202

Whish, R. and Bailey, D., *Competition law*, Oxford University Press, 2021, 10th ed., 627-631

Commission Regulation (EU) 2023/1067 of 1 June 2023 on the application of Article 101(3) of the Treaty on the Functioning of the European Union to certain categories of specialization agreements, OJ 2023, L 143/20

Communication from the Commission - Guidelines on the applicability of Article 101 of the Treaty on the Functioning of the European Union to horizontal co-operation agreements, OJ 2023, C 259/1

Federal Trade Commission, Department of Justice, Antitrust Guidelines for Collaborations Among Competitors, April 2000

See also

Block exemption (regulation), Economies of scale

S

STANDARD-ESSENTIAL PATENT (SEP)

Giuseppe COLANGELO
University of Basilicata

Definition

A patent is deemed to be essential whenever it would be impossible to implement the standard without making use of it. In order to prevent or reduce the risks of patent hold-up and increase the willingness to participate in the development of a standard, Standard Development Organisations (SDOs) typically adopt disclosure and licensing rules. Accordingly, firms taking part in a standardization initiative must disclose the existence of any patent that might be considered essential to the developing standard (SEP), and agree to license their SEPs on fair, reasonable, and non-discriminatory (FRAND) terms. The economic meaning and the legal implications of FRAND commitments has proven to be extremely controversial.

Commentary

Once a technology is included into a standard, the patent owner of that technology will benefit from an increase of the patent value, thus it might be incentivized to behave opportunistically trying to influence the design of the standard to boost its ex post benefits. Indeed, while during the early stage of definition there are competing technologies that might be included into the standard, once the technology is chosen, implementers are locked into the standard. Further, implementers frequently face large investments into their product before the standard is defined. Therefore, once the standard is set, a hold-up problem may arise since holders of patents that cover the standard (SEPs) can leverage their positions by demanding a royalty that reflects the value of the technology as well as the value associated with investments made by producer to implement the standard.

However, at the same time, licensees may also engage in strategic practices refusing to agree on patent holders' offers and exacerbating litigation in order to escape the payment of royalties or depress prices (reverse hold-up or hold-out).

To address these concerns, SDOs adopt disclosure and licensing rules. The first set of rules aims at identifying in due advance patents that should be considered essential to the standard, allowing the SDO to avoid risks of patent ambushes, namely the non-disclosure of patents or patent applications, which are later claimed to be relevant for the adopted standard. The second set of rules requires SEPs holders to submit FRAND commitments to prevent another risk of patent hold-up, that is the extent of ex post opportunism and monopoly pricing by SEP holders. Indeed, by requiring licensing on FRAND terms, the goal is to make SEPs available at a price equivalent to what patents would have been worth in the market prior to the time they were declared essential.

Although the violation of such rules may belong to a merely private contracting problem, the potential competitive implications have also suggested a call for antitrust intervention. Notably, with regards to disclosure rules, the deceptive strategy pursued by SDO participants has been investigated as a potential antitrust violation both in the U.S. and the EU and usually sanctioned by mandating a royalty-free license or a maximum royalty rate (determined according to the FRAND commitment). More controversial is the meaning and the scope of the FRAND commitment as licensing rule. Indeed, notwithstanding a significant flow of litigation and new emerging insights, there is still limited knowledge about the enforcement of SEPs, namely what a FRAND royalty rate actually is, whether a FRAND commitment implies a waiver of general legal remedies (in particular, injunctions), whether the licensing of SEPs under FRAND terms is a competition issue or whether a violation of a FRAND pledge just amounts to a breach of contract.

The relevance of antitrust for FRAND commitments is strictly related to the economic consequences of hold-up and hold-out and the priority that one intends to assign to these two problems from a policy perspective. While hold-up proponents claim that the risk of opportunistic behavior is so severe to require antitrust intervention, a different strand of literature contend that licensing of SEPs should be addressed by contract law as hold-up risk can be considered as the effect of sunk investments already made by implementers on negotiation power. When it comes to remedies, the hold-up theory would require antitrust authorities and courts to pose limitations to injunctive reliefs in favor of FRAND-encumbered SEPs holders. This approach is based on the reasoning that the patent holder that accepts a FRAND commitment voluntarily agrees to a liability rule since it considers his interest adequately satisfied by FRAND terms, thus giving up either to injunctive relief connected to the property rule or any compensation of damages (*Apple v. Motorola*, 2012).

In the EU, in the attempt of striking a balance between hold-up and hold-out risks, *Huawei* (2015) delivered a "willing licensee test" using the threat of antitrust liability and patent enforcement as levers to discipline both parties in order that they converge towards a mutually agreeable FRAND royalty level.

FRAND commitments and the legal issues involved have also raised the attention of the Asian jurisdictions, determining a progressive international convergence on how parties should behave when licensing SEPs. Hence, antitrust evolved in the international landscape heavily restricting SEP owners' freedom to pursue their patent rights. Precisely, if there are FRAND-encumbered SEPs and alleged infringers are willing licensees, then a no-injunction rule applies.

However, in 2019, the U.S. Department of Justice (DoJ), along with the Patent and Trademark Office (PTO) and National Institute of Standards and Technology (NIST), rejected the no-injunction rule considering hold-out as an even more serious impediment to dynamic innovation than hold-up. Moreover, updating its previous IEEE's Business Review Letter, the DoJ stated that concerns over hold-up as a real-world competition problem have largely dissipated. The new approach was ultimately embraced by the Ninth Circuit in *Qualcomm* (2020). Similarly, in Europe, national courts have recently recognised the limited role of antitrust in these kinds of disputes and the importance of ensuring SEP rights enforcement against infringers by endorsing an "unwilling licensee" standard for injunctive relief (see *Sisvel v. Haier*, 2020; and *Unwired Planet*, 2020).

The advent and the increasing diffusion of the Internet of Things (IoT) along with the development of 5G add complexity to the current practice of SEP licensing. Differently from the past, new standard implementers, even if belonging to industries not strictly related to mobile devices, have to deal with the intellectual property complexities of the ecosystem of mobile communications. For instance, the automotive industry is taking central stage as the ecosystem in which the issue of FRAND licensing levels is raised to the highest degree. In light of these dynamics, there is a new highly debated issue concerning if a SEP holder should be asked to grant a FRAND licence to any requiring implementer, including component makers (so-called "licence-to-all" approach), or if they should be allowed freely to target the supply chain level at which the licence is to be granted ("access-for-all").

Moreover, as the rise of the IoT and the evolution of many industries hinge on advanced mobile telecommunication standards (4G and 5G) to ensure interoperability and technical compatibility, SEP licensing has become a matter of geopolitics. Indeed, despite the national nature of patents, the global reach of markets for technology inevitably leads to transnational litigation over SEPs and, because of the uncertainty around the meaning and the scope of FRAND commitments, litigants are increasingly eager to request (and courts appear prone to issue) anti-suit injunctions (ASIs), that is orders restraining a party from pursuing foreign proceedings or enforcing a judgment obtained in foreign proceedings.

Finally, the policy towards SEPs is currently at the centre of significant changes. In the EU, the Commission is expected to deliver a legislative initiative aimed at enhancing SEPs enforcement and licensing, notably by promoting transparency and providing clarity on various aspects of FRAND. Further, the UK Government recently released a summary of the views gathered as part of its innovation strategy to investigate whether the SEPs ecosystem is functioning efficiently and effectively and striking the right balance for all entities involved. In the meantime, the new U.S. administration has promoted a relevant policy shift by withdrawing the 2019 Policy Statement on remedies for FRAND-encumbered SEPs.

Bibliography

BORGOGNO, O. and COLANGELO, G., "SEPs licensing across the supply chain: an antitrust perspective" (2021) 11 *Queen Mary Journal of Intellectual Property* 484

GALETOVIC, A. and HABER, S., "The Fallacies of Patent-Holdup Theory" (2017) 13 *Journal of Competition Law & Economics* 1

LEMLEY, M. A. and SHAPIRO, C., "Patent Holdup and Royalty Stacking" (2007) 85 *Texas Law Review* 1991

MELAMED, D. and SHAPIRO, C., "How Antitrust Law Can Make FRAND Commitments More Effective" (2018) 127 *Yale Law Journal* 2110

SIDAK, G., "The Meaning of FRAND, Part I: Royalties" (2013) 9 *Journal of Competition Law & Economics* 931

See also

Compulsory license, FRAND, Intellectual Property, Licensing, Patents

S

STATE ACTION DEFENCE

Joseph WILSON
McGill University

Definition

State action defence (SAD) is asserted by an antitrust defendant when its challenged anticompetitive conduct is a result of following a state policy, which must be *clearly articulated and actively supervised* by the state itself. The concept is invoked when a legally valid state policy formulated at any level of government to regulate certain conduct conflicts with the national competition law. SAD is recognized in a number of the nation-states with competition laws, in one form or another. (Also referred to as: *Parker doctrine, Grant of implied immunity, State Compulsion Defence, or Regulated Conducted Defence*).

Commentary

The state action defence finds its origin in a 1941 case, *Brown v. Parker*, before a United States district court challenging the enforcement of a marketing plan adopted under the California Agricultural Prorate Act of 1933. The case involved conflict between a state regulatory scheme and federal antitrust laws, which was settled by the Supreme Court keeping in view the U.S. federal form of government in which the "States" are sovereign. The Court noted that the Sherman Act was designed "to suppress combinations to restrain competition and attempts to monopolize by individuals and corporations" and the Act "makes no mention of the state as such, and gives no hint that it was intended to restrain state action or official action directed by a state."(*Parker*at 351) The Court held that since it was the state, acting through the Commission, which adopted and enforced the program, and had extensive official oversight, the Sherman Act did not apply. Later decisions of the Supreme Court enlarged the scope of immunity to the FTC Act (*Ticor*) and the Clayton Act (*Phoebe*).

An entity may invoke SAD only if "the actions in question are an exercise of the State's sovereign power." (*Omni* at 374) State agencies are not simply by their governmental character sovereign actors for the purposes of state-action immunity. There must be "more than a mere facade of state involvement, to ensure the States accept political accountability for anticompetitive conduct they permit and control." (*NCSB Dental Examiners*, at 505). The Supreme Court in later cases allowed the private parties to claim state action immunity. (*Southern Motors* (1985) & *Patrick* (1988)).

Substantive Test

When determining whether the anticompetitive acts of private parties, state agencies or officials regulating the conduct of private parties, are entitled to immunity, the Court in *California Retail Liquor Dealers Ass'n. v. Midcal.* (1980) postulated a two prong test. First, the challenged restraint must be "one clearly articulated and affirmatively expressed as state policy"; and second, the policy was "actively supervised by the state" itself. In a later case the Court, however, exempted the local governmental entities to prove the second prong of the test. (*Phoebe Putney*)

Clearly Articulated State Policy

The clear articulation requirement is satisfied where "the displacement of competition [is] the inherent, logical, or ordinary result of the exercise of authority delegated by the state legislature." (*Phoebe Putney* at 1013) Thus, in *Hallie*, the U.S. Supreme Court found the Wisconsin statutory law, which permitted cities to limit their service to surrounding unincorporated areas, affirmatively contemplated the alleged anticompetitive effects complained of "because it was "clear" that they "logically would result" from the grant of authority." (*Phoebe* at 1013).

Grants of general corporate power that allow governmental entities to participate in a competitive marketplace are held to be used without raising federal antitrust concerns. In Phoebe, the Court noted that "while the Law does allow the Authority to acquire hospitals, it does not clearly articulate and affirmatively express a state policy empowering the Authority to make acquisitions of existing hospitals that will substantially lessen competition" in violation of the Clayton Act. (*Phoebe* at 1012). Compulsion is not a substantive element to prove clear articulation. "A state policy that expressly *permits*, but does not compel, anticompetitive conduct may be 'clearly articulated'" (*Southern Motor* at 1729).

Actively Supervised by the State

The active supervision requirement is designed to ensure that the state-action doctrine will shelter only the particular anticompetitive acts of private parties that, in the judgment of the state, actually further state regulatory policy. (*Hallie* at 47). Regulatory bodies "controlled by active market participants" must also satisfy the active supervision prong. (*NCSB Dental Examiners*, at 510).

To ensure that the state exercise ultimate control over the challenged conduct, the state officials must: (i) review the substance of the anticompetitive decision, not merely the procedures followed to produce it; (ii) have the power to veto or modify particular decisions to ensure they accord with state policy; (*Patrick*, at 1663) and (iii) not itself be an active market participant. (*NCSB Dental Examiners*, at 510). Judicial review of action, where such review exists, falls far short of satisfying the active supervision requirement. (*Patrick*, at 1665) The so-called negative option, where prices/rates submitted by private rate-setting bureaus become effective unless the State rejected them within a specified period, fails to meet the "active supervision" requirement. (*Ticor*, at 2179).

In European Union, Articles 101 and 102 TFEU apply only to anti-competitive conduct engaged in by undertakings on their own initiative. If anti-competitive conduct is required of undertakings by national legislation or by a legal framework created by that legislation or by irresistible pressure imposed by the national authorities, Articles 101 and 102 do not apply. (*Ladbroke Racing* paras 33 to 35). Compulsion is a necessary element to successfully assert State action defence and it may be exercised by a third country. *Polskie* para 64).

In Pakistan, the Competition Commission of Pakistan in the *Karachi Stock Exchange (KSE)* case addressed the issue of implied immunity from competition law. KSE argued that its "act of placing the price floor on the share prices had the *tacit approval* of the securities regulator, *i.e.,* the Securities and Exchange Commission of Pakistan (SECP). To resolve the regulatory conflict, the Commission employed the tests used in the EU and the U.S. The Commission found there was no compulsion from the SECP to place the floor, and as to the powers delegated to KSE by SECP, it noted that "regulatory responsibility sufficient to trigger immunity when in the hands of an administrative agency may not be sufficient when conferred on an industry organ as a self-regulatory regime." (*KSE*, para 64).The Commission thus rejected the claim of KSE, as there was no *Clear articulation or active supervision by the State organ.*

In India, the Supreme Court of India, in *Dalmia Cement (Barat) Limited v. Union of India*, addressed the constitutionality of the Jute Packaging Materials Act, 1987. The Act prevented the manufacturers and distributors of certain commodities to use the bags of their choice, fixed the price of Jute bags, and restrained competition in the market of bags for packing commodities.

The Court first looked at the Statement of Objects and Reasons and the Preamble of the Act, and noted that *"in unmistakable terms,"* the Act intended to provide livelihood to rural agricultural families and industrial workers. "Parliament *avowedly intended* to protect the interests of the persons involved in jute production." (*Dalmia* para 24) Second, the Court noted that "when the orders passed under Section 3 are subject to modification by Parliament, Parliament preserved to itself a great salutary control over executive exercise of power under Section 3(1)." (*Dalmia* para 31) The Court, in upholding the provisions of the Jute Act and directions made pursuant to it, essentially employed the *clear articulation (in unmistakable terms)* and *actively supervised (salutary control over executive exercise)* test. (*Dalmia* para 52)

See also

State Mesure

S

STATE AID (COMPATIBILITY)

Fabrizio DI BENEDETTO
Intesa Sanpaolo

■ Definition

Article 107(1) TFEU prescribes that State aids, as defined in that provision, are forbidden within the internal market. However, TFEU contains derogations from this prohibition; derogations are restrictively interpreted. Certain State aids may be compatible when they pursue public interests that prevail over the protection of competition within the internal market. This compatibility test is predominantly carried out by the European Commission, which is exclusively competent over State aids, according to Article 108 TFEU. The main derogations can be found under: (i) Article 107(2) TFEU; (ii) Article 107(3) TFEU; (iii) the third subparagraph of Article 108(2) TFEU; (iv) and Commission Regulation (EU) No 651/2014 (infra, General Block Exemption Regulation or GBER).

■ Commentary

(i) Article 107(2) contains a list of State aids that are considered de jure compatible with the internal market. Those aids must be notified by Member States to the Commission; however, the role of the latter is limited to a formal assessment regarding the presence of the conditions set out by the Treaty.

For instance, Article 107(2)(a) declares that an "aid having a social character, granted to individual consumers, provided that such aid is granted without discrimination related to the origin of the products concerned" is compatible. All three conditions must be met. According to the General Court in P & O European Ferries (Vizcaya) v Commission (2003), with reference to the third condition "it must be ascertained whether consumers benefit from the aid in question irrespective of the economic operator supplying the product or service" (paragraph 163).

Article 107(2)(b) provides that an "aid to make good the damage caused by natural disasters or exceptional occurrences" is compatible. Three cumulative conditions must be satisfied: to be exceptional, an occurrence must: (1) be unforeseeable or difficult to foresee; (2) have significant scale/ economic impact; (3) be extraordinary. Moreover, according to the Court of Justice in Spain v Commission (2004), there must be a causal link between the exceptional occurrences and the damages compensated by the State (paragraph 37).

(ii) Article 107(3) encompasses State aids that may be considered compatible with the internal market by the Commission after a notification by Member States. Aids falling under the scope of Article 107(3) are subject to a wider Commission's discretion than those under Article 107(2).

For example, pursuant to Article 107(3)(b), the Commission may declare compatible with the internal market an aid to remedy a serious disturbance in the economy of a Member State. As stated by the General Court in Freistaat Sachsen and Others v Commission (1999), the serious disturbance in question "must affect the whole of the economy of the Member State concerned, and not merely that of one of its regions or parts of its territory" (paragraph 167). Moreover, aids under Article 107(3)(b) must be appropriate, necessary, and proportionate.

Article 107(3)(c) allows the Commission to declare compatible aids to facilitate the development of certain economic activities or of certain economic areas, provided that they do not adversely affect trading conditions to an extent contrary to the common interest. Regarding the second condition, the Court of Justice in Austria v Commission (2020) held that it entails "weighing up the positive effects of the planned aid for the development of the activities that that aid is intended to support and the negative effects that the aid may have on the internal market" (paragraph 101). That is the very heart of State aid compatibility assessment, which aims at balancing internal market integrity with other relevant public interests.

(iii) The third subparagraph of Article 108(2) according to the third subparagraph or Article 108(2), in exceptional circumstances the Council, on application by a Member State, may unanimously decide that an aid which that State is granting or plans to grant is compatible, in derogation from other Treaty or regulation provisions. This is the only case where the Council takes on the Commission's competence over State aid assessment for notifiable aids. In this regard, the Court of Justice in Commission v Council (2013) held that "the respective powers of the Council and the Commission are allocated in such a way that, first, the primary competence to act lies with the Commission, the Council having power to act only in exceptional circumstances. Second, the Council's competence, which enables it to derogate, in its decision, from certain Treaty provisions on State aid, must be exercised within a specific time frame [i.e., three months from the application]. Third, as soon as the

Commission or the Council has adopted a final ruling on the compatibility of the aid in question, the other of those two institutions may no longer adopt a contrary decision" (paragraph 50). In a case where the Council doesn't take a decision within the mentioned deadline, the Commission shall decide on the case.

(iv) The General Block Exemption Regulation Commission Regulation (EU) No 651/2014 declares compatible certain categories of aid in application of Articles 107 and 108. Consequently, if the conditions set out in the GBER are met, Member States are exempted from the notification requirement when granting such aids. The fields covered by the GBER are the following: regional aids, aids to small and medium enterprises, aids for environmental protection, aids for research and development, training aids, employments aid for disadvantaged workers, aids to make good the damage caused by certain natural disasters, social aids for transport in remote regions, aids for broadband infrastructures, aids for culture, aids for sport and recreational infrastructures, aids for local infrastructures.

Measures falling under the Commission Regulation (EU) No 1407/2013 (i.e., the de minimis Regulation) "can be deemed not to have any effect on trade between Member States and not to distort or threaten to distort competition" (recital 3).

Bibliography

Buendia Sierra, J. L., "Making the (Hinkley) Point about Compatibility Control" (2021)20 *European State Aid Law Quarterly* 1

Nicolaides, P., Kekelekis, M. and Kleis, M., *State Aid Policy in the European Community: Principles and Practice* (2nd edn, Kluwer Law International 2008), Chapter II

Nogueira de Almeida, J., "The Common Principles of Compatibility of State Aid Laid down in the New General Block Exemption Regulation (Regulation No. 651/2014)" (2014) 57 *Boletim Ciencias Economicas* 69

Nowak, A., "Evidence Requirements for State Aid Compatibility Assessment" (2018) 17 *European State Aid Law Quarterly* 212

See also

Market economy investor, State aid (notion)

S

STATE AID (EXISTING AID)

Tomasz CHRÓSTNY
Polish Competition Authority

■ Definition

Generally, State aid is any intervention by public authority, which confers selective economic advantage to undertaking. According to article 107 (1) TFEU, any aid granted by a Member State or through State resources in any form whatsoever which distorts or threatens to distort competition by favouring certain undertakings or the production of certain goods shall, in so far as it affects trade between Member States, be incompatible with the internal market. Articles 107 to 109 contain the EU rules on state aid. Whereas, as a general rule, new state aids must be notified to the Commission, "existing aid" is subject to different procedural rules.

■ Commentary

There are a number of categories of "existing aid". Article 1(b) Council Regulation (EU) 2015/1589 of 13 July 2015 laying down detailed rules for the application of Article 108 of the TFEU defines existing aid as:

- all aid which existed prior to the entry into force of the TFEU in the respective Member States, that is to say, aid schemes and individual aid which were put into effect before, and are still applicable after, the entry into force of the TFEU in the respective Member States;
- authorised aid, that is to say, aid schemes and individual aid which have been authorised by the Commission or by the Council;
- aid which is deemed to have been authorised pursuant to Article 4(6) of Regulation (EC) No 659/1999 or to Article 4(6) of Regulation (EU) 2015/1589, or prior to Regulation (EC) No 659/1999 but in accordance with this procedure;
- aid with regard to which the limitation period has expired pursuant to Article 17 of Council Regulation (EU) 2015/1589;

- aid which is deemed to be an existing aid because it can be established that at the time it was put into effect it did not constitute an aid, and subsequently became an aid due to the evolution of the internal market and without having been altered by the Member State (where certain measures become aid following the liberalisation of an activity by Union law, such measures shall not be considered as existing aid after the date fixed for liberalisation).

Within the framework of the State aid control system, the treatment of State aid differs depending on whether the aid is existing or new. While existing aid may, in accordance with Article 108(1) TFEU, be implemented until the Commission establishes that it is incompatible, Article 108(3) TFEU provides that measures containing new aid or modifying existing aid must be notified to the Commission. According to Article 108 (1) TFEU, existing aid schemes are subject to constant review by the Commission, which may propose to Member States appropriate measures required by the progressive development or by the functioning of the internal market. The review takes place in cooperation with the Member States which must provide the Commission with all necessary information for the review.

In its judgment in case T-131/21 (Judgment of 21 June 2023, Região Autónoma da Madeira v European Commission) the General Court stated that, in accordance with Article 108(1) TFEU, existing aid may be implemented as long as the Commission does not find it incompatible with the internal market. By contrast, Article 108(3) TFEU requires that plans to grant new aid or to alter existing aid must be notified to the Commission and may not be put into effect before a final decision is adopted under the procedure laid down in Article 108(2) TFEU. [para 75]. It follows that an authorised aid scheme, which is existing aid, is no longer covered by the decision authorising it and, therefore, constitutes new aid whenever the Member State concerned implements that aid scheme on the basis of rules that are substantially different from those laid down in the authorised draft aid scheme [para 76]. An existing aid scheme that has been substantially amended after it was authorised by the Commission loses its classification as existing aid. [para 77].

Article 4(1), of Regulation 794/2004 defines modification of an existing aid as any change other than changesof a purely formal or administrative nature which do not affect the compatibility of the aid with the internal market. This is because a change that is not purely formal or administrative may have an impact on the outcome of the original assessment.

Where the Commission considers that an existing aid is found to be incompatible with the internal market as the result of a review under article 108 (1) TFEU, it shall inform the Member States concerned of its preliminary view and give the Member State the opportunity to submit its comments within a period of 1 month. Where, in the light of the information submitted by the Member State, the Commission concludes that the existing aid scheme is not, or is no longer, compatible with the internal market, it issues a recommendation proposing either a substantive amendment of the aid scheme, the introduction of a number of procedural requirements or the abolition of the aid scheme (art. 22 of Regulation No 2015/1589). Where the Member State accepts the proposed measures, it is bound to implement them. If the appropriate measures are refused, the Commission opens a preliminary examination procedure for new aid (art. 23 of Regulation No 2015/1589). It may ultimately adopt an incompatibility decision, which willbe valid for the future.

When Member States amend or adjust State aid measures after they are approved by the Commission, the changes can turn an existing aid into new aid and the new aid has to be notified to the Commission, otherwise it is deemed to be illegal. Whilst some changes are cosmetic or insignificant, the others may be more substantive and impact on their compatibility with the internal market.

There are numerous cases of the Court of Justice confirming that any amendment that is capable of affecting the compatibility of an approved measure with the internal market must be re-notified to the Commission for the assessment.

Essentially, measures intended to grant aid or alter existing aid constitute new aid. In particular, where the alteration affects the actual substance of the original scheme, the latter is transformed into a new aid scheme. However, there can be no question of a substantive alteration where the new element is clearly severable from the original scheme (Joined Cases T-195/01 and T-207/01 Government of Gibraltar v Commission). The emergence of new aid or the alteration of existing aid cannot be assessed according to the scale of the aid or, in particular, its amount in financial terms at any moment in the life of the undertaking if the aid is provided under earlier statutory provisions which remain unaltered. Whether aid may be classified as new aid or as alteration of existing aid must be determined by reference to the provisions providing for it (Judgment of the Court of 9 August 1994. – Namur-Les Assurances du Crédit SA v Office National du Ducroire and the Belgian State). Whether a change to existing aid is minor, and, as such, would not have to be notified, depends on whether the alterations affect "basic features of the previous system of aids". A "substantial alteration" will be present in the case where changes are made to one or more of those basic features, be the latter subjective, objective or temporal (Opinion of Advocate General Campos Sánchez-Bordona).

In other joined cases C-915/19 to C-917/19 (Eco Fox and others) the Court of Justice on 28 October 2021, interpreted the meaning of an amendment that does not affect the compatibility of State aid. It is an amendment that changes features of the aid measure, such as the criteria for allocating aid among beneficiary companies, that are not taken into account by the Commission in its assessment.

A trivial example would be a change in the address of the granting authority. This is because Commission decisions ignore the address of the granting authority as it would have no relevance whatsoever to the compatibility of the aid. The Court of Justice also concluded that a modification of a preferential tax regime for biodiesel authorised by the Commission should not be considered as new aid subject to the notification obligation, when this modification consists in changing, with retroactive effect, the criteria for allocating the quotas of biodiesel benefiting from a preferential rate of excise tax, insofar as the modification does not affect the constituent elements of the aid scheme, as assessed by the Commission for the purposes of its compatibility the internal market.

As stated in the doctrine, the regime of "existing aid" has two practical consequences. First, any finding of incompatibility of existing aid can lead only to the prohibition of the further disbursement of such aid, implying that no recovery can be ordered for the period preceding its finding of incompatibility. This is because the current State aid rules limit the possibility of recovery to "unlawful aid" which is a different category of aid from "existing aid". Secondly, national courts have no competence to deal with "existing aid" (see: Cheynel, Bejamin, Alteration to an Existing State Aid and Obligation of Notification to the Commission, EStAL 3/2019, p. 404). Thus,the importance of the distinction between new aid and "existing aid" is that the latter enjoys better legal protection. It benefits from a less intrusive system of state aid control, in particular without a risk of recovery (see: Roebling, Georg. Existing aid and enlargement. Competition Policy Newsletter. No 1/2003, p. 33).

The doctrine stresses that the notion of existing aid (as other notions in the State aid field) is still evolving by the case-law of the EU courts. It should be an objective concept but as judgments reveals, it may also be influenced by a subjective analysis regarding State aid compatibility (see: Kekelekis, Mihalis. Stretching the Concept of Existing Aid Alterations and the New Role of National Courts in State Aid Proceedings. EStAL 2/2017, p. 291).

The problem of existing aid is crucial during every new accession to the EU because of integration of the acceding country into the Community's unique system of State aid control. Generally, under the Accession Treaty rules, all aid measures that predate accession and continue to be operated thereafter would automatically qualify as "existing aid" measures within the meaning of Article 108(1) of the TFEU.

Bibliography

Cheynel, B., Alteration to an Existing State Aid and Obligation of Notification to the Commission. *European State Aid Law Quarterly* 3/2019

Kekelekis, M., Stretching the Concept of Existing Aid Alterations and the New Role of National Courts in State Aid Proceedings. *European State Aid Law Quarterly* 2/2017

Roebling, G., Existing aid and enlargement. *Competition Policy Newsletter*. Number 1 – Spring 2003

See also

State aid (notion)

S

STATE AID (NOTIFICATION)

Phedon NICOLAIDES
Maastricht University

■ Definition

Notification is the process by which Member States submit state aid measures to the European Commission for assessment before they implement them. Notification is required of all new aid measures, except if they comply with "block exemption" regulations. The Commission assesses the compatibility of the proposed aid with the internal market. The notification process ends either with authorisation, in case the aid is compatible, or prohibition, in case it is incompatible.

■ Commentary

Article 108(3) TFEU requires Member States to inform the Commission of "any plans to grant or alter aid". The purpose of this requirement is to enable the Commission to assess the compatibility of a proposed aid measure with the internal market. Individual awards within the context of already approved aid schemes, measures that existed before the accession of a Member State to the European Union or measures that became state aid as a result of the evolution of the internal market are exempt from notification.

Exempt from notification are individual awards within the context of already approved aid schemes, measures that existed before the accession of a Member State to the European Union or measures that became state aid as a result of the evolution of the internal market.

Council Regulation 2015/1589 – the so-called procedural regulation – lays down in much more detail than Article 108 TFEU the procedure by which Member States notify aid measures to the Commission and how the Commission may treat notified or non-notified measures.

If the Commission does not have any doubts about the compatibility of the aid, it authorises the measure. If, by contrast, it has "serious doubts" about its compatibility or it encounters "serious difficulties" in assessing the compatibility, it must open the "formal investigation procedure".

The decision to open the formal investigation is published in the Official Journal of the EU and any "interested party" may submit comments. An interested party is any undertaking that can be affected by the proposed aid. The formal investigation can end either with a positive decision authorising the implementation of the aid or a negative decision prohibiting the implementation of the aid. In some cases the investigation may also end with a "no aid" decision, if the Commission concludes that the measure in question does not satisfy all of the criteria of Article 107(1) TFEU.

The notification procedure is a bilateral procedure between the Commission and Member States. Potential beneficiaries and their competitors do not have access to file. Nevertheless, they may challenge a Commission decision before the General Court of the EU.

The Commission is required by Regulation 2015/1589 to complete its assessment of a notified measure within two months. However, if it asks the Member State concerned for clarification or additional information, the two-month period starts afresh.

To assist Member States to notify measures that the Commission may declare compatible with the internal market, the Commission encourages Member States to have "pre-notification" contact. A pre-notification meeting is an informal meeting in which Member States may indicate to the Commission their plans and receive from the Commission non-binding advice on how their envisaged aid measures may need to be adjusted so that when they are formally notified they can be quickly approved.

An aid measure that is implemented without prior notification to the Commission or does not fall within the scope of a block exemption regulation is automatically "illegal" or "unlawful". National courts are obliged to suspend illegal aid measures.

If the Commission becomes aware of an illegally implemented measure and assesses its compatibility with the internal market, it is not bound by the two-month deadline to conclude that assessment. However, it is required by the case law to conclude within "reasonable time", although EU courts have not defined any precise deadline. The length of reasonable time depends on the complexity of the case.

If the Commission finds that aid granted illegally is incompatible with the internal market, it must order the recovery of the full amount of the aid plus interest from the moment it was granted. Within the period defined by the Commission, the Member State concerned must inform the Commission of the measures that it intends to take to secure the complete recovery of the aid. There is no EU law laying down specific provisions on the recovery of incompatible aid. For this reason, recovery is effected on the basis of national law. The Court of Justice has held that Member States are required to take all necessary steps for the immediate and effective recovery of the aid.

Bibliography

HANCHER, L., OTTERVANGER, T., VAN SLOT, P., *EU State Aids*, Sweet & Maxwell, 2021

NOWAK-SALLES, A., The Optimal Assessment Rule for EU State Aid Procedure, *World Competition*, 2020, vol. 43(1), pp. 87-106

Council Regulation of 13 July 2015 laying down detailed rules for the application of Article 108 of the Treaty on the Functioning of the European Union, OJ L 248, 24 September 2015, pp. 9-29

See also

State aid (existing aid), State aid (notion)

S

STATE AID (NOTION)

Anthony ABI HANNA
European Court of Justice

Definition

Under Article 107(1) TFEU, State aid is any direct or indirect measure taken by State authorities and through State resources which grants an economic advantage on a selective basis to certain undertakings or to the production of certain goods, distorts or threatens to distort competition on the internal market and which affects trade between Member States. State aids are incompatible with the internal market unless they meet the exemption criteria provided for by Articles 106(2), 107(2) and 107(3) TFEU, are de minimis because they do not exceed a certain amount, or fall within the scope of the General Block Exemptions Regulation.

Commentary

The TFEU rules on State aid, provided for in Articles 107 109 TFEU, relate to distortion of competition through State resources. These rules are adjacent in the Treaty to the competition rules that are applicable to undertakings. Both State aid rules and the rules on competition are enforced by DG Competition of the European Commission. Measures that meet the criteria of Article 107(1) TFEU are, in principle, incompatible with the internal market, unless they fall under the exemptions of Articles 106(2), 107(2) and (3) TFEU, are below the turnover thresholds in the de minimis regulation (Regulation (EU) 1407/2013), or fall within the scope of General Block Exemptions Regulation (GBER, Regulation (EU) 651/2014). The cumulative criteria of Article 107(1) TFEU are as follows:

The concept of undertakings

Article 107(1) TFEU applies to State aid that is granted to an "undertaking". This concept covers any entity, irrespective of whether it is established under private or public law and the way it is financed, that is engaged in an economic activity, which consists of offering goods or services on a market (Höfner and Elser (1991)).

The range of actors that can qualify as undertakings is large.

State resources and imputability

The measures must emanate from the State or through State resources and be imputable to the State. The notion of State encompasses public bodies, agencies and undertakings that could be assimilated to a public authority. Certain aids granted by private undertakings or entities unrelated to the public sector but financed through public resources may constitute a State aid if there is a sufficient direct link between the granting body and the public budget. Such link can be established by demonstrating the existence of a degree of sufficient control by the State on the transferred resources, or if the State played an active part in the decision-making process of granting the measure (Air France v Commission (1996). The Court of Justice has established a joint assessment of the use of public resources and State imputability, even though they are distinct in the phrasing of the Treaty (PreussenElektra (2001) and Stardust Marine (2002)).

Form of aid and economic advantage

The Court of Justice established in 1994 (Banco Exterior de España) that the concept of economic advantage goes beyond than that of a direct grant or subsidy. Any intervention which can mitigate the charges that are normally incurred by an undertaking and have the same effect as direct subsidies may confer an economic advantage. Whether a direct or indirect form of aid, a measure must grant, according to SFEI (1996), an economic advantage to the undertaking that would not have been obtained under normal market and business conditions or without State intervention. If the State acted as a normal market economy operator, no advantage is granted.

The object of the measure is irrelevant, as State aid law has an effects-based approach. The economic advantage granted must lead to the improvement of the economic situation of the concerned undertaking, or amount to a relief from an economic burden on certain undertakings or the production of certain goods and products, whether intended or not. The economic advantage can therefore amount to a direct positive effect or take the form of, inter alia, exemption of charges, levies, certain types of indemnities or tax rulings.

The notion of selectivity

Selectivity is the most complex element to assess in practice and it is under constant scrutiny and evolution in the European case-law. When a measure granting an economic advantage concerns one particular undertaking, it is inherently selective.

The Commission notice on the notion of State aid distinguishes between material and geographic selectivity. Material selectivity can be either de jure or de facto. On the one hand, a measure is selective de jure when it legally and expressly aims at favoring and conferring an economic advantage to specific undertaking or types of undertakings. On the other, it is de facto selective when it seems prima facie to be of general application but, given its individual characteristics, has the effect of favoring certain undertakings or sectors of an economy to the detriment of others. A de facto aid could also be the result of abuse of administrative discretionary power with the effect of distorting schemes of general application. Difficulties in assessing selectivity arise in the framework of tax measures, hence the necessity of applying a threefold assessment of the measures at stake (see for instance, Commission v Gibraltar and UK (2011) regarding offshore companies, Fiat v Commission, regarding individual aids, and Magnetrol v Commission, regarding aid schemes). Namely, (i) the relevant reference system should be identified, in order to determine whether (ii) a derogation granting an advantage inaccessible to other undertakings in a comparable situation exists (therefore the measures are prima facie selective), and, if that is the case, whether (iii) the derogation is justified by the nature or the general scheme of the system (World Duty Free Group SA and others (2016)). Concerning geographic selectivity, measures taken towards a limited part of a given Member State's territory, concerning only certain regions or local areas are not necessarily selective, especially if they meet three cumulative autonomous criteria: measures are not considered as aid if they are granted by an (i) institutionally, (ii) procedurally and (iii) financially autonomous body (Portugal v Commission (2006)).

Effect on trade and distortion of competition between Member States

To be unlawful, the State aid measure must affect trade and distort or threaten to distort competition between Member States. These two conditions are distinct and not complementary, but they are most often jointly examined and considered inextricably linked. In Philip Morris (1980) the Court defined an aid as distorting or threating to distort competition when it is liable to improve the competitive position of the concerned undertaking on the market. In the same way as it applies to the effect on trade condition, both are based on actual or potential threat or harm. No proof of actual effects on competition or trade is required, as it suffices that the aid is likely or capable of having this effect (Banco Exterior de España (1994)), regardless of whether it has been implemented or not. However a distortion of competition and an effect on trade cannot merely be presumed; the potential effect must be established based on foreseeable factors (AITEC v Commission (1995)).

Bibliography

Bacon KC, K. (ed.), *European Union Law of State Aid* (3rd edn, Oxford, 2017), Chapter 2, The Definition of State Aid

Hofmann, H. C. H. and Micheau, C., *State Aid Law of the European Union* (Oxford University Press, 2016), Part II, Chapters 1, 3 and 4

Quigley, C., *European State Aid Law and Policy* (4th Edn, Hart Publishing, 2022), Chapters 1, 2 and 8

Säcker, F. J. and Montag, F. (eds.), *European State Aid* (1st edn, Beck, Hart, Nomos, 2016), Chapter 2

Commission Notice on the notion of State aid as referred to in Article 107(1) of the Treaty on the Functioning of the European Union (OJ 2016, C 262/1)

See also

Market economy investor, Privatization, State aid (compatibility), State aid (existing aid), State aid (notification), State aid (unlawful aid), State measure

S

STATE AID (UNLAWFUL AID)

Maciej SZPUNAR, Léa BERTHIAU-JEZEQUEL
European Court of Justice

Definition

Pursuant to article 1(f) of Regulation (EU) 2015/1589 of 13 July 2015 laying down detailed rules for the application of Article 108 of the TFEU, an unlawful State aid can be defined as "new aid put into effect incontravention of Article 108(3) TFEU". In other words, an aid is unlawful when it is put into effect in violation of the notification obligation or of the standstill clause. An unlawful aid is examined by the Commission following a procedure distinct from the procedure regarding notified aid, and must be recovered when it is found that the aid in question is not compatible with the internal market.

Commentary

Article 108(3) TFEU provides that Member States must notify the Commission of any plans to grant or alter aid – the notification obligation – and must refrain from putting the proposed aid into effect pending a final decision of the Commission on its compatibility with the internal market – the standstill clause. Any aid put into effect in violation of these obligations must be considered unlawful. The definition of unlawful aid is stated in article 1(f) of Regulation 2015/1589, which is itself a codification of an established Court case law, since the case *Saumon* (C-354/90, 1991, paragraph 11). The unlawfulness of aid has several consequences.

First, the examination procedure conducted by the Commission has special characteristics, in comparison with the procedure regarding aids that have been notified. Articles 12 to 16 of Regulation 2015/1589 lay out the essential features of this procedure.

It starts with the Commission initiative. The Commission can act upon any information at its disposal, although the procedure usually starts following a complaint filed by a competitor of the beneficiary of the aid. In order to conduct its assessment, article 12 of Regulation 2015/1589 provides that the Commission can request information from the Member State concerned, and from any other Member State, from an undertaking, or association of undertakings, once the formal investigation procedure is initiated. In that regard, the procedure regarding unlawful aids is similar to the procedure to procedure regarding notified aid.

However, the procedures differ in a number of other aspects. In relation to unlawful aids, the Commission has extended powers and can adopt interim measures. According to article 12 of Regulation 2015/1589, when a Member States does not respond to the request for information or only provides insufficient information, the Commission can issue an "information injunction," by which the Member State is required to provide specific information in an appropriate period of time.

Moreover, given the potential negative effects of an aid put into effect on competition within the internal market, the Commission also has the power to order the suspension of the aid, pursuant to Article 13 of Regulation 2015/1589 (see, for instance, Commission decision on the 26th May 2014, C(2014) 3192, in the *Micula* case). Both the information injunction and the suspension injunction have been codified in Regulation 2015/1589. Finally, in specific cases, the Commission can adopt a decision requiring the Member State provisionally to recover any unlawful aid.

Considering the severe implications of such a decision – especially on the undertaking already benefiting from the measure at stake – and the fact that it is an exception to the general rule according to which the Commission cannot order State aid to be repaid solely on the ground that it is unlawful, provisional recovery injunction can only be issued if three criteria are fulfilled. There must be no doubt that the measure at stake is an aid, there must be an urgency to act, and there must be a serious risk of substantial and irreparable damage to a competitor. Suspension injunctions and provisional recovery injunctions stay in force until the Commission adopts a final decision on the compatibility of the measure. Non-compliance with such injunctions entitles the Commission to refer the matter directly to the Court and to obtain a declaration that the failure to comply constitutes an infringement of the TFEU.

Another distinction with the procedure regarding notified aids lies in the time limits imposed on the Commission to conduct its assessment. It is clear from both the case law (*HGA e.a. v. Commission* (C-630/11 P to C-633/11 P, 2013), paragraphs 74 and 75) and Article 15(2) of Regulation 2015/1589 that when a Member State has not respected the notification obligation or the standstill clause, the Commission should not be bound by time limits. However, this must not be understood as exempting the Commission from any time limits. Indeed, article 12 of Regulation 2015/89 states that the Commission must examine any complaint "without any delay", and it is established in the case-law of the General Court that the Commission cannot prolong indefinitely the preliminary investigation of State measures (see, recently, *Navieras Armas v. Commission* (T-108/16, 2018), paragraph 60).

The procedure ends with a final decision of the Commission, considering that the measure at stake is not an aid, that it is compatible with the internal market, or that it is incompatible with the internal market. In the latter case, the aid cannot be upheld and must be recovered from its beneficiary. The Commission is under an obligation to order the recovery of aid which it declares to be incompatible with the common market unless the recovery would be contrary to a general principle of EU law (*Mediaset v. Commission* (2011), paragraph 124). The purpose of the obligation to recover incompatible aid is to re-establish the previously existing situation. The Court has specified that that objective is attained once the recipient has repaid the aid in question, where appropriate with default interest, and thus forfeited the advantage which it had enjoyed over its competitors on the market (*Commission v. Italy* (C-348/93, 1995), paragraphs 26 and 27).

Secondly, the notion of unlawful State aid has relevance outside the scope of the Commission examination of the measure. In the *Lorenz* case (120/73, 1973, paragraph 8), the Court has established that Article 108(3) TFEU has a direct effect and gives rise to rights in favor of individuals, which national courts are bound to safeguard. National courts, therefore, have a role to play in relation to unlawful aids. Faced with an unlawful aid, they must pronounce measures appropriate to remedy the unlawfulness of the implementation of the aid, in order that the aid does not remain at the free disposal of the recipient during the period remaining until the Commission makes its decision (*CELF* (2010), paragraph 30). To that end, they must ensure that the measures, which they take with regard to the validity of the contested acts make it possible for the objective of restoring the competitive situation existing prior to the payment of the aid in question to be achieved (*Residex Capital IV* (2011), paragraph 45).

Bibliography

Buendia Sierra, J.-L., *State intervention and EU competition law*, Oxford, Oxford University Press, 2020

Picod, F., « Aides d'État – régime procedural », Fascicule 1532, *JCl Europe traité*, 2014

Signes de Mesa, J.-I. and de Moncuit, A., *Droit procédural des aides d'État*, Bruxelles, Bruylant, 2019

Vogel, L., *European State aid law*, Bruxelles, Bruylant, 2020

Articles 12 to 16 of Regulation 2015/1589 of 13 July 2015 laying down detailed rules for the application of Article 108 of the TFEU

See also

State aid (notion), State aid (notification),

S

STATE MEASURE

Liana JAPARIDZE
University of Sussex

■ Definition

Markets sometimes require state interventions to function effectively. However, such interventions may also harm the competitive process. Therefore, many countries prohibit – to various degrees – state measures of anti-competitive character. In the EU, a state measure is usually prohibited if it harms competition by itself (see definition of "State Aid") or amplifies the anti-competitive effects of a private measure. Such amplification is not permitted for anti-competitive agreements (under *INNO* doctrine, also called "useful effects" or "effects utile" doctrine) or for the abuse of dominance (under a combination of articles 106(1) and 102 TFEU). In the USA, state measures are regulated somewhat differently under the "state action doctrine".

■ Commentary

Markets sometimes require state intervention for multiple legitimate reasons: for example, to remedy market failures, support dynamic competition (for example, by introducing a patent system), and to counter information asymmetries that might result in sub-optimal market outcomes. Hence, state measures regulating market competition are not uncommon worldwide. However, these measures need scrutiny under competition law because they can significantly interfere with competitive processes on various markets. A few examples of such harmful interference include the imposition of product prices, the introduction of discriminatory tax cuts, and the raising of market entry barriers via regulation. To ensure that such interventions do not occur, many countries prohibit – to various degrees – state measures of anti-competitive character.

In the EU, a state measure can be declared anti-competitive in two scenarios. First, measures that are anti-competitive by themselves – i.e.

on a stand-alone basis – might be subject to scrutiny under the State Aid law (so-called "state aid measures"). Second, a state measure can be prohibited as anti-competitive if it amplifies an anti-competitive action undertaken by a market participant or participants. Such prohibition prevents the states from "facilitating anti-competitive behaviour by adopting measures that have the same effect on the market as the undertakings would have achieved themselves" (*BEB v KEVR*, para 52).

EU law defines state measures quite broadly. The term "state" denotes any state institution/administrative body. The term "measure" refers to any instrument emanating from the state, "even of a legislative or regulatory nature" (Case C-2/91, *Meng*, summary judgment, para 1). Some examples of such measures include state legislation, ministerial decrees, decisions by various administrative bodies under state supervision, and acts by regional/municipal organs. "Measures" may also include recommendations if the latter can prompt undertakings to infringe competition law. Importantly, when adopting a particular measure, the adopting body should act within its public powers.

Any state measure described above can be prohibited by joint application of Article 4(3) TEU, Protocol 27 annexed to the TEU, and Article 101 TFEU if such a measure encourages undertakings to engage in anti-competitive agreements, reinforces the effects of such agreements, or delegates to undertakings the powers that enable the latter to interfere with the process of market competition with their collusive actions. A "pure" state measure, without any correlated anti-competitive agreement, will not fall within this prohibition (although it might be qualified as a "state aid measure" under article 107 TFEU). Such regulation of the state measures was developed under the *INNO* doctrine (also called "useful effects"/"effects utile" doctrine). The doctrine takes its name from the case *INNO v ATAB* (1977), where the Court of Justice of the EU (CJEU) clarified that the joint reading of the three above-mentioned legal norms obliged the Member States to take any appropriate measure – or refrain from any measure thereof – to ensure the maintenance of undistorted competition on the EU Internal Market. Hence, the Court elaborated a doctrine that prohibited member states from enacting or maintaining any measure jeopardizing the "useful effects" of the EU competition rules by weakening market competition. In subsequent years, CJEU prohibited various state measures under this doctrine, including pieces of legislation facilitating price-fixing among competitors or approving/enhancing effects of price-fixing agreements; ministerial decrees that declared binding production quotas established by associations of undertakings; and decisions delegating state powers of price-fixing to private bodies while giving the leeway in terms of price ranges to be fixed.

Another route of prohibiting anti-competitive state measures is via the combined reading of articles 106(1) and 102 TFEU. Article 106(1) TFEU prohibits Member States from enacting or maintaining in force any measure contrary to the competition rules when dealing with public undertakings (i.e. undertakings under state's direct or indirect control) or undertakings with State-granted special and exclusive rights. Taken together with Article 102, Article 106(1) TFEU prohibits state measures that make such undertakings abuse their dominant position merely by exercising their public powers or special/exclusive rights or "where such rights are liable to create a situation in which that undertaking is led to commit such abuses" (*Ambulanz Glöckner*, para 39). The latter situation includes scenarios where state measures facilitate the abuse or prompt undertakings to abuse. Some examples of anti-competitive state measures under articles 106(1) and 102 TFEU include acts creating statutory monopolies that are not able to meet the market demand; statutes equipping dominant/monopoly undertakings with regulatory powers that create a conflict of interest (i.e. an undertaking becomes both a regulator and a competitor on the market); statutes extending the dominance of an undertaking to another market; and acts distorting competition by creating unequal market opportunities.

In the USA, the assessment of anti-competitive state measures has developed somewhat differently from the EU. The critical distinction between the two approaches is that the former views regulating anti-competitive state measures as a means of maintaining the Internal Market, while the latter looks at the same measures from the constitutional dynamics between the federal and state governments. Consequently, in the USA, the case law recognizes the "state action doctrine", according to which federal antitrust laws do not apply to state measures under two cumulative conditions. First, the restriction of competition should stream from the state – i.e. the state should allow the anti-competitive activity of private parties to happen, with the explicit aim to disapply federal antitrust regulation in a particular area/on a specific market. Second, such a restriction of competition should be closely controlled by the state – i.e. where state measures weaken competition, this should happen for the sake of public interest (as ensured by the state's adequate control mechanisms) and not for private benefits (*California Retail Liquor Dealers case)*. In practice, the "state action doctrine" means that when the two conditions are met, although the federal government acknowledges the limitation of competition by state measures, it won't annul or disapply the latter due to the division of powers between the federal and state governments.

Bibliography

JONES, A., SUFRIN, B. and DUNNE, N., *Competition Law: Text, Cases and Materials* (8th edition, Oxford University Press, 2023), Chapter 8

VAN DE GRANDEN, J. W. and RUSU, C. S., *Competition Law in the EU: Principles, Substance, Enforcement* (Edward Elgar 2021), Chapter 11

WHISH, R. and BAILEY, D., *Competition Law* (10th end, Oxford University Press 2021), Chapter 6

See also

State action defence, State aid (notion)

S

STATEMENT OF OBJECTIONS (SO)

Sabine ZIGELSKI
German Competition Authority

Definition

A statement of objections is an essential step in any proceeding that leads to an act or decision by a competition authority with adverse effects on a natural or legal person. It forms an integral part of any defendant's right to be heard in order to exercise their right to an effective defense. The statement of objections informs the defendants of all objections raised against them, including the relevant facts and evidence an intended decision or charge is based on, the legal provisions the authority relies on, its legal assessment and the envisaged consequences.

Commentary

The term "statement of objections" is commonly used in the European Union's enforcement context, but the concept as such is universal. It is anchored in the right to defense, which is a basic principle in any jurisdiction adhering to the rule of law and guaranteeing its subjects due process rights. In this context, the statement of objections is an essential procedural safeguard to ensure that a person or an undertaking accused of a legal violation can exercise their right to be heard, as part of an effective defense. This will further include rights of access to file in some form and at some stage before a final decision is taken, and the opportunity to present arguments in the person's or undertaking's defense.

In the European Union, the right to be heard and the subsequent obligation to issue a statement of objections is established in Art. 41 of the Charter of Fundamental Rights of the European Union – the Right to Good Administration – with a pre-dating history in the relevant case law. In the U.S., such a right goes back to the Fifth Amendment to the U.S. Constitution. As expressed in Mullane v. Cent. Hanover Bank Tr. Co., "An elementary and fundamental requirement of due process in any proceeding which is to be accorded finality is notice reasonably calculated, under all the circumstances, to apprise interested parties of the pendency of the action and afford them an opportunity to present their objections." Most jurisdictions' laws will reflect in some way this fundamental legal principle also known as "audi alteram partem" – "listen to the other side" or "let the other side be heard as well", meaning that each party is entitled to a fair hearing and given the opportunity to respond to evidence presented against them.

The indispensable nature of a statement of objections as part of the due process requirements of both administrative and criminal competition enforcement proceedings is further evidenced by two rather recent global initiatives to which major jurisdictions have subscribed: the 2021 OECD Recommendation on Transparency and Procedural Fairness in Competition Law Enforcement and the 2020 ICN Framework for Competition Agency Procedures (CAP). Art. 5 of the OECD Recommendation asks to "inform parties and offer them opportunities to engage meaningfully in the competition law enforcement process, with due regard to the effectiveness of the investigation". Similarly, the ICN CAP includes as principle (h) the "notice and opportunity to defend".

The European Union´s approach and principles relating to a statement of objections can serve as a good example for its integration and practical implementation in an adversarial competition enforcement procedure. Art. 27 of EU Regulation 1/2003 stipulates the "Hearing of Parties, Complainants and Others" and requires that "The Commission shall base its decisions only on objections on which the parties concerned have been able to comment". In practice, a statement of objections needs to inform the undertakings concerned of all the facts and documents on which the Commission intends to rely in its final decision. It must further set out the legal assessment clearly, providing the undertakings concerned with the opportunity to contest the legal conclusions concerning the alleged infringements, and identify all documents used as evidence in support of the objections. Finally, the statement of objections needs to indicate all intended consequences of the envisaged enforcement action, for example the intended fines, periodic penalty payments or remedies. Regarding the fines, it has to indicate the essential facts and matters of law which may result in the imposition of a fine. Regarding remedies, the statement of objections has to be sufficiently detailed to allow the parties to defend themselves as to the necessity and proportionality of the remedies envisaged. Art. 18 of the EU Merger Regulation (Reg. 139/2004) imposes equivalent obligations on the European Commission in merger cases.

For the right to be heard to be exercised effectively, the statement of objections needs to be sent in a timely manner, allowing for sufficient time for the parties to review allegations and evidence and to respond. In turn, the competition authority should also have sufficient time to consider arguments and objections by the parties properly before issuing a final decision. If the arguments brought in the parties' defense trigger additional investigations and adjustments of the evidence being used and the legal conclusions drawn, a new/updated statement of objections will have to be issued in case the objections are changed but would still result in an adverse decision.

In line with the fundamental nature of this due process step, the omission of a statement of objections or its improper or incomplete nature can lead to the invalidity of the decision at hand, regardless of its substantive merits.

From an enforcement practitioner´s perspective, the statement of objections should be embraced as an opportunity to further test and improve an authority´s envisaged decision and course of action. It is not to be seen as a "necessary evil" or additional burden in an already fraught procedure. If used properly, the statement of objections will elicit a meaningful response by the affected parties, which allows the competition authority to correct factual mistakes or erroneous legal assessments before it may have to defend its decision in court. As a result of this hearing process, the final decision stands a better chance of holding up in court.

Bibliography

Yoo, C. S. and Wendland, H. M., Hendrik M., Procedural Fairness in Antitrust Enforcement: The U.S. Perspective (2019); All Faculty Scholarship. 2049

European Commission; Antitrust Manual of Procedures (2019), Chapter 11

ICN Framework for Competition Agency Procedures (CAP) (2020)

OECD; Recommendation of the Council on Transparency and Procedural Fairness in Competition Law Enforcement (2021)

See also

Access to the file

SUNK COSTS

Cindy CHANG, Jonel MARI IBARRA
Competition and Consumer Commission of Singapore

■ Definition

Sunk costs refer to costs that a firm has to incur to enter or to continue to participate in a market, which are not recoverable upon exit from the market. Sunk costs can be considered as a type of fixed cost that possess little to no resale value. Examples of sunk costs include: investment in highly specialised production processes, bespoke software systems, research and development and brand advertising, marketing and other promotion costs. Sunk costs can be further categorised as either (i) exogenous sunk costs i.e. sunk costs that are inherent due to the nature of the industry (e.g. investments in specialised assets); or (ii) endogenous sunk costs i.e. sunk costs that are determined by incumbents (e.g. advertising expenditure necessary for prospective entrants to overcome brand loyalty cultivated by incumbents).

■ Commentary

Sunk costs as barriers to entry

Given that sunk costs cannot be recovered upon exit, they increase the risks associated with entering a market. The likelihood of recouping sunk entry costs is an important determinant of barriers to entry. Generally, the higher the sunk costs, the higher the entry barrier.

It is notable that sunk costs give rise to an asymmetry between an incumbent and prospective entrant(s). An incumbent (which has already sunk its costs) needs only to cover its marginal costs to make it more profitable for it to continue its operations than for it to exit the market. On the other hand, a prospective entrant is likely to enter the market only if the expected profit from being in the market exceeds its sunk costs of entry.

The nature of competition in the market post-entry plays a large role in determining the likelihood of sunk cost recoupment. For example, in a market which involves high sunk costs and where players can compete aggressively on price, it would be difficult for a new entrant to recoup its sunk entry costs, particularly in light of the aforementioned "asymmetry" which exists between it and the incumbent. As set out in paragraph 285 of the European Commission's Guidelines on Vertical Restraints: "*…Where entry requires high sunk costs, the threat of fierce competition by incumbents post-entry may deter such entry, as potential entrants cannot justify the risk of losing their sunk investments*".

Further, sunk costs can be utilised strategically by an incumbent to deter entry into the market. For example, the incumbent may strategically invest in excess capacity to ensure that it has the capabilities to respond quickly to any new market entry. Often, the incumbent's act of incurring the higher sunk costs can in and of itself deter entry as it signals to potential entrants that the incumbent can – and will – respond aggressively should they choose to enter the market. Other examples would be for the incumbent to engage in costly advertising and aggressive promotional strategies to build up brand loyalty; or to invest in extensive research and development. In order to successfully enter and remain in the market, a prospective entrant would likely be compelled to advertise heavily as well to overcome the brand loyalty fostered by the incumbent; or to match the incumbent's research and development efforts.

Sunk costs in competition law assessments

Sunk costs is often an important feature in competition law assessments. For example, high sunk costs (and more generally, substantial barriers to entry) suggest a lower level of competitive threat posed by potential entrants, and so an incumbent with a high market share is more likely to be dominant. Further, where sunk costs of entry are high such that the threat of potential entry (or re-entry) into the market is low, a dominant firm may have more of an incentive to engage in exclusionary practices such as predatory pricing to price their existing competitors out of the market.

In its 2009 infringement decision against Intel for abuse of a dominant market position, the European Commission found that Intel held a dominant position in the worldwide market for x86 central processing units ("CPUs"). In arriving at this conclusion, the Commission found, *inter alia*, that there were significant barriers to entry arising from the sunk investment in research and development and production facilities required to supply x86 CPUs. These sunk costs, in tandem, resulted in significant economies of scale which meant that the minimum efficient scale for a new entrant would be high relative to overall market demand. The Commission additionally noted that there were significant barriers to expansion as any increase in output would require additional sunk costs into new properties, plants and equipment, as well as several years' lead time.

Similarly, in merger cases, it is important to consider whether potential entrants would be able to competitively constrain attempts by the merged entity to exercise its market power post-merger. Generally, the higher the sunk costs of entry, the less likely that the merged entity would be constrained by the threat of new entry.

In *Ryanair/Aer Lingus III,* the European Commission found that barriers to entry with respect to the routes operated by the merger parties were high, given that, amongst other things, establishing an airport base required significant upfront investment such as installing and operating ground services in an airport where no facilities existed before, marketing and brand-building. Entry involved a significant level of sunk costs as these costs cannot be fully recovered upon market exit. In particular, the Commission found that this was especially the case for the Irish airports of Dublin, Cork and Shannon, where the merger parties had their own established bases, which deterred possible new entrants and made entry at these airports unlikely. In concluding that the merger was likely to significantly impede effective competition on 46 routes to and from Ireland, the Commission found that there would not be entry or expansion by competitors on these routes which would be likely, timely and sufficient to provide competitive constraints offsetting the effects of the merger.

Sunk cost fallacy

In theory, sunk costs should not influence a firm's decision on whether or not to remain in the market. It would be rational for a firm to continue producing as long as its revenues cover its marginal costs. Conversely, if its revenues do not cover marginal costs, it would not be rational for the firm to remain in the market simply because it had incurred significant sunk costs in entering the market. Any entry costs (such as market research and investments in highly specialised assets) which are not recoverable (i.e. which have already been sunk) should no longer be taken into account in the firm's decision making. Sunk cost fallacy occurs when firms suffer from "loss aversion" and attach value to sunk costs – resulting possibly in irrational behaviour.

Bibliography

BELLEFLAME, P. and PEITZ, M. (2015), Industrial Organization, Markets and Strategies, 2nd edn, *Cambridge University Press*

MOTTA, M. (2004), *Competition Policy, Theory and Practice*, Cambridge University Press, Cambridge

NIELS, G., JENKINS, H., and KAVANAGH, J. (2023), *Economics for Competition Lawyers*, 3rd edn, Oxford University Press

PINDYCK, R. (2008), *Sunk Costs and real Options in Antitrust Analysis, Issues in Competition Law and Policy* 619 (ABA Section of Antitrust Law 2008)

SCHMALENSEE, R. (2004), *Sunk Costs and Antitrust Barriers to Entry*, American Economic Association

SUTTON, J. (1991), Sunk Costs and Market Structure: Price Competition, Advertising, and the Evolution of Concentration, The MIT Press

WHISH, R. and BAILEY, D. (2021), *Competition Law*, 10th edn, Oxford University Press

See also

Barriers to entry, Economic analysis

S

SUSTAINABILITY

Margaux SEAGER, Tudor N. PANA
Concurrences

Definition

Competition law serves as a crucial instrument for promoting sustainability by ensuring that markets operate efficiently, leading to both environmental protection and societal well-being. This is achieved by fostering innovation, preventing anticompetitive behaviours that hinder sustainable practices, and encouraging collaboration among market participants to address shared environmental challenges. Through fair competition, businesses are encouraged to adopt eco-friendly practices, promoting responsible conduct that not only benefits the environment but also enhances their reputation, enabling sustainable growth within their respective industries. Additionally, it acts as a safeguard against monopolistic tendencies, ensuring a dynamic marketplace that aligns with principles of sustainable management and social responsibility.

Commentary

Sustainability through innovation

Sustainability thrives in a competitive market as businesses strive to introduce the most innovative and environmentally friendly practices. This drive for innovation in sustainability is often accelerated by competitive pressures, encouraging companies to not only comply with the necessary standards but to surpass them in pursuit of market differentiation and consumer preference. Indeed, market forces play a significant role in driving eco-innovation. The rise in consumer demand for sustainable products has led companies to innovate to meet these new preferences. A case in point is the development of renewable energy technologies, such as solar and wind power, which have been bolstered by both consumer interest and lately numerous supportive governmental policies.

Several countries, such as Germany, Spain, the UK, China, and Japan, have embraced Feed-in Tariffs (FiTs) to stimulate renewable energy growth.

Succinctly, FiTs are policy mechanisms that accelerate investments in renewable energy. A FiT establishes a long-term contract between an energy generator and a utility company. The terms of the contract define a set price that the utility will pay for energy generated by the renewable resource over a period of time (typically 20 years). In some cases, the contract may also include an annual recalibration to account for inflation. These FiTs not only encourage diverse energy market participation but also drive innovation in sustainable technologies. By offering incentives for green energy production, they catalyse advancements in renewable sectors, aligning with competition law's objectives.

Barriers to sustainability

This is not a classic barrier to entry approach, but more of a barrier to becoming sustainable. Thus, fair competition is the key to overcoming anticompetitive barriers, allowing businesses to freely embrace sustainable practices without facing unjust market restrictions, due to overly complicated legislation.

Moving on to a few practical examples, under the Brazilian Antitrust Law, the Administrative Council for Economic Defense (CADE) actively dismantles barriers to fair competition, particularly in the agricultural sector. They achieve this by promoting transparency and market access, supporting sustainable certification programmes, and promoting private-public partnerships. This approach not only facilitates entry for smaller businesses but also promotes sustainable farming practices and environmental conservation.

In South Korea, the Korea Fair Trade Commission (KFTC) employs the Monopoly Regulation and Fair Trade Act to combat abuses of market dominance, especially in industries like electronics and automotive. KFTC fosters an inclusive market for innovation by ensuring larger companies do not hinder sustainable technology development. Notably, this approach extends to the fintech sector. The integration of fintech has the potential to advance sustainability goals through green finance initiatives and eco-friendly investment platforms.

These regulatory actions by both CADE and KFTC serve as examples of how competition law can be strategically used to remove market barriers and enable sustainability, particularly through emerging sectors like fintech. Alongside these measures, unified efforts play an increasingly major role, as further elaborated.

Sustainability through collective efforts

Competition law promotes joint action by market players to address sustainability challenges collectively. Certain jurisdictions have explored exemptions in antitrust laws for collaborations focused on environmental protection.

For instance, in Australia, the Competition and Consumer Act 2012 allows companies to seek authorisation from the Australian Competition and Consumer Commission (ACCC) for conduct that may otherwise breach competition laws, if the public benefits (i.e., protecting the environment) outweigh the anti-competitive detriments.

Similarly, in Europe, this approach is reinforced through the 2023 EU Guidelines on horizontal cooperation agreements. They recognise that certain collaborations between competitors, especially those aimed at environmental sustainability, can be beneficial in specific circumstances (see Articles 5 "Efficiencies", 6 "Ancillary Restraints", and 10 "Environmental Agreements" of the Guidelines). These are a legal basis for competitors to work together on research and development, standard-setting, and joint production initiatives that have a positive environmental impact. However, there is a clear difference between promoting collaborative efforts in favour of sustainability and openly anti-competitive collaborations. This is best illustrated in the European Commission's decision, the BMW, Daimler, and Volkswagen emissions collusion case. These manufacturers were fined for restricting competition in the development of emission-reducing technology. Contrastingly, in T-Mobile/Tele2 Netherlands (2020) and Veolia Environnement/SITA France (2021), the General Court and the EU Commission respectively approved the merger and the joint venture, acknowledging potential environmental benefits, as per Article 5 of the Guidelines.

Collaborative efforts towards sustainability require a unified international approach to address global challenges effectively and ensure a smooth transition to a more environmentally conscious future. As the interconnectedness of economies and ecosystems becomes increasingly apparent, no single country or organisation can tackle these issues in isolation. Therefore, fostering collaboration and coordination on an international scale is essential. As Simon Holmes points out in his book "Competition Law, Climate Change & Environmental Sustainability", there is much more that businesses can do within the current legal frameworks, if we are to fight climate change and move towards a more sustainable future, at the necessary pace. While there is room for improvement in existing legislations and government actions, urgent focus is required to catalyse convergent efforts towards sustainability.

The global dimension

Achieving sustainability hinges on a concerted international effort that integrates competition law with environmental standards. The linchpin lies in forging a global consensus on these standards within competition law frameworks. By establishing uniformity, we level the playing field for multinational corporations across jurisdictions, advancing consistent enforcement of eco-friendly practices. An integral part of this is the adoption of global standards, such as the UN Global Compact's principles, the OECD Guidelines for Multinational Enterprises, as well as the UN Sustainable Development Goals. These are aimed at encouraging businesses to work together in areas such as climate action, green energy, or responsible production, mandating the necessity of a common approach, in line with competition law considerations.

Integrating these principles into international trade agreements furthers the commitment to sustainable economic growth, and developing nations, in particular, stand at a crucial juncture. Often experiencing rapid industrialisation and economic expansion, they have the opportunity to shape their competition laws with environmental goals in mind from the outset. Providing support to these countries in drafting legislation that incorporates said goals is thus crucial for inclusive progress, and for the avoidance of long-term ecological damage.

However, non-uniform regulations across different countries create imbalances and can disadvantage developing economies trying to compete on a global market. Stringent environmental regulations in one country could increase production costs, making it difficult to compete with producers in other countries with laxer regulations, even if the latter's practices are less sustainable. This highlights the need for cross-border harmonisation of environmental standards and competition law principles, without impeding the development aspirations of emerging economies.

Sustainability regulations are reshaping markets, creating exciting "green" opportunities while requiring compliance that can impact competition. In this emerging field, dominant players could exploit new markets, strict costs could disadvantage smaller players, standardisation might stifle innovation, while greenwashing risks misleading consumers, highlighting once again the crucial role of competition law. Accurately defining markets, carefully evaluating mergers, tackling abuse of dominance, and protecting consumers from misleading claims are key areas of focus. To navigate these challenges, continuous dialogue, flexible regulations, and strong enforcement are pivotal.

Bibliography

Holmes, S., Middelschulte, D. and Snoep, M., *Competition Law, Climate Change & Environmental Sustainability* (Concurrences 2021)

Jenny, F. Competition Law and Policy and Sustainability. OECD Competition Committee (2023)

Këllezi, P., Kobel, P. and Kilpatrick B., *Sustainability Objectives in Competition and Intellectual Property Law* (Springer Nature 2024)

Nowag, J. Sustainability & Competition Law and Policy – Background Note. (OECD 2021)

2023 EU Guidelines on horizontal cooperation agreements (EU Commission)

See also

Environmental protection

S

SWITCHING COSTS

Adriana HERNANDEZ PEREZ
Fundação Getúlio Vargas

Aldo GONZALEZ
University of Chile

Definition

People or companies experience switching costs when they must incur a specific expense – monetary or not – to change from one supplier to another. This happens when, for instance, individuals face learning costs, must pay a penalty or need to invest in a new equipment to change supplier. Similarly, customers also experience switching costs when they lose benefits due to loyalty programs by migrating to another provider. Also, when individuals must forego an investment (previously) made in the current supplier or once having built a relationship with a supplier, individuals may find it harder to change, which entails switching costs. For a company, switching costs may arise when it is costly to change the methods of production.

Commentary

The concept of switching costs is very important in economics and competition policy because it helps characterizing how intense competition is in a market. In antitrust analysis, it is usually applied to access the level of rivalry between competitors in the event of a merger or to evaluate a dominant position. When individuals face high switching costs to change from one supplier to another, incumbent suppliers retain significant market power over their customer base, which, in turn, allows them to charge a higher price or decrease the (costly) quality of services. One important corollary is that profits increase with the magnitude of people's switching costs.

The analysis of switching costs implies that there are *repeated purchases* of (identical or not) goods or services from one initial supplier, usually referred to as the incumbent. The framework of analysis, then, is essentially *dynamic* as companies consider this feature when designing their competitive strategies. Typically, companies will compete aggressively to be the first in the market, expanding the client base in the first period, to price higher afterwards, a behavior referred in the academic literature as "bargains-then-ripoffs". When switching costs are prevalent, the competition for market share instead of profits makes sense.

In equilibrium, this aggressive competitive behavior compromises overall (intertemporal) profits, as bargains in the first period eat up the second period profits. Therefore, the analyses of a company's competitive behavior must consider whether below cost pricing in one period may be an anticipation to higher prices in the future. In a dynamic perspective, such strategy does not necessarily harm consumers, depending on the pace of innovation in the market.

Switching costs may differ across individuals as some consumers may find easier (or cheaper) than others to switch to a different supplier. In these cases, competition for consumers may be less aggressive because, while consumers that have low migration costs are happy to accept introductory bargain offers, they are also happy to leave before profits are extracted from them. In such cases, the entrant companies start offering freebies and engaging many customers, but lose when they start raising prices.

In merger analysis, determining the customers' switching costs is a necessary step to understand how competition would take place after a transaction. If switching costs arc low, it is possible that customers would easily change supplier if market prices (quality) increased (decreased) post operation. However, high switching costs limit the ability of customers to change suppliers, which, in turn, makes price increases more profitable post-merger.

In the context of conduct, as high switching costs leverage companies' market power, it is expected that companies will be incentivized to develop instruments or contracts to "artificially" elevate customers' switching costs. Cashbacks, frequent-flyer programs, and loyalty contracts are examples of commercial offers that create pecuniary switching costs since they emulate quantity discounts or bundling as past purchases enable discounts on future transactions. Having already bought at a high price, these arrangements allow individuals to buy cheaper units subsequently (as in non-linear pricing).

In a less subtle strategy, long term contracts that lock in customers to one supplier for a long (exclusive) period create switching costs. It is important to consider that none of such strategies is anticompetitive *per se*. Such practices are usually analyzed according to the specificities of the case, where the rule of reason is applied.

Digital platforms present features that may impose switching costs on users. For example, in platforms with recommendation systems, sellers are rated by purchasers when selling their goods or services. This is the case of a property owner renting his home through Airbnb or a driver offering rides through Uber. It is expected that a property owner would prefer changing to a new platform if, for instance, Airbnb raises its fee or degrades the quality of its services. However, if this seller has a well-stablished reputation in Airbnb, this means that he will have to start all over again building its reputation in a new platform. If this is a costly endeavor, then the user will face a cost to migrate to the new platform.

Borrowers experience a similar problem in the credit market as their incumbent bank has better information about their credit risks than other banks unrelated to the borrowers. In such cases, a customer may find it harder to shop around for credit with competitive interest rates since alternative financial institutions would have little knowledge of his credit worthiness. In such instances, the incumbent bank will hold an important market power over its customer base. In the credit market, the recommended public policy prescription to mitigate this asymmetry is the adoption of data portability between rivals, under the consent of the "data subject".

The 2023 U.S. Merger Guidelines highlight that labor markets are marked by significant switching costs, attributed to the challenges involved in searching for, applying to, interviewing for, and adjusting to new employment. Furthermore, the guidelines note that numerous jobs necessitate specific investments, whether in terms of scope or geographic location. This situation potentially grants companies a dominant position over their employees.

The European guidelines for defining the relevant market consider switching costs as an element to help delineate the frontiers of the product market on the demand side analysis. According to these guidelines, when customers encounter considerable difficulties in switching from product A to product B, it suggests that these products may not be part of the same relevant market.

The Horizontal Merger Guidelines of both Chile and Brazil take into account switching costs as a factor in defining the relevant market when examining cases.

Bibliography

Farrell, J. and Klemperer, P., "Coordination and lock-in: Competition with switching costs and network effects." *Handbook of industrial organization* 3 (2007): 1967-2072

Klemperer, P., "Competition when consumers have switching costs: An overview with applications to industrial organization, macroeconomics, and international trade." *The review of economic studies* 62.4 (1995): 515-539

Brazil, Conselho Administrativo de Defesa da Concorrência (2016), Guide for Horizontal Merger Review

Chile, Fiscalia Nacional Economica (2021), Guía para el Análisis de Operaciones de Concentración Horizontales

European Commission. (2018). Guidelines on market analysis and the assessment of significant market power under the EU regulatory framework for electronic communications networks and services

See also

Abuse of dominant position, Barriers to entry, Economic analysis, Market Power

T

TECHNOLOGY TRANSFER

Luis Jose DIEZ CANSECO NÚÑEZ, Robert VENERO PERALTA,
José Carlos GONZÁLES CUCHO
Díez Canseco

Definition

Technology transfer is the process by which knowledge, skills, methods, among others, are transferred for the purpose of disseminating technology and scientific progress; this type of process can take place between governments, educational institutions and companies. The Commission Regulation (EC) 772/2004, on the application of Article 81(3) of the Treaty, defines technology transfer agreements as those that consist of the granting of technology licenses, which include, among others, know-how, patents and software copyright. The aforementioned regulation states that these types of agreements generally have a positive impact on competition and economic efficiency.

Commentary

Although technology transfer is not usually an issue directly addressed by competition rules, in the European Union it is possible to find Commission Regulation (EC) 772/2004, on the application of Article 81(3), which, although not currently in force, establishes valid criteria at the time of analyzing a technology transfer agreement. On 1 May 2014, this Regulation was replaced by the Commission Regulation (EU) 316/2014 on the application of Article 101(3) of the Treaty on the Functioning of the European Union. This new Regulation has practically the same purposes as the previous one, that is, to seek a balance between the promotion of competition and the benefits that can be obtained from technology transfers; to this end, this new Regulation establishes assumptions in which it can be assured that a technology transfer cannot be sanctioned for a possible breach of competition law.

Similarly, in the United States there are the Guidelines for the Licensing of Intellectual Property, which is a document prepared by the Department of Justice and the Federal Trade Commission in order to clarify doubts regarding the application of competition rules with respect to technology transfers.

Both documents agree in that they explicitly recognize that technology transfer agreements tend to have a positive impact on competition, since they protect the economic incentives of researchers and facilitate the dissemination of knowledge, which also prevents resources from being spent on duplicate research that will obtain the same results.

In this sense, although a technology transfer agreement may contain clauses that restrict competition (such as exclusivity or prohibitions on resale), the main purpose of these clauses is usually to protect the value of new scientific knowledge and to protect investments made in research, and could therefore be considered legitimate.

Although this is a positive view of technology transfer agreements, this does not mean that, in practice, there have not been cases in which the authorities have considered that the form in which such agreements have been entered into is anti-competitive. This is because, as mentioned, many times these agreements have clauses aimed at restricting competition. In this sense, it is not difficult for a patent or software license agreement to include among its clauses various restrictions, which may range from prohibiting the sharing of technology with third parties to limiting the commercialization of products.

This does not mean that technology transfer agreements will be considered anti-competitive per se by the competition authorities; rather, depending on the form the agreement takes, it could constitute anti-competitive conduct punishable in different jurisdictions, including the European Union and the United States.

Although it is not possible to establish a general rule to indicate whether a technology transfer agreement is anti-competitive, there are several factors that must be taken into consideration. The first of these is the market power of the companies that participate in the agreement; in this sense, if they have a great deal of market power, it is more likely that the restrictions to competition included in the agreement will be considered unlawful. Similarly, if these restrictions are excessive or extend over a long period of time, they are also more likely to be considered unlawful. Conversely, if the restrictions on competition accompanying an anticompetitive agreement are proportionate to the efficiencies generated by the agreement, or if they are indispensable for the implementation of a lawful agreement, they are more likely to be considered lawful by the competition authorities.

An emblematic case can be seen in Microsoft (2001). This case analyzed the limitations that Microsoft imposed on computer manufacturers and users of the Windows operating system, limiting their ability to uninstall Internet Explorer. According to Microsoft, these limitations were necessary, since they encouraged the development of new software technologies and also favored consumers, since it allowed them to have a web browser free of charge. However, the U.S. courts rejected Microsoft's arguments, due to the major restrictions to competition that these meant, since, due to Microsoft's market power in the operating systems market, they restricted the entry of new companies that could offer alternative services to Internet Explorer.

On the other hand, in the European Union there is GlaxoSmithKline (2009). In this case, GlaxoSmithKline, a British pharmaceutical company, when selling drugs to Spanish wholesalers, required them to refrain from exporting such drugs to other European Union countries. In this regard, the justification given by GlaxoSmithKline was that such restriction sought to protect the sales made by such company to other countries of the European Union, due to the fact that, due to internal regulations of each country, the prices of medicines could have large differences from one country to another; in view of this situation, GlaxoSmithKline sought to prevent Spanish wholesalers from exporting cheaper medicines to the United Kingdom than the pharmaceutical company.

When analyzing this case, the purposes pursued by the European Community regulations were taken into consideration, among which, in addition to protecting competition and consumers, the creation of a common market stands out. The limitations imposed by GlaxoSmithKline on Spanish wholesalers, despite the justifications it may have had, had the main effect of breaking with the common market by establishing barriers to exports that were contrary to the Community spirit. For this reason, the Court of Justice decided that the export prohibition imposed was unlawful.

For the above reasons, when designing a technology transfer agreement, it must be taken into consideration that any restriction to competition included in the agreement must be justified and proportional to the purposes sought by the agreement. Likewise, the economic efficiencies must be weighed against the restrictions to competition that the agreement would generate.

Bibliography

BAUMGARTNER, A. M., "Antitrust Issues in Technology Transfer: A Comparative Legal Analysis of Patent Licenses in the EU and the U.S." (2013) *Transatlantic Technology Law Forum* No. 18

U.S. Department of Justice and the Federal Trade Commission, "Antitrust Guidelines for the Licensing of Intellectual Property" (2017)

WIPO, "Survey on Technology Transfer Agreements and Antitrust" (2013)

*Dario Morales and Camila Chamorro – Díez Canseco associates – have also helped in the preparation of the definition above

See also

Anticompetitive practices, Block exemption (regulation) Know-how, Patents, Market Power

T

TIPPING

Marcela MATTIUZZO
VMCA Advogados

Definition

Tipping refers to the process by which a competitive market reaches a critical point of user adoption and shifts from a market with many suppliers to a market with one or few suppliers. Tipping is a phenomenon that most frequently occurs in markets with strong network effects, especially multi-sided platforms. Tipping happens when a product/service becomes more valuable as more users coalesce around it (network effects) and eventually the product/service becomes so popular that it gains an advantage that may make it difficult for other suppliers to compete. Therefore, tipping is frequently used to describe the convergence toward a product standard or category.

Commentary

Competition authorities are increasingly concerned that certain markets, particularly digital platform markets, are especially prone to tipping. There is a concern that once a market has tipped there is a "winner-takes-all" phenomenon that inevitably leads to market failure. There is still no established and objective test to identify markets prone to tipping, features that strengthen or mitigate tipping, or whether or not a market has reached a tipping point.

Tipping is most common in markets where there are strong network effects. Network effects exist where the inherent value of a product or service increases as the number of people using the same product or service increases. Those could be direct network effects, when having more consumers within the same category (or market side) crates more value to the same group or indirect network effects – particularly on multi-sided platforms – where increases in usage in one side of the platform reflects in increased value to the other side, or across the platform (cross-platform network effects). Several factors may contribute to these network effects, including positive feedback loops and switching costs. For example, a company can use the data of its existing users to identify and address gaps in its services in order to attract even more users. Similarly, subscription costs and the hassle of moving between different accounts may also make users reluctant to switch between services. As a result, a company that gains an early lead in adoption may corner the market.

While regulators are interested in stopping a market from tipping before it occurs, the reality is that it is immensely difficult to predict who the incumbent will be in any given market, when tipping will occur, or if it will be short-lived and temporary or withstand long-term effects. Moreover, tipping may reflect a capture of value of investments in new technology and innovation, as well as the inauguration of new, previously unexplored, markets for products and services. Constant innovation, as well as distinct dimensions of competition within and between digital platforms ought to inform policy and enforcement actions related to market tipping.

Tipping markets may still be contestable markets. Market contestability depends on several factors, including the level of maturity (e.g., if a market is expanding, stable or declining); product/service-level preferences and room for innovation; and the characteristics of network effects (e.g., if they are local; if they affect national or international audiences, if they are age or demographic-specific etc.). If markets are expanding (e.g., increasing users or subscribers), competitors or entrants may capture new groups of consumers. When a product/service can be provided in different means, bundles, conformations or arrangements, competitors or entrants may direct innovative efforts to launch alternative modes of consumption. In markets that tipped because of specific network effects, tipping is unlikely to be prolonged; also, tipping might occur within local markets or internal divisions within a relevant market, and it might not constraint some level of competitive pressure or contestability.

It is relevant to differentiate market tipping and anticompetitive market entrenchment. While tipping is mostly related to structural features, and thus regarded as a possible market failure, anticompetitive entrenchment derives from a dominant firm's illegal strategy to artificially maintain its market power and obstruct competition. That is the case, for example, of a dominant firm that adopts cross-market exclusivity dealings that effectively lock-in substantial groups of consumers, cancelling any remaining contestability (as per above); or that of a dominant platform that introduces default rules that unduly benefit its own products/services and move users away from other competitor-users of the platform. Market entrenchment or entrenched (e.g., incontestable) market power is not per se illegal in virtually all jurisdictions. Entrenchment theories of competitive harm are subject to a rule of reason (or effects-based) assessment, that confronts possible constraints to competition to efficiencies deriving from said conduct.

Therefore, a tipping market may be prone to anticompetitive behaviour but does not necessarily result in anticompetitive conduct. Tipping may be used as an indication of strengthened dominance, reinforcing a plaintiff's abuse of dominance claim, but is far from sufficient as legal basis for conviction. Indeed, the United States' Sherman Act (15 U.S.C. Section 2) prohibits monopolization, but only if monopoly power is acquired or maintained through unlawful means. Likewise, Article 102 of the Treaty on the Functioning of the European Union makes it illegal to abuse an already-existent dominant position. For example: in *Microsoft* (2008) the European Commission condemned the company's tipping of the media player market because it was only possible given that Microsoft leveraged its dominant position in PC operating systems and tied Windows to Windows Media Players.

Following this trend, the Brazilian Competition Authority (CADE) has been referencing market tipping precisely as an indicator of great market power in cases involving digital platforms, highlighting that the companies subject to investigation enjoyed "winner-takes-all benefits", as stated in the *iFood* (2023) and *Gympass* (2022) cases, but applied traditional theories of harm to assess the anticompetitive effects of exclusivity agreements in both cases (both closed after settlement agreements).

Ongoing policy discussions suggest *ex ante* intervention could be used to prevent market tipping. German legislators have introduced recent changes to the country's Competition Act, which provides a standing to sue dominant platforms in digital markets against abusive tipping that, e.g., prevents competitors to capture network effects, creating serious competitive harm to the market. The German case is a distinctive example of *ex ante* interventions toward tipping.

Bibliography

Bedre-Defolie, Ö and Nitsche, R., When Do Markets Tip? An Overview and Some Insights for Policy, *Journal of European Competition Law & Practice*, Volume 11, Issue 10, December 2020, Pages 610–622

Oxera, Tipping: should regulators intervene before or after? A policy dilemma, April 28, 2021

Petit, N. and Moreno Belloso, N., A Simple Way to Measure Tipping in Digital Markets, ProMarket, April 6, 2021

Stucke, M. E. and Grunes, A. P., Big Data and Competition Policy 107 (2016)

See also

Economies of scale, Ecosystem failures, Market Power, Network effect, Online Platforms

T

TRADE SECRETS

Jorge L. CONTRERAS
University of Utah

■ Definition

A trade secret is information that has commercial value to an organization due to its secrecy, is not known outside of the organization, and the continuing secrecy of which the organization has taken reasonable measures to protect. Trade secrets may include information embodied in documents, electronic records, products and other media, as well as information known to individuals. The EU and some other jurisdictions exclude from the definition of trade secrets trivial information or experience/skills gained by employees during the normal course of their employment and information that is generally known among, or is readily accessible to, persons within the circles that normally deal with the kind of information in question.

■ Commentary

A Form of Intellectual Property

Though information, per se, has often been considered to be beyond the reach of property law, trade secrets have, at least in the U.S., been recognized as a form of intellectual property (see *Kewanee v. Bicron* (U.S. 1974), *Rockwell v. DEV* (7th Cir. 1991), *U.S. v. DuPont* (D. Del. 1953)).

Codification of Trade Secrecy Laws

Prior to the 1970s, the unauthorized acquisition and use of another's secret information in the United States and Europe was actionable under a variety of common law and statutory theories including property, contract, bailment, trust, unfair competition, and unjust enrichment (Bone, 1998; Graves, 2013). Article 10bis of the 1967 revision of the Paris Convention for the Protection of Industrial Property requires member states to provide protection against acts of unfair competition, which include "any act of competition contrary to honest practices in industrial or commercial matters", but the Convention does not mention secret information specifically.

In 1979, after a decade of deliberation, in the U.S. the National Conference of Commissioners on Uniform State Laws adopted the text of the Uniform Trade Secrets Act (UTSA), a model statute proposed for adoption in the individual U.S. states. As of May 2023, the UTSA has been adopted, in some form, by all U.S. states except New York (which continues to recognize trade secrets under its common law). At the U.S. federal level, the 1996 Economic Espionage Act (EEA) created criminal liability for the theft of trade secrets, though relatively few prosecutions have been brought. Given perceived inadequacies of the EEA, in 2016 Congress enacted the Defending Trade Secrets Act (DTSA) (18 U.S.C. § 1836 et seq.), a general civil trade secrecy statute modelled on the UTSA.

In 2016, the European Union also adopted a trade secrecy directive in order to harmonize inconsistent national regimes (Directive No. 2016/943, Directive on the protection of undisclosed know-how and business information (trade secrets) against their unlawful acquisition, use and disclosure). Trade secrets are also addressed, albeit briefly, in Article 39 of the WTO's Agreement on Trade-Related Aspects of Intellectual Property Rights (TRIPS), on which the EU Directive is largely based (Niebel et al. 2018).

Trade Secrets Distinguished from Other Confidential Information and Know-How

While all trade secrets are confidential, not all confidential information qualifies for trade secret protection (Graves, 2013). For example, trade secrets must generally have commercial value. Accordingly, private information held by organizations concerning, for example, employee health conditions or retirement savings, or much of the personal information contained in corporate email correspondence, would often fail to qualify as trade secrets. In addition, information that may be accessible from sources outside the organization may still be considered confidential by an organization and thus subject to contractual confidentiality obligations without legal trade secret status.

Protection Measures

In most jurisdictions, a condition for trade secrecy protection is that the owner took reasonable measures to ensure the continued secrecy of trade secret information. Yet few statutes offer significant guidance regarding the types of measures that will qualify as reasonable. Among the measures recommended by commentators to preserve the trade secret status of an organization's information are: establishing a written policy detailing the organization's means for handling trade secrets, identifying and documenting trade secrets, valuing and classifying trade secrets based on their relative values, appropriately marking documents containing trade secret information, implementing trade secrecy procedures in employee and third party agreements, designating a trade secret protection officer, implementing physical and technical security measures to limit access to secret information, tracking access and use of trade secret information and conducting thorough entry and exit interviews of employees (Nachtrab 2019).

Duration

Unlike other forms of intellectual property that have specified durations (e.g., 20 years for patents, and the life of the author plus 70 years for copyrights), trade secrets have no defined expiration. Rather, they retain their protected status for so long as the necessary conditions for trade secrecy are satisfied. It is for this reason that the famous formula for Coca-Cola has allegedly remained a trade secret for more than 130 years.

Misappropriation

Most trade secrecy laws give the owner of a trade secret a civil remedy for the unauthorized acquisition, use or disclosure of a trade secret (often referred to as "misappropriation"). Under the USTA and DTSA, misappropriation may be found if information is acquired by "improper means", which includes "theft, bribery, misrepresentation, breach or inducement of a breach of a duty to maintain secrecy, or espionage through electronic or other means." Article 39(1) of the TRIPS Agreement and the EU Directive speak, rather, in terms of the acquisition of information in a manner that is "contrary to honest commercial practices," which includes "breach of contract, breach of confidence and inducement to breach, and includes the acquisition of undisclosed information by third parties who knew, or were grossly negligent in failing to know, that such practices were involved in the acquisition."

Permitted Acquisitions and Disclosures of Trade Secrets

In general, the following means of acquiring information are not considered to constitute trade secret misappropriation: independent invention; "reverse engineering" (starting with a known product and working backward to find the method by which it was developed); discovery under a license from the owner of the trade secret; observation of an item in public use or on public display; or from published literature. Article 5 of the EU Directive sets out additional exceptions when a trade secret is acquired or disclosed (a) in support of the right to freedom of expression and information, including freedom and pluralism of the media; (b) for revealing misconduct, wrongdoing or illegal activity; (c) by workers to their labor representatives; or (d) for the purpose of protecting a legitimate interest recognised by the EU or national law.

Compulsory Licensing of Trade Secrets

Trade secrets are not covered by the compulsory licensing provisions of Article 31 of the TRIPS Agreement, which relates solely to patents. Beginning in 2020, trade secrets attracted significant global attention in the debate over manufacturing technology for COVID-19 vaccines. Commentators observed that, even without patent barriers, the manufacture of advanced biological products would not be feasible without significant transfers of secret manufacturing knowledge by current producers (Levine and Sarnoff, 2023). These observations led to calls for governmental intervention and potential compulsory disclosures of manufacturing know-how (ibid.).

Bibliography

BONE, R. G., "A New Look at Trade Secret Law: Doctrine in Search of Justification," (1998) 86 *California Law Review* 241

LEVINE, D. S. and SARNOFF, J. D., "Compelling Trade Secret Sharing" (2023) 74 *Hastings Law Journal* 987

NACHTRAB, K., "Protecting Organizational Trade Secrets In View Of The EU Trade Secrets Directive" (2019) 54(3) *Les Nouvelles* 232

NIEBEL, R., DE MARTINIS, L. and CLARK, B., "The EU Trade Secrets Directive: all change for trade secret protection in Europe?" (2018) 13 *Journal of Intellectual Property Law & Practice* 445

TAIT GRAVES, C., "Trade Secrecy and Common Law Confidentiality: The Problem of Multiple Regimes" (2013) in Rochelle C. Dreyfuss & Katherine J. Strandburg, *The Law and Theory of Trade Secrecy: A Handbook of Contemporary Research* 75 (Edward Elgar)

See also

Unfair competition, Intellectual property, Compulsory licensing

T

TRADEMARK

Virender CHANDEL
National Law University Delhi

■ Definition

Article 15(1) of TRIPS Agreement defines a trademark as any sign or any combination of signs possessing distinctiveness in terms of capability to distinguish goods or services of one undertaking from those of other undertakings. Such signs can be in diverse forms including words, letters, combinations of colors, numbers, or any combination of these forms. The fundamental condition for any sign to be eligible for trademark protection is distinctiveness. A sign may possess distinctiveness inherently or acquire it through use. This harmonized definition of trademark is found with some variations in national laws of all members of the World Trade Organization.

■ Commentary

The conditions of trademark registration and enforcement vary in national laws according to relevant public policies.

Signs/Marks

The U.S federal law 15 U.S. Code § 1127 and section 9 of Restatement (Third) of Unfair Competition, 1995 define a trademark as including any word, name, symbol, or device, or any combination thereof. In Qualitex Company v. Jacobson Products Company (1995) the U.S. Supreme Court stated that a sign on account of its ontological status can't be denied trademark protection if the sign has distinctiveness. Thus, non-conventional signs such as scent, flavor, color, moving images etc. can also qualify for trademark protection if they are able to carry a meaning. In the EU, EUTM Directive and EUTM Regulations define a trademark as consisting of any signs including personal names, shapes, or packaging of goods. In Ralf Sieckmann v. Deutsches Patent- und Markenamt (2002), the European Court of Justice ruled that any sign can be subject matter of trademark protection including signs which cannot be visually perceived but can be represented. In

Dyson Ltd v Registrar of Trade Marks (2007), the ECJ restricted what constitutes a sign and ruled that a claimed sign not capable of being perceived by one of the five senses is not a sign.

Distinctiveness

A sign devoid of distinctiveness is not a trademark. TRIPS Agreement does not define the term "distinctiveness" but refers to it in the context of the ability of a sign to "distinguish" goods/services of one undertaking from others. In U.S. law, the definition of trademark explicitly requires two functions of a trademark "to indicate source" and "to identify and distinguish" goods on which it is affixed. The EU definition of trademark explicitly refers to one function of a trademark which is the capability of a sign to distinguish goods/services. However, in Koninklijke Philips Electronics v. Remington Consumer Products (2002), the ECJ, relying on jurisprudence and the preamble of the directive, ruled that the essential function of a trademark is to identify the origin of goods and to enable a consumer to distinguish the goods from other goods. Thus, in contrast to the TRIPS Agreement, the distinctiveness of signs in U.S. and EU laws can be understood in the terms of capability to distinguish goods/services (differential distinctiveness) and indicate source/origin of goods on which they are applied (source distinctiveness). Some commentators emphasis that differential distinctiveness facilitates source distinctiveness.

Similarly, article 9 of Trademark Law of the People's Republic of China requires a trademark to be readily distinguishable. As per section 9(1) a) read with section 2(1)(zb) of Trade Mark Act, 1999 (India) "distinctiveness" is capability of a sign to distinguish goods/services. The source distinctiveness is not a statutory requirement, but it assists consumers in differentiating products (ITC v. Phillip Morris (2010). Source distinctiveness of an infringing mark cannot be used as a defense to infringement action. (Stiefel Laboratories v. Ajanta Pharma (2014)).

Spectrum of Distinctiveness

In EU, distinctiveness is assessed by reference to the associated goods, the perception of an average consumer and the overall impression of a sign (Mag Instrument v. Office of Harmonisation in the Internal Market (2004). A sign should be perceived as an indication that goods come from a single source, that it is a "badge of origin". In addition to it, a sign should not be descriptive and generic. In a classic American case Judge Friendly classified signs into four categories in an ascending order reflecting how much a sign is distinctive: (1) generic; (2) descriptive; (3) suggestive; and (4) arbitrary and fanciful. Generic signs are the antithesis of trademarks and cannot be trademarked under any circumstances. These marks identify a category or class name of associated goods instead of source of goods. Whether a sign is generic can be ascertained by asking the genus of the concerned goods or service and whether the relevant public understands the sign to refer to that genus (H. Marvin Ginn Corp. v. International Ass'n of Fire Chiefs (1986).

Descriptive signs connote the immediate idea of characteristics of the associated goods. Neither generic nor descriptive signs can serve to distinguish and identify the source of goods; therefore, they are not inherently distinctive. Non-conventional signs like colors are also not inherently distinctive because either they are a part of features of goods or functional in nature. In the U.S., a color sign can never be inherently distinctive (Wal-Mart Stores, Inc. v. Samara Brothers, Inc. (2000). In the EU, a color per se is not inherently distinctive except in exceptional circumstances where the number of goods or services to which the sign is applied are restricted (Libertel Grope BV v. Benelux-Merkenbureau (2003).

Suggestive signs when applied to goods, requires some imagination to reach a conclusion as to the characteristics of the goods (In re N.C. Lottery (2017). Whether a sign is descriptive or suggestive can be ascertained if there is incongruity in the sign. Arbitrary and fanciful signs have no relationship with the associated goods and are distinctively stronger than suggestive signs (Nautilus Grp. v. Icon Health & Fitness (2004). These three types of signs are inherently distinctive due to their intrinsic nature which serves to identify a particular source.

Acquired Distinctiveness/Secondary Meaning

Some signs not inherently distinctive may acquire distinctiveness if they develop a secondary meaning in the minds of the public identifying the source of the product instead of the product itself. Secondary meaning can be acquired through consistent and extensive use of the sign causing a consumer to understand the sign has come to identify associated goods as originating from a particular undertaking. The legal issue here is whether a relevant class of people identifies goods as originating from a particular undertaking. In answering this issue, several factors must be considered such as geographical area, market share, length, and intensity of use (Windsurfing Chiemsee Produktions v Walter Huber (1999). In the U.S., signs having acquired distinctiveness have a lesser degree of trademark protection in comparison to inherently distinctive signs (TCPIP Holding Co. v. Haar Communications, Inc. (2001).

Bibliography

Beebe, B., *Trademark Law: An Open-Source Casebook* (Version 9, 2022)

Bently, L. and Sherman, B., *Intellectual Property Law* (6th ed, Oxford University Press 2022)

Pires de Carvalho, N., *The TRIPS Regime of Trademarks and Designs* (4th edition, Wolters Kluwer, 2018)

See also

Intellectual property right, Copyright, Intellectual property

T

TWO-SIDED MARKET

Arno RASEK
German Competition Authority

Definition

The term "two-sided market" is used to emphasize that the demand for a product or service is characterized by two or more distinct customer or user groups – the two "sides" – and where at least one of these groups cares significantly about the involvement of another group (so-called "indirect network effects" or "cross-group externalities"). The product or service is thus some kind of platform or intermediation service connecting the distinct user groups, i.e. sellers and buyers, or readers, authors and advertisers. Examples include physical and digital marketplaces (i.e. stock exchanges, shopping malls), traditional and modern media (i.e. newspapers, broadcasters, social media), as well as software platforms or payment systems.

Commentary

The term "two-sided market" originates from the economic literature and does not bear any direct legal consequence in competition law. The term rather offers an intelligible label for the economic phenomenon of indirect network effects that scholars only since the early 2000s have described in concise economic models. The wide dissemination of the term is mainly attributed to *Rochet & Tirole* (2003). Nowadays, the term "multi-sided" is often used instead of "two-sided", and/or the term "platform" instead of "market". Many, if not most, platforms have more than two distinct customer/user groups. The number and identity of the different platform "sides" is not necessarily a universal characteristic of the business activity at stake but may result from a deliberate choice made by the platform operator. The platform's competitors may differ across these platform sides. For each side of a platform a separate relevant market may be defined, for example a reader market and an advertising market.

The presence of indirect network effects between user groups affects the price setting mechanism and the competitive interaction in these markets. When cross-group externalities are significant, this may have relevant consequences for the suppliers' incentives and thus for the competitive analysis. When user group A places higher value on the participation of user group B than vice-versa, it will be rational for the platform operator to offer lower prices to user group B, and this may go as far as offering the service for free to users B or even rewarding them for their participation with payments or other benefits. This means that in some cases one or several user groups will not be charged for the platform service. The presence of significant indirect network effects should be reflected in all parts of the competition law analysis, i.e. market definition, market power analysis and effects analysis. Price-cost tests developed for identifying predatory pricing or excessive pricing in one-sided markets will not yield reliable results when applied without modification for multi-sided platforms. Other things being equal, positive bidirectional network effects between the two or more sides tend to increase both market power and the magnitude of anticompetitive effects.

Although the economics of indirect network effects are nowadays common-sense among economists, practitioners and courts still struggle with their application in competition law. So far, the three most relevant issues concerned zero-price markets, defining separate markets for each "side" or not, and implications of the increased analytical complexity for the burden of proof.

It can be frequently observed that the platform operator charges only one customer group while the service is offered for free to another customer group ("zero-price markets"). There has been some debate as to whether free-of-charge offers should be considered as (part of) an antitrust market, and some courts even decided that they should not. However, the economic answer, and therefore also the sensible competition law answer to this question seems rather clear. In multi-sided markets, where the provision of a free service is part of a business activity pursuing commercial purposes, zero-pricing should not hinder a relevant market to be defined. With positive indirect network effects, setting a price of zero for one customer group may make perfect sense for the platform provider if it finds it preferable to charge another customer group. There may be competition for non-charged users, and this competition can be restricted through mergers, abusive practices or a cartel. The seminal "zero-price market" case is *Facebook* where the German Federal Court of Justice decided that inadequate privacy conditions by a dominant provider can be exploitative vis-à-vis private users even though the service is offered to them for free.

As multi-sided platforms involve distinct groups of customers, there are in principle two alternative market definition options: defining separate markets for different customer groups or defining a single market encompassing all customer groups. As a first step, the competitive landscape on each "side" of the platform should be identified one after the other. In comparing the competitive forces on each of these sides, it is easy to assess whether the set of relevant product substitutes/competitors, the single- or multi-homing of the customer groups or the geographic scope differ across platform sides. In case of significant differences, typically separate markets should be defined. Conversely, if these factors do not differ across market "sides", a single market encompassing all customer groups can be defined. In particular, this may be the case where the different groups are inseparably linked by a platform interaction, for example a transaction platform or a matching platform.

Effects analysis is more complex in multi-sided markets compared to single-sided markets. While there is broad agreement that, in principle, multi-sided markets may require more scrutiny from antitrust authorities than one-sided markets, there is a question on whether and how established antitrust tests and their implications for the allocation of the burden of proof remain valid in platform settings. In a controversial ruling, the U.S. Supreme Court decided in *Ohio v. American Express* that in case of a transaction platform it was not sufficient for the plaintiff to show harm on one transaction platform side. Legislation to reverse this decision is currently being discussed in the U.S.

While the term two-sided market can be viewed as synonymous to the terms "platform" and "multi-sided market", it should be distinguished from the more recent concept of "digital ecosystems". A digital ecosystem can be understood as a broader conglomerate of several distinct services/platforms whereas the term "multi-sided market" refers to one service/platform only.

Bibliography

Belleflamme, P. and Peitz, M., *Industrial Organization: Markets and Strategies* 2nd edn, Cambridge University Press 2015, Chapters 20-23

Rochet, J. and Tirole, J., Platform Competition in Two-Sided Markets, *Journal of the European Economic Association*, 1(4), 2003, p. 990-1029

Wismer, S., Bongard, C. and Rasek, A., Multi-Sided Market Economics in Competition Law Enforcement, *Journal of European Competition Law & Practice*, 2017, 8(4), p. 257–262

OECD, Rethinking Antitrust Tools for Multi-Sided Platforms, 2018

See also

Market Power, Online platforms, Network effect

U

UNDERTAKING (NOTION)

Carsten KÖNIG
University of Cologne

■ Definition

The concept of undertaking has a number of legal consequences that should be taken into account when applying it. First, in Viho (paras. 13-18), the ECJ clarified that Article 101(1) TFEU (then Article 85(1) of the EC Treaty) normally does not apply to agreements between different members of the same undertaking, since all members are engaged in the same economic activity and are therefore not in competition with each other. This echoes the US Supreme Court's decision in Copperweld v. Independence Tube (1984), according to which a parent company cannot conspire with its wholly owned subsidiary for the purposes of Section 1 of the Sherman Act because they cannot be regarded as separate economic entities. Second, in Case C-542/14 VM Remonts (paras. 23-24), the ECJ clarified that employees are considered to be part of the economic unit that is the undertaking and that their anti-competitive behaviour is therefore imputed to the undertaking to which they belong. Undertakings are therefore strictly liable for the conduct of all their employees (including those lower down the hierarchy), irrespective of the concepts of attribution in the laws of the Member States. Third, a parent company may be liable for an infringement of competition law by a subsidiary, even if it had no knowledge of the infringement and could not have prevented it. What matters is that the subsidiary does not decide independently on its market conduct, but is subject to a decisive influence exercised by the parent company. In Akzo (para. 60), the ECJ established a legal presumption of control where the parent company holds 100% of the shares in the subsidiary. Fourth, a subsidiary may be liable for an infringement committed by a parent company, and a sister company may be liable for an infringement committed by another sister company. According to the ECJ in Sumal (paras. 42-44), this follows from the fact that it is the undertaking as an economic unit that infringes competition law, so that all members of the unit are automatically responsible for the infringement. This consequence of the economic unit is particularly advantageous for private plaintiffs, who have a wider choice of potential defendants and jurisdictions. Fifth, the EU courts believe that even fundamental procedural rights, such as the principle of personal responsibility and the principle that the penalty must be specific to the offender and the offence, apply primarily to the undertaking and not to its individual members (e.g. Siemens Österreich para. 56). However, this approach seems questionable, as the economic unit that is the undertaking does not have legal capacity and therefore cannot be a bearer of fundamental rights. Sixth, the application of the concept of undertaking may have a significant impact on the calculation of fines imposed under Article 23 of Regulation 1/2003. This is because many of the relevant factors, such as the value of sales in the affected markets, the total worldwide turnover or a history of previous infringements, have to be assessed differently when looking at a group of companies rather than a single legal entity.

■ Commentary

The notion of undertaking is not defined in the EU Treaties or in secondary legislation. Instead, the understanding of the term is shaped by the case law of the European Court of Justice (ECJ). The Court emphasises that the drafters of the Treaties chose to use the concept of an undertaking to designate the addressees of Articles 101 and 102 TFEU, and not the concepts of a company or a legal person, which are used in other provisions of the Treaties. Moreover, the Court has held that the concept of undertaking is an autonomous concept of EU competition law for which neither principles of company law nor concepts of the Member States are relevant. The concept of undertaking not only defines the scope of Articles 101 and 102 TFEU, but also determines who is liable for fines under Article 23 of Regulation 1/2003 and for damages under the Courage jurisprudence and Article 3 of the Damages Directive 2014/104. The latter was originally held in Skanska (para. 47) and later confirmed in Sumal (para. 38). However, this does not alter the fact that fines and damages can only be enforced against natural and legal persons, as only they have the legal capacity and assets to satisfy the claims. In the case of fines, the European Commission has discretion as to which members of the undertaking, i.e. the economic unit, it holds liable; in the case of damages, claimants are free to choose.

The common definition of an undertaking as an entity engaged in an economic activity means two things. First, there are very few organisational requirements. The Courts require a "unitary organisation of personal, tangible and intangible elements" (e.g. Sumal para. 41), but this has never been a problem. The entity must include at least one natural or legal person, but can otherwise range from a one-person company to a multinational group of companies. Public bodies such as local authorities or states are also covered, provided that they carry out an economic activity. Second, it is the activity that is ultimately decisive. It must be economic, which means that the entity must pursue a specific economic aim on a long-term basis. Simple cases involve the supply of a product or service on a market. Non-economic activities include, for example, the exercise of sovereign functions by public authorities (e.g. tax collection, pollution control, flight security and airspace management). However, the Courts are strict and consider public services to be economic if they can be provided by private parties in competition (e.g. employment services, management of transport infrastructure, health care, ambulance services).

The concept of undertaking has a number of legal consequences that should be taken into account when applying it. First, in Viho (paras. 13-18), the ECJ clarified that Article 101(1) TFEU (then Article 85(1) of the EC Treaty) normally does not apply to agreements between different members of the same undertaking, since all members are engaged in the same economic activity and are therefore not in competition with each other. This echoes the U.S. Supreme Court's decision in Copperweld v. Independence Tube (1984), according to which a parent company cannot conspire with its wholly owned subsidiary for the purposes of Section 1 of the Sherman Act because they cannot be regarded as separate economic entities.

Second, in Case C-542/14 VM Remonts (paras. 23-24), the ECJ clarified that employees are considered to be part of the economic unit that is the undertaking and that their anti-competitive behaviour is therefore imputed to the undertaking to which they belong. Undertakings are therefore strictly liable for the conduct of all their employees (including those lower down the hierarchy), irrespective of the concepts of attribution in the laws of the Member States.

Third, a parent company may be liable for an infringement of competition law by a subsidiary, even if it had no knowledge of the infringement and could not have prevented it. What matters is that the subsidiary does not decide independently on its market conduct, but is subject to a decisive influence exercised by the parent company. In Akzo (para. 60), the ECJ established a legal presumption of control where the parent company holds 100% of the shares in the subsidiary.

Fourth, a subsidiary may be liable for an infringement committed by a parent company, and a sister company may be liable for an infringement committed by another sister company. According to the ECJ in Sumal (paras. 42-44), this follows from the fact that it is the undertaking as an economic unit that infringes competition law, so that all members of the unit are automatically responsible for the infringement.

This consequence of the economic unit is particularly advantageous for private plaintiffs, who have a wider choice of potential defendants and jurisdictions. Fifth, the EU courts believe that even fundamental procedural rights, such as the principle of personal responsibility and the principle that the penalty must be specific to the offender and the offence, apply primarily to the undertaking and not to its individual members (e.g. Siemens Österreich para. 56). However, this approach seems questionable, as the economic unit that is the undertaking does not have legal capacity and therefore cannot be a bearer of fundamental rights. Sixth, the application of the concept of undertaking may have a significant impact on the calculation of fines imposed under Article 23 of Regulation 1/2003. This is because many of the relevant factors, such as the value of sales in the affected markets, the total worldwide turnover or a history of previous infringements, have to be assessed differently when looking at a group of companies rather than a single legal entity.

Finally, it should be noted that the expansive approach of the EU Courts in interpreting the concept of undertaking is often attacked by the companies concerned and their lawyers, and is also frequently criticised in the academic literature. A common objection is that the Courts do not sufficiently respect the rights of individual legal entities and individuals. In addition, the Courts are criticised for arguing in a self-referential, formalistic manner and for not sufficiently explaining the functions of a broad interpretation of the concept of undertaking.

Bibliography

ARAUJO BOYD, M., *The Notion of Undertaking in EU Competition Law*, PhD thesis, University of Glasgow, 2023

BAILEY, D. and ODUDU, O., The Single Economic Entity Doctrine in EU Competition Law, 51(6) *Common Market Law Review* 1721-1757 (2014)

JONES, A., SUFRIN, B. and DUNNE, N., *Jones and Sufrin's EU Competition Law: Text, Cases, and Materials* (8th edn, Oxford University Press 2023), Chapter 4

KOENIG, C., The Boundaries of the Firm and the Reach of Competition Law: Corporate Group Liability and Sanctioning in the EU and the U.S., in Marco Corradi and Julian Nowag (eds), *Intersections Between Corporate and Antitrust Law* (Cambridge University Press 2023), pp. 63-85

WHISH, R. and BAILEY, D., *Competition Law* (10th edn, Oxford University Press 2021), Chapter 3

See also

Public undertaking, Services of General Economic Interest (SGIE), Competition policy

U

UNFAIR COMPETITION

Rod SIMS
The Australian National University

Definition

Unfair competition is conduct by a market participant which gains or seeks to gain an advantage over its rivals through misleading, deceptive, dishonest, fraudulent, coercive or unconscionable conduct in trade or commerce.

Commentary

Dishonest, inequitable, deceptive, fraudulent or coercive commercial and trade practices have long been proscribed by legislators or sanctioned by Courts of law in many jurisdictions. This jurisprudence is reflected in the concept of unfair competition in the 1883 Paris Convention for the Protection of Industrial Property, which has as its object [among others] "the repression of unfair competition" constituted by "any act of competition contrary to honest practices in industrial or commercial matters."

The Paris Convention specifies certain acts as requiring prohibition, including false allegations discrediting a competitor, and indications or allegations in the course of trade which are liable to mislead the public as to the nature, the manufacturing process, the characteristics, the suitability for their purpose, or the quantity, of the goods.

Over 170 countries are now parties to the Paris Convention. Its obligations have usually been implemented in national and sub-national legislation by the parties. In jurisdictions with codified laws, those codes are used to incorporate unfair competition provisions. For example, in France, the Consumer Code has provisions dealing with prohibited commercial practices such as unfair commercial practices and deceptive marketing practices. This legislation often sits apart from and is administered or enforced by agencies separate from competition agencies. In other jurisdictions unfair competition is dealt with alongside antitrust or competition law and is enforced by a common agency; Australia, New Zealand, Canada, Colombia, Chinese Taipei, Denmark, Kenya, Panama, Peru, the United States, Singapore, and Vietnam are examples of this approach.

Unfair Competition laws in Australia

In Australia, sections 33 and 34 of the Australian Consumer Law (ACL), which is part of the *Competition and Consumer Act 2010* (Cth), implement part of the Paris Convention by prohibiting conduct by a corporation in trade or commerce that is liable to mislead the public about the nature, manufacturing process (in respect of goods), characteristics, suitability for purpose or quality of goods or services.

The ACL is a national law which has been also incorporated into the law of each Australian state and territory. Much of the conduct addressed by the ACL could lead to an "unfair competitive advantage' in a market. It deals with business to consumer transactions, as well as businesses to business transactions.

Many of the concepts which are embodied in the ACL are based on equitable principles developed by the English Court of Chancery over centuries, and subsequently applied and developed by the Australian Courts. Misleading or deceptive conduct is prohibited generally by section 18 (but without penalty, although other remedies including damages can be granted); and specific forms of false or misleading conduct or unfair practices are prohibited and subject to penalty, without requiring intention or fault. This can be seen to reflect the notion of fraud in equity, in which many activities regarded as fraudulent were not done with an intention to cheat and deceive.

The equitable concept of unconscionable conduct is also the subject of ACL prohibitions which attract a penalty and other remedies. One of the ACL provisions dealing with unconscionable conduct simply adopts the equitable concept of unconscionable conduct: where one party has a special disadvantage of which the stronger party takes unconscientious advantage. The other form of proscribed statutory unconscionable conduct is not limited by the unwritten law and involves an evaluative inquiry as to whether the conduct is beyond conscience in all of the circumstances.

Unfair contract terms in standard form contracts with consumers and small businesses are rendered void by the ACL, although at present the ACL does not prohibit or penalise a corporation which includes and relies on those terms.

Other specific unfair practices that may constitute a form of unfair competition are prohibited by the ACL, including:

1. offering rebates, gifts and prizes with the intention of not providing them (section 32);
2. bait advertising (section 35);
3. wrongly accepting payment when not intending to supply the goods or services paid for (section 36); and

4. the use of physical force or undue harassment and coercion in connection with the sale or possible sale of or payment for goods or services or land (section 50).

Unfair competition in Europe

In the European Union, the Unfair Commercial Practices Directive 2005/29/EC regulates unfair trading practices which then requires corresponding laws to be passed that incorporate it into each member state's legal system. The Directive is concerned mainly with the standards of behaviour required of traders. Proscribed conduct includes a general prohibition on unfair business to consumer commercial practices in Articles 3 and 5 and then more specific prohibitions. It is important to note that it does not seek to harmonise within the European Union commercial practices which, although not harming consumers, may hurt competitors and business customers.

Complementary directives also tackle "unfair competition'. They are Directive 93/13/EEC of 5 April 1993 on unfair contract terms in consumer contracts and a recent directive that is being implemented called the Enforcement and Modernisation Directive (EU) 2019/2161.

Unfair competition in the United States

In the United States unfair competition is governed by state and federal statute law as well as the common law, with unfair competition recognised as a tort giving rise to a cause of action. United States Law also has specific prohibitions contained in state statutes reflecting the Uniform Deceptive Trade Practices Act (UDTPA). That legislation prohibits three specific types of representations: (1) false representations that goods or services have certain characteristics, ingredients, uses, benefits, or quantities; (2) false representations that goods or services are new or original; and (3) false representations that goods or services are of a particular grade, standard, or quality.

United States Federal Law includes "unfair competition' provisions in the Federal Trade Commission Act (FTC Act) and rules made under that law. Section 5(a) of the FTC Act provides that "unfair methods of competition" and "unfair or deceptive acts or practices in or affecting commerce… are… declared unlawful."

The FTC explains that: "Deceptive" practices are defined in the Commission's "Policy Statement on Deception" as involving a material representation, omission or practice that is likely to mislead a consumer acting reasonably in the circumstances. An act or practice is "unfair" if it "causes or is likely to cause *substantial injury* to consumers which is not *reasonably avoidable* by consumers themselves and *not outweighed by countervailing benefits* to consumers or to competition." 15 U.S.C. Sec. 45(n).

In addition, the Commission enforces a variety of other consumer protection statutes that prohibit specifically defined practices. These statutes generally specify that violations are to be treated as if they were "unfair or deceptive" acts or practices under Section 5(a); many also provide that violations are to be treated as if they were violations of a trade regulation rule issued under Section 18 of the FTC Act (and thus subject to civil penalties)."

Other jurisdictions

Many jurisdictions now have statutes that address unfair competition. Usually, those statutes define the conduct as including misrepresentation, deception, fraud, unfairness and unconscionable conduct in business affairs and particularly in dealings with competitors. Apart from those jurisdictions already described, others with such a law include Germany, Japan, China, Turkey, India, Korea, Canada, Peru, Kenya.

Conduct outside the scope of this definition

Conduct which also amounts to a cartel, an abuse of dominance or some other form of horizontal or unilateral anti-competitive behaviour is covered by other definitions. Conduct leading to competitive advantage conferred or obtained as a consequence of government regulation or state aid may be regarded as "unfair competition" in some jurisdictions, but there are often separate regulatory regimes in place to promote "competitive neutrality" or govern "state aid".

Bibliography

Coorey, A., *Australian Consumer Law*, Lexis Nexis

Henning-Bodewig, F., *International Handbook on Unfair Competition*, Hart, 2013

FTC Policy Statement on Deception, 1983

Guidance on the Implementation/Application of Directive 2005/29/EC on Unfair Commercial Practices, European Commission Staff Working Document, 2016

Outline of the Japanese Unfair Competition Prevention Law – published by the Japan Patent Office

Paris Convention for the Protection of International Property

Summary of the Unfair Commercial Practices Directive 2005/29

Summaries of the statutes giving the FTC enforcement powers

See also

Abuse of dominant position, Cartel, Consumer protection, Competition policy

U

UNIVERSAL SERVICE

Yusuke TAKAMIYA
Mori Hamada & Matsumoto

Navneet SHARMA
CUTS International

Gokul PLAHA
Independent antitrust law and policy researcher

■ Definition

Universal service is an ex-ante public intervention setting general interest requirements representing the right of all users to access certain essential services and a corresponding obligations imposed on service providers to offer the services under certain conditions. The core principles of a universal service include quality, affordability, geographical reach, and equal access. The core practices include openness in management, price-setting, and funding and scrutiny by bodies independent of those operating the services. The concept of universal service is typically used in the (economic) context of the liberalization of network industries like telecommunications, postal services, and electricity.

■ Commentary

European Union

It is often said that the concept of universal service obligation (USO) originated in the United Kingdom and made its way into the European Union's political-legal order in the 1980s.

In European Union (EU) law, a universal service is a service of general economic interest (SGEI). Set out in secondary law instruments, its origins lie in the European Community (EC) law. According to Article 1 of Protocol on Services of General Interest (SGI(s)) no. 26 annexed to the Treaty of Lisbon and Article 36 of the Charter of Fundamental Rights, promoting universal access to essential services is deemed to be a value of the EU and a common public service obligation.

The 2007 Communication on SGI observes that universal service requirements are essential to promote the well-being of socially and economically vulnerable groups as well as geographical access. Operating as a "minimum set of rights and obligations," they are a derogation from the normal market mechanism.

Where heavily regulated markets are being liberalized, a USO guarantees access to the service at an affordable price and maintenance in quality (and, where necessary, improvement) for every person.

Universal service is compatible with the principle of subsidiarity, i.e., while basic principles can be stipulated at the Community level, implementation can be left to Member States through national regulators with clearly delineated powers and duties. The European Commission (Commission) has highlighted the importance of sanctioning powers in monitoring the enforcement of USOs.

The concept of universal service ensures that general interest requirements such as political, social, economic, and technological developments are factored in. First developed in the context of sectors such as telecommunication, electricity, and postal sectors (before being extended to others like energy), it has allowed public interest requirements such as economic efficiency, technological progress, environmental protection, transparency and accountability, consumer rights and specific measures regarding disability, age or education to be addressed. The Commission has officially acknowledged the role of USOs in reducing disparity in living conditions and opportunities in the Member States.

The concept of USO is relatively vague. Citizens may find it challenging to claim their right of access against a service provider that fails to discharge a USO.

According to the Green Paper on Services of General Interest (2003), Member States can decide that the net costs of the provision of an SGI, including universal service, should be recovered from beneficiaries by means of levies on undertakings. A funding mechanism (like a universal service obligation fund) should ensure that market participants contribute toward financing universal service and not to any other activity. For some services, including telecommunications and postal services, Member States require service provision at a uniform tariff throughout their territory.

United States

In the United States, the term "universal service policy" is most commonly used in the context of the telecommunications sector. They refer to government policies aimed at promoting the affordability of telephone services and network access.

The term first emerged in the context of "dual service" telephone network – contemporary, non-interconnected telephone exchanges in the same community. An alternative to that system, "universal service policy," meant consolidating the competing telephone exchanges into a local monopoly, thereby enabling interconnection telephone connectivity among all users. Universal service did not mean subsidizing telephone penetration or affordability through government policy.

Today, however, the Federal Communications Commission (FCC) describes universal service as the principle that all American citizens should have access to communication services. Universal service is also the name of a fund and the category of FCC programs and policies designed to implement that principle. Moreover, it is described as the cornerstone of the Communications Act of 1934, under which the FCC was established.

The Telecommunications Act of 1996 expanded the scope of the term "universal service" to include access to both telecommunications and advanced services, such as high-speed internet, at just, reasonable, and fair rates. It focused on increasing access to rural areas and for low-income consumers.

The Essential Air Service (EAS) program of the United States Department of Transportation guarantees that small communities that were served by certificated air carriers before airline deregulation maintain a minimal level of scheduled air service.

The United States Postal Service operates under a universal service obligation with respect to the entire population of the United States.

Universal service obligation funds exist for each of those sectors.

Japan

In Japan, universal service is often mentioned in the context of telecommunications and postal services.

Like other countries, various markets categorized as social infrastructure services have been deregulated during and after the 1980s to achieve greater competition and fairness. Such services are important to ensure minimum standards of wholesome and cultured living – as mentioned in the Constitution of Japan. Sectoral regulatory regimes like the Telecommunications Business Law and laws relevant to postal services stipulate that access to such services must be provided at reasonable prices throughout the territory of Japan.

USOs are usually imposed on undertakings that were statutorily approved monopoly companies in their sectors in the period before deregulation. The concept of USOs was first introduced in the regulations when statutorily monopolized sectors were deregulated.

Occasionally, monopoly companies allege that regulatory obligations imposed on them in the period after deregulation are more burdensome than USOs. They contend that those regulatory obligations obstruct them from competing freely and fairly with their competitors. Such disputes actually occur in the telecommunication sector in particular. These days, even basic financial services are sometimes mentioned in the context of universal service. In particular, mergers of local financial institutions in the same prefectures have put a spotlight on the importance of universal service for people residing in the isolated islands.

In this regard, USOs often raise difficult political questions as well as issues from a competition policy perspective.

India

In India, like the United States, the term "universal service" is chiefly used in the context of the telecommunications sector.

The term was introduced about 200 years ago in the postal sector via the Rowland Hill Reforms of 1837.

The Telecom Regulatory Authority Act (TRAI) Act, 1997 states that the TRAI has the duty to ensure the compliance of universal service obligations, i.e., world-class services at affordable prices.

Another sector where such obligations apply is the airline sector. They are intended to increase access to uneconomical routes and regions that witness less air traffic.

In the postal sector, India Post, the national postal system, bears the USO to offer basic postal and financial services to residents in urban, rural, remote, and inaccessible areas.

Funds earmarked for the implementation of USOs exist for each of those sectors.

Bibliography

GALLO, D., *Public Services and EU Competition Law: The Social Market Economy in Action*, Taylor & Francis (2022), Chapter 4

WEHLANDER, C., "Services of General Economic Interest (SGIE) as a Constitutional Concept of EU Law (Series: Legal Issues of Services of General Interest)", *Springer & T.M.C Asser Press* (2016), Chapter 5

ZHU, L., "Services of General Economic Interest (SGIE) in EU Competition Law: Striking a Balance Between Non-economic Values and Market Competition", *Springer & T.M.C Asser Press* (2020) Chapter 5 and Chapter 6

See also

Services of general economic interest

U

UPSTREAM MARKET

J. Nicolás OTEGUI NIETO
Tetra Pak

Definition

Economically speaking, an upstream market is one at a previous stage of the value/production/distribution chain where a given product or service is found. For example, the manufacture of grey cement is the upstream market of the downstream market for the manufacture of ready mixed-concrete. Grey cement, among other raw materials, is one of the materials utilized for the manufacture of ready-mixed concrete. Upstream markets are normally vertically related to downstream markets. In the present example, the product market of grey cement is vertically related to that of ready-mixed concrete, which in turn is also related vertically to other upstream product markets, e.g. aggregates.

Commentary

The economic notion of upstream (and downstream) markets is a very important in competition law. It is one of the economic tools that companies, practitioners, competition authorities and tribunals have to assess whether a proposed acquisition is compatible with the applicable merger control regulation, and / or to assess whether an infraction has occurred (e.g. in certain types of abuse of dominance).

In the merger control realm we can find countless decisions from national competition authorities and the European Commission whereby regulators approve transactions subject to commitments. Most of the commitments offered by merging parties or requested by competition authorities try to address concerns that normally occur in upstream or downstream product markets. In *Veolia/Suez* (case M.9969, 14th December 2021), the European Commission imposed several commitments in relation to several upstream markets to avoid potential foreclosure effects. The economic analysis of the situation of vertically related upstream markets was essential to ascertain whether or not the proposed transaction could hamper competition in the markets related to the treatment, processing, and recollection of various types of waste and or water in France (among many other geographies). In that case, several third parties showed concerns over the proposed transaction when replying to the market test that the European Commission conducted in relation to the product markets related (among others) to the management of non-hazardous and municipal and industrial water activities in France. It can be seen in the text of the decision how the analysis of the upstream markets was of the utmost importance when assessing whether or not the commitments offered by the merging parties addressed the potential issues found in relation to the vertical integration of markets up and downstream.

Moreover, the analysis of the relevant upstream markets in merger cases can also assist competition authorities in determining whether or not two apparently differentiated product markets are part of the same upstream market. In *General Electric/Honeywell* (case M.2220, 3rd July 2001), the European Commission decided to declare the proposed transaction as incompatible with the, by then known, common market and the EEA Agreement. In this case, the analysis of the upstream market helped to understand that two jet engines with very different technical specifications, that were produced to fit into two different aircraft configurations (one for aircraft equipped with two engines and another for aircraft equipped with four engines), were in reality part of the same upstream market given the fact that the demand for those engines was dependent on the demand of the aircraft they were ultimately fit in (ultimately competing against each other). Therefore, the proposed transaction would have entailed the merger of the two main suppliers of jet engines for large regional aircraft (and not for aircraft fitted with two or four engines).

Likewise, competition authorities also use the upstream market analysis to ascertain whether or not a given behavior from a dominant player can configure a type of abuse of dominance. This tool is extremely useful when determining whether or not a dominant firm in the upstream market for raw materials necessary for the production of goods in a given downstream market, abused its position where normally the dominant upstream undertaking also competes with its customers. These types of cases were numerous in the pharmaceutical industry where some patent holders of active molecules compete with their customers in the production of a given medication downstream. Another good example can be found in cases where a vertically integrated dominant firm holds an essential facility necessary for its customers to compete downstream with the integrated firm. Examples of the latter include cases related to train or port services, where a dominant vertically integrated firm controls a port or maintenance warehouses that are indispensable for its downstream customers/competitors.

In *Commercial Solvents v Commission* (1974) the Court of Justice made it clear that when a vertically integrated dominant undertaking playing in both the upstream and downstream markets refuses to supply a raw material essential for its customers/competitors, putting them on the verge of elimination from the downstream market, this is an abuse of dominance in the shape of a refusal to supply. In the case at hand Commercial Solvents produced and sold several chemical compounds (upstream market) that could be refined into the basic element needed to produce several anti-tuberculosis medicaments (downstream market). After a chance of control in the upstream supplier, the company decided to start developing the same medicaments that its customers produced and sold in the downstream market. When the competing drug was developed and received governmental approval to be sold, the upstream company canceled the contract whereby it undertook to supply these chemical compounds to its main customer/competitor. The latter found that it was impossible to procure these chemical compounds in the upstream market from another producer since the upstream company held at that point in time the worldwide monopoly on those compounds. The European Commission (at that point in time the Commission of the European Communities) decided to impose a sanction on the upstream company, stating that this was an abuse of a dominant position, this decision was upheld by the Court of Justice of the European Communities (today the Court of Justice of the European Union).

As we can infer, the economic concept of upstream (and also downstream) market plays a very important role in competition law. It helps in defining the playing field for behavioral conduct and assessing whether or not conduct is an abuse of dominance.

Likewise, in the realm of merger control, this is a fundamental tool of analysis for competition authorities to ascertain whether a given transaction would be compatible with the current regulatory framework, or whether the resulting merged entity could hamper competition in the affected markets downstream. It also guides merging parties in the process of determining which remedies appropriately address the concerns raised by national competition authorities and or the European Commission in order to obtain clearance with commitments.

Bibliography

Bailey, D. and Rose, V. (eds.), *Bellamy and Child: European Union Law of Competition* (7th edn. Oxford University Press 2013), Chapter 10

Levy, N. and Cook, C., *European Merger Control Law: A Guide to the Merger Regulation* (2015 release, Lexis Nexis), Volume I, Chapter 8

See also

Downstream market

V

VARIABLE COSTS

Jaime BARAHONA
Court for the Defense of Free Competition

Definition

Variable Costs refers to the value of the economic costs of a company strictly related to production which vary with the magnitude of output. The concept of economic costs is conceived in relation to efficient production, that is, incurring in minimum possible cost or expenditure.

Commentary

A first aspect that has to be commented is that when referring to costs, from an economic perspective, it is differentiated from the accounting one. The economic costs are not necessarily the sum of expenditures made by a company, which in the event that it is inefficient, may exceed those necessary to carry out production. Economic costs can be referred to the minimum expenditures necessary to carry out the business or economic activity of the company.

It is most relevant, specially from a competition law stance, to understand that any concept of cost must be conceived in relation to efficient production or performance, that is, incurring the minimum possible cost. The Variable Cost refers to that part of the cost that is strictly related to production. The contrast, naturally, is that the company may incur in costs that are not necessarily linked to production, which may occur during a period of time in which the company has technical or contractual limitations to adjust. These fixed costs are incurred in a lump in order for any output to be provided and do not vary with changes in the magnitude of the production level. Thus, the Variable Cost, as a distinctive part of the total cost of a company, is a concept that acquires relevance only in a period in which the firm does not have the capacity to adjust completely and that we call short term. In the long run, all costs may be conceived as variable. This leads to consider that another way to define Variable Costs is any cost that is not fixed. An item of cost is not fixed or variable by nature. It must be determined, therefore, whether, in the course of analysis of a defendant firm´s cost structure, a specific value does or not vary according to the quantities produced.

For the purpose of competition law analysis and ultimately for the proper adjudication of cases, the Variable Cost definition has been most relevant mainly for the assessment of predation and also exclusionary conduct when assessed by means of below cost pricing theories (volume discounts or rebates, leading to exclusivity).

In this regard, the Average Variable Cost (AVC), defined as the Variable Cost per unit of product, has been conceived as a fundamental variable in antitrust practice for the attribution of predatory prices, made explicit in an article by Areeda and Turner (1975) when explaining the price-cost test that is appropriate to determine when there is a below cost pricing strategy that may be predatory. Although in that same work the authors indicate that it is the comparison with the marginal cost that should conceptually dominate any idea of AVC to determine when a price can be predatory, Baumol (1996) has argued that what is conceptually correct is the focus on the AVC. Although using the AVC, for practical and conceptual advantage, has been regarded as the most pertinent form of measurement of this variable, there is still discussion mainly in litigation before the courts on the proper value to be compared.

A corollary of the distinction between variable and fixed costs is that a company that decides to stop producing at a certain moment, will only be able to avoid or finish incurring its variable costs, those associated with production, but it will not be able to do so with fixed costs. Another corollary, which is directly associated with Areeda and Turner's contribution, is that if a firm faces a price that is higher than its AVC, even in the event that this price is lower than its average total cost (which includes the fixed-cost component), the company has incentives to continue producing than to stop. Consequently, only when a company faces a price that is lower than its AVC, then the incentives would lead not to pursue its activity and stop production.

These last comments requires us to introduce a case that depicts the price-cost analysis that has been done in the EU system: Akzo Chemie BV (1991). The Court confirmed that predatory pricing was caught by then Article 82 TFEU [current Article 102] and provided two tests to deem prices as predatory. First, a presumption of a "predatory intent" when it is found that a firm had priced below average variable cost. According to the tribunal, such a firm "has no interest in applying such prices except that of eliminating competitors so as to enable it to subsequently raise its prices by taking advantage of its monopolistic position…". The second test provided by the Court consisted of regarding prices as abusive when they are below average total costs but above average variable costs, insofar they are deemed as part of a plan for eliminating a competitor.

Other cases and findings related to predatory pricing that required cost analysis include Tetra Pak (1996) and the Post Danmark cases (2012, 2015). In Post Danmark I the ECJ held that the efficient competitor test is a required element of the test for predation and that the use of incremental costs instead of AVC was a more suitable strategy. In Post Danmark II, the Court held that pricing below average total costs but above AVC is in itself not a violation. Lately, a thorough analysis related to cost analysis can also be found in Qualcomm [2019].

Turning to the U.S. legal system, the applicable cost test for predation was put to analysis in the Brooke Group case (1993). The Supreme Court provided an analytical framework and held that a plaintiff must prove the alleged predator's prices were "below an appropriate measure of its rival's costs" and that the suspected predator had a dangerous probability of recouping its investment in below-cost prices.

Finally, there is a leading case that cannot be excluded in this commentary: the American Airlines case brought forward after implementing a price strategy against low-cost carriers in the Dallas-Fort Worth airport hub (U.S. v. AMR). The judge ruled that the Department of Justice should have compared American Airlines' price against route-wide AVC and an accusation of "sacrifice" of profit (behavior that would be irrational without its exclusionary effect) was not sufficient.

Bibliography

Areeda, P. and Turner, D., Predatory Pricing and Related Practices under Section 2 of the Sherman Act, 88 *Harv. L. Rev.* 637 (1975)

Baumol, W. J., "Predation and the Logic of the Average Variable Cost Test." *The Journal of Law & Economics* 39, no. 1 (1996): 49–72

De La Mano, M., Durand, B., A Three-Step Structured Rule of Reason to Assess Predation under Article 82, 12 December 2005, DG Competition - European Commission, Office of the Chief Economist, Discussion Paper

See also

Economic analysis, Economic efficiency, Economies of scale, Marginal costs

V

VERTICAL AGREEMENT

Amber DARR
University of Manchester

■ Definition

A vertical agreement is an agreement or arrangement between two or more undertakings operating at different levels of the production or distribution chain and producing complementary, rather than competing, products or services. Such an agreement may be entered into, for example, between the manufacturer of a component and the producer of a product that uses that component, or between a producer and its distributors. Vertical agreements stipulate the conditions under which undertakings at different levels of the production and distribution chain may buy or sell goods or services.

■ Commentary

Mature competition regimes, leading amongst them the European (EU) and United States (U.S.) regimes, evaluate vertical agreements, on the touchstone of their impact on economic efficiency and consumer welfare. These regimes recognise that most vertical agreements aim to improve distribution and reduce prices for consumers and are, therefore, pro-competitive. These regimes also appreciate that vertical agreements need to be examined more carefully when one or both parties to the agreement enjoy a degree of market power.

Under the EU regime, vertical agreements, like their horizontal counterparts, are assessed under Article 101 of the Treaty on the Functioning of Europe (the TFEU). Where Article 101(1) is infringed the agreement will be unlawful unless it is exempt under the Vertical Block Exemption Regulation (the VBER) or otherwise meets the requirements of Article 101(3) on an individual basis. The VBER, first issued by the EU Commission in 1999 and revised in 2010 and, most recently in 2022, stipulate that vertical agreements are exempt from the operation of Article 101 unless the individual market share of parties to the agreements exceeds 30% or if the agreements contain a "hardcore restriction" (Article 4) or any excluded restriction that cannot be severed from the agreement (Article 5).

It is important to note that a vertical agreement that contains a hardcore restriction is not automatically restrictive "by object" and may in theory, avail of the benefit of Article 101(3). This, in turn, means that it is not only necessary for the EU Commission to examine agreements containing hardcore restrictions on a case-by-case basis under Article 101(1) but also to consider whether they satisfy the four conditions of Article 101(3) no matter how unlikely or rare that may be in practice. For instance, although EU courts have historically recognised the hardcore restrictions of absolute territorial restrictions (ATP) and resale price maintenance (RPM) to be by their very nature injurious to competition, the 2023 judgment of the Court of Justice of the European Union (CJEU) in Super Bock has clarified that mere finding that an agreement contains a hardcore restriction such as RPM does not automatically mean that it is prohibited under Article 101(1) unless it satisfies the "by object" test laid down in Cartes Bancaires. The CJEU further clarified that the anticompetiitve object of the agreement needs to be demonstrated by considering the formal agreement and its purpose as well as its economic and legal context. If this test is not met, the agreement may still be anti-competitive based on its effects on competition.

The U.S. antitrust regime evaluates vertical agreements primarily under section 1 of the Sherman Act 1890 which is also the provision it invokes for the assessment of horizontal agreements. Although the U.S. courts had initially adopted a formalistic approach towards vertical agreements, they now increasingly rely on economic theory to argue for the procompetitive effects of even the most egregious vertical restraints including ATP and RPM. This is evident from the decisions of the U.S. Supreme Court in Continental TV, Inc v GTE Sylvania, Inc. in which it overruled earlier decisions to hold that ATP provisions were to be tested by the rule of reason, and Leegin Creative Leather Products Inc v PSKS, Inc, in which it clarified that RPM provisions caused anticompetitive harm only if either party possessed market power.

This shift from treating certain vertical agreements as per se illegal to evaluating them under the rule of reason means that the U.S. antitrust authorities consider even the most egregious vertical restraints to have presumptive legality which needs to be successfully rebutted by the claimant for the agreements to be declared illegal. Therefore, claimants challenging vertical restraints in the U.S. must first establish their actual or likely anticompetitive effects before the defendant may be required to justify them. After hearing both sides, the U.S. antitrust authorities weigh the anticompetitive harms of such agreements against their procompetitive benefits (especially where they consider these restraints to be reasonably necessary to achieve these benefits) and where the benefits outweigh the harms, the U.S. antitrust authorities may hold the vertical agreements to be lawful.

In recent years the UK competition regime appears also to have moved towards a more economic approach in addressing hardcore restrictions. Until 2005, the UK government had excluded all vertical restraints (other than RPM) from the ambit of Chapter 1 of the UK Competition Act 1998 which is largely modelled on Article 101 TFEU, after which, however, the UK Competition and Markets Authority (CMA) largely followed the EU approach towards these agreements. In 2022 when the CMA was fully focused on enforcing the UK Competition Act, it issued the Vertical Agreements Block Exemption Order (VABEO) just as the EU was also moving towards the new VBER. While the scheme of the VABEO is broadly similar to that of the VBER, para 8.8 of the VABEO Guidance allows for a consideration of the procompetitive effects of hardcore restrictions and para 8.21 offers examples of circumstnances in which RPM may be justified. The CMA's approach towards hardcore restrictions though more permissive than that of the EU, still falls short of the approach prevalent in the U.S.

The move towards examining procompetitive effects of even hardcore restrictions in vertical agreements now becoming more evident in the mature competition regimes of the EU and the UK, had already existed in emerging competition regimes perhaps due to the training and support provided by U.S. authorities. In India, for instance, all vertical agreements irrespective of the nature of restraints they contain, are addressed under section 3(4) of the Indian Competition Act 2002 (as amended in 2023), in terms of which it is incumbent upon the Competition Commission of India (CCI) to establish (rather than presume), with reference to factors listed in section 19(3), whether the agreement causes or is likely to cause "an appreciable adverse effect on competition in India". In practice, the CCI has not only considered the procompetitive effects of hardcore restrictions such as RPM, but also in cases such as Ghanshyam Dass Vij v. Bajaj Corp Limited and others (2013) and Jasper Infotech Pvt Limtied v. Kaff Appliances (India) Pvt. Ltd (2014) has concluded that vertical agreements containing RPM clauses did not have an appreciable adverse effect on competition in India.

The variation amongst them notwithstanding, the approaches towards vertical agreements discussed here these have all been informed by the underlying principle of consumer welfare, interpreted, particularly in the U.S. context, as the price offered to end consumers. Recently, however, in suing pesticide giants Syngenta and Corteva for paying their distributors to exclude the more affordable generic options for essential farming products, the U.S. Federal Trade Commission (FTC) appears to have expanded the scope of consumer to include the intermediate consumer and to consider welfare beyond the narrow confines of the neoclassical price theory, and even more importantly to have revived an interest in vertical agreements. In this matter which is likely to proceed to trial after in January 2024 Syngenta and Corteva lost a motion to dismiss the FTC's complaint the FTC argues that by introducing illegal Pay-to-Block Schemes in their agreemetns with their distributors these companies inflate prices for farmers (the intermediate consumers) which, in turn, raises prices for end consumers and suppresses competition and innovation in the pesticide market. It remains to be seen whether the FTC's move will resonate with the competition regimes particularly of emerging economies that are characterised by small farmers, input providers or component manufacturers and will motivate them to address a wider range of vertical restraints especially if these have only an indirect affect on the price offered to end consumers.

Bibliography

De La Mano, M. and Jones, A., "Vertical agreements under EU competition law: proposals for pushing Article 101 analysis, and the modernization process, to a logical conclusion" in Healey, Jacobs, Smith eds *Research Handbook on Methods and Models of Competition Law* (Edward Elgar Publishing 2020)

Gerber, D. J., *Gerber Competition Law and Antitrust: A Global Guide* (Oxford University Press 2020), Chapter 5

Jones, A., Sufrin, B. and Dunne, N., *Jones and Sufrin's EU Competition Law: Text, Cases, and Materials* (8th edn, Oxford University Press 2023), Chapter 11

Jones, A., "Vertical Agreements" in Rodger, Whelan, and MacCulloch eds *The UK Competition Regime* (Oxford University Press 2021)

Sokol, D. D., "The Transformation of Vertical Restraints: Per se illegality, the rule of reason, and per se illegality" *Antitrust Law Journal*, 2014, Vol. 79, No. 3 (2014), pp. 1003-1016

See also

Absolute territorial protection, Exclusive purchasing agreement, Exclusive distribution, Selective distribution, Vertical restraints (or restrictions)

V

VERTICAL RESTRAINTS (OR RESTRICTIONS)

Sandra MARCO COLINO
The Chinese University of Hong Kong

■ Definition

The term vertical restraints refers to the restrictions of competition contained in vertical agreements. These agreements take place between firms operating at different levels of the production or distribution chain. The most common vertical restraints relate to the supply, distribution, production, purchase and sale of goods; however vertical restraints will also be found in the services sector. Typical vertical restraints concern the number of buyers a seller will trade with within a specified territory, the suppliers a buyer is allowed to purchase from, and the conditions (price, location, customers) under which the goods can be resold.

■ Commentary

The extent to which vertical restraints may be anticompetitive is a highly-debated matter. In many instances the restrictions in a vertical agreement are justifiable: indeed they may be pro-competitive. For example when a distributor is required to invest in stocking, promoting and advertising a particular brand of goods, it will likely seek protection from "free-riders" who could profit from the expense incurred by the distributor by selling the same product for less. In principle the distributor could be protected from the free rider by a grant of exclusivity over a specific territory or customer group, or by the imposition of minimum resale prices.

An advantage of these restraints is that, in the absence of market power, they may boost inter-brand competition (for example, between a Canon printer and a HP printer), even though intra-brand competition (between providers of the same Canon printer) might be lessened. The Chicago School of economics generally sees these restrictions as efficient. Nonetheless, their efficiency is not always guaranteed. For instance, if consumers do not benefit from the additional advertising costs, because they are already familiar with the product, they might prefer to pay less and skip the promotional expenses.

While even exclusive dealers will not have control over price if providers of competing goods from other brands cover the same market, concerns arise in situations where market power exists and there is little or no price competition. The most controversial restriction is minimum resale price maintenance (RPM), where sellers impose a price below which their buyers are not allowed to re-sell. In addition to having a direct impact on consumer prices, it may also help implement a price-fixing cartel. Competition authorities tend to take a strict line on RPM, and many examples of fines for this practice can be found. In 2018 four electronics manufacturers were recently fined by the European Commission for imposing minimum prices on their online retailers (Commission decisions *Asus, Denon & Marantz*, and *Pioneer*, 2018).

In the EU, the Court of Justice has confirmed that vertical restraints might fall foul of Article 101(1) of the Treaty on the Functioning of the European Union (TFEU) (*Consten and Grundig*, 1996). While in most cases an effects analysis is required to determine whether vertical restraints have an anti-competitive impact on competition, certain restrictions are considered to be anti-competitive "by object", examples being minimum RPM and provisions that confer absolute territorial protection on a distributor. The inclusion of the latter in the "by object" category is because of the threat territorial restraints pose for single market integration, the main goal of the TFEU.

The basic EU rules are contained in the block exemption regulation for vertical agreements (the "VBER"), Regulation 2022/720 which entered into force on 1 June 2022 and replaced Regulation 330/2010. For the block exemption to apply, the market share of each of the parties to the agreement must not exceed 30%. Moreover, agreements must not contain what are referred to as "hardcore restrictions": these are set out in Article 4 of the VBER and include minimum RPM; territorial restrictions (although it is possible, under certain circumstances, to prohibit active sales outside the buyers' allotted territories, and to prevent wholesalers from selling to end customers); restrictions of cross-supplies in selective distribution systems; and restrictions on the sale of components (suppliers of these should be allowed to sell to end users, repairers and other service providers). If a vertical agreement does not meet the conditions of the VBER, and falls within the scope of Article 101(1) TFEU, then it must comply with the requirements of the legal exception contained in Article 101(3) TFEU to be lawful. The VBER is accompanied by *Guidelines on vertical restraints* which were published on the Official Journal of the European Union on 30 June 2022. These extensive guidelines (and the VBER itself) reflect adaptations required to the rules on vertical restraints to accommodate the widespread digitalisation of markets in recent years and the crucial role of e-commerce in the modern economy.

In 1911 the U.S. Supreme Court confirmed that contracts between non-competitors could fall within the scope of Section 1 of the Sherman Act (*Dr Miles*). Certain restrictions, such as exclusive dealing or RPM, were considered per se illegal. Over the years, the analysis shifted, spurred principally by the acceptance of the postulates of the Chicago School of economics. In 1977, the case *GTE Sylvania* introduced a reasonableness test for non-price territorial restraints. Twenty years later, maximum RPM was placed under the rule of reason analysis following *Khan*. The landmark *Leegin*case did the same for minimum RPM in 2007, proclaiming that "[v]ertical price restraints are to be judged according to the rule of reason." However, the laws of some U.S. states still consider minimum RPM to be per se illegal. While the reasonableness assessment does not equate to per se legality, it has become remarkably difficult for plaintiffs to win cases in which the lawfulness of vertical restraints is in dispute.

In the People's Republic of China, the Anti-Monopoly Law (AML) expressly prohibits agreements that "[fix] the price of commodities for resale to a third party", or "[restrict] the minimum price of commodities for resale to a third party" (Article 14). However, Article 15 AML contains a significant list of broadly construed exemptions. Originally, the approach towards minimum RPM was somewhat incoherent. The administrative agencies – the State Administration for Market Regulation (SAMR) and its predecessors, as well as some regional watchdogs – treated minimum RPM as illegal unless it fell within one of the exemptions of the AML (*Kweichow Maotai*, or *Wuliangye*). The courts however appeared to apply a rule of reason-style analysis before coming to a conclusion as to their compatibility with Article 14 (*Johnson & Johnson*, 2013, and *Gree*, 2018). In 2019, the Supreme People's Court finally confirmed that these restrictions should generally be regarded as illegal, provided the exemptions of the law do not apply (*Yutai*). The parties may however show that the practice bore no anticompetitive effects and escape illegality. The amendments to the Anti-Monopoly Law that entered into force in August 2022 largely follow the *Yutai* approach.

Bibliography

COMANOR, W. S., "Vertical Price-Fixing, Vertical Market Restrictions, and the New Antitrust Policy" (1985) 98 *Harvard Law Review* 983

KAPLOW, L., "The Meaning of Vertical Agreement and the Structure of Competition Law" (2016) 80 *Antitrust Law Journal* 563

LAO, M., "Free Riding: An Overstated, and Unconvincing, Explanation for Resale Price Maintenance", in Robert Pitofsky (ed.), *How the Chicago School Overshot the Mark: The Effect of Conservative Economic Analysis on U.S. Antitrust* (Oxford University Press 2008) 199

MARCO COLINO, S., Building a Coherent Legal Framework for Vertical Price Restrictions in China, *Competition Policy International*, 30 September 2022

MARCO COLINO, S., *Competition Law of the EU and UK* (8th edn, Oxford University Press 2019), chapters 8, 9 and 10

MARCO COLINO, S., *Vertical Agreements and Competition Law: A Comparative Study* (Hart 2010 - new edition expected in 2023)

See also

Absolute territorial protection, Exclusive distribution, Exclusive purchasing agreement, Resale Price Maintenance (RPM), Selective distribution, Vertical agreement, White clause

W

WHITE CLAUSE

Or BROOK
University of Leeds

Definition

White clauses are provisions listed in a block exemption regulation (BER), declaring that certain contractual clauses enjoy a safe haven. Such clauses are presumed to be permissible forms of cooperation under Article 101 TFEU, either because they do not restrict competition in the meaning of Article 101(1) or because they satisfy the conditions for an exemption under Article 101(3). While white clauses used to be an inherent component of the EU's BERs, they were criticised as overly formalistic and unduly favouring certain forms of cooperation. The new generation of effects-based BERs adopted since the late-1990s, no longer include white clauses.

Commentary

BERs were originally introduced to EU competition law in the 1960s to tackle the Commission's administrative burden of responding to notifications under the old enforcement regime of Regulation 17/62. BERs allowed the Commission to automatically discharge certain categories of agreements from the prohibition of Article 101 TFEU, without engaging in a detailed case-by-case analysis.

The inclusion of a list of white clauses in the old generation of BERs (also known as the list of "permitted practices") helped the Commission to achieve this aim. Such lists detailed the types of provisions that could be included in an agreement without infringing Article 101 TFEU. They did not only include restrictions that were presumed to fulfil the conditions of Article 101(3) TFEU, but also restrictions that do not normally restrict competition in the meaning of Article 101(1) TFEU (Italy v Commission, 405-406). When an agreement was notified to the Commission, therefore, the analysis essentially consisted of a "pigeon-holing" exercise; verifying that the agreement only contained white clauses and did not include provisions from the "grey" or "black" list of hardcore restrictions.

That design facilitated a formalistic competition law analysis. In particular, the safe haven of the white clauses applied irrespective to the market power held by the undertakings. When an agreement was found to contain only white clauses, the Commission was not required to define the relevant market or calculate the market share held by the undertakings. Carrying significant administrative benefits, such a formalistic approach eased the burden of notification and provided undertakings with strong legal certainty as to the validity of their agreements.

Considerations of administrative efficiency have also justified a rigid interpretation of the list of white clauses. Undertakings had very little wiggle room to decide how to design their agreements. Even if a single term fell outside the list of white clauses due to trivial or technical details, the agreement would not enjoy the safe haven of the BER (Delimitis, para 34-42). Similarly, when faced with doubts as to the scope of protected practices, the Commission called to rely on the "system and aims" pursued by the BERs. A flexible interpretation of their terms, according to the Commission, "would not be justified in an effort to avoid anticipated difficulties of a practical nature, i.e., a large number of notifications" (Commission's competition annual report of 1991, 89).

Alongside these administrative benefits, the list of white clauses had the effect of influencing business relationships and shaping the EU's industrial policy. The possibility of enjoying an automatic group exemption encouraged undertakings to draft – or modify – their agreements to comply with the list of white clauses. Indeed, the Council's Enabling Regulations, which entrusts the Commission to adopt BERs, explicitly declare that "it is desirable" that the Commission would use BERs to exempt agreements "if they are modified in such manner as to fall within a category defined in an exempting regulation" (see the Preamble of the Enabling Council Regulation 19/65 on Vertical Agreements; Enabling Council Regulation 2821/71 on Standardisation, R&D and Specialisation agreements; and Enabling Council Regulation 1534/91 on Insurance).

The power to influence the design of commercial transactions contributed to furthering the integration of the single market. BERs have functioned as a tool to harmonise the design of agreements across the common market, going beyond their original administrative purpose (Sufrin, 931). This reason too, was invoked by the Commission in support of the formalistic approach of the BERs up until the mid-1990s (see, for example, Commission's competition annual report of 1987, 33; annual report of 1990, 44 49; annual report of 1991, 93; annual report of 1992, 163).

In parallel, the number of white clauses in each BER has grown substantially, reaching a peak in Regulation 240/96 on Technology Transfer Agreements of 1996 (Goyder, 142). This trend left undertakings more freedom to devise their agreements.

Towards the turn of the millennium, there was a growing feeling of unease about the implications of white clauses. Pointing to the "straitjacket effect" of the BERs, commentators warned that the list of white clauses – and the formalistic analysis they facilitated – have obliged undertakings to artificially alter their agreements to comply with the permitted forms in a manner that benefitted neither themselves nor their consumers. This, in turn, carried the risk of the undue stifling of innovation across the EU and deterring undertakings from concluding pro-competitive agreements just because they were not specifically mentioned in the list of white clauses (Korah, Hawk).

Accepting this line of criticism, Regulation 2970/1999 on Vertical Restraints of 1999 – and the BERs adopted subsequently – abolished the category of white clauses. Under the new generation of BERs, all practices that are not explicitly excluded by the list of hardcore restrictions are exempted, as long as the market share held by the undertakings does not exceed a certain threshold. Shifting to an effects-based approach to the BERs, undertakings are expected to have more flexibility to tailor their agreements according to their commercial needs.

Replacing the old lists of white clauses with a market share threshold, nevertheless, bears a price in terms of legal certainty. While the new generation of BERs are clearly more in tune with an effects-based approach to competition law and policy, they require undertakings to define the relevant market and estimate their market shares. Somewhat paradoxically, just as EU competition law shifted to the self-assessment regime of Regulation 1/2003, the application of the BERs has become less certain.

Bibliography

Albors-Llorens, A. and Goyder, J., *Goyder's EC Competition Law* (5th edn, Oxford University Press 2009), chapter 5

Brook, O., *Non-Competition Interests in EU Antitrust Law: An Empirical Study of Article 101 TFEU* (Cambridge University Press 2022), chapter 4

Hawk, B. E., "System Failure: Vertical Restraints and EC Competition Law" (1995) 32 *Common Market L. Rev.* 973

Korah, V., "The Future of Vertical Agreements under EC Competition Law (1998) 19 *European Competition Law Review* 8

Sufrin, B., "The evolution of Article 81 (3) of the EC Treaty" (2006) 51(4) *The Antitrust Bulletin* 915, at 930-933

See also

Block exemption (Regulation), Hardcore restrictions, Vertical restraints (or restrictions)

WITHDRAWAL (OF THE BENEFIT OF A BLOCK EXEMPTION)

Kristian HELGE STRATON-ANDERSEN
Gorrissen Federspiel

Definition

Withdrawal of a block exemption refers to the disapplication of the exemption in individual instances, specifically targeting an agreement, decision, or concerted practice by one or more undertakings. This is distinct from the non-application of the block exemption, which affects all undertakings within the relevant market, or the complete repeal or amendment of the block exemption. Withdrawal has legal implications solely for the designated parties and their existing agreements going forward as of the time of the decision.

Commentary

Within the EU, block exemption regulations are Community acts adopted by the Commission and/or the Council that produce effects erga omnes. Agreements, decisions, or concerted practices benefiting from a block exemption are presumed to satisfy the conditions for an individual exemption under Article 101(3) TFEU. Specific agreements, decisions, or concerted practices may nonetheless have effects that are anti-competitive and do not meet the conditions for an individual exemption. Regulation 1/2003 empowers the Commission, and in some instances, a National Competition Authority (NCA), to withdraw the benefit of a block exemption in individual cases. Previously, withdrawal was specifically provided for in each block exemption, but now it follows from Article 29 of Regulation 1/2003. The competition authority in question is responsible for demonstrating to the requisite legal standard that the agreement, decision, or concerted practice infringes Article 101(1) TFEU and does not satisfy the conditions of Article 101(3) TFEU.

The Commission may, acting on its own initiative or in response to a complaint, withdraw the benefit of a block exemption when it finds, in a particular case, that an agreement, decision, or concerted practice has effects that are incompatible with Article 101(3) TFEU (see article 29(1) of Regulation 1/2003). Since the withdrawal of a block exemption is an exclusive prerogative of the Commission, if it receives a complaint, it is obliged to adopt a formal decision either withdrawing the exemption or rejecting the complaint (Automec, paragraph 75).

An NCA may withdraw the benefit of a block exemption for the territory of the member state when it finds, in a particular case, that an agreement, decision, or concerted practice has effects that are incompatible with Article 101(3) TFEU, and the relevant market is no broader than the territory of the member state in question (see article 29(2) of Regulation 1/2003). If the relevant market is broader, only the Commission will have jurisdiction. The withdrawal is subject to national procedural rules; however, according to Article 11(4) of Regulation 1/2003, no later than 30 days before adopting such a decision, the NCA must inform the Commission. Before Regulation 1/2003, NCAs had withdrawal powers only in respect of vertical agreements (see Article 1(4) of Council Regulation (EC) 1215/1999). The courts of the Member States have no power to withdraw the benefit of block exemption regulations unless they have been designated as a competition authority pursuant to Article 35(1) of Regulation 1/2003, and act in that capacity.

Each block exemption, along with its associated guidelines, provides non-exhaustive examples of situations that might warrant withdrawal, where the legal standard is always that of Article 101(3) TFEU. In the Research and Development block exemption, withdrawal is notably warranted when the agreement restricts third-party R&D or market access, the parties do not exploit the results, there is limited effective competition, or the agreement substantially restricts innovation (see Article 10(2) of Commission Regulation (EU) 2023/1066). In the Specialisation block exemption, withdrawal is particularly warranted in instances of weak competition and high concentration concerning the individual market share of third parties, links between third parties due to parallel specialisation agreements, and links with third parties (see Article 6(2) of Commission Regulation (EU) 2023/1067).

The Technology Transfer block exemption prompts withdrawal, especially in scenarios of reduced innovation incentives and hindered market access, for example, due to the cumulative effect of parallel networks of agreements (see Recital 17 and Article 6(1) of Commission Regulation (EU) No 316/2014). The Vertical block exemption regulation triggers withdrawal considerations for highly concentrated markets, especially in online intermediation services, due to parallel networks of agreements (see Article 6(1) of Commission Regulation (EU) 2022/720). Lastly, the Motor Vehicle block exemption indicates withdrawal circumstances, notably when there are cumulative effects of vertical agreements, including single branding obligations and minimum purchasing obligations (see paragraphs 35 and 37 of the 2023 supplementary guidelines).

Decisions to withdraw the benefit of a block exemption only have effects ex nunc, meaning that agreements, decisions, or concerted practices will be exempt until the date the withdrawal becomes effective. The decision applies only to its addressees and the specifically identified agreement, decision, or concerted practice. Denying certain undertakings the benefit of a block exemption for future dealings contradicts the principle of equal treatment (see Langnese-Iglo, paragraphs 208-209, and on appeal paragraph 74; Scholler, paragraphs 162-163). The latter is now possible via a decision of non-application of the block exemption (see further the individual block exemption).

Withdrawals by the European Commission remain rare. It happened in Langnese-Iglo (Regulation 1984/83 concerning exclusive purchasing agreements). In Eco System/Peugeot (Regulation 123/85 concerning motor vehicles), withdrawal would automatically take place if the parties did not terminate the infringement within the deadline. In Tetra Pak I (Regulation 2349/84 concerning patent licensing agreements), the Commission had threatened to withdraw the protection if the company did not, which it did, amend its agreement.

Bibliography

Ortiz Blanco, L. (ed.), *EU Competition Procedure* (4th edn., Oxford University Press 2022), Chapter 14

Tuytschaever, F. and Wijckmans, F., *Vertical Agreements in EU Competition Law* (3rd edn, Oxford University Press 2018), Chapter 2

See also

Block exemption (regulation)

TABLE OF CONTENTS

THE EDITORS

Deborah **HEALEY**

Deborah Healey is a Professor at UNSW Law and a Director ot the Herbert Smith Freehills China International Business and Economic Law Centre. She is also a member of the Centre for Law, Markets and Regulation. Her research and teaching focus on competition law and policy in Australia, China, Hong Kong and the ASEAN nations and she has written widely in them over a long period of time. She is a regular visitor to those jurisdictions to research and teach. Within the area of competition law, she is particularly interested in the role of government in the market, both in Australia and internationally; merger regulation; competition in banking and finance; and the digital economy. Deborah has undertaken substantial research in the development of the Anti-Monopoly Law of China against the background of its political economy and has written widely alone and with Chinese co-authors and in material translated into Chinese. She has consulted with, and completed research projects for, UNCTAD, OECD and ASEAN, She is a Non-Government Adviser to the International Competition Network and a member of the Law Council of Australia Competition Law Committee.

Richard **WHISH**

Richard Whish is Emeritus Professor of Law at King's College London; in 2014 he was appointed QC Honoris Causa. He was a non-executive director of the Office of Fair Trading in the UK from 2003 to 2009, and a non-executive director of the Singaporean Energy Markets Authority from 2005 to 2011. He is the co-author, with David Bailey, of Competition Law, 9th edition 2018 (OUP), and the author of many other books, articles, case-notes and book reviews on various aspects of international competition law and policy. *In order to honor Richard Whish, Concurrences has published a Liber Amicorum Tribute, Richard Whish KC (Hon): Taking Competition Law outside the Box.*

William E. **KOVACIC**

Before joining George Washington University Law School in 1999, Professor Kovacic was the George Mason University Foundation Professor at the George Mason University School of Law. From January 2006 to October 2011, he was a member of the Federal Trade Commission and chaired the agency from March 2008 to March 2009. He was the FTC's General Counsel from June 2001 to December 2004. In 2011 he received the FTC's Miles W. Kirkpatrick Award for Lifetime Achievement. From August 2013 to March 2022, Professor Kovacic served as a Non-Executive Director with the United Kingdom's Competition and Markets Authority. From January 2009 to September 2011, he was Vice-Chair for Outreach for the International Competition Network. At GW, Professor Kovacic has taught antitrust, contracts, and government contracts. He is co-editor (with Ariel Ezrachi) of the Journal of Antitrust Enforcement. Professor Kovacic graduated with a bachelor's degree from Princeton University in 1974, and received his J.D. from Columbia Law School in 1978 where he was a Harlan Fiske Stone Scholar. In order to honor William E. Kovacic, Concurrences has published a Liber Amicorum Tribute, William E. Kovacic: An Antitrust Tribute (Vol. I & II).

Pablo **TREVISÁN**

Pablo Trevisán is a lawyer, founder of the IDC – Instituto de Derecho de la Competencia, and partner at Estudio Trevisán Abogados SC. He was the main drafter of the Argentina Competition Act 27,442, enacted in 2018. Between 2015-20, he was a Commissioner at the CNDC – Comisión Nacional de Defensa de la Competencia (Argentina). He holds a Master of Laws (LLM) from the LSE – London School of Economics & Political Science (UK), has been Visiting Research Fellow at Fordham School of Law (US), and completed a PhD in Law at UCA – Pontificia Universidad Católica Argentina "Santa María de los Buenos Aires" (Argentina), where his thesis (pending) is on "Private Enforcement and Damages Actions in Competition Law". He is a Member of the Institute for Consumer Antitrust Studies' International Advisory Board (US), and has chaired the Competition Commission of the Colegio de Abogados de la Ciudad de Buenos Aires (2012-17). In the past, he was General Counsel at a bank. He is speaker, author and professor, covering the topics of his expertise at UCA, Universidad AUSTRAL, Universidad Torcuato Di Tella (UTDT), UCEMA, CEDEF, ESEADE, Fordham (US), Loyola (US), LSE (UK), and other institutions.

e-Competitions

Antitrust Case Laws e-Bulletin

e-Competitions Bulletin

CASE LAW DATABASE

e-Competitions is the only online resource that provides consistent coverage of antitrust cases from 85 jurisdictions, organized into a searchable database structure. e-Competitions concentrates on cases summaries taking into account that in the context of a continuing growing number of sources there is a need for factual information, i.e., case law.

- 26,000 case summaries
- 4,000 authors
- 85 countries covered
- 30,000 subscribers

SOPHISTICATED EDITORIAL AND IT ENRICHMENT

e-Competitions is structured as a database. The editors make a sophisticated technical and legal work on all articles by tagging these with key words, drafting abstracts and writing html code to increase Google ranking. There is a team of antitrust lawyers – PhD and judges clerks – and a team of IT experts. e-Competitions makes comparative law possible. Thanks to this expert editorial work, it is possible to search and compare cases by jurisdiction, legal topics or business sectors.

PRESTIGIOUS BOARDS

e-Competitions draws upon highly distinguished editors, all leading experts in national or international antitrust. Advisory Board Members include: Sir Christopher Bellamy, Ioanis Lianos (UCL), Eleanor Fox (NYU), Frédéric Jenny (OECD), Jacqueline Riffault-Silk (Cour de cassation), Wouter Wils (King's College London), etc.

LEADING PARTNERS

- Association of European Competition Law Judges: The AECLJ is a forum for judges of national Courts specializing in antitrust case law. Members timely feed e-Competitions with just released cases.
- Academics partners: Antitrust research centres from leading universities write regularly in e-Competitions: University College London, King's College London, Queen Mary University, etc.
- Law firms: Global law firms and antitrust niche firms write detailed cases summaries specifically for e-Competitions: Allen & Overy, Baker McKenzie, Cleary Gottlieb Steen & Hamilton, Jones Day, Norton Rose Fulbright, Skadden, White & Case, etc.

www.ingramcontent.com/pod-product-compliance
Ingram Content Group UK Ltd.
Pitfield, Milton Keynes, MK11 3LW, UK
UKHW020129290926
15471UKWH00003B/370

9 781939 007056